VIRGINIA

MICHAELA RIVA GAASERUD

Contents

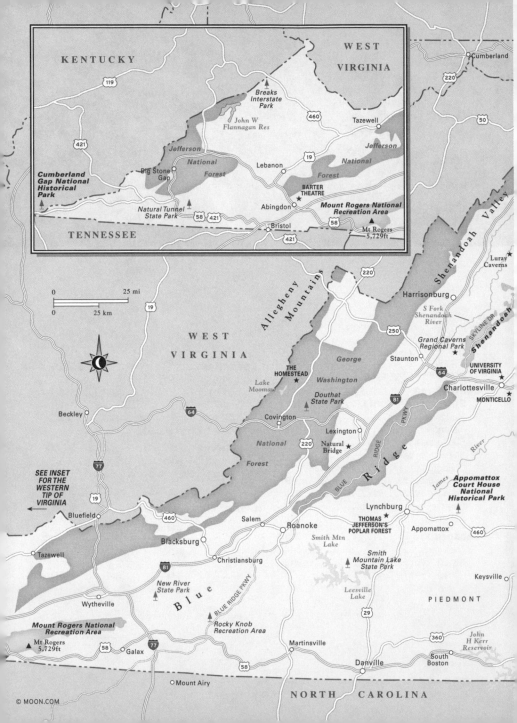

KENTUCKY

WEST VIRGINIA

Cumberland

119

220

460

50

Breaks Interstate Park

John W Flannagan Res

Tazewell

421

Jefferson

National

19

Jefferson

National

Big Stone Gap

Forest

Lebanon

Forest

Cumberland Gap National Historical Park

BARTER THEATRE

Natural Tunnel State Park

58 421

Abingdon

Mount Rogers National Recreation Area

TENNESSEE

Bristol

58

Mt Rogers 5,729ft

421

Luray Caverns

220

250

Harrisonburg

Allegheny Mountains

Shenandoah Valley

S Fork Shenandoah River

SKYLINE DR

0   25 mi

0   25 km

19

WEST

VIRGINIA

George

Staunton

Grand Caverns Regional Park

64

Shenandoah

THE HOMESTEAD

Washington

UNIVERSITY OF VIRGINIA

Lake Moomau

Douthat State Park

81

Charlottesville

MONTICELLO

Beckley

64

Covington

220

Lexington

BLUE RIDGE PKWY

Natural Bridge

Ridge

River

SEE INSET FOR THE WESTERN TIP OF VIRGINIA

77

National

Forest

James

Appomattox Court House National Historical Park

19

Bluefield

460

Salem

Roanoke

THOMAS JEFFERSON'S POPLAR FOREST

Lynchburg

Smith Mtn Lake

Appomattox

460

Tazewell

Blacksburg

81

Christiansburg

New River State Park

Blue

BLUE RIDGE PKWY

Smith Mountain Lake State Park

Leesville Lake

Keysville

29

PIEDMONT

Wytheville

Ridge

Rocky Knob Recreation Area

360

John H Kerr Reservoir

Mount Rogers National Recreation Area

58

77

Martinsville

Mt Rogers 5,729ft

Galax

58

Danville

South Boston

© MOON.COM

Mount Airy

NORTH CAROLINA

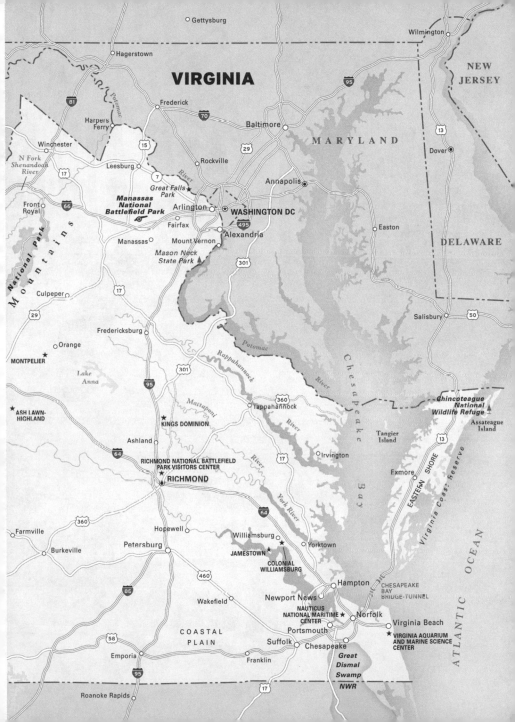

Virginia

Virginia embodies history like few other states in the Union. From the first permanent English settlement in the New World at Jamestown and the heady days of the Founding Fathers in Williamsburg, through the end of the American Revolution at Yorktown and the tragedy and heroism of the Civil War, many of the major events that shaped this country happened in the Old Dominion. Most of the buildings, battlefields, and artifacts involved are now preserved and on display in a host of world-class parks, museums, and historic homes such as George Washington's Mount Vernon and Thomas Jefferson's Monticello.

Virginia not only connects the storied past and thriving present—it's also a bridge between the mountains and the sea. Home to one of the most scenic roads in the country, Shenandoah abounds with spectacular ridgeline vistas, lush forests, and otherworldly caverns. On the Atlantic Ocean at the mouth of the Chesapeake Bay, Virginia Beach is one of the East Coast's premier resort destinations, with a bustling boardwalk and a bevy of great seafood restaurants. Detached from the rest of the state, the Eastern Shore is a time-warped land of unspoiled marshes, fishing towns, and the famous ponies of Chincoteague. Virginia offers the best of the many worlds it bridges— and then some.

Clockwise from top left: Natural Bridge State Park; downtown Lexington; Luray Caverns; Mabry Mill; Ridge Trail, Old Rag Mountain; Fredericksburg & Spotsylvania National Military Park.

7 TOP
EXPERIENCES

1 **Hit the Trail:** The area along the **Blue Ridge Parkway** offers ample hiking opportunities along with some of the best scenery on the east coast (page 303).

2 **Go Back in Time in Colonial Williamsburg:** Immerse yourself in colonial life at the largest living history museum in the world (page 168).

3 **Take a Road Trip on Skyline Drive:** This stunning 105-mile route runs along the mountain ridges of **Shenandoah National Park** (page 234).

^
^ ^
^

4 **Visit Presidential Homes:** Get unique insights into the lives of the founding
fathers at George Washington's **Mount Vernon** (pictured, page 122) and Thomas
Jefferson's **Monticello** (page 293).

5 **Tour Historic Battlefields:** More major battles in the Civil War took place in Virginia than in any other state. Today, history buffs can walk in the footprints of the soldiers who fought there (page 21).

6 **Feast on Local Cuisine:** No trip would be complete without sampling the local crustacean cuisine or enjoying authentic Virginia country ham (page 23).

7 **Explore the National Mall:** The two-mile stretch from the **Lincoln Memorial** (pictured) to the **U.S. Capitol** has some of the country's most iconic monuments, including the **Washington Monument** and the **Vietnam Veterans Memorial** (page 34), as well as 11 **Smithsonian** museums and galleries (page 38).

Planning Your Trip

Where to Go

Washington DC

Washington DC is nestled between Virginia and Maryland on the banks of the Potomac River. Best known for politics, government, and **monuments and museums,** the city is also home to universities, nightlife, art, theater, and sports. One of the largest (and cleanest) cities in the country, Washington DC offers trendy neighborhoods, **upscale shopping,** the **National Cathedral,** the **National Zoo,** and professional sports arenas. The nation's capital is easy to navigate, especially with the help of landmarks such as the **Washington Monument** and the **U.S. Capitol.**

Northern Virginia

From the busy halls of the **Pentagon** in **Arlington** and the trendy streets of historic **Old Town Alexandria** to the quaint alleyways of **Middleburg,** Northern Virginia is a cornucopia of culture, history, business, outdoor recreation, culinary delights, and shopping. It is a central corridor for the technology industry, yet houses key attractions such as **Mount Vernon,** the plantation home of **George Washington.** Northern Virginia's residents make up roughly one-third of the entire state population.

Coastal Virginia

Visiting Coastal Virginia is a great way to take a break from everyday stresses and learn about history or relax on the beach. **Colonial Williamsburg,** a living museum that vividly displays what life in colonial times was like, is one of the most popular historical attractions in the country. Just a short drive away are the resort area of **Virginia Beach** and the sleepy seaside communities on **Virginia's Eastern Shore.** The region offers port towns, battleships, and

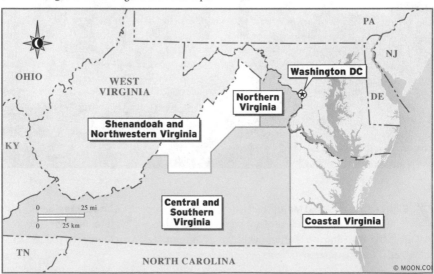

© MOON.CO

Virginia Beach

beautiful clean beaches all within a short drive of one another.

Shenandoah and Northwestern Virginia

Shenandoah National Park and Northwestern Virginia form a very special part of the Blue Ridge Mountains. The area is known for its stunning vistas, and picturesque rivers and streams criss-cross the region and loosely connect the towns that sit on the park's doorstep. Take a scenic drive along **Skyline Drive**, white-water raft down the **Shenandoah River,** spend an afternoon underground in mysterious **Luray Caverns,** or take a hike on the famous **Appalachian Trail.** Choose adventure or opt to relax—there is no wrong answer.

Central and Southern Virginia

Sprawling Central and Southern Virginia offer some of the most beautiful countryside in America. Awesome mountain vistas, rolling foothills, and enchanting fall foliage can be found in this region, especially along the **Blue Ridge Parkway.** The site of many colleges and universities including the **University of Virginia,** the region was also home to famous Americans such as **Thomas Jefferson** and **James Monroe.** The state capital, **Richmond,** and historic **Fredericksburg, Charlottesville,** and **Roanoke** are key destinations in this vast region.

tree-lined drive at James Monroe's Highland

When to Go

If you have the luxury of choosing your time to visit, **late spring** (May and June) and **fall** (September and October) are usually the **best times** to explore Virginia. The weather is most pleasant, and there are fewer tourists to compete with. Although **summer** is the **prime tourist season,** unless your plans involve some beach time or a stay in a mountain retreat, the humidity can be a bit overwhelming. The fall foliage in the state is some of the most spectacular in the country. A drive through the Blue Ridge Mountains in October can lead to some of the most stunning scenery in the East. If your focus is on historical sites and museums, the **winter** months (with the exception of the holiday season) can mean **short or no wait times** for popular attractions. Just be prepared for some sites to be closed or to have shorter hours.

The Best of Virginia

Virginia encompasses a large amount of land. It can take six hours to drive from Washington DC to the southern end of Virginia and six hours to drive from Lexington to the Eastern Shore. A 10-day trip provides the opportunity to hit most of the highlights in the state and to get a good feel for all Virginia has to offer.

Washington DC makes a good starting point for exploration of Virginia. It is conveniently located to Northern Virginia and is easy to get to by air, train, bus, and car. Spend a couple of days at the beginning of your trip exploring this marvelous city. For more suggestions on seeing DC, see page 28.

Northern Virginia
DAY 1

From Washington DC, drive across the Potomac into Northern Virginia. Stop by **Great Falls Park** for a picnic near the impressive falls overlook. Continue on to **Middleburg** and have dinner at **The Red Fox Inn and Tavern** in the historic downtown area before checking into one of the lovely country inns or the **Salamander Resort and Spa** for the night.

Shenandoah National Park
DAY 2

Drive 45 minutes west to **Front Royal,** the gateway to **Shenandoah National Park.** Enter the park on the famed **Skyline Drive.** Spend the rest of the day meandering down the northern section of Skyline Drive to **Luray.** Be sure to stop along the way for a short hike and to take in the sights along this stunning section of road. Overnight in Luray.

Luray and Lexington
DAY 3

Start your day by touring the incredible **Luray Caverns.** Then drive an hour and 40 minutes south on I-81 to historic **Lexington** and tour the

Great Falls Park

Old Town Alexandria

Virginia Military Institute, or take the four-hour scenic route along the southern portion of Skyline Drive and the **Blue Ridge Parkway.** Overnight in Lexington.

Charlottesville
DAY 4
Drive a little over an hour northeast to scenic **Charlottesville.** Visit **Monticello,** Thomas Jefferson's home, then tour a neighboring vineyard. Pick a restaurant on the hip downtown mall in Charlottesville for dinner before spending the night at either **The Clifton** or **Keswick Hall.**

Virginia Beach
DAY 5 AND 6
Make the three-hour drive to **Virginia Beach** early so you can enjoy a day on the Atlantic. Visit the **Virginia Aquarium & Marine Science Center** and walk the famous boardwalk. Enjoy fresh seafood at one of the local restaurants and spend the night in a hotel right on the Atlantic Ocean. Take a rest day the following day and soak in the beach atmosphere. Spend another night in Virginia Beach.

Williamsburg
DAY 7
Drive 1.25 hours northwest to **Colonial Williamsburg.** Lose yourself in U.S. history by dedicating the day to exploring this unique living museum. Visit the **historic buildings,** shop in the authentic **colonial shops,** snack on a sweet potato muffin from **Raleigh Tavern Bakery,** talk to the costumed interpreters, and have a refreshment in a colonial tavern. Dine in **Merchants Square** and spend the night in one of several hotels run by the **Colonial Williamsburg Foundation.**

Richmond
DAY 8
Drive an hour northwest to the capital city of **Richmond.** Spend the day touring **Capitol Square** and the **Science Museum of Virginia.** For a splurge, overnight in the **Jefferson Hotel.**

Best Scenic Drives

Skyline Drive

FALL FOLIAGE

Skyline Drive (page 234)

Starting point: Front Royal, VA
Ending point: Waynesboro, VA
105 miles; 3 hours

Virginia is known for having one of the most spectacular leaf displays in the country, and Skyline Drive in Shenandoah National Park showcases the best of the best.

Blue Ridge Parkway (page 303)

Starting point: Waynesboro, VA
Ending point: Cherokee, NC
469 miles total, 217 in Virginia; 6 hours in Virginia

The Blue Ridge Parkway begins where Skyline Drive ends. The most scenic portion is the 114 miles between Waynesboro and Roanoke.

HISTORICAL ROOTS

Colonial Parkway (page 167)

Starting point: Yorktown, VA
Ending point: Jamestown, VA
23 miles; 35 minutes

This parkway was designed to unify the "Historic Triangle" of Williamsburg, Jamestown, and Yorktown, while preserving the area's scenery and wildlife.

SALTY AIR

Chesapeake Bay Bridge-Tunnel (page 211)

Starting point: South Hampton Roads, VA
Ending point: Eastern Shore, VA
20 miles; 30 minutes

This engineering masterpiece, which spans the mouth of the Chesapeake Bay, takes vehicles over a series of bridges and through two-mile-long tunnels.

MOUNTAIN TOWNS

Virginia's Western Highlands (page 256)

Starting point: Monterey, VA
Ending point: Covington, VA
55 miles; 1.25 hours

Take scenic Route 220 through iconic mountain towns such as Warm Springs and Hot Springs, where the famed Omni Homestead Resort is located.

Fredericksburg

DAY 9

Drive an hour north to historic **Fredericksburg.** Tour the **Fredericksburg & Spotsylvania National Military Park** and then dine in the historic Old Town area. Spend the night at the lovely **Richard Johnston Inn.**

Old Town Alexandria

DAY 10

On your final day, drive north about an hour to historic **Old Town Alexandria.** While away the day shopping and dining in Old Town and enjoying the ambiance of this bustling colonial town. Spend the night in a lovely hotel—**Morrison House, The Alexandrian,** or **Lorien Hotel & Spa**—or head back across the Potomac River to Washington DC. For more suggestions on seeing Old Town Alexandria, see page 105.

Battles and Brews

Virginia has a colorful history. At 122 conflicts, the most Civil War battles by far were fought in Virginia than in any other state, but the region also has notoriety for its Revolutionary War past, colonial history, and of course, the development of our nation's government. This five-day itinerary starts in New Market and ends in Yorktown. The 283-mile trip covers some of the most significant historical cities in the state and includes refreshing stops in some of the best local pubs.

Day 1

Start in **New Market** off I-81 in the northwestern part of the state. Visit the **New Market Battlefield,** where Union troops were forced out of the Shenandoah Valley. Then head to scenic Luray for dinner and delightful beverages at **Moonshadows Restaurant.** Spend the night in Luray.

Day 2

Head northeast about one hour and 20 minutes to the **Manassas National Battlefield Park** and explore the site of two major Civil War battles. Continue on to the old town area of Manassas and have a beer and a cheesesteak at the **Philadelphia Tavern.** Spend the night in Manassas.

Day 3

Drive one hour south to Fredericksburg and spend the day touring the **Fredericksburg & Spotsylvania National Military Park.** Spend a relaxing evening at the **Kenmore Inn** and have a drink in the historic pub and bar.

Day 4

Drive 1.5 hours south to **Petersburg** and visit the **Petersburg National Battlefield,** where the longest single Civil War military event took place. After your visit, continue driving an hour southeast to Colonial Williamsburg. Have dinner and a brew in a historic **colonial tavern** and overnight in Williamsburg.

Day 5

End your trip by driving 20 minutes southeast to Yorktown and take in the **Yorktown Battlefield,** where the last major battle of the Revolutionary War was fought. The battlefield is part of the **Colonial National Historical Park.** Stop in the **Yorktown Pub** for a beer, oysters, and hush puppies. Spend the night in Yorktown at the **Hornsby House Inn.**

Virginia hosted more major Civil War battles than any other state and more than 2,000 "military events" during the war. This was due in part to the relocation of the Confederate Capital near the beginning of the war from Montgomery, Alabama, to Richmond. As such, only a mere 150 miles separated Washington DC and Richmond, and Virginia often found itself in the center of conflict. By the time General Lee surrendered in 1865, a large portion of Virginia had been scarred or destroyed by war.

Many of the battlefields in Virginia are now protected as national historical sites and parks, and visitors from across the nation come to pay tribute, participate in battle reenactments, and see firsthand the land that played such an important role in shaping our country's history. Many beautiful and haunting monuments, statues, and exhibits now stand on these hallowed grounds to help both interpret the history of each battle and to serve as reminders of the many young lives lost there. Key Civil War battlefields in Virginia include:

Manassas National Battlefield Park

- **Fredericksburg & Spotsylvania National Military Park (1862-1862):** the second-largest military park in the world and the site of four Civil War battles (page 263)

- **Manassas National Battlefield Park (July 21, 1861 and August 28-30, 1862):** the site of the First Battle of Bull Run, the first major land battle in the war, and the Second Battle of Bull Run, the biggest simultaneous mass assault of the Civil War (page 134)

- **Petersburg National Battlefield (June 1864-April 1865):** the site of the longest single Civil War military event, lasting more than nine months and producing 70,000 casualties (page 288)

- **Richmond National Battlefield Park (1861-1865):** a collection of 12 individual sites that preserve more than 1,900 acres of Civil War history (page 277)

- **New Market Battlefield State Historical Park (May 15, 1864):** the site of the only occasion in American history when college cadets were responsible for victory in combat, forcing Union troops out of the Shenandoah Valley (page 246)

Virginia is for Lovers

Virginia's official slogan is "Virginia Is for Lovers." What better way to explore the state than to stay in some of the best romantic getaway spots with your special someone. This 261-mile itinerary starts in Middleburg and travels through some of the state's most beautiful areas, ending in Roanoke.

Day 1

Start off your romantic retreat in Virginia hunt country. Book a room at the beautiful **Goodstone Inn & Restaurant** in **Middleburg.** Spend the day exploring the downtown area, then take a stroll around the inn's property or take advantage of the on-site spa. Dine at the inn's restaurant.

Day 2

Drive two hours southwest to **Charlottesville** and stay at the award-winning **Keswick Hall.** Spend the day visiting Thomas Jefferson's home at **Monticello** or sampling wine at a local vineyard, then return to the Hall for dinner and a relaxing evening on the patio.

Day 3

Begin the day by driving two hours southwest to the **Hot Springs** area. Check into **The Omni Homestead Resort,** soaking in the fabulous amenities at its 2,000-acre high-end, self-contained campus. Play a round of golf, visit the spa, or take a dip in the spring pools—there is plenty to do before settling down to a romantic dinner with your sweetheart at one of the wonderful resort restaurants.

Day 4

The final day begins with a 1.5-hour drive south to **Roanoke.** Book a room at the historic **Hotel Roanoke & Conference Center**—the restored Tudor hotel was built in 1882 and has welcomed many famous guests. Spend the day exploring the sites and museums in downtown Roanoke. Dine at the hotel's on-site **Regency Room** before turning in for the night. This hotel is the perfect nightcap to four days of romance in beautiful Virginia.

Monticello, home of Thomas Jefferson

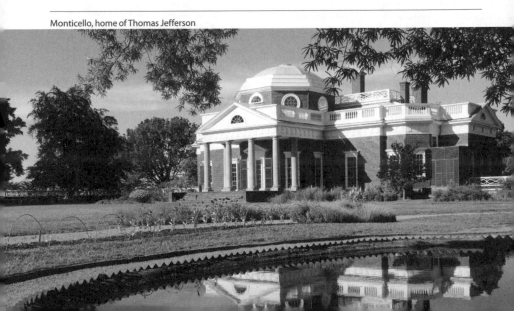

Virginia Eats

Virginia's colonial past, agricultural history, and proximity to water are all evident in the local cuisine. In the 17th century, Virginia settlers learned how to smoke meat from the native residents. To this day, Virginia country ham has an international reputation. Peanuts, which were a popular plantation crop, have remained a staple in the Old Dominion. As one of the nation's top six producers of apples, Virginia makes sure to save room for dessert. And although seafood is not unique to Virginia, it has certainly found a special place here, since it is harvested regionally.

- **The King's Arms Tavern** (page 175) in Colonial Williamsburg, is known for their signature peanut soup. They also serve other southern traditional dishes and decadent dessert.

- **The Red Fox Inn and Tavern** (page 155) is a historic tavern in the heart of Middleburg that serves traditional Virginia-style food using cooking techniques such as roasting, smoking, and braising. If you've never tried peanut soup, this is the place to order it.

- Authentic Virginia ham (country ham) can be enjoyed at **The Homeplace Restaurant** (page 329) in Catawba. It is served family style with one or two other meats, and scrumptious side dishes.

- **Tim's Rivershore Restaurant & Crabhouse** (page 137) in Dumfries offers a beachy atmosphere and waterfront dining on the Potomac River. This super casual crab house is a party spot in the summer with live music and a boating crowd.

- **The Crazy Crab Restaurant** (page 166) in the Reedville Marina is a small, family-owned restaurant on the waterfront. The seafood can't get any fresher, as you can literally see the owner walk outside and harvest it.

- The **Crab Shack** (page 192) sits on the James River in Newport News and has great views throughout its window-lined dining room and

Tim's Rivershore Restaurant & Crabhouse

deck. It offers fresh seafood and a casual atmosphere.

- The folks at **AW Shucks Raw Bar & Grill** (page 201) in Norfolk believe that any meal can include seafood. They are famous for burgers topped with lump crab, and the portions are huge.

- **Four Brothers Crab House & Ice Cream Deck** (page 218) is out on Tangier Island, the "Soft Crab Capital of the World." A trip to this isolated island in the middle of the Chesapeake Bay requires a 12-mile ferry ride.

- Winchester, the state's top apple packaging location at the northern tip of the Shenandoah Valley, is often called "The Apple Capital of the World." Stop at **Marker-Miller Orchards** (page 230), a "pick-your-own" orchard, which begins September 1.

Washington DC

Awe-inspiring Washington DC, nestled between

Virginia and Maryland on the banks of the Potomac River, is best known for government, politics, and museums. Stunning marble monuments dominate the landscape and are a constant reminder of our country's powerful beginnings, while stately government buildings act as the working engine guiding our nation.

One of the largest cities in the nation, Washington is also home to several universities, trendy neighborhoods, professional sports arenas, and attractions such as the National Zoo. The city boasts tremendous nightlife, art, theater, and upscale shopping. On average, around 21 million visitors come to DC annually.

Although much of the city is historic and upscale, there are also parts

Highlights

Look for ★ to find recommended sights, activities, dining, and lodging.

★ **Washington Monument:** This 555-foot-tall monument is a tribute to America's first president and a focal point of the National Mall (page 34).

★ **Lincoln Memorial:** This stunning Doric-style monument sitting on the banks of the Potomac River is a grand memorial to President Abraham Lincoln (page 34).

★ **Vietnam Veterans Memorial:** This moving memorial honors those who fought and died or went missing in action during the Vietnam War (page 35).

★ **National Museum of African American History and Culture:** The only national museum dedicated to African American history and culture, this popular museum is the 19th and most recent Smithsonian Institution Museum (page 38).

★ **National Museum of Natural History:** The most visited natural history museum in the world, this treasure features more than 126 million specimens in 325,000 square feet of exhibit space (page 39).

★ **National Air and Space Museum:** It features the largest collection of air- and spacecraft in the world (page 41).

★ **White House:** Tour the home and workplace of the president of the United States (page 42).

★ **Jefferson Memorial:** Sitting on the shore of the famous Tidal Basin is this stunning

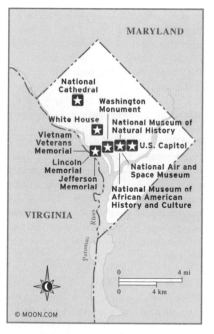

memorial to the author of the Declaration of Independence (page 43).

★ **U.S. Capitol:** The grand neoclassical-style Capitol Building is the official meeting site for the U.S. Congress (page 47).

★ **National Cathedral:** This massive Gothic cathedral in Upper Northwest DC is the sixth-largest cathedral in the world (page 58).

of Washington DC that are impoverished, comprising mostly minority demographics. Many of these residents face homelessness and unemployment. These areas exist side by side with the affluent and wealthy. In a strange way, Washington DC does truly represent the country, even if its residents don't have voting representation in Congress.

ORIENTATION

The city is divided into four quadrants, with the U.S. Capitol sitting in all four. The Capitol Building, however, doesn't sit in the center of the city, which means that the quadrants are not equal in terms of square mileage. The majority of the city and the lion's share of the attractions are in the northwest quadrant of Washington. The city is laid out in a grid pattern of lettered and numbered streets, so it is relatively easy to navigate, especially with the help of large landmarks like the Washington Monument and the Capitol Building.

If you asked 10 people how they would divide up the city to explain it to a visitor, you would get 10 different answers. Some would do it simply by quadrants, others by key neighborhoods, and still others by the sights themselves. For the sake of this guide, we are going to divide the city by popular tourist areas so that we can include key areas where many of the popular sights are located, as well as popular neighborhoods where you can find a tremendous selection of food, nightlife, and festivals.

The National Mall

Many people are surprised to learn that the National Mall is a national park and administered by the National Park Service. It is part of an area known as the National Mall and Memorial Parks unit. The exact boundaries of the mall have always been difficult to define, but according to the National Park Service, it is "the area encompassed by Constitution and Pennsylvania Avenues NW on the north, 1st Street on the east, Independence and Maryland Avenues on the south, and 14th Street on the west." It may be easier to visualize by saying that the Mall is basically the entire three-mile stretch between the Lincoln Memorial at the west end and the U.S. Capitol at the east end. The Washington Monument is a focal point of the Mall and sits just to the west of its center. Often, many areas just outside the Mall's official boundaries are still considered to be "on the Mall."

A plan for the National Mall originally designed in 1791 by Pierre L'Enfant laid out a "Grand Avenue," but it was never carried out. The Mall served several other purposes prior to reaching its current state. During the Civil War, the land was utilized primarily for military purposes—drilling troops, the production of arms, and even slaughtering cattle. Permission was even given to the railroad in the late 1800s to lay tracks across part of the Mall.

The National Mall is the primary tourist area in Washington DC, and visitors should plan on spending a significant amount of time here. Simply put, it is packed with monuments and lined with museums. (Some are even underground.) The Department of Agriculture is also on the Mall. When you set out to explore, wear comfortable walking shoes and be sure your camera is charged.

Capitol Hill

Capitol Hill is the political center of the country. It is home to the U.S. Congress and also the largest historical residential neighborhood in the city. Geographically, Capitol Hill is literally a hill that rises as you approach the Capitol from the west. The U.S. Capitol is on the crest of the hill.

Capitol Hill sits in both the southeast and northeast quadrants of the city. To the north is the H Street Corridor, to the south is the Washington Navy Yard, to the east is

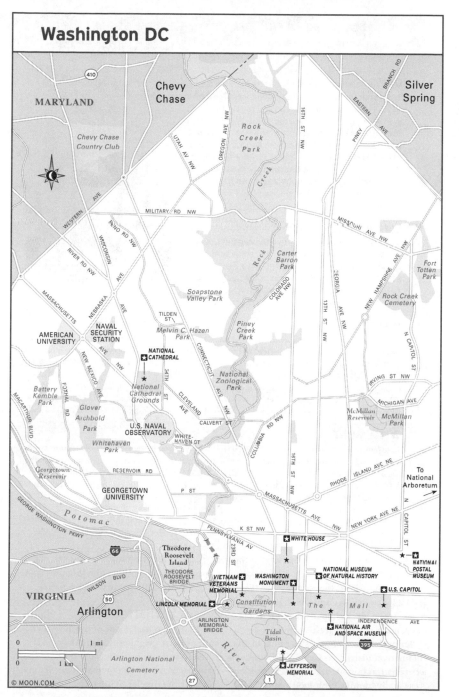

Washington DC

DAY 1

Begin your trip with a day dedicated to the **National Mall.** Put on your walking shoes and start with a bird's-eye view of the city from the top of the **Washington Monument,** then walk through the **National World War II Memorial** on your way to the **Lincoln Memorial.** Choose several of the many beautiful **war memorials** to visit, such as the **Korean War Memorial** and the **Vietnam Veterans Memorial.** Pick up lunch at a local food truck and find a nice bench in **West Potomac Park** to rest your feet. Ride Metrorail up to Capitol Hill and spend the afternoon on a tour of the **U.S. Capitol.** When your feet can take no more, catch a cab or car service to Dupont Circle for dinner, and then walk east on M Street to enjoy some of the city's nightlife at the rooftop bar at **Ozio Restaurant and Lounge.** Spend the night in the nearby **Hotel Tabard Inn** or, if you feel like splurging, at the **Hay-Adams,** overlooking the White House.

National World War II Memorial

DAY 2

On your second day in DC, plan to visit some of the **Smithsonian Institution** museums. After breakfast at the inn, if you're feeling spry, walk the 10 or so blocks down to the National Mall or else take a cab or car service. Pick and choose your favorites such as the **National Air and Space Museum** and the **National Museum of Natural History.** Grab lunch inside one of the museums when you need a break, or sample another one of DC's great food trucks outside. When you've overloaded on museums, walk to the **P.O.V. Roof Terrace and Lounge** at the W Washington D.C. Hotel and have a cocktail, then go for a late dinner at the **Old Ebbitt Grill.**

WITH MORE TIME

Take Metrorail into **Old Town Alexandria** for a day in one of the country's oldest port cities. Stroll the historic streets to window-shop in the many **boutiques** and then take a tour of the **Gadsby's Tavern Museum.** Have lunch at **Gadsby's Tavern** and then visit the **Torpedo Factory Art Center,** with three floors of galleries and studios. If you still have energy, take a walking tour of Old Town and then get off your feet for a relaxing dinner at **The Majestic.** After dinner, take Metrorail, cab, or car service back to DC and take a **nighttime tour of the National Mall** to see the monuments lit up. Spend one last night in the nation's capital.

the Anacostia River, and to the west is the National Mall.

Many politicians, their staff, journalists, and lobbyists live on Capitol Hill. Residential streets are lined with homes from different periods, many of which are historic.

Pennsylvania Avenue is the hub of the commercial district on Capitol Hill and offers restaurants, bars, and shops. The oldest continually running fresh-food market in the city, called **Eastern Market,** is just east of the Capitol Building. This popular shopping spot is housed in a 19th-century brick building.

District Wharf

The District Wharf is one of the newest and most popular neighborhoods in the city. It is a trendy, mile-long area located south of the National Mall on the Potomac River waterfront. At the time of writing, the first phase

The Capitol Architect: Pierre L'Enfant

Washington DC owes a great portion of its inspiring design to Pierre Charles L'Enfant (1754-1825), a French-born American architect and civil engineer. L'Enfant came to America to fight in the Revolutionary War and later became George Washington's number one city planner. L'Enfant designed Washington DC from scratch. He dreamed up a city that was to rise out of a mix of hills, forests, marshes, and plantation land into an extravagant capital city with wide avenues, beautiful buildings, and public squares.

L'Enfant's city included a grand "public walk," which is seen today in the National Mall. His city plan was based on European models, but incorporated American ideals. The design was created from the idea that every citizen is equally important. This is shown in the Mall design, since it is open in all corners.

of the wharf was completed and the neighborhood was already fully established and thriving with dining, shopping, residential and commercial real estate, live music venues, and many events and festivals. Parking can be tricky in this area, with just a few parking garages.

Downtown

"Downtown" may sound a bit broad, but the term actually refers to the central business district in Northwest Washington DC. Geographically, the area is difficult to clearly define, but it is generally accepted as being bordered by P Street NW to the north, Constitution Avenue NW to the south, 4th Street NW to the east, and 15th Street NW to the west.

Some notable areas included in the downtown district are the **K Street Corridor,** which used to be known as the Power Lobbying Corridor and still houses many law firms and businesses (although most of the lobbying firms have relocated to other parts of the city); **Federal Triangle** (bordered by 15th Street NW, Constitution Avenue NW, Pennsylvania Avenue NW, and E Street NW), a triangular area that is home to 10 large federal and city buildings; and **Judiciary Square** (bounded by H Street NW to the north, Pennsylvania Avenue to the south, the I-395 access tunnel to the east, and 6th Street NW to the west), a small neighborhood housing federal and municipal courthouses and offices.

The area also includes the **Penn Quarter** neighborhood, which extends roughly between F and H Streets NW and between 5th and 10th Streets. The name "Penn Quarter" is relatively new. This once sketchy area had new life breathed into it with the opening of the **Capital One Arena** (7th and F Streets) in 1997, which was originally called the MCI Center (and later the Verizon Center) and is home to the **Washington Capitals** professional hockey team and the **Washington Wizards** and **Washington Mystics** professional basketball teams. Now the area is a bustling arts and entertainment district with galleries, museums, restaurants, hotels, and shopping.

At its northern boundaries, Penn Quarter overlaps with the small historic neighborhood of **Chinatown.** Chinatown runs along H and I Streets NW between 5th and 8th Streets NW. It has roughly 20 authentic Asian restaurants and small businesses and is known for its annual Chinese New Year celebration as well as its signature Friendship Arch built over H Street at 7th Street.

Dupont Circle

Dupont Circle is a historic district in Northwest Washington DC. It is technically also the traffic circle at the intersection of Massachusetts Avenue NW, Connecticut Avenue NW, New Hampshire Avenue NW, P Street NW, and 19th Street NW, as well as a park and a neighborhood.

Choosing the Location of the Nation's Capital

Prior to 1800, the newly formed Congress met in several locations in the mid-Atlantic region. Where to establish the permanent federal government became a highly contested topic that went unresolved for many years. Finally, on July 16, 1790, President George Washington was officially put in charge of selecting a location for the permanent capital and appointing three commissioners to oversee its birth. Washington chose a 10-square-mile piece of land from property in both Virginia and Maryland sitting on both sides of the Potomac River.

The old myth is that DC was built on a swamp. This isn't exactly true. The area was a tidal plain but encompassed tobacco fields, cornfields, woods, waterside bluffs, and wetlands along the river. Washington DC is rich with waterways (the Potomac River, Anacostia River, Rock Creek, and others), but most of the land designated for the city was not marshy.

Congress met in the new location for the first time on November 17, 1800, and the move was completed in 1801. In 1846, land that formerly belonged to Virginia (on what is now the Virginia side of the Potomac River) was returned to Virginia. It is said that George Washington never felt comfortable calling the capital Washington, so instead he referred to it as "The Federal City."

The neighborhood of Dupont Circle lies roughly between Florida Avenue NW to the north, M Street NW to the south, 16th Street NW to the east, and 22nd Street NW to the west.

Dupont Circle is often considered the center of Washington DC's nightlife. It is home to many people in their 20s and also a popular neighborhood among the gay and lesbian community. There are many multilevel apartment buildings and row houses that have been split into apartments here.

Northwest of Dupont Circle along Massachusetts Avenue is an area of the city where many foreign embassies are located. This is commonly referred to as **Embassy Row.** Although less than half of the more than 175 embassies in DC are in this area, it has one of the largest concentrations (most are between Scott Circle and Wisconsin Avenue). Many of the embassies were formerly the homes of wealthy families who made their fortunes from the railroad, mining, banking and publishing industries and even politics in the late 1800s. You'll recognize the embassies by the country flags flying out front.

Georgetown

Georgetown has long been known as a trendy yet historic neighborhood with excellent shopping, food, and nightlife. It sits on the Potomac River in Northwest DC, west of downtown and upriver from the National Mall. The area can be loosely defined as being bordered by the Potomac River to the south, Glover Park to the north, Rock Creek to the east, and Georgetown University to the west.

The intersection of M Street and Wisconsin Avenue is the hub of the commercial area, where high-end stores, top-notch restaurants, bars, and The Shops at Georgetown Park are located. Washington Harbor is also a popular area of Georgetown and offers waterfront dining on K Street, between 30th and 31st Streets. The historic Chesapeake & Ohio Canal (C&O Canal) runs between M and K Streets.

Georgetown is home to many politicians and lobbyists and is traditionally one of the most affluent neighborhoods in Washington. Famous people who have lived here include Thomas Jefferson, Francis Scott Key, Alexander Graham Bell, John F. Kennedy, John Kerry, Bob Woodward, and Madeleine Albright.

Many movies have also been filmed in the neighborhood. One of the most notable was the 1973 horror flick *The Exorcist,* which was set here and filmed here in part. Other films include *St. Elmo's Fire* (1985), *No Way Out* (1987), *True Lies* (1994), *Enemy of the State*

(1998), *Minority Report* (2002), *The Girl Next Door* (2004), *Wedding Crashers* (2005), and *Transformers* (2007).

Georgetown is not directly accessible by the Metrorail, Washington DC's subway system, but the local DC Circulator bus runs from 19th Street and N Street at the Dupont Metrorail station (on the Dupont-Georgetown-Rosslyn route) to the Rosslyn Metrorail station in Arlington, and it stops along M Street in Georgetown. The Union Station-Georgetown route also stops in Georgetown as it runs from Union Station to Georgetown along K Street. It also has stops on M Street.

Adams Morgan

Adams Morgan is a lively neighborhood in Northwest DC centered on the intersection of 18th Street and Columbia Road. This culturally diverse neighborhood is north of Dupont Circle, south of Mt. Pleasant, east of Kalorama, and west of Columbia Heights. It is considered to be the center of the city's Hispanic community.

Adams Morgan is known for its thriving nightlife. It has more than 40 bars, a great selection of restaurants, nightclubs, coffeehouses, galleries, and shops (most are located along 18th Street). Cuisine from all parts of the globe can be found, from Ethiopian to Caribbean.

Adams Morgan is a popular neighborhood for young professionals and has many 19th- and early 20th-century apartment buildings and row houses.

Upper Northwest

Some of the country's wealthiest people live in the Upper Northwest section of Washington DC. It is a very pretty part of the city that is largely residential with many suburban-looking tree-lined streets. Although the sights are somewhat spread out, many are accessible by Metrorail.

Just a half mile north of Georgetown is **Glover Park,** a neighborhood of apartment buildings and row houses that were built in the 1920s and '30s. Much of the area's nightlife is found in Glover Park, although compared to neighboring Georgetown, it caters to a slightly older clientele and is less crowded. Glover Park is also slightly west of the **U.S. Naval Observatory** (home to the nation's **Master Clock**) and the vice president's mansion (1 Observatory Circle).

Northeast of Glover Park is **Woodley Park,** which has some key attractions such as the **National Cathedral** and the **National Zoo.** Farther north are **Cleveland Park, Van Ness,** and **Tenleytown,** along Wisconsin and Connecticut Avenues. Each has its own local restaurants, bars, and shopping. To the west is **American University.**

Southwest of American University is a lesser-known neighborhood called the **Palisades,** on the western border of the city along the Potomac River and C&O Canal. This is an elite neighborhood with a few good, high-end restaurants.

Farther north and right on the Maryland state line is **Friendship Heights,** which is technically part of **Chevy Chase.** Friendship Heights has notable wealth and is known for its upscale stores along Wisconsin Avenue and a mall called the **Chevy Chase Pavilion.**

Metrorail's Red Line operates throughout Upper Northwest. The stops are easy to navigate because the stations are named after neighborhoods and sights. The National Cathedral, Glover Park, and the Palisades do not have Metrorail service.

U Street Corridor

The U Street Corridor is a residential and commercial neighborhood in Northwest Washington DC that extends for nine blocks along U Street between 9th and 18th Streets. In the 1920s, this part of the city was known as "Black Broadway" and was one of the largest African American communities in the country. Several famous jazz musicians lived in the neighborhood, including Duke Ellington and Jelly Roll Morton. Others frequented the area's jazz clubs.

Today the U Street Corridor is home to

The National Mall

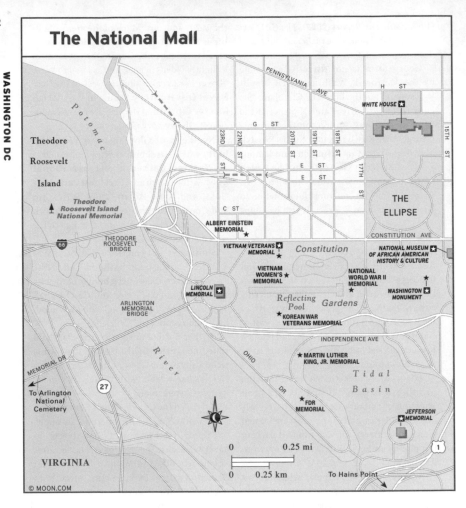

restaurants, nightclubs, music venues, and shops. The intersection of 9th and U Streets is known as "Little Ethiopia" for its concentration of Ethiopian businesses and restaurants.

PLANNING YOUR TIME

Washington DC encompasses approximately 68 square miles, so it is easy to get from one attraction to the next. The truth is, Washington DC has so much to offer, it could take weeks to feel that you've exhausted your opportunities for exploration. That's why it is best to focus on a few key areas when familiarizing yourself with the city and to come prepared with a plan of action or at least a list of the top sights you'd like to see.

The National Mall and Memorial Parks are where most of the key monuments and museums are located. This is an area most first-time visitors focus on to see known landmarks such as the Washington Monument, Lincoln and Jefferson Memorials, and several Smithsonian museums. This area can be explored in a long weekend, but allow more time if you want to visit each of the museums.

Most people spend their first trip to

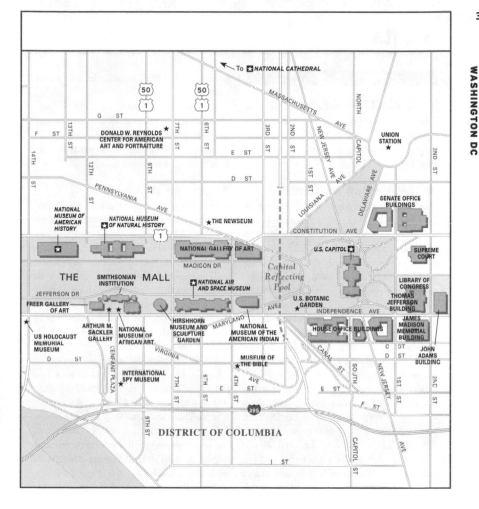

Washington DC exploring the National Mall and visiting the government buildings on Capitol Hill. Repeat visitors, or those with ample time, then branch out to explore some of the wonderful neighborhoods in Northwest DC, spending time in Georgetown, Dupont Circle, Adams Morgan, and other key locations to get more of the flavor of the city and to take in the zoo or National Cathedral.

Above all, be realistic about what you and any travel companions can take in during a day. Three or four top sights a day can be more than enough if they include walking through museums and taking tours.

If you are planning to stay in Washington DC and not stray far from the city limits, there is no need to have a car during your visit. Many of the sights, restaurants, and hotels are accessible by public transportation or a short cab or car-service ride, and parking can be expensive and sometimes difficult to find.

Sights

THE NATIONAL MALL

The National Mall (www.nps.gov/nacc) is open 24 hours a day. National Park Service rangers are available to answer questions at most of the sights daily 9:30am-10pm.

★ Washington Monument

The Washington Monument (2 15th St. NW, 202/426-6841, www.nps.gov/wamo, daily except July 4 and Dec. 25, 9am-5pm with longer summer hours, free but ticket required) is one of the most easily recognized landmarks in the country. This slender, 555-foot-tall stone structure is centrally located on the Mall (east of the Reflecting Pool and the Lincoln Memorial) and is a great landmark with which to orient yourself when touring the Mall.

The Washington Monument is a tribute to the first U.S. president and also the world's tallest true obelisk. Made of marble, granite, and bluestone gneiss, its construction spanned 36 years. Work started in 1848 but was interrupted by several events between 1854 and 1877, including the Civil War. If you look closely at the monument, you can tell that about 150 feet up (a little more than a quarter of the way) the shading of the marble differs slightly. This was due to the long break in construction. The capstone was finally set in 1884, and the monument was dedicated in early 1885. It opened to the public in 1888.

The Washington Monument, upon its completion, was the world's tallest structure. It only held this distinction for one year, however: The Eiffel Tower took over the honor after it was completed in Paris, France.

Visitors can take an elevator to the top of the monument to enjoy stunning views of the city. From the viewing windows, the White House can be seen to the north, the Jefferson Memorial to the south, the Capitol Building to the east, and the Lincoln Memorial to the west.

Although admission is free, advance reservations can be made at www.recreation.gov (877-444-6777) with a reservation fee of $1.00 per ticket. Reservations can be made 90 days in advance and are non-refundable.

★ Lincoln Memorial

A stunning tribute to America's 16th president is the Lincoln Memorial (off 23rd St. NW, 202/426-6841, www.nps.gov/linc, 24 hours, free). This grand limestone and marble monument was built in the Greek Doric style on the western end of the National Mall across from the Washington Monument. It has 36 exterior columns, which represent the number of states that existed at the time of Lincoln's death. The monument was dedicated in 1922.

Inside the memorial is a huge sculpture of Abraham Lincoln and inscriptions from two of his best-known speeches (the Gettysburg Address and his second inaugural address). The sculpture was created by Daniel Chester French, an acclaimed American sculptor of the late 19th and early 20th centuries, and carved by the Piccirilli brothers, who were well-known marble carvers at the time. The memorial is one of the most recognized landmarks in Washington DC and has been the site of many famous speeches, including Martin Luther King Jr.'s "I Have a Dream" speech.

Albert Einstein Memorial

Where else but on the National Mall can you sit with one of the greatest scientific minds of all time? Just north of the Lincoln Memorial is the bronze Albert Einstein Memorial statue sculpted by Robert Berks. It is set in a group of trees on the southwest side of the grounds of the National Academy of Sciences (2101 Constitution Ave. NW). Einstein is seated and

Secrets of the Lincoln Memorial

the Lincoln Memorial under construction in 1920

Many myths surround the Lincoln Memorial. Some say Abraham Lincoln is buried under the monument or entombed inside it, but this is false (Lincoln is buried in Springfield, Illinois). Others think the 57 steps leading up to the statue chamber represent Lincoln's age when he died, but in reality, he was only 56.

One question that is repeatedly asked throughout the local community is what, if anything, lies underneath the memorial? Given that the structure was built on tidal marsh from the Potomac River that was once actually under water, it might make sense that nothing could be under it, but the rumor that something exists there is actually true.

Underneath the Lincoln Memorial is a cavernous area with dirt floors and concrete walls. Hanging from the ceiling beneath where Lincoln sits are hundreds of stalactite formations. The stalactites are long, slender, and pale in color, and they are growing in this artificial cave as the result of water slowly dripping through the monument, which started when it was built.

Other interesting features in the underbelly of the monument are cartoon drawings that were sketched on several support columns by the workers who built the monument. One of the drawings depicts characters from the old *Mutt and Jeff* cartoon, which started running in 1907 and was the first daily newspaper comic strip.

Tours of the cavernous area ceased after 9/11, but this author can vouch for its existence, since in the 1970s and '80s, local children were treated to a tour on elementary school field trips.

has papers with mathematical equations in his lap symbolizing his scientific achievements.

War Memorials

★ **VIETNAM VETERANS MEMORIAL**

One of the most visited war memorials is the **Vietnam Veterans Memorial** (Constitution Ave. between 21st St. and 23rd St., 202/426-6841, www.nps.gov/vive, www.thewall-usa.

com, 24 hours, free). This moving memorial honors U.S. service members who fought and died in the Vietnam War and also those who are missing in action. There are three parts to the memorial: the **Three Soldiers Statue,** the **Vietnam Women's Memorial,** and the **Vietnam Veterans Memorial Wall.**

The focal point of the memorial is the Vietnam Veterans Memorial Wall. Completed in 1982, it is actually two 246-foot-long walls that are sunken into the ground and have the names of more than 58,000 service members who died in the war etched into them in chronological order. (The exact number changes each year as names are added.) When visitors look at the wall, they can see their reflections next to the etched names, symbolically linking the past and present. There is a path along the base of the wall so visitors can walk along it, read names, and, if desired, make pencil rubbings of a particular name.

The memorial is at the west end of the National Mall, adjacent to the Lincoln Memorial in West Potomac Park. It is open to the public 24 hours a day, and park staff conduct free daily interpretive programs throughout the day and are available to answer questions between 9:30am and 10pm daily.

NATIONAL WORLD WAR II MEMORIAL

The **National World War II Memorial** (17th St. between Constitution Ave. and Independence Ave., 800/639-4992, www. wwiimemorial.com, www.nps.gov/nwwm, 24 hours, free) honors the more than 400,000 people who died in World War II, the 16 million people who served the United States during the war in the armed forces, and the millions of people who provided support from home. The memorial contains 56 pillars and two triumphal arches arranged in a semicircle around a fountain and plaza. A Freedom Wall sits on the west side of the memorial bearing more than 4,000 gold stars on it, each representing 100 Americans who lost their lives in the war. An inscription in front of the wall reads, "Here we mark the price of freedom." The memorial opened to the public in 2004 and is administered by the National Park Service. It is on the east end of the Reflecting Pool, between the Washington Monument and the Lincoln Memorial.

KOREAN WAR VETERANS MEMORIAL

The beautiful and haunting **Korean War Veterans Memorial** (17th St. SW, 202/426-6841, www.nps.gov/kwvm, 24 hours, free) is also in West Potomac Park, southeast of the Lincoln Memorial. Erected in 1995, it is dedicated to service members who served in the Korean War. The memorial was designed in the shape of a triangle intersecting a circle with walls depicting images of land, sea, and air troops who supported the war. The focal point, however, is 19 larger than life-size stainless steel statues designed by Frank Gaylord within the walled triangle. The seven-foot-tall figures represent a patrol squad with members from each branch of the armed forces making their way through the harsh Korean terrain, represented by strips of granite and bushes. The figures are dressed in full combat gear and look incredibly lifelike. The memorial is lit up at night, and when the figures are reflected on the surrounding wall, there appear to be 38 soldiers, which represents the 38th parallel dividing the two Koreas.

National Gallery of Art

The **National Gallery of Art** (4th St. and Constitution Ave. NW, 202/737-4215, www. nga.gov, Mon.-Sat. 10am-5pm, Sun. 11am-6pm, free) first opened in 1937 when Andrew W. Mellon donated funding and a large art collection from multiple collectors for the enjoyment of the people of the United States. The gallery traces the development of Western art from the Middle Ages to current times through paintings, prints, drawings, sculpture, photographs, and other media. The only portrait in the Western Hemisphere painted by Leonardo da Vinci is housed in this museum. The gallery is a campus that includes the original museum building (the West Building), which features sculpture galleries with over 900 works or art; the newer East

1: Vietnam Women's Memorial designed by Glenna Goodacre 2: the East Building of the National Gallery of Art 3: Washington Monument and the Capitol behind the Reflecting Pool

Building, which contains a collection of modern paintings, drawings, prints, offices, and research centers; and a 6.1-acre outdoor sculpture garden (open year-round) that offers an ice-skating rink from mid-November through mid-March.

TOP EXPERIENCE

Smithsonian Institution Museums

Washington DC is known for its incredible museums. The most noted are those that are part of the **Smithsonian Institution** (www.si.edu), the largest museum and research complex in the world. The Smithsonian Institution was founded in 1846 and is administered by the U.S. government.

Oddly, the founding donor of the institution was British chemist and mineralogist James Smithson, who had never even been to the United States. An amateur scientist, Smithson inherited a large estate and in turn had no heirs to leave it to. His will stipulated that his estate would be donated to the founding of an educational institute in Washington DC.

The Smithsonian Institution was established as a trust, and it functions as a body of the U.S. government, although separate from the legislative, executive, and judicial branches. Funding for the museums comes from contributions, the institution's own endowment, memberships, government support, and retail and concession revenues. The Smithsonian employs approximately 6,300 people.

The majority of the Smithsonian museums, 19 in fact, are in DC, and many of them are architectural and historical landmarks. Nine research centers and the National Zoological Park are also part of the Smithsonian collection in Washington DC. Most of the Smithsonian facilities are open to the public daily except for December 25, with free admission.

The Smithsonian family also stretches to other parts of the country, including Virginia, Maryland, New York City, and Arizona. There are also many other museums that are affiliated with the organization.

First-timers to Washington DC will want to visit at least one of the major Smithsonian museums, but will most likely fill their dance card with several of the "biggies" on the National Mall (of which there are 11). Visitors should be aware that most of the museums on the National Mall do not offer dedicated parking facilities and require visitors to pass through security screenings upon entry.

SMITHSONIAN CASTLE

Information on the Smithsonian can be found on the south side of the Mall at its headquarters, called the **Smithsonian Castle** (1000 Jefferson Dr. SW, 202/633-1000, www.si.edu, daily 8:30am-5:30pm, free). This sandstone building, which opened in 1855, looks like something out of a fairy tale and houses an exhibit hall, administrative offices, and Smithson's remains (which were laid to rest in a crypt under the castle).

★ NATIONAL MUSEUM OF AFRICAN AMERICAN HISTORY AND CULTURE

The much anticipated **National Museum of African American History and Culture** (1400 Constitution Ave. NW, 844/750-3012, www.nmaahc.si.edu, daily 10am-5:30pm, free, timed-entry pass required) opened to rave reviews and throngs of visitors in 2016 and has been going strong ever since. As the only national museum dedicated to African American history and culture, this incredible museum houses more than 37,000 artifacts and is the 19th Smithsonian Institution museum. The 350,000-square-foot building itself is an architectural masterpiece and has sustainable features in its construction and operation. It features five aboveground stories and three below ground. Powerful and poignant exhibits explore all facets of the African American experience and illustrate the nation's journey from slavery through segregation and the Civil Rights movement, right up to the current day. There are countless exhibits, both permanent and temporary, with items such as Nat Turner's bible, artwork from Charles Alston and Henry O. Tanner, Michael Jackson's fedora, and a Southern plantation cabin. Many special tours and events are offered at the museum (check their website for the latest). Due to the museum's popularity, timed-entry passes during peak times are required.

The museum is also home to the popular **Sweet Home Café** (daily 10am-5pm), which offers authentic selections that showcase African American culture and current food traditions with a focus on locally sourced ingredients.

NATIONAL MUSEUM OF AMERICAN HISTORY

The **National Museum of American History** (Constitution Ave. NW, between 12th St. and 14th St., 202/633-1000, www.americanhistory.si.edu, daily 10am-5:30pm, free) is devoted to exhibits explaining the cultural, social, scientific, technological, military, and political development of the United States. The museum has three floors housing more than three million artifacts. Wings on each floor represent a different theme, each of which is represented by a large, significant, landmark object. Some examples include the 1865 Vassar Telescope in the west wing of the first floor, which is focused on science and innovation; a Civil War draft wheel in the east wing of the third floor, which is focused on political history; and a statue of George Washington in the west wing of the second floor, which focuses on American lives.

Some museum highlights include the Star-Spangled Banner, George Washington's uniform, Thomas Jefferson's lap desk, Archie Bunker's chair from the TV series *All in the Family,* Dorothy's ruby slippers from *The Wizard of Oz,* and the inaugural dresses worn by all the first ladies. The museum also houses the Warner Bros. Theater, which features films, lectures, and concerts.

The one-hour guided tours offered are a good way to see the highlights quickly if you have a full docket of sights to get to on the same day. There is no public parking at the museum. Visitors riding Metrorail can use either the Smithsonian Mall or Federal Triangle stop.

★ NATIONAL MUSEUM OF NATURAL HISTORY

Another favorite Smithsonian creation is the **National Museum of Natural History** (10th St. and Constitution Ave. NW, 202/633-1000, www.mnh.si.edu, daily 10am-5:30pm, free). It first opened its doors in 1910 and is said to be the most visited natural history museum worldwide. The main building encloses 325,000 square feet of exhibit space and is overall the size of 18 football fields. The museum collections include more than 126 million specimens.

Visitors can expect to see plants, animals, fossils, rocks, meteorites, and cultural artifacts including "Henry," the iconic 13-plus-foot-tall African elephant (the largest ever killed by humans), the jaws of a giant prehistoric shark, the stunning Hope Diamond (which is 45.52 carats), and David H. Koch Hall of Fossils (dinosaur hall). There's also a live butterfly pavilion (adults $7.50, children 2-12 $6.50, seniors 65 and over $7). The museum is also home to the largest group of scientists (approximately 185) dedicated to studying the history of the world. Visitor concierges are available to answer questions throughout the museum and can be identified by their green vests. There is no public parking at the museum. Visitors riding Metrorail should exit at the Smithsonian station (Mall exit) on the Blue and Orange Lines.

NATIONAL MUSEUM OF THE AMERICAN INDIAN

The **National Museum of the American Indian** (4th St. and Independence Ave. SW, 202/633-1000, www.americanindian.si.edu, daily 10am-5:30pm, free) opened in 2004 and is the first national museum focused exclusively on Native Americans. The five-story,

250,000-square-foot limestone building sits on more than four acres of what is made to look like wetlands. The museum features approximately 825,000 items that represent more than 12,000 years of history and 1,200 indigenous American cultures. It also offers exhibits, film screenings, public programs, cultural presentations, and school programs.

★ NATIONAL AIR AND SPACE MUSEUM

An overwhelming favorite in the Smithsonian family of museums is the **National Air and Space Museum** (Independence Ave. SW at 6th St. SW, 202/633-2214, IMAX 866/868-7774, www.airandspace.si.edu, daily 10am-5:30pm, free, IMAX and planetarium entry extra). This incredible museum features the largest collection of air- and spacecraft in the world and is also a center for research on historic aviation, spaceflight, planetary science, geophysics, and terrestrial geology. The exhibit space of 21 galleries and more than 160,000 square feet of floor space opened in 1976. Most of the hundreds of aircraft, spacecraft, rockets, missiles, and other aviation artifacts on display are originals.

Some highlights you can expect to see include the *Spirit of St. Louis*, the Apollo Lunar Module, a DC-3 airplane, a real lunar rock, and the *Star Trek* starship *Enterprise* studio model.

Another great attraction located inside the National Air and Space Museum is the **Albert Einstein Planetarium** (adults $9, youth 2-12 $7.50, military and seniors 60 and over $8). Several shows are offered daily and take visitors through the night sky with a first-of-its-kind SkyVision dual digital projection system and digital surround sound.

Other favorite attractions in the museum include the **Lockheed Martin IMAX Theater** (IMAX shows adults $9, youth 2-12 $7.50, military and seniors 60 and over $8,

feature films adults $15, youth 2-12 $13.50, military and seniors 60 and over $14), flight simulators, and an observatory (located on the southeast terrace). One of the best museum shops is also here, and dining facilities are offered on-site.

Free 90-minute museum tours are offered daily at 10:30am and 1pm. There is no public parking at the museum, but several public pay lots are nearby. Metrorail riders should use the L'Enfant Plaza stop and exit at Maryland Avenue.

HIRSHHORN MUSEUM

Many people think the **Hirshhorn Museum and Sculpture Garden** (700 Independence Ave. SW, 202/633-1000, www.hirshhorn. si.edu, daily 10am-5:30pm, free) looks like a giant spaceship parked near the Mall. The design is an open concrete cylinder (231 feet in diameter) standing on four large supports. The idea behind this structure was for it to provide a sharp contrast to everything else around it. It succeeded. This modern art museum, which opened in the 1960s, houses one of the premier collections of contemporary paintings and sculptures in the country focusing on the post-World War II era. A sculpture garden is located outside the museum.

NATIONAL MUSEUM OF AFRICAN ART

The **National Museum of African Art** (950 Independence Ave. SW, 202/633-4600, www.africa.si.edu, daily 10am-5:30pm, free) is part of a quadrangle complex behind the Smithsonian Castle. The building is mostly underground and contains the largest public collection of African art in the nation with approximately 9,000 artifacts. Pieces include sculpture, jewelry, musical instruments, maps, films, and photographs.

FREER GALLERY OF ART AND ARTHUR M. SACKLER GALLERY

The **Freer Gallery of Art** and the subterranean **Arthur M. Sackler Gallery** (1050 Independence Ave. SW, 202/633-1000, www.

1: Smithsonian Castle 2: National Museum of African American History and Culture 3: "Henry" the Elephant at the National Museum of Natural History 4: National Air and Space Museum

freersackler.si.edu, daily 10am-5:30pm, free) together form the national collections of Asian art. They contain the largest Asian art research library in the country (inside the Sackler Gallery) as well as art from all parts of Asia. Their collection of American art includes pieces by well-known artists such as Winslow Homer, Augustus Saint-Gaudens, and John Singer Sargent.

The Freer Gallery features Asian collections spanning 6,000 years that date back to the Neolithic era. Specific collections include stone sculptures from ancient Egypt, Chinese paintings, Persian manuscripts, and Korean pottery.

The Freer's most famous exhibit is the **Peacock Room in Blue and White,** which was the dining room of a mansion in London owned by Frederick Leyland in the late 1800s. The room was designed for display of Leyland's blue and white Chinese porcelain. Artist James McNeill Whistler consulted on the room's colors in 1876 and 1877 and painted intricate patterns of blue and gold that looked similar to peacock plumage. Charles Lang Freer bought the room in 1904, shipped it to his home in Detroit, Michigan, and began filling the shelves with ceramics from Japan, Korea, China, Iran, and Syria. Today, blue and white Chinese porcelains dating back to the Kangxi period (1662-1722) are again displayed in the Peacock Room, as they were in the 1870s.

The Sackler Gallery contains a founding collection of approximately 1,000 items that were donated by American psychiatrist, entrepreneur, and philanthropist Arthur M. Sackler. The collection has both ancient and contemporary items including South and Southeast Asian sculpture, Chinese jade, and Middle Eastern ceramics. The museums are on the south side of the Mall.

MALL CAROUSEL

It may come as a surprise that the Smithsonian operates the **Mall Carousel** (12th St. and Jefferson Dr. SW, 202/633-1000, www. nationalcarousel.com, daily 10am-5:30pm, $3.50). This favorite children's thrill ride with the blue and yellow awning is in front of the Smithsonian Castle. It offers three minutes of fun on faded painted ponies that were built in the 1940s. The carousel was originally at the Gwynn Oak Amusement Park in Maryland prior to coming to the Mall.

WHITE HOUSE AREA
★ White House

Not technically part of the National Mall, the **White House** (1600 Pennsylvania Ave. NW, 202/456-1111, www.whitehouse.gov, free) sits nearby on Pennsylvania Avenue and can be seen from Constitution Avenue. The White House is easily the most recognized residence in the country as the home and workplace of the president of the United States.

The site for the White House was chosen by George Washington in 1791, but John Adams was the first president to live there in 1800. (Mrs. Adams is said to have hung their wash in the East Room.) The house suffered a fire set by the British during the War of 1812, but it was rebuilt and has undergone several renovations since then. The White House currently has 6 levels, 132 rooms, and 35 bathrooms.

It is possible to take a self-guided tour of the White House (the only presidential home in the world that is open to the public), but requests must be made through your member of Congress. Tours are available Tuesday-Thursday 7:30am-11:30am and Friday-Saturday 7:30am-1:30pm. Requests can be made up to three months in advance but must be made at least three weeks in advance. There is no charge for the tour, but it is advised to make a reservation early since space is limited. Citizens of foreign countries may request a tour through their individual embassies in Washington DC. All visitors are required to present current government-issued photo identification or a passport.

The **White House Visitor Center** (1450 Pennsylvania Ave. NW, www.nps.gov, daily 7:30am-4pm, free) is in the Commerce Building. It offers an information booth, exhibits, restrooms, drinking fountains, and a first-aid area.

Presidential Firsts

- **Andrew Jackson** was the first president to ride in a train.
- **James Polk** was the first president to have his photograph taken.
- **Millard Fillmore** was the first president to have a bathtub with running water.
- **Rutherford B. Hayes** was the first president to have a telephone in the White House.
- **Benjamin Harrison** was the first president to have a Christmas tree in the White House.
- **Theodore Roosevelt** was the first president to ride in a car. He was also the first to travel outside the country while in office.
- **Calvin Coolidge** was the first president to be heard over radio.
- **Franklin D. Roosevelt** was the first president to fly in an airplane and the first to appear on television.

Lafayette Square

Lafayette Square (H St. between 15th St. and 17th St. NW, www.nps.gov, 24 hours, free) is a seven-acre park across Pennsylvania Avenue from the White House (it is also known as **Lafayette Park**). The park was designed as part of the White House grounds—and was originally named President's Park—but was separated when Pennsylvania Avenue was built in 1804. Lafayette Square has a checkered past. It has been home to a racetrack, a slave market, a graveyard, and a soldier encampment during the War of 1812. It's no wonder the park is said to be the most haunted location in the city. Today, the park offers green grass and five large statues: an equestrian statue of President Andrew Jackson and four of Revolutionary War heroes. The closest Metrorail stop is McPherson Square. The park is maintained by the National Park Service.

President's Park South

President's Park South, which is more commonly referred to as **The Ellipse,** is a 52-acre park that sits just south of the White House. Technically, the Ellipse is the name of the street that runs the circumference of the park. The park is a large grassy circle that is open to the public and is the site of various events. If you hear locals say they are at or on the Ellipse, they mean they are in the park bordered by Ellipse Road.

TIDAL BASIN AREA
The Tidal Basin

The Tidal Basin is a 107-acre reservoir in **West Potomac Park** that sits between the Potomac River and the Washington Channel (a two-mile-long channel that empties into the Anacostia River). Several major memorials are adjacent to the Tidal Basin, including the Jefferson Memorial, the Martin Luther King Jr. Memorial, and the Franklin Delano Roosevelt Memorial. The Tidal Basin is best known as the center of the National Cherry Blossom Festival; it is lined with many Japanese cherry trees.

★ Jefferson Memorial

Although it was only built in 1942, the **Thomas Jefferson Memorial** (16 E. Basin Dr. SW, 202/426-6841, www.nps.gov/thje, 24 hours, free), which sits on the south shore of the Tidal Basin in West Potomac Park, is one of the most recognized memorials in DC. This neoclassical building dedicated to our third president is built on land that once served as a popular bathing beach along the Potomac River.

OUT OF THE MOUNTAIN OF DESPAIR,
A STONE OF HOPE

THE STRUCTURE
OF WORLD PEACE
CANNOT BE THE
WORK OF ONE MAN,
OR ONE PARTY,
OR ONE NATION...
T MUST BE A PEACE
WHICH RESTS ON
THE COOPERATIVE
EFFORT OF THE
WHOLE WORLD.

ELEANOR ROOSEVELT,
FIRST UNITED STATES DELEGATE
TO THE UNITED NATIONS

1

2

The memorial building is made up of circular marble steps, a portico, a circular colonnade, and a shallow dome open to the elements. Inside stands a 19-foot-high bronze statue of Thomas Jefferson designed by Rudulph Evans, looking north toward his former residence, the White House. The statue was added to the memorial four years after its dedication. Many of Jefferson's writings are inscribed on the memorial.

The site of the Jefferson Memorial is adorned with many Japanese cherry trees, which were a gift from Japan in 1912. The trees are world famous for their beautiful spring blossoms and are the centerpiece for the annual National Cherry Blossom Festival.

Martin Luther King, Jr. Memorial

One of the newest memorials is the **Martin Luther King, Jr. Memorial** (1850 West Basin Dr. SW, 202/426-6841, www.nps.gov/mlkm, 24 hours, free) in West Potomac Park southwest of the National Mall. The memorial sits on four acres and was unveiled in 2011.

The design of the memorial is based on a line from King's "I Have a Dream" speech: "Out of a mountain of despair, a stone of hope." A 30-foot-high relief of the civil rights leader is called the *Stone of Hope,* sculpted by Lei Yixin, and stands just past two pieces of granite symbolizing the "mountain of despair." Additionally, a 450-foot-long wall includes inscriptions of excerpts from many of King's speeches. Martin Luther King Jr. is the first African American to be honored with a memorial near the National Mall. He is also only the fourth person to be memorialized who was not a U.S. president.

Franklin Delano Roosevelt Memorial

The **Franklin Delano Roosevelt Memorial** (400 West Basin Dr. SW, 202/485-9880, www.

1: Marin Luther King, Jr. Memorial carved by sculptor Lei Yixin 2: statue of First Lady Eleanor Roosevelt sculpted by Neil Estern

nps.gov/frde, 24 hours, free) sits on more than seven acres and consists of four outdoor rooms, one for each of FDR's office terms. Running water is an important component of the memorial, as are sculptures depicting scenes with FDR. Each of the rooms contains a waterfall, and the sculptures become larger and more detailed in consecutive rooms. The intention was to show the increasing complexities faced by FDR during his presidency as related to the Depression and war. This is the only memorial to include a depiction of a first lady: Eleanor Roosevelt is depicted in a bronze statue standing before the United Nations emblem.

There is, in fact, another FDR Memorial. FDR was said to have told his trusted friend and Supreme Court justice Felix Frankfurter, "If they are to put up any memorial to me, I should like it to be placed in the center of that green plot in front of the Archives Building. I should like it to consist of a block about the size [of this desk]." Because of this, the first FDR memorial was erected in the 1960s on the corner of 9th Street and Pennsylvania Avenue. It is a simple memorial that met his wishes and consists of a small block of stone that reads, "In Memory of Franklin Delano Roosevelt 1882-1945."

U.S. Holocaust Memorial Museum

The **U.S. Holocaust Memorial Museum** (100 Raoul Wallenberg Pl. SW, 202/488-0400, www.ushmm.org, daily 10am-5:30pm, free) is dedicated to the interpretation of Holocaust history. Its goal is to help leaders and citizens "confront hatred, prevent genocide, and promote human dignity." This museum, perhaps more than most, is of international interest: Visitors from more than 100 countries have walked through its doors since it first opened in 1993. The museum houses more than 12,750 artifacts including prisoner uniforms, a casting of a gas chamber door, and religious articles. Its collections include 1,000 hours of archival footage and 80,000 photographs. It also has information on 200,000 registered survivors, a library, and archives.

Permanent exhibits that show a chronological history of the Holocaust can be accessed on the first floor. A free pass must be obtained for the permanent exhibits March-August but not during the rest of the year. The passes are available at the museum on the day of your visit or can be reserved online. Entrance to other exhibits and memorial spaces is from the first, second, and concourse levels. There is a café on the 15th Street side of the building. This museum can be overwhelming for young children and is best for teenagers and adults.

Bureau of Engraving and Printing

As its web address indicates, the **Bureau of Engraving and Printing** (14th St. and C St. SW, 202/874-2330, www.moneyfactory.gov, Mon.-Fri. 8:30am-6pm, free) is a huge money factory. It produces U.S. currency notes and literally prints billions of dollars each year. Fresh money is delivered to the Federal Reserve System (the nation's central bank). Visitors can take guided tours or walk along the gallery to view the production floor where millions of dollars are being printed. The free 40-minute tour includes a film and explanation of the production process. No ticket is required for tours September-February. Tours run every 15 minutes between 9am and 10:45am and between 12:30pm and 2pm. During peak season (Mar.-Aug.), free tickets are required for tours. Tickets can be obtained at the ticket booth on-site (which opens at 8am) and are for the same day only. Plan to be in line between 6:30am and 7am for the best chance of getting tickets. One person may get up to four tickets.

SOUTH OF THE NATIONAL MALL
International Spy Museum

Enter the world of espionage at the only public museum in the country dedicated to professional spies. The **International Spy Museum** (700 L'Enfant Plaza SW,

Who is Featured on U.S. Paper Currency

- $1 bill: George Washington (1st U.S. president)

- $2 bill: Thomas Jefferson (3rd U.S. president)

- $5 bill: Abraham Lincoln (16th U.S. president)

- $10 bill: Alexander Hamilton (1st secretary of the treasury)

- $20 bill: Currently Andrew Jackson (7th U.S. president)

- $50 bill: Ulysses S. Grant (18th U.S. president)

- $100 bill: Ben Franklin (statesman)

202/393-7798, www.spymuseum.org, Sun.-Thurs. 9am-7pm, Fri.-Sat. 9am-8pm, adults $24.95, youth 7-12 $14.95, children 6 and under free, seniors/military/law enforcement/intelligence community/college students $19.95) is a fantastic and intriguing museum that enjoyed a vast expansion when it moved in 2019 from its former location in Penn Quarter to L'Enfant Plaza between the National Mall and District Wharf. This remarkable museum houses the largest collection of international artifacts geared toward the secret world of spies. Exhibits focus on some of the most secretive missions across the globe and strive to educate the public about their role in historic events.

The museum features artifacts created specifically for intelligence services (think lipstick pistols, disguises, and Enigma cipher machines) and first-person accounts from distinguished intelligence professionals. It brings an elusive world to life through state-of-the-art interactive exhibits designed to challenge visitors and doesn't shy away from the darker side of the profession. Their

Undercover Mission even tests visitors' spy skills as they go on a mission through the museum and tracks their performance on interactives. The end result is a "debrief" and access to a special website for further engagement. Plan on spending a minimum of two hours here.

Museum of the Bible

The **Museum of the Bible** (400 4th St. SW, 866/430-6682, www.museumofthebible.org, daily 10am-5pm, adults $24.99, children 7-17 $14.99, children 6 and under free, seniors/military/first responders/students $19.99) opened its doors in 2017 in a massive 430,000-square-foot building just south of the National Mall. The museum uses advanced technology to engage visitors of all ages in a personal experience with the Bible and features both permanent and temporary exhibits. Artifacts span 3,500 years of history, and the museum is also focused on education and research. The sixth floor is home to **Manna** (daily 11am-4pm, $6 18), a "fast casual" restaurant featuring Mediterranean dishes made from seasonal ingredients.

CAPITOL HILL
★ U.S. Capitol

The centerpiece of Capitol Hill is none other than the grand neoclassical-style **U.S. Capitol** (1st St. and E. Capitol St., 202/226-8000, www.visitthecapitol.gov, Mon.-Sat. 8:30am-4:30pm, free) itself, which sits on 274 acres at the east end of the National Mall. The Capitol Building is the official meeting location of the U.S. Congress. First-time visitors to the city should take the time to tour this national icon and view our elected officials hard at work.

The Capitol Building comprises a central dome towering above a rotunda, flanked by two wings. The building technically has two fronts, one on the east side and one on the west side. The north wing houses the U.S. Senate chamber and the south wing is for the U.S. House of Representatives chamber. Public galleries sit above each so visitors can watch the proceedings. Each of the many rooms in the Capitol is designated with either an "S" for those on the Senate side of the rotunda or "H" for those on the House side.

George Washington laid the cornerstone of the Capitol in 1793. The Senate wing was completed in 1800 (Congress held its first session there the same year), and the House wing was completed in 1811. Since its original construction, the building has undergone many expansions, renovations, and even a rebuilding after it was partially burned by the British during the War of 1812. The Capitol, in its early days, was used for other purposes in addition to government functions. In fact, church services were held there on Sundays until after the Civil War.

Underground tunnels and a private subway connect the Capitol Building with the Congressional office buildings. The Senate office buildings are located to the north on Constitution Avenue, and the House office buildings are located to the south on Independence Avenue. The public may only ride the subway when escorted by a staff member with appropriate identification.

Visitors to the Capitol enter through the three-level underground **U.S. Capitol Visitor Center** (beneath the east front plaza at 1st St. and E. Capitol St., 202/226-8000). The center is a security checkpoint, and visitors should be prepared to wait in line for screening before entering. The center also offers educational exhibits, restrooms, and a food court. The visitors center is open Monday-Saturday 8:30am-4:30pm, but the Capitol Building itself can only be visited on an official tour. Tours are free and can be arranged in advance through the Advance Reservation System (www.visitthecapitol.gov) or through the office of a senator or representative. Tours are given Monday-Saturday 8:40am-3:20pm and last one hour. They include the **Crypt, Rotunda,** and **National Statuary Hall**. Those wishing to watch the House or Senate in session must obtain a pass from their senator or representative's office. International visitors can obtain a ticket at

Capitol Hill

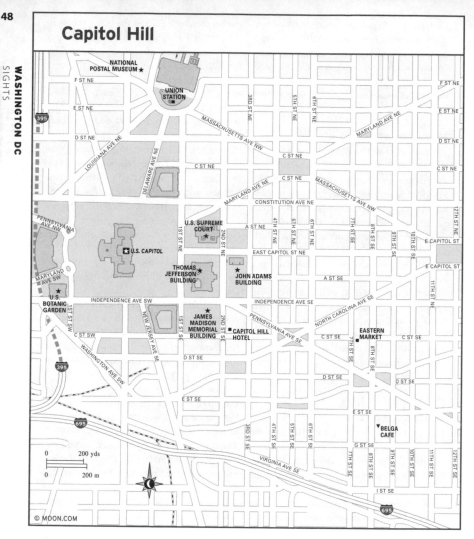

the Capitol with valid photo identification. Plan to arrive 45 minutes before a scheduled tour to allow enough time to get through security.

Summerhouse

The **Summerhouse** (on the west front lawn of the U.S. Capitol Building on the Senate side, www.aoc.gov, 24 hours, free) is a little oasis hidden in a group of trees. This small, decorative, hexagonal brick building offers a cool

place for visitors to rest. It was constructed around 1880 and is anchored by a fountain that once offered spring water. There are nice benches here with seating for 22 that are covered by a tile roof.

U.S. Supreme Court

Behind the U.S. Capitol Building on 1st Street (between E. Capitol St. and Maryland

1: U.S. Botanic Garden 2: U.S. Capitol

DC's Skyline: Onward and Upward?

Unlike most large cities in the country, Washington DC has a low skyline. When the first skyscrapers were going up in the late 1800s elsewhere in the world, DC residents became concerned that if tall buildings were constructed in the city, Washington would lose its European feel. So in 1899, Congress passed the Heights of Buildings Act, which limited the vertical reach of buildings in the nation's capital to no more than 130 feet. This act was later amended (in 1910) to allow buildings to be 20 feet higher than the width of the adjacent street. The only exception is on Pennsylvania Avenue between 1st and 15th Streets. More than 100 years later, the act is now being reviewed for possible revision because the inability to expand the skyline upward has limited the city's tax base and potential for growth.

Ave.) is the **Supreme Court of the United States** (1 1st St. NE, 202/479-3000, www. supremecourt.gov, Mon.-Fri. 9am-4:30pm, free). The Supreme Court is the highest court in the nation, and the current building was completed in 1935 (court was previously held in the Capitol Building). The main entrance faces the Capitol Building and welcomes visitors with a 252-foot-wide oval plaza. Fountains, benches, and flagpoles are on either side of the plaza. Marble columns support the pediment on the Corinthian-style building.

The court building is open to the public during the week, and visitors are encouraged to listen to a variety of courtroom lectures when the Supreme Court is not sitting. Lectures are scheduled every hour on the half hour and begin at 9:30am. The final lecture of the day starts at 3:30pm. A calendar is online with the daily lecture schedule. Visitors can also take in exhibits focused on the work of the Supreme Court, the justices' lives, and the architecture of the Supreme Court building. When the court is sitting, visitors are welcome to see our justice system in action by attending oral arguments. Seating, which is limited and granted on a first-come, first-served basis, is available for an entire argument or for a three-minute viewing. Prior to the beginning of a session, two lines form in front of the courthouse outside on the plaza. One line is for those wishing to sit in on the entire argument, and the other is for those wishing to witness a three-minute sample.

All visitors are required to pass through a security screening that includes X-raying personal items and walking through metal detectors.

Library of Congress

It's hard to imagine that the original collection of books held by the **Library of Congress** (www.loc.gov) went up in flames during the War of 1812 when the British set fire to the Capitol Building where the collection was kept. Fortunately, Thomas Jefferson had a rather substantial collection of personal books with more than 6,500 volumes that he agreed to sell to Congress to rebuild the collection.

Today the Library of Congress, which is a research library and the country's oldest federal cultural institution, is contained in three government buildings on Capitol Hill and one building in Virginia. It is also the largest library in the world. Its collections include upward of 32 million cataloged books, 61 million manuscripts, more than one million U.S. government publications, one million newspapers from all over the world, and more than 120,000 comic books. Its publications are printed in 470 languages.

The main library building is the beautiful **Thomas Jefferson Building** (10 1st St. SE, between Independence Ave. and E. Capitol St., 202/707-8000). This is the oldest building in the complex, having opened in 1897. This building is a feast for the eyes with its murals, mosaics, sculptures, and impressive main reading room containing 236 desks sitting under a 160-foot dome. A visitor center is located at the west front entrance (Mon.-Sat. 8:30am-4:30pm). Free one-hour guided tours are available, during which visitors can learn about the building's architecture and symbolic art. Tours are given Monday-Friday 10:30am-3:30pm and Saturday 10:30am-2:30pm.

The other two library buildings on Capitol Hill are the nearby **John Adams Building** (2nd St. SE, between Independence Ave. and E. Capitol St.) and the **James Madison Memorial Building** (Independence Ave. SE, between 1st St. and 2nd St.). The latter is home to the **Mary Pickford Theater,** which is the "motion picture and television reading room" of the library.

The library primarily exists as a research tool for answering inquiries from members of Congress through the Congressional Research Service. The library is open to the public, but only library employees, members of Congress, and other top-level government officials can actually check books out.

U.S. Botanic Garden

A lovely contrast to memorials, office buildings, and monuments, the **U.S. Botanic Garden** (100 Maryland Ave. SW, 202/225-8333, www.usbg.gov, daily 10am-5pm, free) is the oldest continuously operating garden of its type in the country. Just southwest of the Capitol, this national greenhouse opened in 1850 and has been in its current location since 1933. Major attractions at the garden include a rose garden, butterfly garden, the First Ladies' Water Garden, the Lawn Terrace, and an outdoor amphitheater. The garden houses nearly 10,000 living specimens; the oldest are more than 165 years old.

Smithsonian National Postal Museum

A lesser-known Smithsonian Institution museum is the **National Postal Museum** (2 Massachusetts Ave. NE, 202/633-5555, www.postalmuseum.si.edu, daily 10am-5:30pm, free). Located near Union Station,

the museum contains exhibits of stamps and philatelic items, mail-delivery vehicles, and historical artifacts from America's postal system.

DOWNTOWN
National Archives

Only in Washington DC can you see the original Declaration of Independence, the Constitution, and the Bill of Rights. These powerful documents live in the Rotunda for the Charters of Freedom at the **National Archives Building** (700 Pennsylvania Ave. NW, visitors' entrance on Constitution Ave. between 7th St. and 9th St. NW, 866/272-6272, www.archives.gov, daily 10am-5:30pm, extended summer hours, free). They can be viewed by the public daily, but are then lowered into the vault for safekeeping after hours.

Also known as Archives I, the National Archives Building is the headquarters for the National Archives and Records Administration, an independent agency of the U.S. government that is responsible for preserving historical records. Countless additional documents are on permanent exhibit in the public vaults, including treaties, photographs, telegrams, maps, and films. Interactive exhibits allow visitors to get close to some of the most interesting documents.

Reynolds Center

The revitalized Penn Quarter area of downtown gets more and more hip each year as space is renovated and new attractions move in. A prime example is the Smithsonian's **Reynolds Center** (8th St. and F St. NW, 202/633-1000, www.americanart.si.edu, daily 11:30am-7pm, free), which covers an entire block in the Chinatown neighborhood in what was one of the first patent office buildings. The Reynolds Center is officially named the **Donald W. Reynolds Center for American Art and Portraiture,** and it consists of two Smithsonian museums, the **Smithsonian American Art Museum** and the **National Portrait Gallery.** The massive Greek Revival building dates back to 1836 and originally

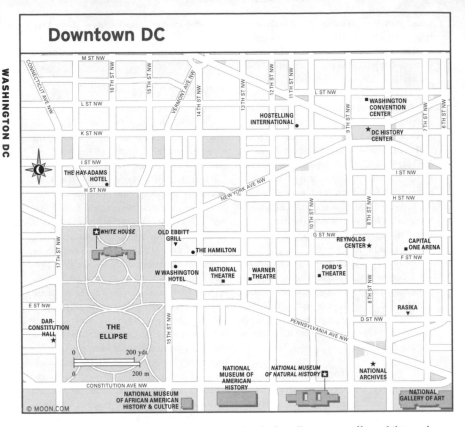

Downtown DC

took 31 years to construct. The Smithsonian American Art Museum features a wide variety of American art and houses works by significant artists such Georgia O'Keeffe, Albert Bierstadt, and Nam June Paik. The National Portrait Gallery contains images of many famous Americans. The museums are above the Gallery Place-Chinatown Metrorail station on the Red, Yellow, and Green Lines.

National Building Museum

If architecture, building, and design intrigue you, the **National Building Museum** (401 F St. NW, 202/272-2448, www.nbm.org, Mon.-Sat. 10am-5pm, Sun. 11am-5pm, adults $16, youth 3-17/students/seniors 60 and over $13) is a must-see. As the country's leading cultural institution committed to interpreting the impact and history of the built environment, this

family-friendly museum offers exhibits, public programs, and festivals. The museum itself is a spectacular building with an impressive Great Hall that contains 75-foot Corinthian columns and a 1,200-foot terra-cotta frieze. Exhibits include *House & Home,* which provides a tour of familiar and surprising homes, and *Play Work Build,* an exploration exhibit that allows children and adults to fill an exhibition wall with virtual blocks and then knock them down.

DC History Center

The **DC History Center** (801 K St. NW, 202/516-1363, www.dchistory.org, Tues.-Sat. 10am-5pm, Sun. noon-5pm, free), located in the Carnegie Library on Mount Vernon Square, opened in 2019 and features exhibits on the history of Washington DC. It is run

Dupont Circle

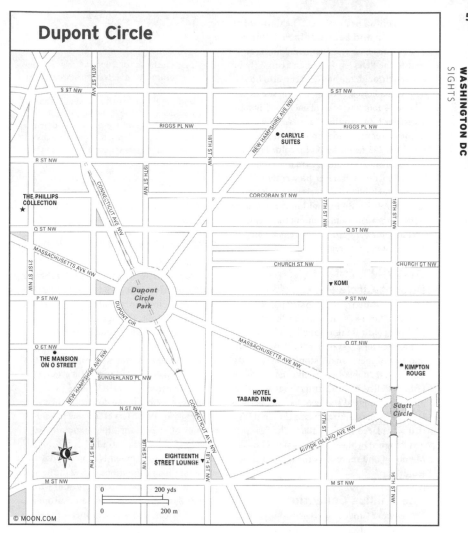

© MOON.COM

by the Historical Society of Washington, D.C. and includes three exhibit areas, the Kiplinger Research Library, and the DC History Center Store. The city's flagship Apple store is also in the building.

Ford's Theatre

Still a thriving theatrical venue, the famous **Ford's Theatre** (511 10th St. NW, 202/347-4833, www.fords.org, daily 9am-4:30pm, $3) is the site where President Lincoln was

assassinated on April 14, 1865. It is also a historical site with a museum focusing on Abraham Lincoln's presidency, assassination, and legacy. Artifacts featured in the museum include the contents of Lincoln's pockets on the day he died, the single-shot .44-caliber derringer that John Wilkes Booth used to kill Lincoln, and two life masks. The **Petersen House** (516 10th St, NW, 202/347-4833, daily 9:30am-5:30pm), where Lincoln died, is located across the street and can also be visited with a Ford's Theatre ticket. The **Center for Education and Leadership** (514 10th St., 202/347-4833, daily 9:30am-5:30pm) is adjacent to the Petersen House and can only be entered through the house. It can also be visited with a Ford's Theatre historic site ticket. It has a 34-foot tower full of books on Lincoln, accessible by a winding staircase. The books in the tower are made from aluminum and represent 205 real titles on Lincoln. This unusual work of art symbolizes that the last word about Lincoln will never be written. There are also exhibits that teach about the hunt for John Wilkes Booth and Lincoln's funeral train. A theatrical audio tour of the theater is available for $5. Ford's Theatre is located in the Penn Quarter area.

DUPONT CIRCLE
Dupont Circle Park
Maintained by the National Park Service, **Dupont Circle Park** has been the location of many political rallies, and it is also a gathering place for chess players to challenge one another on permanent stone chessboards. The central double-tiered white marble fountain, installed in 1920, offers seating; it replaced a memorial statue of Samuel Francis Du Pont, a rear admiral during the Civil War, that was placed there in 1884. The fountain was designed by the cocreators of the Lincoln Memorial and represents the sea, stars, and wind.

The Phillips Collection
The Dupont Circle neighborhood is home to the original late 19th-century Renoir painting *Luncheon of the Boating Party*. It lives at **The Phillips Collection** (1600 21st St. NW, 202/387-2151, www.phillipscollection.org, Tues.-Sat. 10am-5pm, Sun. noon-6:30pm, adults $12, 18 and under free, students/seniors 62 and over $10), an intimate impressionist and modern art museum founded in 1921 by Duncan Phillips. The museum includes the founder's former home and extensive new galleries. Other featured works (there are more than 3,000) include pieces by Vincent van

I Got You Babe

Just southwest of Dupont Circle on New Hampshire Avenue is a small, triangular wedge of land that memorializes pop star and politician **Sonny Bono.** Officially called Sonny Bono Park, the patch of grass has benches and a plaque (that draws a striking resemblance to a manhole cover) honoring the late statesman, who died in a ski accident in 1998.

Gogh, Claude Monet, Pablo Picasso, Georgia O'Keeffe, and Winslow Homer.

GEORGETOWN
Dumbarton Oaks
The **Dumbarton Oaks Research Library and Collection** (1703 32nd St. NW, 202/339-6400, www.doaks.org, museum Tues.-Sun. 11:30am-5:30pm, free, gardens Tues.-Sun. Nov. 1-Mar. 14 2pm-5pm, free, Mar. 15-Oct. 31 2pm-6pm, adults $10, children 2-12 $5, seniors 60 and over and military $8) is a gorgeous, historic, and romantic estate museum and garden. It was a private estate for many years before being donated to Harvard University in 1940. The estate was the site of a series of important diplomatic meetings in 1944 that laid the foundation for the development of the United Nations. Today the museum offers exhibitions of Byzantine and pre-Columbian art (including more than 12,000 Byzantine coins); Asian, European, and American art; and European furnishings. The 10-acre park boasts a fine example of a European-style formal garden, with more than 1,000 rosebushes, an herb garden, and stone fountains.

Georgetown University
Georgetown is anchored by the 104-acre campus of **Georgetown University** (37th St. and

1: Ford's Theatre 2: people relaxing around the Dupont Circle fountain 3: shops along M Street in Georgetown

Georgetown

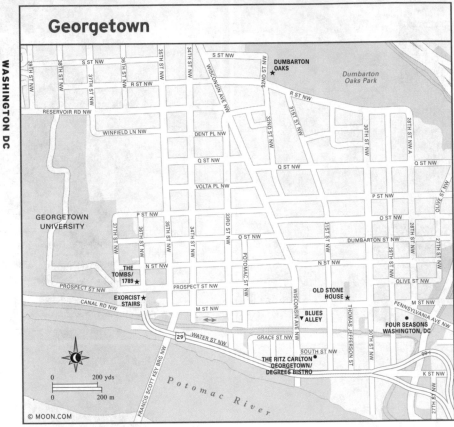

O St. NW, 202/687-0100, www.georgetown. edu). Noted for its law school in particular, this private research university offers nine graduate and undergraduate schools with a total enrollment of around 17,000 students. Georgetown was established in 1789 and is the oldest Catholic and Jesuit university in the country. Notable alumni include President Bill Clinton, actor Bradley Cooper, and the late U.S. Supreme Court justice Antonin Scalia.

Old Stone House

The oldest standing building in DC, and also the city's last pre-Revolutionary colonial building still on its original foundation, was built in 1765 and is simply called the **Old Stone House** (3051 M St. NW, 202/426-6851, www.nps.gov, Wed.-Sun. noon-5pm, free). This excellent example of vernacular architecture was constructed in three phases and served many purposes throughout the years including being a hat shop, tailor's shop, locksmith shop, and even a used-car dealership. The house was renovated in the 1950s and turned into a museum by the National Park Service. Today, visitors can learn the history of the house from park rangers and view the home's kitchen, bedrooms, and parlor, all authentically furnished to reflect the daily lives of average Americans in the 18th century. The Old Stone House is said to be haunted by countless spirits.

Adams Morgan and Upper Northwest

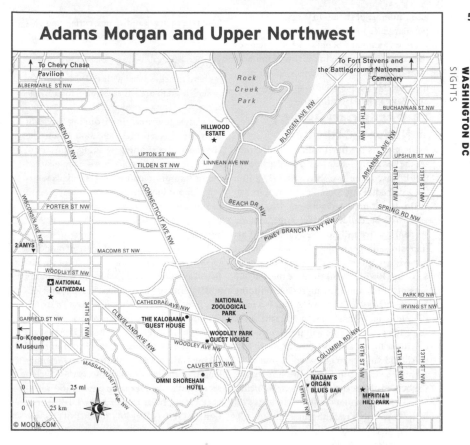

To Chevy Chase Pavilion

ALBERMARLE ST NW

Rock Creek Park

To Fort Stevens and the Battleground National Cemetery

BUCHANNAN ST NW

BLADGEN AVE NW

18TH ST NW

14TH ST NW

HILLWOOD ESTATE ★

RENO RD NW

UPTON ST NW

TILDEN ST NW

LINNEAN AVE NW

ARKANSAS AVE NW

UPSHUR ST NW

13TH ST NW

CONNECTICUT AVE NW

BEACH DR NW

WISCONSIN AVE NW

PORTER ST NW

SPRING RD NW

PINEY BRANCH PKWY NW

2 AMYS ▼

MACOMB ST NW

WOODLEY ST NW

✚ NATIONAL CATHEDRAL ★

34TH ST NW

CATHEDRAL AVE NW

NATIONAL ZOOLOGICAL PARK ★

PARK RD NW

IRVING ST NW

GARFIELD ST NW

CLEVELAND AVE NW

THE KALORAMA ● GUEST HOUSE

To Kreeger Museum

WOODLEY AVE NW

WOODLEY PARK ● GUEST HOUSE

COLUMBIA RD NW

16TH ST NW

14TH ST NW

13TH ST NW

MASSACHUSETTS AVE NW

CALVERT ST NW

OMNI SHOREHAM HOTEL ●

MADAM'S ♪ ORGAN BLUES BAR

15TH ST NW

MERIDIAN HILL PARK ★

0   25 mi

0   25 km

© MOON.COM

Exorcist Stairs

One of the most notable movie scenes filmed in Georgetown was the climactic scene in *The Exorcist,* where the priest hurls himself out the window of a house and down a steep staircase to his death to rid himself of the devil. The famed staircase is still part of the Georgetown landscape and has 75 steps that connect Prospect Street with M Street. There are three landings on the staircase, and the entire length of the stairs is equal to the height of a five-story building. For filming purposes, a fake front was constructed on the house located at the top of the steps to make it appear that the bedroom in the movie overlooked the staircase. In real life, the home is set back a healthy distance from the top of the stairs. It

is not uncommon to see Georgetown students running the stairs. Hoya athletes are known to run it 10 or more times. The steps are located at the end of 36th Street.

ADAMS MORGAN
Meridian Hill Park

Meridian Hill Park (15th, 16th, W, and Euclid Sts. NW, free) is a 12-acre urban park maintained by the National Park Service. It is near Adams Morgan in the Columbia Heights neighborhood. The park was built in the early 1900s and sits on a hillside. It is well landscaped and includes dramatic staircases, benches, and concrete walkways. The focal point of the park is a 13-basin cascading waterfall fountain in a formal garden. There are also a number of statues in the park. This is a popular place to steal some relaxation in the summer, and many people take advantage of this secret little garden in the city. Drummers form circles on Sunday afternoons in the summertime, but people come to spread a blanket and play catch nearly all year.

UPPER NORTHWEST
★ National Cathedral

Many visitors are filled with awe when they see the beautiful Gothic **National Cathedral** (3101 Wisconsin Ave. NW, 202/537-6200, www.cathedral.org, Mon.-Fri. 10am-5pm, Sat. 10am-4pm, Sun. 12:45pm-4pm, adults $12, youth 5-17 $8, children under 5 free, seniors/students/active military/veterans $8). This imposing edifice, which is the sixth-largest cathedral in the world, is hard to miss. It took 83 years (1907 to 1990) to carve the 150,000 tons of stone, and this impressive building has a few tricks up its sleeve. A tour is a must (they offer more than a dozen different ones), since the great docents will provide you access to the towers and crypt, which are off limits should you try to go there on your own. Although the regular tours are impressive, the behind-the-scenes tour (adults $27, children 11 and up/seniors/military/students $23) is the best. You'll walk through hidden hallways, get a close look at the stunning stained glass windows, and learn the cathedral's secrets (like how Darth Vader lives high on the northwest tower in the form of a grotesque that was sculpted after a public competition was held to suggest designs for grotesques and gargoyles). You'll also get a grand view from the cathedral's roof. Be ready for stair climbing, heights, and close quarters. Participants must be at least 11 years old. Reservations can be made online.

Organ demonstrations are given on most Mondays and Wednesdays at 12:30pm. They are impressive and loud. Regular Episcopal worship services are held at the cathedral; a schedule is posted on the website. A café (Mon.-Fri. 7am-6pm, Sat.-Sun. 8am-6pm) is located in the Old Baptistry building next to the cathedral, where the public can purchase light fare such as sandwiches, coffee, and pastries. Parking is available under the cathedral.

Rock Creek Park

It's hard to believe that with all DC has to offer in such a small area, there's room for a 1,754-acre park. **Rock Creek Park** (202/895-6000, www.nps.gov/rocr, open during daylight hours, free) is a prime recreation area in the city that offers running, walking, equestrian, and cycling trails, a golf course, a professional tennis stadium, a nature center and planetarium, an outdoor concert venue, playground facilities, wildlife, and cultural exhibits. The park is administered by the National Park Service.

Visitors can enjoy a real sense of outdoors in this urban park, which consists of woods, fields, and creeks and is home to wildflowers and wildlife such as coyotes, beavers, and fox. The park borders Upper Northwest DC to the east and has long stretches of roads (including Rock Creek Pkwy. and Beach Dr.) that are closed to cars on weekends. Fifteen miles of hiking trails, a bike path that runs the entire length of the park and connects the Lincoln Memorial to the Maryland border, and horseback riding from **Rock Creek Park Horse Center** (5100 Glover Rd., 202/362-0117, www.rockcreekhorsecenter.com, lessons starting $55 per hour, one-hour trail rides $45) are just some of the activities available to visitors. The park's **Nature Center** (5200 Glover Rd., 202/895-6070, Wed.-Sun. 9am-5pm) is a good place to start your exploration. Another attraction is the **Peirce Mill** (2401 Tilden St. NW, at Beach Dr., 202/895-6070, Apr.-Oct. Fri.-Sun. 10am-4pm, Nov.-Feb. Sat.-Sun. noon-4pm, Mar. Sat.-Sun. 10am-4pm, free). It is the only existing water-powered gristmill in DC.

The park is relatively safe for a city park, but it is still advisable to enjoy it with a friend. Leashed dogs are allowed in the park. It is good to keep in mind that on weekdays

---

1: National Cathedral 2: the 22 Corinthian sandstone columns in the National Arboretum

Rock Creek Parkway is one-way going south 6:45am-9:30am and one-way going north 3:45pm-6:30pm.

National Zoological Park

The Smithsonian's **National Zoological Park** (3001 Connecticut Ave. NW, 202/633-4888, www.nationalzoo.si.edu, daily Oct. 1-Mar. 14, grounds 8am-5pm, visitor center and exhibit buildings 9am-4pm, daily Mar. 15-Sept. 30, grounds 8am-7pm, visitor center and exhibit buildings 9am-6pm, free), commonly called the National Zoo, is one of the oldest zoos in the country. The 163-acre park is near the Woodley Park Metrorail station on the edge of Rock Creek Park. The zoo, founded in 1889, is constantly undergoing updates and renovations. Hundreds of animals are tucked into habitats along hillsides, in the woods, and in specially built temperature-controlled animal houses. Since entrance to the park is free, many local residents use the several miles of nicely paved pathways on their regular walking or running routes.

Well-known residents include giant pandas from China, great apes, elephants, Komodo dragons, and much more. Many of the species at the zoo are endangered. Unique exhibits include the Elephant Walk, where Asian elephants can take daily treks for exercise, and a skywalk for orangutans, where a series of high cables and towers allow them to move between two buildings and over spectators below. Another favorite is the American Trail, which features sea lions, wolves, eagles, and other animals native to North America. The zoo also features a Think Tank, where visitors can learn how animals think through a series of interactive displays that are available to the zoo's orangutans at their leisure. The best time to visit the zoo is on weekday mornings when there are fewer crowds and the animals are more active. Although it is free to enter the zoo, there is a parking fee of $25.

Hillwood Estate, Museum & Gardens

Those in the know are fans of the wonderful

Hillwood Estate, Museum & Gardens

(4155 Linnean Ave. NW, 202/686-5807, www. hillwoodmuseum.org, Tues.-Sun. 10am-5pm, suggested donation adults $18, college students $10, children 6-18 $5, seniors $15, children under 6 free), the former home of prominent businesswoman, philanthropist, and heiress to the Post Cereal fortune Marjorie Merriweather Post. This stately and luxurious home with a Georgian-style facade was purchased by Post in 1955 and used for entertaining and to house her abundant collections of French and Russian art, including an extraordinary collection of Fabergé eggs. The artwork is rivaled by the exquisite French- and Japanese-style gardens, where visitors can relax after taking a tour. One-hour guided tours and self-guided tours are available with the suggested donation. A café and gift shop are on-site.

Kreeger Museum

The **Kreeger Museum** (2401 Foxhall Rd. NW, 202/337-3050, www.kreegermuseum. org, Tues.-Sat. 10am-4pm, suggested donation adults $10, students/seniors/military $8) is a private museum that often passes under the radar of tourists due to its Foxhall neighborhood location and small size. This little gem of an attraction features 19th- and 20th-century sculptures and paintings by many world-renowned artists such as Monet, Picasso, Rodin, and van Gogh. It also offers works by local artists and traditional African art. The building is the former home of David and Carmen Kreeger and sits on more than five acres of sculpture gardens and woods.

Battleground National Cemetery

One of the smallest national cemeteries in the nation is the **Battleground National Cemetery** (6625 Georgia Ave., 202/895-6000, www.nps.gov, daily dawn-dusk, free). It is the burial ground for 41 Union soldiers who died in the 1864 Battle of Fort Stevens, the sole Civil War battle to take place in DC. The engagement marked the end of a Confederate effort to act offensively against the national capital. The battle is the only one in Civil War history during which the U.S. president (Abraham Lincoln) came under direct fire. Lincoln rode out to observe the fight and was fired on briefly by sharpshooters (he was then ordered to take cover). After the battle, a one-acre plot of farmland was seized and used to bury the dead. That night, Lincoln came to the site and dedicated it as a national cemetery. Visitors can see grave markers, four monuments to the units that fought in the battle, and a marble rostrum that has eight Doric columns. The rostrum is the site of the annual Memorial Day services at the cemetery. The National Park Service manages the cemetery.

Nearby **Fort Stevens** (1339 Fort Stevens Dr., www.nps.gov, daily dawn-dusk, free), the actual site of the battle, is partially restored and is also maintained by the National Park Service. It was part of a series of fortifications constructed around Washington DC during the Civil War. Visitors can see much of the fort still intact, including the cannons (now facing urban streets). You can even stand on the spot where then future Supreme Court justice Oliver Wendell Holmes is said to have shouted at President Lincoln, "Get down, you fool!" when he was shot at.

NORTHEAST DC
National Arboretum

Northeast of Capitol Hill (2.2 miles from the Capitol Building) is a little-recognized attraction that first opened in 1927: the **National Arboretum** (3501 New York Ave. NE, 202/245-2726, www.usna.usda.gov, daily 8am-5pm, free). This lovely 446-acre campus has more than nine miles of roads that connect many gardens and plant collections where there is always something in bloom. Seventy-six staff members and more than 140 volunteers oversee the arboretum, which was created to "serve the public need for scientific research, education, and gardens that conserve and showcase plants to enhance the environment." Parking areas are available near many of the major collections, and bike racks

are also on hand. The original 22 columns from the east side of the Capitol Building found a home here when the Capitol was enlarged in the 1950s; they now sit on display in a field. The **National Bonsai & Penjing Museum** (daily 10am-4pm, free) is also located on the arboretum grounds, as is a gift shop. Leashed pets are welcome, and there are public restrooms in the administrative building.

TOURS

A great way to see the city is to take an organized tour. There is a wide variety to choose from, including trolley tours, boat tours, and walking tours.

Trolley, Bus, and Boat Tours

One of the most popular motorized tours in the city is given by **Old Town Trolley** (844/356-2603, www.trolleytours.com, daily 9am-5pm, $45). This lively narrated tour covers more than 100 points of interest and offers a "hop on-hop off" format where guests can get off at 17 stops and pick up another trolley (which stops at each location every 30 minutes) at their leisure. Sights include the Lincoln Memorial, the White House, Smithsonian Institution museums, and many more. No reservations are required, and visitors can board and reboard all day. Tickets can be purchased online or at the sales desk in **Union Station** (50 Massachusetts Ave. NE, stop #4) and at the **Washington Welcome Center** (1005 E St. NW, stop #1).

Old Town Trolley also offers a 2.5-hour **Monuments by Moonlight** tour ($40.50) that allows visitors to see the illuminated monuments and memorials. Stops include the FDR Memorial, Iwo Jima Memorial (in Arlington, Virginia), the Lincoln Memorial, and Vietnam Veterans Memorial. This narrated tour includes some fun ghost stories as well. The tour leaves nightly from Union Station.

Another popular tour is the **DC Ducks Tour** (855/969-0828, www.dcducks.com, adults $45, children 12 and under $33).

Guests explore the city on both land and water in a "Duck," a unique vehicle that is part bus, part boat. Ninety-minute trips start at Union Station (50 Massachusetts Ave. NE), drive to the National Mall, and end with a cruise along the Potomac River. The tours are narrated by "wise-quacking" captains who offer a wealth of historical facts and corny jokes.

Another "hop on-hop off" tour is the **Open Top Big Bus Tour** (877/332-8689, www.bigbustours.com, daily 9am-5pm, one-day pass adults $50, children 5-15 $40, 2-day pass adults $60, children 5-15 $50). Guests can take in two routes around the city from a double-decker bus with an open-air top deck. Tickets can be purchased online and on any of their buses.

For a view from the water, sign up for a cruise with **Potomac Riverboat Company** (703/684-0580, www.potomacriverboatco.com). They offer several sightseeing tours leaving from different locations around the region, including their 60-minute "Monument Tour from the Wharf" (950 Wharf St., adults from $20, children from $14).

Walking Tours

Free guided walking tours of DC's monuments are available through **DC by Foot** (202/370-1830, www.freetoursbyfoot.com/dc, free but tips appreciated). These unique tours feature animated, energetic tour guides who work purely on tips. Because of this, they do their best to entertain you while providing unique stories about Washington's most famous residents. Private tours are also available.

Ghost tours are a good way to get in touch with the spirits of the city. Several tour operators offer walking tours around some of the most haunted sites in the city. **Washington Walks** (202/484-1565, www.washingtonwalks.com) offers **Most Haunted Houses** tours (Oct. Fri.-Sat. at 7:30pm, $20). Two-hour walking tours begin at the corner of New York Avenue and 18th Street NW. This is just one of many walking tours they offer throughout the year.

Recreation

SPECTATOR SPORTS

The nation's capital is home to many professional sports teams and hosts countless sporting events throughout the year.

The **Washington Nationals** baseball team, which came to DC in 2005, plays at **Nationals Park** (1500 S. Capitol St. SE, 202/675-6287, www.mlb.com). The stadium sits on the banks of the Anacostia River in the Navy Yard neighborhood and seats approximately 41,500 people. The Washington Monument and Capitol Building can be seen from the upper stands.

The **Capital One Arena** (601 F St. NW, 202/628-3200, www.capitalonearena.com) in Penn Quarter is home to the city's professional hockey team (the NHL's **Washington Capitals**), two pro basketball teams (the NBA's **Washington Wizards** and the WNBA's **Washington Mystics**), and Georgetown University's men's basketball team (the Georgetown Hoyas).

DC's professional soccer team, the **D.C. United,** received a brand-new home in 2018 at **Audi Field** (100 Potomac Ave. SW, www.audifielddc.com), two miles south of the U.S. Capitol. The **Washington Redskins** (www.redskins.com) NFL football team plays at **FedExField** in Landover, Maryland.

Other professional sporting events make their way annually to DC. The **Citi Open** (www.citiopentennis.com) tennis tournament is part of the U.S. Open Series. Professional players from around the globe compete for

1: Josh Gibson statue, designed by sculptor Omri Amrany, outside of Nationals Park 2: paddleboarding on the Potomac River near Key Bridge, Georgetown

Run DC

Runners and triathletes make their way to Washington DC regularly to partake in many annual races. These are just a few of the numerous events scheduled throughout the year.

- **Rock 'n' Roll DC Marathon & Half Marathon** (Mar., www.runrocknroll.com)

- **Credit Union Cherry Blossom Ten Mile Run** (Apr., www.cherryblossom.org)

- **Capitol Hill Classic 10K** (May, www.capitolhillclassic.com)

- **Komen Global Race for the Cure 5K** (Sept., www.info-komen.org)

- **Army 10-Miler** (Oct., www.armytenmiler.com)

- **Marine Corps Marathon** (Oct., www.marinemarathon.com)

more than $1.8 million in this world-class event. The nine-day tournament is held at the tennis center in Rock Creek Park at the end of July and beginning of August.

The **Washington International Horse Show** (www.wihs.org) is a yearly championship event held at Capital One Arena at the end of October. Approximately 600 horses and riders compete for more than $400,000 in prize money and titles. The event includes show jumping, dressage, equitation, hunters, barrel racing, and terrier races.

CANOEING AND KAYAKING

Those interested in paddling a canoe or kayak on the Potomac River are in for a treat. Viewing the city from the calm of the river puts it in a whole new perspective. Rentals are available at several locations, including the **Key Bridge Boathouse** (3500 Water St. NW, 202/337-9642, http://boatingindc.com) and **Thompson Boat Center** (2900 Virginia Ave. NW, 202/333-9543, http://boatingindc. com). Rentals are $16 per hour for a single and $22 per hour for a double kayak. Canoes are $25 per hour.

BIKING

Another great option for getting around the city on two wheels is joining **Capital Bikeshare** (www.capitalbikeshare.com) for a day, three days, a month, or a year.

Members gain access to more than 1,800 bikes in 350 locations throughout the city (including Arlington and Alexandria in Virginia). Twenty-four-hour memberships are $8. Passes can be purchased at kiosks at each bike station.

An 11-mile rail-to-trail route called the **Capital Crescent Trail** starts in Georgetown on K Street. The trail runs parallel to the C&O Canal Towpath for the first three miles but then goes through upscale neighborhoods in Northwest DC. The initial seven miles between Georgetown and Bethesda, Maryland, are paved, but an additional four miles of unpaved trail (mostly crushed stone) can be ridden to Silver Spring, Maryland. The two trails are connected by a tunnel under downtown Bethesda.

Bike Tours

Year-round daily bike tours around Washington DC are offered by **Fat Tire Tours** (502 23rd St. NW, 202/626-0017, www.fattiretours.com, starting at $42). Comfortable beach cruisers are used in the tours, and riders can expect to see sights such as the Lincoln Memorial, White House, Vietnam Veterans Memorial, and the Capitol Building.

Another popular bike tour company is **Bike and Roll Washington DC** (202/842-2453, www.bikeandrolldc.com). They offer seasonal guided tours by bike (three hours, adults $44, children 12 and under $34) and Segway (2.5 hours, $64) from their National Mall location (955 L'Enfant Plaza SW) and year-round tours from their Union Station location (50 Massachusetts Ave. NE, 202/962-0206).

ICE-SKATING

A great way to impress a date on a cold winter night is by going ice-skating at the **National Gallery of Art Sculpture Garden and Ice Skating Rink** (700 Constitution Ave. NW, 202/216-9397). Skate in the shadows of some of the city's most well-known buildings and in view of many of the garden's wonderful sculptures. This enchanting rink is especially romantic at night.

PLAYGROUND

For the coolest playground in town, visit **Turtle Park** (Friendship Park, 4500 Van Ness St. NW, 202/282-2198) in Upper Northwest. The focal point is a huge sandbox with turtle sculptures for climbing on and a "sprayground" for cleaning off the sand and cooling off. There are also ball fields in the park and a recreation center.

Entertainment and Events

THEATER

The premier theater in Washington DC is the **John F. Kennedy Center for the Performing Arts** (2700 F St. NW, 202/467-4600, www.kennedy-center.org). This incredible venue is a landmark on the banks of the Potomac River and first opened in 1971. It hosts more annual performances than any other facility in the country, with approximately 2,000 theater, dance, musical, and multimedia performances each year. There are three primary theaters within the center. The **Concert Hall** seats approximately 2,400 guests and is the largest performance space in the center. It features seven Hadeland crystal chandeliers (courtesy of Norway) and a 4,144-pipe organ (a gift from the Filene Foundation of Boston). The Concert Hall is also home to the **National Symphony Orchestra.** The **Opera House,** with its unique red and gold silk curtain (a gift from Japan), seats approximately 2,300 guests and features a Lobmeyr crystal chandelier (courtesy of Austria). It is the primary venue for opera, ballet, and large-scale musical performances and home to the **Washington National Opera,** the **Suzanne Farrell Ballet,** and the yearly **Kennedy Center Honors.** The **Eisenhower Theater** seats approximately 1,163 guests and hosts smaller-scale operas, plays, and musicals. In addition, **The REACH** was unveiled in 2019 as an open-stage living theater and immersive learning center. It complements the Kennedy Center's mission and vision of an inclusive, interactive, and accessible modern arts center.

The historic **National Theatre** (1321 Pennsylvania Ave. NW, 202/628-6161, www.thenationaldc.com) playhouse is the oldest theater venue in DC. It is three blocks from the White House and has entertained many presidents since its founding in 1835. In fact, Abraham Lincoln's son Tad was attending a production of *Aladdin and the Wonderful Lamp* at the National Theatre at the time his father was assassinated in Ford's Theatre. Today the theater is known for hosting mostly Broadway musicals.

Originally built as a movie palace in 1924, the **Warner Theatre** (513 13th St. NW, 202/783-4000, www.warnertheatredc.com) was then called the Earle Theatre and hosted live vaudeville and silent movies. During the 1940s the theater showed movies exclusively and was renamed for its owner, Harry Warner of Warner Bros. fame. The theater suffered in the 1970s, but was revived shortly after as a concert venue. After major renovations between 1989 and 1992, the theater reopened with theatrical, dance, and musical productions and has since hosted great performers such as Frank Sinatra. It is a landmark in the Penn Quarter neighborhood.

Nearby, **Ford's Theatre** (511 10th St. NW, 202/347-4833, www.fords.org) is most famous as the location of the assassination of President Lincoln in 1865. Following his death, the theater closed. After a long stint as a warehouse and an office building, it finally reopened more than 100 years later in 1968 and again began to host performances. Today it is an active venue with a full schedule of plays and musicals.

A well-known regional theater company in DC is the **Shakespeare Theatre Company** (202/547-1122, www.shakespearetheatre.org). This highly regarded company presents primarily Shakespearean productions but also offers works by other classic playwrights. The company manages the **Harman Center for the Arts,** which consists of two venues in Penn Quarter: the **Landsburgh Theatre** (450 7th St. NW) and **Sidney Harman Hall** (610 F St. NW).

For more-experimental, cutting-edge performances, catch a production by the **Woolly Mammoth Theatre Company** (641 D St. NW, 202/393-3939, www.woollymammoth. net). They develop and produce new plays and pride themselves on being "Washington's most daring theatre company."

In Southwest DC, **Arena Stage at the Mead Center for American Theater** (1101 6th St. SW, 202/488-3300, www.arenastage. org) takes the title of being the largest not-for-profit theater in the city. It features a broad range of performances, including the classics and new-play premiers as well as educational programs.

A unique performance venue is the **Carter Barron Amphitheatre** (4850 Colorado Ave. NW, 202/426-0486, www.nps. gov/rocr) in Rock Creek Park. The beautiful, 4,200-seat outdoor amphitheater is operated by the National Park Service and offers a range of performances including concerts, theater, and dance. Many are provided at no charge.

The historic **AMC Uptown 1** (3426 Connecticut Ave. NW, www.amctheatres. com) is a single-screen movie theater in the Cleveland Park neighborhood run by AMC Theatres. The theater first opened in 1936 and has been the site for many Hollywood movie premieres. The curved, 70-foot-long and 40-foot-high screen is considered to be the best in the DC area, and the theater can seat 850 people.

ARENAS AND HALLS

There are several large performance arenas in the city. **Capital One Arena** (601 F St. NW, 202/628-3200, www.capitalonearena. com) was formerly the Verizon Center and anchors the Penn Quarter neighborhood. It is home to several professional sports teams (Washington Capitals, Washington Wizards, and Washington Mystics) but also hosts numerous concerts and other large-scale performances. **Audi Field** (100 Potomac Ave. SW, www.audifielddc.com) opened in 2018 as the home field for the D.C. United professional soccer team. This state-of-the-art arena is located southeast of the District Wharf. **Robert F. Kennedy Memorial Stadium (RFK)** (2400 E. Capitol St. SE, 202/587-5000, www.eventsdc.com) is the former home of the Washington Redskins and now hosts concerts, conventions, and other events.

Historic **DAR Constitution Hall** (1776 D St. NW, 202/628-1776, www.dar.org), near the White House, was built in 1929 by the Daughters of the American Revolution as a venue for their annual convention. This 3,200-seat hall, which formerly only hosted classical shows and opera, is now a concert venue for rock, pop, hip-hop, and soul.

The 2.3 million-square-foot **Walter E. Washington Convention Center** (801 Mt. Vernon Pl, NW, 202/249-3000, www. dcconvention.com) offers 703,000 square feet of event space, 77 meeting rooms, and the largest ballroom in the city. It hosts countless events throughout the year in the downtown area.

U Street Corridor

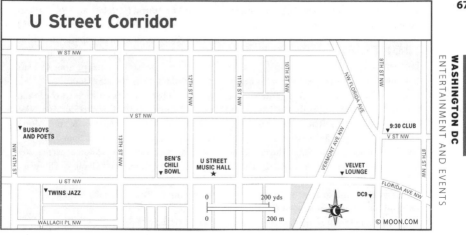

MUSIC VENUES

The most recent addition to the DC music scene is **The Anthem** (901 Wharf St. SW, 202/888-0020, www.theathemdc.com), on the District Wharf. This gorgeous, 6,000-seat concert venue hosts well-known rockers, hip-hop artists, and other stars in its acoustically optimized environment. Food and drinks are available in the arena (no cash), and shows sell out early. Recent shows include The Raconteurs, Jenny Lewis, and Tame Impala. A much more intimate music space (150 seats) and also on the Wharf is **Pearl Street Warehouse** (33 Pearl St. SW, 202/380-9620, www.pearlstreetwarehouse.com). They feature everything from rock to bluegrass music.

The **U Street Corridor** can be called the center of the music scene in Washington DC. Once the haunt of legends such as Duke Ellington, the area carries on his legacy through venues such as **Twins Jazz** (1344 U St. NW, top floor, 202/234-0072, www.twinsjazz.com), which offers live jazz five to six nights a week. This unassuming club with red interior walls looks like someone's home on the outside. It also features Ethiopian, Caribbean, and American food.

The **U Street Music Hall** (1115 U St. NW, 202/588-1889, www.ustreetmusichall.com) is a live-music and DJ dance club. It features a cork-cushioned, 1,200-square-foot dance floor.

For a broader range of music options, the popular **9:30 Club** (815 V St. NW, 202/265-0930, www.930.com) hosts everyone from Echo and the Bunnymen to Corey Smith. This unassuming venue is on the corner of 9th and V Streets. Shows are general admission and standing room only. They have four full bars and a coffee bar and also serve food.

The **Black Cat** (1811 14th St. NW, 202/667-4490, www.blackcatdc.com) hosts a variety of local, national, and international independent and alternative bands. They offer two stages and are a cash-only establishment.

Two small venues that highlight primarily local bands are the **Velvet Lounge** (915 U St. NW, 202/462-3213, www.velvetloungedc.com) and **DC9** (1940 9th St. NW, 202/483-5000, www.dc9.club).

Other areas of the city host great musical artists as well. An intimate venue for hearing live jazz is **Blues Alley** (1073 Wisconsin Ave. NW, 202/337-4141, www.bluesalley.com) in Georgetown. This local landmark consistently delivers quality jazz and a fun atmosphere. They serve food, but the main attraction is the music.

Two blocks from the White House, **The Hamilton** (600 14th St. NW, 202/787-1000, www.thehamiltondc.com) hosts visionary musical performers in an intimate setting.

NIGHTLIFE
Downtown

For the chance to rub elbows with celebrities, professional athletes, and young, hip Washingtonians, grab a drink at the downtown **P.O.V. Roof Terrace and Lounge** (515 15th St. NW, 202/661-2437, www.povrooftop.com, Sun.-Thurs. 11am-midnight, Fri.-Sat. 11am-2am) at the W Washington D.C. Hotel. This rooftop bar and terrace is one of the top hot spots in DC and has phenomenal views of the city through 12-foot-tall windows. They serve premium-brand liquor and a tapas menu. No sneakers or athletic wear is permitted; collared shirts are preferred. Expect a wait to get in on weekends.

Perfect martinis and a more relaxed atmosphere can be found across from the White House at the **Off the Record Bar** (800 16th St. NW, 202/638-6600, www.hayadams.com, Sun.-Thurs. 11:30am-midnight, Fri.-Sat. 11:30am-12:30am) at the Hay-Adams hotel.

Just a little west of downtown and a little south of Dupont Circle on M Street is **Ozio Restaurant and Lounge** (1813 M St. NW, 202/822-6000, www.oziodc.com, Tues.-Thurs. 5pm-2am, Fri. 5pm-3am, Sat. 6pm-3am, Sun. noon-2am). This huge, multilevel club is somewhat upscale and often has a business crowd. They have great martinis, cigars, and a lively rooftop lounge.

Dupont Circle

One of the most exclusive nightlife spots in the city is the **Eighteenth Street Lounge** (1212 18th St. NW, 202/466-3922, www.18thstlounge.com, Tues.-Thurs. 5pm-2am, Fri. 5pm-3am, Sat. 9pm-3am, Sun. 9pm-2am), in the former home of Teddy Roosevelt. This restored row house mansion is classy, and you must be dressed appropriately to enter. There are high ceilings, a dance floor, retro decor, and multiple rooms, each with its own theme and bar.

The **Bar Rouge** (1315 16th St. NW, 202/232-8000, www.rougehotel.com, daily 5pm-10pm) in the Kimpton Rouge is a popular choice for happy hour and evening cocktails. This sleek, modern lounge has good happy hour specials on weekdays. They also serve food.

A lively Latin American scene can be found at **Café Citron** (1343 Connecticut Ave. NW, 202/530-8844, www.cafecitrondc.com, Mon.-Tues. 7pm-2am, Wed.-Thurs. 5pm-2am, Fri.-Sat. 5pm-3am), a two-level lounge that features salsa and other international music. This place can get rowdy on weekends, and they are known for having outstanding mojitos.

Georgetown

A sophisticated place to grab a drink at pretty much any time is the **Degrees Bistro** (3100 S St. NW, 202/912-4100, www.ritzcarlton.com, daily 5pm-midnight), in the Ritz-Carlton Georgetown. This relaxing lounge brings a bit of New York City to the nation's capital with its chic decor, dependable drinks, and great potential for people watching.

A Georgetown favorite since 1962, **The Tombs** (1226 36th St. NW, 202/337-6668, www.tombs.com, Mon.-Thurs. 11:30am-1:30am, Fri. 11:30am-2:30am, Sat. 11am-2:30am, Sun. 9:30am-1:30am) is a casual bar and local hangout for students at Georgetown University. This place served as the inspiration for the setting of *St. Elmo's Fire.* Owned by the Clyde's family of restaurants, it is located in the basement of upscale restaurant 1789. If you're in the mood for good burgers, beer, and a college crowd, or if you're just a fan of *St. Elmo's Fire,* this is the place for you.

If you're looking for live music and an inviting bar scene, check out **Gypsy Sally's** (3401 K St. NW, 202/333-7700, www.gypsysallys.com, Vinyl Lounge Tues. 6pm-midnight, Wed.-Sat. 6pm-2am, Sun.-Mon. if there is a show in the Music Room; Music Room open on show nights only). Not quite your typical nightlife spot, it's located in a renovated old building below the Whitehurst Freeway where K Street gives way to a recreation trail. Folk bands draw a casual,

Best Rooftop Bars

There may be no better way to soak up the vibe of the city than by grabbing a cool drink on a summer evening at a rooftop bar. Following are some of the most popular DC bars and lounges with a bird's-eye view:

- The **DNV Rooftop Bar** (1155 14th St. NW, 202/379-4366, www.viceroyhotelsandresorts.com) is in The Donovan hotel in Thomas Circle at the intersection of Massachusetts Avenue, Vermont Avenue, 14th Street, and M Street NW. This lively poolside lounge offers chaise lounges, a full-service bar, small plates, brunch, panoramic views, and great martinis.

- For stunning views of the Potomac River and the District Wharf, stop in **Whiskey Charlie** (975 7th St. SW, 202/488-2500, www.whiskeycharliewharf.com). This trendy rooftop bar sits atop the Canopy by Hilton Washington, DC hotel. They offer full bar service and food.

- Take in views of Embassy Row and the Dupont Circle neighborhood from the **Sky Bar** at the **Beacon Bar and Grill** (1615 Rhode Island Ave. NW, 202/872-1126, www.bbgwdc.com). They offer full bar service and light fare.

- A lively rooftop bar located in a Mexican restaurant in the U Street Corridor is **El Centro D.F.** (1819 14th St. NW, 202/328-3131, www.eatelcentro.com). Their two-level rooftop has two bars and 200 types of tequila.

- Another U Street neighborhood favorite is **Marvin** (2007 14th St. NW, 202/797-7171, www.marvindc.com). Their rooftop beer garden offers more than 30 Belgian ales and blondes.

- The largest open-air seating area in Adams Morgan is at **Perry's Restaurant** (1811 Columbia Rd. NW, 202/234-6218, www.perrysam.com). They have good happy hour specials, views of the city, and a fun rooftop atmosphere.

- One of "the" places to go in DC is the **P.O.V. Roof Terrace and Lounge** (515 15th St. NW, 202/661-2437, www.povrooftop.com) at the W Washington D.C. Hotel. This rooftop bar and terrace is one of the top hot spots in DC and has phenomenal views of the city through 12-foot-tall windows.

down to earth crowd that isn't afraid to have a few drinks and dance. When a show is going on, you must have tickets to visit the Music Room, but the Vinyl Lounge upstairs (with views of the Potomac River) is open for dinner and drinks.

Adams Morgan

Adams Morgan is known as one of the city's top nightlife areas. It has the largest concentration of bars, restaurants, and nightclubs of any neighborhood in the city. Be aware that on weekend nights, the streets can be so packed with people that it is hard to move around.

One of the best-known bars is **Madam's Organ Blues Bar** (2461 18th St. NW, 202/667-5370, www.madamsorgan.com, Sun.-Thurs. 5pm-2am, Fri.-Sat. 5pm-3am), which offers a diverse crowd, nightly live music, and

dancing. This is a dive-type bar with a slightly older crowd than the frequent college or just-out-of-college patrons that inhabit many of the establishments in Adams Morgan.

Club Heaven and Hell (2327 18th St. NW, 202/667-4355, www.clubheavenandhelldc.com, Sun.-Thurs. 5pm-1:30am, Fri.-Sat. 5pm-3am) has the largest dance floor in Adams Morgan. They have three floors—Heaven, Purgatory, and Hell—with DJs spinning top 40, hip-hop, and retro music.

Bossa Bistro and Lounge (2463 18th St. NW, 202/667-0088, www.bossadc.com, Tues.-Thurs. 5:30pm-2am, Fri.-Sat. 5:30pm-3am, Sun. 5:30pm-2am) is a cozy neighborhood restaurant that serves Brazilian food and offers live music (such as jazz and international) four nights a week and DJs on other nights. In contrast to many options in

Adams Morgan, this is an intimate place to relax in a low-key, dimly lit interior with food and atmosphere.

Habana Village (1834 Columbia Rd. NW, 202/462-6310, www.habanavillage.com, Tues.-Wed. 5pm-11pm, Thurs. 5pm-midnight, Fri.-Sat. 5pm-3am, Sun. 5pm-10pm) is a Cuban restaurant and dance club offering live music and dance lessons.

Upper Northwest

Although Upper Northwest is not the most happening nightlife spot in the city, it does offer some friendly, comfortable options for those not looking to see or be seen.

Atomic Billiards (3427 Connecticut Ave. NW, 202/363-7665, www.atomicbilliards.com, Sun.-Thurs. 4pm-2am, Fri.-Sat. 4pm-3am), in the Cleveland Park neighborhood, is a funky, futuristic-looking pool hall. They also have shuffleboard and darts. They serve good beer on tap but don't have a kitchen. They are located in the basement.

Another basement bar with pool, table tennis, shuffleboard, beer, and sandwiches is **Breadsoda** (2233 Wisconsin Ave. NW, 202/333-7445, www.breadsoda.com, Sun.-Thurs. noon-2am, Fri.-Sat. noon-3am). Tuesdays are tacos-and-ping pong night in this cozy, 1970s-style subterranean bar.

U Street Corridor

Made-to-order drinks are created at **The Gibson** (2009 14th St. NW, 202/232-2156, www.thegibsondc.com, Mon.-Sat. from 6pm), just off U Street. This interesting establishment could be called a modern-day speakeasy. Call ahead and make a reservation at the bar or at one of their booths or tables, then ring the bell when you arrive at the nondescript, tenement-style building. A professional mixologist will concoct something special for you, or you can order a drink off the small menu. Don't expect to eat (they don't serve food), and above all, don't stay longer than your allotted two hours—there's sure to be someone waiting to take your spot.

EVENTS

The nation's capital hosts countless events year-round. Whether it's a festival, athletic event, or holiday celebration, there is something going on nearly every day of the year.

Restaurant Week (www.ramw.org, lunch $22, dinner $35) happens twice a year, in January and August. Two hundred of the most popular restaurants in DC offer prix fixe lunch and dinner menus. The event is sponsored by the Restaurant Association of Metropolitan Washington. Reservations are recommended.

Chinese dragon dances, live music, and a parade are just some of the festivities during the 15-day annual **Chinese New Year Celebration** (H St. NW between 5th St. and 9th St.) in the Chinatown area of downtown DC. Beginning with the new moon on the first day of the Chinese New Year and ending with the full moon, this late-January or early February celebration brings the area's culture to life with a bang of fireworks. The Gallery Place-Chinatown Metrorail stop will put you in the right place for this free event.

The yearly **Washington Auto Show** (www.washingtonautoshow.com, $5-42) is a large event that brings more than 600 new vehicles from both domestic and overseas automakers to the Washington Convention Center. The show is held for 10 days in April and draws hundreds of thousands of visitors.

The coming of the Easter Bunny brings the annual **White House Easter Egg Roll** (www.whitehouse.gov), a tradition that started back in 1878 when President Rutherford B. Hayes opened the White House grounds to local children for egg rolling on the Monday after Easter. Successive presidents have continued this long-standing event, which takes place on the South Lawn.

Washington's signature event is the annual **National Cherry Blossom Festival** (www.nationalcherryblossomfestival.org). This three-week event coincides (ideally) with the blooming of the hundreds of Japanese cherry trees that were given to the United States in 1912 by Japan. The trees are planted all around the Tidal Basin and, when blooming, are a spectacular sight to see. Unfortunately, this huge event means gridlock on the highways and congestion on the sidewalks, but it is a great time to photograph the city. There's a parade, a kite festival, concerts, a 10-mile footrace, and much more. The festival is held late March-mid-April.

Memorial Day is big in Washington DC as thousands descend on the city for a day of remembrance. Many family-friendly events are held throughout the city, and the free **National Memorial Day Concert** (www.pbs.org) is held on the West Lawn of the U.S. Capitol. The concert features patriotic themes to honor Americans who have served our country during times of conflict. Other events include the **National Memorial Day Parade** (www.americanveteranscenter.org).

June brings the annual **Capital Pride** (www.capitalpride.org) event celebrating the gay, lesbian, bisexual, and transgender communities. There are more than 50 educational and entertainment events including a street festival and parade.

The **DC Jazz Festival** (www.dcjazzfest.org) is also held in June and features more than 100 jazz performances throughout the city. Major jazz artists from around the globe participate in this 12-day celebration. Venues include clubs, museums, hotels, and restaurants.

The **Smithsonian Folklife Festival** (www.festival.si.edu) takes place annually during the last week in June and the first week in July. It is held outdoors on the National Mall. The festival is a living-heritage exposition with music, crafts, and artistry. The festival is free to attend.

There's no better place to celebrate the Fourth of July than the National Mall. **America's Independence Day Celebrations** include a parade along Constitution Avenue (www.july4thparade.com), concerts, and a spectacular fireworks display over the Washington Monument.

The premier running event in DC is the annual **Marine Corps Marathon** (www.marinemarathon.com). Known as "The People's Marathon," this 26.2-mile race was first held in 1975 and now has 30,000 participants each October.

Another completely different type of race is the annual **High Heel Race** in Dupont Circle. Each Tuesday before Halloween at 9pm, nearly 100 drag queens sporting elaborate outfits sprint down 17th Street NW over the three blocks between R and Church Streets. The event has been held for more than 30 years and draws thousands of spectators.

During the first week in December, the **National Christmas Tree Lighting** (www.thenationaltree.org) is a special event that takes place on the Ellipse. The president attends the lighting, which is surrounded by additional highlights such as military band concerts and performances by celebrities. A separate event is held annually for the lighting of the national menorah (www.afldc.org).

Shopping

Washington DC has great neighborhood shopping with unique stores and boutiques. Some of the stores are geared toward high-end consumers, but there are also many "finds" if you know where to look.

CAPITOL HILL

Traditional retail shopping can be found on Capitol Hill at **Union Station** (50 Massachusetts Ave. NE, www.unionstationdc.com), which has more than 65 stores, including national retailers such as Ann Taylor, The Body Shop, Jos. A. Bank Clothiers, and Victoria's Secret. A handful of specialty boutiques are also represented, such as **Lost City Art** (202/289-6977), which offers Indonesian statues, masks, murals, jewelry, and household items.

Eastern Market (225 7th St. SE, www.easternmarket-dc.org) is a prime destination in DC for fresh food and handmade arts and crafts. Since 1873, the market has been a community hub on Capitol Hill. It offers several shopping spaces: The **South Hall Market** (Tues.-Fri. 7am-7pm, Sat. 7am-6pm, Sun. 9am-5pm) is an indoor space featuring 13 merchants offering a large variety of food, such as produce, baked goods, meat, and dairy products. The **Weekend Farmers' Line** is an open-air space that is open on weekends and offers fresh local produce and snacks. Those searching for local crafts and antiques can find them at the **Weekend Outdoor Market.** Vendors in this area carry ethno-specific handcrafts, vintage goods, and arts and crafts. There is also a farmers market on Tuesdays.

DISTRICT WHARF

The development of District Wharf includes an ever-growing selection of national retail shops and trendy boutiques. The list is evolving and can be found at: www.wharfdc.com/shops.

A Beautiful Closet (20 District Square SW, 202/488-1809, Mon.-Tues. 11am-6pm, Wed. 11am-7pm, Thur.-Fri. 11am-8pm, Sat. 11am-9pm, Sun. 11am-7pm) is a boutique that sells clothing, jewelry, home décor, and fair trade goods from around the world.

Politics and Prose Bookstore (70 District Square SW, 202/488-3867, Daily 10am-10pm) is an independent bookstore featuring a large variety of books, gifts, and stationary. They also host book signings and other events.

DOWNTOWN

The revitalized Penn Quarter area features more than just museums, the Capital One Arena, and cool new restaurants. The neighborhood has plenty of shopping and features some of the best-known national retailers, such as Pottery Barn and Urban Outfitters.

1: people shopping for art 2: the National Cherry Blossom Festival drawing visitors to the Tidal Basin

A selection of trendy individual shops is also here, such as **Fahrney's Pens** (1317 F St. NW, 202/628-9525, www.fahrneyspens.com, Mon.-Fri. 9:30am-6pm, Sat. 10am-5pm), a pen store with a long DC tradition, and **Pua Naturally** (400 7th St. NW, 202/347-4543, www.puanaturally.com, by appointment only: Tues.-Fri. 1pm-6pm, Sat. 1pm-5pm, closed Sun.-Mon.), a retail clothing studio that works with a cooperative of master tailors, block printers, and seamstresses in Nepal and India.

DUPONT CIRCLE

Lively Dupont Circle features an eclectic choice of gift shops, clothing stores, bookstores, and art galleries. If you're looking for a quirky gift, one-of-a-kind handcrafts, greeting cards, or chocolate, stop in **The Chocolate Moose** (1743 L St. NW, 202/463-0992, www.chocolatemoosedc.com). Serious antiques lovers will be intrigued by the offerings at **Geoffrey Diner Gallery** (1730 21st St. NW, 202/904-5005, www.dinergallery.com). They have items from the 19th and 20th centuries, contemporary fine art, European and American crafts, and Tiffany lamps.

GEORGETOWN

Everyone from first ladies to celebrities has made their way down M Street looking for a special find. Georgetown offers great antiques, cool clothing, and unique local boutiques. Most of the stores can be found along M Street and Wisconsin Avenue. The famous mall **Georgetown Park** (3222 M St., www.georgetownpark.com) has been transformed from an enclosed mall to one where tenants front M Street and Wisconsin Avenue. It offers a mix of retail and restaurant space.

UPPER NORTHWEST

The best shopping in Upper Northwest is in the Friendship Heights neighborhood, along the Maryland state border. **Chevy Chase Pavilion** (5335 Wisconsin Ave. NW, www.chevychasepavilion.com, Mon.-Sat. 7am-11pm, Sun. 7am-9pm) is a shopping mall that features national chains such as J. Crew, World Market, and Old Navy. It is across Wisconsin Avenue from another small, upscale mall, **Mazza Gallerie** (5300 Wisconsin Ave. NW, www.mazzagallerie.com, Mon.-Fri. 10am-8pm, Sat. 10am-7pm, Sun. noon-6pm).

Mazza Gallerie features stores such as Neiman Marcus and Saks Fifth Avenue. There is also a movie theater at the mall and a parking garage. The shopping district is accessible by Metrorail on the Red Line at the Friendship Heights stop.

Food

THE NATIONAL MALL
Asian Fusion
For a trendy night out, dine at **The Source** (575 Pennsylvania Ave. NW, 202/637-6100, www.wolfgangpuck.com, Tues.-Thurs. 11:30am-2:30pm and 5:30pm-10pm, Fri. 11:30am-2:30pm and 5:30pm-11pm, and Sat. 11:30am-3pm and 5:30pm-11pm, $31-60). This popular Wolfgang Puck restaurant is adjacent to the Newseum and was a date-night choice for Michelle and Barack Obama. The Source offers a seven-course tasting menu for $135, and the lower-level lounge offers small plates and a dim sum brunch on Saturday. The modern dining room on the second floor offers a contemporary Asian menu. Floor-to-ceiling windows and a polished tile floor give the space an inviting atmosphere, and there is plush leather seating. A beautiful wine wall with more than 2,000 bottles is a focal point. A seasonal patio is available for outdoor dining.

CAPITOL HILL
American
A Capitol Hill classic is the **Tune Inn** (331 Pennsylvania Ave. SE, 202/543-2725, Mon.-Fri. 8am-2am, Sat.-Sun. 8am-3:30am, $5-13). This historic burger-and-beer bar is quirky: The decor is a symphony in taxidermy (complete with a deer rump and a beer-drinking black bear), but the beer is cheap (by DC standards) and the burgers are tasty.

For delicious, Southern-inspired cooking, dine at **Art and Soul** (415 New Jersey Ave. NW, 202/393-7777, www.artandsouldc.com, Mon.-Fri. 7am-10:30am, 11:30am-3:30pm,

and 5:30 pm-10pm, Sat.-Sun. 7am-3pm and 5:30 pm-10pm, $24-44). They are known for their fried chicken sandwich, and they have a lovely, dog-friendly patio for nice weather.

Belgian
The intimate **Belga Café** (514 8th St. SE, 202/544-0100, www.belgacafe.com, lunch Mon.-Fri. 11am-4pm, brunch Sat.-Sun. 9am-4pm, dinner Mon.-Thurs. 4pm-10pm, Fri.-Sat. 4pm-11pm, and Sun. 4pm-9:30pm, $15-38) serves waffles (with savory or sweet toppings) that will make your knees weak, and their dinner entrées are delicious renditions of items such as mussels (flecked with bacon and steamed in red ale), truffle macaroni and cheese, and Flemish beef stew. They also have a nice beer list. The place is small (the first floor of a row house), and there is exposed brick inside with an open kitchen (read: the noise level is high). There is usually a wait, but the staff is friendly (even to children), and on nice days there is added seating outside.

DISTRICT WHARF
Asian
Go on a funky culinary journey through Southeast Asia at **Kaliwa** (751 Wharf St. SW., 202/516-4739, www.kaliwadc.com, daily lunch from 11:30am, dinner from 5:30pm, $15-24). This visually appealing, waterfront restaurant offers selections from Korea, Thailand, and the Philippines, all described in their native language (a glossary is available for translations). Dishes are meant to be shared and are served when ready. They recommend patrons

order 2-3 items per person. The decor features soaring ceilings, wooden tables, and exotic chandeliers.

Seafood

A taste of coastal Spain can be enjoyed at **Del Mar** (791 Wharf St. SW, 202/525-1402, www.delmardc.com, Sun.-Thurs. 5pm-10pm, Fri.-Sat. 5pm-10:30pm, $30-75), courtesy of DC culinary legends Fabio and Maria Trabocchi. Throw in a dramatic water view and delightful cocktails and you have a reason to celebrate (bring on the paella!). Authentic seafood dishes from Mallorca headline the menu with tapas, stews, and grilled fish. Their dress code is upscale casual.

Hank's Oyster Bar (701 Wharf St. SW, 202/817-3055, www.hanksoysterbar.com, Mon.-Thurs. 11:30am-10pm, Fri. 11:30am-11pm, Sat. 11am-11pm, Sun. 11am-10pm, $14-32) is located on the waterfront and offers indoor and outdoor seating. They are known for their happy hour specials at the bar, but they also offer a good variety of "New England Beach fare" (mostly seafood) dishes. They seem to have a knack for hiring friendly staff. If you like lobster, try the lobster deviled eggs or the lobster roll. They have several other locations around DC and in Old Town Alexandria.

DOWNTOWN

American

It's hard to pass up an opportunity to dine at **Old Ebbitt Grill** (675 15th St. NW, 202/347-4800, www.ebbitt.com, Mon.-Fri. 7:30am-1am, Sat.-Sun. 8:30am-1am, $9-37), the oldest saloon in Washington DC. This historic restaurant is near the White House and was frequented by presidents such as Grant, Cleveland, and Theodore Roosevelt. Currently part of the Clyde's restaurant group, this old favorite is always bustling with political personalities, journalists, and theater patrons. It's a casual, fun place but shows its long history through marble bars and mahogany booths outfitted in velvet. They have an oyster bar and a menu of burgers, pasta, steak, and seafood. They also serve breakfast during the week and brunch on weekends.

Indian

Upscale Indian cuisine can be found at ★ **Rasika** (633 D St. NW, 202/637-1222, www.rasikarestaurant.com, lunch Mon.-Fri. 11:30am-2:30pm, dinner Mon.-Thurs. 5:30pm-10:30pm and Fri.-Sat. 5pm-11pm, $19-36) in Penn Quarter. This fabulous restaurant is one of the best in the area for modern Indian cuisine. A personal favorite for an entrée is the lamb Roganjosh (although the black cod is also spectacular). They also offer a four-course tasting menu for $60, a six-course tasting menu for $75, and a pretheater three-course menu before 6:30pm for $37. This restaurant is red hot on the popularity list, and a reservation is highly recommended. They have a second location at 1190 New Hampshire Avenue NW.

Italian

The vintage-style pizzeria bistro **Matchbox** (750 E St. NW, 202/289-4441, www.matchboxrestaurants.com, Mon.-Thurs. 11am-10:30pm, Fri. 11am-1am, Sat. 10am-1am, Sun. 10am-10:30pm, $10-35) is a favorite in the Penn Quarter neighborhood for pregaming before an event at Capital One Arena. They are known for their incredible pizza and also for their mini-burger appetizers topped with onion straws, but they also offer a full menu of sandwiches and entrées. The atmosphere in this multilevel hot spot is fun, lively, and slightly funky. There are 11 other locations throughout the DC area (in DC, Virginia, and Maryland).

Spanish/Portuguese

The toughest reservation in town and a meal that will blow you away (first when you taste the food and again when you see the bill) is ★ **Minibar by José Andrés** (855 E St. NW, 202/393-0812, www.minibarbyjoseandres.com, Tues.-Sat. seatings at 6pm, 6:30pm, 8:30pm, and 9pm, $275). This "culinary

Food Truck Culture

food trucks on the National Mall

Food trucks have always been part of the lunch scene in Washington DC, but today their quality and diversity have elevated them to noteworthy status.

Dangerously Delicious Pies (www.pieshopdc.com) was the first truck to spawn a brick-and-mortar eatery (at 1339 H St. NE), although the majority of the trucks are stand-alone businesses. Dangerously Delicious Pies serves both sweet and savory pie slices out of its bright red truck. **Himalayan Soul Food** made a name for itself with delicious, generously stuffed dumplings, while the **BBQ Bus** (www.bbqbusdc.com) serves up tender ribs and pulled pork. Even more specialized is **Ball or Nothing,** (www.ballornothingdc.com), which serves meatballs and boldly states, "our balls are for everyone." This local favorite offers traditional meatballs, veggie meatballs, wild boar meatballs, and interesting sides such as mascarpone polenta and roasted peach and spinach salad.

So how do you find these rolling treasures? These meals on wheels can be found on many major roads in the business and tourist areas of the city. Some have their own websites that give their location schedule and others use Twitter to provide their up-to-the-minute whereabouts. Many can also be found on **Food Truck Fiesta** (www.foodtruckfiesta.com), a website geared toward tracking the trucks. When in doubt, try the truck with the longest line. It doesn't take long for word to spread about a great food truck find.

journey" of molecular gastronomy comprises a preset 20-plus-course tasting menu (1-2 bites each) that is a combination of art and science. There is no menu; you simply eat what is served that evening (examples include beech mushroom risotto with truffle, pillow of PB&J, grilled lobster with peanut butter and honey, and apple meringue "pigs" with bacon ice cream).

Seatings are small, just six guests at each of four seatings a night. Guests move through different rooms during the meal. The serving team walks guests through each course (plan on staying about 2-3 hours) and shares the beauty of the ingredients that were selected for each and the technique behind their creation. The $275 price tag does not include drinks, tax, or gratuity. Optional drink pairings are available. Reservations open in two-month periods starting one month prior and can be made online. This is truly a once-in-a-lifetime dining experience.

Turkish/Greek

Another creation of chef José Andrés is the very popular **Zaytinya** (701 9th St. NW, 202/638-0800, www.zaytinya.com, Sun.-Mon. 11am-10pm, Tues.-Thurs. 11am-11pm, Fri.-Sat. 11am-midnight, small plates $7-20). They serve a large and delicious menu of tapas in a casual setting. This is a good choice for both vegetarians and meat eaters. Menu examples include pan-roasted dorado, Turkish-style *pastirma* (cured beef), and knisa lamb chops. They also offer a chef's experience for $65. There is a bar overlooking the dining room for people watching. This is a good place to try some of the creations of one of DC's most famous chefs.

DUPONT CIRCLE
Asian

A tiny restaurant with a big following. That's **Little Serow** (1511 17th St. NW, www.littleserow.com, Tues.-Thurs. 5:30pm-10pm, Fri.-Sat. 5:30pm-10:30pm, $54), a quirky, highly regarded, northern Thailand-inspired restaurant with very limited seating (no parties larger than four). No need to ponder over the menu—the only choice is a family-style fixed-priced menu that changes every Tuesday and normally includes pork, seafood, and nuts (with no substitutions). The food is spicy, flavorful, and notably different from other local Thai restaurants. Come ready to wait. Patrons line up at the door as early as 4:30 (there are no reservations). If there's a wait when you arrive, the friendly staff will text you when your table is ready. The restaurant is hard to find because there is no visible sign outside.

For fast-casual food that's part Chinese and part Korean, stop at **Chiko** (2029 P St. NW, 202/331-3040, www.chikodc.com, Sun.-Thurs. 11am-10pm, Fri.-Sat. 11am-11pm, $15-18). Try their well-known Orange-ish Chicken, Smashed Salmon, or the delightful Pork and Kimchi pot stickers. Service is first-come, first-served, but reservations are available at their small Kitchen Counter that include interaction with their cooks, multiple courses of

their well-known dishes, and a front-row seat to their open kitchen ($50 per person, excluding beverages, tax, and tips).

Greek

Tucked inside a normal-looking row house is one of the best culinary outposts in the city. ★ **Komi** (1509 17th St. NW, 202/332-9200, www.komirestaurant.com, Tues.-Sat. 5:30pm-9:30pm, $165) serves a preset multicourse dinner for $165 per person. The experience starts with several light dishes and progresses to hearty fare and finally dessert. Wine pairing is offered as an option for an additional $85. They do not even have a printed menu. This intimate eatery is steered by a young chef named Johnny Monis, who prepares incredible Greek dishes inspired by family recipes. The menu is different every night, making this the perfect find for foodies—foodies with deep pockets, that is.

GEORGETOWN
American

Timeless quality can be found at **1789** (1226 36th St. NW, 202/965-1789, www.1789restaurant.com, Mon.-Thurs. 5pm-10pm, Fri.-Sat. 5pm-11pm, Sun. 5pm-10pm, $32-59, five-course tasting menu $105), open since 1962. Part of the Clyde's family of restaurants, 1789 is tried-and-true with starched linen tablecloths and candlelight. The restaurant has three floors and six rooms for dining, each with a unique name, ambience, and a common theme of antiques and equestrian decor. Jackets used to be required but are now preferred. The restaurant serves a diverse menu of seafood, steak, pork, duck, and a few vegetarian selections. The food is high quality and consistent, and the service is impeccable. This is a lovely spot for a date or a business dinner.

Just east of Georgetown on M Street, the **Blue Duck Tavern** (1201 24th St. NW, 202/419-6755, www.blueducktavern.com, Mon.-Thurs. 6:30am-10:30am, 11:30am-2:30pm, and 5:30pm-10:30pm, Fri. 6:30am-10:30am, 11:30am-2:30pm, and 5:30pm-11pm,

Sat. 6:30am-10:30am, 11am-2:30pm, and 5:30pm-11pm, Sun. 6:30am-10:30am, 11am-2:30pm, and 5:30pm-10:30pm, $26-52) is a traditional American restaurant that is known for hosting power players from DC's political scene. It also prides itself on using simple, flavor-enhancing cooking methods such as smoking, braising, and roasting. The restaurant is known for both its food and its lovely atmosphere. Handmade wood furnishings and an open kitchen help give it a warm, gathering-place-type feel, although with a contemporary flair. The food sounds simple, with selections such as beef ribs, organic chicken, and halibut, but the dishes are elegantly prepared and beautifully served.

Farmers Fishers Bakers (3000 K St. NW, Washington Harbor, 202/298-8783, www.farmersfishersbakers.com, Mon.-Wed. 7:30am-10:30am and 11am-10pm, Thurs. 7:30am-10:30am and 11am-11pm, Fri. 7:30am-10:30am and 11am-midnight, Sat. 9am-midnight, Sun. 9am-10pm, $12-34) is part of the Farmers Restaurant Group and is a modern, upscale, casual option in Washington Harbor. The restaurant group supports American family farmers and sources regionally and seasonally when possible. Farmers Fishers Bakers offer an in-house bakery, full bar with 24 beer taps, a sushi counter, and a patio with views of the water. Guests are greeted outside in winter with a fire pit, and the inside decor features several different themes for varying dining experiences. The menu is large and includes pizza, sandwiches, salads, and seafood. Their burger with blue cheese and a side of potato salad is a good choice on any day.

Bakery

Many people have heard of **Georgetown Cupcake** (3301 M St. NW, 202/333-8448, www.georgetowncupcake.com, Mon.-Sat. 10am-9pm, Sun. 10am-8pm, under $10), made famous by the reality television series *DC Cupcakes,* but they may not know about a nearby gem called **Baked & Wired** (1052 Thomas Jefferson St. NW, 703/663-8727,

www.bakedandwired.com, Mon.-Thurs. 7am-8pm, Fri. 7am-9pm, Sat. 8am-9pm, Sun. 8am-8pm, under $10), south of the C&O Canal between 30th and 31st Streets. This little independent bakery sells great coffee and a large variety of freshly made bakery items including more than 20 types of cupcakes with names such as Chocolate Cupcake of Doom and Pretty Bitchin'. They turn out amazing baked goods amid a fun, inviting atmosphere. Look for the pink bicycle outside, and don't forget to take home some Hippie Crack (homemade granola) for later.

Italian

The place to celebrity-spot in Georgetown is **Café Milano** (3251 Prospect St. NW, 202/333-6183, www.cafemilano.com, Mon.-Tues. 11:30am-11pm, Wed.-Sat. 11:30am-midnight, Sun. 11am-11pm, $17-75). Political VIPs and visiting Hollywood stars frequent this upscale Italian restaurant, as do local Georgetown socialites. The southern coastal Italian cuisine is consistently good, but diners come more to people watch and enjoy the pleasant atmosphere afforded by the floor-to-ceiling windows and open sidewalk patio. There is normally a sophisticated crowd, and good wine is flowing.

Another great choice for Italian is **Filomena Ristorante** (1063 Wisconsin Ave. NW, 202/338-8800, www.filomena.com, daily 11:30am-11pm, $15-47). This well-known restaurant opened in 1983 and serves authentic, delicious Italian cuisine. You can even see the pasta being made on the way in. Many celebrities and dignitaries have dined here, including Bono from U2 and President Clinton. Seating is a little close together, but the excellent food will make you overlook this. Portions are large, and the service is friendly and attentive. Personal favorites include the Linguini Cardinale and Gnocchi Della Mamma.

ADAMS MORGAN
American
Mintwood Place (1813 Columbia Rd. NW, 202/234-6732, www.mintwoodplace.

com, Tues.-Thurs. 5:30pm-10pm, Fri. 5:30pm-10:30pm, Sat. 10:30am-2:30pm and 5:30pm-10:30pm, Sun. 10:30am-2:30pm and 5:30pm-9pm, $17-34) has a pleasant, modern-farmhouse ambience and a lovely patio. They offer a unique menu of American food with some French influence (such as trout, chicken liver mousse, and a cheeseburger) with lovely presentation. This is a great place to try something new and maybe impress a date. The restaurant is small, and some of the tables are close together, but it has a casual, neighborhood feel despite its chunky price tag.

Italian

Al Volo Osteria (1790 Columbia Rd. NW, 202/758-0759, www.cucina-alvolo.com, Sun.-Thurs. 5pm-10pm, Fri.-Sat. 5pm-11pm, $9-20) is a popular Italian restaurant in a somewhat funky neighborhood. If you're a fan of good, house-made pasta, this is the place to go. The pasta is incredibly fresh, and diners have an open view to the kitchen. The menu is familiar (pick a pasta, pick a sauce, or order pizza and salad), but with some fresh healthy choices (red beet fusilli, cherry tomato sauce, etc.). This is a casual place where the focus is on the food.

Vegetarian

A vegetarian hot spot that the rest of us can also enjoy, the **Amsterdam Falafelshop** (2425 18th St. NW, 202/234-1969, www.falafelshop.com, Sun.-Mon. 11am-midnight, Tues.-Wed. 11am-2:30am, Thurs. 11am-3am, Fri.-Sat. 11am-4am, under $5-15) is known for its perfectly crisp, yet soft, balls of fried chickpeas placed inside pita bread or in a bowl. The concept is simple: You order your falafel, they make it for you in under five minutes, and then you decide which of the 21 toppings and sauces you want from the garnish bar. The shop is open late and also offers sides and desserts.

UPPER NORTHWEST
American

A traditional greasy-spoon breakfast joint

is **Steak 'n Egg** (4700 Wisconsin Ave. NW, 202/686-1201, www.osmanandjoes.com, 24 hours, $7-18). It offers all the wonderful eggs, sausages, hash browns, and biscuits you could ask for, with ultracasual 24-hour-diner charm. As the name implies, they also have steak, as well as burgers, sandwiches, shakes, and good coffee.

Going to the zoo? Even if you are not, stop at ★ **Duke's Counter** (3000 Connecticut Ave. NW, 202/733-4808, www.dukesgrocery. com, Mon.-Thurs. 11am-10pm, Fri. 11am-midnight, Sat. 10am-midnight, Sun. 10am-10pm, $8-15), a wonderful, British-inspired gastropub located across the street from the National Zoo entrance in Woodley Park. They serve scrumptious, overstuffed sandwiches with names such as Fired Up Chicken and Italian Stallion, alongside items such as hummus, curry poutine, and avocado toast. The menu was put together with great care and includes seasonal cocktails. They have a cool, copper-topped bar (open late) and a seasonal patio.

German

Take it from a German girl who has eaten her way through the Old Country: Some of the best traditional German fare in the entire DC area is served at **Old Europe** (2434 Wisconsin Ave. NW, 202/333-7600, www.old-europe.com, Wed.-Thurs. 11:30am-2:30pm and 5pm-9pm, Fri.-Sat. 11:30am-2:30pm and 5pm-10pm, Sun. noon-3:30pm and 4pm-8pm, $15-27). They have all the favorites including schnitzel, sauerbraten, and brats, all served in a lively, homeland atmosphere. The menu is wide-ranging and includes a good selection of traditional side dishes (potato pancakes, red cabbage, potato dumplings). They also have German wine, beer, and spirits (have you ever seen Jägermeister on a printed menu?).

Italian

DC's most popular pizzeria is easily ★ **2 Amys** (3715 Macomb St. NW, 202/885-5700, www.2amyspizza.com, Mon. 5pm-10pm, Tues.-Thurs. 11am-10pm, Fri.-Sat.

11am-11pm, Sun. noon-10pm, $7-15). This gourmet Italian restaurant specializes in authentic Neapolitan pizza. The incredible smell alone will make your mouth water when you walk into this hopping, noisy establishment. The cute bar area is a great place to wait for your table. Although they make other menu items just as well, the focus here is really on the pizza, which lives up to the hype. It is actually one of the few restaurants in the country certified by the D.O.C. (Denominazione di Origine Controllata), an Italian entity that specifies the legally permitted ingredients and preparation methods required to make authentic Neapolitan pizza.

Japanese

It's hard to imagine that good sushi can be found in DC at a decent price, but **Kotobuki** (4822 MacArthur Blvd. NW, 202/625-9080, www.kotobukidc.com, Tues.-Thurs. noon-2:30pm and 5pm-9:30pm, Fri.-Sat. noon-2:30pm and 5pm-10:30pm, Sun. 5pm-9:30pm, $12-30) is that needle in a haystack. It is a tiny restaurant (above another one owned by the same people), and there is usually a line for a table, but the prices are good, the fish is fresh, and the sushi is authentic.

Seafood

In the Palisades neighborhood is **BlackSalt Fish Market & Restaurant** (4883 MacArthur Blvd. NW, 202/342-9101, www.blacksaltrestaurant.com, Mon.-Thurs. 11:30am-2:30pm and 5:30pm-9:30pm, Fri. 11:30am-2:30pm and 5:30pm-10pm, Sat. 11:30am-2:30pm and 5pm-10pm, Sun. 11am-2pm and 5pm-9pm, $17-69), a well-known spot serving New American seafood. The seafood is extremely fresh, and they offer innovative combinations such as Thai Coconut & Galangal Seafood Stew, Cumin Spiced Tuna, and Tempura Fried Dungeness Crab Salad. They also offer a five-course tasting menu for $90 and a seven-course tasting menu for $120. Wine pairings are $50 and $70. There's an adjoining seafood market that sells some of the best fish in the city.

U STREET CORRIDOR
American

A long-standing tradition on U Street is ★ **Ben's Chili Bowl** (1213 U St. NW, 202/667-0909, www.benschilibowl.com, Mon.-Thurs. 6am-2am, Fri. 6am-4am, Sat. 7am-4am, Sun. 11am-midnight, under $10). This historic eatery opened in 1958 and has seen a lot of changes through its windows. It has weathered the rise, fall, and rebirth of the U Street Corridor and could well be the only business on this stretch of street that survived both the riots of 1968 following the assassination of Martin Luther King Jr. and the construction of the Metrorail Green Line. Ben's is "Home of the Famous Chili Dog," which is what has drawn people (including Barack Obama and the Travel Channel's Anthony Bourdain) through its doors and to its red barstools for decades. They serve breakfast and a "main menu" the rest of the day, but chili dogs are available anytime they're open. The staff is smiling and friendly, and celebrities and regular folks are all treated equally.

Busboys and Poets (2021 14th St. NW, 202/387-7638, www.busboysandpoets.com, Mon.-Thurs. 7am-midnight, Fri. 7am-1am, Sat. 8am-1am, Sun. 8am-midnight, $7-26) is a local gathering place and restaurant with a loyal following. It now has seven locations. It is known as a progressive establishment and also as a community resource for artists, activists, and writers. The 14th Street location is large and serves breakfast daily until 11am. The rest of the day they offer soup, sandwiches, panini, pizza, and entrées (after 5pm) with a Southern flair (think catfish, shrimp and grits, and pasta). They offer vegetarian, vegan, and gluten-free selections as well, and there is a progressive bookstore on-site.

Greek

Fantastic gyros are what all the hype is about at **The Greek Spot** (2017 11th St. NW, 202/265-3118, www.greekspotdc.com, Mon.-Fri. 11am-10:30pm, Sat. noon-10:30pm,

$7-18). This is a very casual "fast-food" restaurant that makes tasty Greek meals in a hurry. They serve lamb and beef gyros, vegetarian gyros (made with soy steak strips), chicken souvlaki, and other sandwiches and burgers. The food is tender and inexpensive and has developed quite the local following. They also prepare and deliver takeout orders.

Accommodations

Where you book a room in Washington DC will likely depend on your itinerary. If you are primarily touring museums and monuments, then make a reservation near the National Mall, Capitol Hill, or in the downtown area. If you prefer new accommodations with a water view, then the District Wharf is a good choice. If you desire the charm of the historic neighborhoods this city has to offer, then a room near Dupont Circle, in Upper Northwest, or in Georgetown could be a good option.

Accommodations in Washington DC run the gamut in price range. However, choice hotels near the popular attractions are pricey year-round, and some are downright outrageous. An alternative for booking a room is to stay across the Potomac River in nearby Arlington or Alexandria, Virginia. It can be less expensive, yet still convenient to the city's major attractions by car, bus, or Metrorail.

THE NATIONAL MALL
Under $100
Reservations for a hostel stay can be made months in advance with **Hostelling International-Washington DC** (1009 11th St. NW, 202/737-2333, www.hiusa.org, $30-119). Accommodations are close to the National Mall, Metrorail, and many of the popular DC attractions. This former hotel has 250 beds and offers shared, dorm-style lodging and some semiprivate rooms. Bathrooms are shared, and there is a kitchen and laundry facility on-site. There is also high-speed Internet.

CAPITOL HILL
$100-200
If you want to stay on Capitol Hill, the

Capitol Hill Hotel (200 C St. SE., 202/543-6000, www.capitolhillhotel-dc.com, $134-262) offers lovely boutique accommodations in a residential neighborhood. This is the closest hotel to the Capitol Building and is about one block from the Capitol South Metrorail stop. All 153 rooms are suites with kitchenettes or kitchens. Continental breakfast is included, as well as bike rentals. They also have wine and cookies in the afternoon on weekdays. Valet parking ($50) is available, and the hotel is pet friendly ($150). Their decor appropriately includes vintage political-cartoon art and cherry blossom designs. This hotel is a great value for the location.

DISTRICT WHARF
$200-300
A good hotel choice right on the wharf is the **Hyatt House Washington DC/The Wharf** (725 Wharf St. SW, 202/554-1234, www.hyatt. com, $215-660). This new hotel is in the center of the District Wharf neighborhood and offers terrific river views. It is one mile from the National Mall and about a 10-minute walk to the L'Enfant Plaza Metrorail station. The hotel has 237 guest rooms, a fitness center, and outdoor pool. Free breakfast is included, and the hotel is pet friendly. Another hotel located right on the Wharf is the **InterContinental Washington DC/The Wharf** (801 Wharf St. SW, 202/800-0844, www.wharfintercontinentaldc.com, $265-442). This modern, luxury hotel boasts great waterfront views of the Potomac River in the heart of the Wharf neighborhood. During the summer, the majority of the rooms are around $300.

DOWNTOWN

$100-200

One of the best values in the city is the ★ **Hotel Tabard Inn** (1739 N St. NW, 202/785-1277, www.tabardinn.com, $125-325), five blocks from the White House on a pretty, tree-lined street. The hotel has 35 uniquely designed rooms in three town houses. The houses were built between 1880 and 1890. Rates vary depending on the size of the room and whether it has a shared or private bathroom. Reservations are taken for specific price categories, not for specific rooms. There are no televisions in the guest rooms.

All rates include a guest pass to the Washington Sports Club gym and a $15 food and beverage credit. Free wireless Internet is also available throughout the inn. The inn is known for having live jazz. Valet parking is $39 per day.

Over $300

For a presidential stay in DC, book a room at the ★ **Hay-Adams** (800 16th St. NW, 202/638-6600, www.hayadams.com, $289-2,039) at 16th and H Streets NW. This beautiful downtown hotel has 145 guest rooms and 21 luxury suites. Some of the rooms offer stunning views of local landmarks such as the White House and Lafayette Square. The Hay-Adams was built in 1928 in the Italian Renaissance style and has the appearance of a large private mansion. It sits on the land where the homes of Secretary of State John Hay and historian Henry Adams (author and relative of John Adams and John Quincy Adams) once stood.

The hotel has hosted many important political figures and was the choice for President Obama and his family in the weeks leading up to his first inauguration in 2008.

Visitors taking in the National Mall sights will enjoy the convenient location of this hotel, situated near the White House, downtown attractions, and the Metrorail. The hotel features beautiful, traditionally decorated rooms with molded ceilings, quality furnishings, ample space, comfortable beds,

and wonderful amenities such as fluffy bathrobes. The food at the hotel is also excellent.

The service at the Hay-Adams is outstanding, and from the moment you walk through the front door, it is obvious you will be well taken care of. The hotel's slogan is, "Where nothing is overlooked but the White House," and they mean it.

If you're traveling to DC for the full historical experience and you'd like to indulge in famous accommodations, then the ★ **Willard InterContinental Hotel** (1401 Pennsylvania Ave. NW, 202/628-9100, www.ihg.com, $189-3,989) is a good choice. The Willard is more than 150 years old and is considered to be one of the most prestigious hotels in the city. It is one block from the White House and has been called the "Residence of Presidents" because it has hosted nearly every U.S. president since Franklin Pierce stayed there in 1853. Other famous guests include Martin Luther King Jr. (who stayed there during the time he delivered his famous "I Have a Dream" speech), Charles Dickens, Mark Twain, and Buffalo Bill. The hotel even has its own little museum.

The Willard is beautifully restored and has a grand lobby, comfortable rooms, and outstanding service. The hotel has 12 floors, 335 guest rooms, and 41 suites. It also has a wonderful on-site restaurant.

Another beautifully restored historic hotel is **The Jefferson** (1200 16th St. NW, 202/448-2300, www.jeffersondc.com, $300-594), located roughly halfway between the White House and Dupont Circle. Built as a luxury apartment building in 1923, the beaux arts building was converted to a hotel in 1955 and underwent major renovations in 2009, which included incorporating modern-day features (such as a chef's kitchen and spa) into the original framework. The hotel maintains a large collection of antiques, artwork, and original signed documents. It has 95 guest rooms and suites and

---

1: Ben's Chili Bowl 2: Willard InterContinental Hotel 3: restaurants and specialty shops in Union Station

three on-site restaurants. They also have an Executive Canine Officer (ECO) named Lord Monticello (Monti)—a rescue dog that lives at the hotel. The hotel is dog friendly ($50 fee) and provides dog beds, bowls, treats, and a map of nearby dog-friendly establishmentc and walking routes.

Off Lafayette Park near the White House is the lovely **Sofitel Washington DC Lafayette Square** (806 15th St. NW, 202/730-8800, www.sofitel.accorhotels.com, $206-618). This sophisticated hotel is art deco with a modern flair. The rooms are beautifully appointed and feature soft lighting and fluffy linens. There is also a comfortable lounge area for guests and an on-site restaurant. The location is perfect for touring the city since it is near the National Mall, downtown attractions, and the Metrorail. Ask for a room facing south or east (or simply ask to face the White House).

DUPONT CIRCLE
$100-200

A trendy boutique hotel in the Dupont Circle neighborhood is the 137-room **Kimpton Rouge** (1315 16th St. NW, 202/232-8000, www.rougehotel.com, $103-236). This popular Kimpton hotel has a modern design, a fitness room, good amenities, and is pet friendly. Red is their signature color, which seems to be worked in everywhere. Their rooms are well outfitted with stocked minibars, high-speed Internet, 37-inch plasma televisions, Aveda bath products, and voicemail. Ten rooms feature kitchenettes and entertainment areas. There is a great bar on-site, and approximately 75 restaurants are within walking distance. They also have a state-of-the-art fitness center. The staff is exceptional. Pets are welcome.

$200-300

A wonderful Kimpton hotel in the Dupont Circle neighborhood is the ★ **Kimpton Carlyle Hotel** (1731 New Hampshire Ave. NW, 202/234-3200, www.carlylehoteldc. com, $122-675). This art deco hotel has 170 rooms with ample space, sitting areas, fully equipped kitchens, and Tempur-Pedic beds. The eight-story offering is on a residential street, three blocks from the Dupont Circle fountain. There is a restaurant on-site, a fitness center, free bike use, Tesla and universal charging stations, a daily wine hour, and valet parking ($48). The hotel is pet friendly.

Over $300

The most imaginative hotel in the city is **The Mansion on O Street** (2020 O St. NW, 202/496-2000, www.omansion.com, $375-25,000), just southwest of Dupont Circle. This one-of-a-kind boutique hotel consists of four 1892 townhomes linked to form a luxury inn complex containing guest rooms, a ballroom, multiple dining rooms, conference rooms, and many surprises. Each accommodation has its specialty: It could be a rainforest shower, pirate's tub, tanning room, a shower made from an English telephone booth, extensive gardens with fountains and a barbecue, an aquarium, or a bathroom that's so incredible that legendary jazz musician Miles Davis decided to have dinner in it. That's just the tip of the iceberg at this ultracreative mansion. There's a museum on-site that is equally creative and changes displays daily. There are more than 100 rooms, 70 secret doors, and hidden passageways to explore. Everything in the mansion is for sale, so if you really like something, for a price, it can be yours. Many famous people have stayed in this eclectic world of fantasy, including Kim Basinger, Hillary Clinton, and Sylvester Stallone. Reservations are only taken online.

GEORGETOWN
$200-300

Charming inn accommodations can be found at **The Avery Georgetown** (2616 P St. NW, 202/827-4390, www.averygeorgetown.com, $159-364). This beautiful neighborhood inn offers 15 colorful yet elegant guest rooms with modern furnishings. Amenities include pillow-top mattresses, Netflix, Hulu, and minibars stocked with complimentary refreshments.

Over $300

For a five-star stay in Georgetown, make a reservation at the **Four Seasons Washington, DC** (2800 Pennsylvania Ave. NW, 202/342-0444, www.fourseasons.com, $680-1,925). This high-end hotel is known for its spacious rooms and suites. It is also the only five-star, five-diamond luxury hotel in the city. The Four Seasons is a contemporary hotel with a warm and welcoming ambience. The professional staff is truly exceptional and tends to every guest personally. There is a fitness center, a pool, steam rooms, a sauna, and an aerobics studio on-site. Babysitting is also available. This is a very busy hotel when special events are going on in the city, yet even when the hotel is full, it never feels crowded, and the service is spot-on. The hotel is in a romantic Georgetown neighborhood, yet is convenient to the National Mall and all the city attractions.

UPPER NORTHWEST
$100-200

The **Kalorama Guest House** (2700 Cathedral Ave. NW, 202/588-8188, www.kaloramaguesthouse.com, $109-239) is actually two Victorian town houses—the main house and a nice brick town house—in Upper Northwest with 10 guest rooms total. Located in a cute neighborhood less than a block from the National Zoo, it is a good bargain for the area. Don't expect many amenities in the rooms (no telephone and no television). Some of the rooms have shared bathrooms, but you can fall asleep listening to the sound of monkeys howling in the distance at the zoo and wake to a freshly made continental breakfast in the main house.

$200-300

★ **Woodley Park Guest House** (2647 Woodley Rd. NW, 202/667-0218, www.dcinns.com, $220-292) is one of the nicest bed-and-breakfasts in DC. In a historic neighborhood in Upper Northwest, they offer 15 comfortable and quiet guest rooms and exceptional service. The owners are truly service-oriented, and they help make the city feel personal and accessible. This is a wonderful choice in a quiet location for both business and leisure travel. The rooms have free wireless Internet, and a delicious, fresh continental breakfast is served daily.

The **Omni Shoreham Hotel** (2500 Calvert St. NW, 202/234-0700, www.omnihotels.com, $224-1,353) is a luxurious landmark built in 1930. It has 836 guest rooms, some of which have wonderful views of Rock Creek Park. This historic hotel hosted its first inaugural ball in 1933 (for Franklin D. Roosevelt) and has hosted inaugural balls for each president that followed during the 20th century (Bill Clinton even played his saxophone there during his ball in 1993). At one time, it was the number one choice for accommodations for dignitaries and the rich and famous and has housed such notables as the Beatles and emperors. The hotel offers rooms and suites of varying sizes and prices, with the lower-end rooms being quite affordable and the upper-end suites being very expensive. An elegant restaurant is located in the hotel. The rooms have free wireless Internet, and there is an outdoor heated pool, a fitness center, and more than 100,000 square feet of meeting space.

The Ghost Suite

It's no secret that the **Omni Shoreham Hotel** (2500 Calvert St. NW, 202/234-0700, www.omnihotels.com, $224-1,353) in Upper Northwest DC has some pretty peculiar things going on in Suite 870. The grand and historic hotel, which was built in 1930, originally had an extravagant apartment on the eighth floor where a minor shareholder in the property lived with his family and housekeeper. Shortly after they moved into the apartment, the housekeeper was found dead in her bed in the apartment. Not long after, the family's adopted daughter (the only child in the family) also died mysteriously in the apartment amid rumors of suicide or a possible drug overdose.

The family remained in the apartment for 40 years and finally moved out in 1973. The once extravagant apartment was in shambles when they left and was closed off to the rest of the hotel and abandoned. Once the apartment was empty, guests in neighboring rooms began reporting disturbances. Televisions and lights would go on and off, doors would slam shut, people would feel breezes as if someone had walked by, and many reports of loud noises (including someone playing the piano) were reported coming from the apartment. Many of the strange sounds were reported to be coming from Room 864, which was the housekeeper's bedroom.

In 1997 the hotel decided to renovate the apartment and turn it into a presidential suite. During construction, a worker fell from the balcony to his death. Upon completion of the suite's restoration, the hotel appropriately named it "The Ghost Suite."

It is reported that to this day many guests claim seeing a little girl running through the halls and an older woman in a long dress roaming around alone.

Information and Services

VISITORS INFORMATION

Additional information on Washington DC can be found at www.washington.org or by stopping by the **Washington Welcome Center** (1005 E St. NW, 202/347-6609, daily 9am-8pm).

MEDIA

The most widely circulated daily newspaper in Washington DC is the *Washington Post* (www.washingtonpost.com), featuring world and local news and with an emphasis on national politics. The *Washington Times* (www.washingtontimes.com) is another daily newspaper that has a wide following.

Weekly and specialty newspapers include the *Washington City Paper* (www.washingtoncitypaper.com), an alternative weekly newspaper, and the *Washington Informer* (www.washingtoninformer.com), a weekly newspaper serving the DC area's African American population.

EMERGENCY SERVICES

In the event of an emergency, call 911.

The **Metropolitan Police Department** (202/727-9099, www.mpdc.dc.gov) is the municipal law-enforcement agency in Washington DC. It is one of the 10 largest police forces in the country.

There are no fewer than 10 hospitals in the city. Some of the ones ranked highest nationally include **MedStar Washington Hospital Center** (110 Irving St. NW, 202/877-7000, www.whcenter.org), **MedStar Georgetown University Hospital** (3800 Reservoir Rd. NW, 202/444-2000, www.medstargeorgetown.org), and **George Washington University Hospital** (900 23rd St. NW, 202/715-4000, www.gwhospital.com).

Getting There

AIR

Three major airports serve Washington DC. **Ronald Reagan Washington National Airport (DCA)** (703/417-8000, www.flyreagan.com), just outside the city in Arlington, Virginia, is serviced by the Blue and Yellow Lines of the Metrorail. Taxi service is available at the Arrivals curb outside the baggage claim area of each terminal. Rental cars are also available on the first floor in parking garage A. A shuttle operates outside each baggage claim area to the rental car counter. It is a 15-minute drive to downtown Washington DC from the airport.

Washington Dulles International Airport (IAD) (703/572-2700, www.flydulles.com), 27 miles west of the city in Dulles, Virginia, is a 35-minute drive from downtown Washington DC. Bus service between Dulles Airport and the Metrorail at the Wiehle Avenue Station in Reston (Silver Line) is available through the **Silver Line Express Bus Service** (703/572-7661, $5 one way, children under 2 free). Tickets can be purchased at the ticket counter in the main terminal at Arrivals door 4. Buses depart approximately every 15-20 minutes. Passengers going from the Wiehle Avenue Metrorail station should exit at the north side of the station to board the bus. Tickets can be purchased from the bus driver. **Metrobus** (202/637-7000, www.wmata.com) operates an express bus (Route 5A) between Dulles Airport and the L'Enfant Plaza Metrorail station in Washington DC. Passengers can board the bus at the airport at the Ground Transportation curb (on the Arrivals level) at curb location 2E. Car services such as Uber and Lyft are also available. An extension of Metrorail's Silver Line is planned and will provide a one-seat ride to downtown Washington DC from Dulles Airport in the future.

Baltimore/Washington International Thurgood Marshall Airport (BWI) (410/859-7111, www.bwiairport.com), 32 miles from Washington DC near Baltimore, Maryland, is approximately 50 minutes by car to Washington DC. It is serviced on weekdays by MARC commuter trains at the BWI Marshall rail station. Free shuttles are available from the station to the airport terminal. Shuttle stops can be found on the lower-level terminal road. Metrobus service is available between BWI and the Greenbelt Metrorail station (Green Line) on the **BWI Express Metro.** Bus service is available seven days a week with buses running every 40 minutes.

Washington Dulles Taxi and Sedan (703/554-3509, www.washingtondullestaxisedan.com) provides taxi and sedan service for passengers at all three airports. Shuttle service is also available from all three airports through **SuperShuttle** (800/258-3826, www.supershuttle.com).

CAR

Arriving in Washington DC by car is fairly common. Several major highways lead into the city, such as I-395 from the south in Virginia, I-66 from the southwest in Virginia, and I-295 from the northeast in Maryland. US 50 is the only primary road that runs through the city (on the eastern side) and connects Virginia and Maryland. Most hotels have some provision for parking, although it may come at a significant cost. There is also public parking on some streets and at many public garages throughout the city.

TRAIN

Amtrak (800/872-7245, www.amtrak.com) provides service to Washington DC through beautiful **Union Station** (50 Massachusetts Ave. NE, www.unionstationdc.com) on Capitol Hill. Amtrak connects with the **Maryland Area Rail Commuter (MARC)** system (410/539-5000, www.mta.maryland.gov), a service that runs Monday-Friday and connects Union Station with the Baltimore area, southern Maryland, and northeastern West Virginia; and with **Virginia Railway Express** (703/684-1001, www.vre.org), a service that runs weekdays only between Fredericksburg, Virginia, and Union Station and Manassas, Virginia, and Union Station.

BUS

A **Greyhound** (202/289-5141, www.greyhound.com) bus station is located at Union Station (50 Massachusetts Ave. NE). There is a second station in Dupont Circle at 1610 Connecticut Avenue NW.

Getting Around

METRORAIL

Washington DC and the surrounding area has a clean, reliable, and generally safe subway system called the **Metrorail** (202/637-7000, www.wmata.com) that is run by the **Washington Metropolitan Area Transit Authority (WMATA)**. The Metrorail system is commonly known as "The Metro" and provides service to more than 600,000 customers a day. The system is number two in the country in terms of ticket sales and serves more than 90 stations throughout DC, Virginia, and Maryland. Visit the WMATA website for current delays and alerts.

There are six color-coded rail lines: Red, Orange, Blue, Yellow, Green, and Silver. The system layout is easy to understand (most stations are named for the neighborhood they serve), and getting from one station to another normally requires no more than a single transfer. Metrorail stations are marked with large "M" signs at the entrance that have colored stripes around them to show which line they serve. A complete list of fares and a map of each train line can be found on the website (fares are $2.25-6 during peak hours). Metrorail opens at 5am on weekdays, 7am on Saturdays, and 8am on Sundays. It closes at 11:30pm Monday-Thursday, 1am Friday-Saturday, and 11pm on Sunday. Bicycles are permitted during nonpeak hours. It is important to note that doors on each train do not operate like an elevator door and will not reopen if you stick your arm or hand in them as they close. Never stand in the way of a closing door.

Permanent, rechargeable farecards called **SmarTrip** cards can be purchased online and at Metrorail stations. Riders can recharge their cards online. SmarTrip holders receive a discount on Metrorail and Metrobus service (the cards can be used for both).

METROBUS

WMATA also runs **Metrobus** (202/637-7000, www.wmata.com, $2-4.25) service from Metrorail stops and throughout the city. They operate 325 routes to 11,500 bus stops in Washington DC, Virginia, and Maryland. For a complete listing, visit the website. Bicycle racks are provided on Metrobuses and can accommodate two bikes. Permanent, rechargeable farecards called **SmarTrip** cards can be purchased online and at Metrorail stations. Riders can recharge their cards online. Metrobus accepts SmarTrip or cash.

The **DC Circulator** (202/671-2020, www.dccirculator.com, hours vary by route, free) is a free local bus service with six bus routes to key areas in the city. Some of the areas it serves include Georgetown, Dupont Circle, Rosslyn (in Arlington, Virginia), Union Station, the Navy Yard Metrorail stop, Adams Morgan, and the Potomac Avenue Metrorail stop.

TAXIS AND PRIVATE TRANSPORT

Some neighborhoods in the city, such as Georgetown and Adams Morgan, are not serviced by Metrorail, so traveling by taxi or car service can be an easy way to reach these areas and is also a good alternative for direct transport between two locations. Fares are charged on a meter on a distance-traveled basis. There are many taxi services throughout the city. Sixteen companies can be booked through **DC Taxi Online** (www.dctaxionline.

com). Standard taxi fares in Washington DC are $3.50 for the first eighth of a mile, with each additional mile costing $2.16. Hourly wait rates are $25.

Uber (www.uber.com) and **Lyft** (www.lyft.com) are hugely popular and easily accessible throughout Washington DC and are hailed over the Internet. Charges for the services are made directly to your credit card for a quick and easy transaction. These are fast, cost-effective, and easy ways to travel around the city. Rates are quoted on their websites.

Northern Virginia

Just across the Potomac River from the nation's capital, Northern Virginia is a cornucopia of culture, history, outdoor recreation, culinary delights, and shopping. While most of Northern Virginia is shaped by its proximity to Washington DC, the region also includes rolling hunt country, vineyards, and palatial estates in its western reaches, as well as beautiful views of the Blue Ridge Mountains.

Northern Virginia includes four counties (Arlington, Fairfax, Loudoun, and Prince William) as well as the independent cities of Alexandria, Fairfax, Falls Church, Manassas, and Manassas Park. The regional population comprises roughly one-third of the entire population of Virginia. As a central corridor for government contractors and the technology industry, the area tends to be upscale.

Highlights

Look for ★ to find recommended sights, activities, dining, and lodging.

★ **Arlington National Cemetery:** More than 300,000 plain white headstones stand in neat rows as a somber tribute to those who have served our nation. This is also the site of the Tomb of the Unknowns and the eternal flame at John F. Kennedy's grave site (page 94).

★ **Torpedo Factory Art Center:** This 82-studio art center in Old Town Alexandria hosts three floors of galleries in a former torpedo factory (page 105).

★ **Great Falls Park:** A 77-foot waterfall drops into Mather Gorge on the Potomac River, acting as an impressive backdrop to a park full of outdoor activities (page 119).

★ **National Air and Space Museum Steven F. Udvar-Hazy Center:** This Smithsonian Institution museum features an awe-inspiring aviation hangar that displays historic aircraft on three levels (page 120).

★ **George Washington's Mount Vernon:** Get a window into Washington's private life and the world of an 18th-century plantation (page 122).

★ **Wolf Trap National Park for the Performing Arts:** This unique venue is the nation's only national park created for the performing arts (page 127).

★ **Manassas National Battlefield Park:** This site of two major American Civil War battles is a great place for die-hard historians. The park

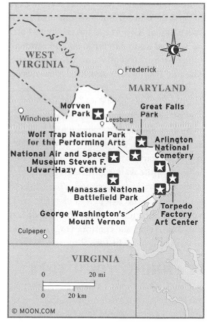

encompasses more than 5,000 acres of fields, woods, and streams (page 134).

★ **Morven Park:** Once home to Virginia governor Westmoreland Davis, this historic estate features the original mansion, two museums, an equestrian center, historic gardens, sports fields, and hiking trails (page 144).

The densely populated areas of Arlington and Alexandria abut Washington DC and border the Potomac River. Arlington is known for its national landmarks, military memorials, and trendy restaurants and shopping areas, while Alexandria is best known for its historic Old Town area, which supports a diversity of shops, excellent restaurants, and perhaps the ghosts of our country's founding fathers, who once walked the city's streets and gathered in its taverns.

Fairfax is the most populous jurisdiction in Virginia, but Loudoun has been growing steadily over the past few decades as new neighborhoods and business parks slowly take over what used to be mostly rolling hills and horse farms.

The second-largest county in Virginia, Prince William, is 35 miles from Washington DC and 20 miles from Washington Dulles International Airport. Its proximity to both has spurred a surge in business and residential growth in recent years. Bordering the Potomac River to the south of Alexandria, the county is rich in Civil War history and is home to Marine Corps Base Quantico.

Northern Virginia attracts entrepreneurs, politicians, advocates, artists, environmentalists, immigrants, and nomads from all corners of the earth. A variety of languages can be heard while walking through nearly any public area, and neighborhoods are as diverse as the people who live in and visit the area. Northern Virginia combines cosmopolitan and countryside, and continues to grow while preserving its deep historical roots.

PLANNING YOUR TIME

Any part of Northern Virginia can be visited in a day trip from Washington DC. The entire area can be covered in a busy few days, but four or five days will give you time to get a real feel for all it offers.

If you plan to stay in Virginia, where you sleep will depend on your priorities. Sights are spread throughout Northern Virginia, so it's best to pick your accommodations based on the atmosphere you like. If you want to stay where restaurants and shopping are within walking distance, consider Old Town Alexandria. If a cozy bed-and-breakfast is more your style, make a reservation in hunt country in Middleburg. Whatever you choose, the biggest consideration for your schedule will be traffic. The Washington DC area is notorious for highway congestion, and this is true year-round.

To avoid the heaviest traffic, don't travel during rush hour, which unfortunately can span many hours each weekday. The best time to travel on weekdays, especially if you are driving I-495 (the Beltway) or I-66, is between 10am and 3pm. Also, if you plan on arriving in the area or leaving the area on a Friday, avoid major arteries (I-495, I-66, and I-95) after 3pm. Friday-afternoon traffic will taint your view of the area. Another thing to be mindful of is high-occupancy/toll (HOT) lane restrictions. These require a minimum of two or three people to be in the car to use the roadway or specific lanes or you must pay a toll during specific times of day (and the toll amount will depend on the volume of traffic). Several major arteries such as I-66, I-395, I-95, and the Dulles Toll Road have these restrictions during prime commuting hours; for a listing of restrictions, visit www.virginiadot.org. The good news is that drivers around Northern Virginia are generally courteous.

Some public transportation is available in Northern Virginia through the **Washington Metropolitan Area Transit Authority** (WMATA) (www.wmata.com), which operates **Metrobus** and **Metrorail** service, although coverage isn't extensive in all parts of Northern Virginia. It is often more convenient to move around by car if that is an option.

Limited county bus transportation is also available in Arlington County, Alexandria, Fairfax County, and Loudoun County,

---

Previous: George Washington's Mount Vernon; Civil War cannons at Manassas National Battlefield Park; Great Falls Park

Northern Virginia

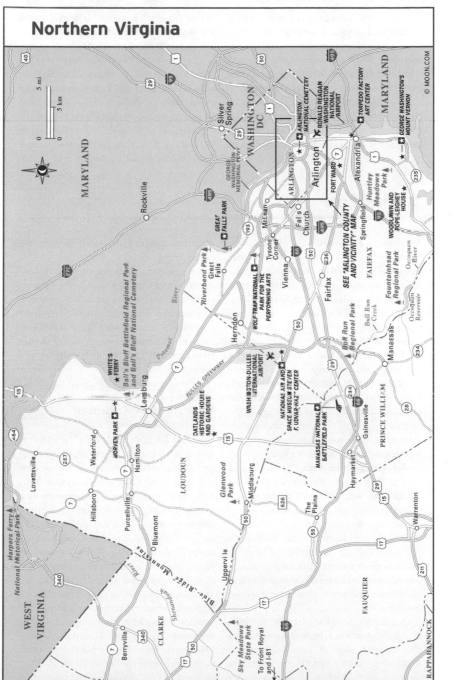

through the Arlington Transit (ART), Alexandria Transit Company (DASH), Fairfax Connector, and Loudoun County Transit, respectively. These services are geared toward commuters; so again, driving is usually the quickest and easiest way to see the sights.

Two major airports service the Northern Virginia area. The first is **Ronald Reagan Washington National Airport** (703/417-8000, www.flyreagan.com) in Arlington. Metrorail's Blue and Yellow Lines connect to this airport. The second is **Washington Dulles International Airport** (703/572-2700, www.flydulles.com) in Dulles, Virginia.

The **Leesburg Executive Airport (JYO)** (1001 Sycolin Rd., Leesburg, 703/737-7125, www.leesburgva.gov), owned and operated by the city of Leesburg, is one of the two busiest general aviation (GA) airports in Virginia. This airport is 35 miles from Washington DC and is a reliever airport for Washington Dulles International Airport.

Arlington

Arlington is the closest Virginia suburb to Washington DC. Just across the Potomac River from the capital, Arlington encompasses 26 square miles, is easily accessed from DC by four bridges and by public transportation (11 Metrorail stops and bus service), and has more than 234,000 residents.

Because of its proximity to the nation's capital, Arlington supports many federal buildings, national agencies, and memorials. Between this and the numerous businesses that call Arlington home, it sometimes seems like an extension of Washington DC rather than part of Virginia. Arlington contains more office space than downtown Los Angeles. Business centers in Arlington include the areas of Ballston, Clarendon, and Crystal City (where Amazon's East Coast headquarters will be located), but hotels, restaurants, and attractions are spread out all over Arlington County.

Arlington is a highly diverse community. Approximately 27 percent of the county's residents speak a language besides English at home. This contributes to a wonderful array of authentic food establishments from around the globe.

Originally slated to be part of Washington DC, Arlington was trimmed from the city plan in 1847 when it was established as Alexandria County. In 1920, the name was changed to Arlington, after the George Washington Parke Custis estate honoring the earl of Arlington.

Arlington is a place you will want to step in and out of during a visit to the nation's capital, but unless you are attending a specific event or coming for work, you don't need to plan an entire week there. It is so easily accessible that you can pick and choose your activities and see the highlights in a day or two.

SIGHTS
★ Arlington National Cemetery

The most famous cemetery in the nation is **Arlington National Cemetery** (1 Memorial Dr., 877/907-8585, www.arlingtoncemetery. mil, Apr.-Sept. daily 8am-7pm, Oct.-Mar. daily 8am-5pm, free). The cemetery is a sprawling 624-acre site where more than 400,000 soldiers from every U.S. military conflict are buried. The uniform white tombstones form an orderly quilt across the rolling green fields of the cemetery and are meticulously maintained. Called "Our Nation's Most Sacred Shrine," as the resting place for many generations of our nation's heroes, the cemetery grows daily: On average, more than two dozen funerals are held each weekday. In 1948, a group of women formed the Arlington Ladies, a volunteer group whose members attend services for all veterans and ensure that

Arlington County and Vicinity

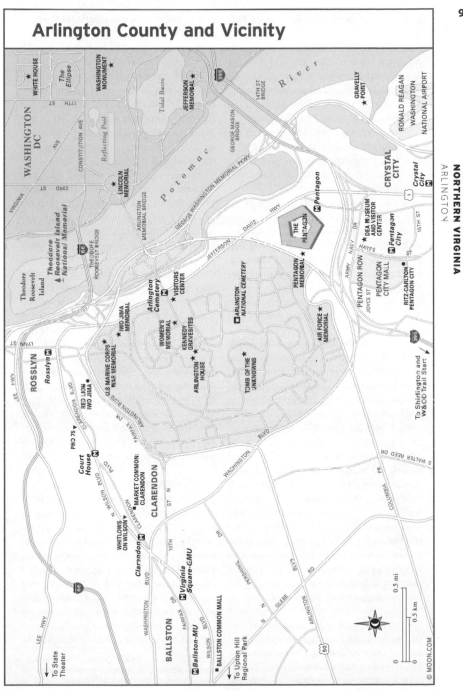

© MOON.COM

no member of the armed forces is ever buried alone.

A welcome center marks the entrance to Arlington National Cemetery and is always open when the cemetery is. Maps, grave locations, guidebooks, and other information on the cemetery can be obtained at the center, and there are restrooms and a bookstore.

Interpretive bus tours of the cemetery depart continuously from the welcome center. Tickets can be purchased at the center (adults $15, children 3-11 $7.25, senior 65 and over $11, uniformed military free).

Private cars are not allowed in the cemetery except by special permission, but parking is available off Memorial Drive in a paid parking garage, and there is a dedicated stop for the cemetery on the Metrorail Blue Line. Please remember that this is not a park but an active cemetery.

There are several key sights within Arlington National Cemetery that are well worth a visit.

The first and the best known is the **Tomb of the Unknowns.** The tomb houses the remains of unidentified American soldiers from World Wars I and II and the Korean War. Remains of a Vietnam War soldier were also housed in the tomb until they were identified in 1998 through DNA testing and relocated. That crypt remains empty but serves as a symbol. The Medal of Honor was presented to each of the interred soldiers, and these medals, along with the U.S. flags that draped their caskets, are displayed to the rear of the tomb in the Memorial Amphitheater. The tomb is guarded around the clock by the 3rd U.S. Infantry, and the changing of the guard is a popular tourist attraction. Guard changes occur every 30 minutes during the summer and every hour during winter.

Another popular sight at Arlington National Cemetery is the **Women's Memorial** (www.womensmemorial.org), an elegant semicircular retaining wall built of stone at the main entrance to the cemetery. This is the only major national memorial honoring American servicewomen. The memorial is open to the public every day (8am-5pm) except Christmas Day.

A short walk uphill from the Women's Memorial is the eternal flame and burial site of **John F. Kennedy.** This is one of the most-visited graves in the cemetery. **Jacqueline Kennedy Onassis** is buried next to him, and **Robert F. Kennedy** was laid to rest nearby in a grave marked (at his request) with only a single white wooden cross and excerpts from two of his civil rights speeches.

Another sight to visit while in Arlington National Cemetery is the **Arlington House, The Robert E. Lee Memorial** (321 Sherman Dr., Fort Myer, 703/235-1530, www.nps.gov/arho, daily 10am-4pm, free). This former home of George Washington Parke Custis, whose daughter married Robert E. Lee, is actually a national park and maintained by the National Park Service. The Greek revival-style mansion, which underwent a major renovation in 2019, sits on land that was once part of a 1,100-acre plantation where the Lee family lived for three decades before the Civil War. Expect to see period furnishings inside the home and to learn the interesting story of how the home was lost by the family during the Civil War. The site is the highest in Arlington National Cemetery and offers terrific views of Washington DC. The house is open for self-guided tours and is a 10-minute walk from the cemetery welcome center.

Iwo Jima Memorial

The **Iwo Jima Memorial,** also called the **U.S. Marine Corps War Memorial** (Arlington Ridge, 703/289-2500, www.nps.gov/gwmp, open 24 hours, free) stands to honor those Marines who died in defense of the United States. This awe-inspiring memorial is a 32-foot-tall granite and bronze sculpture created in the likeness of a Pulitzer Prize-winning photograph depicting the raising of the American flag on Iwo Jima (a small island off the coast of Japan) in March 1945,

1: headstones at Arlington National Cemetery **2:** Iwo Jim Memorial designed by sculptor Felix de Weldon and architect Horace W. Peaslee

near the end of World War II. The sculpture illustrates the U.S. flag being raised by five Marines and a Navy hospital corpsman. The detail in the memorial is stunning, and its enormous size adds to its inspirational appeal. This off-the-beaten-path memorial is definitely worth seeking out. It's a half-mile walk from the Rosslyn Metrorail station and slightly farther from the Arlington Cemetery Metrorail station.

National 9/11 Pentagon Memorial

The **National 9/11 Pentagon Memorial** (1 N. Rotary Rd., Pentagon, 301/740-3388, www. pentagonmemorial.org, open 24 hours, free) is a haunting, thought-provoking memorial dedicated to the 184 people who lost their lives at the Pentagon in the terrorist attacks of September 11, 2001. This two-acre memorial is just outside the Pentagon and is made up of 184 benches, one for each of the men and women who died on the plane that hit the building or inside the building. Illuminated fountains run beneath each bench. If you look at the side of the Pentagon building, it is easy to tell where the plane crashed: The stone replaced in the repair is slightly different in color from the rest of the building. The memorial is open all the time and can be accessed from the Pentagon stop on the Yellow or Blue Line on the Metrorail. Restrooms are available daily 7am-10pm.

Air Force Memorial

The **Air Force Memorial** (1 Air Force Memorial Dr., 703/979-0674, www.afdw. af.mil, daily 8am-8pm, free) is a sight that's visible from a considerable distance. Its three elegant, stainless steel and concrete spires stretch 270 feet toward the sky, honoring the service and lives of the men and women of the U.S. Air Force.

Drug Enforcement Administration Museum and Visitors Center

The **Drug Enforcement Administration**

Museum and Visitors Center (700 Army Navy Dr., 202/307-3463, www.deamuseum. org, Tues.-Sat. 10am-4pm, free) is a learning center dedicated to educating the public about drugs, addiction, law enforcement, and the history of drugs in the United States. It does so through a series of displays that discuss the impact of federal law enforcement on the evolving nature of licit and illicit drug use in the country.

RECREATION

Trails

There are many paved bike trails throughout Northern Virginia, and several go through Arlington. The 18-mile **Mount Vernon Trail** runs between Theodore Roosevelt Island (an 88-acre island and national park that sits in the Potomac River near the Roosevelt Bridge) and George Washington's Mount Vernon. The trail runs along the George Washington Memorial Parkway and passes by Gravelly Point Park and Ronald Reagan Washington National Airport and goes into Old Town Alexandria.

The **Four Mile Run Trail** is a 6.2-mile paved path that begins at **Bluemont Junction Park** (744 N. Emerson St.) and runs toward the Mount Vernon Trail and Ronald Reagan Washington National Airport. The **Washington & Old Dominion Trail** also begins in Arlington in the Shirlington area and runs west 45 miles to Purcellville, Virginia. One offshoot of the trail is the **Martha Custis Trail,** which intersects the Washington & Old Dominion Trail at mile marker 4. The Martha Custis Trail heads directly into Washington DC through Arlington on a four-mile paved path parallel to Route 66. There are a handful of climbs and some winding turns, but nothing too difficult. For a detailed map visit www. bikewashington.org.

Trail runners will enjoy the **Potomac Heritage Trail.** It begins on the west side of Theodore Roosevelt Island at the parking lot and runs 10 miles to the west end of the I-495 bridge. It passes through woods along the river, crosses small cliff tops, and spans a few streams. It is blazed in blue.

Hiking in Washington & Old Dominion Railroad Regional Park

The **Washington & Old Dominion Trail** (www. wodfriends.org) is known as Virginia's skinniest park. It's hard to believe that a regional park can be 45 miles long and just 100 feet wide, but this popular trail is exactly that. It begins at the intersection of Shirlington Road and Four Mile Run Drive in Arlington (just two blocks north of I-395) and follows an old rail route west through Falls Church (crossing over State Route 7) and into Vienna. A bridle path parallels the trail starting in Vienna, and the two paths continue through Reston, Herndon, Ashburn, and Leesburg before ending in the cute town of Purcellville on 21st Street.

Washington & Old Dominion Trail

Trains followed this route for more than 100 years (1859-1968), but today it is widely used for biking, running, walking, and inline skating. The asphalt trail is predominantly rolling, although there are many nice flat sections. There are few true hills, but the trail does gain in overall elevation heading west.

Proper trail etiquette includes staying to the right side of the path as you travel and making yourself known to slower traffic as you pass on the left. A simple "Passing left" callout is enough to warn people when you are going around them on the trail.

There are several rest areas. The largest is the Smiths Switch Station in Ashburn. This stop offers two portable toilets, a covered rest area, and vending machines. Another unofficial but extremely popular stop is at the Ashburn Road crossing at the **Carolina Brothers Pit Barbeque** restaurant and shop (20702 Ashburn Rd., 703/729-7070, www.carolinabrothers.com, Mon.-Thurs. 10:30am-7pm, Fri.-Sat. 10:30am-8pm, Sun. 10:30am-7pm, $6-20). It's hard to ignore the smell of their barbecue cooking, and they have a wonderful outdoor area with tables and umbrellas and numerous bike racks. They also sell drinks and snacks. There are several more porta-potty stops along the trail, including in Reston and Leesburg. As the trail passes through Vienna, it borders a Whole Foods Market where many people like to stop as well. There's also a community center in Vienna with public bathrooms.

For additional information and trail maps, visit **NOVA Parks** (www.novaparks.com) or the **Arlington County Department of Parks and Recreation** (703/228-4747, www.parks.arlingtonva.us).

Parks

Gravelly Point Park (George Washington Pkwy., daily dawn to dusk, free) is a very popular spot for plane-watching. Its proximity to the runways at Ronald Reagan Washington National Airport offers spectacular close-up views of planes as they approach and depart from the airport. The park sits directly on the Potomac River and offers a boat launch, picnic tables, and plenty of open spaces on which to throw down a blanket. A bike path also runs around the park. There's a three-hour limit on parking (which is enforced), so set your cell phone alarm if you plan to nap. This is also a great spot for watching the fireworks on the National Mall on the Fourth of July, but you'll have to get here early to find parking. The entrance to the park is only available from the northbound lanes of the parkway.

Upton Hill Regional Park (6060 Wilson Blvd., 703/534-3437, www.novaparks.com) is a popular family recreation area with a large outdoor water park, a playground, a miniature golf course, and batting cages for both baseball and softball. There is a basic snack bar with reasonable prices. Each activity in the park has its own hours of operation, so it's best to consult the website.

Theodore Roosevelt Island (703/289-2500, www.nps.gov/this) is a beautiful island in the Potomac River accessed off the northbound lanes of the George Washington Memorial Parkway. There are wooded trails and a 47-foot-tall monument to Roosevelt. Ranger tours are available to learn about the local wildlife. The views are beautiful if you can ignore the noise from the planes taking off and landing at Ronald Reagan Washington National Airport.

Another family recreation area is **Bluemont Park** (601 N. Manchester St., 703/228-6525, www.parks.arlingtonva.us). This 70-acre park offers many family activities including picnicking, horseshoes, fishing, a playground, a basketball court, a baseball field, tennis, volleyball, a playground, and disc golf.

For a complete list of Arlington County parks, visit www.parks.arlingtonva.us.

Canoeing and Kayaking

There are two good launch areas on the Potomac River in Arlington. The first is **Columbia Island Marina** (202/347-0173, www.boatingindc.com) off the George Washington Parkway, and the second is **Gravelly Point Park** (George Washington Pkwy.).

Four-hour guided "D.C. Monument Tour" kayak trips on the Potomac River are available through **Potomac Paddlesports** (301/881-2628, www.potomacpaddlesports.com, $95). Trips leave from Columbia Island Marina in Arlington.

ENTERTAINMENT AND EVENTS
Theater
The **Signature Theatre** (4200 Campbell Ave., 703/820-9771, www.sigtheatre.org), in

the shopping area of Shirlington, is a professional nonprofit theater company that features contemporary performances. Although it runs many traditional productions, it is widely known for its musical theater and inventive twists on lesser-known works. A top regional theater with an interesting design, set among a great selection of restaurants and shopping, the Signature Theatre has become a popular destination for the entire metropolitan area. Tickets are reasonably priced but can be difficult to obtain at the last minute.

The State Theatre in nearby Falls Church (220 N. Washington St., Falls Church, 703/237-0300, www.thestatetheatre.com) used to be an old-time movie theater, complete with balcony seating. In recent years, the theater has been renovated as a prime venue for concerts and comedy. There are several levels of seating and standing areas (including the balcony). Food and beverages are served, and table seating can be reserved. This is a fun venue with first-rate entertainment. Parking can be difficult, so plan to arrive early.

After seeing a performance at the **Synetic Theater** (1800 S. Bell St., 703/824-8060, www.synetictheater.org) you may reevaluate the whole theater experience. The goal of this award-winning company is to be the premier American physical theater—in short, this means they perform without speaking. Known for their Shakespeare productions, the theater uses movement, acrobatics, dance, music, and a number of other communication forms to create a very distinct form of theater, telling classic stories in an untraditional way.

Nightlife
The **Arlington Cinema & Drafthouse** (2903 Columbia Pike, 703/486-2345, http://acdh.arlingtondrafthouse.com) is a tradition in Northern Virginia. It opened its doors in 1985 and has served up dinner and a movie (with a full bar) ever since. The theater also offers live entertainment and broadcasts sporting events. This venue is also available for rent for private parties.

A local institution on Wilson Boulevard

is **Whitlows on Wilson** (2854 Wilson Blvd., 703/276-9693, www.whitlows.com, Mon.-Fri. 11am-2am, Sat.-Sun. 9am-2am). This historic venue, which was originally located in Washington DC (in 1946), features rock, reggae, hip-hop, dance, and blues shows many nights. They have food and drink specials throughout the week. Be sure to look around for reclaimed items such as the bowling lane bar top, booths from St. Patrick's Catholic Church, and chairs from the old Arlington County courthouse.

Another local favorite on Wilson Boulevard is **Galaxy Hut** (2711 Wilson Blvd., 703/525-8646, www.galaxyhut.com, daily 5pm-2am). This funky dive bar opened in 1990 as Arlington's first craft beer bar. They have 28 taps and live music Sundays and Mondays ($5).

Drinks and board games. That's really all you need to know about **The Board Room** (925 N. Garfield St., 703/248-9439, www.theboardroomva.com, Mon.-Fri. 4pm-2am, Sat. Sun. 11am-2am). This unique, mostly 21-and-over venue offers dozens of board games to play ($2 or you can bring your own), an extensive bar menu, and food. This is a fun place with many special events (wine tasting, happy hour, trivia, etc.). The entrance is around the corner from the street address. This venue also houses the intimate **Ms. Peacock's Champagne Lounge** (929 N. Garfield St., www.mspeacockschampagne.com, Wed.-Thurs. 6pm midnight, Fri.-Sat. 6pm-1am), a speakeasy-style lounge with an upscale feel and extensive champagne and cocktail list.

Festivals

There are a number of annual festivals held in Arlington. One of the most popular is the **Ballston Quarterfest** (www.quarterfestballston.org), a food, drink, and entertainment festival held each May along Wilson Boulevard. Admission to this lively street festival is free, but tickets must be purchased for the street pub and restaurant crawl. The **Feel the Heritage** event in February at

the **Charles Drew Community Center** (3500 23rd St. S, www.parks.arlingtonva.us) celebrates African American culture with live music, vendors, children's activities, food, and a hall of history.

The **Arlington County Fair** (www.arlingtoncountyfair.us) is also popular. It is one of the largest free annual events on the East Coast and draws over 50,000 people each August. The fair is held at the **Thomas Jefferson Community Center** (3501 S. 2nd St.). Shuttle service is available from nearby Metro stations.

SHOPPING

There are six primary shopping areas in Arlington. **Ballston Quarter** (4238 Wilson Blvd., www.ballstonquarter.com) is a four-level enclosed mall at the corner of Glebe Road and Wilson Boulevard. The mall includes national stores such as Macy's, a movie theater, a health club, and many smaller shops. The **Market Common Clarendon** (2800 Clarendon Blvd., www.marketcommonclarendon.com) is at the Clarendon Orange Line Metrorail stop. It is primarily an outdoor shopping mall (with garage parking) that has national name brand retailers such as Crate & Barrel, Barnes & Noble, and Ann Taylor along with local boutiques. There is also a Whole Foods Market in the shopping center.

Fashion Centre at Pentagon City (1100 S. Hayes St., www.simon.com) is a large mall with many national retailers such as Apple, Macy's, Nordstrom, and Banana Republic. **Pentagon Row** (1201 S. Joyce Street, www.pentagonrow.com) also offers shopping and restaurants in a central plaza with outdoor cafés and ice-skating in winter. It is off I-395 (a parking garage is available) near the Pentagon City Metro station on the Yellow and Blue Lines.

The **Village at Shirlington** (2700 S. Quincy St., www.villageatshirlington.com) has become a popular gathering place because of its great choices of restaurants and small shops. It is an outdoor mall, but garage parking is available. If you are in the Crystal City area, there are plenty of restaurants and shops between 12th and 23rd Streets near the Crystal City Metro stop in an area known as the **Crystal City Shops** (1750 Crystal Dr. and 2100 Crystal Dr., www.thecrystalcityshops. com). Many retailers and restaurants are located below ground along a unique network of walkways.

FOOD

Arlington is known for its diversity of wonderful food. Many eateries serve authentic fare from around the globe and do so at a reasonable price.

American

★ **The Lost Dog Café** (5876 Washington Blvd., 703/237-1552, www.lostdogcafe.com, Mon.-Sat. 11am-11pm, Sun. 11am-10pm, $7-26) is a local favorite for three reasons: great food, great beer, and its ties to the Lost Dog & Cat Rescue Foundation (founded by the restaurant owners). The restaurant is a lively, friendly, and casual café and gourmet pizza deli that serves a creative and delicious assortment of specialty pizzas, sandwiches, salads, and pasta. Menu items have names such as Kujo Pie (tomato sauce with pesto, artichoke hearts, grilled chicken, fresh tomatoes, mozzarella, and basil) and Dog Collars (onion rings). The bar stocks more than 200 types of beer, and the staff is knowledgeable and helpful. The decor is completely done in "dog"—although due to health regulations, no dogs are allowed inside. A portion of the proceeds goes to the foundation, but the food alone is reason to come. Consult the website for additional locations.

For classic diner food, try **Metro 29 Diner** (4711 Lee Hwy., 703/528-2464, www. metro29diner.com, daily 6am-midnight, $5-30). This local institution was featured on the TV show *Diners, Drive-ins and Dives*. They provide a monster menu of delicious homemade food and serve it up fresh in their 12,000-square-foot restaurant. All food is made from scratch; they even make their gravy in house and fresh challah bread for their French toast. They serve breakfast, lunch, and dinner, and they're open late. The service is friendly, and the place has a true diner feel.

Asian

A good Thai option is **Thai Square** (3217 Columbia Pike, 703/685-7040, www. thaisquarerestaurant.com, Mon.-Thurs. 11:30am-10pm, Fri. 11:30am-10:30pm, Sat. noon-10:30pm, Sun. noon-10pm, $9-18). This plain, no-frills restaurant built a reputation on its food. Street parking can be tough, but the service is good and the specials delicious. If you like spicy Thai food, this is an especially good choice.

Some of the most flavorful and creative Chinese food in the area is made at the legendary ★ **Peking Gourmet** (6029 Leesburg Pike, Falls Church, 703/671-8088, www. pekinggourmet.com, Sun.-Thurs. 11am-10:30pm, Fri.-Sat. 11am-11pm, $12-50) in nearby Falls Church. The gallery of celebrity photos hanging on the wall speaks volumes regarding the clientele at the restaurant, and it's not unusual to have VIPs in house. The signature dish is the Peking duck, which is nothing short of amazing. It arrives whole and is expertly carved tableside. Other must-try dishes include the chicken and garlic shoots (when available) and the crispy beef. Hands down, this is *the* best Chinese restaurant in Northern Virginia, and as such, it is crowded—so be sure to make a reservation.

If you're craving pho and only pho, stop by **Pho 75** (1721 Wilson Blvd., 703/525-7355, daily 10am-9pm, under $10). It is one of the original pho restaurants in the area, and they know pho. The soup is hot, delicious, and reasonably priced.

French

If you're feeling the itch for French food, try **La Cote d'Or Café** (6876 Lee Hwy., 703/538-3033, www.lacotedorarlington.com, lunch Mon.-Fri. 11:30am-3pm, brunch Sat.-Sun. 11am-3pm, dinner Sun.-Thurs. 5pm-9pm,

Fri.-Sat. 5pm-10pm, $23-38), a family-owned restaurant that is named after the Burgundy region in France. They serve delicious bistro-style French food—crepes, filet, and seafood—and a carefully selected wine list. The service is friendly and attentive, and you can expect an overall pleasant dining experience in a comfortable, French-country atmosphere.

Italian

As the name suggests, **The Italian Store** (3123 Lee Hwy., 703/528-6266, www.italianstore.com, Mon.-Fri. 10am-9pm, Sat. 10am-8pm, Sun. 11am-6pm, $7-25) is a casual authentic takeout pizzeria and sandwich store combined with an Italian market. Simply put, this place is fabulous. Fresh ingredients, homemade pasta, and Italian wines are just part of the recipe for success. This is a very popular carryout restaurant and is geared toward that, so if you come during peak lunch hours, be prepared to wait. There's a second location at 5837 Washington Boulevard.

Middle Eastern

For a quick meal or to curb a late-night appetite, stop in **Kabob Palace** (2315 S. Eads St., 703/486-3535, open 24 hours, $9-20) in Crystal City. The kabobs are tender and flavorful (the lamb is especially juicy), and the sides are authentic and delicious. Their rice is tasty and fluffy, and their mango lassi is refreshing. The clientele is diverse and lively, and the service is usually good.

Turkish

Yayla Bistro (2201 N. Westmoreland St., 703/533-5600, www.yaylabistro.com, Sun.-Thurs. 11am-9pm, Fri.-Sat. 11am-10pm, $10-25) has a dedicated following. They serve authentic, Turkish food in an elegant and relaxed setting. The menu includes spreads, salads, flatbreads, and delicious grilled meat (such as filet mignon, lamb, and salmon). They also offer a nice selection of Turkish wine.

Treats and Coffee

After trying the **Best Buns Bread Company** (4010 Campbell Ave. 703/578-1500, www.greatamericanrestaurants.com, Mon. 6am-7pm, Tues.-Fri. 6am-8pm, Sat. 7am-8pm, Sun. 7am-7pm, under $15) in Shirlington, you will look for an excuse to come back, maybe even the same day. Whether you're craving sweets, bread, or a sandwich, this is the place to go. They are part of the Great American Restaurants group, which includes **Carlyle Grand Café** (4000 Campbell Ave., 703/931-0777, www.greatamericanrestaurants.com, Mon.-Thurs. 11:30am-10:30pm, Fri. 11:30am-11:30pm, Sat. 10:30am-11:30pm, Sun. 9:30am-10:30pm, $13-28) next door. Carlyle Grand serves flavorful American food such as salads, sandwiches, and seafood in a lively environment. They also have a wonderful brunch menu on weekends.

For a good cup of joe, try the **Java Shack** (2507 N. Franklin Rd., 703/527-9556, Mon.-Sat. 7am-7pm, Sun. 8am-7pm, under $10), just off of Wilson Boulevard. It's pet friendly, people friendly, casual, a little quirky, and best of all, it serves good coffee and tea. The atmosphere is very relaxing, which is rare to find in the hubbub of Northern Virginia. The porch is especially pleasant for catching up with friends on a nice day.

Farmers Markets

Arlington has many wonderful farmers markets, and some are year-round. For a list of markets and locations, visit www.arlingtonva.us.

Arlington has several good farmers markets: the **Arlington County Farmers Market** (2100 Clarendon Blvd., Sat. May-Dec. 8am-noon, Jan.-Apr. 9am-noon), the **Clarendon Farmers Market** (3140 Wilson Blvd, 703/812-8881, Apr.-Dec., Wed. 3pm-7pm), the **Columbia Pike Farmers Market** (corner of S. Walter Reed Drive and Columbia Pike, www.columbia-pike.org/fm/, year-round Sun. 9am-1pm), and the **Crystal City Farmers Market** (Crystal City Drive between 18th and 20th Streets, www.crystalcity.org, Mid-May-Oct. Tues. 3pm-7pm).

ACCOMMODATIONS

Spending the night in Arlington can often be a less expensive alternative to staying in Washington DC. There are mostly large chain hotels in Arlington, but there are a few lesser-known alternatives that shouldn't be overlooked.

$100-200

There are few reliable hotels priced under $200 a night in peak tourist season in Arlington. The **Red Lion Hotel Rosslyn Iwo Jima** (1501 Arlington Blvd., 703/524-5000, www.redlion.com, $99-108) is a consistent option. The hotel is reasonably priced, especially for its location: It's minutes from the Iwo Jima Memorial, a short drive to Ronald Reagan Washington National Airport, and walking distance to the Rosslyn Metro stop. It is also convenient to many Washington DC attractions. There are 141 rooms, and they have complimentary bike rentals. The rooms are older and aren't fancy, but they are comfortable and have free wireless Internet. There is also on-site parking.

The ★ **Hilton Garden Inn Arlington/Shirlington** (4271 Campbell Ave., 703/820-0440, www.hiltongardeninn3.hilton.com, $133-193) is nicely located in a neighborhood of shops, restaurants, and theaters. It is also convenient to Washington DC. The rooms are amply sized and have comfortable beds. The service is friendly and professional. There are 142 rooms, and standard amenities come with each, including free high-speed Internet, a fitness center, a business center, and a swimming pool. The hotel also offers complimentary shuttle service to Ronald Reagan Washington National Airport and the Pentagon City Metrorail stop.

$200-300

The **Residence Inn Arlington Courthouse** (1401 N. Adams St., 703/312-2100, www.marriott.com, $121-409) is a modern, ecofriendly, 176-room hotel in Courthouse Village by the Courthouse Metrorail stop on the Orange Line. Many shops and restaurants are within easy walking distance, and pizza delivery is available to your room. Suites are pleasantly decorated and include wireless Internet and full kitchens. There is also a fitness center and a beautiful indoor pool with a lifeguard. Breakfast is included. There is on-site parking and the hotel allows pets, both for an additional fee.

If you need to stay near Ronald Reagan Washington National Airport, the 161-room **Hampton Inn & Suites Reagan National Airport** (2000 Richmond Hwy., 703/418-8181, www.hamptoninn3.com, $140-308) is a good option. They offer quick shuttle service to the airport and are close to the Metro. Rooms are spacious and include amenities such as free wireless Internet, flat-screen televisions, microwaves, and refrigerators. The beds are comfortable and the bathrooms are modern. Parking is available for $25 per day.

Le Meridien Arlington (1121 19th St. N., 703/351-9170, www.lemeridienva.com, $87-369) is a boutique hotel in the Rosslyn area of Arlington. It has 154 guest rooms and is nicely appointed with comfortable modern furniture. The staff is friendly, and the hotel is convenient to the Rosslyn Metrorail stop and a short walk to Georgetown. The on-site gym is above normal hotel standards, and there is a parking garage available. Book a room with a view of Georgetown across the Potomac River, and take advantage of happy hour on the large patio. The lobby is located on the 4th floor of the building, which can be a little confusing when checking in. There is also a charge for in-room wireless Internet. Le Meridien is a Marriott hotel.

Over $300

The **Ritz-Carlton, Pentagon City** (1250 S. Hayes St., 703/415-5000, www.ritzcarlton.com, $202-5000) is minutes from the Pentagon City Metrorail station. This hotel is consistent in offering a comfortable stay with great beds and attentive service, and they are top-notch for hosting conferences. The location itself is a draw, just minutes from downtown Washington DC and steps from shopping and restaurants. There are 366 guest rooms, and the hotel is pet friendly (for an additional fee).

INFORMATION AND SERVICES

For additional information on Arlington, contact the **Arlington Convention and Visitors Service** (1100 N. Glebe Rd., 800/677-6267, www.stayarlington.com, Mon.-Fri. 8am-5pm).

GETTING THERE AND AROUND

Arlington is just southwest of Washington DC on the other side of the Potomac River. It is a short drive across the Potomac River via the Memorial, Roosevelt, Francis Scott Key, and 14th Street Bridges or a short ride on **Metrorail** (202/637-7000, www.wmata.com).

If you plan to stay in Arlington and tour DC, Metrorail is a great way to get there. Service between Washington DC and Arlington is provided via the Orange, Blue, and Yellow Lines. Key stops in Arlington include Ronald Reagan Washington National Airport (Blue and Yellow), Pentagon City (Blue and Yellow), and Clarendon (Orange).

Regional **Metrobus** (202/637-7000, www. wmata.com) service is available in Arlington and also connects Arlington with DC. A list of the routes serving Arlington can be found at www.arlingtontransit.com. **Arlington Transit (ART)** (703/228-7433, www. arlingtontransit.com, $2) provides supplemental bus service to the regional Metrobus system by covering neighborhoods within Arlington County not served by Metrobus. **Ronald Reagan Washington National Airport** (703/417-8000, www.flyreagan.com) is in Arlington and is the primary arrival and departure point for air travel to Washington DC.

Old Town Alexandria and Vicinity

One of the country's oldest port cities, Old Town Alexandria has a long and vibrant history. Founded in 1749, the town sits on the banks of the Potomac River and offers scenic views of Washington DC and National Harbor.

Old Town Alexandria was an important shipping port because it was the last good anchorage on the river before the falls upstream. Homes, taverns, shipyards, and public warehouses quickly sprang up along the waterfront, and many of our country's founding fathers walked its streets, frequented its taverns, and worshipped in its churches. Teams of horses and oxen rolled hogsheads (large wooden barrels) of tobacco, the primary export at the time, down the streets of Old Town to the waterfront. Soon hemp and wheat joined it in the export trade to England.

The town is well preserved through meticulous restoration efforts and looks much the same as it did when George Washington and Robert E. Lee walked its cobblestone streets. More than 4,000 buildings from the 18th and 19th centuries still stand today, giving the city an authentic colonial feel. Other famous residents have included Jim Morrison and Mama Cass. Stroll along the waterfront on a summer evening and enjoy live music or dine in one of the many unique restaurants. This is an area you can see in one day, but you may choose to return again and again.

SIGHTS
★ Torpedo Factory Art Center

The **Torpedo Factory Art Center** (105 N. Union St., 703/746-4570, www.torpedofactory. org, daily 10am-6pm and Thurs. until 9pm, free) contains three floors of galleries and studios where visitors can see artists at work and purchase original artwork. The center has 82 studios, seven galleries, an art school, and a museum that provides a unique window into Alexandria's history called the **Alexandria Archaeology Museum** (3rd fl., 703/746-4399, www.alexandriava.gov, Tues.-Fri. 10am-3pm, Sat. 10am-5pm, Sun. 1pm-5pm, free). The art center is on the Old Town waterfront, in a former factory that actually produced torpedoes (U.S. Naval Torpedo Station) after World War I. A torpedo that was made in the factory is displayed in the main hall of the building. Today, more than 165 visual artists practice their trade here and encourage visitors to observe them at work. Two workshops are also located inside the Torpedo Factory.

Carlyle House

The beautiful **Carlyle House Historic Park** (121 N. Fairfax St., 703/549-2997, www.novaparks.com, Tues.-Sat. 10am-4pm, Sun. noon-4pm, adults $5, children 6-12 $3, children under 6 free) is the historic home of British merchant John Carlyle. It was built in 1753 and quickly became the focal point of the political and social circles in Alexandria. One of the first private homes built in Old Town, it is the only 18th-century Palladian home built of stone. Tours of the house provide a good window into life in Alexandria prior to the Revolutionary War. Many special events are held at the house throughout the year.

Gadsby's Tavern Museum

The **Gadsby's Tavern Museum** (134 N. Royal St., 703/746-4242, www.alexandriava.gov, Nov.-Mar. Wed.-Sat. 11am-4pm, Sun. 1pm-4pm, Apr.-Oct. Tues.-Sat. 10am-5pm, Sun.-Mon. 1pm-5pm, adults $5, children 5-12 $3, children under 5 free) includes two 18th-century brick buildings named after John Gadsby: a tavern (circa 1785) and a hotel (built in 1792). Just after the development of Alexandria in the late 1700s, the Gadsby buildings became the center of life and business in Alexandria. Prominent people who visited the establishment included George Washington, Thomas Jefferson, John Adams, James Madison, James Monroe, and the Marquis de Lafayette. The tavern and hotel were restored as a museum that now serves to educate visitors on the history, architecture, and social customs of the colonial period. The short, informative tours are truly fascinating and really give visitors a sense of the history of the period and the people who walked the tavern's halls.

Old Town Alexandria

Old Town Alexandria

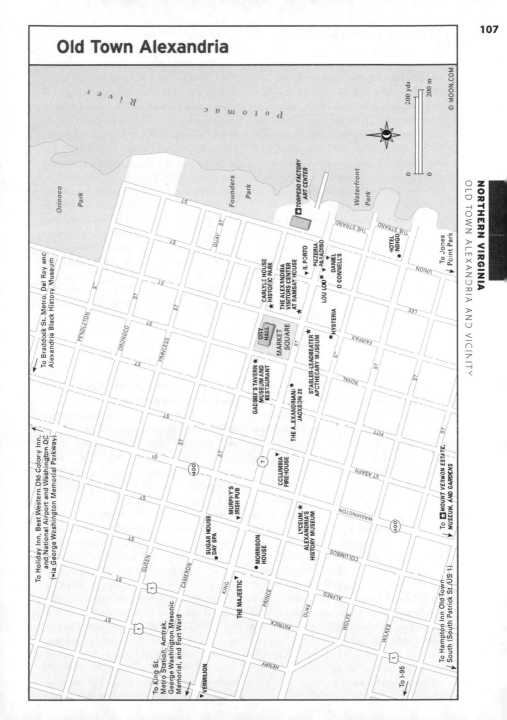

Stabler-Leadbeater Apothecary Museum

An easily overlooked gem is the **Stabler-Leadbeater Apothecary Museum** (105-107 S. Fairfax St., 703/746-3852, www.alexandriava.gov, Nov.-Mar. Wed.-Sat. 11am-4pm, Sun. 1pm-4pm, Apr.-Oct. Tues.-Sat. 10am-5pm, Sun.-Mon. 1pm-5pm, adults $5, children 5-12 $3, children under 5 free). Founded in 1792, the apothecary business operated for nearly 150 years; famous customers included Martha Washington and Robert E. Lee (who purchased paint for his home). A short video tour explains an interesting collection of medicine bottles, pill machines, and containers of native-grown cures, but take the guided tour. The guides take their time telling interesting stories of this family business and its customers. Globes filled with colored water stand in the window as some of the first "open" and "closed" signs. The museum is small and plain on the outside, but it's very authentic. Tours are approximately 30 minutes.

Lyceum, Alexandria's History Museum

Lyceum, Alexandria's History Museum (201 S. Washington St., 703/746-4994, www.alexandriava.gov, Mon.-Sat. 10am-5pm, Sun. 1pm-5pm, $2) is, just as its name suggests, a museum dedicated to Alexandria's history. It is housed in an attractive building on South Washington Street fronted by four tall columns. The structure has served as a Civil War hospital, private home, and the nation's first Bicentennial Visitor Center. The museum is simple but has exhibits on the history of Alexandria, especially during the Civil War, and offers lectures, concerts, school programs, and rental space. There is a gift shop that sells items related to Alexandria including books, maps, and note cards. Several self-guided walking tours of Alexandria begin at the Lyceum. For more information on these, visit www.visitalexandriava.com.

Alexandria Black History Museum

The **Alexandria Black History Museum** (902 Wythe St., 703/746-4356, www.alexandriava.gov, Tues.-Sat. 10am-4pm, $2) is a museum devoted to Alexandria's African American heritage. There are two exhibit galleries in the museum, one of which houses the Robert H. Robinson Library, which opened in 1940 after a sit-in at the segregated Alexandria Library in 1939; it was the first African American library in the area. The other gallery features local history exhibits. A 1797 Free Black Register is one of the most interesting items in the museum and is part of an exhibit that teaches about an area that had both a free black community and enslaved community that existed at the same time. There is also a reading room, art exhibits, and concerts at the museum. The nearby **African American Heritage Park** (Duke St.) is also part of the museum and contains the first African American burial ground in Alexandria, which dates back to the 19th century.

George Washington Masonic National Memorial

A hard-to-miss memorial is the **George Washington Masonic National Memorial** (101 Callahan Dr., 703/683-2007, www.gwmemorial.org, daily 9am-5pm, adults $18, children 12 and under free), which sits on top of a hill overlooking Alexandria. The memorial was constructed by American Freemasons and is perhaps the most recognized landmark in Alexandria, with its multifloor tower and observation deck sitting on top of a temple. The entire structure is slightly more than 330 feet tall and was designed as a memorial "lighthouse" to George Washington, who was a Mason. The building was started in 1922, but the interior was not finished until 1970. It also serves as a research and community center and meeting site for Masonic organizations. Tours are offered daily at 9:30am, 11am, 1pm, 2:30pm, and 4pm and last one hour. The tours include access to the observation area (where there is a panoramic view of Alexandria), so a tour is recommended. The museum is a bit dark inside but displays some of George Washington's personal belongings. The memorial is approximately four blocks from the King Street Metrorail station.

Fort Ward Park and Museum

A great place to relax on a nice day and learn a little history is the **Fort Ward Park and Museum** (4301 W. Braddock Rd., 703/746-4848, www.alexandriava.gov, museum Tues.-Sat. 10am-5pm, Sun. noon-5pm, park daily 9am-sunset, free). This fort was constructed during the Civil War by Union troops to protect Washington DC from Confederate forces. It is the best-preserved fort of the system of Union forts and batteries built for that purpose. Since approximately 90 percent of the fort's original walls are intact and much of the fort was restored to its original form, it is easy to see the design. There is a small museum with Civil War collectibles and exhibits and a nice open park with picnic spots and walking paths.

Tours

There are many guided tours available in Old Town. Some of the most popular tours are walking nighttime ghost tours, such as those hosted by **Footsteps to the Past** (703/683-3451, www.visitalexandriava.com, Mar.-Nov., $15) and **Alexandria Colonial Tours** (703/519-1749, www.alexcolonialtours.com, $10-15), where tour guides dressed in period costumes tell chilling historical stories and legends. There are also guided and self-guided bike tours from **Bike and Roll DC** (202/842-2453, www.bikeandrolldc.com, starting at $34) and seasonal sightseeing cruises with **The Potomac Riverboat Company** (703/684-0580, www.potomacriverboatco.com, starting at $20). Foodies will embrace the three-hour food-focused walking tours offered by **DC Metro Food Tours** (202/851-2268, www.dcmetrofoodtours.com, $65).

RECREATION

TopGolf

If you're looking for something different to do, try **TopGolf Alexandria** (6625 S. Van Dorn St., 703/924-2600, www.topgolf.com, starting at $25). TopGolf is a golf entertainment complex where guests can play different point-scoring golf games using personalized microchipped golf balls. The games are similar to bowling and darts but use golf balls and clubs. No golf experience is necessary.

Parks

CAMERON RUN REGIONAL PARK
Cameron Run Regional Park (4001 Eisenhower Ave., 703/960-0767, www.novaparks.com, fees vary per activity) may be showing its age, but it's still a fun place to take the kids for a day of water fun (wave pool and waterslides), minigolf, and batting cages.

FORT HUNT PARK
Located near the Potomac River, **Fort Hunt Park** (8999 Fort Hunt Park, 202/439-7325, www.nps.gov/gwmp) once belonged to George Washington's estate (Mount Vernon), and batteries in the park defended the river during the Spanish-American War. Today, the park is a favorite for family and corporate picnics, offering lovely open fields and hardwood trees. There is a paved loop that is friendly to cyclists, walkers, and runners, and a pavilion hosts summer concerts.

HUNTLEY MEADOWS PARK
Wildlife-watching is possible in the middle of suburban Northern Virginia at **Huntley Meadows Park** (3701 Lockheed Blvd., 703/768-2525, www.fairfaxcounty.gov, free). This 1,425-acre park offers great wetland wildlife-viewing from its half-mile boardwalk trail and observation tower. The park is a noted birding area, with more than 200 species, and also supports beavers, frogs, and dragonflies. A visitors center has exhibits, and there are two miles of hiking trails.

RIVER FARM

The headquarters of the American Horticultural Society (AHS) is at **River Farm** (7931 E. Boulevard Dr., 703/768-5700, www.ahsgardening.org, free). River Farm was one of George Washington's five farms. The 25-acre site is beautifully landscaped and includes a circa 1757 home that now houses the AHS. The largest specimen of an Osage orange tree in the country is at River Farm; it is said to have been a gift to the Washington family from Thomas Jefferson (Jefferson received Osage orange seedlings from the Lewis and Clark expedition of 1804-1806). There is no charge for admission to the farm and the house, but donations are appreciated.

Boating

You can launch a boat or kayak from **Belle Haven Marina** (1201 Belle Haven Rd., 703/768-0018, www.saildc.com) or learn to sail at their sailing school. Located on the Potomac River, their sailing school was founded in 1975, and they run the largest full-time sailing program on the Potomac. Boats are available for rent.

Biking

Old Town Alexandria is a very bike-friendly area. There are many bike-friendly businesses that encourage employees and guests to ride bikes to their facilities. The 18-mile **Mount Vernon Trail** runs between Theodore Roosevelt Island (an 88-acre island and national park that sits in the Potomac River near the Roosevelt Bridge) and George Washington's Mount Vernon. The trail passes right through Old Town Alexandria but can be a little tricky since it runs along the street. For a map of the trail, visit www.bikewashington.org. Bikes can be rented from **Big Wheel Bikes** (2 Prince St., 703/739-2300, www.bigwheelbikes.com, $7 per hour or $35 per day).

Golf

The **Greendale Golf Course** (6700 Telegraph Rd., 703/971-6170, www.fairfaxcounty.gov, open year-round, $31-40) is an 18-hole regulation golf course covering 148 acres. The terrain is rolling with asphalt cart paths. The course was designed to be challenging with water hazards and tight fairways. The facility includes a putting green, clubhouse with food service, club rentals, cart rentals, and golfing supplies. Golf lessons are also available.

The nine-hole, par-35 **Pinecrest Golf Course** (6600 Little River Tpke., 703/941-1061, www.fairfaxcounty.gov, open year-round, $20-23) is a challenging executive golf course. The course is narrow and includes hills and ponds. It is geared toward both novice golfers and serious players.

Day Spas

Old Town has many salons and day spas. If you are looking for a massage or any number of professional spa services, visit the **Sugar House Day Spa & Salon** (111 N. Alfred St., 703/549-9940, www.sugarhousedayspa.com). They are in a cute row house on North Alfred Street and offer a warm, professional atmosphere with high-quality (female only) massage therapists. Another good option is **Fountains Day Spa** (422 S. Washington St., 703/549-1990, www.fountainsdayspa.com), in a yellow house on Washington Street and offering high-quality massages and a large variety of other spa services. For waxing and other specialty salon services, **Aida Spa** (1309 King St., 2nd Fl., 703/535-7875, www.aidaspaoldtown.com) is the place to go. The owner specializes in skin care, face-and-body treatments, and makeup.

ENTERTAINMENT AND EVENTS

Music and Theater

The Birchmere (3701 Mount Vernon Ave., 703/549-7500, www.birchmere.com, $20-115) is a legendary concert hall seating approximately 500 people that hosts nationally known bands in many genres including folk, jazz, bluegrass, country, and rock. There is table seating at the main stage with food service.

The bandstand includes a dance area. The theater offers a casual, intimate atmosphere with decent food. Parking is a little tricky, so consult the website for directions.

Other good choices for an evening of live music are **Basin Street Lounge** (219 King St., 703/549-1141, www.219restaurant.com), a sophisticated and intimate establishment above the 219 Restaurant that hosts live jazz and blues nightly, and **Murphy's A Grand Irish Pub** (713 King St., 703/548-1717, www.murphyspub.com). Murphy's serves traditional Irish food, has a good selection of beers on tap, and has live music most nights. It has a lively pub atmosphere and friendly patrons and servers.

The Little Theatre of Alexandria (600 Wolfe St., 703/683-0496, www.thelittletheatre.com) was founded in 1934 and is one of just a handful of community theaters in the United States with its own building. Many famous people have sat in its audience including President Harry S. Truman, Lady Bird Johnson, and President George W. Bush. The theater hosts a seven-show season.

Festivals and Events

Old Town hosts numerous festivals and events throughout the year. Following are just some of the fun experiences visitors can participate in. Visit www.visitalexandriava.com for a full list of events.

The **Alexandria Film Festival** (www.alexfilmfest.com) is an annual tradition in November that celebrates the work of both established and emerging filmmakers from around the world. Dozens of films, including independents, shorts, documentaries, animation, and features, are shown in multiple locations around Alexandria.

Those fortunate enough to be in Old Town Alexandria during **Alexandria Restaurant Week** (www.visitalexandriava.com) are in for a treat. For 10 days in August, more than 70 area restaurants offer special menus at discounted prices. It's a great time for visitors to sample the variety of cuisine available in Old Town and for residents to try new establishments.

The **Alexandria King Street Art Festival** (www.artfestival.com) is an annual street festival that takes place on King Street in September. Voted one of the top 100 art festivals in the United States by *Sunshine Artist Magazine,* the juried festival features pieces from artists selected for the quality and originality of their work. Paintings, sculpture, jewelry, photography, and ceramics are just some of the types of art visitors can expect to see. The show stretches down several blocks of King Street to the waterfront.

SHOPPING

Old Town Alexandria is a shopaholic's dream. Block after block of award-winning boutiques, national-brand stores, and specialty shops can exhaust even the most fit shopper. Whether you're looking for clothes, souvenirs, antiques, artwork, or something unusual and funky, you can participate in a tradition of buying and sharing bounty that started back in colonial times. The primary shopping area stretches 11 blocks from the Potomac River up King Street.

Imagine Artwear (1124 King St., 703/548-1461, www.imagineartwear.com) has been a fixture in the community since 1988. They sell contemporary crafts, clothing, jewelry, and other accessories created by American artists. This store is a local favorite, as is **Lou Lou** (132 King St., 703/299-9505, www.loulouboutiques.com). Lou Lou sells jewelry and accessories at reasonable prices. They offer a wide variety of colors and designs.

For the little ones and moms to be, **529 Kids Consign** (122 S. Royal St., 703/567-4518, www.529kidsconsign.com) is a consignment boutique that specializes in high quality kids and maternity wear for "hip moms and cool kids."

To search for a particular type of store, visit www.visitalexandriava.com.

Bring Fido

Old Town Alexandria is extremely dog friendly. Specialty shops cater specifically to our canine friends, and many others put out water bowls and treats in front of their doorways.

HOTELS

Many hotels in Old Town allow dogs in their rooms. The Kimpton hotels, in particular, have a history of being pet friendly and include added amenities for dogs such as honor bars stocked with pet treats, pet bedding, and pet bowls. Some dog-friendly hotels include:

- **Morrison House—A Kimpton Hotel** (116 S. Alfred St., 703/838-8000, www.morrisonhouse.com)

- **Hotel Indigo** (220 S. Union St., 703/721-3800, www.hotelindigooldtownalexandria.com)

- **Residence Inn by Marriott Alexandria Old Town South at Carlyle** (2345 Mill Rd., 703/549-1155, www.marriott.com)

- **Westin Alexandria** (400 Courthouse Sq., 703/253-8600, www.westinalexandria.com)

- **The Alexandrian Old Town Alexandria** (480 King St., 703/549-6080, www.marriott.com)

- **Holiday Inn & Suites Alexandria-Historic District** (625 1st St., 703/548-6300, www.ihg.com)

- **Lorien Hotel & Spa—A Kimpton Hotel** (1600 King St., 703/894-3434, www.lorienhotelandspa.com)

- **Sheraton Suites Alexandria** (801 N. Saint Asaph St., 703/836-4700, www.sheratonsuitesalexandria.com)

DINING

Dog-friendly dining is also fairly common in Old Town Alexandria. By law, pets are not permitted inside restaurants, but many dining spots have seasonal seating outdoors where well-behaved dogs are permitted to join their owners. Following are examples of dog-friendly restaurants, but others can be found by looking for outdoor cafés where other dogs are sitting or establishments that have water bowls outside their doors. If you are uncertain, be sure to ask the host or hostess about the restaurant's policy.

FOOD
American

★ **The Majestic** (911 King St., 703/837-9117, www.themajesticva.com, Mon.-Thurs. 11:30am-midnight, Fri. 11:30am-1am, Sat. 10am-1am, Sun. 10am-midnight, $16-30) is a small gem of a restaurant right in the heart of Old Town. It serves American comfort food and has a history dating back to 1932. The decor is modern and inviting and makes for a fun place to gather with friends, family, or business associates. Step off the street right into the bar and grab a drink while you wait for a table. It is obvious that great care goes into designing each menu item, so don't hesitate to ask your server for more details. Seafood is a specialty here, but you may find it prepared with a new twist such as with an unusual spice or paired with a nontraditional side. The seared scallops are a personal favorite, or the Majestic Burger with its delightful bacon jam. No matter what you choose save room for dessert. If you're lucky to see their coconut cake on the menu, be sure to order it. It is fresh, moist, and just plain out of this world.

- Doggie Happy Hour is a regular event at **Jackson 20** (480 King St., adjacent to the Alexandrian Hotel, 703/549-6080). It is held seasonally on Tuesdays (5pm-8pm) and is a popular Old Town tradition.

- **Vola's Dockside Grill** (101 N. Unions St., 703/935-8890) is known for their dog-friendly atmosphere and has a menu just for furry patrons with three selections that actually sound pretty good (including a 5 oz. sirloin).

- Other restaurants that allow furry friends on their outdoor patios include **Haute Dogs and Fries** (610 Montgomery St., 703/548-3891) and **The Dairy Godmother** (2310 Mount Vernon Ave., 703/683-7767), where they offer puppy pops.

PET-SUPPLY STORES

There are several specialty pet-supply stores in Old Town Alexandria and the vicinity where you can purchase gourmet treats, toys, food, and other supplies:

- **The Dog Park** (705 King St., 703/888-2818, www.thedogparkva.biz)

- **The Olde Towne School for Dogs** (529 Oronoco St., 703/836-7643, www.otsfd.com)

- **Nature's Nibbles** (2601 Mount Vernon Ave., 703/931-5241, www.naturesnibbles.com)

OLD TOWN ATTRACTIONS

Several Old Town Alexandria attractions allow dogs to accompany their owners:

- **Potomac Riverboat Company** (105 N. Unions St., 703/684-0580, www.potomacriverboatco.com) offers 45-minute canine harbor cruises on Saturdays from June to mid-September. Tickets are $24.99 for adults and $15.75 for children 2-11. Children under 2 and dogs ride free.

- The **Torpedo Factory Art Center** (105 N. Union St., 703/746-4570, www.torpedofactory.org) allows well-behaved dogs on leashes.

- **Footsteps to the Past** (724/272-8433, www.visitalexandriava.com) offers dog-friendly guided walking tours of Alexandria.

- The **Alexandria Visitors Center at Ramsay House** (221 King St., 703/746-3301) allows dogs to visit with their owners.

Virtue Feed & Grain (106 S. Union St., 571/970-3669, www.virtuefeedgrain.com, Mon.-Sat. 11:30am-1am, Sun. 10am-1am, $9-32) is housed in a historic brick building on South Union Street that was used as a feed house on the waterfront in the 1800s. They serve a casual menu of burgers, tacos, and entrees such as salmon, shrimp and grits, and steak. The interior is a symphony in reclaimed materials such as wood, brick, and the original concrete floors, with large newly added windows. The two-level space is lively and includes a unique porch with wraparound windows on the second level for private parties. Save room for dessert—they have a scrumptious peanut butter pie.

Gadsby's Tavern (138 N. Royal St., 703/548-1288, www.gadsbystavernrestaurant.com, brunch Sun. 11am-3pm, lunch Mon.-Sat. 11:30am-3pm, dinner daily 5:30pm-10pm, $22-30) offers a rare historical dining experience and one that's unique to Old Town Alexandria. Situated next door to Gadsby's Museum, the tavern has served patrons since the late 1700s. Dine in a space once frequented by George Washington, Thomas

Jefferson, John Adams, James Madison, and James Monroe. The attentive staff is dressed in period attire, and the cozy, candlelit decor depicts the colonial period, but this is not a theater. Great attention is given to both the menu and the dining experience. There is a nice selection of steaks, chops, and seafood, including George Washington's Favorite, which is grilled breast of duck with scalloped potatoes, corn pudding, *rhotekraut* (red cabbage), and a port wine orange glaze.

Another one-of-a-kind dining experience can be had at the **Columbia Firehouse** (109 S. Saint Asaph St., 703/683-1776, www.columbiafirehouse.com, brunch Sat.-Sun. 11am-3pm, lunch Tues.-Fri. 11:30am-3pm, dinner Mon. 5:30pm-9pm, Tues.-Thurs. 5:30pm-10pm, Fri.-Sat. 5:30pm-11pm, Sun. 4:30pm-9pm, $15-39). The restaurant was once a firehouse (built in 1883) and is now a historical, well-preserved eatery in the heart of Old Town. This modern American brasserie and bar still shows its firehouse roots with original exposed brickwork. There is a varied menu of pub food and more-intricate dishes that includes a raw bar, salads, sandwiches, steak, and daily specials. If you're a fan of mussels, the Firehouse serves them three delicious ways. Perfect for foodies, families, and friends, this is an upbeat establishment with a comfortable feel.

It would be difficult to suggest restaurants in Old Town without including **Vermilion Restaurant** (1120 King St., 703/684-9669, www.vermilionrestaurant.com, brunch Sat.-Sun. 10:30am-2:30pm, lunch Mon. and Wed.-Fri. 11:30am-3pm, dinner Mon.-Thurs. 5:30pm-10pm, Fri.-Sat. 5:30pm-11pm, Sun. 5pm-9pm, $19-32). They serve contemporary American food at its finest for lunch and dinner, with entrées such as wild halibut, crusted lamb, and ricotta gnocchi. The menu is small but done well. They also offer a four-course tasting menu for $72. The restaurant is committed to locally grown goods.

French

BRABO Brasserie (1600 King St., 703/894-3440, www.braborestaurant.com, brunch Sunday 11am-2:30pm, dinner Mon.-Thurs. 5pm-10pm, Fri.-Sat. 5pm-11pm, Sun. 5pm-9pm, $23-44), adjacent to the Lorien Hotel & Spa, initially attracts guests with its warm but elegant atmosphere, but keeps them coming back for the exquisite cuisine. Pan-seared sea bass, lamb shank, and Shrimp Boudin Blanc are just some of the entrées created by the award-winning chef. The service is

Virtue Feed & Grain

impeccable, and there's even a communal table for those wishing to mingle. There's also a tasting room and market.

★ **Le Refuge Restaurant** (127 N. Washington St., 703/548-4661, www.lerefugealexandria.com, lunch Mon.-Sat. 11:30am-2:30pm, dinner Mon.-Sat. 5:30pm-10pm, $25-40) is one of the best-kept secrets in Alexandria. This small, family-owned French country bistro feels more like Paris than Virginia. The menu includes favorites such as beef Wellington, bouillabaisse, and rack of lamb as well as daily specials. The setting is cozy and even a bit snug, but the food and service are excellent. They also offer a three-course prix fixe lunch for $22 and a three-course prix fixe dinner for $35.

Irish

What could be more Irish than a restaurant called **Daniel O'Connell's** (112 King St., 703/739-1124, www.danieloconnells.com, daily 11am-1am, $10-17)? This lively spot on King Street serves up traditional Irish fare with a few interesting modifications. Try an Irish Egg Roll or the Dublin Nachos to start your meal. Follow with some classic fish-and-chips, a Guinness burger, or corned beef and cabbage. The menu changes regularly, which is refreshing for an Irish pub, and everything is served with a wide Irish smile. The old brick building gives the restaurant an authentic Old Town feel, and after one too many Guinness stouts, it can be difficult to find your way through the maze of rooms and staircases to the restroom. If you're lucky enough to score a rooftop patio seat overlooking King Street on a nice evening, plan to stay for a while—you won't want to give up your table.

Another fun Irish pub is **Murphy's Irish Pub** (713 King St., 703/548-1717, www.murphyspub.com, Mon.-Sat. 11am-2am, Sun. 10am-2am, $10-15). They offer warm pub fare and entertainment nightly.

Italian

Made-from-scratch Italian cooking can be found at **Il Porto Italian Ristorante**

(121 King St., 703/836-8833, www.ilportoristorante.com, Mon.-Thurs. 11am-10pm, Fri.-Sat. 11am-11pm, Sun. 11am-10pm, $19-30). This Old Town classic opened in 1973 and has a steady following. Traditional pasta dishes are flavorful and filling, as are other Italian staples such as chicken parmigiana and fresh seafood selections.

If you're in the mood for pizza, try **Pizzeria Paradiso** (124 King St., 703/837-1245, www.eatyourpizza.com, Mon.-Thurs. 11:30am-10pm, Fri.-Sat. 11:30am-11pm, Sun. noon-10pm, $12-21), the King Street outlet of a small local chain. The pizza is some of the best in the area and is made with fresh ingredients. The beer list is impressive, and the staff is very friendly and attentive. There is a long list of available toppings, including some less traditional options such as roast lamb, potatoes, hot cherry peppers, and capers.

Treats

One cupcake bakery that does a particularly good job is **Lavender Moon Cupcakery** (116 S. Royal St., 703/683-0588, Sun.-Thurs. 11am-8pm, Fri.-Sat. 11am-9pm, under $10). The selections vary daily, but some sample flavors include s'mores, flourless chocolate, lemon, passion fruit, and blood orange Dreamsicle.

Farmers Markets

There are several farmers markets in Old Town Alexandria and the vicinity. Some are seasonal and some are held year-round. The **Old Town Farmers' Market** (301 King St., Sat. 7am-noon, year-round) is the oldest farmers market in the nation held continuously at the same location. George Washington sent produce grown at Mount Vernon to this market. Other farmers markets include: **Del Ray Farmers Market** (corner of East Oxford Ave. and Mount Vernon Ave., Sat. 8am-noon, year-round); **Four Mile Run Farmers & Artisans Market** (4109 Mount Vernon Ave., Apr.-Oct. Sun. 9am-1pm,); and **West End Farmers Market** (Ben Brenman Park, 4800 Brenman Park Dr., May-Oct. Sun. 8:30am-1pm).

Sidetrip: A Taste for Del Ray

Just northwest of Old Town Alexandria, along Mount Vernon Avenue, is Del Ray, a hip little neighborhood full of coffee shops, art galleries, specialty food stores, and cafés. This trendy little pocket of Northern Virginia has a population of mostly young families, working couples, and singles who can be seen walking the streets with their dogs or strollers or working on their laptops behind café windows.

This pleasant neighborhood didn't always have a laid-back vibe; in fact, not long ago (during the early aughts), it was a place you may have only heard about on the nightly news. In recent years, Del Ray has blossomed into a friendly, funky place to live where eateries now dominate the main thoroughfare and real estate prices have skyrocketed. Also a great place to visit, Del Ray has many good options to satisfy the palate.

One of the most well-known eateries in Del Ray is **The Evening Star Café** (2000 Mount Vernon Ave., 703/549-5051, www.eveningstarcafe.net, brunch Sat.-Sun. 10am-2:30pm, dinner daily from 5:30pm, $14-26). They offer a modern twist on classic Southern cooking. Try their chicken and succotash, flat iron streak, or chicken-fried oysters.

Just off Mount Vernon Avenue, **Del Ray Café** (205 E. Howell Ave., 703/717-9151, www.delraycafe.com, Sun.-Thurs. 8am-2:30pm and 5pm-9pm, Fri.-Sat 8am-2:30pm and 5pm-10pm, $21-32) is a farm-to-table French-American café serving breakfast, lunch, and dinner in a cute house with a red-roofed porch. This is an especially good choice for breakfast—try the crab eggs Benedict or one of the organic omelets.

If you're craving food from south of the border, **Los Tios Grill** (2615 Mount Vernon Ave., 703/299-9290, www.lostiosgrill.com, Sun.-Thurs. 11am-10pm, Fri.-Sat.11am-11pm, $7-25), a Tex-Mex and Salvadoran restaurant, and **Taqueria Poblano** (2400-B Mount Vernon Ave., 703/548-8226, www.taqueriapoblano.com, Mon. and Wed.-Fri. 11am-3pm and 5pm-10pm, Sat. 11am-10pm, Sun. 10am-9pm, $4-18), a Mexican restaurant, are both known for their good food and margaritas.

For a good Philly cheesesteak, try **Al's Steakhouse** (1504 Mount Vernon Ave., 703/836-9443, www.alssteak.com, Mon.-Wed. 10am-8pm, Thurs.-Sat. 7am-8pm, Sun. 7am-4pm, $6-20). The plain brick exterior is easy to miss, but locals know this is the best place for a Philly fix.

Cheese lovers won't want to miss **Cheesetique** (2411 Mount Vernon Ave., 703/706-5300, www.cheesetique.com, Mon.-Fri. 11am-10pm, Sat.-Sun. 10am-10pm, $6-11), an artisan cheese shop with a wine and cheese bar. Sample cheese, take home cheese, or order from a menu of cheese-influenced selections.

For dessert try the **Dairy Godmother** (2310 Mount Vernon Ave., 703/683-7767, www.thedairygodmother.com, Sun.-Mon. noon-9pm, Wed.-Sat. noon-10pm, under $10). This funky frozen-custard shop was made famous when the Obama family stopped in for dessert back in 2009.

ACCOMMODATIONS

As with most of Northern Virginia, accommodations in Old Town Alexandria consist mostly of chain hotels. However, there are a few good boutique hotels that offer unique lodgings right in Old Town.

$100-200

Reasonably priced accommodations near Old Town Alexandria can be found at the **Holiday Inn Express & Suites Alexandria-Fort Belvoir** (6055 Richmond Hwy., 571/257-9555, www.alexandriafortbelvoirhotel.com, $113-128). This hotel offers 144 spacious rooms and friendly service. Rooms have large flat-screen televisions and comfortable beds. There is a small indoor pool and fitness center. Breakfast is included, as is high-speed Internet, and there is free shuttle service to the Huntington Metrorail station as well as free on-site parking.

If you don't have a car and you want to be convenient to the Metrorail and have easy access to shops and restaurants, try the **Hampton Inn Alexandria-Old Town/King Street Metro** (1616 King St., 703/299-9900, www.hamptoninn3.hilton.com, $123-189). This 80-room hotel one block from the King Street Metrorail station offers comfortable rooms, free Internet, complimentary breakfast, a fitness center, and an outdoor pool. The local trolley stops right outside the door, so guests can easily go shopping and dine at local restaurants. Parking is available for a fee, but it is not the most convenient.

$200-300

The Alexandrian (480 King St., 703/549-6080, www.thealexandrian.com, $155-366) is part of Marriott's Autograph Collection. This stunning red brick hotel has a fantastic location on King Street. It offers 241 guest rooms and luxury suites. Rooms are spacious, and the staff is gracious and accommodating. There is a 24-hour fitness center and indoor heated pool. The hotel is dog friendly, and they host doggie happy hours during the summer. Self-parking ($32) and valet parking ($38) are both available for a nightly fee.

The modern ★ **Hotel Indigo** (220 S. Union St., 703/721-3800, www.hotel indigooldtownalexandria.com, $122-354) is a delightful, InterContinental Hotels Group boutique hotel with a water view. During construction of the hotel, opened in 2017, a 50-foot ship from the 18th century was discovered during excavation. The hotel is conveniently located near King Street and the water taxi (perfect for those taking in a Nats game). It features a fitness center, outdoor patio, and is pet friendly. The rooms are simple but well appointed and feature Aveda products. The staff is terrific. Opt for an eastern-facing (waterfront) room toward the south side of the building. Self-parking is available across the street for $25 and valet for $34. There is an on-site restaurant overlooking the river.

The **Morrison House** (116 S. Alfred St., 703/838-8000, www.morrisonhouse. com, $203-334) is another lovely hotel in Marriott's Autograph Collection in Old Town Alexandria. This hotel is decorated with federal-style reproduction furnishings such as four-poster beds and is housed in a stately brick building near King Street. The hotel underwent a multimillion-dollar facelift in 2016. The 45 guest rooms and three suites are comfortable, and the common areas have a nice open feel. The staff is very friendly and accommodating, and guests are made to feel welcome. The hotel is pet friendly, and valet parking is available for $38 per night.

The **Residence Inn Alexandria Old Town** (1456 Duke St., 703/548-5474, www. marriott.com, $136-440) delivers consistently high-quality service and 240 comfortable guest suites. The hotel is geared toward extended stays: All suites offer a full kitchen and separate living and dining areas. It is approximately two blocks to the King Street Metrorail station and within walking distance of many Old Town attractions. Shuttle service is available to the Metro and waterfront. A plentiful breakfast is included, and there is an indoor pool and fitness center. Two-bedroom suites are available, and parking is available for a fee. Last-minute weekend deals are sometimes available on the website. The hotel is pet friendly.

A Kimpton hotel, the **Lorien Hotel & Spa** (1600 King St., 703/894-3434, www. lorienhotelandspa.com, $170-305) is less than two blocks from the Metrorail. This modern, well-appointed boutique hotel offers a friendly atmosphere and 107 very comfortable guest rooms. This award-winning establishment offers many extras, such as a welcome glass of wine, and first-class service. As the name implies, there's a full-service spa on-site (the only hotel spa in Old Town). Book a corner room if you like a lot of windows. This is a quiet hotel within walking distance of the waterfront. It is also pet friendly.

INFORMATION AND SERVICES

A good place to begin your exploration of Old Town Alexandria is at **The Alexandria Visitors Center at Ramsay House** (221 King St., 703/746-3301, www. visitalexandriava.com, Sun.-Wed. 10am-6pm, Thurs.-Sat. 10am-8pm). They offer maps and brochures and sell tickets to some local attractions and tours. If you plan to visit multiple sights, consider purchasing the **Alexandria Key to the City** museum pass ($15). This visitor pass provides admission to nine historic sites and includes dozens of discounts at area shops, restaurants, and attractions (including 40 percent off admission to Mount Vernon).

GETTING THERE

Old Town Alexandria is approximately seven miles south of Washington DC on the opposite side of the Potomac River. It is accessible by the George Washington Memorial Parkway and I-495 (Beltway).

Old Town is accessible by **Metrorail** (202/637-7000, www.wmata.com). The Yellow and Blue Lines both stop at the **King Street Metro station,** which is on King Street near the George Washington Masonic Memorial.

Amtrak (800/872-7245, www.amtrak. com) has a train station in Alexandria at 110 Callahan Drive.

GETTING AROUND

The Alexandria Transit Company's **DASH** (703/746-3274, www.dashbus.com, $1.75)

bus system provides reliable service in Alexandria and offers service between Metrobus stops, Metrorail, and the Virginia Railway Express. There is service from the King Street Metro stop down King Street to Market Square every 15 minutes or so. The fare is $1.75, and exact change is required. A detailed schedule and route map are available on the website.

The free **King Street Trolley** (www. visitalexandriava.com) is another good way to get around Old Town. This fleet of hybrid trolleys runs every 15 minutes between North Union Street and the King Street Metro station (daily 10am-10:15pm) with 20 stops along Old Town's main shopping and restaurant district.

Round-trip water taxis are also available through **The Potomac Riverboat Company** (211 N. Union St., 703/684-0580, www.potomacriverboatco.com, unlimited daily pass adults $30, children $17) between Old Town Alexandria, the Gaylord National Hotel in National Harbor, Maryland, The Wharf in DC, and directly to Washington Nationals baseball games in DC.

Fairfax County

Fairfax County encompasses 395 square miles and is the largest county in Virginia by population, with more than 1.1 million residents. Nearly a quarter of the jobs in the county are technology related, giving it the largest concentration of technology jobs in the country. It is also a very diverse county, with approximately one-half of the residents speaking a language other than English at home. Fairfax County is a suburban area of Washington DC with a large population of commuters. As the popularity of telecommuting grows, more and more people are able to work from home, but don't let that fool you into thinking the phenomenon has lessened highway congestion during rush hour.

Fairfax County contains half of the DC area's Fortune 500 companies and is also home to many government intelligence agencies, including the Central Intelligence Agency, National Reconnaissance Office, and the National Counterterrorism Center.

Visitors will find a densely populated area with pleasant neighborhoods, parks, and many strip malls. There are countless good restaurants, excellent shopping, and a diversity of outdoor recreation opportunities in Fairfax County. Depending on your focus, Fairfax County can be explored in a day or two and is easily accessible from Washington DC for dining and events.

SIGHTS

Near the Beltway

I-495 is a 64-mile highway that runs around Washington DC and through Virginia and Maryland; it is commonly known as the **Capital Beltway** or just the **Beltway**. It runs through much of the eastern portion of Fairfax County.

OLD TOWN FAIRFAX

Although the city of Fairfax formally includes just a six-square-mile area, many of the surrounding neighborhoods share a Fairfax address and are within Fairfax County. Established in 1742, the city of Fairfax was the site of several Civil War events and then remained mostly a residential community of farms and homes until the 1950s and '60s. At that time it experienced a rapid population growth that leveled off some in the 1970s but has since resumed. **Old Town Fairfax** is a good starting point for exploration, with its quaint shops and restaurants. The **Civil War Interpretive Center at Historic Blenheim** (3610 Old Lee Hwy., 703/591-0560, www.fairfaxva.gov, Tues.-Sat. 10am-3pm, free) is a 12-acre attraction with an interpretive center and several historic buildings, including the Blenheim farmhouse, built in 1859. The house contains the largest and best-preserved Civil War inscription examples in the country, which were left on a wall by more than 100 Union soldiers while they occupied the Fairfax Courthouse in 1862 and 1863. The inscriptions include art and poetry and provide good insight into the lives of the soldiers during the war. The interpretive center features an illustrated timeline of events that took place during the Civil War in Fairfax. There is also a lecture hall and gift shop. Guided tours are offered at 1pm Tuesday through Saturday.

The **Fairfax Station Railroad Museum** (11200 Fairfax Station Rd., Fairfax Station, 703/425-9225, www.fairfax-station.org, Sun. 1pm-4pm, adults $4, children 5-15 $2, children 4 and under free), in nearby Fairfax Station, is a rebuilt train depot and museum that preserves a time in Civil War history when wounded soldiers were transported from the depot to hospitals in Washington DC and Alexandria. It later became a hub for commerce in the county and a center for social activity. The station remained open until 1973. Numerous items were donated to the museum, including a refurbished caboose and a railroad-crossing gate from Norfolk Southern.

The **National Firearms Museum** (11250 Waples Mill Rd., Fairfax, 703/267-1600, www.nramuseum.org, daily 9:30am-5pm, free), a National Rifle Association institution, contains a diverse collection of civilian and military firearms and accessories.

MEADOWLARK BOTANICAL GARDENS

Meadowlark Botanical Gardens (9750 Meadowlark Gardens Ct., Vienna, 703/255-3631, www.novaparks.com, June-Aug. daily 10am-8pm, Apr. and Sept. daily 10am-7pm, Mar. and Oct. daily 10am-6pm, May daily 10am-7:30pm, Nov.-Dec. daily 10am-4:30pm, Jan.-Feb. daily 10am-5pm, adults $6, children 6-17 and seniors 55 and over $3, children under 6 free) is a 95-acre property with large ornamental garden displays and unusual native plant collections. A network of walking trails provides access. There are three gazebos at the gardens that can be reserved for private use. A beautiful glass atrium looks out over the park and can be rented for weddings and receptions. During the holidays, they offer a brilliant light display that can be enjoyed along the walking trails.

Western Fairfax County

Western Fairfax County borders Loudoun County to the west and Prince William County to the south.

★ GREAT FALLS PARK

Great Falls Park (9200 Old Dominion Dr., Great Falls, www.nps.gov/grfa, daily 7am-dark, individual fee for entering on foot, horse, or bicycle $7, children under 15 free, vehicle fee for one vehicle and all passengers

$15) is one of Northern Virginia's prime outdoor destinations. In this 800-acre national park, the Potomac River plunges 77 feet into Mather Gorge over a series of jagged rocks. The falls are impressive to say the least and especially so after heavy rain. Three well-placed and -maintained overlooks provide spectacular views of the falls. There is a visitors center (daily 10am-4pm), plenty of picnic areas, and wooded trails for hiking, mountain biking, and horseback riding. Great Falls Park is also a popular area for rock climbing and whitewater kayaking. Admission pass is good for seven consecutive days.

COLVIN RUN MILL

A leisurely afternoon can be spent at **Colvin Run Mill** (10017 Colvin Run Rd., Great Falls, 703/759-2771, www.fairfaxcounty.gov, Wed.-Mon. 11am-4pm, parking and grounds free, tours adults $8, students 16 and over with ID $7, children and seniors $6). This historic mill and general store harkens back to a time when things were a bit simpler. Take a tour of the restored mill that was built in 1811 and learn about the large waterwheel and how grain was ground. Visit the general store and purchase stone-ground cornmeal, grits, penny candy, and books. This is a lovely park with plenty of picnic space and interesting seasonal activities.

★ NATIONAL AIR AND SPACE MUSEUM STEVEN F. UDVAR-HAZY CENTER

The **National Air and Space Museum Steven F. Udvar-Hazy Center** (14390 Air and Space Museum Pkwy., Chantilly, 703/572-4118, www.airandspace.si.edu, daily 10am-5:30pm, free, $15 parking before 4pm) is owned by the Smithsonian Institution and is the companion museum to the Air and Space Museum on the National Mall. The two sites together are the crown jewel of the Smithsonian and display the largest collection of space and aviation artifacts in the world. The awe-inspiring aviation hangar building allows for the display of aircraft on three levels. Thousands of artifacts may be viewed on the hangar floor and from elevated skywalks and include helicopters, experimental aircraft, and retired spacecraft and airplanes. The soaring ceilings and open design of the hangar allow visitors to fully appreciate the size and significance of the items. Exhibits include the Lockheed SR-71 Blackbird (the fastest jet in the world), the *Enola Gay*, the de Havilland Chipmunk aerobatic airplane, and the space shuttle *Discovery*. Visitors can also watch planes take off and land at Washington Dulles International Airport from the Donald D. Engen Tower, which provides a 360-degree view of the airport. The Udvar-Hazy Center is less crowded than the Air and Space Museum in DC but can still pack in the people on summer weekends. Other features in the museum include an IMAX theater and gift shop. The only dining option inside the center is a McDonald's and McCafé, so if this doesn't suit your palate, make plans to eat at a local restaurant. All visitors must go through security screening when entering.

SULLY HISTORIC SITE

Also in Chantilly is the **Sully Historic Site** (3650 Historic Sully Way, Chantilly, 703/437-1794, www.fairfaxcounty.gov, Mar.-Dec. Wed.-Mon. 11am-4pm, Jan.-Feb. Wed.-Mon. 11am-3pm, tours for adults $8, students 16 and over with ID $7, children 5-15 and seniors 65 and over $6), which is in the National Register of Historic Places. The main house was built in 1799 by Robert E. Lee's uncle Richard Bland Lee, a politician who served in the Virginia House of Delegates and was the first Northern Virginia representative in the U.S. House of Representatives. The home is a combination of Georgian and federal architecture, and the historic grounds also include original outbuildings. Guided tours are given on the hour and focus on the early life of the Richard Bland Lee family. On-site programs

---

1: Great Falls Park **2:** National Air and Space Museum Steven F. Udvar-Hazy Center **3:** George Washington's whiskey distillery and gristmill **4:** George Washington's Mount Vernon

reflect Fairfax County history through the 20th century. There is a gift shop.

Southern Fairfax County

TOP EXPERIENCE

★ GEORGE WASHINGTON'S MOUNT VERNON

George Washington's Mount Vernon (3200 Mount Vernon Memorial Hwy., Alexandria, 703/780-2000, www. mountvernon.org, Apr.-Oct. daily 9am-5pm, Nov.-Mar, daily 9am-4pm, adults $20, youth 6-11 $12, children 5 and under free) is one of the premier attractions in Northern Virginia and is the most popular historic estate in the country. Sitting on the banks of the Potomac River eight miles south of Old Town Alexandria, this picturesque manor was George Washington's plantation house.

The land surrounding Mount Vernon became the property of the Washington family in 1674. George Washington built his mansion in stages between 1757 and 1778. Prior to its construction, a smaller house built for Washington's half-brother Lawrence, who died in 1752, occupied the site. George Washington became the sole owner of the estate in 1761 and intended to be primarily a tobacco farmer (although his military career ended up substantially interfering with this plan). The plantation started out with tobacco as the staple crop, but later grew wheat, grain, and corn.

Visiting Mount Vernon: Once you purchase your ticket to Mount Vernon, you enter through the orientation center, where a bronze statue of George, Martha, and two of George's step-grandchildren immediately greets you. Be sure to pick up a brochure and map of the estate and then watch the orientation movie in one of the two adjacent theaters. From the orientation center, you will take a walkway that continues to the idyllic Bowling Green, the expansive lawn that surrounds the mansion and outbuildings. Plan on a minimum of three hours for your visit.

The home is constructed of wood and underwent several renovations during Washington's lifetime. The style is loosely considered to be part Georgian and British Palladian, although with classical influences. The house is somewhat modest as far as historic estates go. It has a five-part Palladian design that features a central mansion connected by two curved colonnades to the servants' hall and kitchen. The riverfront facade has a commanding view of the Potomac, and its exterior pine boards were beveled and then coated with layers of white paint and sand to make the house appear to be made of brick. The stunning red roof and its large cupola are distinguishing features.

Mount Vernon's interior has been meticulously restored to appear as it did in 1799, during the final year of George Washington's life. As such, the rooms are painted in their original vibrant colors, including some in bright shades of blue and green. The interior, as with the exterior, is rather modest but is adorned with original pieces.

The estate is a great place to learn about George Washington's life and times. Tours are self-guided, but spirited costumed interpreters are on hand to reveal stories behind every room in the mansion including how and where George Washington died and who his houseguests were (such as the famous French nobleman the Marquis de Lafayette).

In addition to the mansion with original furnishings, the nearly 50-acre estate (which at one time was over 8,000 acres) includes a dozen original structures and Washington's tomb (where he and Martha Washington are buried).

George Washington designed the outbuildings, gardens, and lanes running through the estate to be both practical and aesthetically pleasing. The outbuildings supported the work of the plantation, and more than a dozen are open to the public, including the kitchen, smokehouse, slave quarters, stable, outhouses, and a blacksmith shop. The estate is still a working farm, much as it was when Washington lived here. Costumed interpreters are featured in many of the buildings and give live demonstrations of the work performed in them. Three miles south of Mount Vernon on Route 235 is George Washington's whiskey distillery and gristmill (Apr.-Oct. daily 10am-5pm, included with general admission). They are still functioning today as they did in the 18th century and produce authentic products.

Four gardens on six enclosed acres can be visited at Mount Vernon. Staff test new plant varieties and provide beautiful flowers for display. Gardens and groves walking tours ($10 in addition to general admission) are offered daily and last approximately 60 minutes.

If you are in town in May or October, partake in the Mount Vernon Wine Festival & Sunset Tour. This twice-yearly event celebrates wine history in Virginia with exclusive evening tours of the mansion and cellar. Live jazz is played on the east lawn, and don't be surprised if George and Martha make a special appearance. Tickets sell out quickly and are $42-52.

Getting There: Mount Vernon is accessible by Metrorail and bus. Those arriving by Metrorail (202/637-7000, www.wmata.com) can take the Yellow Line to the Huntington Station and then exit onto Huntington Avenue on the lower level. From there, take the Fairfax Connector (703/339-7200, www.fairfaxcounty.gov) bus 101 on the Fort Hunt Line to Mount Vernon.

If arriving by car, take the George Washington Memorial Parkway all the way to its southern terminus. Bicycle is another great way to arrive. Cyclists can take the scenic Mount Vernon Trail, which runs near the western bank of the Potomac River and offers great views of the water, to the estate.

Another fun option is to arrive by boat through The Potomac Riverboat Company (703/548-7655, www.potomacriverboatco.com, round-trip adults $50, children $39, including admission to Mount Vernon). Boat trips depart from Old Town Alexandria, Virginia, and National Harbor, Maryland.

WOODLAWN AND POPE-LEIGHEY HOUSE

The Woodlawn Estate and the Pope-Leighey House (9000 Richmond Hwy., Alexandria, 703/570-6902, www.woodlawnpopeleighey.org, Fri.-Mon. 11am-4pm, combined tickets for adults $20, students K-12 $11, seniors 62 and over and active military $18) are two historic homes that share a National Trust for Historic Preservation site. Woodlawn Estate (individual tickets for adults $10, students K-12 $6, seniors 62 and over and active military $8) is a historic plantation home that was originally part of George Washington's Mount Vernon Estate. It is located three miles west of Mount Vernon. The home was built between 1800 and 1805 for George Washington's nephew, Lawrence Lewis, and his bride, Martha Washington's granddaughter, Nelly Parke Custis, as a wedding gift. The main mansion is made of brick and has sandstone trim. It has 86 windows (many that are larger than four feet wide by eight feet tall) and looks imposing with its formal facade. The 126-acre estate originally contained 2,000 acres. The home has since had several owners, including playwright Paul Kester, who moved in with his 60 cats. Take a tour of this beautiful residence and be sure to ask your docent a lot of questions. Guides are very knowledgeable about the estate, and participant interaction can really enhance the experience.

The Pope-Leighey House (individual tickets for adults $15, students K-12 $7.50, seniors 62 and over and active military $12), a modest house with an exterior made of cypress, is a Frank Lloyd Wright home that was originally built in Falls Church, Virginia, in 1939. When a highway expansion threatened the home, it was given to the National Trust for Historic Preservation and moved to the Woodlawn grounds. The home now resides permanently on the grounds and can be toured. The two homes are a bit of an odd combination, but both are beautiful. Areas of the estate can be rented for special events, and the site also houses a nonprofit farm called the Arcadia Center for Sustainable Food & Agriculture.

GUNSTON HALL

Another popular historic plantation is **Gunston Hall** (10709 Gunston Rd., Mason Neck, 703/550-9220, www.gunstonhall.org, daily 9:30am-5pm, grounds open until 6pm, adults $10, children 6-18 $5, seniors 60 and over $8), former home of George Mason. The statesman authored the Virginia Declaration of Rights and was one of his era's most influential figures. He was one of the first people to call for American liberties such as religious tolerance and freedom of the press. Although Mason helped frame the U.S. Constitution, he declined to sign the document because it did not abolish slavery and lacked a bill of rights. Mason's home was built between 1755 and 1759 and originally sat on 5,500 acres. It was a tobacco and corn plantation. It is famous for its intricate Georgian architecture and extraordinary interior that represents Gothic, French modern, Chinese, Palladian, and classical styles. Many details, such as the carvings in its Palladian Room, were created by an indentured servant named William Bernard Sears, whom Mason brought from London to work on Gunston Hall. The estate now includes 550 acres of surrounding land on the Potomac River and has reconstructed outbuildings, a 250-year-old boxwood-lined walkway, and hiking trails down to the water. Guided tours are offered daily every half hour 9:30am-4:30pm.

RECREATION
Parks
MASON NECK STATE PARK
Mason Neck State Park (7301 High Point Rd., Lorton, 703/339-2385, www.dcr.virginia. gov, $10) is in southern Fairfax County approximately 20 miles from Washington DC. This 1,825-acre park sits on a peninsula and is bordered by Pohick Bay to the north, Belmont Bay to the south, and the Potomac River to the east. The park offers endless opportunities for outdoor recreation, including more than four miles of unpaved hiking and biking trails and three miles of paved trails and elevated walkways above marsh areas for wildlife-watching. Fresh- and brackish-water fishing is accessible in the park (with a valid Virginia or Maryland fishing license), and cartop boat-launch facilities are available. Kayaks and canoes can be rented on-site. The park is also a birdwatcher's paradise. It has resident bald eagles and migratory tundra swans and ducks. A visitors center offers exhibits, a gift shop, and a meeting room. The entrance to the park is off Gunston Road and is shared by the 2,277-acre **Elizabeth Hartwell Mason Neck National Wildlife Refuge** (703/490-4979, www.fws. gov, free), which was the first national wildlife refuge specifically established for the protection of bald eagles and also features one of the East Coast's largest heronries.

ALGONKIAN REGIONAL PARK
Algonkian Regional Park (47001 Fairway Dr., Sterling, 703/450-4655, www.novaparks. com, free admission, activities have individual charges) sits on the banks of the Potomac River and offers trails, a boat launch, picnic facilities, cabin rentals, fishing, ball fields, a large water-park complex, miniature golf, and an 18-hole, par-72 golf course. Kayak tours and other scheduled events take place during the summer months.

BULL RUN REGIONAL PARK
Bull Run Regional Park (7700 Bull Run Dr., Centreville, 703/631-0550, www.novaparks. com, $8) is a spacious, scenic park with open fields, woodland trails, a water park, and a public shooting center. The park hosts festivals and special events throughout the year and can accommodate thousands of people at a time.

LAKE FAIRFAX
Lake Fairfax (1400 Lake Fairfax Dr., Reston, 703/471-5414, www.fairfaxcounty.gov, free for county residents, otherwise $10) is a 476-acre park featuring an 18-acre lake, a water park (The Water Mine), campgrounds, ball fields,

mountain biking trails, picnic areas, seasonal fishing, boating, a carousel, and a playground. Nominal fees are charged for the water park, carousel, boating, and camping.

FRYING PAN FARM PARK

Frying Pan Farm Park (2709 W. Ox Rd., Herndon, 703/437-9101, www.fairfaxcounty. gov, free) is a living-history farm (Kidwell Farm) with animals, wagon rides, horse-show facilities, and a country store. Visitors can view farm animals such as cows, goats, pigs, rabbits, and horses and learn about what Virginia farm life was like in the early to mid-20th century. Beginner horseback riding lessons are also offered.

Mountain Biking

Wakefield Park (8100 Braddock Rd., 703/321-7080, www.fairfaxcounty.gov, free) has some of the best mountain biking trails in Northern Virginia. They are great for beginner and intermediate riders with some more challenging sections. The trails are part of a larger network of county trails, including the **Cross County Trail** system. There's also a skate park at Wakefield where they hold skateboarding and BMX classes. Wakefield Park also offers night riding from dusk to 10:30pm year-round on Monday, Tuesday, and Thursday nights. Otherwise the park is open dawn to dusk.

Another premier mountain biking park is **Fountainhead Regional Park** (10875 Hampton Rd., Fairfax Station, 703/250-9124, www.novaparks.com, free). Miles of trails were developed in this park along the Occoquan Reservoir by mountain bikers for mountain bikers. These are technical trails, full of tight turns, steep climbs, stream crossings, and log hops. It's one of the best mountain biking areas in the Washington DC region. Call ahead for trail conditions.

Great Falls Park (9200 Old Dominion Dr., Great Falls, www.nps.gov/grfa, individual fee for entering on foot, horse, or bicycle $7, children under age 15 free, vehicle fee for one vehicle and all passengers $15) also offers nice nontechnical mountain biking with great views of the Potomac River. Nature lovers looking for a moderate ride can pedal to the right (when looking at the river) to pick up a few miles of dirt carriage roads and trails. There are some steep climbs, loose gravel, and rocks but nothing too technical. There are also single-track trails in the park if you head to the left of the parking lot. These trails lead to Riverbend Park and offer some hills. Obtain a trail map from the visitors center before you head out.

Many Fairfax County parks allow mountain biking on their trails. Additional information on the following trails can be obtained from the **Fairfax County Park Authority** (www.fairfaxcounty.gov). **Clarks Crossing** (9850 Clarks Crossing Rd., Vienna) offers 3.2 miles of natural trails connecting to the W&OD Trail. The **Colvin Run Stream Valley** trail (Hunter Mill Rd. and Rte. 7, Reston) is a lovely, 3-mile natural trail that runs between Hunter Mill Road and Route 7. The **Fred Crabtree** park trail (2801 Fox Mill Rd., Herndon) offers 2 miles of wooded trails. **Lake Fairfax Park** offers a challenging network of wooded trails in Reston.

Trails

There are many hiking, running, and walking trails in Fairfax County. Most parks in the area offer some kind of recreational trails. To download trail maps in Fairfax County, visit www.fairfaxcounty.gov.

Golf

The premier public golf course in Fairfax County is **Westfields Golf Club** (13940 Balmoral Greens Ave., Clifton, 703/631-3300, www.westfieldsgolf.com, $89-109). This award-winning, nationally recognized course was designed by Fred Couples and is considered enjoyable for novices yet challenging for experienced players. The course incorporates natural wetlands, beech and oak trees, and rolling hills. The atmosphere is inviting and professional, and the service is outstanding. The complex includes a clubhouse, pro shop, driving range, putting green, fitting studio, and restaurant.

Another great course is the **Laurel Hill Golf Club** (8701 Laurel Crest Dr., Lorton, 703/493-8849, www.fairfaxcounty.gov, $39-99). This is an exciting 18-hole course that was built on land that once housed the DC Department of Corrections facility at Lorton. This course, run by the Fairfax County Park Authority, was ranked in the top 10 municipal courses nationwide and has hosted several notable tournaments.

Pleasant Valley Golfers' Club (4715 Pleasant Valley Rd., Chantilly, 703/222-7900, www.pleasantvalleygc.com, $40-88) is another Fairfax County Park Authority course, but it is managed independently and is considered higher-end. The well-respected 18-hole course also offers a driving range.

The **Reston National Golf Course** (11875 Sunrise Valley Dr., 703/620-9333, www.restonnationalgc.com, $29-84) is one of Northern Virginia's classic golf courses. It was designed by Ed Ault and is home to the Nike Golf Learning Center, a leading golf-instruction program. Reston National offers a driving range and putting and chipping greens. Unsubstantiated legend says that the land the course was built on was once owned by Hugh Hefner. Whether or not this is true, an aerial view of the course does strike a stunning resemblance to the Playboy bunny symbol.

An older course with a lot of character is the **Algonkian Regional Park Golf Course** (47001 Fairway Dr., Sterling, 703/450-4655, www.novaparks.com, $29.50-48). This 18-hole, par-72 course offers long, straight, flat, tree-lined fairways on the front nine and hills and water holes on the back nine. Electric and pull carts are available. No metal spikes are allowed.

Rock Climbing

Great Falls Park (9200 Old Dominion Dr., Great Falls, www.nps.gov/grfa) is a rock climber's paradise with more than 200 climbing routes on the Virginia side of the river. Most climbs are around 50 feet and overhanging. Trad climbing is not recommended, so bring plenty of rope for toprope anchors. The fall is the best time to climb; the water is low, and the climbs offer sun until late in the day.

Canoeing and Kayaking

There are several good launch sites for private canoes and kayaks in Fairfax County. **Algonkian Regional Park** (47001 Fairway Dr., Sterling, 703/450-4655, www.novaparks.com, shore launch $6, ramp $7) has a nice boat ramp on the Potomac River. Paddlers should paddle upstream. **Mason Neck State Park** (Gunston Rd., Mount Vernon, 703/339-2385, www.dcr.virginia.gov, $7 admission, $5 launch) is another good spot to launch and offers paddlers several places to paddle, including Pohick Bay, Belmont Bay, and the Potomac River. Canoe and kayak rentals are available on-site and a cartop launch is provided. **Fountainhead Regional Park** (10875 Hampton Rd., Fairfax Station, 703/250-9124, www.novaparks.com, free) offers a launch site on the Occoquan Reservoir (shore launch $6, ramp $7), kayak rentals ($13 per hour), and canoe rentals ($11 per hour).

Fishing

Burke Lake Park (7315 Ox Rd., Fairfax Station, 703/323-6600, www.fairfaxcounty.gov) has a 218-acre lake with wonderful largemouth bass fishing, making it a popular spot. The park offers shoreline fishing, four fishing bulkheads, a fishing pier, bait and tackle sales, rowboat rentals, and a boat launch.

Lake Fairfax Park (1400 Lake Fairfax Dr., Reston, 703/471-5414, www.fairfaxcountry.gov) offers spring trout fishing in its 18-acre lake and year-round fishing for catfish, bass, sunfish, black crappie, bluegill, and bullhead. Other good fishing spots include **Fountainhead Regional Park** (703/250-9124, www.novaparks.com) and **Riverbend Park** (8700 Potomac Hills St., Great Falls, 703/759-9018, www.fairfaxcounty.gov).

ENTERTAINMENT AND EVENTS

Music and Theater

★ WOLF TRAP NATIONAL PARK FOR THE PERFORMING ARTS

There are few performance venues in the country that compare to the **Filene Center** at **Wolf Trap National Park for the Performing Arts** (1645 Trap Rd., Vienna, 703/255-1868, www.wolftrap.org). This beautiful, indoor/outdoor amphitheater is set on 130 acres of rolling hills and woods, just 20 miles from Washington DC and 3 miles from the Beltway. It is the country's only national park dedicated to the performing arts. It offers a full lineup of concerts, musicals, dance, and other types of performances through the summer from well-known artists and performance companies. Bring a picnic and eat on the lawn before or during the show (many lawn seats are available), or enjoy one of the on-site eateries (reservations are required). October-May, **The Barns at Wolf Trap,** two 18th-century barns that were relocated from upstate New York, offer indoor performances, making this an interesting and inspiring year-round venue. Free parking is available at the park for performances, and the **Wolf Trap Express Shuttle** offers round-trip service

($5) from the West Falls Church Metrorail station to the Filene Center for most performances. Shuttle service begins two hours prior to showtime and runs every 20 minutes. Return shuttle service leaves 20 minutes after the end of each show but no later than 11pm.

EAGLEBANK ARENA

The **EagleBank Arena** (4500 Patriot Circle, Fairfax, 703/993-3000, www.eaglebankarena. com) is on the campus of George Mason University in Fairfax. In addition to hosting campus events, the center features sporting events, concerts, and family performances. Legends such as Bruce Springsteen, Bob Dylan, and the Harlem Globetrotters have performed there.

JAMMIN JAVA

Approximately 15 miles west of Washington DC, in Vienna, Virginia, is **Jammin Java** (227 Maple Ave., 703/255-1566, www. jamminjava.com), a small but important venue in the metropolitan music community. They have live music every night and also hold children's concerts on many mornings. They feature well-known artists such as Ingrid Michaelson, Citizen Cope, and Bon Iver as well as Washington DC favorites such as Bill

Filene Center at Wolf Trap National Park for the Performing Arts

Kirchen and Eddie from Ohio. All concerts are general admission. Tickets can be purchased online.

Festivals and Events

There are many festivals and events that fill the calendar in Fairfax County. One popular venue is the **Reston Town Center** (11900 Market St., www.restontowncenter.com), which hosts festivals throughout the year, including the **Northern Virginia Fine Arts Festival, Pet Fiesta, Taste of Reston,** and **Concerts on the Town** music series held on Saturday nights in the summer. Visit the website for a full schedule and details.

The **Workhouse Arts Center** (9518 Workhouse Way, Lorton, 703/584-2900, www.workhousearts.org) is a vibrant arts center that is housed in a former prison in Lorton. The center is recognized both regionally and nationally for innovative collaborations of visual and performing arts, community engagement, education, and history. The center has galleries, a theater, and six buildings that house artist studios. It supports more than 100 artists, and visitors are encouraged to interact with them. The center hosts many events throughout the year, such as the **Workhouse Brewfest** (Sept.) and the popular **Haunted Trail** (Oct.), and offers more than 800 classes and workshops.

One of the premier festivals in Northern Virginia is the annual **Vintage Virginia Wine Festival** (Bull Run Regional Park, Chantilly, www.vintagevirginia.com, $45), which is held in early June in Centreville. A 20-minute drive from Washington DC, the festival offers wine tasting, local winemakers, more than 100 vendors, food, and entertainment.

Celebrate Fairfax (12000 Government Center Pkwy., Fairfax, 703/324-3247, www.celebratefairfax.com, $10-20) is another popular annual event. It began as the Fairfax Fair and is now the county's largest annual community celebration, entertaining tens of thousands of people during three days in mid-June. The celebration is held on 25 acres and has more than 300 exhibitors sharing food, crafts, and activities. There are also carnival rides, nightly fireworks, and seven stages of live concerts including several big-name bands. Entertainment in the past has included well-known artists such as Third Eye Blind, The Bangles, Rusted Root, and Pat Benatar.

Civil War buffs won't want to miss the **Civil War Encampment Weekend** (3650 Historic Sully Way, 703/437-1794, www.fairfaxcounty. gov, $7-9) at the Sully Historic Site. For two days in August, visitors can watch Civil War reenactors re-create daily life during that era. Daily skirmishes include infantry, artillery, and cavalry. Live music and a fashion show are also part of the festivities.

The **Bull Run Festival of Lights** (Bull Run Regional Park, Chantilly, 703/631-0550, www.bullrunfestivaloflights.com, Mon.-Thurs. $20 per car, Fri.-Sun. $25 per car) is a highlight of the holiday season for thousands of visitors. This six-week festival is a winter wonderland of light displays that can be explored from the comfort of your car. More than 130,000 spectators drive through this 2.5-mile-long holiday wonderland each season.

SHOPPING

You don't have to look far to find shopping in Fairfax County. Strip malls are everywhere, and just about every national chain store imaginable can be found. There are several large malls that are very popular with both visitors and residents.

The most well-known shopping mall in Northern Virginia is **Tysons Corner Center** (1961 Chain Bridge Rd., Tysons Corner, www.tysonscornercenter.com). With more than 300 stores and restaurants, this is a premier destination for serious shoppers. The upscale sister mall to Tysons Corner Center is **Tysons Galleria** (2001 International Dr., McLean, www.tysonsgalleria.com).

The **Reston Town Center** (11900 Market St., Reston, 703/579-6720, www.restontowncenter.com) is a mini city in itself. Many national-brand shops line its streets, and festivals and concerts are scheduled in its center throughout much of the year.

The **Mosaic District** (2910 District Ave., Fairfax, www.mosaicdistrict.com) is an outdoor, upscale shopping and dining district with independent boutiques, upscale national chains, health-minded grocery shopping, and a cinema.

FOOD

Near the Beltway

INDIAN

There are two standout restaurants in the area for Indian food. The first is ★ **Jaipur Royal Indian Cuisine** (9401 Lee Hwy., Fairfax, 703/766-1111, www.jaipurcuisine.com, daily 11:30am-2:30pm and 5:30pm-10pm, $11-20). This very popular restaurant features a delicious and well-priced lunch buffet (weekdays $11.95, weekends $14.95) with plentiful selections that include a variety of vegetarian dishes. Dinner brings a large selection of delightful entrées made from spices that are prepared fresh each day for each individual dish. The decor is authentic and cheerful, and the staff is friendly and helpful with suggestions. Personal favorites include the Mango Prawn Curry, the Malai Kofta, and the Murgh Tikka Masala. If you like your dish hot, be sure to ask for "American hot" unless you're positive you can endure "Indian hot," which is a whole new level of hot. Reservations are a must on weekends.

The second is **Haandi** (1222 W. Broad St., Falls Church, 703/533-3501, www.haandi.com, Sun.-Thurs. 11:30am-2:30pm and 5pm-10pm, Fri.-Sat. 11:30am-2:30pm and 5pm-10:30pm, $12-23). This award-winning restaurant perfects the art of authentic Indian cooking. Although the names of the dishes may sound familiar, the range of flavors, the kitchen's skill with using spices, and the attention to detail are unrivaled. Start with an order of samosas and tantalize your taste buds as you look through the extensive menu of entrées. There are no wrong choices. When in doubt, ask your server for help; they are knowledgeable and eager to help. Reservations are highly recommended.

ITALIAN

Some of the best Italian food in Fairfax is at **Dolce Vita** (10824 Fairfax Blvd., Fairfax, 703/385-1530, www.dolcevitaitaliankitchenandwinebar.com, Mon.-Thurs. 11:30am-9:30pm, Fri.-Sat. 11:30am-10:30pm, Sun. 5pm-9:30pm, $13-41). This cozy little restaurant pairs delicious Italian cuisine with a comfortable, friendly atmosphere. The large, wood-burning brick oven is a focal point in the small dining area, which is decorated with scenes from the Tuscan countryside. The food is mostly traditional Italian fare with an emphasis on fresh ingredients. They also prepare slightly lighter sauces and manage to do so without sacrificing any taste. The restaurant has a huge following with locals and those in the know and can be crowded during peak hours. They also have a wine bar next door with a daily happy hour, wine tastings, and dinner pairings.

MEXICAN

If you're in the mood for Mexican food, try the **Coyote Grille and Cantina** (10266 Main St., Fairfax, 703/591-0006, www.coyotegrille.com, Mon.-Thurs. 11am-9:30pm, Fri.-Sat. 11am-10pm, Sun. 11am-9pm, $8-18) in Fairfax. They offer authentic recipes and a menu refreshingly different from the usual chain fare. The atmosphere is lively, and they have a loyal local client base. Their Southwestern-style entrées include traditional items such as burritos and fajitas and some unexpected twists such as the addition of sweet potatoes in their Fiesta Salad and their Coyote Burger with chipotle dressing. Their heated year-round patio has a margarita bar where they make more than a dozen varieties of scrumptious margaritas. They also have delicious desserts that go beyond fried ice cream and flan (such as a brownie sundae) and full brunch on Sunday.

PERSIAN

Outstanding Persian food is served at **Shamshiry** (8607 Westwood Center Dr., Vienna, 703/448-8883, www.shamshiry.com, Sun.-Thurs. 11:30am-11pm, Fri.-Sat. 11:30am-1am, $6-21), in the Tysons Corner

Local Brews

Even self-proclaimed beer snobs will find something to rave about in Northern Virginia's local beer scene. In recent years, a growing number of new brewers have come onto the radar to compete with the more established breweries. The result is a good selection of locally made beer spread out across much of Northern Virginia.

Founded by former employees of local craft beer pioneer Old Dominion Brewing, the **Lost Rhino Brewing Company** (21730 Red Rum Dr. #142, Ashburn, 571/291-2083, www.lostrhino.com, Tues. 4pm-9pm, Wed.-Thurs. 11:30am-9pm, Fri.-Sat. 11:30am-10pm, Sun. noon-5pm) is a leader in the local brew scene. Named after the surfing term "rhino chaser," which means "someone out to find the best waves, biggest waves, an adventurer," they offer a fantastic selection of artfully crafted beers that just plain taste great. The brewery and tasting room is tucked away in a warehouse in Ashburn, but it's a fun place for a tasting and draws quite a crowd on the weekends. They also have a larger restaurant

Lost Rhino Retreat

with space for events in nearby Brambleton called **Lost Rhino Retreat** (22885 Brambleton Plaza, Ashburn, 703/327-0311, www.lostrhinoretreat.com, Mon.-Thurs. 11:30am-10pm, Fri.-Sat. 11:30am-11pm, Sun. 11:30am-9pm). Try their delicious Barrel-Aged Stout and order a giant Bavarian-style pretzel on the side.

Another brewery with Old Dominion ties is **Old Ox Brewery** (44652 Guilford Dr., Ashburn, 703/729-8375, www.oldoxbrewery.com, Tues.-Thurs. 4pm-9pm, Fri. 2:30pm-10pm, Sat. 11am-10pm, Sun. 11am-7pm), which has a 30-barrel brewhouse. They partner with a local food truck or food vendor to provide a varying menu. The brewery is easily accessible from the Washington & Old Dominion Trail between mile markers 25 and 25.5.

Caboose Brewing Company (www.caboosebrewing.com) entered the market with their cozy **Caboose Tavern** located just off the Washington & Old Dominion Trail in Vienna (520 Mill St. NW, Vienna, 703/865-8580, Mon.-Thurs. 4pm-11pm, Fri. noon-midnight, Sat. 11am-midnight, Sun. 11am-10pm). In addition to brewing great beer, their focus is on health and the environment, and it shows with their community atmosphere and innovative menu, made from mostly sustainably sourced ingredients. Immediate success led to a second, larger location in the Mosaic District of Fairfax called **Caboose Commons** (2918 Eskridge Rd., Fairfax, 703/663-8833, Sun.-Thurs. 7am-11pm, Fri.-Sat. 7am-1pm). Caboose Commons is also a coffeehouse.

The oldest packaging brewery in the area can be found in Alexandria at **Port City Brewing Company** (3950 Wheeler Ave., Alexandria, 703/797-2739, www.portcitybrewing.com, Mon.-Wed. 4pm-9pm, Thurs. 4pm-10pm, Fri. 3pm-10pm, Sat. noon-10pm, Sun. noon-8pm). All of their beers are unfiltered, and you can find their top-notch Port City Porter along with other favorites at distributors throughout the mid-Atlantic. They have food-truck service at their tasting room.

A perfect day in the Virginia countryside might include a visit to **Vanish Farmwoods Brewery** (42245 Black Hops Ln., Leesburg, 703/779-7407, www.vanishbeer.com. Mon.-Wed. noon-9pm, Thurs.-Fri. noon-10pm, Sat. 11am-10pm, Sun. 11am-9pm). This beautiful brewery has one of the best beer menus in the area with more than 20 taps. They also have great pizza and barbeque. If you're into sour ales, try their Juicy Tangerine. Other top picks include their Milk Stout and house IPA (Ghost Fleet). Bring the dog and the kids.

Another great bet for a day outing is **Dirt Farm Brewing** (18701 Foggy Bottom Rd., Bluemont, 540/554-2337, www.dirtfarmbrewing.com, Sat.-Thurs. noon-7pm, Fri. noon-9pm). They pour small-batch, hand-crafted beer produced from ingredients grown on their farm and complement it with a stunning view of the Loudoun Valley. A fresh, seasonal menu is also available.

area. If you're not sure which succulent kabob dish to order, try their specialty Chelo Kabob Shamshiry, a combination of *kubideh* (ground beef) and *barg* (steak). The portions are large and the restaurant is very popular, so go early or plan to wait for a table. They also offer takeout.

VIETNAMESE

Four Sisters Vietnamese Restaurant (8190 Strawberry Ln., Falls Church, 703/539-8566, www.foursistersrestaurant.com, daily 11am-9:45pm, $10-28) is all about delicious food, beautiful ambience, and reasonable prices. This award-winning restaurant offers an extensive and well-planned menu of light and flavorful Vietnamese food. If you aren't sure what to order, they offer dinners for 2, 4, 6, and 10 diners. The selections are wonderful and offer a good sampling of the chef's talents. They also offer a gluten-free menu. Reservations are highly recommended on weekends. Be sure to take note of the flower arrangements in the restaurant—they are made from real, fresh flowers, and they are spectacular.

Western Fairfax County
AMERICAN

One of the Reston Town Center's most noted restaurants is **Passion Fish** (11960 Democracy Dr., Reston, 703/230-3474, www.passionfishreston.com, Mon.-Thurs. 11:30am-10:30pm, Fri. 11:30am-11:30pm, Sat. 4pm-11:30pm, Sun. 10:30am-9pm, $23-48). Elegant, open, and airy, the atmosphere alone (which mimics a classic ocean liner) draws diners looking to enjoy seafood. The menu is primarily seafood, with some interesting twists. Selections from the raw bar, sushi, salads, and succulent entrées sit alongside sweet potato fries, mac and cheese, and jasmine rice with red Thai curry. Steak is also available. A favorite venue for business lunches and dinners, the restaurant also has a sophisticated bar menu and seasonal outdoor seating.

For something leisurely or romantic, try the **Vinifera Wine Bar Bistro** (11750 Sunrise Valley Dr., Reston, 703/234-3550, daily 6:30am-10pm, $19-32), in the Westin Hotel in Reston. It is a great place to bring a date or relax while traveling on business. The trendy spot offers great wine and equally tasty cuisine. Order multiple small plates to accompany wine by the glass, or order a full-size entrée for a bigger commitment. Weather permitting, sit on the patio by a fire pit. There is little noise or street activity, making this a delightful rare find in the area. Even if you aren't on vacation, it will feel like it. They serve breakfast, lunch, and dinner.

Bazin's on Church (111 Church St., Vienna, 703/255-7212, www.bazinsonchurch.com, brunch Sun. 11am-2pm, lunch Tues.-Fri. 11:30am-2pm, dinner Tues.-Thurs. 5pm-10pm, Fri.-Sat. 5pm-10:30pm, Sun. 5pm-9:30pm, $19-38) in Vienna is a contemporary American restaurant specializing in items made from organic and seasonal ingredients. There is also a wine bar with more than 500 selections from around the world. Wine-tasting is available. Dinner entrées include seafood, pasta, and steak, all prepared with unique and delicious recipes. The brunch offers mouthwatering options such as bananas foster French toast and filet sliders. The atmosphere is inviting with large windows, low lighting, and exposed brick walls. This small section of Vienna has a great contemporary feel to it, yet is easy to get to and has free parking. They also offer an extensive gluten-free menu.

If you're looking for a great sandwich or a slice of New York-style pizza, **Santini's** (11804 Baron Cameron Ave., Reston, 703/481-3333, www.mysantinis.com, Mon.-Sat. 9am-10pm, Sun. 9am-9pm, $6-15) in Reston is the place to go. This family-owned New York-style deli is the best sandwich joint in the area. The food is fresh, made to order, and simply delicious. A great place for families and team gatherings, it's also a comfortable spot to grab a beer and watch the game. Santini's offers reasonable prices, fresh food, and friendly, personal service. They also have locations in Sterling, Ashburn, Oakton, McLean, Fairfax, and Chantilly.

Mookie's BBQ (1141Walker Rd., Great Falls, 703/759-2386, www.mookiesbbq.com, Tues.-Thurs. 11am-9pm, Fri.-Sat. 11am-10pm, Sun. 10am-9pm, $10-36) grew out of a competition barbecue and catering company. They serve outstanding barbecue pork, chicken, ribs, and salads.

FRENCH

For a special celebration or a romantic dinner, it is hard to top ★ **L'Auberge Chez François** (332 Springvale Rd., Great Falls, 703/759-3800, www.laubergechezfrancois. com, Tues.-Fri. 11:30am-1:30pm and 5pm-9pm, Sat. 11:30am-1:30pm and 4:30pm-9:30pm, Sun. noon-7:30pm, $75-85). This family-owned restaurant began back in 1954 in Washington DC and relocated to Great Falls in 1975, where it has been a destination in itself ever since. The food and service are simply first-rate, with exceptional attention paid to every detail. But what makes this place special is that regardless of who the famous person may be at the next table, or how many couples are getting engaged that night, the atmosphere is always relaxed and comfortable. Dinner is a six-course prix fixe menu with entrée selections that include seafood, filet, lamb, and their signature chateaubriand for two. Lunch is a four-course prix fixe menu for $45. Reservations are a must and usually are required weeks in advance for prime times, but walk-ins are accepted on the beautiful terrace when the weather is nice. A scaled-down version of the menu is offered on the lower level of the restaurant in the **Jacques' Brasserie and Jacques' Bar Rouge** (Tues.-Fri. 11:30am-1:30pm and 5pm-9pm, Sat. 11:30am-1:30pm and 4:30pm-9:30pm, Sun. noon-7:30pm).

IRISH

The Old Brogue (760C Walker Rd., Great Falls, 703/759-3309, www.oldbrogue.com, Mon.-Thurs. 11am-midnight, Fri.-Sat. 11am-2am, Sun. 10am-10pm, $8-27) is *the* place to go in Great Falls. It's a family-owned institution that began on St. Patrick's Day in 1981. This cozy pub welcomes everyone with an international bar menu, fresh food, traditional Irish fare, and live entertainment. Start with Irish potato skins or some ginger fried calamari. Follow that up with cottage pie or the savory blackened-salmon salad. They also serve Sunday brunch. Everyone is family at the Old Brogue, and it's one of the few places in this fast-paced area where people relax and chat with strangers at the next table.

ITALIAN AND MEDITERRANEAN

If you need a quick, delicious meal for dine in or takeout, stop by **Cafesano** (11130 South Lakes Dr., Reston, 571/257-0854, www. cafesano.com, daily 11am-9pm, $8-18). They offer a wide variety of yummy salads, pasta, kabobs, paninis, wraps, and brick oven pizza with many healthy choices. They also have the best prices in the area for beer and wine. Order at the counter and take your drink and number to your seat. They'll find you when your food is ready. When you're done, take your dishes to the trash and dish bins. There's a second location in Dulles (21305 Windmill Parc Dr., 571/748-7077).

VEGETARIAN

You don't have to be a vegetarian to enjoy **Sunflower Vegetarian Restaurant** (2531 Chain Bridge Rd., Vienna, 703/319-3888, www.crystalsunflower.com, Mon.-Sat. 11:30am-10pm, Sun. noon-10pm, $9-13). In fact, chances are you would never know it was vegetarian just by tasting the food: The tasty Asian-influenced entrées at Sunflower actually mimic meat in texture and taste. The flavors are delicious. First-timers can't go wrong with the local favorite, General Tso's Surprise. The surprise is that there really isn't meat in it, which you'd never guess.

Southern Fairfax County
AMERICAN

★ **Trummer's on Main** (7134 Main St., Clifton, 703/266-1623, www. trummersonmain.com, brunch Sun. 11am-2pm, lunch Sat. noon-2:30pm, dinner

Tues.-Thurs. 5:30pm-9pm, Fri.-Sat. 5pm-10pm, Sun. 5pm-8pm, $19-58) is the hot spot in Clifton. The chef and owner was named one of *Food & Wine Magazine*'s Best New Chefs shortly after Trummer's opened back in 2010, and happy patrons have been coming ever since. Trummer's offers creative American cuisine and handcrafted cocktails (including their signature drink, the Titanic, which is too good to be missed). The ever-changing main plates include seafood, beef, chicken, pork, and vegetarian selections. The chef also offers a daily five-course tasting menu that can be ordered when making your reservation ($86, wine pairing an additional $62). It's imperative to save room for dessert: The pastry chef is nothing short of amazing. The atmosphere is hip and relaxing with high ceilings and many windows. The food presentation is exquisite. The cozy bar with its interesting stone pillars is a great place to meet friends, sample drinks, and try the bar menu.

ACCOMMODATIONS
$100-200

The majority of accommodations in Fairfax County are in national chain hotels. One exception is the **Stafford House** (3746 Chain Bridge Rd., 703/385-9024, www.staffordhouse. net, $129-199) bed-and-breakfast. This comfortable, friendly establishment is a nice change of pace in a convenient location. Each of its two rooms has a private entrance and parking. Breakfast is delivered to your room each morning, and rooms are equipped with many amenities including a fireplace. The owners are very friendly and helpful and contribute to an enjoyable stay.

$200-300

Many hotels in the county are geared toward business travelers and, as such, offer discounted rates on the weekends. The **Residence Inn Tysons Corner Mall** (8400 Old Courthouse Rd., Vienna, 703/917-0800, www.marriott.com, $96-279) is a six-floor, 121-room hotel near Tysons Corner. They offer a free American breakfast daily. This is

an older hotel, but it has been renovated and the staff is friendly and attentive. It is also pet friendly ($75 fee).

The **Hilton McLean Tysons Corner** (7920 Jones Branch Dr., McLean, 703/847-5000, www3.hilton.com, $104-831) is another good option in Tysons Corner. It is convenient to shopping and has modern, attractive decor. There are 458 guest rooms.

One hotel that stands out from the crowd in Fairfax County is the **Westin Reston Heights** (11750 Sunrise Valley Dr., Reston, 703/391-9000, www.westinreston.com, $94-274). It is a modern hotel with 191 guest rooms and a quiet location. There is also a wonderful wine bar on-site.

Another stand out is the **Hyatt Regency Reston** (1800 Presidents St., Reston, 703/709-1234, www.hyatt.com, $113-409), in the beautiful Reston Town Center. It has 518 rooms and anchors the upscale outdoor mall. The interior has modern decor, and free shuttle service is available to and from Washington Dulles International Airport.

Over $300

The **Ritz-Carlton, Tysons Corner** (1700 Tysons Blvd., McLean, 703/506-4300, www. ritzcarlton.com, $169-819) is a high-end option in Tysons Corner with 398 guest rooms, direct access to shopping, and a better-than-average fitness room.

Camping

Camping is limited in Fairfax County, but there are a few parks with nice campgrounds. The first is **Lake Fairfax Park** (1400 Lake Fairfax Dr., Reston, 703/471-5414, www. fairfaxcounty.gov, $28-50) in Reston. Tent and RV camping are available. There are 136 campsites (54 with electrical hookups), a bathhouse, a dump station, picnic tables, grills, and public telephones. Reservations are required, and the campground is open year-round.

The second is the campground at **Burke Lake Park** (7315 Ox Rd., Fairfax Station, 703/323-6600, www.fairfaxcounty.gov,

$28-31). There are 100 wooded campsites (no electric or water hookups), a bathhouse, a dump station, camp store, ice, picnic tables, grills, fire rings, and public telephones. The campground is open mid-April through late October.

Another is **Bull Run Regional Park** (7700 Bull Run Dr., Centreville, 703/631-0550, www. novapark.com, $29-47), which offers RV sites with electric-only service, full-service RV sites, tent sites, group camping areas, and rustic cabins. There are two bathhouses and a camp store. All sites include charcoal grills, picnic tables, and fire rings.

INFORMATION AND SERVICES

The **Fairfax Museum & Visitors Center** (10209 Main St., 703/385-8414, www. fairfaxva.gov, daily 9am-5pm) is in the historic former Fairfax Elementary School, built in 1873. Visitors can pick up information on special events, transportation, restaurants, and lodging. The museum offers exhibits on the history of Fairfax City and walking tours of Old Town Fairfax in the spring and fall. Additional information on the entire county can be found at www.fxva.com.

GETTING THERE AND AROUND

Fairfax County is accessible in some areas by **Metrorail** and **Metrobus** (www.wmata. com), but visitors will greatly benefit from having access to a car.

The city of Fairfax offers the **CUE Bus System** (703/385-7859, www.fairfaxva.gov, Mon.-Fri. 6am-11pm, Sat. 8:30am-8:30pm, Sun. 9:30am-6pm, $1.75) for public transportation around town. Buses accept exact change and SmarTrip cards. Students and seniors can receive discounts. A bus schedule is available on the website.

Additional bus service in the county is provided by the **Fairfax Connector** (703/339-7200, www.fairfaxcounty.gov, $2). This service is countywide. Please consult the website for routes and schedules.

Prince William County

Prince William County is approximately 35 miles southwest of Washington DC. It stretches from the foothills of the Appalachian Mountains to the banks of the Potomac River and contains primarily suburban commuter communities but with a bit more rural feel than neighboring Fairfax County. The county has a number of historical landmarks, including the famous Manassas battlefield. It also offers outdoor recreation along the river and in several large parks.

For many years, the population in Prince William County was focused in Manassas, which was a large railroad junction, and Woodbridge, near the Potomac River. In recent decades the population has expanded significantly throughout the county, making it one of the most populated counties in the state.

SIGHTS
★ Manassas National Battlefield Park

The premier attraction in Prince William County is **Manassas National Battlefield Park** (6511 Sudley Rd., Manassas, 703/361-1339, www.nps.gov/mana, daily dawn to dusk, free, donations accepted). This historic battlefield was established as a national park in 1940 to preserve the site of two well-known Civil War battles: the First Battle of Bull Run (July 21, 1861), which was the first major land battle in the war; and the Second Battle of Bull Run (August 28-30, 1862), which was the biggest simultaneous mass assault of the Civil War and signaled the height of the Confederate army's

1: Civil War cannons at Manassas National Battlefield Park **2:** National Museum of the Marine Corps

power. The battles are also referred to as the First and Second Battles of Manassas. The reason there are two names for each battle is because the North usually named a battle after a nearby body of water (creek, river, or stream) and the South named battles after towns and railroads. So the Confederate army named the battles after Manassas Junction and the Union army named them after the Bull Run stream. It was at this site that Confederate general Thomas J. Jackson was nicknamed "Stonewall" Jackson.

The park encompasses more than 5,000 acres of meadows, woods, and streams. When visiting the battlefield, you can see the site where the battles took place and also visit three buildings: the **Henry Hill Visitor Center,** the **Brawner Farm Interpretive Center,** and the **Stone House.**

The **Henry Hill Visitor Center** (daily 8:30am-5pm) is on Sudley Road near the southern park entrance. It houses exhibits and information on the First Battle of Bull Run that include uniforms from the era, weapons, and field gear. It also offers an electronic battle map that visitors can interact with for a quick lesson in field strategy and tactics. Take the time to watch the 45-minute orientation film offered at the center; it is interesting and informative. It is shown on the hour. There is also a bookstore.

The **Brawner Farm Interpretive Center** (daily 9am-5pm) is the location of the opening phase of the Second Battle of Bull Run. There are exhibits and audiovisual programs that give a detailed overview of the second battle. There is a parking lot off of Pageland Lane on the western side of the park.

The **Stone House** (weekends only 10am-4:30pm) is a two-story brick house that was built in 1848 and served as a hospital during both battles at Bull Run. It is near the intersection of Sudley Road and Lee Highway.

Other attractions in the park include the **Stone Bridge,** which the Union army retreated across after both battles; **Battery Heights,** where Confederate batteries fired on the attacking Union troops at the Brawner Farm; **Matthews Hill,** the site of the opening phase of the first battle; and **Groveton,** the remains of a Civil War-era village. There are many other points of interest in the park as well. A great way to see many of them is by taking a self-guided walking tour of the one-mile **Henry Hill Loop Trail** that begins at the Henry Hill Visitor Center.

More than 900,000 people visit the battlefield yearly. Guided tours running 30 to 45 minutes are available from the Henry Hill Visitor Center.

National Museum of the Marine Corps

The **National Museum of the Marine Corps** (18900 Richmond Hwy., Triangle, 877/635-1775, www.usmcmuseum.com, daily 9am-5pm, free) is in Triangle, adjacent to the **Marine Corps Base Quantico.** The museum was built to serve as an ongoing tribute to U.S. Marines of the past, present, and future. The beautiful, soaring 210-foot design can be seen from I-95, and it is reminiscent of the famous Iwo Jima flag-raising image from World War II. The museum opened in 2006 and continues to expand. It houses interactive exhibits using innovative technology and shows visitors what it is like to be a marine. An example of this is the Legacy Walk, which uses lifelike cast figures of individual marines, photographs, maps, and artifacts to illustrate the evolution of the Marine Corps. Artifacts on display in the museum include aircraft, vehicles, weapons, uniforms, and personal items. A small fee is charged to experience the flight simulator.

Ben Lomond Historic Site

Those looking for a historical site with a new twist will enjoy the **Ben Lomond Historic Site** (10321 Sudley Manor Dr., Manassas, 703/367-7872, www.pwcgov.org, house hours May-Oct. Thurs.-Mon. 11am-4pm, grounds open daily dawn-dusk, adults $5, children under 6 free, active military $3). This is a hands-on historical experience with a focus on medicine. The federal-style manor house, built in 1837, is within five miles of Manassas National Battlefield Park, and it served as both a Confederate and Union hospital during the Civil War. The site includes the main house (where visitors can learn about medical techniques used during the Civil War and even see fake blood), slave quarters, and a smokehouse. Original graffiti written by Union soldiers in 1862 can still be seen on the walls. There is also an heirloom rose garden on the property with rare and antique plants. The garden is one of the largest public rose gardens in the country, with approximately 160 different cultivars. This is a great museum for kids and teenagers. Tours are given on the hour.

Occoquan Waterfront

More than 50 shops and restaurants line the quaint streets along the Occoquan River on the historic **Occoquan Waterfront** (www. occoquanwaterfront.com). The town began as a site for public tobacco warehouses as early as 1734, and its name means "at the end of the water." With a mostly industrial past due to its water access, the town has transformed into a residential community served by small businesses. Antiques stores, galleries, gift shops, and boutiques are just some of the shops visitors will find. Many festivals and events are held throughout the year on the streets and even in the water. Check out the website to see what is happening when you're in town.

RECREATION
Splashdown Water Park

Splashdown Water Park (7500 Ben Lomond Park Dr., Manassas, 703/792-8204, www.splashdownwaterpark.com, 48 inches or taller $16, under 48 inches $12.25, seniors 60 and over $9.50, spectators $9.50) is the largest water park in Northern Virginia. It features five unique water areas and a variety of food options. Some of the fun activities it offers include waterslides, a lazy river, a 25-meter lap pool, bubblers, fountains, cannonball slides, and a beach. They also offer swimming lessons.

Prince William Forest Park

Prince William Forest Park (18170 Park Entrance Rd., Triangle, 703/221-7181, www. nps.gov/prwi, $15 per vehicle for a 7-day pass) is a 15,000-acre all-season destination. It offers hiking, mountain biking, fishing, birdwatching, and cross-country skiing. There are 37 miles of hiking trails (the most extensive hiking network in Northern Virginia) and 21 miles of mountain biking roads and trails. Road biking on a 12-mile scenic stretch of road is also permitted, and the path has light traffic and great natural scenery. The visitors center is open daily March-October 9am-5pm, November-February 8am-4pm.

Leesylvania State Park

Leesylvania State Park (2001 Daniel K. Ludwig Dr., Woodbridge, 703/730-8205, www. dcr.virginia.gov, $10) is in southeast Prince William County, approximately 25 miles from Washington DC. The park is the site of the former Leesylvania Plantation, where General Robert E. Lee's father, Henry Lee III (aka Light Horse Harry), was born. Created in 1992, the park encompasses 542 acres on a peninsula bordered by the Potomac River, Neabsco Creek, and Powells Creek. The park has five hiking trails, including a segment of the **Potomac Heritage National Scenic Trail**. There are also many scenic overlooks to the Potomac River, and the one at Freestone Point is on the remains of a gun battery used by the Confederates in the Civil War. Fishing and boating are popular sports in the park. There is a boat ramp, a cartop launch for canoes and kayaks, and a 300-foot fishing pier. There is a large visitors center with nature displays, information on the history of the park, and a gift shop. Canoe tours, nature walks, guided hikes, and children's fishing tournaments are available. Picnic shelters are also available for rent.

A fun kayaking option is to launch from the park and paddle south on the Potomac River a short way to **Tim's Rivershore Restaurant & Crabhouse** (1510 Cherry Hill Rd., Dumfries, 703/441-1375, www.

timsrivershore.com, $10-31) for a seafood lunch on their deck. The restaurant is visible from the cartop launch, and there's a beach at Tim's to land your kayaks. A short paddle north to Neabsco Creek will take you past a shoreline of cute houses by the railroad tracks.

Largemouth bass are plentiful in the Potomac River near Leesylvania State Park. Other sport fish include catfish, perch, and striped bass. Overnight boating and fishing pier usage are allowed March-October.

Northwest Federal Field at Pfitzner Stadium

The **Northwest Federal Field at Pfitzner Stadium** (7 County Complex Ct., Woodbridge, 703/590-2311) is a minor league baseball stadium and the home field of the Potomac Nationals, a Class A affiliate of the Washington Nationals. The stadium holds 6,000 spectators.

Golf

The **Old Hickory Golf Club** (11921 Chanceford Dr., Woodbridge, 703/580-9000, www.golfoldhickory.com, $57-75) is an upscale golf and banquet facility in Woodbridge. The 18-hole, par-72 course was designed by Tim Freeland and is the sister course to Raspberry Falls in Leesburg. It is a well-maintained course with fast greens.

There are three public golf courses run by the **Prince William County Park Authority.** The first is the **Prince William Golf Course** (14631 Vint Hill Rd., Nokesville, 703/754-7111, www.princewilliamgolf.com, $20-44) in Nokesville. This course was built in the 1960s by local farmers. It is an 18-hole, par-70 course geared toward beginner and intermediate golfers and offers wide fairways and gentle knolls. There is also a driving range, a large putting and chipping green, a practice bunker, and PGA instruction.

The second, **Forest Greens Golf Club** (4500 Poa Annua Ln., Triangle, 703/221-0123, www.forestgreens.com, $25-59) in Triangle, offers resort amenities. This 18-hole, par-72 course was given four stars by *Golf Digest* and

features gently rolling terrain, tree-lined fairways, and protected greens. Designed by architect Clyde Johnston, the course offers an interesting layout with elevated tees, large landing areas, and few blind shots. This facility also includes a driving range, a pro shop, a putting and chipping green, PGA instruction, and a beverage cart on the course.

The third golf course is the 9-hole, par-3 **Lake Ridge Park Golf Course** (12350 Cotton Mill Dr., Woodbridge, 703/494-5564, www.lakeridgegc.com, $12) in Woodbridge. This course is an affordable novice course designed to help improve players' short games.

Bird-Watching

There are two prime birding locations in Prince William County. The first is the **Manassas National Battlefield Park** (6511 Sudley Rd., Manassas, 703/361-1339, www.nps.gov/mana, free, donations accepted), which was named an Audubon Important Bird Area. Park residents include the eastern meadowlark, barn owl, northern harrier, Savannah sparrow, and grasshopper sparrow.

The second is the **Prince William Forest Park** (18170 Park Entrance Rd., Triangle, 703/221-7181, www.nps.gov/prwi, $15 for a 7-day pass), a 15,000-acre national park in Triangle. The park is known as one of the premier birding habitats in Northern Virginia and has residents such as cedar waxwings, warblers, and kingfishers.

ENTERTAINMENT AND EVENTS

Jiffy Lube Live

A bustling venue for summer outdoor concerts is **Jiffy Lube Live** (7800 Cellar Door Dr., Bristow, 703/754-6400, www.livenation.com). This 25,000-capacity pavilion hosts many big-name bands, artists, and other performers. Reserved seating is underneath an overhang and protected from weather, while general admission is out on the lawn. Past performances include the Dave Matthews Band, The Who, Aerosmith, Jimmy Buffett, and Kelly Clarkson. Traffic entering and exiting the pavilion is notorious for being very slow, so plan accordingly.

Hylton Performing Arts Center

The **Hylton Performing Arts Center** (10960 George Mason Circle, Manassas, 703/993-7550, www.hyltoncenter.org) is a modern performing arts center at the Prince William Campus of George Mason University. The center includes 85,000 square feet of performance space including an elegant opera house, a family theater, and an art gallery. Performances include concerts, theater, comedy, dance, and other performing arts. Visit the website for a list of upcoming events.

Fairs and Festivals

The **Occoquan Arts and Craft Show** (www.visitpwc.com) is an annual event held in early June on the streets of historic downtown Occoquan. The show is hosted by the town of Occoquan and has been in existence for more than 50 years. Vendors include local merchants, crafters, and food, and there is live music. During the event, the roads are closed to traffic to make room for vendors and visitors. Information on parking and shuttle service can be found on the website.

The annual **Manassas Heritage Railway Festival** (9201 Center St., Manassas, 703/361-6599, www.visitmanassas.org, $5-6) takes place in June and draws more than 30,000 visitors each year. Enjoy a day of train-oriented activities, including train rides, model train displays, music, train memorabilia vendors, and other performances.

Another popular festival held in Manassas in June is the **Manassas Jazz Festival** (9101 Prince William St., 703/361-6599, www.visitmanassas.org, $25-130). This festival is held on Father's Day on the Manassas Museum Lawn in Old Town Manassas.

SHOPPING

Keeping in step with the rest of Northern Virginia, Prince William County offers a multitude of strip malls with many national retailers. The most well-known shopping area, however, is **Potomac Mills** (2700 Potomac Mills Circle, Woodbridge, 703/496-9330, www.simon.com, Mon.-Sat. 10am-9pm, Sun. 11am-6pm), right on I-95 near Woodbridge. Potomac Mills is the largest outlet mall in Virginia, with more than 200 stores. It is an indoor mall and also offers 25 food retailers and movie theaters.

Manassas Mall (8300 Sudley Rd., Manassas, 703/368-0181, www.manassasmall.com) is a traditional mall with more than 100 stores.

FOOD
American

The ★ **Philadelphia Tavern** (9413 Main St., Manassas, 703/393-1776, www.thephiladelphiatavern.com, daily 11am-2am, $6-16) is the place in Manassas to go for cheesesteaks, brews, and a little bit of everything else. The signature "Build Your Own Original Cheesesteak" is a local favorite. Try it with American cheese and Cheese Whiz. With daily specials like Tuesday's Virginia Beer and Burger Night and Wing Wednesday, every day is a little different at the tavern. Located in the historic district, the building was constructed in 1940 and was formerly a liquor store and storehouse. It was converted to the tavern in the 1990s as a replica of the common corner bar found in Philadelphia neighborhoods.

For casual seafood in a lovely setting, try **Madigans Waterfront** (201 Mill St., Occoquan, 703/494-6373, www.madiganswaterfront.com, daily 11am-10pm, $9-36). Madigans is right on the waterfront in historic Occoquan and offers a large deck with a tiki bar, many seafood selections, steak, pasta, and oysters year-round. They also have a sandwich menu with favorites such as shrimp salad, crab cakes, and an assortment of wraps. If you're looking for a relaxing waterfront setting, Madigans is a good choice.

French

The ★ **Bistro L'Hermitage** (12724 Occoquan

Rd., Woodbridge, 703/499-9550, www. bistrolhermitage.com, Tues.-Wed. 5pm-10pm, Thurs. 11:30am-2:30pm and 5pm-10pm, Fri. 11:30am-2:30pm and 5pm-11pm, Sat. 11:30am-2:30pm and 5pm-11pm, Sun. 11:30am-2:30pm and 5pm-10pm, $26-36) is a cozy French bistro located in Woodbridge but near the charming and historic Occoquan Waterfront. They serve fine French cuisine for brunch, lunch, and dinner. Dinner entrées include many seafood dishes as well as roasted duck, steak, roasted chicken, and veal liver. The restaurant offers delicious, well-presented food, good ambience, and friendly service.

Greek

For great Greek food go to **Katerina's Greek Cuisine** (9212 Center St., Manassas, 703/361-4976, www.katerinasgreekcuisine.com, Sun.-Thurs. 11am-9pm, Fri.-Sat. 11am-10pm, $7-22) in Manassas. This impressive little restaurant combines family recipes with fresh ingredients. If you're not sure what to order, try the Taste of Greece combination dinner or a traditional gyro platter. If someone in your party isn't keen on Greek food, they also offer burgers.

Mexican

Wonderful authentic Mexican food can be found in Haymarket at **El Vaquero West** (14910 Washington St., Haymarket, 703/753-0801, Mon.-Thurs. 11am-10pm, Fri. 11am-11pm, Sat. 11am-10pm, Sun. 11am-9pm, $7-20). People travel from all parts of Northern Virginia to enjoy the white queso and the dozens of freshly prepared menu items (most from family recipes). The chips and salsa are average, but the rest of the food will keep you coming back. The huge burritos are a favorite and come in all varieties. The restaurant is small and very family friendly. The wait staff is extremely nice, and both staff and patrons are lively and always seem to enjoy themselves. Try a Texas-style margarita, which comes in three sizes, and then order your entrée by the menu item number. Don't be thrown by the numbering system;

there really isn't one. You'll understand when you see the menu. The portions are big, the food is consistent, and the prices are very reasonable. This is easily one of the best Mexican restaurants in the region.

Farmers Markets

Haymarket's Farmers Market (Town Hall parking lot, 15000 Washington St., 703/753-2600, www.townofhaymarket.org, Apr.-Oct. Sat. 8am-2pm) is a Virginia-producer-only weekly market featuring fresh produce, specialty items, and baked goods.

ACCOMMODATIONS
$100-200

The **Hampton Inn Manassas** (7295 Williamson Blvd., Manassas, 703/369-1100, www.hamptoninn3.hilton.com, $132-193) is a reasonably priced hotel near I-66. It is approximately 20 minutes from Washington Dulles International Airport. The hotel offers 125 pleasant, clean rooms, a fitness center, and free Internet. Complimentary breakfast is available each morning.

The **Holiday Inn Manassas Battlefield** (10424 Balls Ford Rd., 571/292-5400, www.ihg.com, $128) is convenient to I-66 and the Manassas Battlefield. This modern hotel offers visitors 104 spacious guest rooms with a few extra touches such as nice hair products in the bathrooms and an attentive staff. Breakfast is included each morning with your stay. A pleasant indoor pool and hot tub and small fitness room are also on-site.

The **SpringHill Suites Potomac Mills** (14325 Crossing Pl., Woodbridge, 703/576-9000, www.marriott.com, $103-146) in Woodbridge is conveniently located off exit 158 of I-95 near the Potomac Mills shopping area. There are 98 spacious guest rooms. The hotel is modern, and the staff goes out of its way to make guests comfortable. Breakfast is included, and there is a pool, fitness center, and a free laundry facility on-site. Free high-speed Internet and parking are included.

A good value near I-95 is the **Country Inn & Suites by Radisson, Potomac Mills** (2621

Prince William Pkwy., Woodbridge, 703/492-6868, www.radissonhotels.com, $79-103). This hotel offers 100 nice guest rooms, complimentary coffee, tea, hot chocolate, and friendly service. The rooms have comfortable beds, microwaves, and refrigerators. Breakfast is included. There is also an indoor pool. The hotel is convenient for Potomac Mills shopping.

Camping

Prince William Forest Park (18170 Park Entrance Rd., Triangle, 703/221-7181, www.nps.gov/prwi, $26-80 plus $15 entrance fee) has two campgrounds (some sites can accommodate up to 40 people) and backcountry camping. One campground is open all year. Cabin camping is available in five cabins, four of which were built during the Great Depression and are now listed in the National Register of Historic Places. Cabin rentals are available May-October and can accommodate between 4 and 10 people ($40-60).

INFORMATION AND SERVICES

The **Historic Manassas Visitor Center** (9431 West St., Manassas, 703/361-6599, daily 9am-5pm) is housed in an early 20th-century train depot in the center of town. Another good resource for Manassas information is www.visitmanassas.org.

For additional information on Prince William County in general, visit www.visitpwc.com.

GETTING AROUND

The **OmniRide** (703/730-6664, www.omniride.com, times vary by location, $1.55) is a local bus service in Prince William County. The service is unique because buses are able to alter their routes to accommodate additional service locations when there is available time in their schedules.

NORTHERN VIRGINIA
LOUDOUN COUNTY

Loudoun County

It is hard to believe that at one time Loudoun County was considered the northwestern frontier of Virginia. Loudoun became a county in 1757 during the French and Indian War. It was named after John Campbell, the fourth earl of Loudoun (of Ayrshire, Scotland), who was the commander in chief of the British and colonial troops. Leesburg became the county seat around 1760. When the British invaded Washington DC during the War of 1812, the county clerk in Loudoun hid the Constitution and the Declaration of Independence in a family vault in a home just southeast of Leesburg.

President James Monroe had a home in Loudoun County called Oak Hill. Located in Aldie (13 miles south of Leesburg), it was there that he wrote the Monroe Doctrine in 1823. Oak Hill is currently a private residence and not open to the public.

Loudoun was a divided county during the Civil War. Sitting on the border between the North and the South, it became a thoroughfare of sorts for both Union and Confederate troops. Communities in Loudoun were often stripped of their horses and resources as the troops came through, leaving many residents in dire straits. Some residents began to fight back as members of John Singleton Mosby's partisan rangers, and Mosby became known as the "Gray Ghost of the Confederacy" after experiencing success with his hit-and-run strategy.

After the war, the railroad expanded west through Loudoun and new communities sprang up. The county saw the development of many farms and summer homes for Washingtonians. In the 1960s, the county began to blossom into a full-fledged suburb of Washington DC and experienced a population growth of 600 percent during a 40-year span. Today substantial growth continues, and many homes and businesses are built in the county yearly, making it one of the wealthiest and most populous counties in the state.

Visitors to Loudoun County will find large housing developments and strip malls, but despite incredible growth, the area is also known as "Virginia hunt country" for its history of foxhunting, and many wineries grace its rolling terrain. The historic towns of Leesburg and Middleburg have maintained their charm and should be high on the list of places to visit.

GETTING THERE AND AROUND

Loudoun County Transit (703/771-5665, www.loudoun.gov) provides commuter bus service from Loudoun County to Washington DC, the Pentagon, Crystal City, and Rosslyn (Arlington) for $11 one-way and to the Wiehle-Reston Metrorail station for $1.50 one-way. Service begins at multiple park-and-ride lots throughout Loudoun County. For a map of parking lot locations, visit www.loudoun.gov.

LEESBURG

Leesburg is a historic town 45 miles west of Washington DC and 15 minutes from Washington Dulles International Airport. Its roots stretch back more than 250 years, but this bustling town has seen tremendous growth over the past two decades as suburban sprawl found its way into Loudoun County and then continued to explode. Spend a day or a weekend exploring historic downtown Leesburg, watch a point-to-point horse race sponsored by the Loudoun Hunt, or spend an afternoon shopping at the Leesburg Outlets.

Sights
HISTORIC DOWNTOWN LEESBURG
Leesburg was established in 1758 and is the seat of Loudoun County. At the outbreak of the Civil War, the town was prospering and had approximately 1,700 residents. Leesburg is just two miles south of the Potomac River, which at the time divided the North and South. During the war, the town suffered

frequent raids and fighting in its streets, and it changed hands nearly 150 times. Following the war, Leesburg's proximity to Washington DC helped it recover economically, and it eventually became a primary stop for the railroad. Today, visitors to **Historic Downtown Leesburg** (www.visitloudoun.org) can see beautiful 18th- and 19th-century architecture, walk its brick sidewalks, visit many unique shops, eat in trendy restaurants, and partake in special events and festivals. Blue tourist information signs direct the way to the **visitors center** (112-G South St., 703/771-2617, daily 9am-5pm), which is a great place to begin exploration.

OATLANDS HISTORIC HOUSE AND GARDENS
A National Trust Historic Site and National Historic Landmark, **Oatlands Historic House and Gardens** (20850 Oatlands Plantation Ln., 703/777-3174, www.oatlands.org, mid-Apr.-Dec. daily 10am-5pm, guided tours Thurs.-Sun., house $15, active military $12, gardens only $10) is a lovely example of a Virginia plantation. Just six miles south of downtown Leesburg, Oatlands was built in the early 19th century and was a thriving 3,408-acre wheat plantation. It was owned by George Carter, a descendant of one of Virginia's most well-known families. A large federal-style mansion was started near the southern border of the property but ended up being finished in the 1820s in the Greek revival style. Many outbuildings were added, including a smokehouse, greenhouse, and barn. The plantation prospered until the time of the Civil War, but the family's wealth declined after the war and the plantation became a girls' school and boardinghouse.

In 1897, the mansion and 60 acres were sold to *Washington Post* founder Stilson Hutchins, although he never actually lived there. In 1903, the property was purchased by William and Edith Eustis, who were avid outdoors lovers and saw the potential for restoring the

---

1: Oatlands Historic House **2:** Morven Park

home and neglected gardens and using the property for foxhunting. In 1964, after Edith's passing, her daughters donated the mansion (furnished) and 261 acres to the National Trust for Historic Preservation.

Oatlands is now open to the public April-December. Forty-minute interpretive guided tours of the first floor are available, and self-guided tours of the second floor are encouraged. They also feature the Smokehouse exhibit, which teaches about the lives of the enslaved individuals who are part of the estate's history.

The formal terraced Oatlands Gardens and grounds are open to visitors. These 200-year-old gardens were designed in the Tidewater Virginia style and have multiple terraces carved into a hillside. Box hedges, trees, vegetables, shrubs, and flowers are part of the plantings, and the beautiful stonework was quarried locally. There are also many sculptures in the gardens (thanks to the Eustises' son-in-law, who was the first director of the National Gallery of Art). Be sure to take in the wonderful view of Bull Run Mountain.

Many events are held at Oatlands throughout the year; check their website for information. There's a gift shop on-site but no food facilities. However, there are plenty of places to enjoy a relaxing picnic on the grounds.

★ MORVEN PARK

Morven Park (17195 Southern Planter Ln., 703/777-2414, www.morvenpark.org, grounds open daily 8am-5pm, free) is a special place in Loudoun County. This 1,200-acre estate was home to Virginia governor Westmoreland Davis, who served as governor 1918-1922, for 40 years. The site now offers the original mansion (Governor's Residence), two museums, an equestrian center, historic gardens, sports fields, hiking trails, and beautiful country scenery. Many public events are held at Morven Park throughout the year including Civil War reenactments, equestrian competitions, and festivals. It is also the "forever home" to pardoned White House turkeys.

The **Governor's Residence** is worth a trip itself. It evolved from a fieldstone farmhouse built in 1781 into a beautiful turn-of-the-20th-century mansion. The stately home with its white exterior and columned facade sits on a rise surrounded by a blanket of pristine lawn. It supports an unusual mix of architectural styles that includes a Greek Revival portico, a Jacobean dining room, French drawing room, and a renaissance great hall. The furnishings are also an eclectic mix that includes 16th-century Belgian tapestries and pieces from the Renaissance and neo-Renaissance. A terraced, formal garden sits just behind the house and can be toured at leisure with admission to the Governor's Residence.

Other museums on-site include the **Carriage Museum,** which houses an assortment of antique vehicles, and the **Museum of Hounds & Hunting** (inside the Governor's Residence), which preserves art and memorabilia of foxhunting in Virginia. All-inclusive tours of the Mansion and Carriage Museum are available (Thurs.-Mon. noon-5pm, adults $10, children 6-12 $5, children 5 and under free). No ticket is needed for the Museum of Hounds & Hunting.

Other points of interest include information on Morven Park during the Civil War (offered on the grounds through permanent historical markers and periodic living-history programs, free) and the beautiful parklike grounds surrounding the mansion (free).

The **equestrian center** at Morven Park (41580 Tutt Ln.) hosts local, regional, national, and international equestrian events including horse trials, schooling shows, trail rides, clinics, polo events, races, and dressage events. It includes indoor and outdoor arenas, a series of stunning cross-country courses, and sporting fields. Morven Park is two miles north of downtown Leesburg.

LOUDOUN MUSEUM

The **Loudoun Museum** (16 Loudoun St. SW, 703/777-7427, www.loudounmuseum. org, Fri.-Sun. 10am-4pm, free) is dedicated to Loudoun County's rich and diverse heritage.

It offers educational exhibits that are a little different from other museums since the artifacts displayed are authentic items formerly owned by county residents. The museum's goal is to tell the stories of the people from the county. Exhibits include original documents, photographs, maps, furniture, and toys. There are also exhibits geared specifically toward kids.

GEORGE C. MARSHALL HOUSE

The **George C. Marshall House** (312 E. Market St., 703/777-1301, www. georgecmarshall.org, Sat. 10am-5pm, Sun. 1pm-5pm, adults $15, seniors $10, students $5, active military free) was the home of General George C. Marshall, Chief of Staff of the Army, Special Envoy to China, Secretary of State, Secretary of Defense, and President of the American Red Cross. He was also a Nobel Peace Prize winner in 1953. The home sits on nearly four acres in the Historic District and is a National Historic Landmark. The Marshalls lived in the home between 1941 and 1959, and 90 percent of the belongings in the home were owned by them.

LEESBURG ANIMAL PARK

A fun place to take the kids is the **Leesburg Animal Park** (19270 James Monroe Hwy., 703/433-0002, www.leesburganimalpark. com, Tues.-Sun. 10am-5pm, adults $14.95, children and seniors $10.95, children under 2 free), a 21-acre family petting zoo. It offers an animal-petting and -feeding area with residents such as llamas, bunnies, deer, lambs, pigs, and camels and exotic animal exhibits with animals such as lemurs, gibbons, zebras, porcupines, and tortoises. Kids of all ages can participate in many park activities. They offer pony and camel rides, wagon rides, and other activities, too. The favorite event of the year at the park is their **Pumpkin Village** (www.pumpkinfestleesburg.com), which is open daily between late September and early November. Visitors can enjoy a kids' hay maze, slides, an obstacle course, face and pumpkin painting, and many more seasonal activities.

THOMAS BALCH LIBRARY

The **Thomas Balch Library** (208 W. Market St., 703/737-7195, www.leesburgva.gov, hours vary daily) features collections on Loudoun County, Virginia history, genealogy, military history, and the American Civil War. The library is operated by the town of Leesburg. The library is also a designated Underground Railroad research site.

BALL'S BLUFF BATTLEFIELD REGIONAL PARK

Ball's Bluff Battlefield Regional Park (Ball's Bluff Rd., 703/737-7800, www. novaparks.com, daily dawn-dusk, free) preserves the site where the first Civil War engagement in Loudoun County took place, the Battle of Ball's Bluff, in October 1861. Visitors can enjoy seven miles of marked hiking trails and read interpretive signs that describe the battle. The park surrounds **Ball's Bluff National Cemetery,** the third-smallest national cemetery in the country. A small monument dedicated to a Confederate soldier who was killed in the battle, Clinton Hatcher, may be found in the cemetery. A second memorial is dedicated to the memory of a Union colonel, Edward D. Baker, who was also killed in the battle. Baker was a U.S. Senator at the time he was killed. Efforts are underway to restore the battlefield to its original appearance. Guided tours are available by appointment.

WINERIES

With more than 40 wineries, Loudoun County boasts more wineries than any other county in Virginia. More information can be found at www.visitloudoun.org and the county's Wine Growers Association website (www. loudounwine.com). **Point to Point Winery & Vineyard Tours** are also available through **Point to Point Limousine** (703/771-8100, www.pointtopointlimo.com, from $40 per person).

Stone Tower Winery (19925 Hogback Mountain Rd, 703/777-2797, www. stonetowerwinery.com, Thurs.-Mon. 11am-6pm, tastings $20) is a stunningly beautiful and large winery that sits on over 200 acres. The property consists of multiple buildings including two tasting rooms (one is family friendly and the other is 21 and over). There is also an upscale picnic area. The wines are delicious and the staff delightful. Specialty tours and tastings are offered, and this is a great place to plan an event or bring a group (groups of nine or more require a reservation). A tip from this white-wine lover: Try the sauvignon blanc.

Red-wine lovers shouldn't miss a tasting at **Fabbioli Cellars** (15669 Limestone School Rd., 703/771-1197, www.fabbioliwines.com, daily 11am-5pm, tastings $15). This small, family-owned boutique vineyard and winery grows and makes high-quality red wines (and only red wines). Tastings include a food pairing (chocolate or savory). The staff is very knowledgeable and goes out of its way to make everyone feel welcome. This is an ideal outing for a small group. Groups with more than eight people should make a reservation.

Recreation

GOLF

The **Raspberry Falls Golf and Hunt Club** (41601 Raspberry Dr., 703/779-2555, www.raspberryfalls.com, $35-95) is a beautiful and challenging 18-hole, par-72 course that is open to the public. The award-winning course was designed by Gary Player to evoke the feeling of the British Isles. This is evident in the rolling terrain, stone walls, rambling streams, and bunkers. The course has elevated tee boxes and lush bent grass greens. The course is set against the backdrop of the Catoctin Mountains, and holes 3 and 18 have particularly nice views. This is one of the most popular daily-fee courses in Northern Virginia.

PARKS

If you're looking for a nice short hike with good views of the Potomac River, visit **Red Rock Wilderness Overlook Regional Park** (43098 Edwards Ferry Rd., 703/779-9372, www.novaparks.com, free). This 67-acre park is four miles east of downtown Leesburg and offers a two-mile loop trail through the woods and over hills to a panoramic view of the river. Trail terrain varies from moderate to strenuous in some places. Dogs are allowed on leashes, and there are no restroom facilities in the park.

Entertainment and Events

The **Loudoun Hunt Point to Point Races** are held annually in mid-April at the historic **Oatlands Historic House and Gardens** (20850 Oatlands Plantation Ln., 703/728-0545, www.loudounhunt.com, $40 per car). The races were first held in 1966 and are known for featuring challenging timber and hurdle courses that test the abilities of the local and global competitors.

Classic-car enthusiasts won't want to miss the annual **Leesburg Classic Car Show** (www.leesburgva.gov, free). This event is usually held in May and takes place in downtown Leesburg. More than 200 classic cars are on display, including street rods and muscle cars. The event is free to spectators.

Music lovers will enjoy the free **Acoustic on the Green** (Town Hall Green, 25 W. Market St., www.leesburgva.gov) summer concert series in downtown Leesburg. Concerts are held on Saturday evenings 7pm-8:30pm June-August.

The **Leesburg Air Show** (1000 Sycolin Rd., www.leesburgairshow.com, free) is a much-anticipated free annual air show that is held at the **Leesburg Executive Airport** at the end of September. The show features many types of planes, including experimental aircraft and warbirds from World War II. The show has air performances and tarmac attractions, and food is available for purchase.

Shopping

Historic Downtown Leesburg offers antiques stores, art galleries, and other specialty shops. The primary shopping area is on Market, Loudoun, and King Streets.

Since 1998, the **Black Shutter Antique Center** (1 Loudoun St., SE, 703/443-9579, www.blackshutterantiques.com, Mon.-Sat.,

10:30am-5:30pm, Sun., 12pm-5pm) has offered 20 rooms of antique merchandise in a historic 19th century home. They feature art, furniture, maps, clothing, and books.

In recent years, Leesburg has become synonymous with outlets. People travel from all over the region to shop at the **Leesburg Corner Premium Outlets** (241 Fort Evans Rd., 703/737-3071, www.premiumoutlets. com). The mall houses 110 outlets including stores for designer fashion, shoes, children's clothes, leather, jewelry, housewares, and gifts. There is also a food court, and other national chain restaurants are nearby.

The **Village at Leesburg** (1602 Village Market Blvd., 571/291-2288, www. villageatleesburg.com) is a modern, 57-acre open-air shopping plaza with upscale retailers and restaurants. The anchor store is **Wegmans** food market.

The **Dulles Town Center** (21100 Dulles Town Circle, Dulles, 703/404-7120, www. shopdullestowncenter.com) offers many national-brand stores and restaurants with ample free parking. It is located at the intersection of Route 7 and Route 28, 10 miles east of Leesburg.

Food

AMERICAN

One part wine-tasting, one part farm-to-table experience, **The Wine Kitchen** (7 S. King St., 703/777-9463, www.thewinekitchen.com, Tues.-Thurs. 11:30am-9pm, Fri.-Sat. 11:30am-10:30pm, Sun. 11:30am-9pm, $10-37) is a small, cozy restaurant with a modern vibe. Wine is served with clever and humorous description cards, and the food selection is interesting and beautifully presented. The staff is very knowledgeable about the wine and food and makes excellent recommendations. If you are unsure what to order, try a wine flight.

Tuscarora Mill (203 Harrison St., 703/771-9300, www.tuskies.com, Mon.-Thurs. 11am-10pm, Fri.-Sat. 11am-midnight, Sun. 10am-9pm, $20-48) is a local institution in Leesburg. The food is consistent and delicious, and the warm, historic ambience is inviting.

The owners of this establishment really care about the food and guests at their restaurants (they own another great restaurant in nearby Purcellville called **Magnolias at the Mill,** which is equally wonderful). There's an informal bar area to grab a casual drink (they have a great wine list), and the dining area is good for groups. This is a good place for a date or to visit with friends. Tuscarora Mill is also known for their beer- and wine-pairing dinners. They are fantastic. The chef goes out of his way to prepare delicious and unexpected combinations. Check the website for a schedule.

Lightfoot Restaurant (11 N. King St., 703/771-2233, www.lightfootrestaurant. com, Mon.-Thurs. 11:30am-11pm, Fri.-Sat. 11:30am-midnight, Sun. 11am-9pm, $15-33) serves contemporary food in a great atmosphere. The building is a restored turn-of-the-20th-century bank building with many interesting and original architectural features and artifacts as well as original French posters from the 1920s. There are two bars, one with a grand piano, and an open kitchen with a chef's table. If you are unsure what to order, the onion-and-field-mushroom soup, fried green tomatoes with shrimp, crab cakes, and filet are all excellent choices. There is a private parking lot in back of the restaurant and street parking out front.

ITALIAN

The popular **Fireworks Pizza** (201 Harrison St., 703/779-8400, www.fireworkspizza.com, opens daily at 11am, $10-19) restaurant housed in the former Leesburg Freight Depot has fantastic pizza (try the Smokey Blue Pizza) and a great beer selection. The sandwiches are good too. The ambience is warm and friendly, and on nice days, the porch adds much-needed seating. If you come on the weekend, expect a wait. Great food, a fun vibe, and reasonable prices make this place a gem in the heart of historic Leesburg. Their patio is dog friendly.

TREATS

When your sweet tooth is acting up, stop in **Mom's Apple Pie** (220 Loudoun St. SE,

703/771-8590, www.momsapplepieco.com, Mon.-Fri. 7:30am-6:30pm, Sat. 8am-6pm, Sun. 10am-5pm), at the fork in the road between Loudoun Street and Market Street. As the name implies, they have fantastic pie, cookies, cupcakes, bread, and other baked goods. A Leesburg tradition, this establishment is known for baking natural, preservative-free pies. They even grow much of their own fruit.

FARMERS MARKETS

Leesburg hosts several great farmers markets featuring local producers such as **Shenandoah Seasonal** (www. shenandoahseasonal.com) from Boyce, Virginia.

The **Leesburg Saturday Farmers Market** (Virginia Village Shopping Center on Catoctin Circle SE, 540/454-8089, www. loudounfarmersmarkets.org, Nov.-Apr. 9am-noon, May-Oct. 8am-noon) is open year-round. There is also a seasonal Wednesday market in the same location (May-mid-Sept. 4pm-7pm).

The **One Loudoun Farmers Market** (Atwater Dr., Ashburn, www.eatloco.org) is also open year-round, Saturdays 9am-1pm.

The **Brambleton Market** (Brambleton Plaza, Brambleton, www.eatloco.org) is held seasonally on Sundays 9am-1pm.

Accommodations

There is a wide assortment of national chain hotels in Leesburg. Many are on the newer side as part of the rapid growth in Loudoun County in recent decades. If you're looking for someplace unique, there are several good options.

$100-200

The Country Comfort Bed and Breakfast (19724 Evergreen Mills Rd., 703/926-6994, www.countrycomfortbedandbreakfast.com, $175-200) offers two suites near downtown

Leesburg that are more like apartments. Guests are treated to a scrumptious home-cooked breakfast of their choice delivered each morning. Refrigerators are stocked with sodas, water, juice, and snacks, which are available throughout the stay. The suites have king beds, private bathrooms, a work area, high-speed Internet, and a living/dining area. The Evergreen Suite also has a private deck.

$200-300

The beautiful **Stone Gables Bed and Breakfast** (19077 Loudoun Orchard Rd., 703/303-6364, www.stonegables-bb.com, $225-250) offers four luxurious guest rooms in a rare, fully renovated, stone gabled barn. The property includes 10 acres, a pool, and close proximity to the W&OD Bike Trail. A full hot breakfast is included.

Lansdowne Resort (44050 Woodridge Pkwy., 703/729-8400, www.lansdowneresort. com, $163-699) has 305 guest rooms in the Potomac River valley, approximately four miles east of Leesburg. Amenities at the resort include a golf course, spa, health club, tennis courts, indoor and outdoor pools, and on-site restaurants. This resort offers beautiful grounds, a great view, and a quiet atmosphere. It is a popular location for business conferences.

Information and Services

Visitor information on Leesburg can be found at www.leesburgva.gov and www. visitloudoun.org, or visit the **Loudoun County Visitors Center** (112-G South St., 703/771-2617, www.visitloudoun.org, daily 9am-5pm).

MIDDLEBURG

Middleburg is an oasis in Northern Virginia just 42 miles west of Washington DC. Its stunning landscape, rich Civil War history, and beautifully restored buildings make it a very special place for visitors to explore. The area truly has the look of the English countryside: ribbons of low stone walls wind across lush pastures, and acres and acres of pristine

1: downtown Leesburg **2:** Lightfoot Restaurant **3:** Mom's Apple Pie

The Gray Ghost

Throughout American Civil War history, the operatives of one man in particular continue to fascinate scholars and history buffs alike. Colonel John Singleton Mosby, known as "the Gray Ghost," was a free-thinking man whose dislike for routine military life eventually led him to develop an independent guerrilla group that made forays throughout Loudoun County.

An attorney by profession and a graduate of the University of Virginia, Mosby joined his local militia unit as a private soldier in 1861. With the outbreak of the Civil War, his cavalry unit joined the Confederate forces. Mosby's strength was in scouting and patrolling duties, and he became a member of J. E. B. Stuart's personal staff.

In 1863, with nine men from his regiment, Mosby began guerrilla attacks on isolated Union posts in Northern Virginia and Maryland. Mosby led lightning-quick cavalry strikes aimed at disrupting supply lines and communication.

Mosby's men swelled in numbers and soon became known as "Mosby's Rangers." Many of Mosby's Rangers were volunteers who had never had any formal military training. Many brought their own uniforms and weapons. Their two most important items were their pistols and their horses. They often assembled near a blacksmith's shop so their horses' feet could be tended to.

When things became dangerous, the Rangers would melt into the night. They'd stay with friends or family, or simply camp out in the hills. Loudoun became known as Mosby's Confederacy, and Union commanders were furious with his success. Because of their guerrilla tactics and tendency to keep their spoils, the Rangers were often viewed by Federal officials as criminals rather than soldiers.

On March 9, 1863, Mosby led 29 Rangers through Federal lines at the Fairfax Courthouse and captured General Edwin Stoughton, 33 men, and 58 horses. A sack of gold and silver coins worth $350,000 was also taken, but Mosby was forced to bury it when chased by Union troops. Allegedly, he was never able to recover the loot, and it is still said to be buried between two tall pine trees in a shallow hole between Haymarket and New Baltimore.

By April 1865, Mosby had been promoted to colonel, had been wounded seven times, and was in command of eight companies. His last raid was on April 10, the day after Robert E. Lee surrendered at Appomattox. At that time, he had more than 700 men in his command.

After the war, Mosby continued to practice law in Warrenton. Mosby wrote two books while serving terms as U.S. consul to Hong Kong and assistant attorney in the Justice Department. They are titled *Mosby's War Reminiscences and Stuart's Cavalry Campaigns (1887)* and *Stuart's Cavalry in the Gettysburg Campaign (1908)*. He died on May 30, 1916, in Washington DC.

farmland blanket the foothills of the Blue Ridge Mountains. Middleburg has over 160 historic buildings, and nearly every one has a unique story. Some housed troops during the Civil War, others were shot at, and some hid well-known figures such as John Singleton Mosby (aka the Gray Ghost) and his band of raiders.

Middleburg is horse and hunt country. Many of its residents have family histories in equine sports competitions, and many U.S. Olympic riders live and train in the Middleburg area. As such, equine events and festivals attract visitors from all over the country.

Sights

THE VILLAGE OF MIDDLEBURG

Middleburg was developed in the mid-1700s and was later named for its location midway between Alexandria and Winchester. The town (with a local population of around 850 people) was established in 1787 and has many Civil War roots. It is beautifully preserved as a quaint, colonial island in an otherwise busy Northern Virginia. The main attraction is the village of Middleburg itself. This charming, historic section is lined with family-owned shops, inns, and restaurants and is well worth a day trip from Washington DC or other parts of Virginia and Maryland. Take a stroll down

Washington Street, and you'll feel miles and possibly centuries away from the busy nation's capital, as you become part of the historic landscape. The people are friendly, the pace is relaxed, and the merchandise is often rare and unusual.

NATIONAL SPORTING LIBRARY & MUSEUM

The **National Sporting Library & Museum** (102 The Plains Rd., 540/687-6542, www. nationalsporting.org, Wed.-Sun. 10am-5pm, library free, museum adults $10, youth 13-18 $8, children 12 and under free, seniors 65 and over $8) is a beautiful site dedicated to preserving equestrian, angling, and field sports literature, art, and culture. It is a research facility and art museum (located in two buildings) with more than 24,000 books and pieces of art. Be sure to look closely at the beautiful, haunting horse statue in front of the library. It is a memorial to the horses who lost their lives in the Civil War.

MOUNT DEFIANCE CIDERY & DISTILLERY

Mount Defiance Cidery & Distillery (207 W. Washington St., 540/687-8100, www. mtdefiance.com, Tues.-Sun. noon-6pm, tastings $10-15) is located right on West Washington Street. They create small-batch, handcrafted, classic hard cider and spirits. Their cidery produces farmhouse blends and a single-variety cider but is also known for unique infused and co-fermented ciders (honey, five-pepper, blueberry, etc.). The distillery focuses on classic spirits from both colonial America and Europe, such as apple brandy, apple liqueur, rum, and absinthe. They have a second location called the **Mount Defiance Cider Barn** (495 E. Washington St.).

ALDIE MILL HISTORIC PARK

The **Aldie Mill Historic Park** (39401 John Mosby Hwy., Aldie, 703/327-9777, www. novaparks.com, mid-Apr.-mid-Nov. Sat.-Sun. noon-5pm, free), just east of Middleburg, is a fully operational restored gristmill that dates back to 1807. Visitors can witness live grinding demonstrations, and tours of the mill are available. The mill is a popular location for weddings and events.

WINERIES AND VINEYARDS

Middleburg is on the edge of Virginia wine country and home to a number of outstanding wineries, vineyards, and tasting rooms that are worth visiting for their relaxing atmosphere and, of course, wine.

The beautiful **Boxwood Winery** (2042 Burrland Ln., 540/687-8778, www. boxwoodwinery.com, Nov.-Apr. Fri.-Sun. 11am-6pm, May-Oct. Thurs.-Sun. 11am-6pm) is owned by former Washington Redskins owner John Kent Cooke. They produce red and white wine in the Bordeaux tradition. Tastings by the glass or flight are available by appointment at the winery in Middleburg, but they also have several tasting rooms throughout the Washington DC area (consult their website for current locations).

Chrysalis Vineyards (39025 John Mosby Hwy., Middleburg, 540/687-8222, www. chrysaliswine.com, Mon-Thurs. noon-6pm, Fri.-Sat. noon-8pm, Sun. noon-7pm, tastings $15 for 10 wines) is located just west of Aldie on Route 50 in the Ag District Center. They specialize in unusual French and Spanish grape varietals and also in the native Virginia Norton grape.

Greenhill Winery and Vineyards (23595 Winery Ln., 540/687-6968, www. greenhillvineyards.com, May-Sept. Mon.-Thurs. noon-6pm, Fri.-Sun. noon-7pm, Oct.-Apr. daily noon-6pm, tastings $14) is a beautiful destination winery. They offer a tasting room, club house, and farm store. This is an adults-only winery.

Recreation

HORSEBACK RIDING

It seems like everyone in Middleburg owns a pair of riding boots. Most of the farms are privately owned and don't offer riding to the public, but if you are interested in giving it

The War Horse

There is something beautiful and haunting about the three-quarters life-size bronze sculpture that stands in the courtyard of the National Sporting Library & Museum in Middleburg. It depicts a thin, exhausted, war-weary Civil War horse wearing authentic Civil War-style tack.

This sculpture was created in the mind of Paul Mellon, a well-known American philanthropist, Thoroughbred racehorse breeder, and coheir to the Mellon Bank fortune who lived in nearby Upperville. Mellon was profoundly moved by Robert F. O'Neill Jr.'s book *The Cavalry Battles of Aldie, Middleburg and Upperville, June 10-27, 1863,* which told of human and horse bloodshed during a 17-day period in the American Civil War. After reading the book, Mellon felt compelled to do something for all the horses that died during the war.

To that point no monuments had been erected to honor the war's tremendous equine losses. The idea of a memorial came up one day while Mellon was speaking with the director and others at the National Sporting Library. The idea grew into a vision for an extraordinary bronze sculpture to honor all mules and horses from both the Union and Confederate armies.

Extensive research was conducted on the number of equine fatalities and also on the type of leather tack and gear they wore during battle. Mellon then took the idea to sculptor Tessa Pullan from Rutland, England, whom he had worked with earlier on a statue of his 1993 Kentucky Derby winner, Sea Hero.

A tremendous amount of time was spent consulting with many sources to create a design that was completely authentic. An example is the horse's stance, with his back leg bent, which is how horses stand when they are tired. Another is the scabbard worn by the horse. It is shown without a sword to indicate that the horse's rider was lost in battle. Care was also taken to fit the horse with gear that could have been from either the Union or Confederate side.

More extensive research showed that a realistic estimate of equine losses during the war was between 1,350,000 and 1,500,000, an astonishing and unsettling number. This number is reflected in the inscription at the bottom of the statue.

The library's Civil War horse was completed in 1997 and is now one of the most visited landmarks in the area. Local residents feel a personal attachment to the statue and often place horse blankets over it when the weather is cold.

a try, **Foxrock Stables** (37744 Featherbed Farm Ln., 703/346-4029, www.foxrockstables.com) offers lessons and summer camps.

BIKING

Road cycling and mountain biking are very popular in Middleburg. The beautiful and rolling country roads draw bikers from all over Northern Virginia, and the incredible scenery keeps them coming back. This has caused some friction between the local residents and visiting cyclists. The roads in Middleburg do not have bike lanes, so traffic is shared between bikes and cars. Although there is little traffic compared to the rest of the region, the hairpin turns and low shoulders can create a dangerous situation for both drivers and cyclists. Use extreme caution when biking in Middleburg and be sensitive to traffic. A good resource for finding bike routes in the area is www.mapmyride.com.

HOT-AIR BALLOONING

For high-flying adventure, try a hot-air balloon ride with **Balloons Unlimited** (23217 Meetinghouse Ln., Aldie, 703/327-0444, www.balloonsunlimited.com, adults $225, children 12 and under $125). Rides begin in several locations depending on the weather. Two flights are scheduled daily.

Entertainment and Events

CHRISTMAS IN MIDDLEBURG

One of Loudoun County's largest annual events is **Christmas in Middleburg** (Washington St., 571/278-5658, www.christmasinmiddleburg.org), held annually on the first Saturday in December. This daylong celebration in horse country includes a unique parade with more than 700 horses, llamas, alpacas, and hounds. An assortment of troops, bands, and floats also join the march down Washington Street along with fire trucks and, of course, Santa in a horse-drawn coach. The final phase of the celebration is a wine crawl where adults can enjoy samples from area vineyards and food in local restaurants.

HUNT COUNTRY STABLE TOUR

The **Hunt Country Stable Tour** (www.trinityupperville.org/hunt-country-stable-tour, $30-35, children under 10 free) is a 60-plus-year tradition in Middleburg and neighboring Upperville. This self-driven stable tour takes visitors through some of the most impressive private horse stables in the region. The tour is held over Memorial Day weekend and includes Thoroughbred breeding farms, foxhunting barns, and show hunter barns. A remarkable experience for horse lovers and nonequestrians alike, this is a great way to spend a day in the beautiful Virginia countryside.

UPPERVILLE COLT & HORSE SHOW

The **Upperville Colt & Horse Show** (Upperville Show Grounds, on Rte. 50 between Middleburg and Upperville, 540/687-5740, www.upperville.com, parking $45 for the week) is the longest-running horse show in the country. It was founded in 1853 and is held each year at the **Upperville Show Grounds.** More than 2,000 horses and riders compete each year over seven days at the beginning of June under towering oak trees in a beautiful storybook setting. Young riders on ponies and Olympic and World Cup riders and horses are all part of this well-known event.

THE MIDDLEBURG SPRING RACES AND THE VIRGINIA FALL RACES

The Middleburg Spring Races (www.middleburgspringraces.com) and **The Virginia Fall Races** (www.vafallraces.com) are two annual point-to-point (steeplechase) horse races with a long tradition in Middleburg. Both are held at **Glenwood Park** (36800 Glenwood Park Ln.), less than two miles north of downtown Middleburg. The spring races are in April, and the fall races are in October.

VIRGINIA GOLD CUP RACES

The premier event at the premier equestrian venue in Northern Virginia is the **Virginia Gold Cup Races** (540/347-2612, www.vagoldcup.com) at Great Meadows. This event is held eight miles south of downtown Middleburg in a nearby village called The Plains. The grand point-to-point race is held the first Saturday in May (rain or shine) and brings out the best gourmet tailgates in town. The day of racing dates back to 1922, and now more than 50,000 spectators from all over the Washington DC area descend on hunt country to enjoy this festive eating, drinking, people-watching, and yes, horse-watching event. The race itself is extremely demanding, with horses running more than four miles and jumping over four- to five-foot solid rail fences. The **International Gold Cup Races** are held at the same venue in October. Tickets to both events must be purchased well in advance.

Shopping

The village of Middleburg is an elegant and

historic shopping area right on Route 50 (John S. Mosby Highway). Unique boutiques housed in beautiful old buildings line the streets and offer goods from all over the world. Most stores are individually owned and operated specialty shops with hand-selected merchandise. It is obvious the owners take great pride in these establishments.

Food

AMERICAN

The Red Fox Inn and Tavern (2 E. Washington St., 540/687-6301, www.redfox.com, Mon.-Fri. 8am-10am and 5pm-9pm, Sat. 11am-2pm and 5pm-9pm, Sun. 11am-2pm and 5pm-8pm, $14-60) is a historic tavern in the heart of Middleburg that serves traditional Virginia-style food using cooking techniques such as roasting, smoking, and braising. Hearty breakfasts, relaxing brunch, and cozy candlelight dinners draw people to the tavern from all over the region. The stone fireplace and handcrafted furnishings are a good complement to the seasonal menus featuring traditional Southern and Virginia ingredients. If you've never tried peanut soup, this is the place to order it. The wine list includes both imported and domestic wines and includes many local Virginia wines. The restaurant offers great ambience, consistently good food, and friendly service. There are several additional dining spaces on the property, including the **Night Fox Pub.**

If you're looking for breakfast, a gourmet sandwich, or a picnic to take with you to a winery, or you need to purchase gourmet ingredients, the **Market Salamander** (200 W. Washington St., 540/687-9720, www.marketsalamander.com, Wed.-Thurs. 8am-2pm, Fri.-Sun. 8am-4pm, $8-21) is the place to visit. It is a chef's market, complete with an in-house café, custom cake bakery, and catering services. The market sells produce, prime aged meat, seafood, artisanal cheese, house-baked bread, pastries, wine, and a variety of imported packaged goods. The focal point in the market is the open display kitchen where the chef's daily selections are prepared.

Their menu includes items such as soup, sandwiches, burgers, and crab cakes.

If a local pub is more your style, stop in the **Red Horse Tavern** (118 W. Washington St., 540/687-6443, www.redhorsetavern.net, daily 11am-10pm, $9-15). They offer pub fare and a large patio.

ENGLISH

About eight miles west of Middleburg on Route 50 is **Hunter's Head Tavern** (9048 John S. Mosby Hwy. [Rte. 50], Upperville, 540/592-9020, www.huntersheadtavern.com, Mon.-Sat. 11:30am-9:30pm, Sun. 11am-9:30pm, $11-36). This authentic English pub is in a cute, old crooked house right on the road with a red English telephone box out front. Hunter's Head offers local organic farm meat and produce and was the first restaurant in the country to receive a certified humane designation. Original log cabin walls, "settled" floors, and mismatched wooden tables are all part of the charm. Read the extensive menu off the chalkboard and place your order at the window next to the bar (even if you have reservations, which is advised). The menu includes hearty pub fare and fine-dining options, and the offerings change frequently. If the macaroni and cheese is on the menu, it's worth ordering in spite of the calories. The calamari is also good and very tender. Hunter's Head Tavern has good beer on tap as well, and the desserts are fabulous, so save room.

FRENCH

The Conservatory at Goodstone (36205 Snake Hill Rd., 540/687-3333, www.goodstone.com, Wed.-Sun. 5:30pm-9pm, $50-75, prix fixe menu $79 for two courses, $89 for three, chef's tasting menu $115) deserves accolades. This small restaurant, located in the **Goodstone Inn,** serves outstanding "modern American French country cuisine" in a superb country setting. The chef only uses fresh ingredients, and many of them are sourced from the inn's private organic herb and vegetable gardens. Sample menu items include Icelandic cod, beef tenderloin, and lamb loin.

It is a charming place full of simple elegance for a special date or to just get away from it all.

SEAFOOD

Good seafood and a lively atmosphere can be found at the **King Street Oyster Bar** (1 E. Washington St., 540/883-3156, www. kingstreetoysterbar.com, Mon.-Thurs. 11am-9:30pm, Fri.-Sat. 11am-11pm, Sun. 10:30am-9:30pm, $7-59). This small and very popular restaurant is a fun place to grab a drink and eat good oysters. Don't be surprised if you end up making friends with the people seated next to you—it's that kind of place. There's another (original) location in Leesburg (12 S. King St.).

TREATS

Curb your sweet tooth while helping homeless animals. What could be better? Stop in **Scruffy's Ice Cream & Coffee Parlor** (6 W. Washington St., 540/687-3766, Mon.-Sat. 12pm-6pm, Sun. 12pm-5:30pm, under $10) for some delicious ice cream. A portion of the proceeds benefits local homeless animals at the Middleburg Humane Society. Try the chocolate ice cream or the mango sherbet. This is a small place, but there are a few stools inside and some benches outside.

A wonderful local bakery is the **Upper Crust** (4 N. Pendleton St., 540/687-5666, Mon.-Sat. 7am-4pm, under $15, cash only). They serve breakfast and lunch but are known for their pastries and fresh pies. You'll likely smell cookies baking as you approach. They do not take credit cards.

Accommodations

Middleburg is one of the few places in Northern Virginia where you'll have a good selection of private inns and bed-and-breakfasts to choose from. Truly a stay in the country, a night in Middleburg can make you feel light-years away from the city.

$100-200

The stately **Welbourne** (22314 Welbourne Farm Ln., 540/687-3201, www.welbourneinn. com, $170) is an authentic historical treasure in Virginia hunt country. The house was built in the 1700s and has been in the same family ever since. A stay there will take you back to Civil War times (the owners refer to it as "faded elegance"). There are five primary guest rooms with private baths and fireplaces. Relax in a rocking chair on the back porch, or take a hike around the property. Complimentary cocktails (served each evening at 6:30pm) and a wonderful, hearty breakfast are just some of the amenities that make visitors feel like family. Many dogs and horses live at this 520-acre property, so be prepared for four-legged company. The estate is decorated with family heirlooms and antiques. The property is dog friendly.

Another lovely bed-and-breakfast a few miles from town is the **Briar Patch Bed and Breakfast Inn** (23130 Briar Patch Ln., 703/327-5911, www.briarpatchbandb.com, $150-295). This historic home (built in 1805) was damaged during the Civil War and still shows a few scars today. The main house offers eight guest rooms decorated with antiques and colonial quilts. Six of the rooms can be combined into two-bedroom suites. There is also a small cottage and three "chicken coop" rooms. A good buffet breakfast is served daily, and plentiful snacks are available all day. There are resident horses, and the inn is dog friendly.

$200-300

One of the best-known inns in Middleburg is **The Red Fox Inn and Tavern** (2 E. Washington St., 540/687-6301, www.redfox. com, $239-649). This iconic inn and restaurant sits prominently at the center of Middleburg on the corner of East Washington and North Madison Streets. The tavern is famous as a meeting spot for Confederate colonel John Singleton Mosby and his Rangers. The Red Fox Inn is a complex consisting of several buildings with 16 guest rooms and three cottages. The tavern is located in the main building, and there is event space on the first and second floors. Five of the guest rooms are also in the main building on the upper two levels. The rooms are cozy and cleanly appointed in a colonial style, yet not overstuffed. A hunt country breakfast is served each day. The inn is very convenient to shopping and restaurants in the village.

OVER $300

The charming and luxurious ★ **Goodstone Inn & Restaurant** (36205 Snake Hill Rd., 540/687-3333, www.goodstone.com, $325-895) is a wonderful choice for an upscale country getaway. The inn has a highly regarded restaurant with a noted chef, and the service is friendly and genuine. There is also an on-site spa. The property is large (265 acres) and scenic with views of the Blue Ridge Mountains. The 18 tastefully decorated guest rooms and suites are housed in six buildings around the farm (which actually has farm animals). You can hike around the property on a trail that is several miles long and very relaxing. Canoeing is also available.

The **Salamander Resort and Spa** (500 North Pendleton St., 844/303-2723, www.salamanderresort.com, $475-975 plus a $39 per night resort fee) opened in 2013 and was one of the first luxury resorts in the nation to be LEED (Leadership in Energy and Environmental Design) certified. This stately 168-room resort sits on 340 acres in the heart of Virginia's wine and horse country, just outside the historic district of Middleburg. The modern, spacious guest rooms are 545-575 square feet and include sitting areas and a private balcony or terrace. Guests can enjoy a 23,000-square-foot spa, cooking studio, wine bar, billiards room, pool complex, tennis courts, and a two-acre culinary garden that supplies the resort's restaurant. There is also a full-service, 22-stall equestrian center on-site with an arena, riding trails, and instructional classes.

Information and Services

Middleburg's information center, the **Pink Box** (12 N. Madison St., 540/687-8888, daily 11am-3pm) is a good place to pick up brochures. They also offer information on a self-guided walking tour of the town. Downloadable driving maps are also available from the **Mosby Heritage Area Association** (www.mosbyheritagearea.org).

Coastal Virginia

Coastal Virginia sounds like a simple concept: the place where the Atlantic Ocean meets the land. It's actually much more complicated than that. The Chesapeake Bay is a defining feature along the coast, and the area where it opens into the Atlantic Ocean has developed into one of the world's largest and busiest natural ports. Several large rivers empty into the Chesapeake Bay as well, including the Potomac, Rappahannock, James, and York Rivers.

The coastal region can be divided into five main areas. The first is the Northern Neck, which sits between the Potomac and Rappahannock Rivers, both of which flow into the bay. The Northern Neck is quiet and flat, and farms line the riverbanks. The area is home to several notable historic sites including George Washington's birthplace. The second

Highlights

Look for ★ to find recommended sights, activities, dining, and lodging.

★ **Colonial Williamsburg:** This unmatched living museum takes you back in time. It's one of America's most popular family destinations (page 168).

★ **Historic Jamestowne:** The original site of the Jamestown settlement spans centuries of history. Founded in 1607, it was the first permanent English settlement in the New World (page 178).

★ **Nauticus National Maritime Center:** This nautical-themed science and technology center in Norfolk is also home to the battleship USS *Wisconsin* (page 197).

★ **Virginia Beach Boardwalk:** The most popular beach resort in the state provides access to miles of wonderful sand and surf (page 204).

★ **Virginia Aquarium & Marine Science Center:** Hundreds of exhibits, live animals, and hands-on learning make this amazing aquarium one of the most popular attractions in the state (page 204).

★ **Tangier Island:** This remote island in the middle of the Chesapeake Bay feels like another country. The residents even have their own language (page 215).

★ **Chincoteague National Wildlife**

Refuge: This 14,000-acre wildlife refuge protects a herd of wild ponies and thousands of birds. Enjoy miles of natural beaches and hike or bike through the marsh (page 220).

area is known as the Historic Triangle, which includes the colonial cities of Williamsburg, Jamestown, and Yorktown. These cities sit along the James and York Rivers, which also flow into the Chesapeake Bay. Next is the huge area of Hampton Roads. This is where everything converges. The rivers flow into the bay just to the north, and the Chesapeake Bay flows into the Atlantic Ocean just to the east. The main cities in this area are Newport News, Hampton, and Norfolk. Then we have Virginia Beach. The Virginia Beach resort area is truly on the Atlantic coast. Our final region, Virginia's Eastern Shore, is sandwiched between the Chesapeake Bay on the west and the Atlantic Ocean on the east. It is sparsely populated compared to its mainland neighbors and offers charming historical towns and ample bird-watching and fishing.

PLANNING YOUR TIME

Visiting Coastal Virginia requires some planning, a love of water, and no fear of bridges.

Although there is some public transportation between specific cities, the easiest way to get around is by car. I-64 runs from Richmond down to the Historic Triangle and Hampton Roads areas, while US Route 17 and State Route 3 traverse the Northern Neck. US Route 13 runs the length of the Eastern Shore.

Coastal Virginia is a beautiful region but one that takes days, not hours, to explore. If you are limited on time, select one or two key destinations, such as Williamsburg and Virginia Beach, or maybe spend a day or two on the Eastern Shore. Wherever you decide to go, keep in mind that the area is heavily visited in the summer months, so you will likely have a few thousand close friends to share the experience with, especially in the historic towns and the beachfront areas.

If you are looking for a one of a kind experience, spend a day visiting Tangier Island. This isolated sandbar of a town is 12 miles out in the Chesapeake Bay and almost feels like a different country.

Northern Neck

The Northern Neck is a peninsula bordered by the Potomac and Rappahannock Rivers, not far from the Chesapeake Bay and approximately 75 miles from Washington DC. The Northern Neck is laden with history and was explored as early as 1608 by the famed Captain John Smith. George Washington, who was born here, called the region the "Garden of Virginia" for the tidewater landscape and the many forests and creeks that shape this area of the state.

During the steamboat era between 1813 and 1937, the Northern Neck supported a network of approximately 600 steamboats. These mechanical works of art were used to transport both people and goods throughout the Chesapeake Bay area.

In modern times, the Northern Neck is still rural and supports a thriving, generations-old fishing industry. It is also a popular area for recreational boating and water sports. It offers small-town charm, historical sites, colonial architecture, and marinas. Many establishments are only open seasonally, so if you are traveling during the colder months, a quick call ahead could pay off.

SIGHTS

George Washington's Birthplace

Although the father of our country only lived in the Northern Neck until he was three years old, his birthplace on **Pope's Creek Plantation** (1732 Popes Creek Rd., Colonial

COASTAL VIRGINIA
NORTHERN NECK

Coastal Virginia

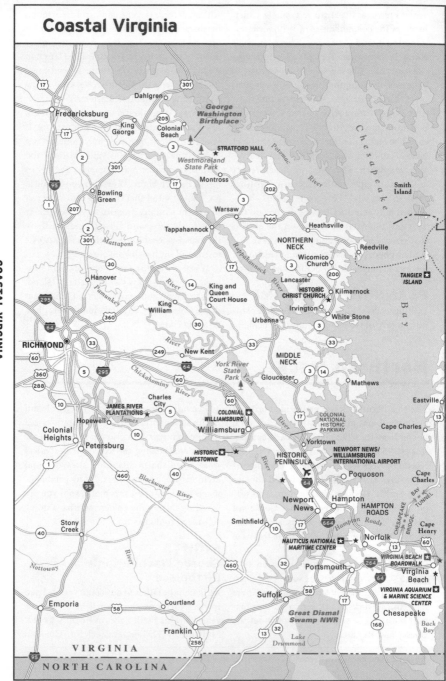

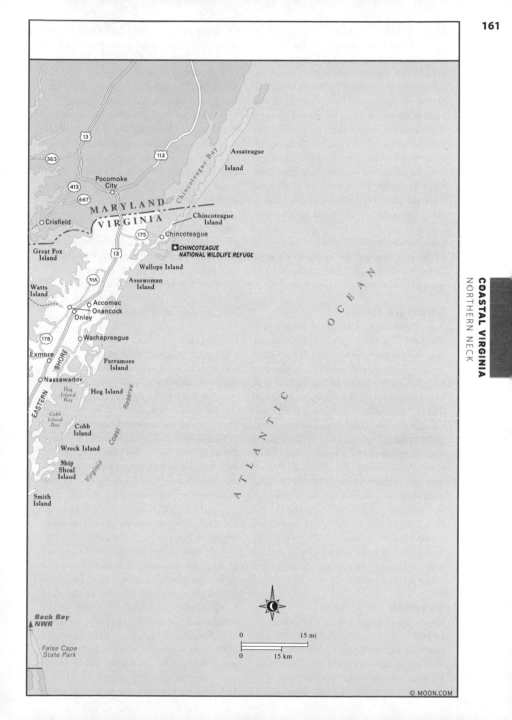

© MOON.COM

Beach, 804/224-1732, www.nps.gov/gewa, daily 9:30am-5pm, shorter winter hours, free) on the banks of the Potomac River is a lovely place to visit. The National Park Service maintains a visitors center with a film, exhibits, and bookstore. The actual house Washington was born in no longer exists (it burned down in 1779), but ranger talks about the historic area are offered throughout the day. There is a reconstructed colonial farm, with animals and tobacco, operated by costumed interpreters. A one-mile nature trail can be accessed from the picnic area. There is also a beach along the river, but no swimming is permitted. Relatives spanning five generations of Washington's family are buried on the site in the Washington Family Burial Ground, including George's father, grandfather, and great-grandfather.

Stratford Hall

Stratford Hall (483 Great House Rd., Stratford, 804/493-8038, www.stratfordhall. org, daily 9:30am-5pm, adults $14, children 6-11 $9, children 5 and under free, seniors over 60 $13) is the birthplace of General Robert E. Lee. The beautiful brick mansion, which sits on 1,900 acres next to the Potomac River, was built in the late 1730s. It is furnished with 18th-century American and English pieces (including Lee's crib). The home has 16 fireplaces. Visitors can take a 60-minute house tour (given daily at 11am, 1pm, and 3pm), walk six nature trails, enjoy the beach overlook, examine exhibits in a visitors center, and browse a gift shop. There are even two on-site cottages for rent. Many events (including photography workshops, kayaking tours, etc.) are held throughout the year, and details can be found on their website.

Reedville

Reedville is a little gem of a town founded in 1867 and a jumping-off point to **Tangier Island** in the Chesapeake Bay. It is known for its thriving Atlantic menhaden-fishing industry (menhaden are small, oily fish found in the mid-Atlantic) and in the early 20th century

was the wealthiest city per capita in the country. (Millionaire's Row, a string of Victorian mansions along the water, attests to this affluence.) Reedville remains a major commercial fishing port in terms of weight of catch, second behind Kodiak, Alaska.

Don't miss the **Reedville Fishermen's Museum** (504 Main St., 804/453-6529, www. rfmuseum.org, Tues.-Sat. 10:30am-4:30pm, Sun. 1pm-4pm, adults $5, children under 12 free, seniors $3) on Cockrell's Creek. There are several parts to the museum: the **William Walker House,** a restored home built in 1875 that represents a waterman's home; the **Covington Building,** which houses temporary exhibits and a permanent collection; and the **Pendleton Building,** which contains a boatbuilding and model shop. In addition, there are two historic boats at the museum, a skipjack and deck boat. Both are in the National Register of Historic Places.

Irvington

The historic village of **Irvington** (www.town. irvington.va.us) was established in 1891 during the steamboat era. A busy port on the well-traveled Norfolk-Baltimore route, the town thrived during the early 1900s. The Great Fire of Irvington destroyed many businesses in June of 1917, coinciding with the decline of the steamboat era. In 1947, the town was put back on the map with the opening of the **Tides Inn Resort,** and today Irvington is a hip little town with boutique shopping, friendly dining, and several key attractions. It's easy to feel the upbeat vibe in Irvington. Stroll down Irvington Road and read some of the fun sayings that are posted on signs in the gardens of shops and restaurants. Keep in mind that many establishments are closed on Monday.

The **Steamboat Era Museum** (156 King Carter Dr., 804/438-6888, www. steamboateramuseum.org, mid-June-mid-Nov. Tues.-Sat. 10am-4pm, shorter hours rest of the year, adults $5, children under 12 and active military free) is a delightful little museum in Irvington that preserves artifacts and information from the steamboat era of

The Steamboat Era

the Steamboat Era Museum

Steamboats came on the scene in the Chesapeake Bay in the early 1800s. As their popularity rose, they quickly became as important to the cities along the bay as the railroad was to the rest of the country. By the mid-1800s, steamboats were used to transport passengers, mail, and goods.

By the turn of the 20th century, nearly 600 steamboats cruised the bay, carrying thousands of passengers to the cities of Norfolk, Virginia, and Baltimore, Maryland, and every place in between. Steamboat excursions became extremely popular, and commerce flourished. Farms grew as their potential for distributing goods expanded, and many canneries were built near the shore. At one time, 85 percent of the world's oyster trade came from the Chesapeake Bay, and these little delicacies were shipped via steamboat.

The 20th century brought the development of the automobile and the slow demise of the steamboat. As cars became affordable and more common, passenger traffic on the steamboats began to dwindle. Still, the boats were used for commerce until the 1930s, when a hurricane in 1933 wiped out many of the Chesapeake Bay wharfs.

The final excursion of a popular steamboat named the *Anne Arundel* was made on September 14, 1937. That day is still celebrated in Virginia as "Steamboat Era Day."

Visit the **Steamboat Era Museum** (156 King Carter Dr., 804/438-6888, www. steamboateramuseum.org, Tues.-Sat. 10am-4pm, closed in winter) in Irvington to learn more about the steamboat era of the Chesapeake Bay. Additional information on the era can be found on the museum's website.

the Chesapeake Bay (1813-1937). Steamboats were a vital mode of transportation along the bay for both goods and people and the lifeline of the economy connecting the region to cities such as Norfolk, Virginia, and Baltimore, Maryland. This is the only museum fully dedicated to the steamboats of the Chesapeake Bay, and the docents are very entertaining and knowledgeable.

The most treasured historic structure in the Northern Neck is arguably the **Historic Christ Church and Museum** (420 Christ Church Rd., Weems, 804/438-6855, www. christchurch1735.org, May-Oct. Mon.-Sat. 10am-4pm, Sun. 1pm-4pm, Apr. and Nov. Mon.-Thurs. by appointment only, Fri.-Sat. 10am-4pm, Sun. 1pm-4pm, Dec. by appointment only, $5). Less than two miles north of

Irvington, the church was finished in 1735 and remains one of the few unaltered colonial churches in the United States. It was a center of social and political activity during colonial times, and Sunday service was a big event. In addition to being a place or worship, it was a place to exchange news and the cornerstone of the community. The detailed brickwork in the tall walls and a vaulted ceiling help make it one of the best-crafted Anglican parish churches of its time. Services are still held there, and the interior boasts a triple-decker pulpit, walnut altar, and high-backed pews. **The Carter Reception Center** houses a museum dedicated to the church and its founder, Robert Carter. Guided tours are available from the center, and there is also a gift shop.

RECREATION
Westmoreland State Park
Westmoreland State Park (145 Cliff Rd., Montross, 804/493-8821, www.dcr.virginia. gov, $7-10 per vehicle) along the Potomac River offers riverfront beaches, hiking trails, a public pool, kayak and paddleboat rentals, a pond, and cliffs housing fossils. It became one of Virginia's first state parks in 1936. This 1,300-acre park also provides camping cabins for rent year-round and 133 seasonal campsites. The Potomac River Retreat is a lodge that is available for rent; it holds 15 overnight guests and up to 40 people for meetings. There is a small camp store, but it's best to bring your own food because they stock only limited drinks and snacks. Dogs and cats are allowed in the park and cabins for an additional fee. Take in the great view of the Potomac from **Horsehead Cliffs,** and don't miss a stroll down Fossil Beach, where you might even find some ancient shark's teeth. There is a visitors center that is open daily 8am-4:30pm.

Westmoreland Berry Farm
If picking berries makes you feel connected to colonial times, stop by the

Westmoreland Berry Farm (1235 Berry Farm Ln., Colonial Beach, 804/224-9171, www.westmorelandberryfarm.com, May-Nov. Wed.-Sat. 9am-5pm, Sun. 10am-5pm). This farm on the banks of the Rappahannock River offers visitors the opportunity to pick their own fruit and berries (depending on what's in season). Or you can browse their country store for fresh produce or have lunch at the country kitchen.

Canoeing and Kayaking
The country's first national water trail, the **Captain John Smith Chesapeake National Historic Trail** (www.nps.gov) includes 3,000 miles of routes through the Chesapeake Bay, Northern Neck, Middle Neck, and their tributaries in Virginia and Maryland. The route was inspired by the regions explored in the 17th century by Captain John Smith.

Kayak rentals are available at **Westmoreland State Park** (www.dcr. virginia.gov, 1 hour $15, 4 hours $45).

Fishing
Captain Billy's Charters (545 Harveys Neck Rd., Heathsville, 804/580-7292, www captbillyscharters.com) runs boat charters for both fishing and cruising from the **Ingram Bay Marina** into the Chesapeake Bay. **Crabbe Charter Fishing** (51 Railway Dr., Heathsville, 804/761-0908, www. crabbescharterfishing.com, $660 for up to six people) is another charter fishing company in the Northern Neck. They offer outings year-round.

Bird-Watching
Bird-watchers have many opportunities to view songbirds, waterfowl, eagles, and wading birds along the **Northern Neck Loop** birding trail (www.dgif.virginia.gov). This driving trail passes by historical sites and through an area known to have the largest population of bald eagles on the Eastern Seaboard.

1: Pope's Creek Plantation 2: The Local in Irvington
3: Stratford Hall

ENTERTAINMENT AND EVENTS

Many of the events in the Northern Neck revolve around water and nature. The **Blessing of the Fleet** is an annual event in Reedville that opens the fishing season on the first weekend of May. There is a parade of boats and the official blessing service.

Mid-September brings the **Reedville Antique and Traditional Small Boat Show** (www.acbs.org), featuring an antique boat parade, while mid-November is the time for the much-anticipated **Reedville Fishermen's Museum Oyster Roast** (www.rfmuseum.org). Tickets go on sale in September and sell out quickly for this mouth-watering event.

Wine enthusiasts will enjoy the **Taste by the Bay: Wine, Food, Arts & Ale** (www.lancasterva.com) held annually in November. It offers tastings and sales from Virginia wineries including some along the **Chesapeake Bay Wine Trail** (www.chesapeakebaywinetrail.com), Virginia craft brews, local restaurant tastings, live music, and art vendors.

FOOD
Reedville

The Crazy Crab Restaurant (902 Main St., 804/453-6789, www.crazycrabreedville.com, Tues.-Fri. 5pm-9pm, Sat. noon-9pm, Sun. noon-8pm, $17-26), at the Reedville Marina, is a casual joint offering an abundance of local seafood choices and a few land-based options. The waterfront view from the restaurant is nice, the atmosphere is fun, and outdoor seating is available.

Cockrell's Seafood (567 Seaboard Dr., 804/453-6326, www.smithpointseafood.com, seasonal Mon.-Thurs. 11am-3pm, Fri.-Sat. 11am-4pm, $8-10) is a seafood deli on the waterfront. The atmosphere is very casual, with diners sitting at picnic tables. They serve delicious crab dishes.

Satisfy your sweet tooth at **Chitterchats Ice Cream** (846 Main St., 804/453-3335, www.chitterchatsicecream.com, $5-10, closed in the off season). This family-oriented ice-cream shop offers delicious homemade ice cream in roughly 20 flavors.

Irvington

The Office Café (4346 Irvington Rd., 804/438-8032, www.theofficeirvington.com, Tues.-Wed. 11am-3pm, Thurs.-Sat. 11am-9pm, $9-14) is a trendy little find in town. The menu offers tasty flatbreads, sandwiches, salads, seafood baskets, and desserts. Try some of their originals, such as the Pastrami Dog, Crabby Dog, or the Drunken Sausage Flatbread. This place is worth a stop.

The Local (4337 Irvington Rd., 804/438-9356, www.thelocalblend.com, Mon.-Sat. 7am-3:30pm, Sun. 7am-2:30pm, under $10) is a good choice for grabbing breakfast or a sandwich at lunchtime. This friendly little restaurant has cute decor and a good selection of sandwiches (both breakfast and lunch) and salads. They also have a coffee bar and a handful of desserts.

ACCOMMODATIONS
$100-200

Ma Margaret's House (249 Greenfield Rd., Reedville, 804/453-9110, www.mamargaretshouse.com, $75-225) is a cozy, 4,000-square-foot home built in 1914 that belonged to the owner's grandparents. It offers several guest suites, a lot of privacy, and a wonderful staff.

$200-300

★ **The Hope and Glory Inn** (65 Tavern Rd., Irvington, 804/438-6053, www.hopeandglory.com, $245-395) is a boutique inn with six rooms and six cottages. Lavish and romantic, with a little sense of humor, the inn was originally a schoolhouse built in 1890. The school had two front doors, one for girls and one for boys. The building now boasts beautifully appointed rooms, lush gardens, and even a moon garden with flowers that only bloom in the evening. There's a spa, meeting facilities, and a dock for boating, kayaking, or canoeing on-site as well as an outdoor pool and an outdoor bath (that is not a typo, there really is a claw-foot tub in an enclosed area outside). Tennis and three golf courses are a short distance away. The town of Irvington, which sits on the Chesapeake Bay, offers trendy shopping and a fun atmosphere.

Wine lovers won't want to miss visiting **The Dog and Oyster,** the Hope and Glory Inn's vineyard. It's named for the establishment's rescue dogs, who guard the grapes from area wildlife, and also in honor of the local oysters, which pair well with the wines. If the weather is nice, enjoy a bottle of wine on the porch.

The **Tides Inn** (480 King Carter Dr., Irvington, 804/438-5000, www.tidesinn.com, $185-530) is a well-known resort bordered by the Potomac and Rappahannock Rivers and the Chesapeake Bay. This romantic waterfront inn hangs on the banks of Carters Creek as a little oasis of red-roofed buildings offering peace and relaxation to visitors of all ages. It features luxurious waterfront accommodations, golf, a marina, and a spa. There is also a sailing school with many options for lessons and family sailing activities. Packages include some geared toward golf, family vacations, and romance. There are also several good restaurants on-site, and the inn is dog friendly.

CAMPING

Westmoreland State Park (1650 State Park Rd., Montross, 804/493-8821, www.dcr. virginia.gov) offers 133 campsites and a handful of camping cabins. Camping sites feature fire-ring grills or box grills. Forty-two sites offer electric and water hookups for $40 per night; sites without these amenities are $30 per night. There is also one group tent site that can accommodate up to 40 people ($148). Camping cabins have a maximum capacity of four and require a two-night minimum stay. Cabins do not have bathrooms, kitchens, heat, air-conditioning, or linens. Bathhouses are available on-site for all campers.

INFORMATION AND SERVICES

For additional information on the Northern Neck, visit www.northernneck.org.

Williamsburg and the Historic Triangle

The "Historic Triangle," as it is known, consists of Williamsburg, Jamestown, and Yorktown. These three historic towns are just minutes apart and are the sites of some of our country's most important Revolutionary War history.

The **Colonial Parkway,** a scenic, 23-mile-long, three-lane road, connects the points of the Historic Triangle. Millions of travelers drive the road between Williamsburg, Jamestown, and Yorktown each year. The parkway is maintained by the National Park Service and was designed to unify the three culturally distinct sites while preserving the scenery and wildlife along the way. The construction of the parkway took more than 26 years and stretched through the Depression and World War II. It was completed in 1957.

The parkway enables motorists to enjoy the surrounding landscape and has a speed limit of 45 miles per hour.

The National Park Service also maintains the **Colonial National Historical Park,** which contains two of the most historically significant sites in the country: the **Historic Jamestowne** National Historic Site (which is jointly administered by Preservation Virginia) and **Yorktown Battlefield.** These sites are connected by the Colonial Parkway.

WILLIAMSBURG

The original capital of the Virginia Colony, Jamestown, was founded in 1607. It was located on the banks of the James River with a deepwater anchorage on a peninsula between the York and James Rivers. By 1638, an area

Colonial Williamsburg

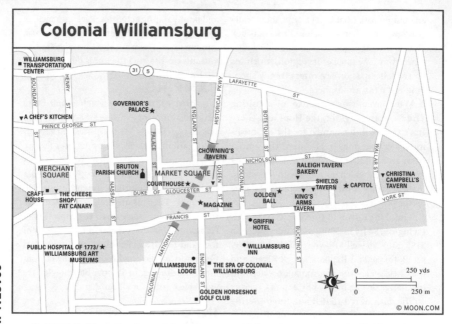

WILLIAMSBURG TRANSPORTATION CENTER

31 5

LAFAYETTE ST

BOUNDARY

HENRY ST

A CHEF'S KITCHEN

GOVERNOR'S PALACE ★

PRINCE GEORGE ST

ENGLAND ST

HISTORICAL PKWY

BOTETOURT ST

PALACE ST

CHOWNING'S TAVERN

NICHOLSON ST

MERCHANT SQUARE

BRUTON PARISH CHURCH

MARKET SQUARE

COURTHOUSE ★

DUKE OF GLOUCESTER ST

QUEEN ST

COLONIAL ST

RALEIGH TAVERN BAKERY

SHIELDS TAVERN ★ CAPITOL

WALLAR ST

CHRISTINA CAMPBELL'S TAVERN

CRAFT HOUSE

THE CHEESE SHOP/ FAT CANARY

NASSAU ST

GOLDEN BALL

KING'S ARMS TAVERN

YORK ST

★ MAGAZINE

FRANCIS ST

GRIFFIN HOTEL

BUCKTROT ST

PUBLIC HOSPITAL OF 1773/ ★ WILLIAMSBURG ART MUSEUMS

NATIONAL

COLONIAL

WILLIAMSBURG LODGE

ENGLAND ST

WILLIAMSBURG INN

THE SPA OF COLONIAL WILLIAMSBURG

GOLDEN HORSESHOE GOLF CLUB

0   250 yds

0   250 m

© MOON.COM

called Middle Plantation (named for its location halfway across the peninsula) was settled about 12 miles away on higher ground. In 1676, Jamestown burned down, and the government seat was temporarily moved to Middle Plantation. The statehouse was rebuilt, but burned down again in 1698. Once again, the capital was relocated to Middle Plantation. Finding the temporary location to be safer and less humid than Jamestown, the House of Burgesses permanently moved the colonial capital there in 1699. A village was planned in the new location, and the name Middle Plantation was changed to Williamsburg in honor of King William III of England.

Williamsburg is one of America's earliest planned cities. It was designed as the capital of the Virginia Colony, which was the most populous of the British colonies in America in 1699. As such, Williamsburg had the oldest legislative assembly in the New World, and a series of elaborate capitol buildings were erected as the city developed into the thriving center of Virginia. Williamsburg remained the capital of Virginia until 1780, when the seat of government was moved to its current location in Richmond.

Today, when people speak of Williamsburg, they most often are referring to the area known now as **Colonial Williamsburg.** This original capital city is the country's prime example of not only the preservation of American colonial history but also its interpretation. However, although Colonial Williamsburg is the best-known attraction in the Williamsburg area, there are many other attractions nearby, including the historic **College of William & Mary** and a number of popular theme parks.

Sights

TOP EXPERIENCE

★ COLONIAL WILLIAMSBURG

Colonial Williamsburg (888/965-7254, www.colonialwilliamsburg.com, adult one-day ticket $44.99, children 6-12 $24.99, adult three-day ticket $54.99, children 6-12 $29.99) is the largest living museum in the country, and it is truly a historical marvel. It is open 365 days a year and run by the private, not-for-profit **Colonial Williamsburg Foundation.**

The museum encompasses the restored 18th-century colonial Virginia capital city, which was the center of politics in Virginia for 80 years, and includes the real city streets and buildings that were erected during that time. There are historical exhibits, taverns, shops featuring original trades, and many other sites within the museum area. Ticketholders gain access to the historical buildings, theatrical performances, more than 20 site tours, 35 exhibitions, and museums. It is free to wander the streets themselves.

Although Colonial Williamsburg is open all year, if you are flexible in choosing when to visit, spring and fall can be the most rewarding. This is when crowds are less dense and the temperatures are the most moderate (plan to do a lot of walking around the city). Summer is the busiest tourist season because school is out of session, and it can also be very hot and humid, especially in August.

It is best to begin your visit at the **Colonial Williamsburg Regional Visitor Center** (101 Visitor Center Dr., 866/691-7063, daily 8:45am-5pm). The staff can help you put together an itinerary for your stay that will allow you to hit the highlights and choose additional sites you are interested in. You can also purchase tickets and learn about events and activities taking place during your time here. The highlights in Colonial Williamsburg can be seen over a weekend, but to really soak in the atmosphere, it can be fun to spend an extra day or two, or to make it your base for exploring other nearby attractions.

Everything within the museum area is neat, clean, well maintained, and historically correct. The staff is dressed in period clothing and plays their roles very seriously. Conversations between staff members and the public are always in character. Visitors become "Residents of the City" and are immersed in history—and can enjoy authentic colonial-era dining and shopping while staying in hotels with all the modern conveniences.

There's a large pedestrian area through the center of the historical enclave along **Duke of Gloucester Street.** President Franklin D. Roosevelt called this road the "most historic avenue in all of America." Horses and horse-drawn carriages are allowed on the street if they are part of the museum.

Market Square, the center of activity in Colonial Williamsburg, straddles Duke of Gloucester Street. Residents went there on a regular basis (if not daily) to purchase goods and socialize. Visitors can experience the same atmosphere along Duke of Gloucester Street, where the official Williamsburg-brand shops are located.

Ticket-holding visitors can explore a variety of historical buildings, such as the reconstructed **Capitol** (daily 9am-5pm), which sits at the east end of Duke of Gloucester Street. The current building is the third capitol to stand on the site, but it is very much the same as the original, completed in 1705. A trip through this tall brick building is like a history lesson on the government in colonial Virginia and the contributions the colony made to the American Revolution. Evening programs in the Capitol include reenactments of political and social events that actually occurred here in the 18th century. One day a year, a naturalization ceremony is carried out at the Capitol for immigrants becoming Americans, carrying on a tradition that began nearly 300 years ago.

The impressive **Governor's Palace,** built between 1706 and 1722 at the end of Palace Green Street off of West Duke of Gloucester Street, was home to seven royal governors, as well as Thomas Jefferson and Patrick Henry. After many decades as a symbol of the power of royal England, the home served as a military headquarters and twice as a wartime hospital (156 soldiers and 2 women are buried in the garden, casualties of the Battle of Yorktown). The original structure burned to the ground in 1781, but the building was reconstructed to its current grandeur in the 1930s. Since then, the home has been furnished with American and British antiques in the colonial revival style. This is perhaps the most popular site in Colonial Williamsburg,

so make it first on your list, early in the day, before the crowds set in.

The **Courthouse** (W. Duke of Gloucester St.) is a focal point of Market Square and one that no doubt struck fear in the hearts of many criminals in its day. Built in 1770, it is one of Williamsburg's original 18th-century buildings, and it housed the municipal and county courts until 1932. The building's T-shaped design is common to many Virginia courthouses, but an octagonal cupola and several other formal design elements (such as a weather vane, arched windows, and a cantilevered pediment) make it distinct in appearance. The signing of the Treaty of Paris (ending the Revolutionary War) was announced at the Courthouse.

A small but fascinating building is the **Magazine** (E. Duke of Gloucester St.). It was constructed in 1715 at the request of Governor Alexander Spotswood, who wanted a solid-brick house in which to store and protect weapons and ammunition. The Magazine is well known for its role in the **Gunpowder Incident** of April 20, 1775, an episode that occurred in the opening days of the Revolutionary War between the royal governor, Lord Dunmore, and the militia (led by Patrick Henry). Lord Dunmore gave orders to remove all the gunpowder from the Magazine and move it to a Royal Navy ship. This led to unrest in Virginia and the movement of Patrick Henry's militia toward Williamsburg to secure the gunpowder for the colonial troops. The matter was resolved peacefully, but Dunmore retreated to a naval ship, thus ending royal governance of the colony. The incident helped move Virginia toward revolution.

Many craftspeople, some of whom have spent years learning the trade, create colonial-era crafts in dozens of shops throughout Colonial Williamsburg. Visitors can watch blacksmiths and armorers shape tools,

weapons, and hardware out of iron and steel at **Anderson's Blacksmith Shop & Public Armoury** (E. Duke of Gloucester St.) or visit the **Wigmaker** (E. Duke of Gloucester St.) to learn the importance of 18th-century wigmakers and barbers and how these trades were essential to the social structure of the day. Other crafters include the **Shoemaker** (W. Duke of Gloucester St.), the **Weaver** (W. Duke of Gloucester St.), and the **Bindery** (E. Duke of Gloucester St.).

A number of historic taverns and restaurants are also located in Colonial Williamsburg and serve authentic colonial-style food. Look for the colonial flags out in front of the buildings. If a flag is out, it means the establishment is open.

More than 20 tours, both guided and self-led, are included in a Colonial Williamsburg admission ticket. The visitors center is the best place to find out what tours are offered on the day(s) you are there and what time they leave.

Active U.S. military receive complimentary admission for a single day once a year for themselves and up to three direct dependents (retired military and veterans receive 50 percent off).

WILLIAMSBURG ART MUSEUMS

Two top-notch art museums, the **DeWitt Wallace Decorative Arts Museum** (325 W. Francis St., 855/776-1765, daily 10am-7pm) and the **Abby Aldrich Rockefeller Folk Art Museum** (326 W. Francis St., 877/848-8039, daily 10am-7pm) are located in the same building and can be reached by walking through the **Public Hospital of 1773** (326 W. Francis St., admission is included with the Colonial Williamsburg ticket). The DeWitt Wallace Decorative Arts Museum opened in 1985, funded by a generous donation from DeWitt and Lila Wallace, the founders of *Readers Digest*. It houses a large collection of American and British art and antiques, including the world's most extensive collection of Southern furniture. The Abby Aldrich Rockefeller Folk Art Museum features a colorful variety of paintings, sculptures, and other

1: Magazine in Colonial Williamsburg 2: garden in Colonial Williamsburg 3: Governor's Palace 4: Shields Tavern

art forms. Each work was created by self-taught artists and shows an imaginative array of details and color selections. There is also a kid-friendly animal-themed exhibit called *Down on the Farm*. While you're there, take in the exhibits at the Public Hospital. It was the first facility in North America dedicated to caring for the mentally ill. In this day and age, the hospital is seen as part jail, part infirmary, and the treatments used in the 18th and 19th centuries are thankfully just part of history.

THE COLLEGE OF WILLIAM & MARY

Early on, Williamsburg developed into a hub for learning. **The College of William & Mary** (200 Stadium Dr., www.wm.edu), which is the second-oldest college in the country, was founded in 1693. It is just west of Colonial Williamsburg and an easy walk from the colonial city. William & Mary turned out many famous early political leaders including Thomas Jefferson, John Tyler, and James Monroe. Today, the 1,200-acre campus is bustling with students. Visitors can enjoy a handful of historical attractions right on campus, including the **Sir Christopher Wren Building,** which was built 1695 and is known for being the oldest college building in the country. It was named for a royal architect, although concrete evidence has not been found that Wren actually designed it.

WILLIAMSBURG WINERY

Wine lovers will want to stop in for a tour and tasting at the **Williamsburg Winery** (5800 Wessex Hundred, 757/229-0999, www.williamsburgwinery.com, Mar. 16-Oct. 31, Sun.-Thurs. 11am-5:30pm, Fri.-Sat. 11am-6:30pm, Nov.-Mar. 15, Sun.-Thurs. 11am-4:30pm, Fri.-Sat. 11am-5:30pm, tastings $10-18), about a 10-minute drive from the Colonial Williamsburg visitors center. The winery is one of Virginia's largest and is part of the Wessex Hundred, a beautiful, 300-acre farm that includes two restaurants and an inn.

BUSCH GARDENS WILLIAMSBURG

Busch Gardens Williamsburg (1 Busch Gardens Blvd., 757/229-4386, www.buschgardens.com, hours vary greatly throughout the year but generally open at 10am during the season, $86.99) is a theme park with rides, re-created European villages, shows, exhibits, and tours. The park is less than five miles southeast of Williamsburg and is owned by SeaWorld Parks & Entertainment. Hair-raising roller coasters, water rides, and special attractions for little kids are just part of the fun at this beautiful park. Test your nerves on the Griffon, a 205-foot dive coaster where brave riders free-fall at 75 miles per hour, or the Verbolten, an indoor/outdoor multi-launch coaster set in Germany's Black Forest. The park's classic ride is the Loch Ness Monster, a 13-story, double-loop roller coaster that made Busch Gardens famous in 1978. This popular park also offers an Oktoberfest Village, a high-tech simulator ride that takes passengers over Europe, and animal attractions such as Jack Hanna's Wild Reserve, where visitors can see and learn about endangered and exotic animals. A combined Busch Gardens Williamsburg and Water Country USA ticket can be purchased for $109.99.

WATER COUNTRY USA

Busch Gardens Williamsburg's sister park, **Water Country USA** (176 Water Country Pkwy., 757/229-4386, www.watercountryusa.com, Memorial Day-Labor Day daily 10am-close, $61.99), is the largest water theme park in the mid-Atlantic. It is approximately three miles southeast of Williamsburg, just north of Busch Gardens. The park offers waterslides, pools, Virginia's first water coaster, and more than 30 rides for kids of all ages as well as restaurants and live entertainment. A combined Busch Gardens Williamsburg and Water Country USA ticket can be purchased for $109.99.

Recreation

GOLF

The **Golden Horseshoe Golf Club** (401 S. England St., 757/220-7696, www. colonialwilliamsburg.com, $52-79) is part of Colonial Williamsburg and offers 45 walkable holes. This scenic course is well maintained and has received accolades from publications such as *Golf Magazine* and *Golfweek*.

The **Kingsmill Resort** (1010 Kingsmill Rd., 757/253-1703. www.kingsmill.com, $60-165) offers three championship 18-hole courses that are open to the public (one of which was ranked in the top 10 for women by *Golf Digest*).

The award-winning **Williamsburg National Golf Club** (3700 Centerville Rd., 757/258-9642, www.wngc.com, $69-89) has two 18-hole courses.

SPAS

The **Spa of Colonial Williamsburg** (307 S. England St., 757/220-7720, www. colonialwilliamsburg.com) is behind the Williamsburg Inn. Enjoy treatments made from botanicals used by the early settlers or a variety of soaks and massages. Packages are available.

HORSEBACK RIDING

If horseback riding seems appropriate while visiting Williamsburg, contact **Lakewood Trails** (2116-A Forge Rd., Toano, 575/566-9633, www.lakewoodtrailrides.com, $75) for one-hour guided trail rides.

GO APE TREETOP ADVENTURE

For something completely different, try a **Go Ape** (5537 Centerville Rd., 800/971-8271, www.goape.com, ages 16 and up $59, ages 10-15 $39) Treetop Adventure. This adventure course is appropriate for ages 10 and up (who are taller than 4 feet, 7 inches) and includes high wires, ladders, tunnels, zip lines, and a lot of treetop excitement. A junior course is available for children under 10 who are 3 feet, 3 inches or taller.

Entertainment and Events

Colonial Williamsburg doesn't shut down after dark. A variety of tours are available, including **The Original Ghost Tour** (345 W. Duke of Gloucester St., text questions to 757/342-6599, www.theghosttour.com, Mar.-Nov. daily 8pm, Jan.-Feb. Fri.-Sat. 8pm, $13). This is a family-friendly, candlelit, walking ghost tour of the town and taverns that offers a relaxing end to a day of sightseeing.

The **Kimball Theatre** (428 W. Duke of Gloucester St., 757/221-2674, www. kimball.wm.edu) is a film and stage venue in Merchants Square, right in the middle of Colonial Williamsburg. It offers programming in alliance with the College of William & Mary, including foreign, classic, and documentary films, along with live concerts.

Outside of the historic center—but only minutes away—visitors can play pool and enjoy live music on some nights at **The Corner Pocket** (4805 Courthouse St., 757/220-0808, www.thecornerpocket.us, Mon.-Tues. 11:30am-1am, Wed.-Fri. 11:30am-2:30am, Sat. 11:30am-2am), an upscale pool hall.

Busch Gardens Williamsburg hosts an annual **Howl-O-Scream** (1 Busch Gardens Blvd., www.buschgardens.com) starting in mid-September and running through October. During Howl-O-Scream, the park becomes a horrorfest for brave souls, featuring scary shows, creepy creatures lurking about the park, and fun characters. It is not advisable to take young children.

The holiday season is a very popular time to visit Colonial Williamsburg. The **Grand Illumination** (www.colonialwilliamsburg. com), held on the Sunday of the first full weekend in December, is an eagerly awaited street festival where the entire historic area is decorated with traditional natural adornments for the season, such as pinecones, evergreen branches, and candles. The area flickers at night by candlelight as carols are sung, concerts are held, and fireworks light up the night.

Shopping

Williamsburg offers endless shops. Strip malls and outlet stores can be found in much of the area surrounding Colonial Williamsburg. For unique souvenirs, try stopping in the **Williamsburg Craft House** (420 W. Duke of Gloucester St., 757/220-7747), run by the Colonial Williamsburg Foundation. Pewter and ceramic gifts, jewelry, and folk art are for sale. Other favorite shops in the historic district include **The Prentis Store** (214 E. Duke of Gloucester St., 757/229-1000), which sells handcrafted leather pieces, pottery, furniture, ironware, and baskets; the **Market House** (102 W Duke of Gloucester St., 888/965-7254), an open-air market on Duke of Gloucester Street that sells hats, toys, and other handmade items; and the **Golden Ball** (406 E. Duke of Gloucester St., 757/229-1000), which sells one-of-a-kind jewelry.

Food

AMERICAN

If you just need to grab a quick sandwich or you'd like to enjoy a gourmet cheese platter and a glass of wine, stop in **The Cheese Shop** (410 W. Duke of Gloucester St., 757/220-0298, www.cheeseshopwilliamsburg.com, Mon.-Sat. 10am-8pm, Sun. 11am-6pm, under $15) in Merchants Square. They make custom cheese plates (from 200 varieties of imported and domestic cheese) at their cheese counter (to the left) and deli sandwiches at the back of the store (try their chicken salad; it has just enough bacon to taste wonderful but not enough to feel guilty). The store also carries fresh-baked bread and a variety of snacks and drinks. Their wine cellar has more than 4,000 bottles of wine. There's seating outside (pay before you exit).

The ★ **Fat Canary** (410 W. Duke of Gloucester St., 757/229-3333, www.fatcanarywilliamsburg.com, daily 5pm-10pm, closed Mon. Jan.-Feb., $29-42) in Merchants Square is named for the wine brought to the New World by ships that stopped in the Canary Islands for supplies. The wine was called a "canary," and this wonderful restaurant knows its wine. Widely considered one of the top dining spots in Williamsburg, The Fat Canary is an upscale restaurant that delivers an interesting menu of mouthwatering entrées such as quail, scallops, lamb, and beef tenderloin. They also have delicious desserts. The restaurant has a romantic ambience with soft pendant lighting and friendly service. This is a great place for a date or to relax after a day touring Colonial Williamsburg. Reservations are strongly suggested.

For a unique dining experience, make reservations at **A Chef's Kitchen** (501 Prince George St., 757/564-8500, www.achefskitchen.biz, Tues.-Sat. seating 6:30pm, $105), in the heart of Williamsburg. This food destination allows guests to learn about the fare they are eating and how it's prepared while being entertained by a talented chef. The fixed-price menu is for a multicourse meal in which recipes are prepared, served, and paired with great wines. Diners sit at elegant long tables in tiered rows. The menu changes monthly, but sample dishes include asparagus and sweet pea soup, scallion and lime Gulf shrimp cake, roast rack of lamb, and strawberries sabayon in a lace cup cookie. This small restaurant only seats 26 people, and it only offers one seating per night, so reservations are a must. Plan for 2-3 hours of dining time.

FRENCH

For an expertly prepared, upscale French meal, make a reservation at **Café Provençal** (5810 Wessex Hundred, 757/941-0317, www.williamsburgwinery.com, Tues.-Sun. 5:30pm-9pm, $26-42). This charming restaurant is located on the 300-acre Wessex Hundred farm (home of the Williamsburg Winery). They feature selections made from their own harvest and also support smaller farms that are dedicated to humanely raising animals and practicing environmental stewardship. Their menu changes seasonally but includes selections such as Juniper Chicken Roulade, filet mignon, and Local Farro Cast Iron Porridge.

TREATS

To satisfy a craving or pick up an afternoon snack, stop in the **Raleigh Tavern Bakery** (410 E Duke of Gloucester St., behind the Raleigh Tavern, 888/976-0916, under $10). They offer a selection of fresh cookies, muffins, rolls, sandwiches, drinks, and other treats. Try the sweet potato muffins and the gingerbread cookies, which are done to perfection and are much better than the peanut butter and chocolate chip cookies. Casual seating is available in the courtyard outside. A cookbook with the recipes is available for purchase, and this writer knows firsthand that almost nothing has changed in this historical little bakery in the past 30 years—but then again, that's the idea here.

The **Jamestown Pie Company** (1804 Jamestown Rd., 757/229-7775, www.buyapie.com, Mon.-Sat. 9am-9pm, Sun. 10am-9pm, $15-32) sells everything round including pizza and dessert pie. Pies are also available to go or ship.

COLONIAL TAVERNS

There are four taverns in the historic area of Williamsburg, and dining in one is a great way to get into the spirit of the town. Costumed servers bring authentic dishes from two centuries ago to wooden tables in flickering candlelight. Don't be hesitant to try some 18th-century staples such as spoon bread and peanut soup. There are a few featured items available in all four taverns, but aside from that, each specializes in its own dishes. Make reservations when you book your hotel, as these restaurants are very popular.

Christiana Campbell's Tavern (101 S. Waller St., 855/263-1746, Tues.-Sat. 5pm-7:45pm, $30-50) is noted as George Washington's favorite tavern. It specializes in seafood dishes. The tavern was re-created from artifacts excavated on-site and from a sketch of the building found on an original insurance policy. George and other famous colonial figureheads often met here for business and pleasure, and private rooms could be reserved alongside public chambers where travelers sometimes shared beds with complete strangers when the tavern was full. The crab cakes are a signature dish.

Chowning's Tavern (109 E. Duke of Gloucester St., 855/270-5114, daily 11:30am-9pm, $12-19) is a casual alehouse where lively singing and other reenactments of 18th-century life are common. All-day pub fare includes pork barbecue sandwiches, ribs, and Brunswick stew. Outdoor seating is available behind the tavern in the garden.

The King's Arms Tavern (416 E. Duke of Gloucester St., 855/240-3278, Thurs.-Mon. 11:30am-2:30pm and 5pm-7:45pm, $23-40) is a genteel tavern serving Southern food and decadent desserts. This chophouse-style tavern offers entrées such as game hen, pork chops, and prime rib. The peanut soup is a signature dish. Their lunch menu offers sandwiches, stew, and fried chicken ($14-17).

Shields Tavern (422 E. Duke of Gloucester St., 855/268-7220, Tues.-Sat. 11:30am-2:30pm and 5pm-7:45pm, $27-34) is the largest of the taverns, and it specializes in comfort food such as fried chicken, blackened catfish, and pork shank. Their lunch menu offers less expensive sandwiches, stew, and hamburgers ($8-17).

Accommodations

If Colonial Williamsburg is the focus of your Williamsburg trip, and you'd like to be immersed in the Revolutionary City, book a room in one of the Colonial Williamsburg Foundation hotels or guesthouses. These are conveniently located near the museum sites and have a historical feel to them. Reservations, especially during the peak summer months, should be made well in advance.

COLONIAL WILLIAMSBURG FOUNDATION

The **Colonial Williamsburg Foundation** maintains several hotels/lodges and 24 guesthouses. Each offers a different atmosphere and price range. Hotel guests have access to a terrific fitness facility located behind the Williamsburg Inn that includes a spa, state-of-the-art fitness room, indoor lap pool, and two gorgeous outdoor pools. Hotel guests also receive the best rate on general admission passes and discounts on special events. Reservations for all are handled through the foundation (855/231-7240, www. colonialwilliamsburghotels.com), and all the hotels are dog friendly. The **Colonial Houses** ($189-989) are individual colonial homes and rooms, each with a unique history. The number of rooms per house varies, but all are decorated with authentic reproductions of period pieces such as canopy beds, and all have modern amenities. Look out over Duke of Gloucester Street, or sleep in the home where Thomas Jefferson lived while attending The College of William & Mary. Some homes are original historic buildings and others are replicas.

The luxurious ★ **Williamsburg Inn** (136 E. Francis St., $449-649) was built in 1937 by John D. Rockefeller Jr., and the decor and furnishings in the lobby are still arranged exactly the way his wife, Abby Aldrich Rockefeller, designed it. This stately, upscale hotel has hosted many heads of state, including President Dwight D. Eisenhower, Queen Elizabeth II, and Sir Winston Churchill. In 1983, the inn welcomed the Economic Summit of Industrialized Nations, hosted by President Ronald Reagan. It is listed in the National Register of Historic Places but offers modern first-class accommodations in its 62 guest rooms. The hotel was the first in the United States to have central air-conditioning. Each elegant and spacious room is furnished similar to an English country estate. The setting and decor are charming, and the service is excellent. Mrs. Rockefeller wished for guests to feel at home in the inn and as such instilled a warmth throughout the staff that still radiates today. Every last detail is attended to in the luxurious rooms, from beautifully tiled, temperature-controlled showers to a fresh white rose in the bathroom (the rose is the official inn flower) and little comforts such as vanity mirrors and nightlights. The hotel is centrally located adjacent to Colonial

Williamsburg. The Golden Horseshoe Golf Club is behind the inn, and daily participatory events such as lawn bowling are offered to guests. There are two restaurants on-site (one formal dining room and a more casual lounge), and the hotel is very family friendly.

The **Williamsburg Lodge** (310 S. England St., 855/294-5683, $227-389) is owned by the Colonial Williamsburg Foundation but is part of Marriott's Autograph Collection. It is decorated in the classic Virginia style. Colorful fabric, leather, and warm woods give this hotel a lodge feel. This 300-room hotel hosts many conferences, and its unique garden gives it a relaxing focal point. The rooms are spacious, the lodge is conveniently located near Colonial Williamsburg, and it's an easy walk to the attractions.

The **Williamsburg Woodlands Hotel and Suites** (105 Visitor Center Dr., $179-199) is next to the visitors center for Colonial Williamsburg. This 300-room hotel offers contemporary rooms in a wooded setting. It is one of the least expensive options of the Colonial Williamsburg Foundation hotels.

The **Griffin Hotel** (302 E. Francis St., $179-269) is located in a natural setting a short walk from historic Colonial Williamsburg and the visitors center.

OUTSIDE COLONIAL WILLIAMSBURG

There are quite a few choices for accommodations outside Colonial Williamsburg. Many are within an easy drive of the historical area.

The **Marriott's Manor Club at Ford's Colony** (101 St. Andrews Dr., 757/258-1120, www.marriott.com, $161-339) is in the private community of Ford's Colony and offers colonial architecture, deluxe guest rooms, and one- and two-bedroom villas. Each villa has a kitchen, living/dining area, washer and dryer, a balcony or patio, and a fireplace. This is a great place for families or groups who need a bit more space or plan an extended stay. Colonial Williamsburg and the College of William & Mary are about a 15-minute drive away, and Busch Gardens is about 20 minutes. There's a spa and golf course in the community, a fitness center, indoor and outdoor pools, and a sport court. Rooms are nicely appointed, and the buildings are spread out on a well-manicured property.

Wedmore Place (5810 Wessex Hundred, 757/941-0310, www.wedmoreplace.com, $155-700) offers 28 individually decorated rooms and suites in a variety of price ranges. Each room is designed after a European province and a different time in history, including all the furnishings and wall hangings. The 300-acre farm is also the site of the Williamsburg Winery and is about a 10-minute drive to the Colonial Williamsburg visitors center. All rooms include continental breakfast.

If you're looking for a kid-oriented hotel, the **Great Wolf Lodge** (549 E. Rochambeau Dr., 757/229-9700, www.greatwolf.com, $229-549) provides endless amusement for the little ones. This Northwoods-themed lodge offers 405 guest rooms and a huge indoor water park complete with waterslides, a wave pool, and a tree house. It is a four-season resort.

The **Kingsmill Resort and Spa** (1010 Kingsmill Rd., 757/253-1703, www.kingsmill.com, $146-479) offers 425 luxurious rooms and suites (with up to three bedrooms) as well as breathtaking views of the James River. It also has golf, a spa, an indoor pool, and summer children's programs. This is a great place for a romantic getaway or to spend time with friends playing golf or taking a spa day.

Camping

There are several good options for camping in Williamsburg. The **Anvil Campground** (5243 Mooretown Rd., 757/565-2300, www.anvilcampground.com, $55-155) is open year-round and offers 77 campsites and two cottages. It has been in operation since 1954 and is close to Colonial Williamsburg with shuttle service available to attractions, restaurants, and shopping. The **Williamsburg KOA Campground** (4000 Newman Rd., 757/565-2907, www.koa.com, starting at $48) is another good option close to Colonial Williamsburg and the theme parks. They offer 180 acres of wooded sites and patio sites (with more than 100 sites total). They also offer bus service to attractions in the peak season. Two additional campgrounds in Williamsburg are the **Williamsburg RV Resort and Campground** (4301 Rochambeau Dr., 757/566-3021, starting at $57), with 158 sites, and the **American Heritage R.V. Park** (146 Maxton Ln., 757/566-2133, www.americanheritagervpark.com, starting at $38), with 103 sites.

Information and Services

The best information on Colonial Williamsburg can be obtained from the **Colonial Williamsburg Foundation** (888/965-7254, www.colonialwilliamsburg.org and www.colonialwilliamsburg.com) and at the **Colonial Williamsburg Regional Visitor Center** (101 Visitor Center Dr., 866/691-7063, daily 8:45am-5pm). For additional information on Williamsburg, contact the **Greater Williamsburg Chamber and Tourism Alliance** (www.williamsburgcc.com) or visit www.visitwilliamsburg.com.

Getting There

Most people arrive in Williamsburg by car. The city is off I-64 approximately 1 hour from Richmond, 1 hour from Norfolk, and 2.5 hours from Washington DC.

The **Newport News/Williamsburg International Airport** (PHF, 900 Bland Blvd., Newport News, www.flyphf.com) is off I-64 at exit 255B. Williamsburg is a 20-minute drive from the airport.

Amtrak (468 N Boundary St., 800/872-7245, www.amtrak.com) offers train service into Williamsburg.

Getting Around

Getting around Colonial Williamsburg

requires a lot of walking. The pedestrian area, where you'll find many of the attractions, is preserved as it was during Revolutionary times when there were no cars. If you are not staying at one of the Colonial Williamsburg hotels, you will want to arrive early during peak season to park outside the pedestrian area. Parking spaces can be difficult to come by, but designated areas are clearly marked. The important thing to remember is not to park in private lots or at the College of William & Mary (even in the summer). Parking restrictions are strictly enforced.

Williamsburg has a reliable bus system called the **Williamsburg Area Transit (WATA)** (www.gowata.org), which offers bus service seven days a week and stops at many of the local hotels. An all-day pass is $3.

Shuttle service between the Colonial Williamsburg Regional Visitor Center and select hotels is available for free to those who have a Colonial Williamsburg ticket. Shuttle tickets can also be obtained at the visitors center.

JAMESTOWN

Jamestown was the first permanent English settlement in America. It was founded in 1607, more than a decade prior to the Pilgrims' arrival at Plymouth. Three small ships carrying 104 men made landfall at Jamestown (which is actually an island) on May 13, 1607. They moored the ships to trees, came ashore the following day, and never left. The newly formed town served as the capital of Virginia during the 17th century.

★ Historic Jamestowne

Historic Jamestowne (1368 Colonial Pkwy., 757/856-1250, www.historicjamestowne.org, daily 9am-5pm, adults $20, children 15 and under free, $10 with receipt from Yorktown Battlefield, discounts given to active military and National Park Pass holders) occupies the site of the original Jamestown settlement on the banks of the James River. It is run by the National Park Service and Preservation

Virginia. The site was also the location of a military post during the American Revolution where prisoners were exchanged from both sides.

Purchase your admission ticket at the visitors center, which shows an informative 18-minute video that is a good start to orienting yourself with the site. From there, continue to "Old Towne," the original settlement site, and explore it on foot. Highlights include the original Memorial Church tower (the oldest structure still standing in the park), a burial ground (many of the first colonists died here), a reconstructed sample of a "mud-and-stud" cottage, and the foundations of several buildings. Another don't-miss sight is the Jamestown Rediscovery excavation, where remains of the original James Fort built in 1607 are being uncovered at an archaeological dig site open to visitors. History programs and children's events are held in the summer months.

Continue on to "New Towne," where you can explore the part of Jamestown that was developed after 1620. The foundations of many homes were excavated in the 1930s and 1950s, and replicas can be seen throughout the site. Next, take a cruise along the Loop Drive, a five-mile wilderness road. Be sure to stop to read the interpretive signs and view the paintings along the route to learn how inhabitants used the island's natural resources, or visit the **Glasshouse** to see artisans creating glass products as glassblowers did back in the early 1600s.

Jamestown Settlement

The **Jamestown Settlement** (2110 Jamestown Rd., 757/253-4838, www.historyisfun.org, daily 9am-5pm with extended summer hours, adults $17.50, children 6-12 $8.25, under 6 free) is one of the most popular museums in Coastal Virginia. It is

1: participants in period costume in Historic Jamestowne 2: navigation tools at Jamestown Settlement 3: Yorktown Battlefield 4: interactive exhibit at the American Revolution Museum at Yorktown

a living museum that re-creates and honors the first permanent English-speaking settlement in the country and takes visitors back to the 1600s. Costumed guides share facts about a Powhatan Village, and there are replicas of the three ships that sailed from England under the command of Captain Christopher Newport and eventually landed at Jamestown. The ships are a highlight of the museum, and the costumed crew does an excellent job of answering questions and showing off every nook and cranny of the ships. The **James Fort** is another main attraction. There, visitors can see authentic meals being prepared, witness arms demonstrations, and even try on armor. Thanksgiving is a great time to visit because special events are held in the museum. Combination tickets can be purchased to other Historic Triangle sites.

Getting There

Jamestown is nine miles southwest of Colonial Williamsburg along the Colonial Parkway.

YORKTOWN

The quaint waterfront village of Yorktown was established in 1691 and is most famous as the site of the historic victory in the American Revolutionary War. It was also an important tobacco port on the York River, where crops were exported from local plantations. During its peak in the mid-1700s, it had nearly 2,000 residents and several hundred buildings. It was a thriving city of primarily merchants, planters, shopkeepers, and indentured servants.

There are many earthworks surrounding Yorktown. These were first built by British troops in 1781, when nearly 80 percent of the town was damaged or destroyed during the Siege of Yorktown. These earthworks were built over with new fortifications by Confederate troops during the Civil War. During the **Siege of 1862,** the Union army was held back by the Confederates for more than a month in this area. After the Confederates left town, Union troops settled in for the rest of the war.

In addition to learning about history, visitors can enjoy art, shopping, special events, and water sports.

Sights
YORKTOWN BATTLEFIELD AND VISITOR CENTER

The **Yorktown National Battlefield** (757/898-2410, www.nps.gov/york) is a national park that marks where, on October 19, 1781, the British army, led by General Charles Lord Cornwallis, surrendered to General George Washington, ending the Revolutionary War. Visitors can see the battlefield, Washington's Headquarters and tent, and the actual surrender field.

The **Yorktown National Battlefield Visitor Center** (1000 Colonial Pkwy., 757/898-2410, reservations 757/898-2411, daily 9am-4:30pm, adults $10 for 7-day pass, children 15 and under free) is a great place to begin your exploration of the battlefield and town. It is a living-history museum where re-creations are staged by historical interpreters in costume. Two self-guided driving tours allow visitors to learn about the Siege of Yorktown at a relaxed pace. An audio tour is available on CD for the drive for $4.95. Guided group tours are also available for a fee (rates vary depending on the number of participants), and reservations should be made two months in advance.

The entrance fee is paid at the visitor centers, where maps are available as well as an informative 15-minute orientation film that should be your first order of business if you're a first-timer to the site. The admission fee at Yorktown includes entrance into historic houses, entrance to the battlefield, and access to a variety of interpretive programs and is good for seven days. Your pass can be upgraded to visit Jamestown Settlement at the Historic Jamestown Visitor Center for an additional $10.

The 84-foot-tall **Yorktown Victory Monument** and the **Moore House,** where the surrender terms were negotiated, are fascinating sites at the battlefield. The Victory

Monument was not erected until 100 years after the end of the war. Its purpose was to "keep fresh in memory the all decisive successes that had been achieved." The four-sided base has an inscription on each side: one for victory, one for a succinct narrative of the siege, one for the treaty of alliance with France, and one for the resulting peace treaty with England. The pediments over the inscriptions feature emblems of nationality, war, alliance, and peace. The monument's podium is a "symbol of the birth of freedom." The column (coming out of the podium) symbolizes the greatness and prosperity of the United States after a century. On top of the monument's shaft is a sculpture of Liberty, which attests to the existence of a nation governed by the people, for the people.

AMERICAN REVOLUTION MUSEUM AT YORKTOWN

Near the battlefield is the **American Revolution Museum at Yorktown** (200 Water St., 757/253-4838, www.historyisfun.org, daily 9am-5pm with extended summer hours, adults $15, children 6-12 $7.50, under 6 free), an informative museum dedicated to the American Revolution that chronicles the entire era beginning with unrest in the colonies and ending with the creation of a new nation. Visitors can view hundreds of artifacts, enjoy interactive exhibits, and take in *The Siege of Yorktown* film on a 180-degree screen.

Outdoor exhibits include the re-creation of a Continental Army encampment featuring live historical interpreters and daily demonstrations that teach about artillery, cooking, and medical treatment of the time. They also include a reconstructed farm that even has an orchard, crop fields, and tobacco barn.

Summer is the best time to visit since there are outdoor living-history exhibits (you might even be asked to help load a cannon), but the museum is wonderful to visit all year.

If you're lucky enough to be here on the Fourth of July, you can experience the **Liberty Celebration** firsthand. What better location to celebrate American's independence than where it all began? The celebration includes a plethora of reenactments, military drills, and food demonstrations. This event complements the **Yorktown Fourth of July Celebration** that takes place in the evening on July 4.

HISTORIC YORKTOWN

Yorktown still has a sparse population of full-time residents. Its streets are lined with historic homes, some more than two centuries old. There's Yorktown Beach, a pleasant sandy beach along the York River, and overall, Yorktown offers a relaxing place to explore history, shop, and dine.

Riverwalk Landing (425 Water St., 757/890-3500, www.riverwalklanding.com) is a pedestrian walkway along the York River. This quaint area includes retail shops and dining. Take a stroll on the mile-long River View path that runs along the York River from Yorktown Battlefield to the Yorktown Victory Center. Riverwalk Landing is a great place to take a walk, go shopping, or grab an ice-cream cone on a hot day.

The **Watermen's Museum** (309 Water St., 757/887-2641, www.watermens.org, Apr.-Dec. 22 Tues.-Sat. 10am-5pm, Sun. 1pm-5pm, closed the rest of the year, adults $5, seniors and students $4, children under 6 and military free) highlights the role that watermen on the Chesapeake Bay's rivers and tributaries had in the formation of our country. This is done through displays illustrating the methods of their trade and craft. Visitors learn what it means to earn a living harvesting seafood from the Chesapeake Bay watershed. The museum offers educational programs and a waterfront facility that can be rented for events.

The **Nelson House** (501 Main St., 757/898-2410, www.nps.gov/york, open as staffing permits, $10) is a prominent 18th-century structure on Main Street. It was built in the Georgian manor style by the grandfather of

Thomas Nelson Jr., one of Yorktown's most famous residents. The younger Nelson was the governor of Virginia in 1781 and the commander of the Virginia militia during the siege. He was also a signer of the Declaration of Independence. Damage from the siege is still evident at the Nelson House. Informal tours are available throughout the year. It's best to call for hours because the house is not open continuously.

Recreation

Yorktown is a waterfront town and outdoor recreation haven. The mile-long **Riverwalk** is a great place for a power walk or to stretch your legs after travel. The two-acre beach near the Riverwalk offers a great location for launching a kayak, swimming, and beachcombing.

There are also kayak and canoe launches at nearby **Old Wormley Creek Landing** (1110 Old Wormley Creek Rd.), with access to Wormley Creek and the York River; **Rodgers A. Smith Landing** (707 Tide Mill Rd.), with access to the Poquoson River and the lower Chesapeake Bay; and **New Quarter Park** (1000 Lakeshead Dr., Williamsburg, 757/890-5840, www.yorkcounty.gov), with access to Queens Creek and the York River.

The **Riverwalk Landing Piers** (425 Water St.) is a pleasant place to enjoy a day of fishing, and visitors can dock their boats there.

For bicycle rentals ($7.50 per hour or $25 for four hours), kayak and stand-up paddleboard (SUP) rentals ($30-45 for two hours), or guided Segway tours ($39 for one hour or $65 for two hours), contact **Patriot Tours & Provisions** (757/969-5400, www.patriottoursva.com).

If sailing on a romantic schooner sounds appealing, **Yorktown Sailing Charter** (757/639-1233, www.sailyorktown.com, adults $37, children 12 and under $25 for two hours) docks its beautiful sailing vessel, the schooner *Alliance,* at the pier at Riverwalk Landing April-October. They offer daily sailing trips during the day and at sunset. Daytime trips leave at either 11am or 2pm.

Sunset cruise times vary by month. Its sister schooner, *Serenity,* offers pirate cruises (adults $37, children 12 and under $25), educational trips, and charters for those looking for a bit of adventure.

Entertainment and Events

The **Lighted Boat Parade** (Yorktown Beach) kicks off the holiday season in early December with a festive procession featuring power- and sailboats adorned with holiday lights. Musical performances and caroling are held on the beach by the light of a bonfire, and hot cider is served. The event is free to the public.

The **Yorktown Wine Festival** (425 Water St. at Riverwalk Landing, tastings $30-35) is held in October and features wines from throughout Virginia. Art and food vendors also share their wares at the festival. Another October festival is the **York River Maritime Heritage Festival** (309 Water St., 757/887-2641, www.watermens.org, free). It offers two days of music, vendors, re-enactors, and crafts.

Shopping

Yorktown's Main Street in the Historic Village is lined with unique shops and galleries. There are antiques stores, galleries, and jewelry and glass shops to name a few. Down by the water at Riverwalk Landing are additional shops featuring colonial architecture and offering art, home items, jewelry, quilts, and clothing.

Auntie M's American Cottage (330 Water St., 757/369-8150, Mon.-Sat. 10:30am-6:30pm, Sun. 11am-6:30pm) sells handcrafted work that is made in America.

Viccellio Goldsmith & Fine Jewelry (325 Water St., 757/890-2162, Sun 12pm-4pm, Mon.-Sat. 10am-6pm) sells unique jewelry made by local master goldsmith and precious metals craftsman J. Henry Viccellio.

Food

The **Carrot Tree Kitchen** (323 Water St., 757/988-1999, www.carrottreekitchens.com, daily 10am-4pm, under $10) is a small, casual lunch spot on the waterfront with delightful food. Don't be turned off by the paper plates and plastic utensils; the Carrot Tree offers delicious lunches of sandwiches and comfort food. Save room for the carrot cake—it's their signature dessert.

The **Riverwalk Restaurant** (323 Water St., 757/875-1522, www.riverwalkrestaurant. net, Mon.-Sat. 11am-9pm, Sun. 10am-8pm, $10-42) provides diners with a scenic view of the York River through large glass windows and a cozy fireplace for cool evenings. The fare is primarily seafood and steak, but they also offer a selection of salads. This is a great place to relax after a day of sightseeing.

If fresh seafood and cold beer right on the beach sound like a good ending to a day of exploration in Yorktown, stop in at the **Yorktown Pub** (540 Water St., 757/886-9964, www.yorktownpub.com, Sun.-Thurs. 11am-midnight, Fri.-Sat. 11am-2am, $9-29). The atmosphere is very casual, but the food and service are good. The pub burger, local oysters, and hush puppies are among the best choices. The place is crowded on the weekends, so plan ahead.

Accommodations

UNDER $200

The **Duke of York Hotel** (508 Water St., 757/898-3232, www.dukeofyorkhotelwaterfro ntyorktownva.com, $149-169) is an older hotel with a great location right on the water. This family-run establishment has all river-view rooms (some have balconies and some open to landscaped grounds), an outdoor pool, and an on-site café and restaurant. The Yorktown Trolley stops in front of the hotel.

The **York River Inn Bed & Breakfast** (209 Ambler St., 757/887-8800, www. yorkriverinn.com, $135-165) sits on a bluff overlooking the York River and offers two rooms, a suite with private bathrooms, and all the hospitality you can imagine from its friendly owner (who is also a knockout breakfast chef). This is a wonderful, colonial-style inn with elegant rooms.

The **Marl Inn Bed & Breakfast**

(220 Church St., 301/807-0386, www. marlinnbandb.com, $115-145) is two blocks from the Riverwalk. This colonial-style home is a private residence and inn offering four guest rooms; rates can be booked with no breakfast or with full breakfast. The owner is a great-grandson of Thomas Nelson Jr. of Nelson House.

$200-300

The ★ **Hornsby House Inn** (702 Main St., 757/369-0200, www.hornsbyhouseinn.com, $149-238) offers five beautiful guest rooms with private modern bathrooms in an exquisite colonial home. The inn is in the heart of Yorktown and offers a great view of the York River. It is also just a short walk from the Yorktown Battlefield. The inn is run by two friendly brothers who grew up in the house and provide exemplary service, wine and cheese, and a delicious fresh breakfast each morning. The owners take the time to eat breakfast with and get to know their guests as well as share the history of their home. They also make recommendations for attractions in the area and the best strategy for enjoying them. The house is beautifully appointed and is a warm and inviting home away from home. Book the Monument Grand Suite and enjoy a private outdoor terrace overlooking the York River and Yorktown Victory Monument.

Information and Services

For additional information on Yorktown, visit www.visityorktown.org and www.yorkcounty. gov.

Getting There and Around

Yorktown is 13 miles southeast of Williamsburg along the Colonial Parkway. The **Yorktown Trolley** (757/890-3500, www.visityorktown.org, daily 11am-5pm, extended service hours June-Aug., free) is a free seasonal trolley service with stops in nine locations around Yorktown. It runs every 20-25 minutes from the end of March until November.

James River Plantations

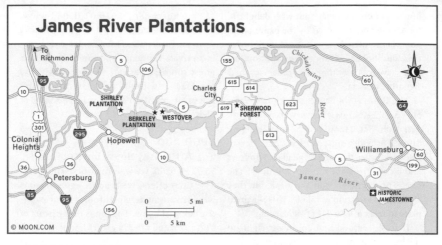

JAMES RIVER PLANTATIONS

Between Richmond and Williamsburg (in Charles City County) along State Route 5 are four stunning plantations that survived the Revolutionary War, War of 1812, and Civil War. These treasures, which span three centuries, are all privately owned National Register properties that are open to the public. For additional information on all four plantations, visit www.jamesriverplantations.org.

Sherwood Forest

Sherwood Forest (State Route 5, 14501 John Tyler Hwy., Charles City, 804/829-5377, www.sherwoodforest.org, grounds open daily 9am-5pm) sounds like a place out of a fairy tale, and it kind of is. This beautiful plantation was the home of President John Tyler for 20 years. The home has been the residence of the Tyler family continuously since he purchased it in 1842.

At more than 300 feet in length—longer than a football field—Sherwood Forest is the longest frame house in the country. The home evolved from a modest 17th-century English-style home (circa 1660) into a substantial 19th-century "Big House" that features a ballroom designed specifically for dancers to engage in the Virginia reel. There is also a resident ghost.

Self-guided walking tours of the grounds are available for $10 per person (children 15 and under free). The tour features 21 numbered stations on 25 acres with information on the 19th-century plantation. The grounds include terraced gardens, quiet woodlands, and lush lawn. A printed guide is available at a kiosk at the main entrance and features descriptions and history information for each station. House tours are only available by appointment and cost $35 for adults and $25 for children.

Westover

Speaking of fairy tales, **Westover** (off State Route 5, 7000 Westover Rd., 804/829-2882, www.westover-plantation.com, grounds open daily 10am-5pm, adults $5, children 7-16 $2, children 6 and under free) could have come straight off the pages of one. William Byrd II, who founded the city of Richmond, built the home in 1730. Westover is known for its architectural details, but kids of all ages will love it for its secret passages and enchanting gardens. The mansion is widely considered to be one of the top examples of Georgian architecture in the country. The house itself is not open to the public, but there are still many interesting things to see on the grounds, which offer wide views of the James River. The icehouse and another small structure to the east of the mansion contain a dry well and passageways leading under the house and down to the river. These were created as an escape route from the house during attacks.

Shirley Plantation

Shirley Plantation (501 Shirley Plantation Rd., 804/829-5121, www.shirleyplantation. com, daily mid-Mar.-Dec. 10am-4pm, house and grounds admission for adults $25, children 7-16 $17.50, seniors 60 and over $22.50, military/veterans $20, children 6 and under free) was the first plantation built in Virginia. It was established in 1613, just six years after Jamestown, and construction was completed in 1738. This property has a legacy of 11 generations of one family (descendants of Edward Hill I) who still own and operate the colonial estate. It has survived attacks, war, and the Great Depression and remains the oldest farm and family-owned business in the United States.

Admission includes a guided house tour that showcases original furnishings, artwork, silver, and hand-carved woodwork. Special architectural features include a "flying staircase" and a Queen Anne forecourt. A self-guided grounds tour features gardens and original outbuildings. Allow at least one hour for your visit. Admission for just the grounds is also available (adults $11, children 7-16 $7.50, seniors and military $9.50, children 6 and under free).

Berkeley Plantation

Berkeley Plantation (12602 Harrison Landing Rd., 804/829-6018, www. berkeleyplantation.com, daily Jan.-Feb. 10:30am-3:30pm, Mar.-Dec. 9:30am-4:30pm, adults $12.50, children 6-16 $7, seniors 60 and over and military $11.50, children 5 and under free) is famous for being the site of the first official Thanksgiving in 1619, although substantiated claims for the first Thanksgiving also belong to locations in Florida, Texas, Maine, and Massachusetts. It is also the birthplace and home of Declaration of Independence signer Benjamin Harrison and President William Henry Harrison. The beautiful Georgian mansion, which was erected in 1726, sits on a hilltop overlooking the James River. The brick used to build the home was fired on the plantation.

Guided tours are conducted in the mansion and feature a nice collection of 18th-century antiques. An audiovisual presentation is included in the tour, as is access to a museum collection of Civil War artifacts and unique paintings by artist Sydney King. Visitors can then tour the grounds on their own and explore five terraces of boxwood and flower gardens. Allow approximately 1.5 hours for the house tour and to roam the gardens.

Hampton Roads

The Hampton Roads region is all about water. In sailors' terms, "Roadstead" means a safe anchorage or sheltered harbor. The word "Hampton" came from an English aristocrat, Henry Wriothesley, who was the third earl of Southampton. Hence, Hampton Roads.

Hampton Roads, which used to be known as Tidewater Virginia, contains one of the largest natural deepwater harbors in the world. The harbor is where the James, Elizabeth, and Nansemond Rivers meet the Chesapeake Bay. Pioneers first settled the area in 1610, after disease struck nearby Jamestown. The area was a throughway for goods from both the colonies and England and, as such, drew merchants and pirates. One of history's most famous pirates, Blackbeard (Edward Teach), plundered the port and waters of Hampton Roads, which was just a short distance from his base in North Carolina.

The port in Hampton Roads is the country's second largest to New York City and is notable for remaining ice-free year-round. It is also the birthplace of the modern U.S. Navy.

Defining the Hampton Roads area can be a bit confusing. Technically, the Historic Triangle is considered part of Hampton Roads, but the coastal cities from Newport News to Virginia Beach are more commonly thought of as the Hampton Roads area.

NEWPORT NEWS

Newport News is a short drive from Williamsburg, Virginia Beach, and the Atlantic Ocean. There are several versions of whom Newport News was named for, but the most widely accepted is that it was named for Captain Christopher Newport, who was in charge of the three ships that landed in Jamestown in 1607. The "news" part of the name came from the news that was sent back to England on the ships' safe arrival.

Sights

THE MARINERS' MUSEUM AND PARK

The Mariners' Museum and Park (100 Museum Dr., 757/596-2222, www.marinersmuseum.org, Mon.-Sat. 9am-5pm, Sun. 11am-5pm, museum admission $1, children 3 and under free, museum and 3D movie $7, children 3 and under free) is one of the largest maritime history museums in the United States. It has more than 60,000 square feet of gallery space showing maritime paintings, artifacts, figureheads, ship models, and small craft from around the world. Exhibits include vessels for warfare, exploration, pleasure, and fishing. A highlight of the museum is the USS Monitor Center, where a full-scale replica of the Civil War battleship USS *Monitor* is housed. In 1862 the *Monitor* battled the CSS *Virginia* in what went down in history as the first engagement of steam-powered iron warships (aka The Battle of the Ironclads). Visitors can learn about the historic encounter in the Battle Theater. The center is also home to recovered parts of the original battleship, which sank off the coast of Cape Hatteras, North Carolina, in December 1862.

The museum offers countless other collections including the **Crabtree Collection of Miniature Ships.** The museum is very kid friendly and offers numerous events, lectures, and even a concert series (check the website for upcoming events). The park (daily 6am-7pm, free) offers a five-mile trail along Lake Maury. There is also boating and hiking.

THE VIRGINIA LIVING MUSEUM

Endangered red wolves, loggerhead turtles, and moon jellyfish are just some of the amazing animals you can get close to at The Virginia Living Museum (524 J. Clyde Morris Blvd., 757/595-1900, www.thevlm. org, daily 9am-5pm, extended summer hours, adults $20, children 3-12 $15). This is a wonderful place to learn about Virginia's natural heritage. Indoor exhibits, outdoor exhibits, four interactive discovery centers, and gardens showcase Virginia's geographical regions and the more than 250 species of plants and animals that live in the state. The 30,000-gallon aquarium is a focal point for kids of all ages. Many hands-on activities are also offered, such as touch tanks and live feedings, and there is even a planetarium.

VIRGINIA WAR MUSEUM

The Virginia War Museum (9285 Warwick Blvd., 757/247-8523, www.warmuseum.org, Mon.-Sat. 9am-5pm, Sun. noon-5pm, adults $8, children 7-18 $6, children under 7 free, seniors 62 and over and military $7) explains the development of the U.S. military from 1775 to modern times. Its many exhibits showcase war efforts throughout our country's history. Weapons, artifacts, and uniforms are displayed from the Revolutionary War through the Vietnam War, and exhibits explain the evolution of weaponry, the role of women in the military, and contributions made by African Americans to military history, as well as provide a tribute to prisoners of war.

Northern Hampton Roads

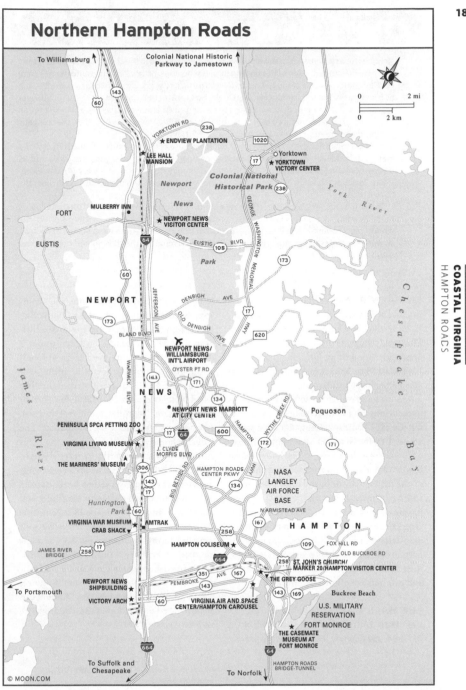

To Williamsburg

Colonial National Historic Parkway to Jamestown

143
60

0   2 mi
0   2 km

YORKTOWN RD

238

★ ENDVIEW PLANTATION

1020

☆ Yorktown

LEE HALL MANSION

17 ★ YORKTOWN VICTORY CENTER

Newport

Colonial National Historical Park

238

York River

News

FORT

MULBERRY INN ●

★ NEWPORT NEWS VISITOR CENTER

GEORGE WASHINGTON MEMORIAL

64

FORT EUSTIS BLVD

105

EUSTIS

Park

173

Chesapeake

60

NEWPORT

JEFFERSON AVE

DENBIGH AVE

17

173

OLD DENBIGH AVE

BLAND BLVD

620

NEWPORT NEWS/ WILLIAMSBURG INT'L AIRPORT

WARWICK BLVD

143

OYSTER PT RD

171

James River

NEWS

134

● NEWPORT NEWS MARRIOTT AT CITY CENTER

Poquoson

PENINSULA SPCA PETTING ZOO ★

17

64

600

HAMPTON

WYTHE CREEK RD

172

171

VIRGINIA LIVING MUSEUM ★

J. CLYDE MORRIS BLVD

THE MARINERS' MUSEUM

306

HAMPTON ROADS CENTER PKWY

NASA LANGLEY AIR FORCE BASE

143
17

BIG BETHEL RD

134

Huntington Park

60

N ARMISTEAD AVE

VIRGINIA WAR MUSEUM CRAB SHACK ▼ AMTRAK

258

167

H A M P T O N

JAMES RIVER BRIDGE

258
17

HAMPTON COLISEUM ★

109

FOX HILL RD

OLD BUCKROE RD

664

258

ST. JOHN'S CHURCH/ MARKER 20/HAMPTON VISITOR CENTER

NEWPORT NEWS SHIPBUILDING ★

351

PEMBROKE AVE

167

THE GREY GOOSE

To Portsmouth

143

VICTORY ARCH ★

60

VIRGINIA AIR AND SPACE CENTER/HAMPTON CAROUSEL

143

169

Buckroe Beach

U.S. MILITARY RESERVATION

★ FORT MONROE

THE CASEMATE MUSEUM AT FORT MONROE

664

64

HAMPTON ROADS BRIDGE-TUNNEL

To Suffolk and Chesapeake

To Norfolk

© MOON.COM

Shipbuilding in Newport News

Newport News is home to the largest privately owned shipyard in the country, **Newport News Shipbuilding** (a division of Huntington Ingalls Industries, https://nns.huntingtoningalls.com) on Washington Avenue along the James River. The facility was built in 1886 for a sum of $7 million and was called the Chesapeake Dry Dock and Construction Company. Its 4,000 employees repaired the many vessels that came to use the ever-growing transportation hub in the Hampton Roads area. The yard produced its first tugboat (named *Dorothy*) in 1891. By 1897, the company had produced three additional tugboats for the U.S. Navy.

Business took off with the onset of the Great Naval Race of the early 1900s. At the start of World War I, shipbuilding was in full swing, and the company constructed six dreadnoughts and 25 destroyers for the U.S. Navy. The company has been going full force ever since, with its achievements including building the first nuclear-powered submarine and the famous ocean liner the SS *United States*.

Today, the company is the largest private employer in Hampton Roads. The 20,000 employees (many of whom are third- and fourth-generation shipbuilders) turn raw steel into some of the world's most complex ships. The shipyard is the country's sole designer and builder of nuclear-powered aircraft carriers and also one of only two companies that design and build nuclear submarines.

ENDVIEW PLANTATION

Endview Plantation (362 Yorktown Rd., 757/857-1862, www.endview.org, Apr.-Dec. Mon. and Thurs.-Fri. 10am-4pm, Sat. 10am-5pm, Sun. noon-5pm, Jan.-Mar. Thurs.-Sat. 10am-4pm, Sun. 1pm-5pm, adults $8, children 7-18 $6, seniors 62 and over $7, children under 7 free) was a privately owned estate that was used briefly as a Confederate hospital during the 1862 Peninsula Campaign. The small, white, T-frame Georgian-style home was later occupied by Federal troops. The house sits on top of a knoll, and a spring flows at the base of the hill. This, coupled with the beautiful rolling farmland that surrounds the place, has made it an attractive location for centuries. The city of Newport News purchased the plantation in 1995 and restored it to its original configuration. School programs are held at the plantation, and guided tours of the house and grounds are offered periodically.

LEE HALL MANSION

Lee Hall Mansion (163 Yorktown Rd., 757/888-3371, www.leehall.org, Apr.-Dec. Mon. and Thurs.-Fri. 10am-4pm, Sat. 10am-5pm, Sun. noon-5pm, Jan.-Mar. Thurs.-Sat. 10am-4pm, Sun. 1pm-5pm, adults $8, children 7-18 $6, seniors $7, children under 7 free) is the only remaining large antebellum plantation on the lower Virginia peninsula. The 6,600-square-foot structure is a blend of several architectural styles, including Italianate, Georgian, and Greek Revival. The primary style, however, is Italianate. The redbrick home was built on a rise in the 1850s and was home to wealthy planter Richard Decatur Lee. Due to the mansion's commanding view, the home served as headquarters for Confederate generals John Magruder and Joseph E. Johnston during the 1862 Peninsula Campaign. Visitors can take a step back in time to the mid-Victorian period and view hundreds of artifacts in the mansion's authentically furnished rooms. Combination admission tickets for Lee Hall Mansion, Endview Plantation, and the Virginia War Museum can be purchased for $21 for adults, children $15, and seniors $18.

1: The Mariners' Museum 2: The Virginia Living Museum in Newport News 3: Victory Arch in Newport News

The Peninsula Campaign of 1862

The Peninsula Campaign of 1862 was an aggressive plan designed by Union forces during the Civil War to outsmart Confederate defenses in Northern Virginia by moving 121,000 troops by sea to the Virginia Peninsula between the York and James Rivers. This would place them to the east of Richmond, the Confederate capital. Having bypassed the Northern Virginia forces, the army, led by General George B. McClellan, would be able to advance on Richmond without meeting entrenched opposition.

The failure of this plan remains a highly debated episode in the war. Union troops moved slowly and never made a serious attack on Richmond, despite their strategic placement. Although they were met by small Confederate forces, McClellan blamed the failure on Washington for not providing men and support for the effort, even though his troops outnumbered the Confederates throughout the campaign.

From the Confederate standpoint, the Peninsula Campaign of 1862 resulted in the emergence of two great commanders, Stonewall Jackson and Robert E. Lee, who jointly kept the Union forces out of Richmond.

PENINSULA SPCA PETTING ZOO

The **Peninsula SPCA Petting Zoo** (523 J. Clyde Morris Blvd., 757/595-1399, www.peninsulaspca.org, Mon.-Sat. 11am-5pm, $3) is a fun place to bring the kids for a hands-on experience with barnyard animals. The zoo is run by the nonprofit Peninsula Society for the Prevention of Cruelty to Animals (SPCA). Visitors can enjoy the company of sheep, goats, chickens, ducks, and other friendly animals.

VICTORY ARCH

The **Victory Arch** (25th St. and West Ave., 757/926-1400, www.nnva.gov) was built in 1919. Troops returning from World War I marched through the arch in victory parades after disembarking from their ships. The arch was reconstructed in 1962, and an eternal flame was added to it on Memorial Day in 1969. Today the arch stands as a memorial to all men and women of the armed forces.

Recreation
PARKS

The **Newport News Park** (13560 Jefferson Ave., 757/888-3333, www.newport-news.org) is one of the largest municipal parks in the country, encompassing nearly 8,000 acres. Boat and bike rentals are available in the park, as are hiking and biking trails, picnicking,

canoeing, archery, disc golf, fishing, and camping. The park's Discovery Center has many hands-on activities and historical artifacts.

Huntington Park-Beach, Rose Garden & Tennis Center (361 Hornet Cir., 757/886-7912, www.newport-news.org) offers a public beach with lifeguards, a playground, baseball, boating, swimming, and tennis.

King-Lincoln Park (600 Jefferson Ave., 757/888-3333, www.nnva.gov) overlooks the Hampton Roads Harbor and provides fishing, tennis, picnicking, playgrounds, and basketball.

Riverview Farm Park (105 City Farm Rd., 757/886-7912, www.newport-news.org) has two miles of multiuse paved trails, a 30,000-square-foot community playground, biking, hiking, and soccer fields.

The Mariners' Museum Park (100 Museum Dr., 757/596-2222, www.marinersmuseum.org) offers a five-mile trail along Lake Maury. There is also boating and hiking.

GOLF

Golfers can get their fix at two local courses: **Kiln Creek Golf Club and Resort** (1003 Brick Kiln Blvd., 757/874-2600, www.kilncreekgolf.com, $33-59) and **Newport News Golf Club at Deer Run**

(901 Clubhouse Way, 757/886-7925, www. nngolfclub.com, $17-38).

FISHING

Fishing enthusiasts will enjoy the **James River Fishing Pier** (2019 James River Bridge, 757/274 0364, adults $9, children 6-12 and seniors 65 and over.$7), which is made entirely of concrete and has LED lights. It is one of the longest fishing piers on the East Coast.

BOATING

Boaters can make the **Leeward Marina** (7499 River Rd., 757/274-2359, www.newport-news. org) a base for exploration of the Hampton Roads Harbor and the Chesapeake Bay.

Entertainment and Events

FERGUSON CENTER FOR THE ARTS

The **Ferguson Center for the Arts** (1 Ave. of the Arts, 757/594-8752, www.fergusoncenter. org) at Christopher Newport University is a performance hall that also houses the university's theater, arts, and music departments. The center contains a 1,725-seat concert hall and a 200-seat studio theater. It offers a wide range of performances. Check the website for upcoming events.

PENINSULA FINE ARTS CENTER

The **Peninsula Fine Arts Center** (101 Museum Dr., 757/596-8175, www.pfac-va.org, Tues.-Sat. 10am-5pm, Sun. 1pm-5pm) is dedicated to the promotion of the fine arts. It offers exhibits, a studio art school, an interactive gallery, educational programs, and hands-on activities for children.

EVENTS

The **Newport News Fall Festival** (www. nnva.gov) is held on the first weekend in October and has been running since 1972. The festival draws 35,000 visitors annually and has more than 150 exhibitors featuring trade demonstrations, crafts, and food.

The **Newport News Children's Festival of Friends** (www.nnva.gov) is held at the beginning of May and offers a variety of themed areas for children. Activities, rides, entertainment, and food are all part of the fun of this popular festival that's been going on since 1990.

Shopping

The **City Center at Oyster Point** (701 Town Center Dr., 757/873-2020, www. citycenteratoysterpoint.com) is an outdoor town center with retail stores, gourmet eateries, spas, and salons.

The **Patrick Henry Mall** (12300 Jefferson Ave., 757/249-4305, www. shoppatrickhenrymall.com) is the largest mall on the peninsula, with more than 120 stores in a single-level, indoor configuration.

Food

AMERICAN

★ **Circa 1918 Kitchen & Bar** (10367 Warwick Blvd., 757/599-1918, Tues.-Sat. 5pm-10pm, $18-32) offers delicious food, a lovely wine list, wonderful specials, seasonal selections, and friendly, professional service. Sample menu items include bison meat loaf, pan roasted sea scallops, and grilled lamb burgers. The restaurant is in the historic, two-block-long Hilton Village neighborhood. The atmosphere is relaxed and comfortable, and separate groups of patrons actually talk to each other. Don't shy away from interacting—you could get a great tip for what to order. This is a small restaurant with only about a dozen tables, so reservations are highly recommended.

Fin Seafood (3150 William Styron Sq., 757/599-5800, www.finseafood.com, daily 11am-10pm, $28-100) is a great choice for a romantic dinner or a large gathering. It is a local favorite for delicious seafood and high-end steaks. They use mostly organic and sustainable produce and proteins, as well as seasonal ingredients.

Second Street American Bistro (115 Arthur Way, 757/234-4448, www.secondst. com, Mon.-Thurs. 11:30am-10pm, Fri.-Sat. 11:30am-11pm, Sun. 11am-10pm, $8-31) is an upscale yet casual restaurant with a wide menu selection, including small plates, pizza, burgers, steak, chicken, ribs, fish, and many desserts. There is also a wonderfully extensive wine list and they offer tasting events.

Brickhouse Tavern (141 Herman Melville Ave., 757/223-9531, www.welcometobrickhouse.com, daily 11am-2am, $8-13) is a casual restaurant serving a variety of pub food, including burgers and pizza. **Chic N Fish** (954 J. Clyde Morris Blvd., 757/223-6517, www.chicnfishva.com, Mon.-Sat. 11am-9pm, $5-25) serves up a little bit of everything including burgers, seafood, and Korean fried chicken.

One of the best views in town is from the **Crab Shack** (7601 River Rd., 757/245-2722, www.crabshackonthejames.com, Sun.-Thurs. 11am-11:30pm, Fri.-Sat. 11am-12:30am, $8-24), on the James River waterfront. This casual seafood restaurant serves sandwiches and entrées in a window-lined dining room or on an outdoor deck.

ITALIAN

For good mid-priced Italian food, try **Al Fresco** (11710 Jefferson Ave., 757/873-0644, www.alfrescoitalianrestaurant.com, Mon.-Fri. 11am-3pm and 5pm-10pm, Sat. 5pm-10pm, $8-27).

Accommodations
UNDER $100
The **Mulberry Inn & Plaza at Fort Eustis** (16890 Warwick Blvd., 757/887-3000, www.mulberryinnva.com, $63-139) is a 101-room hotel offering standard rooms, efficiencies, and studios that can hold up to four people. It is close to I-64 and has amenities such as an outdoor pool, a fitness center, and a business center. Hot breakfast is included, and they are pet friendly.

$100-200
The **Comfort Suites Airport** (12570 Jefferson Ave., 757/947-1333, www.choicehotels.com, $89-170) is the hotel closest to the Newport News/Williamsburg International Airport. It offers all suite accommodations, a free airport shuttle, an indoor pool, and a spacious workout facility.

The **Hilton Garden Inn Newport News** (180 Regal Way, 757/947-1080, http://hiltongardeninn3.hilton.com, $119-129) offers 122 guest rooms, an indoor heated pool and spa, an airport shuttle, and easy access to the city center and military bases.

OVER $200
The **Newport News Marriott at City Center** (740 Town Center Dr., 757/873-9299, www.marriott.com, $187-409) is a 256-room hotel near shopping and many restaurants. It offers a pool and workout facility.

Camping
Year-round camping is available in **Newport News Park** (13564 Jefferson Ave., 757/888-3333, www.nnva.gov, $33-40). This is one of the biggest municipal parks on the East Coast, and it has 188 campsites with hot showers and restroom facilities. The 8,000-acre park is a combination of woods, meadows, and lakes (campsites are wooded).

Information and Services
For additional information on Newport News, visit www.newport-news.org or stop by the **Newport News Visitor Center** (13560 Jefferson Ave., 757/886-7777, daily 9am-5pm), off I-64 at exit 250B.

Getting There and Around
Newport News is located along I-64 and US Route 60.

The **Newport News/Williamsburg International Airport** (PHF, 900 Bland Blvd., www.flyphf.com) is off I-64 at exit 255B. Downtown Newport News is a 15-minute drive from the airport.

Amtrak (9304 Warwick Blvd., 757/245-3589, www.amtrak.com) has a station in Newport News at Huntington Park. Consult the website for schedules and fares.

Newport News, Hampton, Norfolk, and Virginia Beach are connected by **Hampton**

Roads Transit (757/222-6100. www.gohrt. com). Consult the website for schedules and fares.

HAMPTON

Hampton is the oldest continuously inhabited English-speaking community in the United States, with a history dating back to 1607. It is also home to Langley Air Force Base. Hampton was partially destroyed during three major wars—the Revolutionary War, the War of 1812, and the Civil War—but was rebuilt each time and continues to undergo renovations even today. The city now offers an attractive waterfront filled with modern sailing and fishing boats and a variety of attractions for visitors and residents.

Sights
VIRGINIA AIR & SPACE CENTER
The **Virginia Air & Space Center** (600 Settlers Landing Rd., 757/727-0900, www. vasc.org, Mon.-Sat. 10am-5pm, Sun. noon-5pm, extended summer hours, adults $20, children 3-18 $16.50, under 3 free, active military $17, seniors $18, includes IMAX) houses more than 100 interactive exhibits that detail the historic achievements of NASA. Topics include space travel, aircraft development, and communications, as well as a hands-on space gallery. Hampton was the birthplace of the space program in the United States and has played an important role in the 100-plus-year history of flight. Displays include more than 30 historic airplanes, the Apollo 12 command module, a passenger jet, moon rocks, and many replicas.

THE HAMPTON CAROUSEL
The **Hampton Carousel** (602 Settlers Landing Rd., Carousel Park, 757/727-1610, www.hampton.gov, Apr.-Dec. Tues.-Sun. 11am-8pm, $1) was originally built for an amusement park at Buckroe Beach, where it resided between 1921 and 1985. It is now on the waterfront in downtown Hampton, fully restored and protected from the elements. The merry-go-round's 48 horses and chariots

were hand-carved out of hardwood, and it is adorned with original paintings and mirrors. It also still plays the original organ music.

THE CASEMATE MUSEUM AT FORT MONROE
The **Casemate Museum** (20 Bernard Rd., 757/788-3391, www.fortmonroe.org, Tues.-Sun. 10:30am-4:30pm, daily during the summer, free) on the grounds of Fort Monroe shares many exhibits about the fort, which was built in 1834 to protect the Chesapeake Bay, James River, and Hampton River. This is the largest stone fort in the country. The museum contains the prison cell where Confederate president Jefferson Davis was held and also the living quarters of Robert E. Lee while he was stationed there from 1831 to 1834. Other displays include military uniforms and supplies. The grounds at Fort Monroe are open year-round for walking and other outdoor activities.

ST. JOHN'S EPISCOPAL CHURCH
St. John's Episcopal Church (100 W. Queens Way, 757/722-2567, www. stjohnshampton.org) is the oldest English-speaking parish in the United States. The church was founded in 1610, and the current structure was built in 1728. The church was designed in the shape of a Latin cross and boasts beautiful colonial-style brickwork, two-foot-thick walls, and stained glass windows. The church survived the Revolutionary War, the War of 1812, and the Civil War. The silver used for communion dates back to 1618 and is considered to be the most valuable relic in the American Anglican Church. Services are still held here; consult the website for details.

Recreation
Buckroe Beach (N. 1st St., www.hampton. gov) is a wide, sandy, eight-acre beach on the Chesapeake Bay. There is a playground, picnic shelters, a bike path, and certified lifeguards on duty. Concerts are held in the summer months, as is an outdoor family-movie series.

Grandview Nature Preserve (State Park Dr., www.hampton.gov) is a local secret. This nature preserve and beach at the end of Beach Road in Grandview is great for families and allows dogs in the off-season.

Hampton is located at the entrance to the Chesapeake Bay and is a convenient stopping point for boaters. Those traveling by boat can stop at the **Blue Water Yachting Center** (15 Marina Rd., 757/723-6774, www.bluewateryachtcenter.com), which offers daily dockage.

If you don't have your own boat but wish to take a relaxing sightseeing cruise, board the double-decker *Miss Hampton II* (757/722-9102, www.misshamptoncruises.com, adults $27, children 7-12 $17, active military $13.50, retired military and seniors 65 and over $25, 6 and under free, for 2.5-3 hours), a motorized vessel that offers cruising in Hampton Harbor and on the Chesapeake Bay.

Golf enthusiasts can play at the **Woodlands Golf Course** (9 Woodlands Rd., 757/727-1195, www.hampton.gov, $13-19) or the **Hamptons Golf Course** (320 Butler Farm Rd., 757/766-9148, www.hampton.gov, $14-21).

Entertainment and Events

The **Hampton Coliseum** (1000 Coliseum Dr., 757/838-4203, www.hamptoncoliseum.org) is the premier venue in Hampton for concerts, performances, and sporting events. A list of upcoming events can be found on the website. The Coliseum is convenient to I-64 and offers free parking.

The annual **Hampton Jazz Festival** (www.hamptonjazzfestival.com) has been going on since 1968. It is held for three days at the end of June in the Hampton Coliseum. Information on the lineup and tickets can be found on the website.

The **Hampton Cup Regatta** (www.hamptoncupregatta.com) is billed as the "oldest continually run motorsport event in the world." It is held for three days in September in Mill Creek, between Fort Monroe and the East Mercury Boulevard Bridge. Another fun water festival is the **Blackbeard Pirate Festival** (www.blackbeardfestival.com), held at the beginning of June each year. The Hampton waterfront is overrun with pirate re-enactors as visitors are taken back to the 18th century. There is live music, children's activities, vendors, fireworks, and arts and crafts.

Food

Surf Rider Bluewater (1 Marina Rd., 757/723-9366, www.surfriderrestaurant.com, opens daily 11am, $7-30) is a family-owned seafood restaurant in the Blue Water Yachting Center off Ivy Home Road. This is a great place for local seafood, which you can tell by the number of local residents eating here. Their crab cakes are famous, as are the oysters, tuna, and hush puppies.

Venture Kitchen and Bar (9 E. Queens Way, 757/325-8868, www.venturekitchenandbar.com, Mon.-Thurs. 11am-10pm, Fri.-Sat. 11am-midnight, Sun. 10am-10pm, $8-15) offers a little bit of everything. Tapas, pizza, sandwiches, seafood, meatballs, pasta, salads, and more are served in a cozy atmosphere (bar and booths) with friendly service. They also have gluten-free and vegan options plus an extensive cocktail menu.

Another local favorite is **Marker 20** (21 E. Queens Way, 757/726-9410, www.marker20.com, Mon.-Fri. 11am-2am, Sat.-Sun. 10am-2am, $8-25). This downtown seafood restaurant has a large, covered, outdoor deck and inside seating. Enjoy a casual menu of soups, salads, sandwiches, and seafood specials, along with dozens of types of beer.

The cute **Grey Goose** (118 Old Hampton Way, 757/723-7978, www.greygooserestaurant.com, Mon. 11am-3pm, Tues.-Thurs. 11am-8pm, Sat. 10am-9pm, Sun. 10am-2pm, $8-14) serves homemade soups, salads, sandwiches, and bakery items made from fresh ingredients.

1: Virginia Air & Space Center in Hampton 2: Blue Water Yachting Center in Hampton

Accommodations

$100-200

The **Candlewood Suites Hampton** (401 Butler Farm Rd., 757/766-8976, www.ihg.com, $105-120) offers 98 reasonably priced, spacious rooms in a quiet location. The hotel is geared toward extended-stay guests and offers per diem rates for members of the armed services. The service is good, and the staff is caring and friendly. The rooms are well stocked, and there are free laundry facilities on-site.

The **Hilton Garden Inn Hampton Coliseum Central** (1999 Power Plant Pkwy., 757/310-6323, www.secure3.hilton.com, $139-169) is another good value. It offers 149 guest rooms, an on-site restaurant, fitness center, and complimentary parking. It is also pet friendly.

OVER $200

The **Embassy Suites by Hilton Hampton Hotel Convention Center & Spa** (1700 Coliseum Dr., 757/827-8200, www.embassysuites3.hilton.com, $259-589) offers 295 suites with kitchenettes. The hotel has warm decor with an attractive atrium, and the staff provides good, reliable service. There's a restaurant and a nicely appointed fitness center. Spa service is also available.

Information and Services

For additional information on Hampton, visit www.hampton.gov and www.visithampton.com or stop in at the **Hampton Visitor Center** (120 Old Hampton Ln., 757/727-1102, daily 9am-5pm).

Getting There and Around

Hampton is approximately 10 miles southeast of Newport News.

The **Newport News/Williamsburg International Airport** (PHF, 900 Bland Blvd., Newport News, www.flyphf.com) is off I-64 at exit 255B. Hampton is a 20-minute drive from the airport.

Greyhound (2 W. Pembroke Ave., 757/722-9861, www.greyhound.com) offers bus service to Hampton.

Hampton Roads Transit (www.gohrt.com) is a public transit service that serves the Hampton Roads area including Hampton. It currently offers transportation by bus, light rail, ferry, and Paratransit (a service for people with disabilities).

NORFOLK

Norfolk is the second-largest city in Virginia and home to the largest naval base in the world. A longtime navy town, the city has an appealing downtown area and a nice waterfront. The city has undergone a rebirth in recent history that is most evident in the delightful restaurants and shops in the trendy Ghent village, located just northwest of downtown, not far from the Elizabeth River. The city also boasts numerous universities, museums, and a host of other attractions including festivals and shopping.

Sights

CHRYSLER MUSEUM OF ART

The **Chrysler Museum of Art** (1 Memorial Pl., 757/664-6200, www.chrysler.org, Tues.-Sat. 10am-5pm, Sun. noon-5pm, free) is one of Virginia's top art museums, with 50 galleries and 30,000 pieces of artwork including paintings, textiles, ceramics, and bronzes. The art on display spans thousands of years and comes from around the world. A highlight is the glass museum (a museum within a museum) that is entirely devoted to glass art and features 10,000 glass pieces (spanning 3,000 years) and a glass-art studio. Other collections include European painting and sculpture, American painting and sculpture, modern art, a gallery of ancient and non-Western art, contemporary art, photography, and decorative arts.

NORFOLK BOTANICAL GARDEN

Something is always in bloom at the **Norfolk Botanical Garden** (6700 Azalea Garden Rd., 757/441-5830, www.norfolkbotanicalgarden.org, daily 9am-5pm, Apr.-Sept. open until 7pm, $12, children 3-17 $10, seniors/military $10, 2 and under free). This 155-acre garden contains more than 60 different themed areas

Norfolk and Vicinity

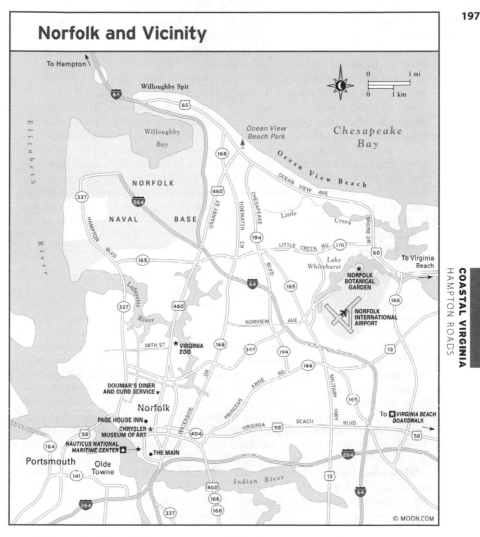

© MOON.COM

and thousands of plants. It is open to visitors year-round. Inside the garden is the three-acre **WOW Children's Garden,** which is geared toward children and families and houses several learning areas.

★ NAUTICUS NATIONAL MARITIME CENTER

The **Nauticus National Maritime Center** (1 Waterside Dr., 757/644-1000, www. nauticus.org, Memorial Day-Labor Day Mon.-Sat. 10am-5pm, Sun. noon-5pm, rest of the year Tues.-Sat. 10am-5pm, Sun. noon-5pm, adults $15.95, children 4-12 $11.50, seniors 55 and over $14.95, military $12.95, 3 and under free) is an incredible interactive science and technology center. They have a great floor plan with a lot of interesting permanent and rotating exhibits including hands-on activities for children (they also offer an escape room). Be sure to catch one of the 3D movies on the third floor.

The **Battleship *Wisconsin*** is one of the prime on-site attractions, and the center features many exhibits related to the ship. It is one of the biggest and also one of the last battleships built by the U.S. Navy. The ship served in World War II, the Korean War, and Operation Desert Storm. Admission to the ship is included with admission to Nauticus, and visitors can take a self-guided tour of the deck. For $35.95 (which includes Nauticus admission), guided **Battleship *Wisconsin* Topside Tours** are available. These tours include the administration area, radio room, main deck with enlisted berthing, the captain's cabin and sleeping quarters, the flag bridge, and the combat engagement center. Participants must be at least eight years old and have the ability to climb stairs to four decks and be comfortable in small spaces. They also offer overnight family/adult stays on the ship during the summer.

The **Hampton Roads Naval Museum** (free admission) is also located inside the Nauticus National Maritime Center on the second floor. The museum is run by the U.S. Navy and details the 237-year history of the Hampton Roads region fleet. Exhibits in the museum include an 18-pounder cannon from 1798, artifacts from the cruiser **CSS *Florida*** and the sloop of war **USS *Cumberland*,** a World War II Mark 7 undersea mine, and a torpedo warhead from a German submarine.

Allow at least 2-4 hours to explore the center and the ship. The facility includes a casual restaurant serving sandwiches, salads, beverages, and snacks.

NAVAL STATION NORFOLK

Norfolk offers a unique opportunity to tour the largest naval base in the world. The **Naval Station Norfolk** sits on 4,300 acres on Sewells Point and is home to 75 ships and 134 aircraft. The 45-minute bus tour leaves from the **Naval Tour and Information Center** (9079 Hampton Blvd., 757/444-7955, www.visitnorfolk.com, adults $10, children 3-11 and seniors over 60 $5, cash only) next to gate 5. The tour rides past destroyers, aircraft carriers, frigates, amphibious assault ships, and the airfield. Tour times change frequently so call for a current schedule.

VIRGINIA ZOO

The **Virginia Zoo** (3500 Granby St., 757/441-2374, www.virginiazoo.org, daily 10am-5pm, ages 12 and over $17.95, 2-11 $14.95, seniors 62 and over $15.95) occupies 53 acres adjacent to Lafayette Park. It opened in 1900 and houses more than 400 animals including elephants, giraffes, orangutans, otters, and birds. The zoo is operated by the City of Norfolk and the Virginia Zoological Society. It offers many educational and children's programs including behind-the-scenes tours.

ST. PAUL'S CHURCH

St. Paul's Church (201 St. Paul's Blvd., 757/627-4353, www.saintpaulsnorfolk.com) is the oldest building in Norfolk, dating back to 1739. A cannonball that was fired into the church on the night before the Revolutionary War began is still lodged in its southwestern wall. Tombstones in the church's historic cemetery date back to the 17th and 18th centuries. Episcopalian services are still held at St. Paul's, and the public is welcome during daylight hours to the churchyard. Self-guided-tour brochures can be found in the vestibule. Guided tours are available upon request.

Recreation
SPECTATOR SPORTS

Harbor Park (150 Park Ave., www.milb.com) is home to the **Norfolk Tides,** the Class AAA affiliate of the Baltimore Orioles. The park is considered one of the best minor league baseball facilities in the country, boasting a practical design and a terrific view of downtown Norfolk. The park opened in 1993 on the Elizabeth River.

The **Norfolk Admirals** (www.norfolkadmirals.com) take to the ice seasonally at the **Scope Arena** to compete in the

1: the Virginia Zoo 2: Nauticus National Maritime Center

ECHL. Consult the website for schedules and tickets.

BEACHES

Beachgoers can enjoy miles of public beach at **Ocean View Beach Park** (100 W. Ocean View Ave., www.oceanviewbeachpark.org). The park offers a boardwalk, bandstand, beach-access ramp for people with disabilities, commercial fishing pier, and open recreation space. There is a bathhouse, and parking is free. Dogs are allowed on leashes in the off-season.

SAILING

A trip with **American Rover Sailing Cruises** (333 Waterside Dr., 757/627-7245, www.americanrover.com, $25-30) is a relaxing way to tour the Hampton Roads Harbor and the Elizabeth River. The *American Rover's* red sails are a distinctive sight in the Hampton Roads area. From April through October, they offer 1.5- and 2-hour narrated cruises. Guests can help out with sailing the ship or just sit back and relax.

Entertainment and Events

Chrysler Hall (215 St. Paul's Blvd., 757/644-6464, www.sevenvenues.com) is the top performing arts venue in the Hampton Roads area. It hosts Broadway shows, concerts, theatrical performances, the **Virginia Symphony** (www.virginiasymphony.org), the **Virginia Arts Festival** (www.vafest. org), and the **Virginia Ballet** (www.vaballet. org).

The **Virginia Opera** (www.vaopera.org, 866/673-7282) performs in three locations throughout Virginia (Norfolk, Richmond, and Fairfax). The Norfolk venue, the **Harrison Opera House** (160 E. Virginia Beach Blvd., 757/627-9545), is a beautifully renovated World War II USO theater that seats just over 1,600 people.

The **Scope Arena** (201 E. Brambleton Ave., 757/644-6464, www.sevenvenues.com) is a 12,000-seat complex that hosts concerts, family shows, and conventions. It is also the home of the **Norfolk Admirals** of the ECHL (East Coast Hockey League).

Norfolk also has a number of quality small venues featuring good nightlife and entertainment. The **NorVa** (317 Monticello Ave., 757/627-4547, www.thenorva.com) is a 1,500-person concert venue that hosts a variety of artists such as Ingrid Michaelson, Citizen Cope, and The Legwarmers. **The Banque** (1849 E. Little Creek Rd., 757/480-3600, www.thebanque.com) is a popular, award-winning country-and-western nightclub and restaurant offering a large dance floor and well-known artists.

Norfolk Festevents (757/441-2345, www.festevents.org) presents 10 months of events annually, including concerts and festivals in **Town Point Park** (on the Elizabeth River in the center of the business district in downtown Norfolk) and **Ocean View Beach Park** (at the end of Granby St. at Ocean View Ave.). One of the most popular events, the **Norfolk Harborfest** is held annually for four days at the beginning of June and attracts more than 100,000 people. This large festival covers more than three miles on the Norfolk waterfront and offers visitors three sailboat parades, tall ships, the largest fireworks display on the East Coast, and seemingly endless entertainment. Another Festevent, the **Norfolk Waterfront Jazz Festival** is a two-day festival held in late August. Tickets are $30-200.

The **Town Point Virginia Fall Wine Festival** is held in Town Point Park for two days in October. More than 200 Virginia wines are featured. Tickets start at $25 and can be purchased online.

Shopping

The **MacArthur Center** (300 Monticello Ave., 757/627-6000, www.shopmacarthur. com) is a large shopping mall with close to 150 retail stores and restaurants. There is also a movie complex.

A trendy shopping area worth checking out is **The Palace Shops and The Palace Station** (301 W. 21st St., 757/622-9999, www.

ghentnorfolk.org) in the historic Ghent neighborhood. This is a trendy, three-block restaurant-and-retail area near downtown Norfolk.

Food

★ **Freemason Abbey Restaurant** (209 W. Freemason St., 757/622-3966, www. freemasonabbey.com, Mon.-Thurs. 11am-9:30pm, Fri.-Sat. 11am-10:30pm, Sun. 9:30am-9:30pm, $8-32) is a local favorite in downtown Norfolk for fresh seafood, steak, and pasta. It is housed in a renovated church built in 1873 and has been a restaurant since 1989. The atmosphere is friendly, elegant, and casual with beautiful decor that retains a church-like feel yet has cozy seating. Try the award-winning she-crab soup. Reservations are highly recommended on the weekends.

Saltine (100 E. Main St., 757/763-6280, www.saltinenorfolk.com, daily 11:30am-3pm and 5pm-close, Sat. 10am-3pm, $8-40) is a terrific seafood restaurant located on the street level in the **Hilton Norfolk The Main** hotel. This hip downtown spot has an inviting atmosphere and exposed brick and tile. They use locally sourced ingredients and offer selections from their raw bar, whole fish, shellfish, and a handful of farm-based entrees.

Seafood lovers can also get their fix at **AW Shucks Raw Bar & Grill** (2200 Colonial Ave., 757/664-9117, www.awshucksrawbar. com, daily 11am-1:30am, $9-25). They seem to be firm believers that any meal can include seafood. Try their burger topped with lump crab, or a po'boy; both are well seasoned, huge, and delicious. Finding the place can be a bit tricky—look on 22nd Street in the plaza rather than along Colonial Avenue. The staff is friendly and attentive, and the atmosphere is social. This is a good choice for reasonably priced, yet tasty food. There are also plenty of nonseafood selections.

Doumar's Barbeque & Curb Service (1919 Monticello Ave., 757/627-4163, www. doumars.com, Mon.-Thurs. 8am-11pm, Fri.-Sat. 8am-12:30am, under $10) is a legendary diner that was featured on the show *Diners,* *Drive-Ins and Dives*. Its origin was an ice-cream stand that opened in 1907 in Ocean View Amusement Park. The business moved to its current location in 1934 and is still owned by the same family. Famous for barbecue and ice cream, they bake their own ice-cream cones in the original cone machine. Take a seat inside the diner, or dine from your car and enjoy their carhop service. This is a fun, genuine, old-school diner that is inexpensive and has a great history.

Accommodations

$100-200

There are many chain hotels in Norfolk. A few stand out for above-average accommodations, good service, and proximity to downtown attractions and the airport, such as the **Courtyard Norfolk Downtown** (520 Plume St., 757/963-6000, www.marriott.com, $149-199) and the **Holiday Inn Express Hotel & Suites Norfolk International Airport** (1157 N. Military Hwy., 757/455-5055, www. ihg.com, $108-210).

In addition to the selection of large chain hotels, there are some very nice bed-and-breakfasts and historic hotels in Norfolk. The **Page House Inn** (323 Fairfax Ave., 757/625-5033, www.pagehouseinn.com, $183-253) is a historic bed-and-breakfast (circa 1899) next to the Chrysler Museum of Art in the Ghent Historic District. This stately redbrick mansion has four guest rooms and three guest suites, decorated with 19th-century furniture, antiques, and art. A delicious full breakfast is served each morning, and refreshments are served each afternoon. The innkeepers are warm and welcoming.

OVER $200

The **Hilton Norfolk The Main** (100 E. Main St., 757/763-6200, www3.hilton.com, $289-2,500) is a wonderful upscale hotel choice in an excellent downtown location. They offer 300 guest rooms, 39 meeting rooms (including a conference center), indoor pool, fitness center, and three restaurants that include a roof lounge. Self-parking is $20, valet $26.

Information and Services

For additional information on the Norfolk area, visit www.visitnorfolktoday.com.

Getting There and Around

Norfolk is 16 miles south of Hampton.

The **Norfolk International Airport** (ORF, 2200 Norview Ave., www.norfolkairport.com) is convenient for those traveling by air to the Norfolk area. It is one mile east of I-64 (exit 279) and just minutes from downtown Norfolk.

The city is serviced by **Amtrak** (280 Park Ave., www.amtrak.com) rail service and by **Greyhound** (701 Monticello Ave., 757/625-7500, www.greyhound.com) bus service.

Norfolk Electric Transit (www.virginia. org) is a free commuting service that links many downtown attractions. It is part of **Hampton Roads Transit,** which also offers additional bus routes around Norfolk (www. gohrt.com, $2) and the **Paddlewheel Ferry** (www.gohrt.com, $2) service on three passenger paddle-wheel boats. Each boat holds 150 passengers and runs between downtown Norfolk (at the Waterside) and Portsmouth. The ferry operates every 30 minutes. Extended service kicks in during peak summer weeks. Passengers are allowed to bring bicycles aboard.

Virginia Beach

Virginia Beach is the state's premier beach destination. It is a thriving, year-round city with more than 442,000 full-time residents and an influx of nearly 19 million visitors annually. *King Neptune* (31st St. and the Boardwalk), a 34-foot-tall bronze statue designed by Paul DiPasquale and cast by Zhang Cong, seems to be the official Virginia Beach greeter. He stands on the boardwalk at the entrance to Neptune Park and invites visitors to enjoy the wonders of the ocean responsibly.

The resort area runs along more than 20 miles of beach, which is maintained and replenished on a regular basis. The area is booming with commercialism and has more than its share of touristy gift shops and oversize hotels but also offers a variety of attractions, events, parks, and wildlife refuges. The farther north you travel, the quieter it gets, and the northern reaches are mostly residential.

The three-mile-long boardwalk is the center of activity, and the aquarium, water sports, fishing, and parks keep visitors coming back year after year. Accommodations are plentiful but also book quickly during the peak summer season, especially those right on the

beach. The beach is busiest not only in the summer but also during March and April, when thousands of college students arrive for spring break. Keep this in mind when planning your trip since it may be best to avoid these windows unless you are joining in the fun.

Tourism in Virginia Beach began with the opening of the first hotel in 1884. The boardwalk was built just four years later. The strip has been growing ever since, and a few historic landmarks, such as the Cavalier Hotel (circa 1927), still stand today.

A population boom in the 1980s resulted in some bad press for the beach area, which experienced some pains from the onslaught of visitors and the hard partying that came with them. Since then, the municipality has made a concerted effort and spent millions of dollars to revamp the beach's reputation as a family resort. They've succeeded on most levels by encouraging more high-end businesses to come to the beach and by making the main thoroughfares more visually pleasing to visitors with fresh lighting and landscaping. The area is now known for its excellence in environmental health,

Virginia Beach

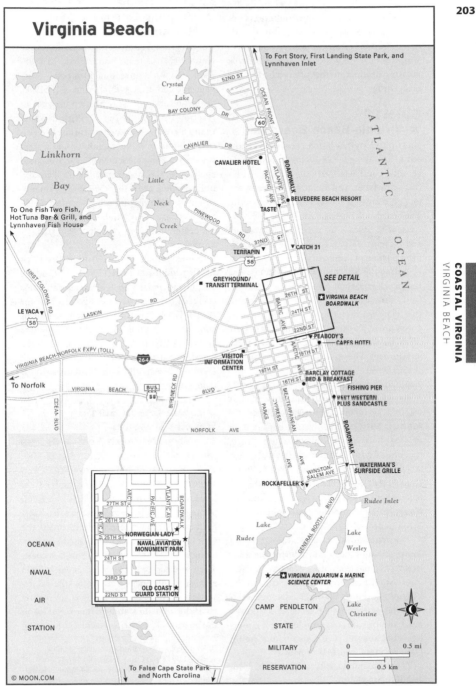

To Fort Story, First Landing State Park, and Lynnhaven Inlet

Crystal Lake

52ND ST

BAY COLONY DR

60

CAVALIER DR

Linkhorn

CAVALIER HOTEL

Little

Bay

Neck

BELVEDERE BEACH RESORT

To One Fish Two Fish, Hot Tuna Bar & Grill, and Lynnhaven Fish House

PINEWOOD RD

Creek

TASTE

32ND ST

CATCH 31

TERRAPIN

58

SEE DETAIL

GREYHOUND/ TRANSIT TERMINAL

26TH ST

VIRGINIA BEACH BOARDWALK

RD

BALTIC AVE

24TH ST

LE YACA

58

LASKIN

22ND ST

PEABODY'S

CAPES HOTEL

VIRGINIA BEACH-NORFOLK EXPY (TOLL)

264

19TH ST

VISITOR INFORMATION CENTER

18TH ST

BARCLAY COTTAGE BED & BREAKFAST

To Norfolk

VIRGINIA BEACH

BUS. 58

BLVD

16TH ST

FISHING PIER

BIRDNECK RD

PARKS AVE

CYPRESS AVE

BEST WESTERN PLUS SANDCASTLE

NORFOLK AVE

MEDITERRANEAN AVE

BOARDWALK

WATERMAN'S SURFSIDE GRILLE

WINSTON-SALEM AVE

ROCKAFELLER'S

Rudee Inlet

GENERAL BOOTH BLVD

Lake Rudee

Lake Wesley

OCEANA

27TH ST

BALTIC AVE

ARCTIC ST

PACIFIC AVE

ATLANTIC AVE

BOARDWALK

26TH ST

NORWEGIAN LADY

NAVAL

25TH ST

NAVAL AVIATION MONUMENT PARK

24TH ST

VIRGINIA AQUARIUM & MARINE SCIENCE CENTER

AIR

23RD ST

OLD COAST GUARD STATION

22ND ST

CAMP PENDLETON

Lake Christine

STATION

STATE

MILITARY

0   0.5 mi

RESERVATION

0   0.5 km

To False Cape State Park and North Carolina

and as more and more sporting events are booked for the beach, it is becoming a destination for the fitness-minded. In a nutshell, Virginia Beach is a modern and affordable vacation destination that offers a little bit of everything.

SIGHTS
★ Virginia Beach Boardwalk

No trip to Virginia Beach is complete without a stroll along the 28-foot-wide boardwalk running parallel to the ocean for three miles (between 1st St. and 42nd St.) on one of the longest recreational beach areas in the world. The boardwalk is perfect for getting some exercise with a view. There are lanes for walkers and bicycles, and many running events utilize a portion of the boardwalk on their route, including the **Shamrock Marathon** (www.shamrockmarathon.com) and the **Rock 'n' Roll Marathon Series** (www.runrocknroll.com). The boardwalk is adorned with benches, grassy areas, play areas, amusement parks, arcades, hotels, restaurants, shops, and other entertainment. There is also a large fishing pier at 15th Street.

A handful of monuments along the boardwalk pay tribute to U.S. military and first responders, including the **Naval Aviation Monument** (25th St.), which pays tribute to Virginia Beach's deep aviation heritage; the **Law Enforcement Memorial** (35th St.), which honors the Virginia Beach Police Department, Sheriff's Office, and state and federal law enforcement agencies; and the **Navy SEAL Monument** (38th St.) honoring Virginia Beach Navy SEALs.

The *Norwegian Lady* statue (16th St.) commemorates the lives lost during the shipwreck of a boat from Moss, Norway. A sister statue stands in Moss. At 13th Street is the **Virginia Legends Walk,** a landscaped walkway that pays tribute to some of Virginia's most famous citizens, including Thomas Jefferson, Robert E. Lee, Captain John Smith, Ella Fitzgerald, and Arthur Ashe.

There are public restrooms at 17th, 24th, and 30th Streets.

★ Virginia Aquarium & Marine Science Center

The **Virginia Aquarium & Marine Science Center** (717 General Booth Blvd., 757/385-3474, www.virginiaaquarium.com, daily 9am-6pm, adults $24.95, children 3-11 $19.95, seniors 62 and over $22.95) is a must-visit attraction in Virginia Beach. With its more than 800,000 gallons of aquariums, live animal habitats, numerous exhibits, and a giant six-story 3-D movie screen ($7.95), you could spend several hours or an entire day here and not get bored. More than 300 species are represented in numerous educational exhibits, and there are many hands-on experiences in the center, including a touch pool of friendly animals.

A great attraction is the **Adventure Park at Virginia Aquarium** (757/385-4947, adults $59, 13 and under $49). It offers adventure for children over five years of age and also for adults. The park is a trail of wooden platforms connected by zip lines and bridges. A play area is also available for younger children. This is a wonderful attraction when you need a break from the beach, and kids of all ages find it compelling.

Virginia Beach Surf & Rescue Museum

The **Virginia Beach Surf & Rescue Museum** (2401 Atlantic Ave., 757/422-1587, www.vbsurfrescuemuseum.org, Tues.-Sat. 10am-5pm, $1, children 6 and under free) houses more than 1,800 artifacts and 1,000 photographs that honor Virginia's maritime heritage. Two galleries relate the history of the U.S. Life-Saving and Coast Guard Services, along with shipwrecks off the Virginia coast. The building itself was constructed in 1903 and is the only one of five original life-saving stations built that year along the Virginia coast that remains standing. It now resides on the boardwalk at 24th Street, and the rooftop

1: *King Neptune* designed by Paul DiPasquale and cast by Zhang Cong 2: The Old Cape Henry Lighthouse 3: Virginia Aquarium & Marine Science Center

"Towercam" enables guests to look at ships in the Atlantic.

The Old Cape Henry Lighthouse

The Old Cape Henry Lighthouse (583 Atlantic Ave., Fort Story, 757/422-9421, www.preservationvirginia.org, Jan.-Mar. 15 daily 10am-4pm, Mar. 16-Dec. daily 10am-5pm, adults $10, students $8, senior 60+ and military $9, under 42 inches tall free) is part of the Fort Story military base. It once protected the entryway to the Chesapeake Bay at the northern end of Virginia Beach. Construction of the lighthouse was authorized by George Washington as one of the first acts of the newly organized federal government, and it was the first federal construction project. Alexander Hamilton oversaw its construction. The lighthouse was completed in 1792. This octagonal sandstone edifice remains one of the oldest surviving lighthouses in the country and is a National Historic Landmark. Visitors can climb to the top of the lighthouse and enjoy commanding views of the Chesapeake Bay and the Atlantic Ocean. Guided tours of the grounds are also available, and there's a gift shop. To reach the lighthouse, you must drive through a security gate at Fort Story. Photo identification is required to enter, and car searches are frequently made.

RECREATION

Parks and Wildlife

First Landing State Park (2500 Shore Dr., 757/412-2300, www.first-landing-state-park.org, $7) is the site where the first permanent English settlers landed in 1607. This 2,888-acre park offers 20 miles of hiking trails, biking, fishing, a boat ramp, and camping.

Mount Trashmore Park (310 Edwin Dr., 757/385-2995, www.vbgov.com, free) is a famous land-reuse park that was built on an old landfill. The 165-acre park was created by compressing multiple layers of waste and clean soil. The park includes playgrounds, picnic areas, volleyball courts, and a large skate park.

Back Bay National Wildlife Refuge (4005 Sandpiper Rd., 757/301-7329, www.fws.gov, $5) includes approximately 9,000 acres of beach, marsh, and woods. It is a haven for many migratory birds. There is both fresh- and saltwater fishing, a canoe and kayak launch, biking, and hiking.

False Cape State Park (4001 Sandpiper Rd., 757/426-7128, www.dcr.virginia.gov, $4) is an ocean-to-brackish-water area that is only accessible by boat, bike, or on foot. The land trail leading in is five miles long. A tram from the Back Bay National Wildlife Refuge visitors center is also available (call for a schedule). Primitive camping is allowed.

Boat Ramps

The **Owl Creek Boat Ramp** (701 General Booth Blvd.) is a free launch facility next to the Virginia Aquarium & Marine Science Center. Other boat ramps include **First Landing State Park** (2500 Shore Dr., www.first-landing-state-park.org), **Bubba's Marina** (3323 Shore Dr., www.bubbasseafoodrestaurant.com), and **Munden Point Park** (2001 Pefley Ln., www.vbgov.com).

Kayaking and Boat Tours

There are many local outfitters in the Virginia Beach area offering seasonal kayak tours, rentals, and ecotours. **Chesapean Outdoors** (757/961-0447, www.chesapean.com) provides an exciting guided dolphin kayak tour ($60) where guests can paddle with bottlenose dolphins at the north end of Virginia Beach. They also offer guided sunset paddle tours ($60) and rentals (SUP, one hour $20, two hours $30; single kayak, one hour $20, two hours $30; tandem kayak, one hour $30, two hours $40). **Kayak Nature Tours** (757/480-1999, www.kayaknaturetours.net) also has guided dolphin kayak tours (2.5 hours, $62) and flatwater guided trips (2.5 hours, $53).

Explore the creeks near the **Virginia Aquarium & Marine Science Center** (www.virginiaaquarium.com) on a guided pontoon boat, or ride along with aquarium

The Great Dismal Swamp

The **Great Dismal Swamp National Wildlife Refuge** (3100 Desert Rd., Suffolk, free) is a 112,000-acre refuge southwest of Virginia Beach. The refuge is primarily forested wetlands and is home to numerous birds and animals. It also encompasses 3,100-acre Lake Drummond, which is the largest natural lake in Virginia. One hundred miles of trails are open daily for hiking, walking, and biking (sunrise to sunset).

Although humans first occupied the swamp as much as 13,000 years ago, there was not much interest in the area until Lake Drummond was discovered by William Drummond (a governor of North Carolina) in 1665. The area was later surveyed, and the state line between Virginia and North Carolina was drawn through it in 1728. The name of the land was recorded as the Great Dismal (dismal was a common term at the time for a swamp). Shortly thereafter, George Washington visited the swamp and developed the Dismal Swamp Land Company, with designs on draining and logging parts of it. The name "great" was likely added to the swamp's name due to its large size. Logging continued in the swamp until 1976, with all parts of the swamp having been logged one or more times.

The dense forests in the swamp have traditionally been a refuge for animals but have also been used by people for a similar reason. The swamp was at one time a haven to people fleeing slavery, and as a result, the swamp was the first National Wildlife Refuge to be recognized officially as part of the Underground Railroad.

Today, more than 200 species of birds live in the refuge either permanently or seasonally. Perhaps an even more impressive fact is that 96 species of butterflies have also been recorded here. More than 47 mammals live in the refuge, including black bears, bobcats, white-tailed deer, river otters, and mink.

For more information, visit www.fws.gov or contact the park headquarters at 757/986-3705.

staff on a 90-minute seasonal dolphin-watching excursion (adults $22.95, children 3-11 $16.95, under 3 free). The aquarium also offers ocean collections boat trips (for the same price), during which a variety of sea creatures are brought aboard, and several other trips (including a Craft Brews Cruise).

Kayaking and SUP tours are also available through **Back Bay Getaways** (757/589-1069, www.backbaygetaways.com, $40-65), and kayak tours are available through **Ocean Eagle Kayak** (757/589-1766, www.oceaneaglekayak.com, $75).

Fishing

The Virginia Beach coastline and inshore waterways are thoroughfares for many species of fish, including tuna, bluefin, blue marlin, Atlantic mackerel, red drum, and flounder. Private fishing charters are available through a number of companies including **Dockside Seafood and Fishing Center** (3311 Shore Dr., 757/481-4545, www.fishingvabeach.com), **Rudee Tours** (200 Winston Salem Ave., 757/425-3400, www.rudeetours.com), **Virginia Beach Fishing Center** (200 Winston Salem Ave., 757/491-8000, www.virginiafishing.com), and **Fisherman's Wharf Marina** (524 Winston Salem Ave., 757/428-2111, www.vabeach.com).

There are also several fishing piers that are great for dropping a line, including the **Virginia Beach Fishing Pier** (15th St.), the **Little Island Fishing Pier** (3820 S. Sandpiper Rd., www.vbgov.com), and the **Sea Gull Fishing Pier** at the Chesapeake Bay Bridge-Tunnel (www.cbbt.com).

Amusement Park

The **Atlantic Fun Park** (233 15th St., 757/422-0467, www.atlanticfunpark.com) has a yesteryear vibe that is nostalgic for parents and pure fun for the kiddies. The park offers thrill rides, family rides, and kiddie rides, including a 100-foot Ferris wheel. Single-ride tickets ($3.30-5.50) or unlimited-ride arm-bands ($24.99-39.99) can be purchased.

ENTERTAINMENT AND EVENTS

Endless entertainment can be found on the Virginia Beach boardwalk, including concerts, athletic events, and performances.

Nightlife

Virginia Beach doesn't sleep when the sun goes down. In fact, in the summer it doesn't seem to sleep at all. Live music can be found at the **Hot Tuna Bar & Grill** (2817 Shore Dr., 757/481-2888, www.hottunavb.com). They offer Top 40 dance music daily. Another dance bar is **Peabody's** (209 21st St., 757/422-6212, www.peabodysvirginiabeach.com). They've been around since 1967 and have one of the largest dance floors in the area.

If a game of pool is more your speed, try **Q-Master II Billiards** (5612 Princess Anne Rd., 757/499-8900, www.q-masters.com). They are the premier billiards room in the region and have 70 tables. They also host competitions.

Those wishing to kick back for some live music (country, reggae, folk, etc.) should check out **Elevation 27** (600 Nevan Rd., 757/716-4028, www.elevation27.com). They offer live entertainment and a large menu from **The Jewish Mother** that includes delicious deli sandwiches. If comedy is more up your alley, catch a show at the **Funny Bone Comedy Club & Restaurant** (217 Central Park Ave., 757/213-5555, www.vb.funnybone.com). They host well-known comics and offer tables with a full dinner and bar menu during the show. Shows are for ages 21 and older.

Events

Some popular annual events include the **American Music Festival** (5th St. and Atlantic Ave., www.beachstreetusa.com, starting at $25), one of the largest outdoor music events on the East Coast. It runs for three days over Labor Day weekend and features local and national artists. Sounds of rock, jazz, country, blues, and R&B flow out to the oceanfront from a huge stage on the beach at 5th Street and from stages in many parks along the water. Another favorite is the **Boardwalk Art Show and Festival** (http://virginiamoca.org), held annually for four days in mid-June. This event began in 1956 and is one of the oldest and best outdoor art shows on the East Coast. It is held on the boardwalk between 17th and 24th Streets.

Those looking for a little something different can take in a **sand wrestling** (www.sandwrestling.com) competition. Sand wrestling, which is also known as beach wrestling, is a version of traditional wrestling. Established as an international style of amateur wrestling in 2005, it is quickly gaining popularity and offers competition for males and females of all ages.

Runners won't want to miss the annual **Shamrock Marathon** (www.shamrockmarathon.com) weekend in mid-March. The Shamrock Marathon has been around since 1973 and is now a premier running event and Boston Marathon qualifier.

FOOD
American

Firebrew Bar & Grill (1253 Nimmo Pkwy., Ste. 117, 757/689-2800, www.fire-brew.com, Mon.-Thurs. 11am-10pm, Fri.-Sat. 11am-11pm, Sun. 11am-9pm, $8-26) is a casual bar and grill with a few twists. Most menu items (flatbread, steak, tacos, etc.) are prepared on an open-flame fire deck, and the restaurant proudly states that they do not use microwaves or fryers. Their extensive bar includes local craft brews and a self-service wine station.

Terrapin (3102 Holly Rd., 757/321-6688, www.terrapinvb.com, Sun.-Thurs. 5pm-9pm, Fri.-Sat. 5pm-10pm, $17-35) supports sustainable organic farmers and is committed to using fresh ingredients with no hydrogenated oils or high-fructose corn syrup. Their menu includes homemade pasta (including a delicious lobster and corn ravioli), selections such as ribeye and chicken for the table, salads, seafood, and a cheeseburger. They also offer an extensive wine menu.

If you're looking for a good place to grab a sandwich, stop in **Taste** (36th St. and Pacific Ave., 757/422-3399, www.taste.online, daily 9am-7pm, $4-14). This pleasant sandwich shop and specialty food store, a block from the beach, has ample seating, good variety, and a friendly atmosphere. They also sell wine, cheese, and other gourmet snacks, and at times there's even a little farmers market outside.

French

★ **Le Yaca French Restaurant** (741 First Colonial Rd., Ste. 107, 757/500-4773, www.leyacawilliamsburg.com, Tues.-Thurs. 11:30am-2:30pm and 5pm-9pm, Fri.-Sat. 11:30am-2:30pm and 5pm-10pm, Sun. 11am-2:30pm and 5pm-9pm, $16-80) is an elegant and delicious departure at the beach from traditional seafood and burgers. This contemporary French restaurant is the second U.S. location (the first is in Williamsburg) and offers traditional French and modern selections for brunch, lunch, and dinner. They offer a prix fixe menu, chef's tasting menu and an à la carte menu. Don't let the strip mall location deter you; this is a great place for a date or celebration. Fresh flowers and delightful service add to the wonderful experience.

Seafood

Catch 31 (3001 Atlantic Ave., 757/213-3472, www.catch31.com, Mon.-Fri. 6am-2am, Sat.-Sun. 7am-2am, $14-49) is inside the Hilton Virginia Beach Oceanfront and is one of the finest restaurants along the main strip. They are known for offering at least 15 types of fresh fish, and their signature dish is the seafood towers that include crab legs, mussels, lobster, and shrimp. The restaurant's high ceilings, ocean-blue walls, and indoor/outdoor bar add to the ambience. If the weather is nice, dine outside on their beachfront terrace. They serve breakfast, lunch, and dinner.

A restaurant popular with Virginia Beach residents is **Rockafeller's** (308 Mediterranean Ave., 757/442-5654, www.rockafellers.com, Mon.-Sat. 11am-10pm, Sun. 10am-10pm, $7-33). This dependable local favorite offers seafood, steaks, pasta, and salads in a large three-story home on Rudee Inlet. Double-decker porches provide lovely seating, or you can dine inside. There's a bar and raw bar and nice views from indoors as well.

Waterman's Surfside Grille (5th St. and Atlantic Ave., 757/428-3644, www.watermans.com, Mon.-Sat. 11am-10pm, Sun. 9am-10pm, $8-35) is one of the few freestanding restaurants left on the strip that isn't connected to a hotel. It offers a lively atmosphere, good seafood, and outstanding cocktails.

ACCOMMODATIONS

$200-300

The **Belvedere Beach Resort** (3603 Atlantic Ave., 800/425-0612, www.belvederebeachresort.com, $209-297) is a privately owned hotel on the oceanfront on the northern end of Virginia Beach. The lightfilled, wood-paneled rooms offer private balconies with views of the beach. The hotel has adult-size bicycles for guest use and direct access to the boardwalk. Rooms are quiet, and the staff is very friendly and helpful. The **Wave Trolley** stops in front of the hotel for easy access to many places on the beachfront. This is not a luxurious resort, but a very pleasant, comfortable choice in a fantastic location. The hotel is open seasonally, normally April through the beginning of October. Minimum stays may be required. Coffeepots are available upon request.

The **Capes Hotel** (2001 Atlantic Ave., 757/428-5421, www.capeshotel.com, $219-329, closed Oct.-Mar.) is a pleasant oceanfront hotel on the boardwalk. It has an indoor pool with a view of the ocean and nicely kept grounds. The hotel is convenient to all the beach attractions. The 59 oceanfront rooms are cozy rather than large, but all are comfortable with an airy feel and good views. The service is also very dependable. There is a small café on-site with an oceanfront patio. This is not a luxurious resort, but it doesn't attempt to be; it's a good value in a great location, with a friendly staff.

Another good value on the beachfront is the **Best Western Plus Sandcastle Beachfront Hotel** (1307 Atlantic Ave., 757/428-2828, www.bestwestern.com, $212-374). This pleasant oceanfront hotel features a heated indoor pool, free breakfast buffet, free parking, and a fitness center. There is also a restaurant on-site.

Over $300

★ **The Cavalier Hotel** (4200 Atlantic Ave., 757/425-8555, www.cavalierhotel.com, $299 and up during off-season, $499 and up in peak season) is a historic hotel that opened in 1927. A Virginia Beach icon and a National Register of Historic Places property, the grand hotel was built on a hill overlooking the ocean and has welcomed 10 U.S. presidents, celebrities such as Frank Sinatra, Judy Garland, and Bette Davis, and international dignitaries. It was also used as a naval training center during World War II. The hotel completed a $70 million renovation in 2017, at which point it became a member of Marriott International's Autograph Collection. Today the hotel portrays the bygone age of grand hotels as it sits majestically above the hubbub of activity on the oceanfront. The Cavalier Hotel offers 85 guest rooms and suites, three restaurants, a spa, a bourbon distillery and tasting room, a museum, ballroom, meeting space, poolside vistas and loggias, a fitness center, and electric-car-charging stations.

The imposing 21-story **Hilton Virginia Beach Oceanfront** (3001 Atlantic Ave., 757/213-3000, www.hiltonvb.com, $349-459) offers oceanfront luxury with amenities such as a rooftop infinity pool, an indoor pool, the Sky Bar, a fully equipped fitness center, and bicycle rentals. There are 289 modern rooms and suites, outfitted with beach decor and offering a choice of city or ocean views. There are several on-site restaurants and convenient parking ($10 for self-park and $16 for valet per day).

Bed-and-Breakfast

The ★ **Barclay Cottage Bed and Breakfast** (400 16th St., 757/422-1956, www.barclaycottage.com, $179-309) is a beautiful B&B offering five comfortable guest rooms. Three rooms have private bathrooms, and two others share bath facilities. Each room is individually decorated with its own colors and theme (such as nautical or floral). The white, two-story, porch-wrapped cottage (complete

The Cavalier Hotel

with rocking chairs) is within walking distance of many attractions and a few blocks from the beach.

House and Condo Rentals

There are several local real estate offices in Virginia Beach that offer rentals for a week or longer. **Sandbridge Realty** (800/933-4800, www.sandbridge.com) is in southern Virginia Beach and offers a property-search feature on its website, as does **Siebert Realty** (877/422-2200, www.siebert-realty.com), which is also in southern Virginia Beach.

CAMPING

First Landing State Park (2500 Shore Dr., 757/412-2300, www.dcr.virginia.gov, $30-46) on the north end of Virginia Beach offers 200-plus beach campsites near the Chesapeake Bay. There are also 20 cabins for rent ($151-173).

INFORMATION AND SERVICES

For additional information on Virginia Beach, visit www.virginiabeach.com or stop by the **Visitor Information Center** on Parks Avenue (2100 Parks Ave., 800/822-3224, daily 9am-5pm) or in First Landing State Park (2500 Shore Dr., 757/412-2300, daily 9am-4:30pm). There are also two kiosks run by the Visitor Information Center that are available from May to September; they are on the Boardwalk at 17th Street and on Atlantic Avenue at 24th Street.

GETTING THERE

Most people arrive in Virginia Beach by car. I-64 connects with the Virginia Beach-Norfolk Expressway (I-264), which leads to the oceanfront at Virginia Beach.

The **Norfolk International Airport** (ORF, 2200 Norview Ave., Norfolk, www.norfolkairport.com) is approximately 17 miles from Virginia Beach. Daily flights are available through multiple commercial carriers.

Rail service does not run to Virginia Beach, but **Amtrak** (800/872-7245, www.amtrak.com) serves Newport News with connecting bus service to 19th Street and Pacific Avenue in Virginia Beach. Reservations are required. Bus service is also available to Virginia Beach on **Greyhound** (971 Virginia Beach Blvd., 757/422-2998, www.greyhound.com).

GETTING AROUND

There are plenty of paid parking lots in Virginia Beach. The cost per day ranges about $7-10. Municipal parking lots are located at 2nd Street, 4th Street, 9th Street, 19th Street, 25th Street, and 31st Street. **Hampton Roads Transit** (www.gohrt.com, $2-4) operates about a dozen bus routes in Virginia Beach.

Virginia's Eastern Shore

Visiting Virginia's Eastern Shore can be a bit like stepping back in time. The long, narrow, flat peninsula that separates the Chesapeake Bay from the Atlantic Ocean has a feel that's very different from the rest of the state. The pace is more relaxed, the people take time to chat, and much of the cuisine centers on extraordinary seafood fished right out the back door.

Traveling from the Virginia Beach area to the Eastern Shore requires passage over and through one of the great marvels of the East Coast. The **Chesapeake Bay Bridge-Tunnel** (www.cbbt.com) spanning the mouth of the Chesapeake Bay is an engineering masterpiece. The four-lane, 20-mile-long bridge-and-tunnel system is a toll route and part of US Route 13. It takes vehicles over a series of bridges and through two-mile-long tunnels that travel under the shipping channels. Five-acre artificial islands are located at each end of the two tunnels, and a fishing pier and restaurant/gift shop were built on one.

Upon arrival on the Eastern Shore, you are greeted by endless acres of marsh, water, and wildlife refuge areas. Agriculture and fishing are the primary sources of revenue on the peninsula, and tourism in the towns provides a nice supplement.

A handful of charming towns dot the coastline on both bodies of water, and most have roots prior to the Civil War. In fact, many beautiful 19th-century homes have been refurbished, as have the churches, schools, and public buildings.

The first town on the southern end of the Eastern Shore is Cape Charles, and the northernmost is Chincoteague Island. Bus transportation runs between the two via **Star Transit** (757/787-8322, www.vatransit.org, Mon.-Fri.).

CAPE CHARLES

Cape Charles is the southernmost town on Virginia's Eastern Shore, 10 miles from the Chesapeake Bay Bridge-Tunnel. The town was founded in 1884 as the southern terminus of the New York, Philadelphia, & Norfolk Railroad. It was also a popular steamship port for vessels transporting freight and passengers across the Chesapeake Bay to Norfolk.

Today, Cape Charles is primarily a vacation town. It is not large, nor is it particularly well known, but this is part of the charm. It offers a quiet historic district, sandy beaches, golfing, boating, and other outdoor recreation.

Sights

The **Historic District** (757/331-3259) in Cape Charles is approximately seven square blocks and boasts one of the largest groups of turn-of-the-20th-century buildings on the East Coast. The area offers a pleasant atmosphere of shops and eateries near the Chesapeake Bay waterfront. State Route 184 runs right into the historic district and ends at the beach.

Cape Charles Beach (Bay Ave., www. capecharles.org) has a pleasant, uncrowded atmosphere and wonderful sunsets over the Chesapeake Bay. The beach is clean, family oriented, and free to the public. The water is generally shallow with little to no waves.

The **Cape Charles Museum and Welcome Center** (814 Randolph Ave., 757/331-1008, www.smallmuseum.org, mid-Apr.-Nov. Mon.-Fri. 10am-2pm, Sat. 10am-5pm, Sun. 1pm-5pm, free, donations appreciated) is a nice place to begin your visit to Cape Charles. It is located in an old powerhouse and has a large generator embedded in the floor. Visitors can view boat models, pictures, and decoys as they learn about the history of Cape Charles.

Kiptopeke State Park (3540 Kiptopeke Dr., 757/331-2267, www.dcr.virginia.gov, daily 6am-10pm, $7) is approximately 10 miles south of the Historic District in Cape Charles. It encompasses a half mile of sandy beach open to the public during the summer. There are no lifeguards on duty, so swimming is at your own risk. There are also hiking trails, a fishing pier, a boat ramp, and a full-service campground. The park is known for its robust bird population. Many bird studies are conducted here by the U.S. Fish and Wildlife Service. Some of the birds encountered in the park include hawks, kestrels, and ospreys.

Recreation

SouthEast Expeditions (239 Mason Ave., 757/331-6190, www.southeastexpeditions. com, starting at $45) offers kayaking tours in Cape Charles. Trips of different lengths are available, and paddlers of all experience levels are welcome. They also rent kayaks (starting at $20) and SUPs (starting at $20).

Golfers will enjoy the beautiful atmosphere and two challenging courses designed by Arnold Palmer and Jack Nicklaus at the **Bay Creek Golf Club** (1 Clubhouse Way, 757/331-8620, www.baycreek.net, $35-120).

A big annual event in October in the Cape Charles area is the **Eastern Shore Birding & Wildlife Festival** (www. chesapeakenetwork.org). The area is one of the most important East Coast migration stops for millions of birds each year, and festivalgoers can observe the spectacle firsthand in early October.

Food

★ **The Oyster Farm Seafood Eatery** (500 Marina Village Circle, 757/331-8660, www.theoysterfarmatkingscreek.com, Mon.,Wed., Thurs., and Sun. 11:30am-9pm, Fri.-Sat. 11:30am-10pm, $14-36) is the top choice for food and ambience in Cape Charles. The modern beachfront building offers a trendy "water-to-table" eating experience in a comfortable waterfront dining room. The food is delicious, with many creative seafood items and land entrées as well. The scene is semi-upscale with a lively clientele. This is a great place to bring the family or relax with friends for an unrushed and tasty meal. There is a beautiful waterfront patio and lawn games for entertainment.

The Bay Creek Resort's **Coach House Tavern** (1 Clubhouse Way, 757/331-8630, www.baycreek.net, Sun.-Thurs. 7am-8pm, Fri.-Sat. 7am-9pm, winter hours Mon. 8am-8pm, Tues.-Thurs. 8am-5pm, Fri. 8am-9pm, Sat. 7:30am-9pm, Sun. 7:30am-8pm, $6-24) is located at the golf clubhouse and overlooks the golf course. The rustic ambience of the beautifully appointed building is due in part to the use of reclaimed wood and bricks from a farmhouse that once stood on the property. The restaurant offers traditional pub fare with exquisite soups and sandwiches. There is patio seating, and the atmosphere is upscale and inviting.

For a quick and casual breakfast, burger, or seafood meal, stop in **Sting Ray's Restaurant** (26507 Lankford Hwy., 757/331-1541, Sun.-Thurs. 6:30am-8pm, Fri.-Sat. 6:30am-8:30pm, $6-30). This restaurant shares a roof with a gas station and offers a full breakfast menu featuring homemade biscuits and omelets. The lunch menu includes hot dogs, burgers, and barbecue, while the dinner menu offers a large variety of local seafood. Order at the counter, and the server will bring the food to your table.

Accommodations

$100-200

The **King's Creek Inn** (3018 Bowden Landing, 757/678-6355, www.kingscreekinn.com, $150-210) is a beautiful historic plantation home that has offered guest accommodations since 1746. The home has been fully renovated and has four guest rooms with private bathrooms. The inn sits on 2.5 acres and overlooks Kings Creek (with access to the Chesapeake Bay). A private dock is available for guest use. The cozy salon offers great ambience for breakfast, or guests can enjoy meals on their balconies. The home has a long and exciting history and some interesting legends that include stories of the Underground Railroad and a possible resident ghost.

$200-300

The **Fig Street Inn** (711 Tazewell Ave., 757/331-3133, www.figstreetinn.com, $175-250) is a year-round boutique bed-and-breakfast offering four comfortable guest rooms with private bathrooms. All rooms have memory foam mattresses, lush towels, flat-screen televisions, wireless Internet, and a jetted tub or gas fireplace. The house has been renovated and is decorated with antiques. The beach and shops are within walking distance.

OVER $300

★ **Bay Creek Resort** (3335 Stone Rd., 757/331-8750, www.baycreek.net, $400-900) is the premier resort community in Cape Charles. The resort offers rentals of vacation homes, villas, and condos in a well landscaped waterfront and golf community on more than 1,700 acres. Golf packages are available, and golf condos offer three-bedroom, two-bath units with garages and a balcony or patio. Single-family homes are also available overlooking the golf course. Those who prefer a water view will enjoy the Marina District. Rental options include single-family villas with views of the Chesapeake Bay or the Kings Creek Marina. One- and two-bedroom suites are also available. Nightly and longer-term stays can be accommodated. A beautiful restaurant is located on the golf course. The staff is extremely helpful and friendly.

The Oyster Farm at Kings Creek (500 Marina Village Circle, 757/331-8660, www.theoysterfarmatkingscreek.com, $219-619) offers beautiful villas, suites, and houses for rent on 39 acres of waterfront property on the Chesapeake Bay and Kings Creek. There is a great on-site restaurant and an events center on the property.

Camping

Camping is available at **Kiptopeke State Park** (3540 Kiptopeke Dr., 757/331-2267, www.dcr.virginia.gov). The park has multiple types of facilities including tent sites ($30-47), cabins ($122-194), and a six-bedroom lodge ($382-488). Minimum stays may apply in the summer. There is a $5 reservation fee.

Information and Services

For additional details on Cape Charles, contact the **Northampton County Chamber of Commerce** (757/678-0010, www.northamptoncountychamber.com).

ONANCOCK

Thirty-eight miles north of Cape Charles is the picturesque town of Onancock. The town sits on the shore of Onancock Creek and has a deepwater harbor. Cute, 19th-century homes with gingerbread trim line the streets, and visitors can shop, visit art galleries, partake in water sports, or just relax and enjoy the tranquil atmosphere. The town was founded in 1680 by English explorers, but its name is derived from the native Algonquian word *au-wannaku*, which means "foggy place."

Onancock was one of the colonies' 12 original "Royal Ports." Its deepwater access to the Chesapeake Bay made it appealing for ships, and its port provided safety during storms. For more than 250 years, Onancock was the trade center on the Eastern Shore and was closely connected (in terms of commerce) to Norfolk and Baltimore.

The homes along Market Street belonged to sea captains who worked on the Chesapeake

Bay. These homes harken back to a time during the steamboat era when Onancock was a stop on the way to bustling Baltimore.

Today, Onancock retains a small working harbor and offers a pretty port of call for recreational boaters. It has modern boats in its harbor, and outdoor enthusiasts paddle colorful kayaks around its waters. Its wharf is also the jumping-off point for a small ferry that goes to and from Tangier Island. The town is a pleasant place to spend a day or two, and about 1,200 people make it their permanent home. There are free parking areas located around town and by the wharf.

Sights

The key sight in Onancock is **Ker Place** (69 Market St., 757/787-8012, www.shorehistory.org, Mar.-Dec. Tues.-Sat. 11am-3pm, admission by donation), one of the finest federal-style manors on the Eastern Shore. John Shepherd Ker was the owner and a renaissance man of his time. He was a successful merchant, lawyer, banker, and farmer. His estate was built in 1799 and originally comprised 1,500 acres. The home is now restored to its original appearance and features period furniture, detailed plasterwork, and rich colors throughout. The headquarters for the **Eastern Shore of Virginia Historical Society** are in the house, and the second floor contains a museum, the society's library, and archives space. A smaller, newer section of the house serves as a welcome center with a museum shop. Visitors can view Eastern Shore artwork throughout the home, and rotating exhibits are displayed regularly. Tours are given on "a loop," and reservations can also be made for private tours.

Recreation

A public boat ramp at the wharf has a launch for canoes and kayaks ($5 launch fee). **SouthEast Expeditions** (209-A Mason Ave., 757/331-6190, www.southeastexpeditions.com) offers kayak and SUP rentals (starting at $20) and tours ($45-125) from the wharf. Guided kayak trips are also offered by two local travel writers and kayak guides through **Burnham Guides** (2 King St., 757/710-5137, www.burnhamink.com). Visitors arriving by boat can dock at the Town Marina but should call the **harbormaster** (757/787-7911) for reservations.

Free self-guided walking tours are a fun way to learn about the town. Pick up a tour brochure at the visitors center (located on the wharf) and learn about Onancock's historic homes and gardens.

Food

Mallards Restaurant (2 Market St., 757/787-8558, www.mallardsvamd.com, Sun.-Mon. 11am-4pm, Tues.-Thurs. 11am-8pm, Fri.-Sat. 11am-9pm, $8-29) is on the wharf. The menu includes fresh seafood, ribs, duck, pasta, and many more delicious entrées. Don't be surprised if chef Johnny Mo comes out of the kitchen with his guitar to play a few tunes. He's a local legend.

The **Blarney Stone Pub** (10 North St., 757/302-0300, www.blarneystonepubonancock.com, Tues.-Thurs. 11am-9pm, Fri.-Sat. 11am-10pm, Sun. 11am-7pm, $11-20) is an Irish pub three blocks from the wharf serving traditional pub fare. It has indoor and outdoor seating and frequent live entertainment.

Accommodations

★ **The Charlotte Hotel and Restaurant** (7 North St., 757/787-7400, www.thecharlotte.com, $140-200) is a boutique hotel with 10 guest rooms. The owners take great pride in this lovely hotel and even made some of the furnishings by hand. There is an award-winning restaurant on-site that can seat more than 30 people, and the American cuisine served is made from products supplied by local watermen and farmers.

The Inn at Onancock (30 North St., 757/787-7711, www.innatonancock.com, $199-239) is a luxurious bed-and-breakfast with five guest rooms, each offering a stylish modern bathroom and feather-top bed. Full-service breakfasts are served in their dining room, or guests can choose to eat on the porch in nice weather. A wine hour is also hosted every evening. Soda and water are available to guests all day.

The **Colonial Manor Inn** (84 Market St., 757/787-3521, www.colonialmanorinn.com, $109-139) offers six spacious rooms decorated with period furnishings. The home was built in 1882 and is the oldest operating inn on the Eastern Shore in Virginia. A delicious full breakfast is served daily.

Information and Services

Additional information on Onancock can be found at www.onancock.com. There is also a small, seasonal visitors center at the wharf.

★ TANGIER ISLAND

Tangier Island is a small 3.5-mile-long island, 12 miles off the coast of Virginia in the middle of the Chesapeake Bay. It was first named as part of a group of small islands called the Russell Isles in 1608 by Captain John Smith when he sailed upon it during an exploration of the Chesapeake Bay. At the time, the island was the fishing and hunting area of the native Pocomoke people, but it was allegedly purchased from them in 1666 for the sum of two overcoats. Settlers were drawn to the island for the abundant oysters and crabs.

The unofficial history of the island states that John Crockett first settled here with his eight sons in 1686. This appears to be accurate since most of the 700 people who live on Tangier Island today are descendants of the Crockett family, and the majority of the tombstones on the island bear the Crockett name. The island was occupied by British troops during the Revolutionary War, and it has also survived four major epidemics, with the most devastating being the Asian cholera epidemic of 1866. So many people died in such a short period of time that family members buried their dead in their front yards. Cement crypts can still be seen in many yards on the island.

There is a tiny airstrip, used primarily for the transport of supplies, but most visitors come by ferry (without their cars). There are no true roads on the island, and golf carts and bicycles are used to get around (you can rent a golf cart or hire one with a driver). A few residents have cars, but they have to receive permission from local authorities.

Tangier Island is only five feet above sea level, and it is known as the "soft-shell crab capital" for its delectable local crabs. It is also known for the unique dialect the people on Tangier Island speak. They converse in an old form of English and have many euphemisms that are unfamiliar to visitors. It is thought that the island's isolation played a role in preserving the language that was spoken throughout the Tidewater area generations ago.

Tangier Island can be toured in a couple of hours. The ferry schedules are such that they allow enough time to cover the sights on the island, grab lunch, and head back the same day. If you enjoy the slow pace of the island, limited overnight accommodations are available, but be aware there is not much, if any, nightlife, and the island is "dry." Addresses aren't frequently used when describing how to get to a place on Tangier Island. Basically, you can see the whole island from any given point. The ferry drops visitors off in the heart of the small commercial area, and if you can't see the establishment you are looking for immediately, take a short walk or ride down the main path and you'll find it. The island residents are also very friendly, so if in doubt, just ask someone walking by.

There are very limited services on Tangier Island. The island hasn't changed much in the last century, and it looks much as it did 30 or 40 years ago. There is a post office and one school that all local children attend (most go on to college elsewhere in the state). There is spotty cell service on the island, but some establishments do offer wireless Internet. More important, there are no emergency medical facilities on the island; however, there is a 24-hour clinic, **The Tangier Island Health Foundation** (www.tangierclinic.org), where a physician's assistant is available.

Many establishments do not accept credit cards, so it's best to bring cash and checks. There is only one ATM on the island (located by **Four Brothers Crab House**).

Sights

TANGIER HISTORY MUSEUM AND INTERPRETIVE CENTER

The **Tangier History Museum and Interpretive Center** (16215 Main Ridge, 757/891-2374, www.tangierisland-va.com, mid-May-mid-Oct. daily 11am-4pm, other times by appointment, $3) is a small museum down the street from the ferry dock. It doubles as the island's vistors center and is worth a visit and the small fee to learn about life on Tangier Island and its interesting heritage. Watch the short movie to begin with, and then view island artifacts and a five-layered painting of the island that illustrates the erosion it has experienced since 1866. Visitors can also learn about the many sayings that are common on the island but completely foreign to those on the mainland, such as "He's adrift," which means, "He's a hunk," and the term "snapjack," which means "firecracker." A handful of kayaks are available behind the museum for visitors to borrow (for free) for exploring the surrounding waterways. There's also a small gift shop on-site (they don't take credit cards).

TANGIER BEACH

At the south end of Tangier Island is the nice, sandy public **Tangier Beach.** Rent a golf cart from **Four Brothers** and head out of the village on the winding paved path and over the canal bridge. The beach is at the very end of the path on the left side of the island. There's a small parking area for carts and a sandy path to the beach. There is no lifeguard on duty so swimming is at your own risk. Bring plenty of water with you since there are also no services at the beach. Water machines and soda machines can be found along the golf

---

1: golf course at Bay Creek Resort in Cape Charles
2: Ker Place in Onancock 3: harbor at Tangier Island
4: Chincoteague Pony Centre

cart paths on the island if you need to pick up beverages on your way. There is also a very small grocery store near the ferry dock with a few bare essentials, but it's best to bring provisions with you.

Recreation

Kayaking the waterways of Tangier Island is a wonderful way to explore the marshes. Kayaks can be borrowed from the Tangier History Museum, and a listing of water trail routes can be found at www.tangierisland-va.com. The marshes also offer a terrific opportunity for bird-watching. Black skimmers, great blue herons, common terns, double-crested cormorants, Forster's terns, clapper rails, and ospreys are just some of the birds living on the island.

Since there are no roads on Tangier—only paved paths—the place is very conducive to casual biking. Bikes can be brought over on the ferry on weekdays only (call ahead to schedule), and a fleet of older-model cruising bikes can be rented from **Four Brothers** on the island. Since the island is only 3.5 miles long, it is easy to cover the entire length by bicycle in a short time.

For a unique local experience, take a **Crab Shanty Tour** (757/891-2269, ask for Ookire). This 30- to 45-minute tour is led by a Chesapeake Bay waterman. Other island tours are available outside the ferry dock. Tour guides wait in golf carts for guests when the ferries arrive, and offer guided tours in their vehicles.

Shopping

There are two small gift shops on Tangier Island: **Wanda's Gifts** (16139 Main Ridge Rd., 757/891-2230) and **Sandy's Place** (16227 Main St., 757/891-2367). Both are on the main path not far from the ferry dock. They sell souvenir T-shirts and trinkets.

Food

Visitors arriving by ferry will likely see the **Waterfront Restaurant** (757/891-2248, mid-May-Nov. 1 Mon.-Sat. 10am-4pm, Sun. 1pm-4pm, under $15) as they depart the ferry. This small, seasonal restaurant is right by the dock and offers a variety of casual food including burgers, fried seafood baskets, and crab cakes.

Four Brothers Crab House & Ice Cream Deck (757/891-2999, www. fourbrotherscrabhouse.com, lunch and dinner daily) will likely be the next establishment you see when you take the short path from the dock to the main path in the small commercial area. While this is the place to rent golf carts, crabbing equipment, and bicycles, they also serve a casual menu of seafood and sandwiches on their deck, along with 60 soft-serve ice-cream flavors. Four Brothers also offers free wireless Internet; however, they do not accept credit cards. Another fun place for ice cream is **Spanky's Place,** just down the path.

A short walk from the ferry terminal is **Lorraine's Seafood Restaurant** (4409 Chambers Ln., 757/891-2225, Mon.-Fri. 10am-2pm and 5pm-10pm, Sat. 10am-2pm and 5pm-11pm, Sun. noon-5pm, under $15). Take a right on Main Street, and the restaurant is on the right. They serve snacks, lunch, and dinner. As at all the restaurants on the island, local, fresh seafood is the specialty, and this place is known for its soft-shell crabs. Lorraine's also delivers to any of the inns on the island.

Across from Lorraine's, **Fisherman's Corner Restaurant** (4419 Long Bridge Rd., 757/891-2900, www. fishermanscornerrestaurant.com, daily 11am-7pm, $6-26) has a long menu with steaks and seafood. Sandwiches and a kids' menu are also available. It's no surprise that fresh crab is a highlight, and their crab cakes contain large, succulent blue crab meat with little filler.

The best-known and oldest restaurant on the island is ★ **Hilda Crockett's Chesapeake House** (16243 Main St., 757/891-2331, www.chesapeakehousetangier. com, daily 7am-9am and 11:30am-5pm, $11-25). They offer an all-you-can-eat breakfast with selections such as scrambled eggs, fried bread, and potatoes. They are most famous, however, for the family-style lunch and dinner. For $22, guests can enjoy unlimited homemade crab cakes, clam fritters, ham, potato salad, coleslaw, pickled beets, applesauce, green beans, corn pudding, and rolls. The family-style setting means you may share a table with other guests.

Accommodations

It is difficult to find more friendly innkeepers than those at the **Bay View Inn** (16408 W. Ridge Rd., 757/891-2396, www.tangierisland. net, $125-150). This family-run bed-and-breakfast offers seven motel-style rooms, two cottages, and two guest rooms in the main house. A scrumptious homemade breakfast is included with your stay. The inn is on the west side of the island and has lovely views of the Chesapeake Bay and decks to watch the sunset. The inn is open year-round. They do not take credit cards.

Hilda Crockett's Chesapeake House (16243 Main St., 757/891-2331, www. chesapeakehousetangier.com, $100-165) is the oldest operating bed-and-breakfast on the island and was established in 1939 as a boardinghouse. It is located in the small commercial area not far from the ferry dock. There are eight guest rooms in two separate buildings.

Renovated in 2018, the **Brigadune Beachside Getaway** (16650 Hog Ridge Rd., 757/891-2580, www. brigadunebeachsidegetaway.com, $155-250) overlooks the bay and offers modern bed-and-breakfast accommodations. Their rooms have private bathrooms, and breakfast is delivered to your door daily.

Those arriving by private boat can rent a slip at the **James Parks Marina** (16070 Parks Marina Ln., 757/891-2581). They offer 25 slips and showers, but no pump-outs. Docking fees start at $25.

Information and Services

For additional information, visit www. tangier-island.com.

Getting There

Getting to Tangier Island is half the fun. Three seasonal ferries travel to and from the island May-October. The first is the **Chesapeake Breeze** (804/453-2628, www.tangiercruise. com, one-way adults $20, children 4-12 $10, 3 and under free, round-trip adult $28, children 4-12 $13, 3 and under free), a 150-person passenger boat that leaves at 10am daily from Reedville for the 1.5-hour trip. The ship heads back to Reedville at 2:15pm. The second is the **Steven Thomas** (410/968-2338, www. tangierislandcruises.com, one-way $20, $27 round-trip for same-day service, $35 for overnight, children 7-12 $12, 6 and under free), a 90-foot, 300-passenger boat that leaves from Crisfield, Maryland, daily (May 15-Oct. 15) at 12:30pm and arrives on Tangier at 1:45pm. The return voyage departs Tangier at 4pm. The third ferry is the **Joyce Marie II** (757/891-2505, www.tangierferry.com, one-way $20, $25 round-trip for same-day service, $30 for overnight, children 6-12 $10, 5 and under $5), a small fiberglass lobster boat that holds 25 people and runs from Onancock, Virginia, to Tangier Island daily May-September. The trip takes 65 minutes. Ferry service is offered twice a day with departures from Tangier Island at 7:30am and 3:30pm and departures from Onancock at 10am and 5pm.

Getting Around

There are no cars on Tangier Island. The best way to get around is by renting a golf cart from **Four Brothers Crab House & Ice Cream Deck** (757/891-2999) or a bicycle. They do not take reservations—rentals are first-come, first-served.

CHINCOTEAGUE ISLAND

Chincoteague Island is 7 miles long and just 1.5 miles wide. It is nestled between the Eastern Shore and Assateague Island. Chincoteague is famous for its herd of wild ponies, and many children and adults first became familiar with the island through the popular book *Misty of Chincoteague*, which was published in 1947. Many local residents made appearances in the movie that followed.

The island is in the far northeastern region of the Eastern Shore in Virginia and has a full-time population of 2,900 residents. It attracts more than one million visitors each year to enjoy the pretty town and to visit the Chincoteague National Wildlife Refuge and the beautiful beach on nearby Assateague Island.

Chincoteague is a working fishing village with world-famous oyster beds and clam shoals. It is also a popular destination for bird-watching. During the summer, the town is bustling with tourists, but in the off-season things slow down considerably and many establishments close.

The town of Chincoteague is accessed via State Route 175. A scenic causeway spans the water and marsh and ends on Main Street, which runs along the western shore of the island. Maddox Boulevard meets Main Street and runs east to the visitors center and Chincoteague National Wildlife Refuge.

Sights
★ CHINCOTEAGUE NATIONAL WILDLIFE REFUGE

The **Chincoteague National Wildlife Refuge** (8231 Beach Rd., 757/336-6122, www.fws.gov, May-Sept. daily 5am-10pm, Apr. and Oct. daily 6am-8pm, Nov.-Mar. daily 6am-6pm, $20 per car for 7-day pass, pedestrians and cyclists free) is a 14,000-acre refuge consisting of beach, dunes, marsh, and maritime forest on the Virginia end of Assateague Island. It was established in 1943, and the area is a thriving habitat for many species of waterfowl, shorebirds, songbirds, and wading birds. The popular herd of wild ponies that Chincoteague is known for also lives in the refuge.

Assateague Island itself extends south from Ocean City, Maryland, to just south of Chincoteague Island. It is a thin strip of beautiful sand beach, approximately 37 miles long. The entire beach is a National Seashore, and the Virginia side is where the Chincoteague National Wildlife Refuge is located.

One of the main attractions is the **Assateague Island Lighthouse,** which visitors can hike to. The lighthouse is painted with red and white stripes and is 142 feet tall. It was completed in 1867 and is still operational. There are also 15 miles of woodland trails for hiking and biking (the wild ponies can often be seen from the trails). The lighthouse is open for climbing (free) spring-fall, but the days it is open change seasonally and with the weather so call ahead for the current schedule. **Refuge Treks** (adults $14, children 12 and under $7) are also available for wildlife viewing. Transportation is provided on a 7-mile service road with stops at select locations.

To get to the refuge, travel east on State Route 175 onto Chincoteague Island and continue straight at the traffic light onto Maddox Boulevard. Follow the signs to the refuge. The entrance is at the end of Maddox Boulevard. The road ends at the Atlantic Ocean, where there's a large parking area for beachgoers. Parts of the beach are open to swimming, surfing, clamming, and crabbing. A visitors center is situated near the beach and is where information and trail brochures can be obtained.

MUSEUM OF CHINCOTEAGUE ISLAND

The **Museum of Chincoteague Island** (7125 Maddox Blvd., 757/336-6117, Tues.-Sun. 11am-5pm, adults $4, children under 12 free) is on Maddox Boulevard just prior to the entrance to the National Wildlife Refuge. The museum was formerly the Oyster and Maritime Museum and is dedicated to sharing the history of the island and to the preservation of the "material culture that reflects the historical progression of the life on Chincoteague Island." One of the most noteworthy exhibits in the museum is the Fresnel lens that was part of the Assateague Island Lighthouse. This lens helped guide ships as far out to sea as 23 miles for nearly 96 years.

CHINCOTEAGUE PONY CENTRE

For those wishing to see the local ponies up close, the **Chincoteague Pony Centre**

(6417 Carriage Dr., 757/336-2776, www. chincoteague-pony-centre.business.site, Thurs.-Sat. and Mon. 10am-5pm, Sun. 11am-4pm, closed Jan.-Feb.) has a herd of ponies from the island in their stable and a field facility for visitors to enjoy. The center offers pony rides, riding lessons, shows, day camps, and a large gift shop.

Recreation

Kayaks can be launched on the beach on Assateague Island, but not in areas patrolled by lifeguards. Kayak tours are available through **Assateague Explorer** (757/336-5956, www.assateagueexplorer. com, $49-59). **Snug Harbor Resort** (7536 East Side Rd., 757/336-6176, www. chincoteagueaccommodations.com) also offers tours ($49) and rents kayaks (single kayak half day $38, full day $48, tandem kayak half day $48, full day $58).

Jus' Bikes (6527 Maddox Blvd., 757/336-6700, www.jus-bikes.com) rents bicycles ($4 per hour or $12 per day), scooters ($15 per hour or $45 per day), surreys ($20 per hour or $75 per day), tandems ($5 per hour or $25 per day), and three-wheelers ($3 per hour or $18 per day).

Fishing enthusiasts can have all their needs met at several fishing and tackle establishments, including **Capt. Bob's Marina** (2477 Main St., 757/336-6654, www. captbobsmarina.net) and **Capt. Steve's Bait & Tackle** (6527 Maddox Blvd., 757/336-0569, www.stevesbaitandtackle.com).

For an interactive cruise, contact **Captain Barry's Back Bay Cruises** (6262 Marlin St., 757/336-6508, www.captainbarry.net). They offer interactive "Hands on Eco-Expedition" (adults $45, children under 1 $40) and "Champagne Sunset Cruises" (adults-only, $45) leaving from the Chincoteague Inn Restaurant at 6262 Main Street. They do not take credit cards.

Entertainment and Events

The premier event on Chincoteague Island is the annual **Wild Pony Swim** (www.

chincoteague.com), which takes place each year in late July. At "slack tide," usually in the morning, the herd of wild ponies is made to swim across the Assateague Channel on the east side of Chincoteague Island (those ponies that are not strong enough or are too small to make the swim are ferried across on barges). The first foal to complete the swim is named "King" or "Queen" Neptune and is given away in a raffle later that day. After the swim, the ponies are given a short rest and are then paraded to the carnival grounds on Main Street. The annual Pony Penning and Auction is then held, in which some foals and yearlings are auctioned off. Benefits from the auction go to support the local fire and ambulance services. The remaining herd then swims back across the channel.

Another big event in town is the **Chincoteague Island Oyster Festival** (8128 Beebe Rd., www. chincoteagueoysterfestival.com, $45, children under 5 free). This well-known event has been happening since 1973 and offers all-you-can-eat oysters prepared every which way imaginable. It is held in early October, and tickets are available online.

Food

AMERICAN

If you like a casual beach environment, eating outside, and lounging in hammocks, then **Woody's Serious Food** (6700 Maddox Blvd., Mon.-Sat. 11am-8pm, Sun. 1pm-8pm, $8-28) is worth checking out. They specialize in barbecue (pulled pork, ribs, chicken, etc.) and offer sides such as corn nuggets. Wash it down with peach tea and you're ready to go. The restaurant is dog friendly, and there are outdoor games for the kids.

For a quick bite to go, stop at the ★ **Sea Star Café** (6429 Maddox Blvd., 757/336-5442, www.seastarcafeci.com, Thurs.-Mon. 11am-6pm, daily July and Aug., $5-10). They have yummy sandwiches and wraps to go (order at the window; be sure to know what you're ordering before going up when there's a crowd). Everything is fresh and made to order, and they have a large vegetarian menu. The café sits back off the road a little and offers a few picnic tables but no restrooms. The menu is handwritten on a chalkboard, and items contain whatever is fresh that day.

SEAFOOD

Seafood is the mainstay on Chincoteague Island, and the local oysters and crabs are especially delicious. Many restaurants are only open seasonally, so finding open eateries in the off-season can pose a bit of a challenge.

AJ's on the Creek (6585 Maddox Blvd., 757/336-5888, www.ajsotc.com, Mar.-Dec. Mon.-Thurs. 11:30am-8:30pm, Fri.-Sat. 11:30am-9:30pm, $15-35) is the longest-operating restaurant on the island under one management. They are one of a few upscale restaurants on the island, and they serve delicious seafood menu items such as crab imperial, shellfish bouillabaisse, crab cakes, and grilled scallops. The restaurant is owned by two spunky sisters originally from Pittsburgh.

Don't let the plain exterior of **Bill's Seafood Restaurant** (4040 Main St., 757/336-5831, www.billsseafoodrestaurant.com, daily from 6am for breakfast, lunch, and dinner, $15-35) fool you. They offer delightful seafood entrées such as lobster tail, scallops, oysters, and crab cakes, as well as pasta selections. This is one of the few restaurants in town that is open all year.

TREATS

The **Island Creamery** (6243 Maddox Blvd., 757/336-6236, www.islandcreamery.net, year-round daily 11am-10pm) is "the" place to go for ice cream. The place is large for an ice-cream joint and offers friendly smiles, samples, and dozens of flavors. It's a popular stop, so the line can be long and parking difficult, but it's worth it.

Accommodations
$100-200

If you're looking for a charming bed-and-breakfast, spend a night at ★ **Miss Molly's**

Inn (4141 Main St., 757/336-6686, www.missmollys-inn.com, $180-240) on Main Street. This beautiful Victorian B&B offers seven delightful guest rooms and five porches with rocking chairs. The home overlooks the bay and has a pretty English garden. Marguerite Henry stayed at the bed-and-breakfast when she wrote the famous book *Misty of Chincoteague*, and the room she stayed in has since been named after her. A full breakfast is included. The sister inn to Miss Molly's is the **Island Manor House Bed and Breakfast** (4160 Main St., 757/336-5436, www.islandmanor.com, $178-253), which offers eight guest rooms and plenty of common areas. This house was built in the popular Maryland-T style, which borrows from both federal and Georgian architecture. Refreshments are available 24 hours a day. They provide a gourmet breakfast each day and easy access to Main Street attractions.

$200-300

The ★ **Hampton Inn & Suites Chincoteague Waterfront** (4179 Main St., 757/336-1616, www.hamptoninnchincoteague.com, $222-309) is known as one of the premier Hampton Inns in the country. Its bayfront location offers beautiful views, and it is close to many shops and restaurants in town. The rooms are well appointed with light wood furniture, and everything is oriented toward the water. The landscaping is appealing, the breakfasts are better than standard chain fare, and there is a boat dock next to the hotel. Amenities include a large indoor heated pool, a fitness center, laundry facilities, a waterfront veranda, and wireless Internet. The staff and owner are also very friendly. Ask for a room on the third floor with a balcony looking over the water, and don't be surprised if you spot dolphins swimming by.

Camping

Camping is available on Chincoteague Island at several campgrounds. The **Chincoteague**

Island KOA (6742 Maddox Blvd., 757/336-3111, www.koa.com, $75) has 550 campsites and 361 utility hookups. Tom's Cove Campground (8128 Beebe Rd., 757/336-6498, www.tomscovepark.com, $36-58) has waterfront campsites near the pony swim, three fishing piers, and a pool. They are open March-November. Pine Grove Campground (5283 Deep Hole Rd., 757/336-5200, www.pinegrovecampground.com, $35-45) offers campsites on 37 acres April-December. There are six ponds on the property.

Information and Services

For additional information on Chincoteague Island, visit www.chincoteaguechamber.com or stop by the Chincoteague Island Visitor's Center (6733 Maddox Blvd., 757/336-6161, Mon.-Sat. 9am-4:30pm).

Getting There

Visitors should arrive on Chincoteague Island by car; the surrounding waters are shallow and difficult to navigate by boat. The closest airport is Wicomico Regional Airport (410/548-4827), which is 52 miles away in Salisbury, Maryland.

Shenandoah and Northwestern Virginia

Bounded to the east by the Blue Ridge

Mountains and to the west by the Appalachians, Northwestern Virginia and the Shenandoah Valley make up one of the prettiest regions in the nation.

From the charming town of Winchester, with its historic homes, apple orchards, and inviting pedestrian area, south to Staunton, one of the oldest cities in the Shenandoah Valley, this area is filled with history and charm. Civil War battlefields, forts, and other military-related structures dot the landscape, and ghosts of fallen soldiers are said to haunt many of the towns.

Nature fans can get their fill of outdoor bliss with stunning mountain vistas, intricate caverns, rolling foothills, and lush forests.

Highlights

Look for ★ to find recommended sights, activities, dining, and lodging.

★ **Museum of the Shenandoah Valley:** This impressive complex in Winchester focuses on the art, history, and culture of the Shenandoah Valley (page 226).

★ **Skyline Drive:** This stunning 105-mile road takes travelers from vista to vista through beautiful Shenandoah National Park (page 234).

★ **Old Rag Mountain:** Enjoy the challenging and rewarding nine-mile hike to the summit (page 235).

★ **Luray Caverns:** Enter a subterranean world of mystery that took more than four million centuries to create (page 243).

★ **New Market Battlefield State Historical Park:** This 300-acre park was the site of a historic 1864 battle that forced Union troops out of the Shenandoah Valley (page 246).

★ **Grand Caverns Regional Park:** Grand Caverns is the oldest continuously operating "show" cave in the country (page 250).

Virginia's pride and joy, Shenandoah National Park, makes up a large part of the region, covering more than 200,000 acres. Its highest point is 4,051 feet. The wide and picturesque Shenandoah River winds through the park, nearly 40 percent of which is protected wilderness. This long, narrow park is home to Skyline Drive, one of the most scenic stretches of road in the nation.

The town of Luray is another prime destination. It is home to the world-famous Luray Caverns, the largest caverns in the eastern United States. This landmark has drawn millions of visitors since it was discovered in 1878. It comprises vast chambers up to 10 stories tall that contain natural columns, stalactites, stalagmites, mudflows, and pools.

Other towns in this region include Harrisonburg, home of James Madison University, and the quaint town of New Market, which is the site of the New Market Battlefield, a 300-acre historical park.

PLANNING YOUR TIME

Shenandoah National Park and northwestern Virginia can be covered by car in a long weekend, but nature lovers will want to allot more time to truly explore the region. The park itself deserves a couple of days to fully appreciate by cruising Skyline Drive, taking a hike or two, and staying at one of the park lodges. If you plan to visit the park to see the fall foliage, keep in mind that Skyline Drive can be very crowded, and you may have to wait in a line of traffic to access it. Those wishing to relax in the Hot Springs area may want to plan on a day or two just for that, especially if you book a room at The Omni Homestead Resort. The cities along I-81—Winchester, New Market, Harrisonburg, and Staunton—can be visited in a few hours each, but you should plan on incorporating a bit more time into your schedule for Luray, especially if you plan to go down into the famous Luray Caverns, which can take at least two hours to tour if you also visit the aboveground attractions.

Winchester

Lying in the northwest corner of the state, Winchester is one of the loveliest towns in Virginia. Founded in 1744, Winchester is also the oldest Virginia city west of the Blue Ridge Mountains. It is the county seat of Frederick County and has a population of around 26,500. It is known mostly for its Civil War history (General Stonewall Jackson had his headquarters here during the winter of 1861-1862), its apple blossoms, acres of orchards, and its charming downtown area with many historic buildings and tree-lined streets.

Although industry has developed in Winchester during the past decades with employers such as Rubbermaid, Kraft, and American Woodmark, many people make the daily commute into Washington DC or the Northern Virginia area and then enjoy their little slice of heaven when they get home.

The downtown area has a very pleasant mall lined with shops and restaurants, with a pedestrian section located on Loudoun Street between Piccadilly and Cork. Winchester is also home to Shenandoah University.

SIGHTS
★ Museum of the Shenandoah Valley

The **Museum of the Shenandoah Valley** (901 Amherst St., 540/662-1473, www.themsv.org, Tues.-Sun. 10am-5pm, adults $10, youth 13-18 and seniors $8, 12 and under free, free to individuals and families on Wed.) is a complex that focuses on the art, history, and culture of

Previous: view from Stony Man Mountain Hike; Skyline Drive; Luray Caverns

Shenandoah and Northwestern Virginia

the Shenandoah Valley and also features historical information on Winchester. The well-landscaped site includes multiple collections on display in three venues. The first is the 18th-century **Glen Burnie House,** which exhibits paintings, furniture, and decorative items. The second is seven acres of gardens, and the third is a 50,000-square-foot museum made up of four galleries.

The museum itself is reason enough to visit the complex. This is an outstanding facility with comprehensive and well-thought-out exhibits. The **Shenandoah Valley Gallery** is where the history of the valley comes to life through multimedia presentations and dioramas. The **Founders Gallery** features rotating exhibits of fine art and antiques. The **R. Lee Taylor Miniatures Gallery** displays the work of more than 70 artists through fully furnished miniature houses and rooms. The fourth gallery is the **Changing Exhibition Gallery,** where a new exhibit is featured every 3-6 months.

The historic house and gardens welcome the public April to October, but the museum is open all year. The hours of operation are the same year-round. The complex can be explored in a few hours. There is a café and gift store on-site.

Stonewall Jackson's Headquarters Museum

Stonewall Jackson's Headquarters Museum (415 N. Braddock St., 540/667-5505, www.winchesterhistory.org, Apr.-Oct. Mon.-Sat. 10am-4pm, Sun. noon-4pm, adults $5, students K-12 $2.50, seniors $4.50) is nestled in a neighborhood on Braddock Street. It is a lovely little Hudson River Gothic Revival-style home that was used by General Jackson over the winter of 1861-1862. Jackson occupied two rooms in the home, including an office on the lower level. The house features a large collection of authentic Jackson belongings, as well as personal items that belonged to his staff. His office remains much as it looked when he used it. Allow about an hour to tour the home.

Winchester

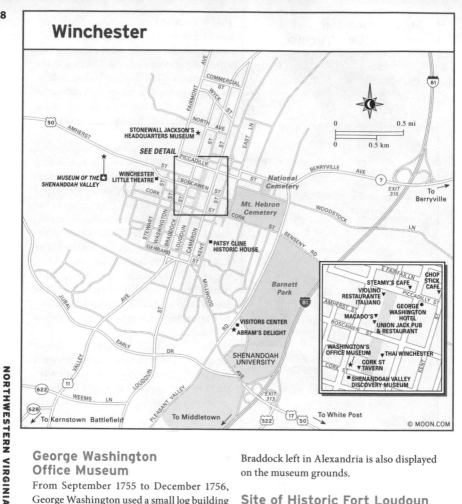

George Washington Office Museum

From September 1755 to December 1756, George Washington used a small log building in Winchester as an office while he supervised the construction of Fort Loudoun on the north side of town. Today, that office is the middle room of the **George Washington Office Museum** (32 W. Cork St. and Braddock St., 540/662-4412, www.winchesterhistory.org, Apr.-Oct. Mon.-Sat. 10am-4pm, Sun. noon-4pm, adults $5, students K-12 $2.50, seniors $4.50). Visitors can see some of Washington's personal items on display, along with surveying equipment and a model of Winchester circa 1755. A cannon that General Edward Braddock left in Alexandria is also displayed on the museum grounds.

Site of Historic Fort Loudoun

During the French and Indian War, Fort Loudoun was George Washington's regimental headquarters. During 1755 and 1756, Washington oversaw the construction of Fort Loudoun from his small office in Winchester. The log fort was considered the "most formidable fort on Virginia's colonial frontier" and was the command center for a series of fortifications. Washington is said to have brought his personal blacksmith from Mount Vernon

1: Museum of the Shenandoah Valley **2:** Abram's Delight

to craft the ironwork at the fort, which housed 14 mounted cannons on half an acre. The fort held barracks for 450 men and had its own well, which remains there still. Today, the fort is no longer standing, but the **Site of Historic Fort Loudoun** (419 N. Loudoun St., 540/665-2046, www.frenchandindianwarfoundation.org, daily 8am-5pm, free) can be visited during daylight hours. A marker between the sidewalk and a fenced yard recounts the fort's history.

Shenandoah Valley Civil War Museum

A nice Civil War exhibit can be found in the Historic Frederick County Court House building in the **Shenandoah Valley Civil War Museum** (20 N. Loudoun St., 540/542-1145, www.civilwarmuseum.org, Mon.-Sat. 10am-5pm, Sun. 1pm-5pm, adults $5, children under 16 free, seniors 62 and over $4.50). The Georgian-style building is located on the downtown mall and in a past life served as a prison, hospital, and Civil War barracks for both armies. One of the unique features of the building is the original graffiti from both Union and Confederate soldiers that is still visible. The museum displays more than 3,000 Civil War items.

Patsy Cline Historic House

Patsy Cline fans will enjoy the **Patsy Cline Historic House** (608 S. Kent St., 540/662-5555, www.celebratingpatsycline.org, Apr.-Oct. Mon.-Sat. 10am-4pm, Sun. 1pm-4pm, adults $8, seniors 65 and over $7, active military with ID free). Cline lived in the little house with her family between 1948 and 1953. The house is furnished with some Cline family personal items and is decorated as it was when the singer lived there. The admission price includes a 45-minute guided tour of the house.

Shenandoah Valley Discovery Museum

The **Shenandoah Valley Discovery Museum** (19 W. Cork St., 540/722-2020, www.discoverymuseum.net, Tues.-Sat.

9am-5pm, Sun. 1pm-5pm, $9, children under 2 free) offers many hands-on exhibits for children. This little museum right near the downtown mall is a fun place to go on a rainy day and is particularly interesting for children under 10. Some activities include moving apples around a packing shed, riding in a mock ambulance, stepping into a kaleidoscope, and playing in a sandbox.

Abram's Delight

The oldest home in Winchester, built in the mid-1700s, is **Abram's Delight** (1340 S. Pleasant Valley Rd., 540/662-6519, www.winchesterhistory.org, Apr.-Oct. Mon.-Sat. 10am-4pm, Sun. noon-4pm, adults $5, students K-12 $2.50, seniors $4.50). The stone house was home to five generations of the Hollingsworth family, spanning 200 years. Tours give visitors a great look into life between the colonial period and the Civil War. The antiques furnishing the home include rope beds that had to be tightened each night by crank (which some believe to be the origin of the phrase, "Sleep tight"). The friendly ghost of Abraham Hollingsworth is said to haunt the house.

RECREATION AND EVENTS

If you visit Winchester during apple season, you'll be missing out if you don't sample the local produce. Stop in at a "pick-your-own" orchard before leaving town. A good place to pick and sample these delights is **Marker-Miller Orchards** (3035 Cedar Creek Grade, www.markermillerorchards.com). Pick-your-own apple time begins September 1.

The premier event in Winchester is the spring **Shenandoah Apple Blossom Festival** (www.thebloom.com). This 10-day event takes place in April/May and features music, parades, parties, celebrities, and a lot of tradition. The first festival was held back in 1924. There is even a 10k race and the coronation of the Apple Blossom Queen. Many local businesses close on the first Friday of Apple Blossom weekend.

Patsy Cline: Winchester's Sweetheart

Patsy Cline Historic House

It is hard to make your way around Winchester without bumping into a photo or poster of Patsy Cline. Patsy was born as Virginia Patterson Hensley in Winchester Memorial Hospital on September 8, 1932. Her family moved around Virginia many times during her early years, but in 1948, after her parents separated, she returned to Winchester with her mother and siblings. "Ginny," as she was known, dropped out of school to help support the family and went to work in a local poultry plant. She later held a number of different jobs around town and began singing in the evenings and on weekends for additional income.

Over the next few years, Ginny's singing career grew as she won contests, was featured on local radio, and sang with several local bands. In 1952, Ginny was hired by a bandleader named Bill Peer to sing on a regional music circuit. He gave her the stage name Patsy.

In 1953 she married Gerald E. Cline and became Patsy Cline. Her big break came in 1954, when she signed a contract with a record company and produced her first titles in Nashville. Her first songs included "Hidin' Out," "Honky-Tonk Merry-Go-Round," "Turn the Cards Slowly," and "A Church." Cline's first single was released in July 1955. Her most recognizable song, a cover of Willie Nelson's "Crazy," was released in 1961.

Cline died in 1963 and is buried in Winchester.

Local theater fans will thoroughly enjoy the **Winchester Little Theatre** (315 W. Boscawen St., 540/662-3331, www.wltonline. org), which produces several shows throughout the year, including dramas, mysteries, comedies, and even musicals. The cast and staging are professional, and it is clear everyone involved is very passionate about their performance. The stage itself is set in an old train station, which adds to the fun.

FOOD

American

One block west of the downtown mall is the appropriately named **One Block West** (25 S. Indian Alley, 540/662-1455, www. oneblockwest.com, Tues.-Thurs. 11am-2pm and 5pm-8:30pm, Fri.-Sat. 11am-2pm and 5pm-9pm, $21-36), which serves creative American cuisine and is known for using very fresh ingredients and local products in its dishes. The chef/owner is very hands-on and speaks with guests, takes reservations, and does much of the cooking. The menu changes daily based on what is available in local markets, generally split between seafood and meat. Sample items include trout, bison, crab cakes, and shepherd's pie. They also offer a seven-course chef's tasting menu ("menu of the moment") for $75.

Grab a mini-burger and dine where Patsy Cline did at the **Snow White Grill** (159 N. Loudoun St., 540/431-5977, Wed.-Thurs. 11am-5pm, Fri.-Sat. 11am-6pm, under $10). This historic burger joint opened in 1949 and hasn't changed much since. Their famous mini-burger is a small ground beef patty with mustard, a pickle, and grilled onions. It's served on a steamed bun just like Patsy had it when she dined here "daily." They also serve sandwiches and ice cream. Grab a seat at the counter (there are no tables) and enjoy the nostalgia. This is the complete 1950s experience—and probably one of the few restaurants in the country with no bathroom.

For a beer and a burger and cozy ambience, try **Union Jack Pub and Restaurant** (101 N. Loudoun St., 540/722-2055, www.theunionjackpub.com, Mon.-Thurs. 11am-11:30pm, Fri. and Sat. 11am-1am, Sun. 11am-11pm, $7-29). This multilevel restaurant serves good pub food, including gluten-free and vegetarian options. The long wooden bar is a focal point, and the friendly staff helps to create the warm atmosphere.

Those of us who were first introduced to **Macado's** (121 N. Loudoun St., 540/323-7162, www.macados.net, Sun.-Thurs. 8am-11:30pm, Fri.-Sat. 8am-12:30am, under $10) in college will always have a soft spot for their massive sandwich menu, nachos (with a side of onion dip), draft beer, and ice cream. This regional chain is known for their college and small-town locations throughout western Virginia. Personal favorites include the Brooklyn Bridge, Custer's Last Stand, Diamond Jim, and the Turkey Trot. They open at 8am but don't have a breakfast menu.

Good coffee and delicious handmade bagels can be found at **Steamy's Cafe** (38 E. Piccadilly St., 530/392-8372, www.steamyscafe.com, Mon.-Fri. 7am-noon, Sat.-Sun. 8am-noon, under $10).

A good lunch stop is **Bonnie Blue Southern Market and Bakery** (334 W. Boscawen St., 540/686-7490, www.bonniebluebbq.net, Mon.-Thurs. 8am-6pm, Fri. 8am-8pm, Sat. 8am-5pm, Sun. 10am-4pm, $9-15), housed in a former gas station at the corner of Boscawen and Amherst Streets. They offer tasty sandwich selections and also carry locally made goods and excellent homemade bakery items. There is only outdoor seating, but it's a fun place to stop on a sunny day. This is more of a market than a restaurant, but they have good food.

Italian

★ **Violino Restaurant** (181 N. Loudoun St., 540/667-8006, www.violinorestaurant.com, Tues.-Fri. 11:30am-2pm and 5pm-9pm, Sat. noon-2pm and 5pm-9pm, $16-35) is known for its delicious northern Italian dishes and hearty sauces. The staff is friendly, professional, and very good at suggesting wine pairings. The food is downright superb, and it is also consistent. The menu includes many specialty dishes such as lobster *pansotti gondoliera* (Mediterranean lobster ravioli sautéed in a lemon parmesan sauce) and *galletto al limone* (grilled Cornish hen marinated and pressed with rosemary, garlic, and lemon). They also offer a wonderful selection of authentic Italian desserts. The restaurant is on the north end of the downtown mall.

Thai

A great little place to grab some Thai food is the **Chop Stick Café** (207 N. Kent St., 540/450-8691, www.chopstickcafe.biz, Mon.-Thurs. 11am-9pm, Fri. 11am-10pm, Sat. noon-10pm, Sun. noon-8pm, $9-14). They serve traditional Thai food, sushi, and even a few burgers. The place is a little cramped, but don't let that fool you: It's friendly, slightly funky on the inside, and even has good music.

They also specialize in home-baked pies—unusual for a Thai place, but they're delicious.

ACCOMMODATIONS

$100-200

Comfortable lodging choices include the **Holiday Inn SE Historic Gateway** (333 Front Royal Pike, 540/667-3300, www.ihg.com, $97-117), just off I-81. This friendly hotel was built in 2008 and has 130 nicely appointed rooms with comfortable beds. There is an indoor pool, fitness center, Internet, and an on-site restaurant.

Another good option is the **Country Inn & Suites Winchester** (141 Kernstown Commons Blvd., 540/869-7657, www.countryinns.com, $80-157). This pet-friendly hotel (additional $20) offers an indoor pool, fitness room, free wireless Internet, and a complimentary breakfast. The hotel is a 10-minute drive from the historic downtown area.

A third comparable option is the **Candlewood Suites Winchester** (1135 Millwood Pike, 540/667-8323, www.ihg.com, $97-117). This extended-stay hotel is near I-81 and offers 70 guest suites with fully equipped kitchens, 32-inch TVs, workspace, and free high-speed Internet. There are also free laundry facilities, a convenience store, and a 24-hour fitness center on-site.

$200-300

The most historic and luxurious hotel in town is ★ **The George Washington Grand Hotel** (103 E. Piccadilly St., 540/678-4700, www.wyndham.com, $129-439). This downtown treasure was built in 1924 and features 90 guest rooms and a unique indoor swimming pool designed to look like a Roman bath complete with columns and statues. The soaring ceilings, beautiful marble floors, antique front desk (the original), and traditionally decorated rooms help make the atmosphere inviting and elegant. The staff is exceptional, and guests are treated with the utmost respect. The hotel restaurant serves breakfast, lunch, and dinner, and there is a bar in the lobby. There is also a spa, fitness room, business center, and high-speed Internet access. The hotel is within walking distance of most downtown attractions and was originally built near the B&O Railroad depot to accommodate train travelers. Famous guests have included Lucille Ball and Jack Dempsey.

INFORMATION AND SERVICES

For additional information on Winchester, contact the **Winchester-Frederick County Convention and Visitors Bureau** (1400 S. Pleasant Valley Rd., 540/542-1326, www.visitwinchesterva.com, daily 9am-5pm).

GETTING THERE AND AROUND

Winchester is 75 miles northwest of Washington DC off US 50 and I-81. The local **Winchester Transit** (540/667-1815, www.winchesterva.gov, Mon.-Fri. 6am-8pm, Sat. 9am-5pm, $1) provides bus service throughout the city during the day.

Shenandoah National Park

Seventy-five miles west of Washington DC is 200,000 acres of protected parkland known as **Shenandoah National Park** (540/999-3500, www.nps.gov/shen, $30 per vehicle or $15 per person, admission good for 7 consecutive days). The park is a popular escape for people living in the densely populated areas of Northern Virginia and Maryland, and for good reason: It offers superb outdoor recreation, stunning mountain scenery, and the lovely Shenandoah River.

The park stretches 105 miles from north to south and has four primary entrances: from Front Royal (via I-66 and US 340), at Thornton Gap (via US 211), at Swift Run Gap (via US 33), and at Rockfish Gap (via I-64 and US 250).

Shenandoah National Park is a prime location for hiking. There are more than 500 miles of trails here, mostly through lush forests. Trail maps are available at entrance stations and visitors centers. The park is also a great place to view wildlife. Some of the resident animals include coyote, black bear, bald eagles, and the timber rattlesnake. Dogs are welcome in the park as long as they are leashed.

TOP EXPERIENCE

★ SKYLINE DRIVE

One of the most beautiful stretches of road in the East, **Skyline Drive** (540/999-3500, www.nps.gov/shen, $30 per vehicle) is the most popular attraction in Shenandoah National Park. This 105-mile road takes travelers from vista to vista along a stunning byway that runs the entire length of the park from north to south. It is the only public road that goes through the park. Access to Skyline Drive is from four entry points: from Front Royal at the northern terminus (near I-66 and US 340), at Thornton Gap (US 211), at Swift Run Gap (US 33), and

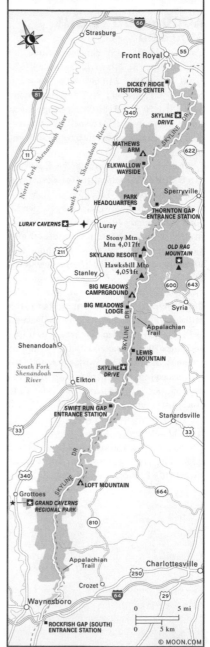

Shenandoah National Park

Strasburg
Front Royal
DICKEY RIDGE VISITORS CENTER
SKYLINE DRIVE
MATHEWS ARM
ELKWALLOW WAYSIDE
Sperryville
PARK HEADQUARTERS
THORNTON GAP ENTRANCE STATION
LURAY CAVERNS
Luray
Stony Mtn 4,017ft
OLD RAG MOUNTAIN
SKYLAND RESORT
Hawksbill Mtn 4,051ft
Stanley
BIG MEADOWS CAMPGROUND
BIG MEADOWS LODGE
Syria
Appalachian Trail
Shenandoah
LEWIS MOUNTAIN
South Fork Shenandoah River
SKYLINE DRIVE
Elkton
SWIFT RUN GAP ENTRANCE STATION
Stanardsville
LOFT MOUNTAIN
Grottoes
GRAND CAVERNS REGIONAL PARK
Appalachian Trail
Charlottesville
Crozet
Waynesboro
ROCKFISH GAP (SOUTH) ENTRANCE STATION

0   5 mi
0   5 km

© MOON.COM

near Waynesboro at Rockfish Gap at I-64 and US 250 (at the southern terminus). Skyline Drive ends where the **Blue Ridge Parkway** begins. It takes approximately three hours to drive the entire road.

The most popular time to visit Skyline Drive is during the fall. Virginia is known for having one of the most spectacular leaf displays in the country, and this route showcases the best of the best. Unfortunately, this can often mean long lines leading into the park when the colors are at their peak, so expect to have a lot of company, especially on a weekend. Inclement weather can also close the road at any time during the year. Call or visit the park's website for a status if the forecast calls for fog, snow, or heavy rain. The road is also closed at night during deer-hunting season (mid-Nov. through early Jan.). Hikers are allowed into the park on foot even if the road is closed.

RVs, camping trailers, and horse trailers are allowed on Skyline Drive but will need to use a low gear. There is also a low tunnel (Marys Rock Tunnel) south of the entrance at Thornton Gap off US 211 that is 12 feet, 8 inches high. The speed limit on Skyline Drive is 35 miles an hour. This is partly because of the curves and steep inclines and partly to protect wildlife in the area.

Mileposts (mp) demarcate the entire length of Skyline Drive on the west side of the road starting with 0.0 in Front Royal. All park maps use these as location references.

There are 75 overlooks along the route. Visitors can see the beautiful Shenandoah Valley to the west and the Piedmont to the east. Wildflowers and other stunning blooms keep the area colorful throughout the warmer months.

HIKING
★ Old Rag Mountain
The most popular hike in Shenandoah National Park is **Old Rag Mountain** (www.nps.gov/shen). It is also the most challenging and dangerous. A day at Old Rag is an experience to remember, as summiting the peak requires a vigorous uphill ascent and many rough areas of scrambling near the top.

The hike is a 9-mile circuit that can take up to seven or eight hours. The route at the top changes periodically but always involves a hefty scramble requiring good upper body strength. Children and shorter adults may need assistance to get through some sections.

Several search-and-rescue missions are required each year at Old Rag, but this shouldn't deter you from the hike. It is a fun way to spend the day, and the views from the top are very rewarding. A safety video on the park website should be viewed prior to your hike. Bring food and water (at least two quarts per person) with you. Arrive early in the morning to ensure you can get a parking space; this is a very popular hike and can be crowded on nice days, especially on weekends.

Most people arrive at Old Rag Mountain from the eastern park boundary near Sperryville. From the intersection of State Route 211 and US 522 in Sperryville, take US 522 south for 0.8 mile. Turn right on State Route 231 and go eight miles. Turn right on State Route 601. Continue three miles, following the signs to the parking lot. Parking can be tough on weekends. Hikers must use the designated parking area at the Old Rag Fee Station and then walk to the trailhead; the small parking lot at the trailhead is not open for public parking. This is not a pet-friendly hike, and pets are not allowed on parts of the trail. A valid Shenandoah National Park entrance pass is required.

White Oak Canyon
At milepost 42.6 on Skyline Drive, just south of Skyland Resort, is the parking lot and trailhead for the popular **White Oak Canyon** hike (www.nps.gov/shen). This moderate hike offers one of the premier waterfall views in the park and treats hikers to spectacular scenery as they walk down a steep gorge past boulders, pools, and six waterfalls (35-85 feet in height). This hike is steep in sections (there is an elevation gain of 1,200 feet), but the trail is well used and maintained. It can also be very

crowded in peak season. Allow four hours for this 4.8-mile up-and-back hike.

Dark Hollow Falls

A scenic, family-friendly hike near Skyline Drive is the 1.5-mile round-trip route to **Dark Hollow Falls.** The trail begins just north of Big Meadows at mile 50.7. The trail follows the Hogcamp Branch stream out of the Big Meadows spring to the falls. The hike to the 70-foot waterfall is downhill, which means it is uphill on the way back. The trail is especially pretty in the spring when the mountain laurel along the path blooms a vibrant pink. The trail is shaded by the tree canopy, keeping it relatively cool in the summer.

FOOD

There are two park-operated dining facilities in Shenandoah National Park. The first is the **Pollock Dining Room** (dinner entrées $9-28) at Skyland Resort. They serve breakfast, lunch, and dinner and offer regional cuisine (such as rainbow trout and beef tenderloin). Be sure to try the Blackberry Ice Cream Pie. The **Mountain Taproom** is also at Skyland Resort and has family-friendly entertainment and adult drinks. Visitors can also purchase boxed lunches to go. Just ask the hostess for a "picnic to go."

The second dining facility is the **Spottswood Dining Room** (dinner entrées $9-29) at Big Meadows Lodge. They are open for breakfast, lunch, and dinner and serve regional cuisine such as roasted turkey and steak. The **New Market Taproom** is also on-site with live music and specialty drinks.

In addition to the two sit-down restaurants, the park operates three **Wayside Food Stops** along Skyline Drive. **Elkwallow Wayside** (mp 24.1, open mid-Apr.-Oct.) has carryout food in addition to groceries, camping supplies, and gasoline. **Big Meadows Wayside** (mp 51.2, open mid-Mar.-mid-Nov.) offers full-service meals (breakfast, lunch, and dinner), groceries, camping supplies, and gasoline. **Loft Mountain Wayside** (mp 79.5, open May-Oct.) provides a snack counter, groceries, camping supplies, and gasoline.

ACCOMMODATIONS

Park-operated lodges and campgrounds in Shenandoah National Park can provide a unique base for exploration. Reservations for prime seasons such as summer and especially during fall foliage (mid-Sept. to mid-Oct.) should be made well in advance. Many places accept reservations up to a year in advance.

Lodges

There are three park-run lodges in Shenandoah National Park. Information on all can be found at www.goshenandoah.com (877/847-1919). **Skyland Resort** (open Apr.-Nov., $135-344) occupies 36 acres at the highest point on Skyline Drive (mp 41.7). The resort sits at an elevation of 3,680 feet and has incredible views of the Shenandoah Valley. It offers 179 rooms, multiunit lodges, rustic cabins, and modern suites for rent in 28 buildings. Skyland Resort is not luxurious; there are no phones or wireless Internet access in the rooms. It is geared toward the enjoyment of the surrounding nature.

Big Meadows Lodge (open mid-May-Oct., $91-197) is near the center of the park at milepost 51.2. This is the largest developed area of the park, and it is named after a beautiful large meadow near the lodge where deer come to graze. The exterior of the main lodge is made of stones cut from Massanutten Mountain back in 1939, while the interior structure was constructed from chestnut trees (now extinct in the area).

The main lodge at Big Meadows has 29 guest rooms. There is a full-service dining room offering breakfast, lunch, and dinner, a taproom with light fare and nightly entertainment, and a gift shop. Five cabins and six multiunit buildings are also near the lodge.

Big Meadows is close to the Shenandoah River and the Shenandoah Valley. There are

1: sun rays on Skyline Drive **2:** Dark Hollow Falls in Shenandoah National Park **3:** view from Old Rag Mountain in Shenandoah National Park

no phones or wireless access in the lodge rooms, but free wireless Internet is available in the Great Room of the main building.

Lewis Mountain (open Apr.-mid-Nov., $138-169) offers cabins for rent in a quiet wooded setting near milepost 57.5. Cabins have electricity, private bathrooms, heat, towels, linens, and an outdoor grill pit. There are no phones or wireless access in the cabins. The Shenandoah River and the town of Luray are nearby.

Camping

Most of Shenandoah National Park is open to backcountry camping (a free permit is required). In addition, there are four seasonal, park-operated campgrounds with a variety of amenities (877/444-6777, www. goshenandoah.com and www.nps.gov/shen) that are open from spring to fall. They are located at milepost 22.1 (**Mathews Arm Campground,** mid-May-Oct., $15), milepost 51.2 (**Big Meadows Campground,** late Apr.-Dec., $20), milepost 57.5 (**Lewis Mountain Campground,** May-Nov., $15), and milepost 79.5 (**Loft Mountain Campground,** mid-May-Oct., $15). Mathews Arm Campground has approximately 178 sites (tent, generator-free, and group sites),

restrooms, water, and a trash and recycle center. Big Meadows Campground has more than 200 sites (tent, generator-free, and group sites), restrooms, showers, and a trash and recycle center. Lewis Mountain Campground has approximately 30 tent sites, restrooms, a camp store, and a trash and recycle center. Loft Mountain Campground has more than 200 sites (tent, generator-free, and group sites), restrooms, showers, and a trash and recycle center. Reservations are taken (and advised) at all the campgrounds except Lewis Mountain Campground, which only operates on a first-come, first-served basis.

INFORMATION AND SERVICES

There are two visitors centers in Shenandoah National Park. **Dickey Ridge Visitor Center** (mp 4.6 on Skyline Dr., 540/999-3500, Apr.-mid-May weekends 9am-5pm, mid-May-Nov. daily 9am-5pm) has an information desk, restrooms, an orientation movie, maps, permits, first aid, and publications. **Harry F. Byrd, Sr. Visitor Center** (mp 51 on Skyline Dr., 540/999-3500, Apr.-mid-May weekends 9am-5pm, mid-May-Nov. daily 9am-5pm) has an information desk, restrooms, publications, maps, permits, and first aid.

Front Royal

The northern gateway to the popular **Skyline Drive** in Shenandoah National Park is **Front Royal** in Warren County. The town has a population of around 15,000.

The Shenandoah River runs through Front Royal, offering opportunities for fishing, canoeing, and tubing. The downtown area is worth a visit in itself, with a **Town Hall** that looks like it came from a movie set, many cute stores, and several first-rate restaurants. The two main roads in downtown Front Royal are Royal Avenue and East Main Street. The Village Commons off of East Main Street house Front Royal's trademark gazebo,

a large red caboose, and the visitors center. Front Royal is also known for a series of elegant murals painted on buildings in the downtown area.

SIGHTS
Warren Rifles Confederate Museum

The **Warren Rifles Confederate Museum** (95 Chester St., 540/636-6982, Apr. 15-Nov. 1 Mon.-Sat. 9am-4pm, Sun. noon-4pm, by

---

1: Gadino Cellars **2:** Luray Singing Tower **3:** gazebo on Main Street in Front Royal

appointment the rest of the year, $5, students and active military free) is in a plain brick home and offers displays of Civil War relics such as weapons, battle flags, uniforms, photos, and rare documents. Memorabilia of famous Civil War players in the Front Royal area (such as Belle Boyd, John S. Mosby, Jefferson Davis, General Robert E. Lee, and General Stonewall Jackson) are also on exhibit. There is a book and gift shop.

Belle Boyd Cottage

Nearly across the street from the Warren Rifles Confederate Museum, in one of the oldest buildings in Front Royal, is the **Belle Boyd Cottage** (101 Chester St., 540/636-1446, www.warrenheritagesociety.org, year-round Mon.-Fri. 10am-4pm, Mar. 30-Nov. 16 also Sat. 11am-4pm, adults $10, children 6-18 $5, 5 and under free). Belle Boyd was a charming female spy who helped Stonewall Jackson capture Front Royal in May 1862. Boyd was well known among Union forces and had been reported no fewer than 30 times, arrested a half-dozen times, and even spent time in jail. For a time during the war, Front Royal was her home base, and she stayed in this cottage owned by her relatives. Visitors can learn more about Boyd's life and her spy adventures.

Skyline Caverns

A wonderful underground experience, **Skyline Caverns** (10334 Stonewall Jackson Hwy., 540/635-4545, www.skylinecaverns.com, June 15-Labor Day daily 9am-6pm, Mar. 15-June 14 and Labor Day-Nov 14. Mon.-Fri. 9am-5pm, Sat.-Sun. 9am-6pm, Nov. 15-Mar. 14 daily 9am-4pm, adults $22, children 7-13 $11, under 6 free) opened to the public in 1939. Visitors are led by professional guides through a maze of living caverns on a one-hour tour. Expect to see magical cave formations, three underground streams, and a 37-foot waterfall. A fun mirror maze is also offered for both children and adults for an additional $6. Skyline Caverns is just southwest of town.

RECREATION

The Shenandoah River is ideal for float trips. A handful of outfitters offer gear and shuttle service for visitors wishing to spend a day on this normally peaceful river. **Front Royal Outdoors** (8567 Stonewall Jackson Hwy., 540/635-5440, www.frontroyaloutdoors.com, open Apr.-Oct.) offers self-guided trips down the river (3-11 miles) in canoes ($50-60), kayaks ($38-60), four-person rafts ($110-120), and six-person rafts ($165-172). They offer three-mile tubing trips (complete with a tube for your cooler) for $25 per person. They also rent stand-up paddleboards and fishing kayaks. **Skyline Canoe Company** (540/305-7695, www.skylinecanoe.com) offers self-guided canoe ($40-55) and kayak ($30-40) trips of 3-12.5 miles. They also offer three-mile tubing trips ($20).

Mountain bikers can challenge themselves on trails that go up to 3,300 feet in elevation, traversing deep valleys and wooded slopes. A popular expert trail is the **Elizabeth Furnace** trail, approximately 11 miles west of Front Royal in **George Washington National Forest** (www.singletracks.com). The 15-mile trail starts with a long uphill climb on a fire road, followed by a long, bumpy ride downhill. It is very challenging and offers many water crossings, outcrops, technical sections, and rock gardens. Another local favorite is the 13-mile network of trails in **Shenandoah River State Park** (350 Daughter of Stars Dr., Bentonville, www.dcr.virginia.gov), 9 miles southwest of Front Royal. The trails are wide and smooth and not nearly as daunting as the Elizabeth Furnace trail, but there are moderate climbs. There are also scenic views of the river.

Equine enthusiasts may enjoy a trail ride with **Royal Horseshoe Farm** (509 Morgan Ford Rd., 540/636-6375, https://royalhorseshoe.com, starting at $35). They offer trail rides for riders of all levels of experience.

Blue Ridge Whiskey & Wine Loop

The Front Royal and Northern Blue Ridge Mountains area is home to many lovely vineyards and wineries. The Blue Ridge Whiskey Wine Loop is a driving tour through scenic country roads with stops at wineries, a whiskey distillery, and other attractions. A map of the tour and recommended stops can be downloaded at the Discover Shenandoah website (www.discovershenandoah.com). Some popular wineries along the tour include:

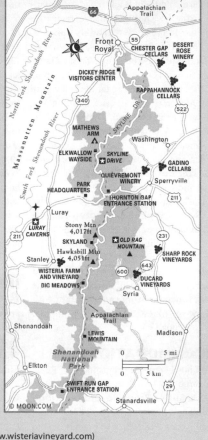

- **Chester Gap Cellars** (4615 Remount Rd., Front Royal, 540/636 8086, www.chestergapcellars.com)

- **Desert Rose Winery** (13726 Hume Rd., Hume, 540/635-3200, www.desertrosewinery.com)

- **DuCard Vineyards** (40 Gibson Hollow Ln., Etlan, 540/923-4206, www.ducardvineyards.com)

- **Gadino Cellars** (92 Schoolhouse Rd., Washington, 540/987-9292, www.gadinocellars.com)

- **Quievremont** (162 Gid Brown Hollow Rd. #335, Washington, 540/827-4579, www.quievremont.com)

- **Rappahannock Cellars** (14437 Hume Rd., Huntly, 540/635-9398, www.rappahannockcellars.com)

- **Sharp Rock Vineyards** (5 Sharp Rock Rd., Sperryville, 540/987-8020, www.sharprockvineyards.com)

- **Wisteria Farm and Vineyard** (1126 Marksville Rd., Stanley, 540/742-1489, www.wisteriavineyard.com)

FOOD

A few restaurants in Front Royal have grabbed the attention of weekend visitors. The first is **Blue Wing Frog** (219 Chester St., 540/622-6175, www.bluewingfrog.com, Wed. and Thurs. 11am-9pm, Fri.-Sat. 11am-10pm, Sun. 10am-9pm, $8-32). They are a bit eclectic, in a good way, starting with the setup. Walk in, grab a menu, find a table, and when you're ready, order at the counter. Then, return to your seat and they'll bring out your food. When you're done, pay up front. The menu changes a lot and offers a lot, from salads and burgers to grilled cheese and steak. Even catfish tacos make an appearance. The restaurant is committed to sustainability, buying local and making as much in house as possible, even their own ketchup and peanut butter.

The popular **Element** (317 E. Main St., 540/636-1695, www.elementonmain.com,

Tues.-Sat. 11:30am-2:30pm and 5pm-9pm, $16-32) offers a delectable menu of salads, veggie selections, seafood, beef, pork, and starters. They also serve lunch. The atmosphere is modern, and there is a full bar and handpicked wine list. The menu changes regularly.

Another favorite is **Ben's Family Cuisines** (654 W. 11th St., 540/551-3147, www.bensfamilycuisines.com, Tues.-Thurs. 11am-9pm, Fri.-Sat. 11am-10pm, Sun. noon-8pm, $10-24). This unassuming family restaurant is a bit hidden in a small brick building in a residential neighborhood. They offer Thai, Cambodian, Vietnamese, Korean, Japanese, and American dishes. All meals are made to order, and the staff is warm and delightful. Try the Ben's Family Pancake Wrap; it is unique and scrumptious.

If you're craving a burger and frozen custard, stop in at **Spelunker's Frozen Custard and Cavern Burgers** (116 South St., 540/631-0300, www.spelunkerscustard.com, daily 11am-10-pm, under $10). They offer dine-in and drive-through service with fun custard flavors of the day. One of the sweetest is The Circus, which is cotton candy custard with rainbow sprinkles, marshmallow topping, and sugar cookies.

ACCOMMODATIONS

Several hotels provide rooms in Front Royal for around $100, such as the **Holiday Inn Hotel & Suites Front Royal Blue Ridge Shadows** (111 Hospitality Dr., 540/631-3050, www.ihg.com, $93-208). The hotel is next to the Blue Ridge Shadows Golf Club and offers 124 guest rooms on seven floors, with free high-speed Internet, a heated indoor pool, a 24-hour fitness center, and a 24-hour business center.

Another good option is the **Hampton Inn Front Royal** (9800 Winchester Rd., 540/635-1882, www.hamptoninn3.hilton.com, $123-177). This pleasant, 102-room hotel is located just off I-66 and is a short drive from town. Guests can enjoy a complimentary breakfast, free wireless Internet, and a fitness room.

For those who prefer to stay in a bed-and-breakfast, the lovely **Woodward House on Manor Grade** (413 S. Royal Ave., 540/635-7010, www.acountryhome.com, $120-225) is a cozy spot with a homey feel. This charming home has six guest rooms and two cabins (all with private bathrooms). A delightful breakfast is served daily, and each room comes with snacks, fresh-baked cookies, and water. The house sits on a hill above town and has nice views.

INFORMATION AND SERVICES

For additional information on Front Royal, contact the **Front Royal-Warren County Visitor Center** (414 E. Main St., 540/635-5788, www.discoverfrontroyal.com, daily 9am-5pm).

GETTING THERE

Front Royal is 70 miles west of Washington DC and is easily accessed from I-66.

Luray

The town of Luray is nestled in the scenic Shenandoah Valley in Page County. The town is less than five square miles and has a population of fewer than 5,000 people. Luray is a western gateway to Shenandoah National Park and is a two-hour drive from Washington DC. The charming downtown area along Main Street is the focal point of Luray and offers visitors a choice of restaurants and shops. The streets are decorated with seasonal flowers, and the lovely Shenandoah Valley scenery is everywhere. Luray is a great day or overnight trip from many areas of Virginia and Maryland and offers small-town charm, friendly residents, outdoor recreation, and the world-famous Luray Caverns.

SIGHTS
★ Luray Caverns

There are many cavern attractions in the Blue Ridge Mountains, but the cream of the crop is **Luray Caverns** (970 US 211 West, GPS 101 Cave Hill Rd., 540/743-6551, www.luraycaverns.com, opens daily at 9am with tours beginning every 20 min., closing hours vary by season: Apr.-June 6pm, June 15-Labor Day 7pm, day after Labor Day-Oct. 6pm, Nov.-Mar. weekdays 4pm, weekends 5pm, adults $28, children 6-12 $15, seniors 62 and over $25, children 5 and under free). This incredible natural wonder has been awing visitors since it was first discovered in 1878. Upon entering the caverns, you are transported into a subterranean world of mystery that took more than four million centuries to create. A series of paved walkways guide visitors through massive cavern "rooms" filled with natural stalagmites, stalactites, and, when the two join, columns or pillars. Some of the chambers have ceilings that are 10 stories high.

There are many attractions along the paved route in the caverns, including the famous **Stalacpipe Organ.** It is considered the world's largest musical instrument and is made up of stalactites covering 3.5 acres. The organ produces symphonic-quality sounds when the stalactites are tapped (electronically) by rubber-tipped mallets. It took 36 years to perfect the organ, but visitors can hear its haunting melodies played on every tour.

The general admission rate includes the entrance fee to the caverns, a cavern tour (tours depart every 20 minutes and are one hour), a self-guided tour of the **Car and Carriage Caravan Museum,** which displays restored cars, carriages, and coaches from 1725 to 1941, and entrance to the **Luray Valley Museum,** which interprets early Shenandoah Valley culture from as far back as precontact native people and includes a Swiss Bible (in the German vernacular) from 1536. Visitors can also enjoy displays of thousands of toys and train-related artifacts at **Toy Town Junction.**

Other attractions at the caverns can be enjoyed for an additional fee, including the **Rope Adventure Park,** a challenging multilevel ropes course with trails consisting of several poles connected by acrobatic elements; the **Stonyman Mining Company Gem Sluice,** a re-created operational mining station; and the **Garden Maze,** a half-mile evergreen-hedge maze.

Another interesting sight opposite Luray Caverns is the **Belle Brown Northcott Memorial,** which is also known as the **Luray Singing Tower.** This beautiful 117-foot-tall bell tower was built in 1937 and contains 47 bells (the largest of which is 7,640 pounds with a diameter of six feet). The tower holds regular recitals from spring through fall.

Luray Zoo

The **Luray Zoo** (1087 US 211, 540/743-4113, www.lurayzoo.com, Apr.-Oct. daily 10am-5pm, Nov.-Feb. Wed.-Sun. 11am-4pm, Mar. daily 11am-4pm until daylight savings time then 10am-5pm, adults $12, children 3-12 $6, seniors age 56 and over $11, children 2 and under free) is a small zoo that rescues exotic animals. The more than 250 animals that live there have all been taken from sad and harmful situations and given a permanent home. The friendly zookeepers interact with both the animals and the visitors and are happy to answer any questions. The zoo's reptile center has one of the largest collections of snakes on the East Coast. There is a petting section of the zoo for children, with animals such as goats, deer, a burro, and a potbellied pig.

RECREATION

Luray is an outdoor town. Tucked in the Shenandoah Valley, Luray offers visitors a wonderful home base for hiking, fishing, canoeing, tubing, and kayaking. **Shenandoah River Outfitters** (6502 S. Page Valley Rd., 540/743-4159, www.shenandoah-river.com) is a great place to rent boats and gear. They rent white-water and flat-water canoes and kayaks ($36-56 per day) and offer 3-4-mile tubing trips ($22). They also rent furnished log cabins ($150-250 per night).

Those wishing to hike can take the **Stony**

Underground Adventures

stalactites, stalagmites, and other formations at Luray Caverns

The mountains of Virginia harbor some of the nation's best caverns. Many are open to the public and can be explored in a couple of hours.

- **Luray Caverns** (page 243) is the granddaddy of all caverns. This awe-inspiring natural wonder in Luray, Virginia, transports visitors into an underground world of mystery and adventure that took more than four million centuries to create (yes, *centuries*).

- **Skyline Caverns** (page 240) near Front Royal, Virginia, offers kids of all ages a magical subterranean experience. With cave formations, three streams, and a 37-foot waterfall, this is another top cavern experience in rural Virginia.

- **Grand Caverns Regional Park** (page 250) near Harrisonburg, Virginia, is the oldest continuously operating "show" cave in the nation. It opened to the public in 1806 and at one time hosted elaborate balls in its 5,000-square-foot "Grand Ballroom."

- **Natural Bridge Caverns,** along the Blue Ridge Parkway, is 34 stories below ground. Visitors can see this natural wonder during a trip to a unique aboveground attraction, **Natural Bridge** (page 313).

Man Mountain Hike (www.hikingupward. com), in Shenandoah National Park. This short (less than four miles) loop hike is pleasant, easy, and offers stunning views of the park. Just under the main peak is a fun rock-climbing area known as **Little Stony Man.** The trailhead is off of Skyland Drive (between mp 41 and 42).

Triathletes can compete in the annual **Luray Triathlon** (luraytriathlon.com), which is held over two days in August and features both international- and sprint-distance races.

FOOD

Moonshadows Restaurant (132 E. Main St., 540/743-1911, www.moonshadowsonmain. com, Thurs.-Mon. 4pm-8:30pm, Sat.-Sun. 10:30am-2:30pm, $12-29) offers an elegant atmosphere (white tablecloths, wood floors, etc.) with delicious food in a beautifully renovated blue house on Main Street. The wonderful food presentation matches flavorful selections such as Brazilian steak, lump crab cakes, jumbo shrimp, and blueberry bread pudding. They also offer a patio/garden dining space. This is a great spot for a date, special occasion, or simply a good meal with friendly service.

Outstanding New York-style pizza, pasta, and delicious cheesesteaks can be found at **Gennaro's Pizza and Italian Restaurant** (402 W. Main St., 540/743-2200, daily 11am-9:30pm, $4-14). The owner is from Napoli, and many of the recipes are family heirlooms.

For a cup of coffee or casual sandwich, stop in the **Gathering Grounds Patisserie and Cafe** (24 E. Main St., 540/743-1121, www. ggrounds.com, Mon.-Thurs. 7am-6pm, Fri. 7am-7pm, Sat. 8am-7pm, Sun. 11am-3pm, $10-15). They serve a variety of egg sandwiches, wraps, quiche, soup, salads, and homemade baked treats (different every day). They also have delicious coffee, frappuccino, chai lattes, smoothies, beer, and wine. The atmosphere is warm and friendly.

A wonderful wine bar and bottle shop right on Main Street is **The Valley Cork** (55 E. Main St., 540/743-1207, www.thevalleycork. com, Thurs.-Fri. 4pm-10pm, Sat. 2pm-10pm, Sun. 2pm-8pm, $6-17). They offer Virginia and international wines (by the glass or bottle), small plates, flatbread, and charcuterie boards. They also feature live music.

ACCOMMODATIONS

There are many cabins for rent in and around Luray. Some overlook the Shenandoah River while others are mountain-view retreats. The **Luray & Page County website** (www. luraypage.com) has an extensive listing of available cabins and is a good resource for private accommodations.

There are also several inns and motels in town. The **Mimslyn Inn** (401 W. Main St., 540/743-5105, www.mimslyninn.com, $150-359) is the premier overnight location in Luray. The colonial-style inn is just a short walk from the historic downtown area and strives to offer "vintage Southern hospitality." Visitors enter the property on a circular driveway leading to a portico lined with columns.

The winding staircase in the lobby is reminiscent of those found in grand homes of the Old South, and each guest is warmly greeted by the attending staff. The inn has 45 guest rooms, each individually decorated. Rooms are available in a variety of sizes in several price ranges. There is a spa, fitness room, and business center on-site as well as a formal dining room and casual tavern.

The **Inn of the Shenandoah** (138 E. Main St., 540/300-9777, www.innoftheshenandoah. com, $140-195) is a nice, three-suite bed-and-breakfast with antique glass windows and European accents. The house has a pretty front porch and second-story balcony. Behind the inn is a renovated farmhouse called the **Cottage of the Inn,** which offers two additional suites.

The **Hotel Laurance** (2 S. Court St., 540/742-7060, www.hotellaurance.com, $185-225) is a boutique hotel offering 12 guest rooms, many with full kitchens. The decor is lovely and modern, and their website has detailed write-ups about each room. This hotel is geared toward hosting small weddings and events.

The very similar **Luray Caverns Motel East** (at the east entrance to Luray Caverns across from the Luray Singing Tower) and **Luray Caverns Motel West** (at the west entrance to Luray Caverns) offer standard accommodations. Both have free wireless Internet and swimming pools. Rates for both range $79-99 per night, and reservations can be made by calling 540/743-6551.

CAMPING

Several local campgrounds are convenient to Luray, including **Yogi Bear's Jellystone Park** (2250 US 211, 540/300-1697, www. campluray.com, camping $76-110, cabins $190-286), which offers camping and cabin rentals three miles east of downtown off US 211 and **Camp Roosevelt** (540/984-4101, www.fs.usda.gov, $10), 8.5 miles northwest of Luray on State Route 675 in the George Washington and Jefferson National Forests.

INFORMATION AND SERVICES

Begin your visit to Luray at the **Luray Train Depot and Visitor Center** (18 Campbell St., 540/743-3915, www.visitluraypage.com, daily 9am-5pm). This lovely building houses knowledgeable staff, brochures, and clean bathrooms amid a parklike setting. It is downtown about a block off Main Street and is within easy walking distance to shops and restaurants.

GETTING THERE

Luray is 93 miles southwest of Washington DC on US 211. US 340 also runs through Luray.

New Market

Fourteen miles west of Luray is the town of New Market. It was established in 1796 and became known for its printing and publishing industry in the early 1800s. During the Civil War, the town was a key thoroughfare in the Shenandoah Valley and witnessed Stonewall Jackson's troops marching through at four different times. The historic Battle of New Market took place in 1864 and is reenacted annually in mid-May.

Visitors to New Market will find a cozy, quiet downtown area on the east side of I-81 and the historic battlefield on the west side of the interstate. Explore the battlefield or take in a show at the **Rouss Center for the Arts** (9357 N. Congress St., 888/341-7313, www. rousscenter.org). They offer theater performances including plays, musicals, and dramatic readings. They also showcase local artists and artwork.

SIGHTS

★ New Market Battlefield State Historical Park

The main attraction in New Market is the **New Market Battlefield State Historical Park** (8895 George R. Collins Pkwy., 866/515-1864, www.vmi.edu, daily 9am-5pm, adults $10, children 6-12 $6, seniors 65 and over $9, children 5 and under free). This 300-acre park occupies the site of a Civil War battle on May 15, 1864, famous for being the only

New Market Battlefield State Historical Park

Destination Dining

Inn at Little Washington

One of the premier dining destinations in Virginia is the famous **Inn at Little Washington Restaurant** (309 Middle St., Washington, 540/675-3800, www.theinnatlittlewashington.com). This extremely high-end restaurant is renowned for its incredible food, scenery, and service. Located in the town of Washington, between Front Royal and Luray and not far off US 211 and US 522, the inn sits on a historic street that hasn't changed much since George Washington himself named the town roads in 1749 (he was only 17 at the time).

The inn was founded in 1978, and the main building (where the restaurant is) occupies the space of a former garage, dance hall, and general store. It has since grown into a campus of sorts, incorporating many additional properties in the village (some dating back to the 1700s) into its accommodations (in addition to nearly a dozen guest rooms and suites located in the main building). There is also a cutting garden (where fresh herbs and vegetables are grown), a walking path, a ballroom, and a gift shop.

The inn describes itself as an "unassuming dark blue building festooned with flags on the corner of Middle and Main Streets." This may be true, but once you step inside and see the crackling fire and tables adorned with silver and crystal, you will know you've entered a very special restaurant that is renowned for its exquisite food. Not only do they purchase food from local farmers, but the inn also has its own gardens and orchards.

Dinner reservations are accepted up to a year in advance. They offer three tasting menus to choose from. Prices vary during holidays and special events, but are generally $238 per person (not including beverages, tax, or gratuity). An optional wine pairing of $170 per person is available. Main course selections can include items such as pan-roasted Maine lobster, juniper-crusted venison loin, and seared rare tuna crusted with mustard seeds, while desserts may include choices such as a Southern butter pecan ice-cream sandwich, lemon-meringue tartlet with toasted pistachios, or cocoa nib napoleon with caramelized bananas.

This is truly a special and memorable dining experience in a beautiful location.

occasion in American history when college cadets were responsible for victory in combat. During the battle, cadets from the Virginia Military Institute in Lexington fought alongside Confederate soldiers to force Union troops out of the Shenandoah Valley.

Today visitors can explore nine structures at the 19th-century **Bushong Farm** that provided shelter to the Bushong family as the battle unfolded around them on their property (primarily in the orchard right behind the house). After the battle, the farmhouse was used as a field hospital for a week (bloodstains can still be seen in the parlor).

Another on-site attraction is the **Virginia Museum of the Civil War.** This museum has information and exhibits on the entire Civil War but focuses on the conflict in Virginia. The museum is housed in the **Hall of Valor,** a monument building dedicated to young people who have served in the military during times of national need. Plan to watch the Emmy Award-winning film *Field of Lost Shoes* during your visit.

The park also offers walking trails, scenic overlooks of the Shenandoah River, and wonderful picnic areas. The park is a National Historic Landmark.

It is important to note that the nearby New Market Battlefield Military Museum, on the way to the battlefield park, is not part of the state-run battlefield facility (despite its official-looking Greek Revival exterior with large white columns). It offers a private collection of relics, many of which are not Civil War related.

FOOD

New Market isn't known as a foodie's paradise, but good comfort food can be found on Congress Street. A local favorite with an old-fashioned ambience is the **Southern Kitchen** (9576 S. Congress St., 540/740-3514, daily 7am-9pm, $5-15). They serve simple, Southern cooking (think country ham, pork barbecue, burgers, and fried chicken) in a friendly atmosphere. Look for the neon sign and crowded parking lot; it is hard to miss in small downtown New Market. They are open for breakfast, lunch, and dinner.

Another popular choice is **Jalisco Mexican Restaurant** (9403 S. Congress St., 540/740-9404, Mon.-Thurs. 11am-10pm, Fri.-Sat. 11am-10:30pm, Sun. 11am-9:30pm, $5-15). This eatery serves traditional Mexican food from an extensive menu. The atmosphere is lively (for New Market), and the place has a friendly vibe. They have good chorizo and a lot of vegetarian options as well as dishes with shrimp.

ACCOMMODATIONS

There aren't many choices for hotels in New Market. There are a few inexpensive chain hotels such as the **Quality Inn Shenandoah Valley** (162 W. Old Cross Rd., 540/740-3141, www.choicehotels.com, $120-125), with 100 rooms and an adjoining restaurant, and the **Days Inn New Market Battlefield** (9360 George Collins Pkwy., 540/740-4100, www.wyndhamhotels.com, $67-84), which has a continental breakfast, free wireless Internet, and a seasonal pool.

Another option is the **Shenvalee Golf Resort** (9660 Fairway Dr., 540/740-3181, www.shenvalee.com, $92). Accommodations here include a guesthouse and motel less than three miles from New Market Battlefield State Historical Park. The 42 rooms are not luxurious, but they offer balconies with golf course or pool views, free Wi-Fi, and minifridges. The guesthouse has four bedrooms, a kitchen, and a mountain view. There is also a restaurant on-site.

The **Rosendale Inn Bed and Breakfast** (17917 Farmhouse Ln., 540/325-4544, www.rosendaleinn.com, $150) is a good choice for a quiet getaway. The historic home was built in 1790 and has two lovely 60-foot verandas (with rocking chairs and benches) and a two-story front porch. Accommodations include four rooms in the main house and a separate cozy cottage that has a fireplace. The owner is an author and has many interesting stories to share about the area. He goes out of his way to make sure each guest has a good experience.

There is a barn on the property that can accommodate guests' horses.

If you'd prefer a bed-and-breakfast that includes the entire house with your stay, the **Jacob Swartz House** (574 Jiggady Rd., 540/740-9208, www.jacobswartz.com, $150) is for you. The house is a lovely historic cottage and renovated cobbler shop that sits on a river bluff. It has a master bedroom and a second loft bedroom as well as a living room (with a woodstove), dining area, and full kitchen (stocked with staples). The house has wireless Internet and is located outside of town on a long country road.

INFORMATION AND SERVICES

Additional information on New Market can be found at www.newmarketvirginia.com and www.shenandoahvalleyweb.com.

GETTING THERE

New Market is 113 miles (approximately two hours) southwest of Washington DC off US 211 and I-81.

Harrisonburg

Harrisonburg, tucked away in the Shenandoah Valley, is part of Rockingham County and has a population of around 50,000. It is best known as the home of **James Madison University.** The historic section of its downtown area includes 10 blocks of locally owned restaurants, galleries, and museums.

Harrisonburg is an active town, due in part to the large population of students that live here much of the year and also to its proximity to the Blue Ridge Mountains. The town was named as a top location for families to "beat nature deficit disorder" by *Backpacker Magazine.*

SIGHTS
James Madison University

James Madison University (JMU) (800 S. Main St., 540/568-6211, www.jmu.edu) is the largest attraction in Harrisonburg. The school was founded in 1908 and offers more than 130 degree programs. With over 21,000 students and 148 buildings on 721 acres, the school dominates the Harrisonburg landscape. JMU has earned many national rankings and recognitions and is considered to be one of the most environmentally responsible colleges.

The beautiful campus is a pleasure to walk around, with the focal point being the large grassy quadrangle on South Main Street, where students can be seen lounging, reading, or playing ball when the weather is nice. This is also the location of the stately **Wilson Hall,** which houses a 1,372-seat auditorium under its red roof and was named after President Woodrow Wilson. It is said that on a clear day, it is possible to see Staunton, Virginia—the birthplace of its namesake—from its cupola.

The campus is split by I-81, with the original buildings on the west side and the newer **College of Integrated Science and Technology** on the east side (along with other academic and resident buildings). A bridge and a tunnel connect the two sides.

A highlight of the campus is the **Edith J. Carrier Arboretum** (540/568-3194, open daily dawn to dusk, free) on University Boulevard. This beautiful, 125-acre landscaped area offers nature trails and guided tours by appointment.

Explore More Discovery Museum

For those traveling with children, the **Explore More Discovery Museum** (150 S. Main St., 540/442-8900, www.iexploremore.com, Tues.-Sat. 9:30am-5pm, open Mon. June 10-Aug. 26, $7.50, children under 1 free) is a great stop that has interactive exhibits geared toward children under 10 on topics such as health, construction, art, science, mechanics, theater, farms, the outdoors, and much more.

Virginia Quilt Museum

The **Virginia Quilt Museum** (301 S. Main St., 540/433-3818, www.vaquiltmuseum.org, mid-Feb.-mid-Dec. Tues.-Sat. 10am-4pm, adults $8, students with ID $5, military, first responders, and seniors over 65 $7, children under 12 free) is a small specialty museum that features a wonderful permanent collection of nearly 300 quilts, antique sewing machines, and a gift store. They also have a handful of rotating exhibits throughout the year. The museum is housed in a pretty home that was built in 1856. Tours are self-guided, but guided group tours can be arranged.

★ Grand Caverns Regional Park

Approximately 15 miles southeast of Harrisonburg is **Grand Caverns Regional Park** (5 Grand Caverns Dr., Grottoes, 540/249-5705, www.grandcaverns.com, Nov.-Mar. daily 10am-4pm, Apr.-Oct. daily 9am-5pm, adults $20, children $11, seniors $18). Discovered in 1804 and opened to the public in 1806, Grand Caverns is the oldest continuously operating "show" cave in the country. The caverns are made up of an impressive network of caves, including Cathedral Hall, one of the most massive underground rooms on the East Coast, as well as the Grand Ballroom, which is 5,000 square feet and literally was the site of balls in the early years after the caverns were discovered. Many famous people have visited the caverns, including Thomas Jefferson and both Confederate and Union soldiers (of which more than 200 signed their names on the cave walls). This is a great attraction for both adults and children. Seventy-minute tours are given on the hour. Admission to the caverns is by guided tour only.

The park also features a pool, minigolf, fitness, cycling and hiking trails, fishing, picnic areas, and **Fountain Cave** (tours offered in May on Sat., June-July Tues., Thurs., and Sat.,

must be at least 12 years old, starting at $50). Fountain Cave was a commercial cave almost 100 years ago and is now open for two-hour tours. There are no lights in the cavern, and guests are given helmets, headlights, knee-pads, and gloves. Exploring is via a rough path from the 1800s or the more adventurous way, which includes crawling and strenuous climbing.

RECREATION

The nearby **Massanutten Resort** (1822 Resort Dr., Massanutten, 540/289-9441, www.massresort.com) is a 6,000-acre, four-season family destination that offers lodging, skiing, snowboarding, snow-tubing, golfing, fishing, mountain biking, a water park, a spa, and hiking around Massanutten Peak as well as panoramic views of the Blue Ridge Mountains. Best known as a ski resort, Massanutten has 14 trails (all with lights for night skiing) with 1,110 feet of vertical drop (lift tickets are $44-77). Massanutten is about 15 miles southeast of Harrisonburg.

Cycling is big in Harrisonburg. Both road biking and mountain biking are popular, and many events are scheduled throughout the year. For information on cycling in the area visit the **Shenandoah Valley Bicycle Coalition** website (www.svbcoalition.org). Mountain bike rentals are available at Massanutten Resort (starting at $50).

FOOD

Fresh local ingredients, beautiful exposed brick walls, white tablecloths, and great food are some of the key ingredients to the success of the ★ **Local Chop & Grill House** (56 W. Gay St., 540/801-0505, www.localchops.com, Mon.-Thurs. 5pm-9pm, Fri.-Sat. 5pm-10pm, $16-34). This wonderful restaurant occupies the former building of Harrisonburg's Old City Produce Exchange, which is perfect for this modern establishment whose menu features fresh, handpicked local and seasonal

1: stunning view from Massanutten Resort **2:** Joshua Wilton House

foods. They specialize in steak and seafood and have a large selection of savory house-made sauces.

Another local favorite is **Vitos Italian Kitchen** (1047 Port Republic Rd., 540/433-1113, www.vitositaliankitchen.com, Sun.-Thurs. 11am-10pm, Fri.-Sat. 11am-11pm, $8-17). This wonderful Italian restaurant is a great place to bring the family. The atmosphere is warm and inviting, the food is delicious, and the staff is friendly. The menu has traditional Italian items, house specials, and pizza. Their house Italian salad dressing deserves accolades on its own.

ACCOMMODATIONS

The **Hotel Madison and Shenandoah Conference Center** (710 S. Main St., 540/564-0200, www.hotelmadison.com, $167-228) is a 230-room hotel with a restaurant, fitness center, indoor pool, and coffee shop. It is connected to a 21,000-square-foot conference center. The rooms and suites are modern and offer downtown or mountain views. On-site parking is $5.

Charming lodgings can be found at the **Joshua Wilton House** (412 S. Main St., 540/434-4464, www.joshuawilton.com, $150-175). This lovely inn and restaurant has five beautiful guest rooms in an elegant Victorian home. Each offers a feather-top queen-size bed, private bathroom, ceiling fan, antique furniture, robes, and free wireless Internet. A continental breakfast is included with each stay. The inn is also known for its restaurant and wonderful seasonally inspired menu. They offer beer- and wine-tasting dinners and more than 100 bottles of wine on their wine list. The Joshua Wilton House is where actor Richard Dreyfuss spent his honeymoon in 2006.

INFORMATION AND SERVICES

For additional information on Harrisonburg, visit the **Harrisonburg Tourism** website at www.visitharrisonburgva.com or stop by **Harrisonburg Tourism and Visitor Services** (212 S. Main St., 540/432-8935, daily 9am-5pm).

GETTING THERE

Harrisonburg sits right on I-81 and is 132 miles (about a 2.25-hour drive) southwest from Washington DC.

Staunton

Founded in 1747, Staunton is the self-proclaimed "Queen City of the Shenandoah." It sits in Augusta County and has approximately 24,000 residents.

The focal point of Staunton is the charming and compact historic downtown area. Beautiful Victorian architecture, unique restaurants, local galleries, and independent shops lend the area to exploration on foot. Staunton was lucky that it escaped destruction during the Civil War, and many of its original 18th- and 19th-century homes still stand today. The city does a wonderful job preserving the town's heritage and visual appeal by disallowing power lines and cell towers within view in the historic districts.

If you hear someone mention the "Wharf," don't look around for water. The Wharf is the neighborhood surrounding the train station. The name dates back to the 19th century when the warehouses in this historic neighborhood resembled those commonly seen in port towns.

Staunton was President Woodrow Wilson's birthplace. It is also the home of **Mary Baldwin University, Stuart Hall School** (a private prep school), and the **Virginia School for the Deaf and Blind.**

Haunted Staunton

There are many stories of hauntings throughout Virginia, a number of which center on towns where Civil War battles were fought. Staunton is no exception, and in fact, seems to have more than its fair share of tales of the paranormal.

The most famous haunting in Staunton is at the train station. This is where a member of an opera troupe, Myrtle Knox, was killed in 1890 when a train carrying her troupe derailed and demolished Staunton's C&O depot. The 18-year-old actress bled to death at the site after multiple injuries. It has been reported many times by eyewitnesses that Knox's spirit now haunts the rail station and was even seen looking through windows at the former Pullman Restaurant (which is now closed). It is interesting to note that the train station has been featured in several movies, including The Love Letter in 1998.

Another well-known haunting is at the Thornerose House at Gypsy Hill. The home was built in 1912. Shortly after, the owner's 10-year-old son became very ill. His dedicated nurse, Caroline, spent day and night by the boy's side trying desperately to keep him alive, but he eventually died. It is said that Caroline now roams the house looking for him. The house served as a bed-and-breakfast for many years, and guests reported meeting Caroline in what was called the Canterbury Room (where she had lived), at which point she would introduce herself and then disappear. She was also known to play tricks on people by stealing their keys and bringing them to her room.

The Selma House was built in approximately 1848 and is the site of another famous Staunton haunting. In 1864, when Union troops were stationed in Staunton, they were said to have chased a young Confederate soldier into the house. He stopped in front of the fireplace, turned toward the door, and was shot and killed. The young man's blood flowed onto the wooden floor and caused a rather disturbing bloodstain that became a permanent mark on the floor despite numerous efforts to remove it. In addition to his blood, the soldier's spirit is said to have never left the house, and is described by the many who have seen him as a "polite man in uniform" who listens intently to conversations going on in the home. One hundred years after his death, he is said to have pushed a woman out of her bed in the middle of the night. The Selma House is a private residence, but it is easily spotted at the top of Selma Boulevard near the park.

Many additional ghost sightings have been reported in Staunton locations, including at the Stonewall Jackson Hotel, Emilio's restaurant, the Clock Tower, Mary Baldwin University, the grounds of the Commonwealth Center for Children & Adolescents, and in private homes.

SIGHTS

Frontier Culture Museum

The **Frontier Culture Museum** (1290 Richmond Rd., 540/332-7850, www.frontiermuseum.org, mid-Mar.-Nov. daily 9am-5pm, Dec.-mid-Mar. daily 10am-4pm, adults $12, students $11, children 6-12 $7, seniors $11.50, under 6 free) is a popular family destination that tells the fascinating story of the thousands of immigrants who settled colonial America. The fun and informative museum explores the lives of people from England, Germany, Ireland, and West Africa and how they all contributed to the success of our country. The museum is a collection of original and reproduced buildings that represent the Old World and America. Each features interpretive signage, period furnishings, food, animals, and living-history demonstrations presented by costumed interpreters.

Woodrow Wilson Presidential Library and Museum

The **Woodrow Wilson Presidential Library and Museum** (20 N. Coalter St., Staunton, 540/885-0897, www.woodrowwilson.org, Mon.-Sat. 9am-5pm, Sun. noon-5pm, adults $15, youth 6-15 $8, over 60 $14, active military $12, under 6 free) tells the story of our country's 28th president. Self-guided tours lead visitors through seven galleries depicting different phases of Wilson's life. A highlight is the president's restored

Pierce-Arrow limousine from 1919. He liked it so much his friends bought it for him when he left office. There is also a state-of-the-art World War I trench experience, a research library, gardens, and a hands-on kids' corner.

At the same address is the **Woodrow Wilson Birthplace.** This wonderfully restored Greek Revival home offers guided tours and a window into what life was like back in 1856, the year Wilson was born. The home contains period furniture and artifacts from the Wilson family. Behind the house is a beautiful Victorian-style garden that was created in the 1930s.

ENTERTAINMENT AND RECREATION

The **Blackfriars Playhouse** (10 S. Market St., 540/851-1733, www. americanshakespearecenter.com) is a widely popular local theater in Staunton. Run by **The American Shakespeare Center,** the theater is said to be the only re-creation of Shakespeare's indoor theater in the world. It may sound small, with just 300 seats, but the performances are greatly entertaining and energetic. Balcony seats are sold as general admission, but offer a terrific view. Aim to get there early (they have entertainment before the show) so you can grab a balcony seat in the front row. This is a fun theater with a relaxed atmosphere.

Gypsy Hill Park (600 Churchville Ave.) is a lovely 214-acre public park with an outdoor gym, walking paths, ball fields, playgrounds, a duck pond, tennis courts, a small train, and an outdoor pool. Pets are allowed, but they must remain on a leash.

FOOD
American

★ **Zynodoa** (115 E. Beverley St., 540/885-7775, www.zynodoa.com, Mon.-Tues. 5pm-9:30pm, Wed.-Sat. 5pm-10:30pm, Sun. 10am-2pm and 5pm-9:30pm, $21-30) offers wonderful contemporary Southern cuisine. This farm-to-table restaurant has an ever-changing menu (depending on what fresh

ingredients are available). They even have their own 50-acre farm from which they harvest many ingredients for their dishes (including fresh eggs). Examples of menu items include wood-smoked pork, blackened wild blue catfish, and double-cut New York strip steak. The service is outstanding; servers are well versed in the details of the menu and are also helpful with suggestions and wine pairings. This is one of the few restaurants open late on Sunday nights.

For great ribs and delicious steak and burgers, stop in the **Mill Street Grill** (1 Mill St., 540/886-0656, www.millstreetgrill. com, Mon.-Thurs. 4pm-9:30pm, Fri.-Sat. 4pm-10:30pm, Sun. 11am-9pm, $8-30). The restaurant is housed in a former turn-of-the-20th-century flour mill. It has a loyal client base and can be crowded on weekends. The menu also includes seafood, pasta, sandwiches, and vegetarian choices. If you happen to be in town during Mardi Gras, they offer jazz entertainment and go all out with their decorations.

The slightly out-of-the-way **Depot Grille** (42 Middlebrook Ave., 540/885-7332, www. depotgrille.com, Sun.-Thurs. 11am-10pm, Fri.-Sat. 11am-11pm, $9-24) is a unique little restaurant in the historic freight-train station in Staunton. The atmosphere is train oriented, cozy, and fun. The main dining room maintains the original hardwood floors from the station, and the dining booths were once church pews. There is also a 40-foot-long Victorian bar that came from a historic luxury hotel in Albany, New York. They offer a lot of variety on their menu (including ribs, chicken, prime rib, salads, sandwiches, and seafood), and there is an enclosed deck with views of the downtown area.

A downtown restaurant offering a flavorful Southern menu is **Byers Street Bistro** (18 Byers St., 540/887-6100, www. byersstreetbistro.com, Sun.-Thurs. 11am-11pm, Fri.-Sat. 11am-midnight, $10-25). This upbeat favorite has a large patio and live entertainment many nights. The menu includes selections such as shrimp and grits, fish tacos, ribs, steak, and gourmet pizza.

Italian

A large dining establishment with a small-restaurant feel is **Emilio's** (23 E. Beverley St., 540/885-0102, www.emiliositalianrestaurant. com, Tues.-Thurs. 11am-9:30pm, Fri.-Sat. 11am-10:30pm, Sun. 11am-8:30pm, $15-27). This wonderful, friendly Italian eatery has terrific food and great ambience with its downtown location, lounge, four fireplaces, and a rooftop patio. Fresh pasta, wonderful specials, wine tastings, and live entertainment many nights in the lounge help make this a fun place to spend an evening.

ACCOMMODATIONS

$100-200

The **Stonewall Jackson Hotel and Conference Center** (24 S. Market St., 540/885-4848, www.stonewalljacksonhotel. com, $129-199) was built in 1924 and has since been fully restored. It has 124 guest rooms, a heated indoor pool, a fitness center, and a business center. The rooms aren't large, but they are comfortable and well appointed. The public areas are nice also. A big plus for this hotel is its location in downtown Staunton, convenient to attractions and dining. The hotel is also pet friendly ($50). Parking is $7.50.

The ★ **Blackburn Inn** (301 Greenville Ave., 540/712-0601, www.blackburn-inn.com, $135-250) is a welcome recent addition to the hotel scene in Staunton. This fully restored, 49-room boutique hotel was formerly the headquarters of the Western State Hospital (originally named the Western Lunatic Asylum), which was one of two key hospitals in Virginia for those with mental illness. The hotel was named after Thomas Blackburn, the original building architect (circa 1828), who worked as an apprentice for Thomas Jefferson. The hospital relocated in the 1970s, and the building became a medium-security prison in 1981. Abandoned in 2002, the property was purchased in 2006, and the renovated hotel opened in 2019. Today guests enjoy rooms with 27 unique floor plans, modern furnishings, tall ceilings, and an incredible spiral staircase on the fourth floor that leads to a cupola with stunning views of Staunton. There is also a fitness room and bistro on-site. The hotel is dog friendly (no extra fee) with complimentary amenities for your best friend (such as bowls, beds, treats, and waste bags).

$200-300

The ★ **Inn at WestShire Farms** (1329 Commerce Rd., 540/248-4650, www. westshirefarms.com, $199-305) is a cozy bed-and-breakfast just north of town. The inn was built prior to the Civil War and has nine guest rooms in two buildings. The main house contains the common areas including an English-style conservatory, living room (with a fireplace and baby grand piano), meeting room, breakfast room, and outdoor patios. A beautifully renovated barn contains eight guest rooms, a common area living room, and decks overlooking the valley. The house and grounds are elegant and well maintained. A delicious full breakfast is served each morning, or guests can opt for a light breakfast or breakfast to go.

INFORMATION AND SERVICES

For additional information about visiting Staunton, go to www.visitstaunton.com or visit the downtown **Staunton Visitor Center** (35 S. New St., 540/332-3971, daily 9:30am-5:30pm).

GETTING THERE

Staunton is located in the Shenandoah Valley off I-81, 28 miles south of Harrisonburg and 36 miles north of Lexington.

Allegheny Highlands

The western reaches of the state toward the West Virginia border include Highland County, Bath County, and parts of Augusta and Allegheny Counties. The Allegheny Mountains spill into West Virginia, and the area is split by river valleys. This region is scenic and sparsely populated. **US 220** from Monterey to Covington is a particularly scenic drive. Part of the enjoyment of a trip to this region can be the drive there and back.

HOT SPRINGS

The village of Hot Springs is in a beautiful area of Bath County that offers visitors a blend of resort atmosphere and natural scenery. Bath County is one of the wealthiest in Virginia, thanks to several resorts that have taken advantage of numerous natural thermal springs. Native tribes originally hailed their healing powers, but wealthy Virginians quickly learned what a wonderful retreat the mountain air and spring waters made. The area became the site of lavish resorts and to this day remains a destination for vacationers.

Hot Springs is quaint and small, and it contains many buildings that have existed for more than 150 years. The population is just over 700 people. During the summer months, Hot Springs hosts a local farmers market, and its **Garth Newel Music Center** (403 Garth Newel Ln., 540/839-5018, www.garthnewel. org) is a popular venue for chamber music, blues, and jazz performances.

Hot Springs is known as home to one of Virginia's premier resorts, ★ **The Omni Homestead Resort** (7696 Sam Snead Hwy., 540/839-1766, www.omnihotels.com, $279-463), off US 220. This enormous, 483-room resort has origins dating back to 1766 and was built around magnificent warm springs. The crystal-clear springs are still a focal point of the resort and maintain a uniform temperature and flow all year long. The mineral content of the springs is also very high, making them easy to float in. The spring pools are named for President Thomas Jefferson, who visited them in 1818.

The resort encompasses 2,000 manicured acres and has impressive stately brick buildings, two premier golf courses, and clay tennis courts. It offers elaborate lodging, dining, and many year-round recreational opportunities. It is also a popular conference site for Virginia businesses.

The resort is nothing short of a self-contained campus, with many restaurants, stores, a first-class European-style spa, and countless guest activities including a trout stream, a shooting club, and a small ski resort.

Additional information on Hot Springs can be found at www.discoverbath.com.

DOUTHAT STATE PARK

About 26 miles southeast of Hot Springs (much less as the crow flies) is one of the oldest state parks in Virginia, **Douthat State Park** (14239 Douthat State Park Rd., Millboro, 540/862-8100, www.dcr.virginia.gov, $7 entrance fee). The park is just under 4,500 acres and offers all of the following: 40 miles of hiking trails; a 50-acre lake for swimming, boating, and fishing; rental cabins ($86-405); camping ($10-40); horseback riding; nature programs; picnic areas; a camp store; laundry facilities; and a restaurant. This is a wonderful park for families and outdoor enthusiasts.

GETTING THERE

The Allegheny Highlands are approximately 200 miles from Washington DC. Much of the trip is on major highways such as I-66 and I-81, but the last 60 miles are in more rural, mountainous areas. This part of the trip is slow going but very scenic.

Central and Southern Virginia

Central and Southern Virginia is teeming with both history and natural beauty. It's a place where breathtaking byways and small country roads lead to state parks and country inns, and Civil War battlefields and presidential homes attest to the land's deep roots and historical importance.

The region encompasses a vast amount of acreage but is much less densely populated than Northern Virginia and Coastal Virginia. This part of the state is home to many colleges and universities, including the University of Virginia and Virginia Tech, and the state capital, Richmond.

From the Civil War battlefields in Fredericksburg to Robert E. Lee and Stonewall Jackson's final resting place in Lexington, Central

Highlights

Look for ★ to find recommended sights, activities, dining, and lodging.

★ **Fredericksburg & Spotsylvania National Military Park:** Hear the story of four important Civil War battles that resulted in more than 100,000 casualties (page 263).

★ **Capitol Square:** This beautifully landscaped 12-acre parcel in the heart of Richmond is home to several state buildings, including the Virginia State Capitol (page 274).

★ **Monticello:** This amazing 5,000-acre plantation was the home of Thomas Jefferson, author of the Declaration of Independence, and the University of Virginia's founder (page 293).

★ **Natural Bridge State Park:** This 20-story solid limestone arch is an impressive natural formation (page 305).

★ **Thomas Jefferson's Poplar Forest:** The president's personal retreat is an architectural masterpiece and the first octagonal house in the country (page 307).

★ **Virginia Military Institute:** The oldest state-supported military college in the country was founded in Lexington, Virginia, in 1839 (page 312).

★ **Taubman Museum of Art:** This popular museum in Roanoke highlights the culture of

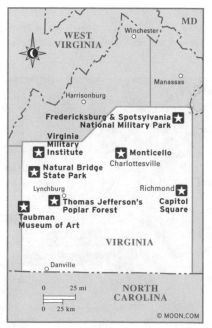

the Roanoke Valley and Southern Virginia (page 326).

Virginia offers visitors many opportunities to learn firsthand about the conflicts fought on the nation's soil and the many soldiers who gave their lives in those wars. Thomas Jefferson also had strong ties to Central Virginia, and his influence can be seen in many places. His home, Monticello, is a popular attraction in Charlottesville and is close to the University of Virginia, which was founded by Jefferson himself.

Southern Virginia is home to the scenic Blue Ridge Parkway and vast tracts of farmland and mountains that provide a deep contrast to the more populated regions of the state. Business suits are traded for fishing waders and limousines for tractors. Visitors can sample a slower pace of life through small towns and historic cities such as Lynchburg and Roanoke and gain an appreciation for the natural beauty of the state.

PLANNING YOUR TIME

You could easily spend weeks exploring Central and Southern Virginia. The drive time alone between Fredericksburg and Abingdon is approximately five hours. Since most of the cities in this region are about an hour away from each other, it is best to focus on a handful of destinations over a few days and to go from one to the next hitting the highlights.

If Civil War history is your passion, then Fredericksburg is a must. If you're fascinated with the accomplishments of Thomas Jefferson, then Charlottesville will be on your list.

If it's beautiful mountain scenery you seek, then a ride down the Blue Ridge Parkway should be on your agenda—especially during the fall. The parkway's Virginia portion stretches 218 miles and can be driven in one day but is best experienced over two days. This allows time to explore the unique sights and towns along the way and take in some of the best scenery the state has to offer.

The best way to move between cities is by car. The highways in Virginia are easy to navigate and are generally in excellent shape. I-95 and I-64 are the primary routes through Central Virginia, while I 81 is the main highway in Southern Virginia.

Fredericksburg

Fredericksburg is a far-reaching suburb of Washington DC and the largest city between Washington and Richmond. It is easily accessed from I-95, and the quaint historic district is a popular day trip from many locations in Virginia.

Fredericksburg is known for its extensive history. It was established in 1728 and named after the Prince of Wales and the father of King George III. Fredericksburg was a prominent port during the colonial era and home to George Washington during his boyhood. It also has an extensive Civil War history due in part to its location halfway between the Union and Confederate capitals.

Although the Fredericksburg area is home to many commuters who drive north for work, it is also home to the **University of Mary Washington** (www.umw.edu) and several large employers (such as GEICO). The city sits within the county lines of Spotsylvania but is an independent city with approximately 28,000 residents.

SIGHTS
Old Town Fredericksburg
Old Town Fredericksburg takes visitors

Central and Southern Virginia

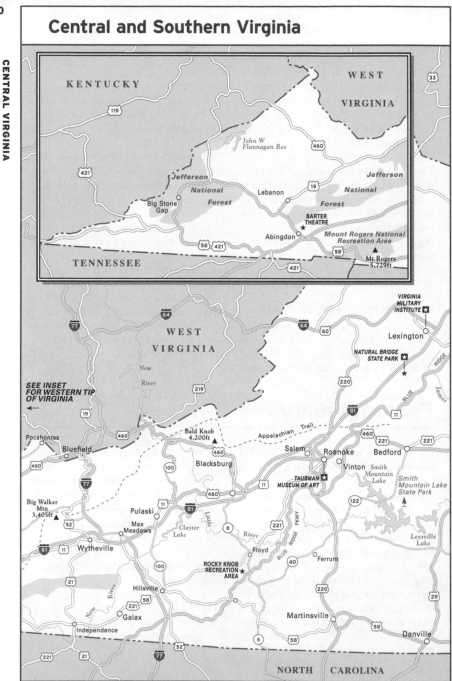

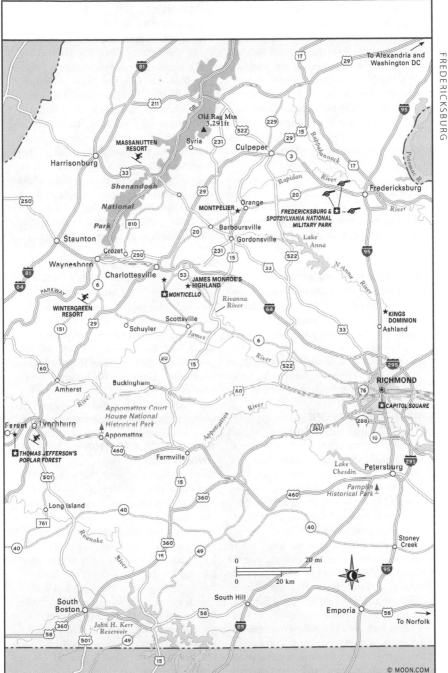

© MOON.COM

back to the Civil War era. The town was built along the Rappahannock River and includes several blocks of tree-lined streets with historic residences from the 18th and 19th centuries. A few of the homes still bear scars from Civil War battles and have cannonballs stuck in their exterior walls.

The 40-block historic district boasts many galleries, restaurants, and shops. It's a lovely place to window-shop, take a walk, grab a bite, and enjoy some of the history in this famous town.

The students from the University of Mary Washington provide much of the workforce for the charming stores and eateries along Princess Anne Street and neighboring roads in the historic district. Most of the businesses are privately owned and operated.

FREDERICKSBURG AREA MUSEUM

The **Fredericksburg Area Museum** (907 Princess Anne St., 540/371-3037, www.famva. org, Thurs.-Tues. 10am-5pm, adults $5, seniors 65 and over $4, military $3, children under 5 free) hosts permanent and changing exhibits that focus on the Fredericksburg region. It features topics on everything from rivers, buildings, and memorabilia to pet ownership.

RISING SUN TAVERN

The **Rising Sun Tavern** (1304 Caroline St., 540/371-1494, www. washingtonheritagemuseums.org, Mar.-Oct. Mon.-Sat. 10am-5pm, Sun. noon-4pm, Nov.-Feb. Mon.-Sat. 11am-4pm, Sun. noon-4pm, adults $7, children 6-18 $3, under 6 free) is a historic site (they do not serve food) that used to be Charles Washington's home (George's younger brother). The home was built in 1760 and made a popular overnight stop for weary travelers. It hosted such famous people as George Mason, James Madison, Thomas Jefferson, and John Paul Jones. The home became a "proper" (high-class) tavern in 1792. Visitors are treated to a lively introduction to tavern life in the 18th century. Costumed interpreters lead the way through the taproom, dining room, and public and private quarters.

HUGH MERCER APOTHECARY SHOP

The **Hugh Mercer Apothecary Shop** (1020 Caroline St., 540/373-3362, www. washingtonheritagemuseums.org, Mar.-Oct. Mon.-Sat. 9am-4pm, Sun. noon-4pm, Nov.-Feb. Mon.-Sat. 11am-4pm, Sun. noon-4pm, adults $7, children 6-18 $3, under 6 free) makes for a fun visit. Hugh Mercer practiced medicine in Fredericksburg for 15 years, and his list of clients included Martha Washington. This shop dates back to 1742, and visitors are treated to lively tours of the reconstructed shop, where they can learn about a variety of natural ingredients (such as leeches, crab claws, and lancets) that were used to cure common ailments.

MARY WASHINGTON HOUSE

The **Mary Washington House** (1200 Charles St., 540/373-1569, www. washingtonheritagemuseums.org, Mar.-Oct. Mon.-Sat. 9am-4pm, Sun. noon-4pm, Nov.-Feb. Mon.-Sat. 11am-4pm, Sun. noon-4pm, adults $7, children 6-18 $3, under 6 free) was purchased in 1772 by George Washington for his mother (Mary Ball Washington). Mary lived in the house for 17 years. Welcoming tour guides dressed in period clothing provide a nice insight into Mary's life and personality.

KENMORE PLANTATION AND GARDENS

On the western edge of Old Town is the **Kenmore Plantation** (1201 Washington Ave., 540/373-3381, www.kenmore.org, Mar.-Oct. Mon.-Sat. 10am-5pm, Sun. noon-5pm, Nov.-Dec. Mon.-Sat. 10am-4pm, Sun. noon-4pm, adults $12, students $6, under 6 free). The estate was built by Betty Washington (George Washington's sister) and her husband, Fielding Lewis. Lewis owned a mercantile business but lost money during the Revolutionary War because he could no longer trade with England. He died while the state of Virginia still owed him the money that he had lent it to build a gun factory in Fredericksburg.

Downtown Fredericksburg

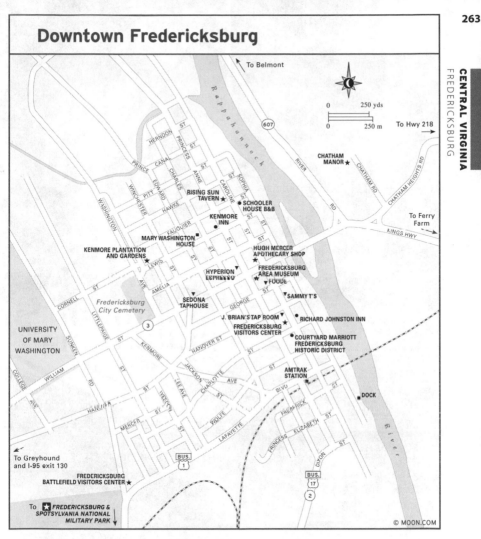

To Belmont

0   250 yds
0   250 m   To Hwy 218

Rappahannock River

607

CHATHAM
MANOR ★

CHATHAM RD

CHATHAM HEIGHTS RD

HERNDON ST

PRINCESS ST

CANAL

PRINCE

CHARLES

EDWARD

PITT

WINCHESTER

ANNE ST

CAROLINE ST

SOPHIA ST

RISING SUN
TAVERN ★

SCHOOLER
HOUSE B&B

KENMORE
INN

To Ferry
Farm

KINGS HWY

WASHINGTON

HAWKE

FAUQUIER

MARY WASHINGTON
HOUSE

KENMORE PLANTATION
AND GARDENS ★

LEWIS

HUGH MERCER
APOTHECARY SHOP ★

HYPERION
ESPRESSO

FREDERICKSBURG
AREA MUSEUM ★

FOODE

AMELIA

Fredericksburg
City Cemetery

SEDONA
TAPHOUSE

GEORGE

SAMMY T'S

CORNELL

LITTLEPAGE

3

J. BRIAN'S TAP ROOM

FREDERICKSBURG
VISITORS CENTER

RICHARD JOHNSTON INN

COURTYARD MARRIOTT
FREDERICKSBURG
HISTORIC DISTRICT

UNIVERSITY
OF MARY
WASHINGTON

SUNKEN

KENMORE

HANOVER ST

COLLEGE

WILLIAM

JACKSON

CHARLOTTE

AVE

AMTRAK
STATION

BLVD

DOCK

River

HANOVER RD

WEEDON

VIOLET

MERCER

LAFAYETTE

PRINCESS ELIZABETH ST

DIXON

FREDERICK ST

To Greyhound
and I-95 exit 130

BUS.
1

FREDERICKSBURG
BATTLEFIELD VISITORS CENTER ★

BUS.
17

2

To ★ FREDERICKSBURG &
SPOTSYLVANIA NATIONAL
MILITARY PARK

© MOON.COM

The Georgian-style brick home sits on three acres and is open for tours. It is elegant inside and out and noted for having stunning decorative plaster ceilings. Tours begin at the **Crowninshield Museum**, to the left of the front gate. Decorative arts and antique furnishings are on display there. Next, guides lead a 45-minute tour of the mansion's first floor and kitchen. The gardens are then available to explore on your own. Visitors who wish to visit both Kenmore and Ferry Farm can purchase a combination ticket for $19 for adults and $8.50 for students.

★ Fredericksburg & Spotsylvania National Military Park

Between 1862 and 1864, four Civil War battles were fought on the streets of Fredericksburg and in the fields and forests surrounding the city. The result was more than 100,000 casualties. The **Fredericksburg & Spotsylvania**

National Military Park (540/693-3200, www.nps.gov/frsp, free) is the second-largest military park in the world. It can take two days to fully explore, or visitors can choose to see specific sights. There are two visitors centers: the **Fredericksburg Battlefield Visitors Center** (1013 Lafayette Blvd., 540/693-3200, daily 9am-5pm) and the **Chancellorsville Battlefield Visitor Center** (9001 Plank Rd., Spotsylvania, 540/693-3200, daily 9am-5pm). Orientation films are available at both locations (ages 10-61 $2, over 61 $1, under 10 free), as are maps to trails and driving tours.

The most important and well-known battle of the four that occurred here was the **Battle of Fredericksburg**, which took place on December 11-15, 1862. The battle was one of the largest (nearly 200,000 soldiers) and deadliest of the war and is known for being the "first major opposed river crossing in American military history." It was also the first time Union and Confederate troops fought right on city streets and as such is considered the first location of urban combat.

The Union's plan for the battle was for General Burnside's command to defeat General Lee's southern flank at Prospect Hill, while also holding the Confederate First Corps at Marye's Heights. The bloody battle raged for several days, eventually resulting in a Confederate victory and Burnside's troops retreating back across the river. Four generals were killed in the battle (two from each side).

The **Fredericksburg National Cemetery** (1013 Lafayette Blvd., 540/373-6122, daily dawn to dusk) was placed on Marye's Heights as the final resting place of more than 15,000 soldiers Approximately 20 percent of the soldiers buried there have been identified.

A driving tour can be made of Prospect Hill and Marye's Heights. The route is five miles long. Directions for self-guided walking trails for a 400-yard walk around the Sunken

---

1: Hugh Mercer Apothecary Shop 2: Mary Washington House 3: a sunny day in charming Fredericksburg

Road, a short loop through the Fredericksburg National Cemetery, and several other short walks can be downloaded at the National Park Service website (www.nps.gov/frsp).

Across the Rappahannock from Fredericksburg is **Chatham Manor** (120 Chatham Ln., 540/693-3200, daily 9am-4:30pm), which served as a hospital during the battle. The home was built between 1768 and 1771. Five of the 10 rooms of this 12,000-square-foot Georgian estate are open for touring (free). Interior exhibits provide information on the home's 15 owners and the mansion's role in the Civil War.

Another Civil War battle that took place near Fredericksburg was the **Battle of Chancellorsville** (Apr. 30-May 6, 1863). It is best known as General Lee's "perfect battle," since his risky move of dividing his army against much greater enemy forces ended in a Confederate victory. During this battle Stonewall Jackson was mortally wounded by friendly fire. He died eight days later at age 39.

The third battle that took place here is the **Battle of the Wilderness** (May 5-6, 1864). This engagement marked the start of the Overland Campaign, known as the bloodiest campaign of the war. It was also the first battle between Robert E. Lee and Ulysses S. Grant.

The fourth was a continuation of the Battle of the Wilderness, known as the **Battle of Spotsylvania Court House**. This conflict marked a sea change in the war: The Union army moved forward to Spotsylvania and continued to push forward for the rest of the war.

Ferry Farm

Ferry Farm (268 Kings Hwy., 540/370-0732, www.kenmore.org, Mar.-Oct. Mon.-Sat. 10am-5pm, Sun. noon-5pm, Nov.-Dec. Mon.-Sat. 10am-4pm, Sun. noon-4pm, adults $9, students $4.50, under 6 free) was George Washington's childhood home. The 80-acre park is in Stafford, across the river from Fredericksburg. It is so named because people (including the Washingtons) used to cross the river by ferry from the farm to reach Fredericksburg. Washington lived

The Angel of Marye's Heights

the Kirkland Monument

During the horribly bloody Battle of Fredericksburg, more than 8,000 Union soldiers were wounded or killed in front of Marye's Heights at the Sunken Road on December 13. As dawn came on the morning of the 14th, many wounded soldiers who were not able to walk to the field hospital lay moaning and crying on the battlefield suffering from their wounds and a lack of water. Both armies had ceased fire and were forced to sit and listen to the agony.

A young soldier from the Confederate army, Richard Rowland Kirkland, finally requested permission to help the wounded Union soldiers by giving them water. He was first denied, but later was given permission at his own risk. The young man collected canteens, filled them with water, and risked his own life walking out on the battlefield. Realizing what he was doing, soldiers from both sides watched in silence and not one shot was fired.

Kirkland spent an hour and a half running between his lines and the wounded, bringing them water, blankets, and warm clothing. Wounded soldiers cried out for water as Kirkland performed his task, and he did not stop until he had helped each one that lay on the Confederate side of the field.

Kirkland was killed in battle only a year later. However, he will always be known as the Angel of Marye's Heights. A statue of him by artist Felix de Weldon (who also created the U.S. Marine Corps War Memorial) was erected in front of the stone wall at the Sunken Road and unveiled in 1965.

there between the ages of 6 and 20, and this is where he is rumored to have chopped down the cherry tree and thrown a penny across the Rappahannock River. Not much remains of the original house, but there is a visitors center where colonial and Civil War artifacts that were found on the property are on display (there is an archaeological lab on-site where scientists work on weekdays). There are also gardens to explore featuring plants commonly grown in the 18th century. Visitors who wish to visit both Kenmore and Ferry Farm can purchase a combination ticket for $19 for adults and $8.50 for students.

Gari Melchers Home and Studio at Belmont

The **Gari Melchers Home and Studio at Belmont** (224 Washington St., Falmouth, 540/654-1015, www.garimelchers.org, Apr.-Oct. daily 10am-5pm, Nov.-Mar. daily 10am-4pm, adults $10, 18 and under free with paying parent – limit 2) is the estate of one of the most sought-after painters of the late 1800s and early 1900s, Gari Melchers. It is in Falmouth, two miles north of Fredericksburg, and visitors can tour the home where Melchers and his wife lived between 1916 and 1932 and enjoy the site's beautiful 27-acre grounds. There are four stunning art galleries with 1,677 paintings and drawings by Melchers and approximately 3,000 of his personal furnishings and decorative objects. There are also gardens and trails to enjoy. The home (originally built around 1790) and studio are one of just 30 artists spaces named in the National Trust for Historic Preservation's Historic Artists' Homes and Studios consortium. Tours of the estate, which run throughout the day, take 90 minutes and include a 12-minute film.

TOURS

Trolley Tours of Fredericksburg (540/898-0737, www.fredericksburgtrolley. com, adults $20, children 5-12 $8, military $18) last 75 minutes and depart from the **Fredericksburg Visitor Center** (706 Caroline St.). Reservations are recommended during the summer months.

Old Towne Carriages (540/371-0094, www.oldetownecarriages.com, starting at $20 for adults, children $10) carries visitors around Fredericksburg in horse-drawn carriages. They offer daily tours in the historic district and can arrange private evening tours. Tours depart from the **Fredericksburg Visitor Center** (706 Caroline St.), and tickets can be purchased there.

Another fun tour is the **Flavors of Fredericksburg** (540/656-7272, www. flavorsoffredericksburg.com, starting at $60) food and history tour. This walking tour through the downtown area stops for tastings at restaurants and shops while providing fun details on historical sites, architecture, and famous historical residents.

RECREATION

Fredericksburg sits on the banks of the Rappahannock River. As such, it lends itself to canoeing, kayaking, and boating in a relaxed and mostly pristine environment. At the southern end of Old Town is **City Dock Park** (207 Sophia St.). The historic dock was in place during George Washington's time, and the boat ramp there offers the best access to the Rappahannock River. Follow the river east along Sophia Street; the road dead-ends at the ramp. Fishing is allowed 24/7. There is a nice parking area in which to leave your car. Be aware that water levels fluctuate a lot on the river. Springtime can bring massive floods, while late summer and fall can offer low, slow-moving water. The Chesapeake Bay can be reached via the Rappahannock River. Head downstream if you are in anything other than a kayak or canoe (away from the railroad bridge). Upstream can be very rocky, especially in low water.

Two local outfitters that can arrange outdoor instruction and rentals are the **Virginia Outdoor Center** (3219 Fall Hill Ave., 540/371-5085, www.playva.com) and **Clore Brothers Outfitters** (5927 River Rd., 540/786-7749, www.clorebros.com).

Mountain bikers can learn about local trails and events by visiting the **FredTrails** website (www.fredtrails.org).

SHOPPING

In the past decade or two, the Fredericksburg area has seen tremendous growth as an exurb of Washington DC. As sprawling housing developments sprang up along the I-95 corridor, so did numerous strip malls. Many national chain stores can be found along State Route 3 and farther north into Stafford County.

Old Town Fredericksburg, however, has remained a fun and charming place to shop. Art galleries and independently owned gift shops and boutiques line the historical streets, offering a nice break from the chain stores and the opportunity to buy one-of-a-kind merchandise. Princess Anne Street is the main shopping area and contains several blocks of stores and restaurants. This is a pleasant area to window-shop or to look for a special Civil War-era gift or items made in Virginia.

Beck's Antiques & Books (709 Caroline St., 540/371-1766, www.becksantiques.com, daily 12pm-5pm) is a serious antique dealer with pieces selected mostly from homes and estates in Virginia.

A combination art gallery, store, and classroom, **Ponshop** (712 Caroline St., 540/656-2215, www.ponshopstudio.com, Mon.-Sat. 10am-6pm, Sun. 11am-5pm) offers artwork, clothing, and handmade pieces created by local artists. They also offer art classes.

FOOD

American

Yummy pub fare with a healthy twist is what **Sammy T's** (801 Caroline St., 540/371-2008, www.sammyts.com, Mon.-Thurs. 11:30am-9pm, Fri.-Sat. 11:30am-10pm, Sun. 11:30am-7pm, $5-20) is known for. A local favorite, this friendly place has a lot of atmosphere and a fun vibe. Sit at the bar and chat with new friends, or grab a table and be treated to good service. They serve a wide variety of dishes and have many vegetarian and vegan entrées. There is an indoor beer garden for events and a few outdoor seats right on Caroline Street.

J. Brian's Tap Room (200 Hanover St., 540/373-0738, www.jbrianstaproom.com, Sun.-Thurs. 11am-10pm, Fri.-Sat. 11am-11pm, $8-22) is a great local eatery in the historic district that's been around since 1961. They have delicious food at reasonable prices and offer a friendly atmosphere in an old building that has a lot of character. They have outdoor seating that is dog friendly (they even provide water bowls). The crab bisque is a winner, but their pizza and sandwiches are also good choices. This is a fine place to grab a drink with friends or enjoy a casual meal.

The **Sedona Tap House** (591 William St., 540/940-2294, www.sedonataphouse.com, Mon.-Thurs. 11am-11pm, Fri.-Sat. 11am-midnight, Sun. 10:30am-10:30pm, $14-32) is part of a small chain of restaurants with several locations in Virginia. They serve a menu of Southwest-inspired selections such as Smoky BBQ Beef Short Rib, crab cakes, pasta, steak, and a large salad menu. Sides include Mexican street corn and bacon succotash. This is a very popular restaurant, but they update their waitlist online.

The popular **Foode** (900 Princess Anne St., 540/479-1370, www.foodefredericksburg.com, Tues.-Thurs. 11am-3pm and 4pm-9pm, Fri.-Sat. 11am-3pm and 4pm-10pm, Sun. 9am-3pm, $16-31) is located in the historic National Bank Building downtown. The menu changes seasonally and highlights local products and produce and organic ingredients. The dinner menu includes items such as Rosie's Buttermilk Fried Chicken, burgers, steak, and shrimp and grits. They also offer signature cocktails and desserts.

Treats and Coffee

Hyperion Espresso (301 William St., 540/373-4882, www.hyperionespresso.com, Mon.-Thurs. 7am-8pm, Fri.-Sat. 7am-10pm, Sun. 8am-8pm, under $10) is the local favorite for coffee lovers. It is a comfortable, unpretentious place to grab a good cup of coffee and a light meal or snack. Sit outside (you can bring your pooch) and watch the world go by. This is a hometown coffee place that will please even the pickiest travelers.

No trip to Fredericksburg is complete without a stop at ★ **Carl's** (2200 Princess Anne St., www.carlsfrozencustard.com, mid-Feb.-late Nov. Sun.-Thur. 11am-11pm, Fri.-Sat., 11am-11:30, under $10). Carl's is perhaps the most famous ice-cream stand in the state and is truly a landmark. Don't be scared off if the line of eager patrons is wrapped around the building (which will no doubt include everyone from your grandmother to police officers, small children, and tattoo-clad bikers). The line will move quickly—just have your money and your order ready when it's your turn at the window.

ACCOMMODATIONS

There are many large hotels in the Fredericksburg area, but in the historic district

1: Sammy T's 2: Carl's 3: historic Kenmore Inn 4: Foode

visitors can choose from among a handful of lovely and historic bed-and-breakfasts.

$100-200

Comfort Suites Fredericksburg South (4615 Southpoint Pkwy., 540/891-1112, www.choicehotels.com, $85-134) is an all-suite hotel offering 85 guest rooms with two double beds or one king bed. All suites have a parlor with a sofa bed. The hotel is near I-95 and a short drive to the historic district. The hotel lobby welcomes guests with a five-story atrium and a large stone fireplace. A complimentary hot breakfast is included, and there is an indoor pool and fitness room.

The **Hampton Inn & Suites Fredericksburg South** (4800 Market St., 540/898-5000, www.hilton.com, $127-150) offers 121 guest rooms and is a five-minute drive from the historic district. There is an indoor pool, and a hot breakfast is included.

The **Schooler House Bed and Breakfast** (1303 Caroline St., 540/287-5407, www.theschoolerhouse.com, $160-175) is a small, Victorian-style home built in 1891. It offers two guest rooms with private fireplaces and bathrooms. Original pine floors and trim are still in place throughout much of the house, and the four fireplaces have restored antique tile. The home is decorated with many antiques (even the wicker furniture on the front porch is antique). A full breakfast is included, as is Wi-Fi. Pets and children are discouraged.

The historic **Kenmore Inn** (1200 Princess Anne St., 540/371-7622, www.kenmoreinn.com, $130-225) offers nine well-appointed guest rooms with private bathrooms in a historic home on Princess Anne Street. The rooms are not terribly large, but they are beautiful and cozy. Luxury rooms are located in the original portion of the home, which was built in 1793. These rooms have high ceilings, hardwood floors, and wood-burning fireplaces. Deluxe rooms are located in an addition that was put on the home in 1933 and have antique furniture and wall-to-wall carpeting. The inn has a comfortable porch with chairs and swings. Some street parking is available. Breakfast is served in the main dining room, and evening meals can be taken in the wonderful restaurant downstairs. Ask for a room in the front of the house.

The ★ **Richard Johnston Inn** (711 Caroline St., 540/899-7606, www.therichardjohnstoninn.com, $165-300) was built in 1770 and during the 1800s was home to Richard Johnston, the mayor of Fredericksburg. The inn has seven guest rooms and two suites, all with private bathrooms. A continental breakfast is served during the week, and a full breakfast is served on weekends. The inn has two pet-friendly rooms. It is located three blocks from the train station, and parking is available on-site.

The **Courtyard Marriott Fredericksburg Historic District** (620 Caroline St., 540/373-8300, www.marriott.com, $185-239) offers 94 comfortable, modern rooms in the historic district.

INFORMATION AND SERVICES

The **Fredericksburg Visitor Center** (706 Caroline St., 540/373-1776, www.visitfred.com, Sun.-Thurs. 9am-5pm, Fri.-Sat. 9am-8pm) provides wonderful information on touring the Fredericksburg area. Maps, brochures, parking information, tickets, and lodging information are just some of the things visitors can learn about from the helpful staff. A short orientation film about the city is shown there.

GETTING THERE AND AROUND

Fredericksburg is about 50 miles south of the nation's capital. A **Virginia Railway Express** (800/743-3873, www.vre.org) and **Amtrak** (800/872-7245, www.amtrak.com) station can be found at 200 Lafayette Boulevard. Commuter service runs to Alexandria and Washington DC.

The local bus system, called the **Fredericksburg Regional Transit (FRED)**

(540/372-1222, www.ridefred.com, $1.25), provides local bus transportation on weekdays year-round and on weekends during the University of Mary Washington school year.

Richmond

Richmond is the capital of the Commonwealth of Virginia. The city is independent, but the Richmond area encompasses part of Henrico and Chesterfield Counties.

The city was founded in 1737 and is significant in both Revolutionary and Civil War history. During the Revolutionary War, Richmond was the site of Patrick Henry's famous "Give me liberty or give me death" speech, and it became the capital of Virginia in 1780. During the Civil War, Richmond was the Confederate capital.

Richmond was known in the early 20th century as home to one of the first successful streetcar systems. It was also a center of African American culture.

Today, Richmond is a vibrant, ever-changing city. Many neighborhoods have undergone major revitalizations over the past decades, although some are still waiting for their turn. Outdoor recreation is gaining popularity, even in the shadow of the downtown buildings. This is due in part to the James River flowing through the city limits and the plethora of activities it invites.

The Richmond economy is fueled by the presence of federal, state, and local government agencies, banking firms, and legal agencies. The U.S. Court of Appeals for the Fourth Circuit and the Federal Reserve Bank of Richmond are located in Richmond. Many private companies, large and small, also call Richmond home.

Richmond is a city of colleges and universities. The University of Richmond (UR), Virginia Commonwealth University (VCU) and its Medical College of Virginia branch, Virginia Union University, and the Union Theological Seminary all call the city home.

Safety can be an issue on the downtown streets after dark. It is best to drive through town at night rather than walk. Many hotels offer shuttles around the city, but if yours does not, drive or call a cab or car service.

SIGHTS

Richmond is carved up geographically into five primary sections: Downtown, the East End, West End, North Side, and South Side. It sounds simple at first, but Richmonders like to further distinguish areas of the city by neighborhood names. This becomes confusing to visitors who have no frame of reference for each neighborhood and is further complicated by the loosely defined boundaries. For simplicity's sake, the sights in this guide are broken out by the directional distinctions, and additional information is provided on specific neighborhoods that are either commonly known or have distinct characteristics that might be of interest to visitors.

Downtown

Downtown, like it sounds, is at the heart of Richmond. The area includes the financial district and several popular neighborhoods such as **Court End,** which sits to the north of Capitol Square and East Broad Street. This neighborhood was developed during the federal era, just after the state capital was moved to Richmond. The area is a combination of historic mansions and modern office space.

Jackson Ward is historically the center for African American commerce and entertainment. It is less than a mile from the capitol, west of Court End and north of Broad Street. Many famous people such as Duke Ellington, Ella Fitzgerald, Lena Horne, Billie Holiday, and James Brown frequented the neighborhood.

Monroe Ward is a historic district (east of the Fan District) that is now home to many

Central Richmond

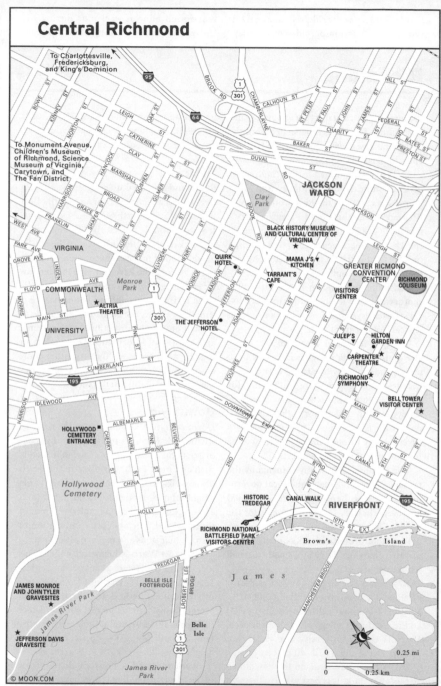

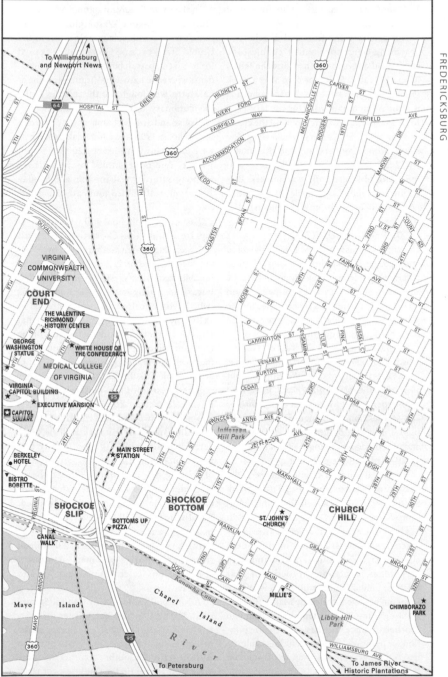

VCU students. The historic **Jefferson Hotel** is located there.

Not far from the financial district is a charming neighborhood of cobblestone streets and alleys that runs along the James River. It is called **Shockoe Slip** after a creek that ran through the area. "Shacquohocan" was an Algonquian word for the large flat rocks that collected at the mouth of the creek, and the word "Slip" refers to boat slips. The neighborhood consists mainly of Italianate-style brick and iron-front structures, including restored taverns and warehouses. It is Richmond's most fashionable district and is now known for its dining and shopping.

★ CAPITOL SQUARE

Capitol Square is a historic 12-acre parcel of grassy, beautifully landscaped public grounds that house government buildings, serve as the site for inauguration and commemoration events, and function as a civic campus for the governing of Virginia. A distinctive cast-iron fence built in 1818 surrounds the grounds.

A giant equestrian statue of George Washington sits at the formal square entrance. It was erected in honor of Washington, but also to hail the role Virginia played in the road to independence. More than 130 paintings and statues honor distinguished American figures inside the buildings in Capitol Square and also outdoors. Living memorial trees are also part of the square's landscape.

The focal point of Capitol Square is the **Virginia Capitol Building** (1000 Bank St., 804/698-1788, www.virginiacapitol.gov, Mon.-Sat. 9am-5pm, Sun. 1pm-5pm, free). It has been the home of the General Assembly since 1788. The stunning, monumental, classical-style structure was the handiwork of Thomas Jefferson, who designed it as the first public building in the New World. Jefferson modeled it after the Maison Carrée, a 1st-century Roman temple at Nîmes in southern France that has been the inspiration for many other capitol buildings, municipal buildings, and courthouses throughout the country.

In the capitol's central rotunda is a marble sculpture of George Washington. It is said to be the most valuable marble statue in the United States because George himself posed for it. Seven portrait busts of other U.S. presidents who were natives of Virginia and one of Lafayette, who fought for the colonies in the Revolutionary War, are also displayed.

House and Senate chambers were added to the capitol in 1904, and additional renovations were made between 2005 and 2007.

Free, one-hour guided tours are held Monday-Saturday 9:30am-4pm and Sunday 1pm-4pm. Self-guided tours are also available daily.

East of the capitol but still within Capitol Square stands the **Executive Mansion** (www.executivemansion.virginia.gov). This federal-era mansion is the oldest continually inhabited governor's residence in the country. It was designed by architect Alexander Parris (who lived in Boston) and was completed in 1813. The home is a Virginia and National Historic Landmark. Rooms in the front of the mansion still retain most of the original ceilings, woodwork, and plaster cornices. Tours are available Tuesday-Thursday.

The latest addition to Capitol Square is the **Virginia Women's Monument** (womensmonumentcom.virginia.gov), the only monument in the country fully dedicated to women that is prominently featured on statehouse grounds. At the time of writing, the monument was still being erected; the fist seven bronze statues of notable Virginia women have been unveiled. Eventually there will be 12 in total. A plaza made of granite features the glass **Wall of Honor,** which has the names of 230 women from four centuries who made significant contributions to the state's history and culture.

Additional buildings in Capitol Square include the neoclassical **Oliver Hill Sr. Building** (Virginia's first state library, to the east of the capitol), the 12-story **Washington Building** (in the southeast corner), and the brick **Bell Tower** (in the southwest corner).

AMERICAN CIVIL WAR MUSEUM

The **American Civil War Museum** (804/649-1861, www.acwm.org) is located on three sites in Richmond and the surrounding region (**Historic Tredegar**, the **White House of the Confederacy**, and the **American Civil War Museum – Appomattox**). It is the result of a merger between the former Museum of the Confederacy and the American Civil War Center at Historic Tredegar. It interprets the American Civil War from the Union, Confederate, and African American viewpoints.

Historic Tredegar (500 Tredegar St., daily 9am-5pm, adults $15, children 6-17 $8, seniors $13, 5 and under free) is located on the James River at the historic Tredegar Iron Works site. A new building contains the museum visitors center, store, exhibits, a theater, and hundreds of artifacts.

The **White House of the Confederacy** (1201 E. Clay St., daily 10am-5pm, adults $12, children 6-17 $6, seniors $10, 5 and under free) was the executive mansion and residence of Confederate President Jefferson Davis between 1861 and 1865. The fully restored home served as the political, social, and military center of the Confederacy. Forty-five-minute guided tours share information on the lives of the people who lived there.

The **American Civil War Museum – Appomattox** (159 Horseshoe Rd., Appomattox, summer daily 10am-6pm, shorter hours the rest of the year, adults $12, 6-17 $6, seniors $10, 5 and under free) interprets both the end of the Civil War and the beginning of a reunified nation. This location features many audiovisual stations and artifacts from the surrender. Parking is free with admission.

A combination admission ticket for the two sites in Richmond (adults $27, 6-17 $14, seniors $23) or all three sites (adults $39, 6-17 $20, seniors $33) is available.

BLACK HISTORY MUSEUM AND CULTURAL CENTER OF VIRGINIA

The **Black History Museum and Cultural Center of Virginia** (122 W. Leigh St., 804/780-9093, www.blackhistorymuseum.org, Tues.-Sat. 10am-5pm, Sun. by appointment, adults $10, students and seniors $8, children 4-12 $6, 3 and under free) is a permanent repository for artifacts as well as visual, oral, and written records that commemorate the accomplishments of African Americans in Virginia. It features detailed exhibits on Richmond's African American history and a gift shop. The museum is housed in the historic Leigh Street Armory.

MAGGIE L. WALKER NATIONAL HISTORIC SITE

The **Maggie L. Walker National Historic Site** (600 N. 2nd St., 804/771-2017, www.nps.gov/mawa, Tues.-Sat. 9am-5pm, free) covers about a quarter of a city block in the Jackson Ward neighborhood. The site is dedicated to Maggie Lena Walker, an inspirational woman who devoted her life to the advancement of civil rights, education, and economic empowerment for African Americans and women. She was the president of a bank, a newspaper editor, and a fraternal leader. Maggie L. Walker's home (which is impeccably preserved) and surrounding buildings are part of the site and make up the exhibit hall and visitor center. Be sure to watch the featured film. Parking can often be found along the surrounding streets.

CANAL WALK

Richmond's **Canal Walk** (14th St. and Dock St., www.rvariverfront.com) was completed in 1999 and stretches for 1.25 miles through downtown Richmond in the Shockoe Slip area along the Haxall Canal and James River and Kanawha Canal. The walk can be accessed from 5th Street, 7th Street, Virginia Street, 14th Street, 15th Street, and 17th Street. Four centuries of history can be explored along the walk as it passes by monuments and exhibits

and also the popular **Brown's Island,** a park that hosts festivals, art exhibits, and concerts.

RICHMOND NATIONAL BATTLEFIELD PARK

The **Richmond National Battlefield Park** (www.nps.gov/rich, daily sunrise to sunset, free) is a collection of 13 individual sites that preserve more than 1,900 acres of Civil War history. The sites are located in Hanover, Henrico, and Chesterfield Counties as well as the city of Richmond. The park tells the story of Richmond's involvement in the war between 1861 and 1865.

The **Tredegar Visitor Center** (470 Tredegar St., 804/226-1981, daily 9am-5pm) is the main visitors center for the park. It is housed inside the former Tredegar Ironworks building, which was an important asset to Confederate troops since it produced their cannons and ammunition. The center offers three floors of displays and an orientation film. The **Chimborazo Medical Museum** (3215 E. Broad St., 804/226-1981, Wed.-Sun. 9am-4:30pm) is another visitors center for the park that contains exhibits that focus on Confederate medical equipment and hospitals. This building is also the park headquarters. One additional visitors center is located in the park: **Cold Harbor Battlefield Visitor Center** (5515 Anderson-Wright Dr., 804/226-1981, Wed.-Sun. 9am-4:30pm), which offers a book store, ranger programs in the summer, and electric map programs that provide information on the 1862 Battle of Gaines' Mill and the 1864 Battle of Cold Harbor.

East End

The East End of Richmond is a collection of neighborhoods loosely defined as the area north of the James River and east of the historic Virginia Central Railroad-Chesapeake & Ohio Railway line.

Church Hill, one of the largest existing

19th-century neighborhoods in the country, is located at the end of Broad Street, a primary east-west road through Richmond. It retains numerous examples of period architecture.

Fulton Hill runs roughly from Gillies Creek to the Richmond city limits. This is an urban neighborhood that is finally seeing renovations after years of neglect, which can be credited in part to the dedication of its community in dealing with criminal activity in the area.

Major nightlife can be found in **Shockoe Bottom,** just east of downtown near the James River. This is one of Richmond's oldest neighborhoods, and although it has a history of flooding from the James River, it has become a hot spot for dining, entertainment, and partying. Just east of Shockoe Bottom is **Tobacco Row,** so named for a group of multistory brick tobacco warehouses and factories producing cigarettes. The buildings were vacated in the 1980s, but many of the warehouses have since been converted into loft apartments, condos, retail space, and offices. The neighborhood sits adjacent to the James River and was the site of two famous Confederate prisons, **Libby Prison** and **Castle Thunder.**

One of the most historic neighborhoods in Richmond is **Union Hill,** an area bordered to the south by Jefferson Avenue, to the north by Venable Street, to the east by 25th Street, and to the west by Mosby Street. Union Hill sits high on a bluff above Shockoe Bottom. Its mix of antebellum, Victorian, classical revival, and modern architecture has landed the neighborhood in the National Register of Historic Places and the Virginia Landmarks Register.

SAINT JOHN'S CHURCH

Saint John's Church (2401 E. Broad St., 804/648-5015, www.historicstjohnschurch.org, Mon.-Sat. 10am-4pm, Sun. 1pm-4pm), in Church Hill, was built in 1741 and served as a place of worship but also as a local meeting hall. When the assembly of the Second Virginia Convention moved from Williamsburg to Richmond, Saint John's was

1: Byrd Park 2: spring color along the Canal Walk 3: Virginia Capitol Building 4: historic Tredegar

its meeting place. In March of 1775, as things heated up between Virginia and England, many prominent historical figures, such as George Washington, Thomas Jefferson, and Richard Henry, attended the meeting where Patrick Henry gave his famous "Give me liberty or give me death" speech. Services are still held in Saint John's Church, and visitors are welcome.

CHIMBORAZO PARK

Chimborazo Park (3201 E. Broad St., open sunrise to sunset), in Church Hill, is the former site of the Chimborazo Hospital, the largest American Civil War hospital. The hospital served the Confederate army between 1862 and 1865. During that time, more than 76,000 soldiers were treated there, and it had a 20 percent mortality rate. The National Park Service now owns the site. The 30-acre park offers a 180-degree view of the city and is home to the headquarters of Richmond National Battlefield Park. There is a small house on the east side of the park that is available to rent for events. The **Church Hill Dog Park** is also located on the east side of the park and includes an area for large dogs and one for small dogs.

West End

The boundaries of the West End are most commonly considered to be north of the James River, west of I-195, and south of Broad Street.

Byrd Park is a residential neighborhood north of a park with the same name and south of the Downtown Expressway. The neighborhood contains row homes from the 1920s and bungalows, ranch houses, Cape Cods, and American foursquare homes from the 1930s and 1940s.

Carytown is a thriving and eclectic cluster of 1920s homes, restaurants, antiques stores, clothing stores, and cafés. The 2800-3500 blocks of Cary Street, west of **Arthur Ashe Boulevard** (a historic street that provides entrance to Byrd Park and divides Carytown and the Museum District from the Fan District), are the most active. The neighboring

Museum District is just north of Carytown. This neighborhood (also known as West of the Boulevard) is home to a number of large institutions such as the **Virginia Museum of Fine Arts** and the **Virginia Historical Society.**

On the eastern edge of the West End of town is the **Fan District.** It is named simply for the "fan" formed by the streets that run west from Belvidere Street. The area is bordered to the north by Broad Street and to the south by I-195. The neighborhood is mostly residential and includes late-19th-century and early 20th-century homes. Historic **Monument Avenue** is located there, as are numerous cafés.

South of Cary Street, west of Belvidere Street, and north of the James River is **Oregon Hill,** a neighborhood of affordable housing that is a popular location for students to live. The Cowboy Junkies rock band released a song in 1992 called "Oregon Hill," the lyrics of which describe this neighborhood.

BYRD PARK

Byrd Park (600 South Blvd., www.richmondgov.com, sunrise to sunset) is a 287-acre public park just south of the Byrd Park neighborhood. It has a one-mile trail, an amphitheater, three small lakes, tennis courts, baseball fields, and a playground. Pedal boats are available for rent during the summer (804/646-0761). The park is named after William Byrd II, whose family owned a large portion of the land in Richmond when it was founded in 1737.

★ VIRGINIA MUSEUM OF FINE ARTS

The **Virginia Museum of Fine Arts** (200 N. Arthur Ashe Blvd., 804/340-1400, www.vmfa.museum, Sat.-Wed. 10am-5pm, Thurs.-Fri. 10am-9pm, free) first opened its doors in the middle of the Great Depression in 1936. Its purpose was to become the flagship art

---

1: Amuse Restaurant at the Virginia Museum of Fine Arts 2: Virginia Museum of Fine Arts

museum in Virginia and to lead an educational network throughout the state to bring the best of world art to Virginia. Today, the museum is state-supported and privately endowed. It has nearly 40,000 items in its permanent collection spanning 6,000 years. The museum is known for its wide range of world art collections and their exceptional aesthetic quality.

The museum building and grounds are lovely, and the exhibits are first-rate. Permanent exhibits cover topics such as African art, American art, ancient art, East Asian art, European art, English silver, Fabergé imperial jewels, and modern and contemporary art. Its holdings include paintings by European masters such as Monet and Goya and American masters such as Winslow Homer.

The Virginia Museum of Fine Arts supplements its collection with stunning temporary exhibitions. Over the years, these have included everything from modernist works from Walter P. Chrysler Jr.'s collection by artists from the School of Paris (a "bold" presentation for its time in the early 1940s) to masterpieces of Chinese art in 1955.

The **Amuse Restaurant** (804/340-1580, Sat.-Wed. 11:30am-4:30pm, Thurs.-Fri. 11:30am-4:30pm and 5pm-8:30pm), located on the upper level of the museum, offers fine dining, a full-service bar, and views of the atrium and sculpture garden. Reservations are available. The museum is located in the Museum District.

VIRGINIA MUSEUM OF HISTORY AND CULTURE

The **Virginia Museum of History and Culture** (428 N. Arthur Ashe Blvd., 804/340-1800, www.virginiahistory.org, daily 10am-5pm, adults $10, children 6-17 $5, seniors 65 and up $8, 5 and under free), in the Museum District, is a research and teaching center for Virginia history as well as a large repository. It offers many award-winning exhibits. Their key exhibition, *The Story of Virginia,* covers 16,000 years of history in the state (prehistoric

to present) and contains over 500 artifacts. The museum has the largest display of artifacts from Virginia.

MONUMENT AVENUE

The most recognized street in Richmond is Monument Avenue. It runs through the northern border of the Fan District and is known as one of the most beautiful boulevards in the world. According to the National Park Service (www.nps.gov) it is "the nation's only grand residential boulevard with monuments of its scale almost unaltered to the present day." The tree-lined street with a large grass median and six grand statues along a 1.5-mile section is a significant example of the "Grand American Avenue"-style of city planning. The first statue was of Robert E. Lee and was erected in 1890. Other famous Americans honored on the street include Civil War figures J. E. B. Stuart, Jefferson Davis, and Stonewall Jackson, as well as Matthew Fontaine Maury (a Richmond native known as the "Father of the Seas") and tennis star Arthur Ashe.

Monument Avenue is lined with beautiful historic homes and churches, and a one-mile segment is still surfaced with original cobblestones. The avenue is listed in the National Register of Historic Places and has been named one of 10 "great" streets in America by the American Planning Association.

HOLLYWOOD CEMETERY

Just west of Oregon Hill is the **Hollywood Cemetery** (412 S. Cherry St., 804/648-8501, www.hollywoodcemetery.org, daily 8am-5pm, free). Jefferson Davis, James Monroe, and John Tyler may be the most famous "residents" in this forever home, but many others, such as J. E. B. Stuart and more than 20 additional Confederate generals, two Supreme Court justices, six Virginia governors, and the very first battle casualty of the Civil War, keep them company. The cemetery sprawls over 135 acres and has stunning views of the James River. Walking, Segway, and private trolley tours are offered April-November.

North Side

The North Side of Richmond has a diversity of residential neighborhoods with a wide mix of architectural styles represented. Portions of Henrico County and Hanover County are broadly regarded as part of the North Side.

The most noted neighborhood on the North Side is **Three Corners,** which sits north of Broad Street and east of Arthur Ashe Boulevard. The triangle-shaped area (hence the name) has notable landmarks situated near each corner. Near the north point is **The Diamond** baseball stadium (3001 N. Arthur Ashe Blvd.), home to the VCU Rams and the Richmond Flying Squirrels (a minor league baseball team). Near the west corner is the **Science Museum of Virginia,** and near the east corner is the **Sauers Vanilla Factory (C.F. Sauer Company),** which displays one of the country's oldest moving lightbulb billboards.

SCIENCE MUSEUM OF VIRGINIA

To the west of Three Corners is the **Science Museum of Virginia** (2500 W. Broad St., 804/864-1400, www.smv.org, daily 9:30am-5pm, exhibits only admission adults $15, youth and seniors $13.50, preschool $10, exhibits and dome show adults $19, youth and seniors $17.50, preschool $14). Housed in the former Broad Street Station (built in 1919) and established in 1970, the museum includes many exciting permanent exhibits on space, electricity, health, and the Earth and also has unique visiting exhibits from around the globe. Some of the things you can expect to see include the world's largest analemmatic sundial (located in the parking lot), the world's first aluminum submarine, the world's first solar airplane, a giant 76-foot-screen movie theater (The Dome), live animals, and the world's largest kugel ball. You can't miss the green copper dome that sits on top of the building. This is a great stop for both children and adults.

South Side

The South Side refers to areas that are south of the James River.

Manchester is both a residential and industrial neighborhood across the James River from the Canal Walk. This is an area of new development where modern homes, loft condos, and businesses are part of the revitalization process.

Westover Hills, an established neighborhood also south of the James River, sits at the intersection of State Route 161 and the Boulevard Bridge. It is home to many restaurants, churches, and businesses.

The **Woodland Heights** neighborhood was built in the early 1900s along the James River. It is listed in the National Register of Historic Places and also in the Virginia Landmarks Register.

RECREATION
Spectator Sports

There are many sporting events throughout the year at the University of Richmond and VCU. A list of events can be obtained through both athletic departments at www.richmondspiders.com and www.vcuathletics.com, respectively.

The **Richmond Coliseum** (601 E. Leigh St., 804/780-4970, www.richmondcoliseum.net) hosts numerous professional and college sporting events such as football, basketball, wrestling, and monster-truck events. A list of events is available on the website.

Five miles north of Richmond, the **Richmond International Raceway** (600 E. Laburnum Ave., 866/455-7223, www.richmondraceway.com) hosts NASCAR racing on weekends in April and September. Additional events are held at the raceway throughout the year.

If horse racing is more your thing, then **Colonial Downs** (10515 Colonial Downs Pkwy., 804/966-7223, www.colonialdowns.com) in New Kent offers a pari-mutuel-betting racecourse with a five-level grandstand and some of the nicest amenities of any track in the country.

Outdoor Recreation

Runners, walkers, climbers, and

The Grand Kugel

kugel ball at the Science Museum of Virginia in Richmond

The word *kugel* is a German term for ball or sphere. A kugel ball is a large, heavy, perfectly spherical sculpture made of granite that is supported by a thin film of water. Although it can weigh thousands of pounds, the ball spins on top of the water due to the lubrication provided by the water.

Kugel balls are found in many parts of the world. One popular kugel ball is at the Science Museum of Virginia in Richmond and is famous for its enormous size. The ball currently on display is actually their second ball; the first, the "Grand Kugel" unveiled in 2003, was carved from South African black granite, was more than eight feet in diameter, and cost approximately $1.5 million. However, shortly after its installation, the Grand Kugel cracked, eventually preventing it from floating. In 2005, a replacement kugel ball was installed. It is recognized as the world's largest floating-ball sculpture by the *Guinness Book of World Records*. The original can be found on display behind the museum.

boaters can enjoy **James River Park** (www.jamesriverpark.org), which includes more than 500 acres of parkland in the city and several islands on the James River. Access to the park is from 22nd Street, 43rd Street, and at Reedy Creek where the park headquarters and a canoe launch are located.

Cyclists will find a lot of company both on and off road in the Richmond area. The **Richmond Area Bicycling Association** (www.raba.org) has information on local group rides for road cyclists, while the **Mid-Atlantic Off Road Enthusiasts** (www.more-mtb.org) has information on local mountain biking.

White-water rafting is a big sport in Richmond. The James River runs right through the city and offers rapids up to Class IV. Visitors can book a guided raft trip through a handful of outfitters including **Riverside Outfitters** (804/560-0068, www.riversideoutfitters.com, starting at $59).

Hot-air ballooning is popular in Central Virginia. When in Richmond, contact **Balloons Over Virginia, Inc.** (804/798-0080, www.balloonsovervirginia.com, from $275) for piloted balloon rides.

Amusement Parks

A half hour north of Richmond off I-95 is one of the mid-Atlantic's favorite theme parks, **Kings Dominion** (16000 Theme

Park Way, Doswell, 804/876-5000, www. kingsdominion.com, June-Aug. daily, late May and Sept.-Oct. weekends, starting at $45). This 400-acre park first opened in 1975 and offers more than 60 rides. It is known for its large collection of roller coasters (12), including classic wooden coasters such as the Grizzly as well as many new steel coasters. The Intimidator 305 plunges riders 305 feet at more than 90 mph. The park holds special events and a fun Halloween Haunt in October. There is also a 20-acre water park on-site.

ENTERTAINMENT AND EVENTS

Tours

Richmond History Tours are provided through the **Valentine Richmond History Center** (1015 E. Clay St., 804/649-0711, ext. 301, www.thevalentine.org, from $15). They offer hundreds of tours by foot, bus, and even with your dog. Professional guides lead all tours.

Performing Arts

The **Dominion Energy Center** (600 E Grace St., 804/592-3330, www. dominionenergycenter.com) is a multistage performing arts venue in the downtown area offering a wide array of performances. The primary venue is the **Carpenter Theatre**, a beautifully renovated grand theater built in 1928.

The **Altria Theater** (6 N. Laurel St., 804/592-3368, www.altriatheater.com) first opened in 1927 as a Shriner facility and was called the Mosque Theater. The City of Richmond purchased the theater in 1940. This popular stage on the VCU campus west of downtown hosts concerts, lectures, comedians, commencements, and fashion shows. It has a seating capacity of 3,600.

The **Richmond Symphony** (612 E. Grace St., 804/788-1212, www.richmondsymphony. com) was founded in 1957 and gives more than 200 appearances each year. Consult the website for a list of upcoming performances.

The **Virginia Opera** (866/673-7282, www. vaopera.org) is the premier opera performance company in Virginia. They offer 40 performances in three markets (Richmond, Fairfax, and Norfolk). Consult the website for a schedule of events.

The largest ballet company in town is the **Richmond Ballet** (407 E. Canal St., 804/344-0906, www.richmondballet.com), one of the best ballet companies on the East Coast. The **Concert Ballet of Virginia** (804/798-0945, www.concertballet.com) is another wonderful local ballet company.

Theater

A beautiful historic movie palace called the **Byrd Theater** (2908 W. Cary St., 804/353-9911, www.byrdtheatre.org) in Carytown was built in 1928 at the astronomical cost of $900,000 (which would be more than $11 million today). Movie tickets were 50 cents. It now shows second-run movies for $4 (big-screen classics $5). The original manager of the theater, Robert Coulter, remained there until 1971 and is rumored to now haunt the theater.

Nightlife

Richmond is an active city with a large population of students and twentysomethings. There's no shortage of nightlife, especially around the Shockoe Slip neighborhood. Establishments in Virginia are required by law to serve food if they serve alcohol, so much of the action can be found in local restaurants. As with many cities, it is safer to drive or take a cab or car service after dark in Richmond.

The **Tobacco Company** (1201 E. Cary St., 804/782-9555, www.thetobaccocompany.com, no cover) is a Shockoe Slip restaurant that includes a classy lounge and bar area featuring dancing on the weekends (Thurs.-Sat. 8pm-2am). They have a dress code.

It is difficult to beat the atmosphere at **Havana 59** (16 N. 17th St., 804/780-2822, www.havana59.net, Mon.-Sat. bar opens at 4:30pm) in Shockoe Bottom. They strive to re-create a feeling of Havana in the 1950s and do a great job with strung lights, wood floors, high ceilings, ironwork, and the famous rooftop bar (where you can salsa dance on Thursday nights). Cigars are allowed on the second floor. You can purchase them there or bring your own. The club is known for delicious drinks and friendly service. Business casual attire is expected.

More than 200 types of bottled beers can be ordered at the **Capital Ale House** (623 E. Main St., 804/780-2537, www.capitalalehouse. com, daily 11am-1:30am) in the heart of downtown Richmond. This classic alehouse, housed in a century-old building half a city block long, also has 51 taps, two cask-conditioned ale hand pumps, and a gaming area with pool tables and darts. They also have a beer garden. This is a great place for serious beer lovers to share their passion with other like-minded souls. There is also a music hall by the same name next door.

A small venue with outstanding, reasonably priced drinks and an atmosphere reminiscent of a speakeasy is **The Jasper** (3113 W. Cary St., www.jasperbarrva.com, daily 5pm-2am). Their slogan is "Full Pours and Honest Prices," and they seem to live up to it.

Events

The **State Fair of Virginia** (www.statefairva. org) in nearby Doswell is a 10-day fair full of tradition. There are rides, food, livestock, music, arts, and even a circus. The fair started back in 1854 and is held annually at the end of September and beginning of October.

SHOPPING

Shopping in Richmond offers everything from quaint boutiques, antiques shops, and specialty stores to upscale modern shopping malls. A unique area to shop is **Carytown,** where nine blocks of West Cary Street (between Thompson Street and Arthur Ashe Boulevard) are alive with stores selling clothing, furniture, jewelry, and toys, along with many independent eateries.

The **Shoppes at Bellgrade** (11400 W.

Huguenot Rd.) include clothing stores, specialty shops, and stores selling athletic gear. Two additional shopping areas are **Shockoe Slip** (E. Cary Street) between 11th and Virginia Streets and **Shockoe Bottom** between Broad and Dock Streets from 14th to 21st Streets.

FOOD
American

The stunning Jefferson Hotel in downtown Richmond is the venue of one of the nicest restaurants in town: ★ **Lemaire** (101 W. Franklin St., 804/649-4629, www. lemairerestaurant.com, daily 5pm-10pm, $12-36). This "Virginia Green Certified" restaurant offers not only farm-to-table-influenced menu items, but also exceptional service. The menu isn't extensive but certainly offers a little of everything (including small plates, burgers, and seafood). The wine list, however, has more than 200 selections, including a significant selection of bottles under $30 and wines offered by the glass. They also have a creative list of cocktails and a lovely lounge to enjoy them in. Ask for a table by the window so you can see both the dining room and the view onto Franklin Street. A great time to go is around the holidays, when the hotel is festively decorated.

For some true Southern-style comfort food and a healthy dose of city atmosphere in downtown Richmond, grab a bite at **Mama J's Kitchen** (415 N. 1st St., 804/255-7449, www.mamajskitchen.com, Sun.-Thurs. 11am-9pm, Fri.-Sat. 11am-10pm, $5-12). Between Clay and Marshall Streets, this feel-good restaurant full of food made from family recipes serves wonderful cocktails and gut-warming selections such as fried chicken, catfish, and mac and cheese. They also have cobbler and ice cream for dessert. Their slogan is "welcome home," and it's easy to see why.

Southern-style cooking can also be found downtown at the upscale **Julep's** (420 E. Grace St., 804/377-3968, www.juleps.net, Mon.-Sat. 5pm-10pm, $25-35). Their "New Southern Cuisine" puts a fancy spin on some old favorites such as shrimp and grits, lacquered duck breast, and petite filet mignon. The restaurant is housed in the historic Shields Shoes building on the first floor. The dress is equivalent to business casual, and you'll want to make a reservation.

The former Tarrant Drug Company building at the corner of Foushee and Broad Streets now houses one of Downtown's most popular eateries. **Tarrant's Café** (1 W. Broad St., 804/225-0035, www.tarrantscaferva.com, Mon.-Thurs. 11am-11pm, Fri. 11am-midnight, Sat. 10am-midnight, Sun. 10am-11pm, $10-30) is a quaint restaurant with an upscale feel. It is quite dark inside but has nice paintings, exposed brick walls, and a hip and pleasant atmosphere. It has a long, full-service bar and two dining areas with booths and tables. Reminders of the building's pharmacy past are in the form of signs noting Prescriptions, Soda, Drugs, and Tobacco. The huge menu includes a number of Italian dishes, Southern comforts, seafood, beef, salads, sandwiches, pizza, and wraps. Portions are generous, the service is excellent, and there's a large Sunday brunch menu.

What do you call a deep-fried, bacon-wrapped jumbo beef hot dog topped with hand-pulled pork, barbecue sauce, and coleslaw? At the **HogsHead Café** (9503 W. Broad St., Henrico, 804/308-0281, www.thehogsheadcafe.com, Tues.-Sat. 11:30am-9pm, $7-32), they call it a "Hog Dog." Build-your-own hot dogs, ribs, barbecue, seafood, and beer served in mason jars—it's all part of the fun atmosphere at this Southern restaurant. The food is authentic, the service is friendly and quick, and the patrons are lively. They also offer takeout and catering.

For those wanting the comfort of a diner with more upscale food, visit **Millie's** (2603 E. Main St., 804/643-5512, www.milliesdiner.com, Tues.-Fri. 11am-2pm and 5:30pm-10pm, Sat.-Sun. 9am-3pm, $19-26), on the edge of Shockoe Bottom (look for the black-and-white dog out front). For starters, don't wait to be given a menu—it's on the chalkboard. You'll most likely have to wait for a table, so plan on

having a mimosa and people watching. Their brunch is legendary (example: lobster in a puff pastry with lightly scrambled egg and hollandaise sauce for $14). The 44-seat restaurant serves upwards of 300 brunch customers on Sunday. The lunch and dinner menu is wonderful too. Be sure to take a look at the vintage jukeboxes (they have an impressive collection of 45s).

French

Those yearning for a little French bistro need look no further than **Bistro Bobette** (1209 E. Cary St., 804/225-9116, www.bistrobobette.com, Mon. 5pm-10pm, Tues.-Fri. 11:30am-2:30pm and 5pm-10pm, Sat. 5pm-10pm, $21-36) in trendy Shockoe Slip. They serve Provençal food in a casual yet elegant atmosphere, and the owners do a wonderful job at making guests feel welcome. The menu stands up to the most seasoned foodie and offers a diverse yet creatively prepared choice of entrées and sides. Fresh ingredients are clearly standard in this establishment and contribute to an overall delightful dining experience.

Greek

Everyone feels like family at a hidden gem called ★ **Stella's** (1012 Lafayette St., 804/358-2011, www.stellasrichmond.com, Mon.-Thurs. 11am-3pm and 5pm-10pm, Fri. 11am-3pm and 5pm-11pm, Sat. 5pm-11pm, Sun. 10am-3pm, $10-30). The modern and traditional Greek cuisine is exquisite, and the atmosphere in this neighborhood establishment makes guests feel like they are visiting friends (there's even a communal table). There is a meze menu (the Greek equivalent of tapas), full entrées, and numerous sides to choose from. There are also delicious desserts. Stella's has many loyal customers, so make a reservation if you plan on dining here on a weekend evening. Parking is on the street.

Italian

No city is complete without a favorite pizza joint. **Bottoms Up Pizza** (1700 Dock St.,

804/644-4400, www.bottomsuppizza.com, Mon.-Wed. 11am-10pm, Thurs. and Sun. 11am-11pm, Fri.-Sat. 11am-midnight, large pizza $13-26) may be under the I-95 overpass, but it serves fantastic pizza with a thick sourdough crust. They have great specialty pies with unique toppings (crab, artichoke, spinach, etc.) and two outdoor decks to enjoy when it's nice out. They reimburse parking fees from the Main Street Parking Lot (see details on their website).

ACCOMMODATIONS
Under $100

The **Candlewood Suites Richmond Airport** (5400 Audubon Dr., 804/652-1888, www.candlewoodsuites.com, $79-103) is a good value near the airport. The hotel caters to a business clientele with a business center, free wireless Internet, complimentary laundry service, and a 24-hour fitness center, but vacationers can also enjoy the apartment-style suites and proximity to the downtown area. Candlewood even offers a library of DVDs that guests can borrow.

$100-200

A pretty little European-style hotel in the Shockoe Slip is the **Berkeley Hotel** (1200 E. Cary St., 804/780-1300, www.berkeleyhotel. com, $144-175). This charming boutique hotel has 55 elegant guest rooms with traditional furniture. Many rooms have great views of downtown Richmond. The service is excellent, and rooms come with free wireless Internet, coffeemakers, terry robes, a morning paper, and access to a health club. Laundry and dry cleaning services are available, as is valet parking.

$200-300

The **Hilton Richmond Downtown** (501 E. Broad St., 804/344-4300, www3.hilton.com, $149-302) is a good choice for staying right in the city. They offer 250 modern rooms and suites in a historic downtown building. Each room has a minifridge, microwave, free wireless Internet, and access to an indoor pool, a

modern fitness center, and a business center. There is a restaurant on-site. Valet parking is available for $27 a day (no self-parking), and the hotel is pet friendly ($100 fee).

A good hotel on the far northwest side of Richmond (near where I-64 and I-295 meet) is the **Hyatt House Richmond-West** (11800 W. Broad St., Henrico, 804/360-7021, www. hyatt.com, $193-252). The hotel can accommodate long stays and offers 134 spotless guest rooms and suites. They provide a complimentary hot breakfast, a 24-hour fitness room, and an indoor heated pool. Next door, the Short Pump Town Center is home to many shops and restaurants.

The **Westin Richmond** (6631 W. Broad St., 804/282-8444, www.marriott.com, $152-304) is a modern hotel with 250 rooms just off I-64 on the west side of town. The hotel has comfortable beds and nice bathrooms (most king rooms have a stand-up shower while most double rooms have a bathtub shower). There is an extra charge for Internet access.

Located a few blocks from Virginia Commonwealth University, **Quirk Hotel** (201 W. Broad St., 804/340-6040, www. destinationhotels.com, $179-239) is a fun boutique hotel occupying the former J. B. Mosby Department Store, built in 1916. The hotel offers 74 guest rooms and has an art-driven theme. The 13-foot ceilings and original wood floors reveal the building's roots, but the rest of the hotel's charm is in the details—for one, the rooms are pink. It may sound unusual (and it is), but it works for this hotel. Rooms are decorated with regional and local artwork. Each floor features a unique papier-mâché portrait of an animal or human and the lobby features art made from used coffee lids (they have their own custom blend of coffee). All the beds are made of reclaimed wood and floor joists. The rest of the details you'll need to see for yourself.

Over $300

★ **The Jefferson Hotel** (101 W. Franklin St., 804/649-4750, www.jeffersonhotel.com, $225-445), located near the state capitol, first opened on Halloween in 1895 and has a long and interesting history. This grand hotel has hosted 12 U.S. presidents, numerous actors, musicians, and politicians, and even had alligators living in the marble pools of its Palm Court for a period of time (the last one died in 1948). The hotel has undergone many changes including the addition of an indoor swimming pool in 2000. The most recent update began in 2013 and included the transformation of the hotel's 262 guest rooms into 181 new rooms and suites.

The public areas in the hotel are tremendous. The center attraction is the 36-step polished marble staircase that many believe was the model for the one shown in *Gone with the Wind*. The staircase leads to the Palm Court, which has a beautiful Tiffany stained glass dome and a life-size statue of Thomas Jefferson. The court had, at one time, a grass lawn surrounding marble pools, but both have long since been removed.

The many amenities in the hotel include a large fitness center, massage treatments, a salon, and an extensive business center. All rooms and suites have high ceilings, marble bathrooms, soaking tubs, and plush bathrobes.

There are two restaurants on-site: the upscale Lemaire and the more casual TJ's.

INFORMATION AND SERVICES

There are three **Richmond Region Visitors Centers** (804/783-7450, www.visitrichmondva.com). The main location is in the **Greater Richmond Convention Center** (405 N. 3rd St., 804/783-7300, daily 9am-5pm). A second is found at the **Richmond International Airport** (804/236-3260, Mon.-Fri. 9:30am-4:30pm, Sat.-Sun. noon-5pm), on the lower level near baggage claim, and the third is inside the **Bass Pro Shops** (11550 Lakeridge Pkwy., Ashland, 804/496-4700, daily 10am-9pm). Staff at each can provide local maps and make hotel reservations.

Another visitors center (that has information on the entire state) is located in the southwest corner of **Capitol Square** inside the Bell Tower (9th St. and Franklin St., 804/698-1788, daily 6am-11pm).

The Jefferson Hotel rotunda lobby and grand staircase

GETTING THERE AND AROUND

Richmond is 98 miles south of Washington DC. The city sits at the intersection of I-95 and I-64.

Air service to Richmond is through the **Richmond International Airport** (RIC, 1 Richard E. Byrd Terminal Dr., 804/226-3000, www.flyrichmond.com), approximately nine miles east of downtown. This is the busiest airport in Central Virginia and has seven carriers that operate approximately 170 daily flights to major domestic cities and connections worldwide.

Amtrak (800/872-7245, www.amtrak.com) provides train service to the **Main Street Station** (1500 E. Main St.) in Shockoe Slip and also the **Staples Mill Road Station** (7519 Staples Mill Rd.). There is a **Greyhound** (804/254-5910, www.greyhound.com) bus terminal at 2910 North Arthur Ashe Boulevard.

The **GRTC Transit System** (804/358-4782, www.ridegrtc.com) provides local bus service in the Richmond area. They offer more than 30 routes and operate daily in the city between 5am and 1am.

PETERSBURG

Petersburg, 25 miles south of Richmond, served as an important supply hub for the Confederate capital during the Civil War. It had five railroad lines and several key roads running through it, and General Grant knew that if he could cut off this resource to General Lee's army, the Confederates would be forced out of Richmond.

Petersburg National Battlefield

The Siege of Petersburg was the longest single Civil War military event. It lasted more than nine months and produced 70,000 casualties.

In June 1864, the Union army began using force against Petersburg, thus beginning a long tough fight for control of the city. By February 1865, General Lee had only 60,000 troops against Grant's 110,000, and finally on April 2, Lee's army was forced out of the strategic location.

Today, visitors to the **Petersburg National Battlefield** (804/732-3531, www.nps.gov/pete) can follow a 33-mile route that includes 13 battlefield sites and three visitors centers. It takes an entire day to fully explore the park.

The **Eastern Front** (5001 Siege Rd., 804/732-3531, ext. 200, daily 8am-8pm, free) visitors center is a great place to begin exploration of the battlefield. It has audiovisual programs and standing exhibits that explain the progression of the siege and its overall impact on the Civil War. Be sure to watch the introductory movie.

At **Grant's Headquarters at City Point** (1001 Pecan Ave., Hopewell, 804/458-9504, daily 8am-5pm, free) visitors can learn about the huge Union supply base and field hospital. There is also information on a plantation that sat on the battlefield before the war overtook the area.

The western side of the tour route is where the **Five Forks Battlefield** (9840 Courthouse Rd., Dinwiddie, 804/469-4093, daily 8am-5pm, free) is located. The Union victory here sealed the fate of Petersburg and Richmond.

The park hosts a number of special events throughout the year including tours, lectures, and living-history demonstrations. Downloadable brochures are available on the website.

Pamplin Historical Park & The National Museum of the Civil War Soldier

Pamplin Historical Park & The National Museum of the Civil War Soldier (6125 Boydton Plank Rd., 804/861-2408, www.pamplinpark.org, daily 9am-5pm, weekends only in winter, adults $15, children 6-12 $8, seniors 62 and over, military, teachers, and students $12, under 6 free) is a 424-acre historical campus that features multiple indoor and outdoor exhibits.

A primary attraction in the park is one of

the nation's best-known Civil War museums, the **National Museum of the Civil War Soldier.** This 25,000-square-foot building features a seven-gallery exhibit called *Duty Called Me Here,* which allows visitors to follow the personal experiences of Civil War soldiers through an MP3 audio player, video, interactive computers, original artifacts, dioramas, and a multisensory battlefield simulator. Another popular feature is the Remembrance Wall, which displays the names of people who "responded to the call of duty during the Civil War."

The **Tudor Hall Plantation** is another popular attraction in the park. Just a short walk from the National Museum of the Civil War Soldier, this 1812 house is fully restored and furnished with period antiques. The house was used by Confederate general Samuel McGowan as his headquarters.

Visitors can also tour the **Field Quarter,** the area of the plantation where the agricultural enslaved people lived. Elements common to field quarters of the time have been re-created to give a sense of slave life at the plantation. Guided tours of the plantation are available. To find out specific tour dates, call 804/861-2408.

Be sure to also make time to visit the **Field Fortifications Exhibit.** This unusual exhibit is the only one of its kind and features 60 yards of re-created late-war field fortifications. Other exhibits in the park include a military encampment, a battlefield center with a theater and fiber-optic battle map, a battlefield walk with three loop trails (0.3-1.25 miles long), and the historic **Banks House,** which served as General Grant's headquarters in 1865. Plan for a minimum of 2-4 hours to explore the park.

Charlottesville

Charlottesville (aka C-ville) is an independent city in the foothills of the Blue Ridge Mountains that is surrounded by, but not included in, Albemarle County. Charlottesville was established in 1762 and encompasses 10.4 square miles.

Charlottesville was home to two U.S. presidents: Thomas Jefferson and James Monroe. James Madison also lived nearby in Orange. Monticello, Jefferson's home, hosts nearly 500,000 visitors each year and is one of the top attractions in the area. Ash Lawn-Highland, James Monroe's home, is just down the road from Monticello. Both Jefferson and Monroe also served terms as the governor of Virginia, during which time each traveled the 71-mile historic **Three Notch'd Road,** a popular east-west route across Virginia, back and forth to Richmond.

Despite the city's small size, there are many attractions and historic sites in and near Charlottesville. Right in town on West Main Street between 6th Street East and 2nd Street

East is the **Downtown Mall.** This beautiful outdoor pedestrian section of the city is one of the longest of its type in the nation. It is a pleasant mix of trees, statues, benches, shops, restaurants, and vendors. There is also a movie theater at the west end. At the east end is the **Sprint Pavilion,** where concerts and the popular free "Fridays after Five" concerts featuring local talent are held. A large white tent marks the pavilion.

The **University of Virginia (UVA)** also calls Charlottesville home. The main grounds of UVA along University Avenue are next to a neighborhood known as **The Corner,** which is an eight-block area (between Chancellor St. and 10th St. NW) full of bars, restaurants, and UVA-related stores. Greek life abounds on nearby Rugby Road and adds to the buzz of social life at the local bars. A commercial district that runs from The Corner to the Downtown Mall along West Main Street is home to more restaurants, bars, and private businesses.

Charlottesville

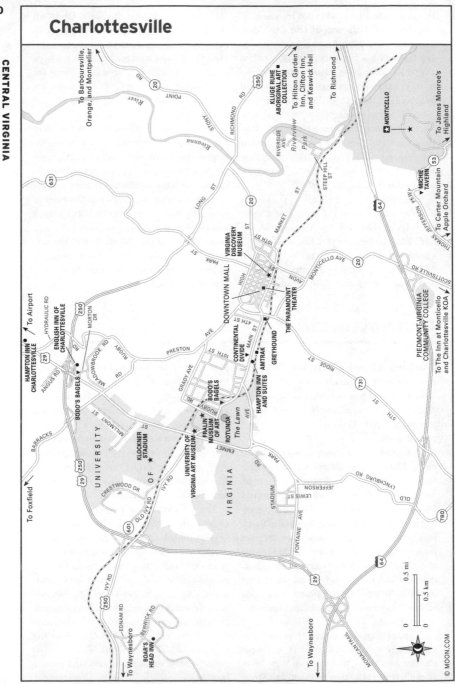

To Barboursville,
Orange, and Montpelier

POINT RIVER RD

20

Stony Point River

Rivanna River

RICHMOND RD

250

KLUGE RUHE
ABORIGINAL ART
COLLECTION

To Hilton Garden
Inn, Clifton Inn,
and Keswick Hall

To Richmond

MONTICELLO

To James Monroe's
Highland

RIVERSIDE AVE

Riverview
Park

STEEP HILL ST

MARKET ST

64

MICHIE
TAVERN

53

To Carter Mountain
Apple Orchard

THOMAS JEFFERSON PKWY

631

LONG ST

20

PARK ST

VIRGINIA
DISCOVERY
MUSEUM

10TH ST

DOWNTOWN MALL

HIGH ST

MONTICELLO AVE

AVON

20

SCOTTSVILLE RD

To Airport

HYDRAULIC RD

ENGLISH INN OF
CHARLOTTESVILLE

250

MORTON DR

HAMPTON INN
CHARLOTTESVILLE

29

ANGUS RD

MEADOWBROOK RD

RUGBY RD

BODO'S BAGELS

PRESTON AVE

GRADY AVE

10TH ST

4TH ST

CONTINENTAL
DIVIDE

MAIN ST

THE PARAMOUNT
THEATER

AMTRAK

GREYHOUND

RIDGE ST

731

5TH ST

PIEDMONT-VIRGINIA
COMMUNITY COLLEGE

To The Inn at Monticello
and Charlottesville KOA

BARRACKS

29 250

UNIVERSITY

MILLMONT ST

KLOCKNER
STADIUM

BODO'S
BAGELS

RUGBY RD

FRALIN
MUSEUM
OF ART

ROTUNDA

The Lawn

HAMPTON INN
AND SUITES

PARK AVE

To Foxfield

CRESTWOOD DR

OF

EMMET ST

UNIVERSITY OF
VIRGINIA ART MUSEUM

IVY RD

VIRGINIA

STADIUM RD

LEWIS ST

JEFFERSON

FONTAINE AVE

LYNCHBURG RD

OLD

780

601

OLD IVY RD

IVY RD

250

EDNAM RD

BERWICK RD

BOAR'S
HEAD INN

To Waynesboro

To Waynesboro

29

64

MONACAN TRAIL

0.5 mi

0.5 km

0

0

© MOON.COM

Across the train tracks from downtown Charlottesville is the Belmont neighborhood. It is a short walk (about 10 minutes) from the east side of downtown. Belmont used to be a farm but has undergone several transformations over the years. It is now an area of great restaurants and the home of the **Bridge Progressive Arts Initiative** (209 Monticello Rd., 434/218-2060, www.thebridgepai.com), a nonprofit inclusive arts organization that provides space to working artists and community programming.

SIGHTS
University of Virginia
The **University of Virginia** (434/924-0311, www.virginia.edu) is one of the top-rated state universities in the nation, with 11 schools in Charlottesville and one in southwest Virginia. The university, founded by Thomas Jefferson, opened in March 1825 with 123 students. Jefferson was heavily involved with the students and faculty for the first year of operation, but he passed away on July 4, 1826. UVA now adds almost 22,000 students to the local population in Charlottesville during the school year.

The main grounds are situated on the west side of Charlottesville. Thomas Jefferson's Academical Village, also referred to as "The Lawn," is its focal point. The Academical Village reflects Jefferson's vision that daily life at college should be infused with learning. He designed 10 pavilions, each focused on a different subject, that had faculty living quarters upstairs and classrooms downstairs and were attached to rows of student housing. The Lawn is a long esplanade with two premier buildings: the elegant early republic-style **Rotunda** (which Jefferson designed, standing 77 feet tall with a diameter of 77 feet) and the stately **Old Cabell Hall** (which faces the Rotunda and has a pediment sculpture that reads, "Ye shall know the truth, and the truth shall make you free.").

The Rotunda is open daily 9am-5pm, and free, guided tours of the Rotunda and Lawn (www.virginia.edu) are offered daily at 10am, 11am, 2pm, and 3pm during the academic year. They depart from the Rotunda's Lower East Oval Room.

THE FRALIN MUSEUM OF ART AT THE UNIVERSITY OF VIRGINIA
The **Fralin Museum of Art at the University of Virginia** (155 Rugby Rd., 434/924-3592, www.uvafralinartmuseum. virginia.edu, Tues., Wed., Fri., and Sat. 10am-5pm, Thurs. 10am-7pm, Sun. noon-5pm, free) is one block north of the Rotunda. It houses a permanent collection of more than 14,000 artifacts. Exhibits include (but are not limited to) 15th to 20th century European and American painting and sculpture, Asian art, American figurative art, and photography. There is a special focus on the "Age of Thomas Jefferson" (1775-1825), and temporary exhibits change often throughout the year.

Kluge-Ruhe Aboriginal Art Collection of the University of Virginia
The **Kluge-Ruhe Aboriginal Art Collection of the University of Virginia** (400 Worrell Dr., 434/244-0234, www.kluge-ruhe.org, Tues., Wed., Fri., and Sat. 10am-4pm, Thurs. 10am-8pm, Sun. 1pm-5pm, free) is the only museum in the nation fully dedicated to Australian indigenous artwork. The museum collaborates with artists, scholars, and art professionals to advance the knowledge of Australia's indigenous people and to provide learning opportunities for the university community. The museum houses one of the premier Aboriginal art collections in the world. It is located approximately three miles east of the UVA campus. Free tours are given on Saturdays at 10:30am.

★ Monticello

Monticello (931 Thomas Jefferson Pkwy., 434/984-9880, www.monticello.org, hours change throughout the year, entrance with tour: adults Mar.-Oct. $29.95/$26.95 online, Nov.-Feb. $25/$23 online, youth June-Aug. online only $17, children 5-11 $10, under 5 free), located on a mountaintop approximately four miles southeast of Charlottesville, is one of the most visited historic sites in the region. The 5,000-acre plantation was the home of Thomas Jefferson, our nation's third president, author of the Declaration of Independence, and the University of Virginia's founder.

Jefferson inherited the land Monticello sits on from his father and began building the house at the age of 26. He maintained and lived in Monticello the rest of his life, always working on and expanding the beautiful home.

Jefferson conceived of his home as a functioning plantation house. Although the design was influenced by Italian Renaissance architecture, it included many elements that were fashionable in late 18th-century Europe and even more elements that were entirely Jefferson's own.

Monticello has one of the most recognized exteriors of any home in Virginia. The large brick structure has a facade adorned by columns and a dramatic octagonal dome. Two large rooms anchor the interior: an entrance hall that Jefferson used to display items of science and a music room. The dome, which sits above the west front of the building, had a room beneath it that is perhaps the most famous part of the house. This "dome room" has yellow octagonal walls and a green wooden floor. Each wall contains a circular window. The top of the dome (the oculus) also has a window that is made of brown glass. The room functioned as an apartment but is said to not have been used much. Visitors are prohibited from entering the room today due to fire regulations.

1: downtown Charlottesville 2: Monticello, the home of Thomas Jefferson

Jefferson never sat idle. He is said to have told his daughter in a letter, "Determine never to be idle . . . It is wonderful how much may be done, if we are always doing." As such, he created many unusual contraptions in his home, and some are still on display today. Fascinated with time, Jefferson put a clock in nearly every room of his mansion. One notable clock is the Great Clock in the entrance hall. He designed the Great Clock to tell both the time and day of the week, and it has both an interior face, which faces the hall, and an exterior face that looks outside over the plantation. The exterior face bears a huge hour hand so enslaved people on the plantation could read it. It also contained a gong that sounded so loudly that the time could be heard three miles away. Another fun invention was Jefferson's clothing rack. Instead of climbing a ladder to reach the top of his tall closet, he created a large spiral rack with 50 arms to hold his clothing. He then turned the rack with a stick to make his outfit selection.

Thomas Jefferson was a terrific gardener and grew many varieties of plants and vegetables. There are three main gardens on the grounds of Monticello for flowers, fruits, and vegetables.

Monticello is the only house in the country included on the UNESCO World Heritage List. Visitors can take a guided, 45-minute tour of the first floor of this beautiful mansion and see original furnishings and personal items that belonged to Jefferson.

Monticello offers tours on a timed-ticketing basis. To ensure you get a tour time that's convenient for you, purchase your ticket online. Be sure to arrive 30 minutes ahead of your ticketed time since it takes 30 minutes to submit tickets and ride the shuttle bus from the ticketing area to the house. Allow two hours for your visit. Tours run throughout the day, and tours of the grounds and gardens are included in the price of the house tour (visitors are welcome to walk the grounds on their own at other times of the year). Interpreters lead these 45-minute walking tours and provide plant identification, stories, and historical insight into the extensive gardens.

Several additional tours are offered, such as the "Behind the Scenes" tour ($49-65) visiting the upstairs of the mansion, and the "Hemings Family Tour" ($28-31), which shows Monticello through the eyes of the best-documented enslaved family in the country.

James Monroe's Highland

James Monroe's Highland (2050 James Monroe Pkwy., 434/293-8000, www.highland. org, Apr.-Oct. daily 9am-6pm, Nov.-Mar. daily 11am-5pm, self-guided and augmented reality [AR] tour $13, guided and AR tour adults $19, youth 6-11 $13, under 6 free) sits 2.5 miles south of Monticello and was formerly called Ash Lawn-Highland. Highland is not a grand mansion like Monticello; instead, it is a 535-acre working farm, a performing arts site, and a historic home museum. James Monroe (fifth President of the United States) and his wife, Elizabeth Kortright Monroe, owned the estate from 1793 to 1826 and lived there most of the time. The estate is now open to the public and displays examples of Victorian and early American architecture, features period craft demonstrations, showcases decorative arts, and is the site of special events and a summer music festival. Original period furnishings are on display in the main house, including some the Monroes had while living in the White House. There are even rumors of a resident ghost.

The College of William & Mary (Monroe's alma mater) maintains the estate, and many events and workshops are hosted there throughout the year.

Virginia Discovery Museum

A great place to bring the little ones is the **Virginia Discovery Museum** (524 E. Main St., 434/977-1025, www.vadm.org, Mon.-Sat. 9:30am-5pm, adults and children $8, under 1 year old free). This children-oriented museum at the east end of the Downtown Mall is small compared to other children's museums in large cities, but it is still a wonderful little attraction, especially on a rainy day. The interactive exhibits are excellent for little kids (under 10) and offer crafts, science, and opportunities to run around. Don't miss the beehive in the back of the museum.

Montpelier

Another presidential home, **Montpelier** (11350 Constitution Hwy., Montpelier Station, 540/672-2728, www.montpelier.org, daily 9am-5pm, adults $22, 6-14 $9, under 6 free, 62 and up and military $21) was home to the "Father of the Constitution," James Madison, and the country's first first lady, Dolley Madison. Madison spent six months in the library of the home performing research and designing the principles for a representative democracy. These ideas first became the "Virginia Plan" and were later used to frame the Constitution.

Today the estate features Madison's mansion, a garden, archaeological sites, and other historical buildings. The Madisons frequently hosted guests at the estate, and the central feature of the compound is their stately brick mansion. Admission tickets include a guided tour of the mansion, highlighting the dining room that was used to host dinner parties, the drawing room, and the presidential library. A self-guided tour of additional exhibits on the second floor of the home, the cellars, gardens, and grounds is also covered by admission. Plan on spending at least two hours at the mansion.

Wineries and Vineyards

October is officially "wine month" in Charlottesville, but any of the 35 local vineyards on the local **Monticello Wine Trail** (www.monticellowinetrail.com) can be enjoyed year-round. Part of the reason for the success of vineyards in this part of the state is the topography. The eroded mountains create wonderful growing conditions, which in turn yield beautifully complex wines. Following are a few vineyards in and around Charlottesville that should be included on any wine tour.

Barboursville Vineyards (17655 Winery Rd., Barboursville, 540/832-3824, www.

1: Jefferson Vineyards 2: tree-lined drive at James Monroe's Highland 3: Montpelier, home of James Madison

Jefferson VINEYARDS ™

Here in 1774, Th. Jefferson and Phillip Mazzei planted Virginia's first commercial vineyards, intending to export their wine back to Europe. The vineyard was abandoned in 1776 with the advent of the Revolutionary War.

Jefferson's effort to grow grapes on a small ____ ____ at Monticello one mile North. ____ original vineyard sites and others ____ replanted in 1981 by Stanley Woodward. ____ ____ ____ sho____ ____ ____ ____ ____ ____ me S____ ____

bbvwine.com, Mon.-Sat. 10am-5pm, Sun. 11am-5pm, $10) is a popular stop on the local wine-tour scene. It's on a beautiful 18th-century estate, less than a half hour from Charlottesville. They were the first in the region to seriously develop European wine varietals and offer daily tastings.

Blenheim Vineyards (31 Blenheim Farm, Charlottesville, 434/293-5366, www.blenheimvineyards.com, daily 11am-5:30pm, $10) was established in 2000 by Dave Matthews, of Dave Matthews Band fame. The vineyard is a family-owned and -operated business 20 minutes southeast of the city. They have two vineyard sites and grow chardonnay, viognier, cabernet franc, petit verdot, and cabernet sauvignon. The timber-frame tasting room has cool glass flooring that allows visitors to look into the tank-and-barrel room below.

Thatch Winery (1650 Harris Creek Rd., Charlottesville, 434/979-7105, www.thatchwinery.com, daily 11am-6pm, $8-15) offers wines that have received state, national, and international awards. They were formerly called First Colony Winery and produce chardonnay, viognier, merlot, cabernet franc, and cabernet sauvignon. They have tastings, a gift shop, a beautiful 2,000-square-foot event room, and picturesque grounds for picnicking.

Jefferson Vineyards (1353 Thomas Jefferson Pkwy., Charlottesville, 434/977-3042, www.jeffersonvineyards.com, daily 11am-6pm, $12) sits on the site between Monticello and James Monroe's Highland where Thomas Jefferson and Filippo Mazzei of Italy first decided to establish a vineyard. The vineyard makes wine entirely from grapes grown in Virginia.

Keswick Vineyards (1575 Keswick Winery Dr., Keswick, 434/244-3341, www.keswickvineyards.com, daily 10am-5pm, $15) specializes in the production of small lots of wine. Their international award winners include viognier, verdejo, chardonnay, cabernet franc, cabernet sauvignon, merlot, petite verdot, syrah, Norton, chambourcin, and touriga.

Their wines are all produced from their own fruit. Tastings are available daily.

Pippin Hill Farm and Vineyard (5022 Plank Rd., North Garden, 434/202-8063, www.pippinhillfarm.com, Tues.-Fri. and Sun. 11am-5pm, Sat. 11am-4:30pm, $13) is a boutique winery and vineyard just outside Charlottesville. It offers a sustainable viticulture program, an exquisite event space, and landscaped gardens. The tasting room features signature wines and food pairings, which can be enjoyed at a beautiful hand-carved bar or out on a stone terrace.

RECREATION
Spectator Sports
There are no professional sports teams in Charlottesville, but a plethora of sporting events take place at **UVA** (434/924-8821, www.virginiasports.com). Whether it's football at **Scott Stadium,** basketball at the **John Paul Jones Arena,** or soccer and lacrosse games at **Klockner Stadium,** you can catch the Wahoo spirit most anytime during the school year.

Spring and fall steeplechases are held annually at **Foxfield** (2215 Foxfield Track, 434/293-9501, www.foxfieldraces.com). A full day of tailgating, people watching, and, of course, horse racing is a tradition on the last Saturday in April and the last Sunday in September. Patrons who drink are encouraged to leave their cars on the property and may do so for up to 48 hours after the race.

Outdoor Recreation
Intermediate and advanced mountain bikers should check out the five-mile single-track trail at **Walnut Creek Park** (4250 Walnut Creek Park Rd., North Garden, www.cambc.org, $4.50), about 10 miles southwest of Charlottesville. This challenging loop runs through a hardwood forest surrounding a 23-acre lake. The trail is twisty, tight, and technical. Less experienced riders may enjoy the easier trail along the water. There are 15 miles of trails in this 525-acre park.

Fishing and boating (electric motors only)

Follow the Brew Ridge Trail

Grapes aren't the only things growing in Charlottesville. Hop vines also love the Central Virginia climate. In fact, once upon a time, Virginia was the hop capital of the world. Albemarle County and nearby Nelson County are home to many small-batch brewhouses that produce a wide variety of handcrafted beers. The Brew Ridge Trail (www.brewridgetrail.com) gives beer lovers a chance to tour a small number of these breweries.

The five breweries along the trail are listed below. Maps of the trail and additional information about upcoming events are available on the trail website.

- **Blue Mountain Barrel House** (495 Cooperative Way, Arrington, 434/263-4002, www. bluemountainbrewery.com)

- **Blue Mountain Brewery** (9519 Critzer's Shop Rd., Afton, 540/456-8020, wwwbluemountainbrewery.com)

- **Devils Backbone Brewing Company** (200 Mosbys Run, Roseland, 434/361-1001, www. dbbrewingcompany.com)

- **Starr Hill Brewing Company** (5391 Three Notched Rd., Crozet, 434/823-5671, www. starrhill.com)

- **Wild Wolf Brewing Company** (2461 Rockfish Valley Hwy., Nellysford, 434/284-5220, www.wildwolfbeer.com)

are popular pastimes on **Beaver Creek Lake** (4365 Beaver Creek Park Rd., www.albemarle. org, $4.50). This 104-acre lake is stocked with sunfish, channel catfish, and largemouth bass. A Virginia state fishing license is required.

Mint Springs Valley Park (6659 Mint Springs Park Rd., Crozet, 434/296-5844, www.albemarle.org, $4.50) in nearby Crozet is a 520-acre park with an 8-acre lake. It offers a beach with swimming during the summer, four hiking trails ranging from 0.5 miles to 1.8 miles, fishing (license required), and boating (electric motors only).

Pick your own apples and peaches (depending on the season) April through December at **Carter Mountain Apple Orchard** (1435 Carters Mountain Trail, 434/977-1833, www. chilesfamilyorchards.com), next to Michie Tavern near Monticello.

ENTERTAINMENT AND EVENTS
Live Music
The music scene in Charlottesville is surprisingly active. The best-known local talent is the Dave Matthews Band. Dave was a bartender

at **Miller's Downtown** (109 W. Main St., 434/971-8511, www.millersdowntown.com, daily 11:30am-2am), a local restaurant where they have a full schedule of live music (jazz and otherwise). It is on the Downtown Mall and used to be a hardware store.

The **Southern Café and Music Hall** (103 S. 1st St., 434/977-5590, www. thesoutherncville.com) is another truly local establishment. They feature locally sourced ingredients on their menu, have local artwork on their walls, and host great live music nearly every night. There's not a bad spot in the house. Visitors enter through a brick patio in this nearly belowground establishment.

The **Jefferson Theater** (110 E. Main St., 434/245-4980, www.jeffersontheater.com) is one of the best live venues in Charlottesville and attracts better-known acts such as Eric Hutchinson and Amos Lee. They have a more advanced sensory experience with improved lighting and sound systems.

The **Paramount Theater** (215 E. Main St., 434/979-1333, www.theparamount.net) is a historic theater on Main Street that first opened in 1931. It became an icon and local landmark immediately and flourished during the Great Depression and even as the era of the American movie palace declined. The venue closed in 1974 but was refurbished and reopened in 2004. It now hosts larger acts as well, such as Gladys Knight and Lyle Lovett.

The **Sprint Pavilion** (700 E. Main St., 434/245-4910, www.sprintpavilion.com) also hosts nationally known talent such as Elvis Costello, Kacey Musgraves, and Dwight Yoakam in an outdoor concert series from spring until fall.

The largest local venue, the **John Paul Jones Arena** (295 Massie Rd., 434/243-4960, www.johnpauljonesarena.com), is a major concert venue featuring talent such as Willie Nelson, Ariana Grande, and Cardi B.

Performing Arts

Charlottesville's number one performance company is **Live Arts** (123 E. Water St., 434/977-4177, www.livearts.org). They are a volunteer theater offering a rounded schedule of drama, comedy, dance, music, and performance arts.

The **Martin Luther King Jr. Performing Arts Center** (1400 Melbourne Rd, 434/466-3880, www.charlottesvilleschools.org) is a 1,276-seat venue run by the Charlottesville City School Division. It hosts student and commercial performances.

Events

The annual **Dogwood Festival** (www.cvilledogwood.com), held each spring in mid-April, is the largest festival in the city and lasts for two weeks. It is a great celebration of the city itself and features fireworks, a carnival, food, and a parade.

The **Virginia Film Festival** (617 W. Main St., 2nd Fl., 434/982-5277, www.virginiafilmfestival.org) is an annual event hosted by the University of Virginia in late October. The festival features more than 70 films and more than 80 guest artists and presenters at a variety of venues. Free panel discussions take place on topics important to both high- and low-budget film processes.

Featured guests in the past have included big-name actors such as Sandra Bullock, Anthony Hopkins, and Sigourney Weaver.

The **Virginia Festival of the Book** (www.vabook.org) draws over 20,000 writers and readers for five days each March to celebrate reading, books, literacy, and literacy culture.

SHOPPING

The Downtown Mall is Charlottesville's premier browsing district and is considered one of the best urban parks in the nation. There are more than 120 independent shops on or near Main Street, with delightful surprises such as rare-book stores, funky boutiques, galleries featuring local artists, craft stores, wine shops, and many others.

Farm-fresh produce can be found seasonally at the **Charlottesville City Market** (www.charlottesvillecitymarket.com). This market, which started in 1973, is held on Saturdays in the parking lot at 1st and Water Streets.

FOOD
American

The ★ **Ivy Inn** (2244 Old Ivy Rd., 434/977-1222, www.ivyinnrestaurant.com, daily 5pm-9:30pm, $11-32) is an elegant restaurant serving "locally inspired seasonal American cuisine." The restaurant is just one mile from UVA in a beautiful home built in 1816; the business itself was established in 1973. The food is excellent. They offer limited choices, but all are done exceptionally well. Examples of the menu include pan-roasted halibut, beef tenderloin, and spinach and ricotta ravioli. The atmosphere is genteel and refined, but not pretentious. The staff is friendly and very knowledgeable about the food and wine list.

For some colonial charm and old-world atmosphere, the **Michie Tavern** (683 Thomas Jefferson Pkwy., 434/977-1234, www.michietavern.com, Apr.-Oct. daily 11:15am-3:30pm, Nov.-Mar. daily 11:30am-3pm, adult $18.95, ages 12-15 $10.95, ages 6-11 $6.95, one child under 6 eats free with each paying adult, vegan/vegetarians $10.95) offers a bountiful lunch buffet in a tavern that was built in 1784. The tavern is a half mile from Monticello and was a popular lodging option for travelers more than 200 years ago. Today they offer a Southern-style buffet lunch with fried chicken, pork barbecue, baked chicken, black-eyed peas, corn bread, stewed potatoes, and other colonial favorites, served by staff dressed in period clothing. The cider ale is wonderful, and the tavern does beer and wine tastings in the evening. The food is served in five dining rooms known as **The Ordinary**. Meals are eaten on steel/pewter plates to add to the experience. A pescatarian option is available with 24 hours notice. Tours of the tavern are also available.

The Local (824 Hinton Ave., 434/984-9749, www.thelocal-cville.com, Sun.-Thurs. 5:30pm-10pm, Fri.-Sat. 5:30pm-11pm, $8-22) showcases the products of local farmers, artisan cheese makers, distilleries, vineyards, and breweries. They serve trout, chicken, beef, and pasta entrées and offer an extensive wine list and a variety of desserts (try the brownie sundae or blackberry cobbler). The brick and wood building dates back to 1912, when it housed a shoe-repair shop (the proprietor lived upstairs in what is now part of the restaurant). The building has served as a church, general store, furniture store, pool hall, motorcycle shop, and photography studio. Start with the crispy shrimp appetizer; it is a unique and delicious dish.

Good burgers, fries, and beer can be found at the Downtown Mall at **Citizen Burger Bar** (212 E. Main St., 434/979-9944, www.citizenburgerbar.com, Sun.-Thurs. 11:30am-10:30pm, Fri.-Sat. 11am-11:30pm, $8-21). This lively spot is a popular choice when students, visitors, and locals crave a meal on a bun (gluten-free buns are available). The portions are large, the food is locally sourced, the beef is grass-fed, and the cheese is made in Virginia. They also offer vegan burgers. Sides such as cheese fries and sweet potato fries are big enough to share. Their bar is well stocked with interesting cocktails and more than 110 types of beer.

Bodo's Bagels (www.bodosbagels.com) serves top-notch bagels at three locations (1418 Emmet St., 434/977-9598; 505 Preston Ave., 434/293-5224; 1609 University Ave., 434/293-6021; all-day breakfast, lunch, and dinner Mon.-Sat., breakfast and lunch Sun., hours vary by location). Their New York-style "water" bagels are simply delicious, and they have great bagel sandwiches, salads, and soups.

Italian

The rustic **Tavola** (826 Hinton Ave., 434/972-9463, www.tavolavino.com, Mon.-Sat. 5pm-10pm, $21-26) is a cozy little Italian restaurant that is big on taste. This isn't a typical American Italian place; the meals are freshly prepared and full of authentic flavor. The atmosphere is lively and fun (aka noisy), but it is charming at the same time and feels like a European bistro. They don't take reservations, so put your name on the list and go to one of the neighboring bars for a drink while you wait. The restaurant is in the Belmont district.

Tex-Mex

The "Get in Here" sign may be the only clue to the entrance to the **Continental Divide** (811 W. Main St., 434/984-0143, Mon.-Thurs. 5pm-10pm, Fri.-Sat. 5pm-10:30pm, Sun. 5pm-9:30pm, $5-14). This little hole-in-the-wall is known for incredible tuna tostadas and the best margaritas in town. The atmosphere is lively and noisy (and not family friendly), so be ready for a party when you finally find the front door. The food is fantastic and cheap, and there's normally a line out the door on weekends. The restaurant is in Midtown across from the Amtrak station.

Turkish

Excellent kabobs are a staple at **Sultan Kabob** (333 2nd St. SE, 434/981-0090, www.sultankebabcville.com, Sun.-Thurs. 11am-9pm, Fri.-Sat. 11am-9:30pm, $5-18). The atmosphere is comfortable, the prices are reasonable, and the staff is friendly. This is a quiet, relaxing place where the food takes center stage. For something different, try the hummus casserole. They also have vegan and gluten-free options.

Treats

For a tasty Italian treat, stop in **Splendora's Gelato** (317 E. Main St., 434/296-8555, www.splendoras.com, Mon.-Thurs. 7:30am-9pm, Fri. 7:30am-10pm, Sat. 9am-10pm, Sun. noon-9pm, under $10) on the Downtown Mall. They offer between 24 and 36 flavors of delectable gelato every day as well as espresso and other desserts.

ACCOMMODATIONS
$100-200

The **English Inn of Charlottesville** (2000 Morton Dr., 434/971-9900, www.englishinncharlottesville.com, $129-159) is an independent hotel with 106 rooms and suites. Built in the Tudor style, this friendly hotel offers free Internet access, a fitness room, an indoor pool, and a free hot breakfast.

The **200 South Street Inn** (200 W. South St., 434/979-0200, www.southstreetinn.com, $135-219) has 19 rooms and suites just two blocks from the pedestrian mall, one mile from the University of Virginia, and four miles from Monticello. The inn is made up of two restored homes, one built in 1856 and the other in 1890. It is decorated with antiques, and many rooms have fireplaces, whirlpool baths, and canopy beds. Larger suites with living rooms are available. All rooms have private baths. Guests can enjoy a continental breakfast in the library or, in nice weather, on the veranda. Cookies are also available around the clock. Rooms are comfortable but lack some of the modern conveniences of large hotel chains. Still, the personal attention given by the innkeepers, the charming atmosphere, and proximity to the downtown area make this a good choice in Charlottesville.

The **Hampton Inn Charlottesville** (2035 India Rd., 434/978-7888, www.hamptoninn3.hilton.com, $140-159) has 123 guest rooms, an outdoor pool, free breakfast, and wireless Internet. The hotel is a few miles from the downtown area, but there are chain restaurants and stores within walking distance. The staff is exceptionally friendly and helpful.

A second Hampton Inn in Charlottesville is the **Hampton Inn & Suites Charlottesville at the University** (900 W. Main St., 434/923-8600, www.hamptoninn3.hilton.com, $169-259). It has 100 guest rooms and suites near UVA and complimentary breakfast.

Over $200

★ **The Clifton** (1296 Clifton Inn Dr., 434/971-1800, www.the-clifton.com, $150-849), formerly the Clifton Inn, is a luxurious inn with 20 guest rooms in five late-18th- and early 19th-century buildings. This romantic establishment sits on 100 acres, with sweeping Blue Ridge Mountain views, and was built and used by Thomas Jefferson's son-in-law, Thomas Mann Randolph Jr., who was also the governor of Virginia (the estate also offers views of Monticello). During the Civil War, the family of Colonel John Singleton Mosby stayed at Clifton after fleeing their home near Middleburg in Northern Virginia. Mosby had a secret hiding area outside the main house where he is said to have left supplies for his family when Union troops were nearby. Today, guests enjoy first-rate service in the serene environment of this charming estate, which underwent major interior renovations with new ownership in 2018. Guests enjoy many amenities such as an infinity pool, private lake, gardens, walking trails, on-site restaurant, bar, and wine cellar.

Two miles west of town is the highly acclaimed ★ **Boar's Head Resort** (200 Ednam Dr., 434/296-2181, www.boarsheadresort.com, $185-325). The 573-acre estate is a destination in itself, with 175 rooms and suites, a fitness club, a spa, 20 tennis courts, a lap pool, golf course, biking, fishing, hiking, and even hot-air-balloon rides. There are also four restaurants and 20 event spaces. The inn is a certified "Virginia Green" establishment.

1: The Clifton entry 2: Ivy Inn 3: Citizen Burger Bar 4: Keswick Hall

Getaway to Wintergreen Resort

condos at Wintergreen Resort

Forty minutes southwest of Charlottesville is **Wintergreen Resort** (39 Mountain Inn Loop, Wintergreen, 434/325-2200, www.wintergreenresort.com). This beautiful, year-round destination is perched on the eastern side of the Blue Ridge Mountains. Unlike traditional mountain resorts, Wintergreen is built at the top of the mountain ridges instead of at the base of the mountain. The elevation is approximately 4,000 feet.

There is a large full-service spa on-site, 40,000 square feet of meeting space, and 300 choices of condos and homes for rent. There is also an aquatics center with indoor and outdoor pools.

Skiing and snowboarding ($39-89 for lift tickets) are popular on the 26 trails (14 of which are lit for night skiing). There is also a 900-foot tubing trail with 12 lanes and a terrain park. There are five chairlifts, and the resort can make snow on 100 percent of its trails.

During the summer, there are 45 holes of championship golf, tennis, hiking on 30 miles of trails, and many family activities such as minigolf, a climbing tower, and a bungee trampoline.

Rooms are decorated with antique furnishings and have beautiful bathrooms with modern conveniences. Premium bath items, plush bathrobes, and high-quality bedding are standard. The service is top-rate. The inn is close enough to downtown attractions to be convenient, but far enough away that you feel like you're out in the country. Rooms are spread out over several buildings. Ask for one in the main inn building.

The award-winning ★ **Keswick Hall** (701 Club Dr., Keswick, 434/979-3440, www.keswick.com, $310-1,000) at Monticello is a 1912 Italianate villa that was turned into a grand resort by the widower of designer Laura Ashley. Guests are welcomed into this extravagant home in a comfortable lounge opening onto a patio that overlooks the 600-acre estate grounds. Guests in its 48 rooms can enjoy access to the Keswick Club, where they can play golf or tennis, swim in the saltwater pool, and use the spa. At the time of writing, the resort was closed for major renovations throughout the entire hotel and was scheduled to reopen in 2020.

INFORMATION AND SERVICES

The **Charlottesville-Albemarle Convention and Visitors Bureau**

(610 E. Main St., 434/293-6789, www. visitcharlottesville.org, daily 9am-5pm) provides visitors with maps and brochures about Charlottesville and the surrounding area. They are on the Downtown Mall.

GETTING THERE AND AROUND

Charlottesville is 115 miles southwest of Washington DC. The main highways running through Charlottesville are I-64, US 250, and US 29.

The **Charlottesville-Albemarle Airport** (CHO, 100 Bowen Loop, 434/973-8342, www.gocho.com) is a public airport with commercial service eight miles north of Charlottesville. Three airlines provide service to six cities, and approximately 25 flights are scheduled daily. Rental cars are available on-site.

Amtrak (800/872-7245, www.amtrak.com) provides service to Charlottesville at 810 West Main Street (not far from the UVA campus), and **Greyhound** (800/231-2222, www.greyhound.com) bus service is also available at 310 West Main Street.

Charlottesville Area Transit (CAT) (434/970-3649, www.charlottesville.org, Mon.-Sat. 6am-11:45pm, times vary by route, $0.75) offers 12 bus routes throughout the city. CAT also provides free trolley services daily from the Downtown Transit Station (615 E. Water St.) along Main Street. It also goes through the grounds of UVA.

Blue Ridge Parkway

The **Blue Ridge Parkway** (www.blueridgeparkway.org) is one of the most popular units of the national park system. The parkway is 469 miles long and connects **Great Smoky Mountains National Park** in North Carolina and Tennessee with **Shenandoah National Park** in Virginia. The parkway was designed during the Great Depression, and its creators took advantage of the beautiful terrain and followed the natural contours of the ridgeline. Gorgeous scenery is the key ingredient to this outstanding park, and visitors can enjoy overlooks of the Blue Ridge Mountains, countless vistas, beautiful old meadows, and picturesque farmland.

A 217-mile stretch of the Blue Ridge Parkway is in Virginia, with the prettiest part being the 114 miles between Waynesboro and Roanoke. This section follows the crest of the Blue Ridge Mountains.

Attractions and landmarks along the parkway are announced by mileposts (mp). Milepost 0 is at the northern end of the parkway at Rockfish Gap. This is also the southern end of Shenandoah National Park. Milepost 218 is at the North Carolina border. The speed limit along the entire Blue Ridge Parkway is 45 miles per hour. Visitors should expect slower traffic during peak foliage time in the fall and also during the summer months.

PLANTS AND ANIMALS

Wildflower meadows, colorful leaves, spotted fawns, and black bear cubs can all be seen at times along the Blue Ridge Parkway. There are millions of varieties of flora and fauna that can be found on this famed stretch of road.

There are more than 130 species of trees growing along the parkway (as many as are found in all of Europe). Some of the most popular types include evergreens such as Virginia pine, white pine, spruce, fir, and hemlock. The altitude along the entire parkway varies from just under 650 feet to 6,047 feet. Because of this, the fall foliage season is rather long since the fireworks of colored leaves burst at slightly different times at each altitude. A current **Fall Color Report** can be heard by calling 828/298-0398 (press 3).

Dogwood, sourwood, and black gum leaves change to deep red, while hickory and tulip tree leaves turn bright yellow. Red maples

Blue Ridge Parkway

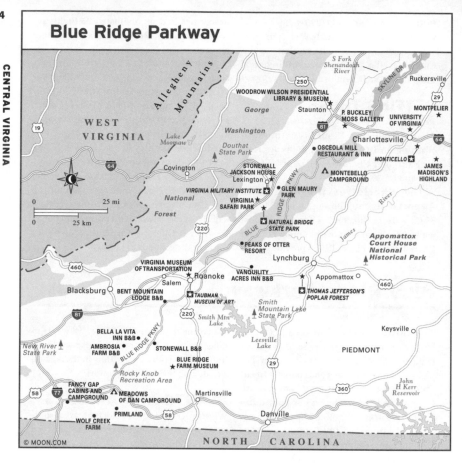

produce multicolored leaves, while sassafras trees add orange leaves to the mix. The fall is an amazing time to explore the parkway. There's nothing quite like the autumn foliage in Virginia, and the Blue Ridge Parkway offers the crème de la crème of this incredible spectacle.

There are many types of flowers along the parkway. The Blue Ridge Parkway website (www.blueridgeparkway.org) has a helpful **Bloom Schedule** that gives tentative blooming periods for many popular flowers. There is also a **Wildflower Report** available on the Parkway Information Line (828/298-0398) during the spring and summer. It should be noted that all plants along

the parkway are protected and should not be picked or destroyed.

Many animals make their home in the wilds along the Blue Ridge Parkway. There are more than 50 species of mammals, 250 species of birds (159 that nest there), 40 species of reptiles, 50 types of salamanders, and 50 species of fish. Many people are interested to know that of the 22 species of snakes living in the region, only two types are venomous: the timber rattlesnake and the copperhead. Both are not aggressive and prefer to avoid contact with people altogether.

Wildlife should be left wild. No matter how friendly they may seem, any animals in the park should not be fed or interacted with.

Picture taking, from a distance, is of course acceptable, but no close contact should be made.

SIGHTS

There are many wonderful attractions along or just off the parkway as it passes close to numerous towns. Locations are best described by their corresponding mileposts. Visitors centers are located at milepoint 5.8 (Humpback Rocks), milepoint 63.6 (James River), milepoint 86 (Peaks of Otter), milepoint 115 (Explore Park), milepoint 169 (Rocky Knob), and milepoint 213 (Blue Ridge Music Center).

Woodrow Wilson Presidential Library and Museum

The **Woodrow Wilson Presidential Library and Museum** (mp 0, 20 N. Coalter St., Staunton, 540/885-0897, www. woodrowwilson.org, Mon.-Sat. 9am-5pm, Sun. noon-5pm, adults $15, youth 6-15 $8, over 60 $14, active military $12, under 6 free) is a historical destination and the former home of Woodrow Wilson. It offers multiple attractions such as the Woodrow Wilson Museum (self-guided tours are available through seven galleries), a state-of-the-art World War I trench experience, a research library, gardens, and a hands-on kids' corner.

Milepost 0 is also where the **P. Buckley Moss Gallery** (329 W. Main St., Waynesboro, 540/949-6473, www.pbuckleymoss.com, Mon.-Sat. 10am-5pm, Sun. noon-4pm, closed Mon. Jan.-Mar.) is located. The gallery is home to the permanent art collection of Virginia artist P. Buckley Moss, who is known for her rural landscape paintings and those depicting life in the Shenandoah Valley. At the museum, visitors can learn about her life and achievements in art.

Stonewall Jackson House

The **Stonewall Jackson House** (mp 45.6, 8 E. Washington St., Lexington, 540/464-7704, www.vmi.edu, daily 9am-5pm, adults $8, youth 6-17 $6, 5 and under free) is the former home of the Civil War general. It has been beautifully restored and contains some original Jackson family furnishings. Guided tours, a garden, and a museum shop are part of the offerings.

★ Natural Bridge State Park

Natural Bridge State Park (mp 61.6, 6477 S. Lee Hwy., Natural Bridge, 540/291-1326, www.naturalbridgestatepark.org and www. dcr.virginia.gov, daily 9am-4pm, extended summer hours, adults $8, children 6-12 $6, under 6 free) is a National Historic Landmark that was once owned by Thomas Jefferson. The 20-story solid limestone rock arch created by nature is an awesome sight and one that has inspired people for generations. A variety of other attractions are also at the Natural Bridge, including the **Caverns at Natural Bridge** (15 Appledore Ln., Natural Bridge, 540/291-2482, daily 9am-4pm, Nov.-mid-Mar. Fri.-Sun. only, adults starting at $18.50, ages 7-17 $12.75, under 7 free), which sit 34 stories below ground. A combo bridge-and-caverns ticket can be purchased for $30 for adults, children 6-12 $19.50.

Virginia Safari Park

Four miles north of the Natural Bridge is the **Virginia Safari Park** (mp 61.6, 229 Safari Ln., Natural Bridge, 540/291-3205, www. virginiasafaripark.com, mid-Mar.-Nov. daily 9am-5pm, extended weekend and summer hours, adults $21.95, children 2-12 $14.95, seniors 65 and over $20.95, under 2 free). This 180-acre drive-through zoo houses more than 1,000 animals that are free to roam in a natural setting. Three miles of roads meander through woods and fields, allowing visitors to see animals such as deer, zebras, elk, antelope, giraffe, camels, and bison. The free-roaming animals literally stick their heads inside your car waiting to be fed. Buckets of feed are available at the entrance to the park. There is also a walk-through area where visitors can feed giraffes, goats, pigs, and baby llamas.

★ Thomas Jefferson's Poplar Forest

Thomas Jefferson's Poplar Forest (mp 86, 1542 Bateman Bridge Rd., Forest, 434/525-1806, www.poplarforest.org, Mar. 15-Dec. 30 daily 10am-5pm, adults $16, teens 12-18 $8, youth 6-11 $4, seniors 65 and over $14, military $14, under 6 free) was Thomas Jefferson's personal retreat. He originally inherited the land from his father-in-law as a working tobacco farm, and it offered him a nice source of income. Ten miles west of Lynchburg, the home is an architectural masterpiece built in 1806 and one of only two that Jefferson designed and constructed for his personal use. It was also the first octagonal house in the country. It was a three-day ride for Jefferson between Monticello and Poplar Forest, but he went there several times a year and stayed from two weeks to two months each visit. Visitors to Poplar Forest learn about life in the early 19th century, the architecture of the home, and its preservation. They also witness ongoing excavation of the property and can see authentic artifacts from the plantation. Admission includes a guided 40-minute tour of the house and a self-guided tour of the grounds.

Virginia Museum of Transportation

Farther south, in Roanoke, is the **Virginia Museum of Transportation** (mp 112.2, 303 Norfolk Ave. SW, Roanoke, 540/342-5670, www.vmt.org, Mon.-Sat. 10am-5pm, Sun. 1pm-5pm, adults $10, youth 13-18, students with ID, and seniors 60 and over $8, children 3-12 $6, under 3 free). This large museum is mostly outdoors and holds more than 50 railway exhibits, road vehicle exhibits, and air exhibits. It is best known for its exhibits on the Norfolk & Western Class J-611 and Class A-1218 modern steam locomotives.

1: Blue Ridge Parkway overlook 2: Stonewall Jackson House in Lexington 3: Thomas Jefferson's Poplar Forest home 4: Natural Bridge State Park

Blue Ridge Farm Museum

For a lesson on farm life, check out the **Blue Ridge Farm Museum** (mp 152, 20 Museum Dr., Ferrum, 540/365-4412, www.ferrum.edu, mid-May-Labor Day Sat. 10am-5pm, Sun. 1pm-5pm, free). The farm takes visitors back to 1800 to experience what life was like on a Virginia German farmstead. Interpreters dressed in period clothing complete numerous farm chores such as cooking, driving oxen, and blacksmith work.

Mabry Mill

The most photographed location on the Blue Ridge Parkway is **Mabry Mill** (mp 176.1). This charming, water-powered mill (built in 1867) is visited by several hundred thousand people each year. The gristmill and sawmill have been restored, and visitors can see a working miller demonstrate the milling process. The mill grounds are lovely and tranquil, although crowded in the summer months, and include interpretive media.

RECREATION

The Blue Ridge Parkway has numerous attractions and recreational opportunities along its winding route. Campgrounds, hiking trails, interpretive centers, and picnic areas are just some of the possibilities for a break when traversing this gorgeous roadway. The famed **Appalachian Trail,** which runs 2,184 miles from Maine to Georgia, meanders along the parkway from Rockfish Gap (at the northern end) down to Roanoke.

Near the northern end of the parkway is a beautiful area known as **Humpback Rocks** (mp 5.8). Visitors can see farm buildings from the 19th century and enjoy numerous hiking trails suitable for all abilities. Interpretive programs in which park rangers demonstrate making local mountain crafts are held during the summer months.

At milepost 64, a section of the **James River** can be explored. Visitors can see one of the restored canal locks from the James River and Kanawha Canal, a prime commercial route in Virginia in the mid-1800s, and also go fishing from a public dock. There are plenty of areas for picnicking.

The popular **Peaks of Otter** area at milepost 86 offers incredible views and an abundance of natural beauty. The area has been a popular tourist attraction since 1834. Ranger programs are offered at the visitors center, and a lovely picnic area along Little Stoney Creek provides tables, grills, and restroom facilities. There are six hiking trails at Peaks of Otter, and Abbott Lake is open to the public for fishing (with a Virginia or North Carolina fishing license).

Virginia's Explore Park (mp 115, Blue Ridge Pkwy., 540/427-1800, www.explorepark. org), located near Roanoke, is a 1,200-acre park with nine miles of mountain bike trails, a one-mile interpretive trail, fishing, canoeing, and kayaking. There is also a Treetop Quest (adults $35, ages 12-17 $29, ages 7-11 $22, ages 4-6 $15) aerial adventure course that has obstacles and zip lines.

The **Smart View Trail** (mp 154.5) is a popular 2.6-mile loop hiking trail around the Smart View Picnic Area. It is a level trail through the woods with nice views.

The beautiful **Rocky Knob** area at milepost 169 offers several great hiking trails of different lengths. The Rock Castle Gorge Trail (blazed in green) is a moderate-to-strenuous 10.8-mile loop with elevation ranges from 1,700 feet to 3,572 feet. Sections are steep and rocky on this National Scenic Trail. The Black Ridge Trail (blazed in blue) is a moderate 3-mile loop hike with good views to the north from the top of Black Ridge. This trail joins the Rock Castle Gorge Trail on the return trip. The Rocky Knob Picnic Area Trail (blazed in yellow) is an easy 1-mile loop walk through mature forest.

ENTERTAINMENT

The **Blue Ridge Music Center** (mp 213, 700 Foothills Rd., Galax, 276/236-5309, www. blueridgemusiccenter.org) is a modern performing arts venue that was constructed for the purpose of promoting historical Blue Ridge music. Old-time and bluegrass music frequently floods the facility and surrounding area. Visitors can take in a show, explore the visitors center, and check out the views of Fisher Peak.

FOOD

At milepost 27 (halfway between Staunton and Lexington) is the **Osceola Mill** (mp 27, 352 Tye River Turnpike, Steeles Tavern, 540/377-6455, www.osceolamill.com, Fri. and Sat. 5pm-10pm, $26-40). This elegant but casual restaurant serves seafood, steak, and veal. The menu varies weekly depending on what is in season. The Mill Stone dining room has huge chestnut beams, original millworks, and views of the mill's waterwheel.

The **Liberty Station Restaurant** (mp 86, 515 Bedford Ave., Bedford, 540/587-9377, www.oldelibertystation.com, Mon.-Thurs. 11am-9pm, Fri.-Sat. 11am-10pm, $9-21) in Bedford is housed in a former railroad station. It serves traditional American food and is known for its cheesecake.

Seven miles from the parkway at milepost 121 is the **Roanoker Restaurant** (mp 121, 2522 Colonial Ave., Roanoke, 540/344-7746, www.theroanokerrestaurant.com, Tues.-Sat. 7am-9pm, Sun. 8am-9pm, $10-17). They serve American home-style food and are open for breakfast, lunch, and dinner. Their menu includes a variety of seafood, salads, and sandwiches at reasonable prices.

If you're looking for food near milepost 164, the **Blue Ridge Cafe** (mp 164, 113 E. Main St., Floyd, 540/745-2147, www. blueridgecafefloyd.com, Mon.-Wed. 6am-4pm, Thurs.-Fri. 6am-8pm, Sat. 7am-8pm, Sun. 7am-4pm, $4-16) is a good stop for traditional diner food. This no-frills place across from the courthouse in Floyd, six miles from the parkway, will satisfy your appetite in a casual, friendly environment. They are open for breakfast, lunch, and dinner.

The **Mabry Mill Restaurant** (mp 176, 266 Mabry Mill Rd. SE, Meadows of Dan, 276/952-2947, www.mabrymillrestaurant.com, May-Oct. Mon.-Fri. 7:30am-5pm, Sat.-Sun. 7:30am-6pm, under $12) offers home-style cooking and is known for its buckwheat pancakes, country ham, and Virginia barbecue. They serve breakfast all day. The restaurant is located next to the **Mabry Mill.**

Not far from milepost 199.5 is **The Gap Deli at the Parkway** (mp 199.5, 7975 Fancy Gap Hwy., Fancy Gap, 276/728-3881, www.thegapdeli.com, Sun.-Thurs. 10am-4pm, Fri.-Sat. 10am-7pm, under $10). They serve a nice variety of sandwiches, wraps, salads, and dessert.

ACCOMMODATIONS

There are many wonderful independent inns, lodges, and bed-and-breakfasts nestled in the mountains along the Blue Ridge Parkway. Most are family owned and operated and offer reasonable rates. Book early when visiting during peak season.

In a town called Steeles Tavern (between Staunton and Lexington) is the **Osceola Mill** (mp 27, 352 Tye River Turnpike, Steeles Tavern, 540/377-6455, www.osceolamill.com, $105-200). They offer bed-and-breakfast accommodations, cabin rentals, and a restaurant. There are four rooms and one individual cabin for rent in a peaceful, beautiful six-acre compound. Another good option near milepost 27 is the **Sugar Tree Inn** (mp 27, 145 Lodge Trail, Vesuvius, 540/377-2197, www.sugartreeinn.com, closed Jan., $148-248). This peaceful log inn offers accommodations in the main lodge (three rooms) and four additional cabins/houses. There are 13 guest rooms total. It has expansive views and wood-burning fireplaces in all guest rooms. A full breakfast is included with your stay.

A nice bed-and-breakfast in Bedford near milepost 86 is the **Vanquility Acres Inn** (mp 86, 105 Angus Terrace, Bedford, 540/587-9113, www.vanquilityacresinn.com, $115-145). This 10-acre farm has wonderful views of the Blue Ridge Mountains, fishing, fireplaces, wireless Internet, and suites with private bathrooms. There are five guest rooms. The better-known **Peaks of Otter Lodge** (mp 86, 85554 Blue Ridge Pkwy., Bedford, 866/387-9905, www.peaksofotter.com, $112-188) sits between two mountains on the parkway and looks over tranquil Abbott Lake. It offers 63 rooms and has a restaurant on-site.

Unique accommodations can be found at the ★ **Depot Lodge Bed and Breakfast** (mp 112.2, Rte. 311, Paint Bank, 540/897-6000, www.thedepotlodge.com, $149-289), about an hour from Roanoke in the Jefferson National Forest. This restored train depot was built in 1909 as the final stop on the Potts Valley Branch line of the Norfolk & Western Railroad. They offer nine guest rooms in the depot and surrounding historic buildings, including cabins, and a romantic restored caboose. There is also an Airstream trailer and two luxurious "glamping" tents.

The **Bent Mountain Lodge Bed and Breakfast** (mp 136, 9039 Mountain View Dr., Copper Hill, 540/651-2500, www.bentmountainlodgebedandbreakfast.com, $120-150) has 10 guest suites with private bathrooms. This 15,000-square-foot lodge is between Floyd and Roanoke (20 minutes away from each). Room rates include continental breakfast. The lodge is pet friendly.

The **Bella La Vita Inn Bed and Breakfast** (mp 161, 582 New Haven Rd. SE, Floyd, 540/745-2541, www.bellalavitainn.com, $149-160) is less than two miles from the Blue Ridge Parkway and offers four delightful European-style guest rooms and in-house massage therapy.

A good overnight stop near milepost 165 is the **Stonewall Bed and Breakfast** (mp 165.2, 102 Wendi Pate Trail SE, Floyd, 540/745-2861, www.stonewallbed.com, $70-130). They have six guest rooms in the main house and two cabins for rent. This lovely three-level log house is in the woods and has a warm and inviting atmosphere.

The **Ambrosia Farm Bed and Breakfast** (mp 171.5, 271 Cox Store Rd., Floyd, 540/745-6363, www.ambrosiafarm.net, $90-135) is housed in a restored log farmhouse that is 200 years old. It now contains four cozy guest rooms. The home has lovely views, porches to enjoy them from, and an on-site pottery studio.

Getaway to Primland

Primland

Primland (2000 Busted Rock Rd., Meadows of Dan, 866/960-7746, www.primland.com, $300-1,890) might be the best-kept secret in all of Virginia. Nestled in the beautiful Blue Ridge Mountains on more than 12,000 acres, this LEED-certified, upscale resort offers complete relaxation, as well as stunning scenery, plentiful activities, great food, and attention to every last detail.

Unpretentious, yet classy in every respect, this unique four-season property is the perfect getaway for a range of occasions, from family vacations to business conferences and even honeymoons. In addition to its luxurious suites, the main lodge offers a formal dining room, a cozy pub, a conference space, a beautiful spa, an indoor swimming pool, a fitness center, a game room, a common space, and a large deck with a fire pit. The lodge also features an observatory with a Celestron CGE Pro 1400 series telescope, and nightly tours of the universe are offered by a local astronomer. Additional accommodations include stunning secluded tree houses, golf-course-view cottages, pinnacle cottages, and individual homes.

The list of amenities and activities available at Primland includes the highly ranked Highland Golf Course, hiking, sporting clays, fly fishing, RTV rides, hunting, kayaking, horseback riding, disc golf, geocaching, nature walks, tree climbing, mountain biking, and an authentic Virginia moonshine experience. They also offer a Tesla charger, a smoking house, and eco-conscious extras throughout the resort.

Just 200 yards from the Blue Ridge Parkway near milepost 174 is the **Woodberry Inn** (mp 174.1, 182 Woodberry Rd. SW, Meadows of Dan, 540/593-2567, www.woodberryinn.com, $99). They offer 16 simply appointed rooms (each with a private bathroom), free wireless Internet, and a restaurant on-site. They are pet friendly.

For stunning upscale accommodations, treat yourself to a stay at ★ **Primland** (mp 177.7, 2000 Busted Rock Rd., Meadows of Dan,

866/960-7746, www.primland.com, $300-1,890). Primland offers 62 units that include lodge rooms, suites, cottages, treehouses, and mountain homes. There is a mile-long list of amenities and activities offered on the premises, including a spa, fitness center, and golf course. Turn east at milepost 177.7 to take Route 58/Jeb Stuart Highway for 4.5 miles to Busted Rock Road.

The **Wolf Creek Farm** (mp 192, 688 Gid Collins Rd., Ararat, 276/952-8869, www.

wolfcreekfarmva.net, $135-160) offers two guest rooms and one cabin for rent in the town of Ararat. It sits on 102 acres and has a fishing lake and swimming pool.

CAMPING

Camping and fishing can be found three miles from the parkway at milepost 27 and the **Montebello Camping and Fishing Resort** (mp 27, 15072 Crabtree Falls Hwy., Montebello, 540/377-2650, www.montebellova.com, $30-46). This full-service campground accommodates RVs, trailers, and tent camping. There's a four-acre lake and cabins on-site.

The **Glen Maury Park Campground** (mp 45.6, 101 Maury River Dr., Buena Vista, 540/261-7321, www.bvcity.org, $22-30) is five miles from the parkway on 315 acres. They have 52 sites and modern facilities. A few miles down the parkway is the **Lynchburg NW/Blue Ridge Parkway KOA** (mp 61.5, 6252 Elon Rd., Monroe, 434/299-5228, www.koa.com, $30-53), sitting just one mile from the parkway and open all year. They have RV and tent camping.

Visitors can pitch a tent at one of 74 tent sites in the **Roanoke Mountain Campground** (mp 120.4, Blue Ridge Dr., Roanoke, 540/342-3051, www.blueridgecampgrounds.com, $16). Facilities include 30 RV/trailer sites, comfort stations, water, flush toilets, and sinks (no showers).

Near milepost 177.7 is the **Meadows of Dan Campground** (mp 177.7, 2182 Jeb Stuart Hwy., Meadows of Dan, 276/952-2292, www.meadowsofdancampground.com, $30). They have full hookups, a separate tent area, a bathhouse, and a dumping station. They also offer log cabin rentals.

The **Fancy Gap Cabins and Campground** (mp 199.5, 202595 Blue Ridge Pkwy., Fancy Gap, 276/730-7154, www.fancygapcabinsandcampground.com, $25-70) is right on the Blue Ridge Parkway in Fancy Gap. They offer tent sites, RV sites, camping cabins ($25-55), and motel rooms ($70) with scenic views. They are pet friendly.

INFORMATION AND SERVICES

For additional information on the Blue Ridge Parkway, visit www.blueridgeparkway.org or stop by one of their visitors centers, located at milepost 5.8 (Humpback Rocks, May-Oct. daily 10am-5pm), milepost 63.6 (James River, June-Oct. Wed.-Sun. 10am-5pm), milepost 86 (Peaks of Otter, May-Oct. daily 10am-5pm), milepost 169 (Rocky Knob, June-Oct. Thurs.-Mon. 10am-5pm), and milepost 213 (Blue Ridge Music Center, June-Oct. daily 10am-5pm).

Lexington

Lexington is a popular tourist stop due to its lovely location in the southern part of the Shenandoah Valley, vibrant military history, and the fact that it is home to **Washington and Lee University** and the **Virginia Military Institute (VMI)**. Lexington is part of Rockbridge County. Buena Vista is the closest town (15-minute drive), and Natural Bridge near the Blue Ridge Parkway is about 20 minutes away.

Many historic residences are preserved along the town's tree-lined streets and in the downtown area, making Lexington a charming mix of homes, shops, and restaurants. There are numerous cozy inns and bed-and-breakfasts to choose from, and many are within walking distance of local attractions.

Two of the most famous Confederate heroes, Robert E. Lee and Stonewall Jackson, are buried in Lexington. Both lived and worked in Lexington, and their legacies live on in this somewhat quiet community.

Lexington was founded in 1777 and was destroyed by fire in 1796. It was quickly rebuilt

Lexington

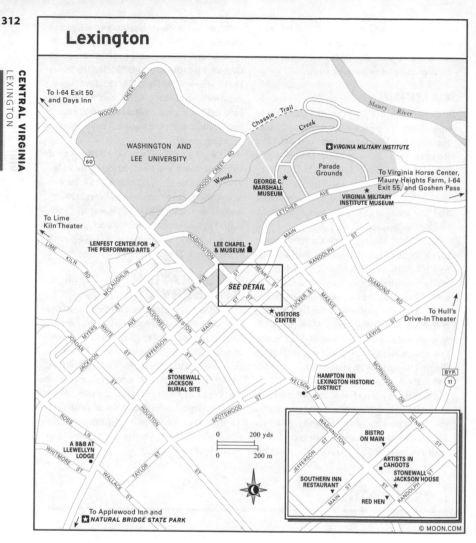

To I-64 Exit 50 and Days Inn

WOODS CREEK RD

Chassie Trail

Maury River

Creek

WASHINGTON AND LEE UNIVERSITY

60

WOODS CREEK RD

Woods

★ VIRGINIA MILITARY INSTITUTE

GEORGE C. ★ MARSHALL MUSEUM

Parade Grounds

To Virginia Horse Center, Maury Heights Farm, I-64 Exit 55, and Goshen Pass

LETCHER AVE

★ VIRGINIA MILITARY INSTITUTE MUSEUM

To Lime Kiln Theater

LIME KILN RD

LENFEST CENTER FOR ★ THE PERFORMING ARTS

WASHINGTON ST

LEE CHAPEL ✝ & MUSEUM ★

MAIN ST

RANDOLPH ST

DIAMOND RD

MCLAUGHLIN ST

LEE AVE

HENRY ST

SEE DETAIL

TUCKER ST

MASSIE ST

LEWIS ST

To Hull's Drive-In Theater

MYERS ST

WHITE ST

MCDOWELL AVE

PRESTON ST

MAIN ST

★ VISITORS CENTER

JORDAN

JACKSON ST

JEFFERSON ST

★ STONEWALL JACKSON BURIAL SITE

NELSON ST

HAMPTON INN LEXINGTON HISTORIC DISTRICT

MORNINGSIDE DR

BYP. 11

ROSS LN

HOUSTON ST

SPOTSWOOD ST

WHITMORE

A B&B AT LLEWELLYN LODGE

TAYLOR ST

WALLACE ST

0   200 yds

0   200 m

WASHINGTON ST

JEFFERSON ST

BISTRO ON MAIN ▼

HENRY ST

ARTISTS IN CAHOOTS

STONEWALL JACKSON HOUSE ★

SOUTHERN INN RESTAURANT ▼

MAIN ST

RED HEN ▼

RANDOLPH ST

To Applewood Inn and ★ NATURAL BRIDGE STATE PARK

© MOON.COM

but was again partly destroyed in 1864 by Union gunfire. Today it is a lovely Southern town, steeped in history, where cadets in uniform can be seen strolling down the streets, and tourists enjoy leisurely meals in local eateries.

SIGHTS
★ Virginia Military Institute

The **Virginia Military Institute** (319 Letcher Ave., 540/464-7230, www.vmi.edu) is the oldest state-supported military college in the country (founded in 1839). Many famous leaders have graced its doorstep, including General Stonewall Jackson, who was a professor there prior to the Civil War. Be sure to check the VMI website for the cadet parade schedule. This is a highlight of any trip to the institute. Cadet-led tours of campus are also available.

One of the most interesting sights on campus is the **George C. Marshall Museum** (340 VMI Parade, 540/463-2083, www.

marshallfoundation.org, Tues.-Sat. 11am-4pm, adults $5, students $2, seniors $3), an informative space dedicated to the life of a legendary five-star general who rose to fame during World War II. The museum follows Marshall's career beginning as a young lieutenant. Visitors can get a dose of military history and learn about the evolving role of the United States military during the 20th century. The museum also illustrates how Marshall learned to be such a strong leader. Items featured in the museum include Marshall's Nobel Peace Prize, a narrated World War II map, and a Jeep from 1943. A good place to begin is by watching the video presentation on Marshall's life. Allow 1-2 hours to visit. The museum is in the southwest corner of campus, and there is plenty of parking behind it.

Another VMI museum is **The Virginia Military Institute Museum** (Jackson Memorial Hall, 415 Letcher Ave., 540/464-7334, www.vmi.edu, daily 9am-5pm, $3 suggested donation) in Jackson Memorial Hall. Visitors can learn about the history of VMI and hear stories of its alumni. Special features include a statue of Stonewall Jackson's horse, his field desk, and his uniforms. There is also an antique firearms collection.

Stonewall Jackson House

The **Stonewall Jackson House** (8 E. Washington St., Lexington, 540/464-7704, www.vmi.edu, daily 9am-5pm, adults $8, youth 6-17 $6, 5 and under free) offers an interesting look at life in Lexington prior to the Civil War. Visitors can learn about many aspects of Stonewall Jackson's life including his time as a professor at the Virginia Military Institute (VMI), his role as a leader in his church, his time as a businessman, and his private affairs. The museum first opened in 1954 and was meticulously restored to its original appearance in 1979. Owned by VMI, the museum contains many of Jackson's personal belongings. Guided tours are available on the hour and half hour.

Stonewall Jackson Burial Site

General Stonewall Jackson was laid to rest in Lexington in May 1863 following his death from pneumonia. His remains were moved to their current resting place in 1890, now known as the **Stonewall Jackson Memorial Cemetery** (314 S. Main St., 540/463-2931) A statue marks his tomb on the south end of Main Street, which is surrounded by grave sites of other prominent Civil War soldiers

Virginia Military Institute

Stonewall Jackson

Thomas Jonathan Jackson was born in western Virginia (in Clarksburg, which is now part of West Virginia) in 1824 and was orphaned at the age of seven. Raised by extended family, Jackson was a constable and a teacher prior to his appointment to the U.S. Military Academy at West Point. After graduation, he served in the U.S. Army and fought in the Mexican-American War before being stationed in New York and Florida.

In 1851 Jackson was appointed as a professor at the Virginia Military Institute in Lexington, where he taught natural and experimental philosophy and was an artillery instructor. Some of his methods are still passed on there today. While in Lexington, he married Elinor Junkin in 1853 and joined the Lexington Presbyterian Church. After only one year of marriage, Elinor died in childbirth. The child was stillborn, and Jackson was suddenly alone.

In 1857, Jackson married Mary Anna Morrison, and the couple bought a home on Washington Street. They lived there quietly until 1861, when Jackson went off to fight in the Civil War just weeks after it began.

Stonewall Jackson's burial site in Lexington

Jackson entered the war as an infantry colonel but was soon promoted to brigadier general. During the First Battle of Bull Run on July 21, 1861, Jackson and his brigade provided reinforcements to Confederate lines that were under heavy Union fire. As other Confederate troops began to flee the battle, Jackson and his troops held their ground. Seeing this, General Barnard E. Bee Jr. yelled, "There is Jackson, standing like a stone wall," and thus, Jackson earned the nickname "Stonewall."

Jackson became known for his superb leadership skills and was promoted to major general. His most noted accomplishment was the Valley Campaign of 1862, during which Jackson's army of 17,000 marched 646 miles in 48 days and won five big victories against forces numbering around 60,000. It is thought of as one of the most brilliant campaigns in history.

In May 1863 at Chancellorsville, Virginia, Jackson's troops won a great victory. During the battle, Jackson was accidentally fired on by Confederate troops. The shots killed two of his aides and seriously wounded the general's left arm and right hand. Doctors in a field hospital decided to amputate his left arm. As Jackson lay in bed, Robert E. Lee looked at him and said, "He has lost his left arm, but I have lost my right."

Weakened by the amputation, Jackson contracted pneumonia and died on May 10.

and citizens. The grounds are open dawn to dusk.

Washington and Lee University

Washington and Lee University (204 W. Washington St., 540/458-8400, www.wlu.edu) is the ninth-oldest institution of higher learning in the United States. It was founded in 1749 as the Augusta Academy. The school has undergone four name changes in the past 250 years and is now named for George Washington (who gave the school its first endowment) and Robert E. Lee (who served as president of the school and is now buried there). It is a private liberal arts school that was originally all male. The first women were admitted to the university's top-ranked law school in 1972, but it wasn't until 1985 that they were allowed in undergraduate programs. The charming campus full of Georgian-style buildings with redbrick facades and multistory porticos is right in downtown Lexington.

LEE CHAPEL & MUSEUM

The **Lee Chapel & Museum** (100 N. Jefferson St., Washington and Lee University, 540/458-8768, www.wlu.edu, Apr.-Oct. Mon.-Sat. 9am-5pm, Sun. 1pm-5pm, Nov.-Mar. Mon.-Sat. 9am-4pm, Sun. 1pm-4pm, $5 suggested donation) was built in 1867 at the request of Robert E. Lee. At the time, Lee was the university president of what was then called Washington College. Lee was a regular at weekday services in the chapel and had his office in the lower level of the building. When he died in 1870, he was buried under the chapel, but his remains were moved in 1883 into a family crypt that was added to the lower level of an addition to the building. Other members of Lee's family are also buried in the crypt, and the remains of his horse Traveller were laid to rest just outside the entrance to the museum. Today the chapel hosts concerts, lectures, and other events in an auditorium on the main level. There is seating for 500 people. The lower level houses an informative museum that discusses the contributions both George Washington and Robert E. Lee made to education and features Lee's office. There is also a museum shop. The museum plays a part in many university events, so it is best to call ahead prior to visiting.

Virginia Horse Center

The enormous **Virginia Horse Center** (487 Maury River Rd., 540/464-2950, www.vahorsecenter.org) is a 600-acre equestrian compound three miles north of downtown Lexington. The beautiful grounds house a coliseum that holds 4,000 spectators, eight barns that hold 1,200 horses, 17 outdoor riding rings, two indoor arenas, a cross-country and combined-carriage-driving course, a campground, and food services. The center hosts many horse events throughout the year but also hosts non-horse-related events such as dog shows, agricultural programs, the Rockbridge Regional Fair and Farm Show, and BMX competitions.

RECREATION

Lexington is surrounded by the **George Washington** and **Jefferson National Forests,** which encompass land in the Appalachian Mountains of Virginia, West Virginia, and Kentucky. The two forests are managed jointly by the U.S. Forest Service. Together at 1.8 million acres they form one of the largest public land areas in the eastern part of the country. Easy access to this large wilderness area provides ample possibilities for outdoor recreation near Lexington.

The seven-mile **Chessie Nature Trail** (www.traillink.com) links Lexington with the neighboring town of Buena Vista. The trail begins at State Route 631 in Lexington and follows the north bank of the Maury River along mile markers on the former Chesapeake & Ohio Railroad route. Travelers can expect to see scenic Virginia countryside along the way and a variety of wildlife and farm animals. Be aware that cattle gates are sometimes closed along the trail.

Local streams are teeming with trout. Expert fly-fishing guides and instruction can be found at **Fly Fishing Adventures** (540/463 3235, www.vatrout.com). They offer fishing trips and instruction for beginners and experienced fly fishers.

Lexington is horse country. The pristine Virginia Horse Center is a prime example of this; however, there are also 65 miles of **horse trails** that wind through the George Washington and Jefferson National Forests near Lexington (https://www.fs.usda.gov). Multiple trailheads with room for trailer parking are located in the forest.

Canoeing, kayaking, and float trips on tubes on the James and Maury Rivers can be arranged April-October through **Twin Rivers Outfitters** (653 Lowe St., Buchanan, 540/254-8012, www.canoevirginia.net). They are a full-service livery in Buchanan (about 25 miles from Lexington) and have been in business since 1978.

Take a shot at some sporting clays at **Quail Ridge Sporting Clays** (336 Murat Rd., 540/463-1800, www.quailridgesportingclub.

com). They offer a challenging course with multiple types of targets at different speeds and distances.

ENTERTAINMENT AND EVENTS

Lexington is a charming city to explore. **Doc's Guide Service** (540/463-4501, $20/hour) specializes in personal historic, Civil War, architecture, and scenic tours. They will meet you anywhere in the area and they're available on short notice.

Starting each Memorial Day and running through Halloween, the **Visitor Center of Lexington** (106 E. Washington St., 540/463-3777, www.lexingtonvirginia.com) offers **Haunting Tales** (540/464-2250, ages 13 and up $15, ages 6-12 $7) tours of Historic Lexington. This 90-minute tour by candlelight follows in the footsteps of Generals Lee and Jackson. Costumed guides reveal ghost stories about the city that will likely raise the hair on your neck or at least make you shiver. Reservations are required, and tours begin at the visitors center.

For those who prefer to let a horse do the walking, the **Lexington Carriage Company** (540/463-5647, www.lexcarriage. com, daily 11am-4:30pm, adults $16, children 7-13 $7, children 4-6 $4, seniors 65 and over $14) offers horse-drawn-carriage tours April through October. Tours last 40-45 minutes and are narrated by a professional guide. Tours pass through historic residential streets and go by the Stonewall Jackson House, Lee Chapel, Washington and Lee University, and the Stonewall Jackson Cemetery. Tours meet across the street from the Visitor Center of Lexington (106 E. Washington St.).

Theatergoers will love the unique **Lime Kiln Theater** (607 Borden Rd., 540/463-7088, www.limekilntheater.org). This beautiful outdoor venue was erected out of the ruins of a 19th-century kiln. The theater is set among the vine-covered stones of the ruins and has two stages (one that is open to the stars). The theater hosts classic theater, concerts, and civic celebrations April to October.

Concerts and theater performances can also be found at the **Lenfest Center for the Performing Arts** (100 Glasgow St., 540/458-8000, www.wlu.edu) at Washington and Lee University. The center hosts more than 250 performances a year by both students and professionals.

Moviegoers can take in the action from the comfort of their cars at **Hull's Drive-in Theater** (2367 N. Lee Hwy., 540/463-2621, www.hullsdrivein.com, adults $7, children 5-11 $3, under 5 free), a seasonal drive-in theater that first opened in 1950. Its first showing was of John Wayne's *The Wake of the Red Witch*.

A yearly celebration is held to honor the birthdays of General Robert E. Lee and General Stonewall Jackson on **Lee-Jackson Day** (www.leejacksonday.webs.com) in mid-January. The celebration actually spans two days and features a variety of speakers, an annual memorial service, a parade, a luncheon, and a ball. Free tours of Jackson's home are also given during the celebration.

Another much-anticipated annual event is the **Balloons Over Rockbridge Festival** (www.lexingtonvirginia.com). This free event lasts for three days over the Fourth of July and is a spectacular gathering of brightly colored hot-air balloons. Visitors can purchase piloted balloon rides during the event.

SHOPPING

Lexington is an antiques collector's dream. There seems to be at least one antiques store on every block. The largest is **Duke's Lexington Antique Center** (1495 N. Lee Hwy., 540/463-9511, www.lexingtonvirginia. com). This impressive 20,000-square-foot space features more than 200 antiques dealers and consignments. It is open 365 days a year and has ample parking for cars and RVs.

A wonderful local gallery run by an artist cooperative is **Artists in Cahoots** (21 W. Washington St., 540/464-1147, www. artistsincahoots.com). The cooperative, which is closed January and February, was founded in 1983, and the gallery features paintings, jewelry, pottery, ironwork, woodwork, furniture, bird carvings, decoys, photography, sculpture, printmaking, fabric art, and more.

FOOD

For comfort food with a Southern touch, dine at the ★ **Southern Inn Restaurant** (37 S. Main St., 540/463-3612, www.southerninn.com, Mon.-Sat. 11:30am-10pm, Sun. 10am-9pm, $8-45). They serve contemporary American food (such as pan-seared sea scallops and roasted duck breast) along with classic American dishes such as meat loaf, rainbow trout, and fried chicken. There is also a good wine list and homemade desserts. The restaurant was established in 1932 but has been updated by the current owners cosmetically, functionally, and with a refreshed menu. A seat at the bar invites a casual evening with locals, as this is a popular place with visitors and residents alike.

Another contemporary American restaurant that is well worth a visit is the **Bistro on Main** (8 N. Main St., 540/464-4888, www.bistro-lexington.com, Tues.-Sat. 11:30am-2:30pm and 5pm-9pm, Sun. 11am-2pm, $8-32), which has a great little bar and serves creative dishes with a variety of influences. Try the shrimp and grits, duck breast with blackberry sauce, or jambalaya; each dish is different, yet delicious. Their brunch menu is also good (a personal favorite is the smoked salmon omelet paired with a Bloody Mary). The atmosphere is comfortable, intimate, and has an upscale feel to it, yet the food is reasonably priced. There is a plate charge for split dishes.

A favorite farm-to-table restaurant right in town is the **The Red Hen** (11 E. Washington St., 540/464-4401, www.redhenlex.com, Tues.-Sat. 5pm-9pm, $24-35). This cozy little restaurant in a little red house serves imaginative, well-planned entrées that have great flavor combinations. The menu changes daily depending on what produce and meat are fresh. Whether it is local steak or fresh beet risotto, there is always something new to try. The wine list is also carefully picked to pair well with the current menu, and they focus on serving natural wines that come from vineyards using organic growing methods. At the time of writing, they charged a $45 reservation fee per person. It's credited to your dining bill, but it's a bit odd.

ACCOMMODATIONS

Lexington is known for its lovely bed-and-breakfasts and inns. There are dozens of them in and around the town. Some offer visitors a piece of history, some offer stunning landscape views, and some offer both. Although there are more than 1,500 rooms to rent, these can fill up quickly when there's an event going on in town or at the area's universities. It is best to book a room as early as possible if you know you'll be competing with many other out-of-town guests.

$100-200

While you explore Lexington, **A Bed and Breakfast at Llewellyn Lodge** (603 S. Main St., 540/463-3235, www.llodge.com, $120-259) is a great place to get spoiled. They offer six guest rooms with private bathrooms, high-speed Internet, and air-conditioning in a charming gray-brick colonial home. The lodge is in a residential area of Lexington, just a short walk from shops, restaurants, and attractions. The innkeepers are experts in hospitality and serve a delicious full breakfast (from a menu). They are also experts on the Lexington area and eager to share their knowledge.

An ecofriendly bed-and-breakfast is the **Applewood Inn & Llama Trekking** (242 Tarn Beck Ln., 540/463-1962, www.applewoodbb.com, $169-255). They offer "green" lodging in a three-story passive-solar home built in 1979. The inn is south of town, at the end of a dirt road in a private setting on 37 acres. They have three lovely rooms with wood floors and private bathrooms, as well as a two-bedroom cottage. One room comes with a private hot tub. Guests can use the pool and kitchen. The inn also offers guided llama trekking, which can be arranged at the house. Treks last about two hours.

The **Comfort Inn Virginia Horse Center** (62 Comfort Way, 540/463-7311, www.choicehotels.com, $89-152) offers clean, comfortable rooms at a good value near the Virginia Horse Center. They have 80 guest rooms, a small heated indoor pool, a sundeck, and a picnic area for guest use.

$200-300

The ★ **Brierley Hill Bed and Breakfast** (985 Borden Rd., 540/464-8421, www.brierleyhill.com, $159-425) offers six guest rooms/suites and two cottages, all with private bathrooms. The inn was built in 1993 specifically as a bed-and-breakfast and was named after the antique clock that hangs in the foyer. Located just outside Lexington, the B&B has wonderful views of the Shenandoah Valley landscape, and the house is meticulously maintained. They serve wonderful gourmet breakfasts and afternoon cookies and lemonade, and the staff is very friendly.

The **Hampton Inn Lexington—Historic District** (401 E. Nelson St., 540/463-2223, www.hamptoninn3.hilton.com, $144-269) is an unusual chain hotel that is in part a historic manor house called the Col Alto Mansion. There are 10 rooms in the restored manor house and 76 hotel rooms. The hotel sits on seven acres and is within walking distance of many attractions in downtown Lexington. The grounds are nicely kept, and there are beautiful old trees on the property. There is a fitness center and outdoor pool for guest use, free high-speed Internet, and free breakfast.

CAMPING

Lake Robertson Park (106 Lake Robertson Dr., 540/463-4164, www.co.rockbridge.va.us, $30-35) offers 53 tent and full hookup camping sites. The 581-acre park has a lake, boat rentals, tennis courts, a swimming pool, a picnic pavilion, and hiking trails. Pets are welcome, and there is a laundry facility on-site.

Lee Hi Campground (2516 N. Lee Hwy., 540/463-3478, www.leehi.com, $15-35) has 15 tent sites and 50 full hookup sites, a bathhouse, restaurant, playground, laundry facility, and a dump station. Pets are welcome.

The **Virginia Horse Center** (487 Maury River Rd., 540/464-2950, $25-40) also offers camping. They have more than 90 campsites with hookups and four campgrounds.

INFORMATION AND SERVICES

Lexington has a great **Visitors Center** (106 E. Washington St., 540/463-3777, www.lexingtonvirginia.com, daily 9am-5pm). They provide an information video, a small museum, and very helpful employees.

GETTING THERE AND AROUND

Lexington is in central Virginia off I-81 and I-64, 185 miles southwest of Washington DC, approximately 55 miles east of the West Virginia border, and 50 miles north of Roanoke. There is no direct air or rail service to Lexington.

Lynchburg

Lynchburg is a city of 50 square miles in the foothills of the Blue Ridge Mountains and along the James River. It sits near the geographic center of Virginia.

Lynchburg was settled in 1757 when 17-year-old John Lynch began a ferry service across the James River to a 45-acre parcel of land he owned. In 1786, he was granted a charter for the town, and in 1805 Lynchburg was incorporated.

Early Lynchburg relied on tobacco and iron as its primary sources of revenue. Due in part to Lynch's ferry system, the town became one of the largest tobacco markets in the country. During the Civil War, Lynchburg was a major storage depot and burial spot for soldiers. Many Confederate generals were laid to rest here. Lynchburg was the sole major city in Virginia that was not overtaken by the Union during the Civil War.

Lynchburg is nicknamed the "City of Seven Hills," and each hill has a historical reference behind its name, including Franklin Hill, which was probably named after Ben Franklin, and College Hill, which was named after a military college that existed prior to the Civil War.

Lynchburg is also known as the core of Virginia's conservative religious community and is sometimes referred to as the "Buckle in the Bible Belt." Jerry Falwell's Liberty University is here, as are more than 130 places of worship. As such, many businesses (including restaurants) are closed on Sunday. The city is also considered to have a strong network of safe neighborhoods and good schools, and its residents enjoy a high quality of life.

SIGHTS
Historic Districts

Lynchburg has five historic districts. **Court House Hill** overlooks the James River and downtown Lynchburg. The main street, Court Street, is home to the historic **City Court House,** a Greek Revival building that is the main attraction in this small district. Many churches with distinctive steeples also line the street, which is otherwise a mix of government and private offices. **Daniel's Hill** is a linear district that contains high-traffic Cabell Street. The area was developed for residential use in the 1840s and overlooks the James River and Blackwater Creek.

The most diverse historical district is **Diamond Hill.** This 14-block area contains a large variety of architectural styles including Georgian revival and colonial revival homes. The district is bounded by steep hills and the Lynchburg Expressway. Major streets in the district include Washington Street, Church Street, Harrison Street, and Grace Street. Diamond Hill is the largest historic district and encompasses more than 100 historic structures. Most of the homes were built during the late 19th and early 20th century. The area is well maintained, and extensive renovations are apparent throughout its streets.

Federal Hill offers views toward downtown. The primary street is Federal Street. Many houses in the district were constructed in the 1820s, and the area is known for the fine craftsmanship of its buildings. Many of the homes in the district face maintenance issues but retain most of their original character.

One of the best-preserved neighborhoods in Lynchburg is the historic **Garland Hill** district. The district begins off 5th Street and runs along tree-lined Madison Street to its end overlooking Blackwater Creek and includes Harrison and Clay Streets. The neighborhood was built between the early 19th century and the early 20th century and includes architectural styles such as Gothic Revival, Victorian, and Queen Anne. The area was home to many distinguished residents who worked in the tobacco industry.

Lynchburg

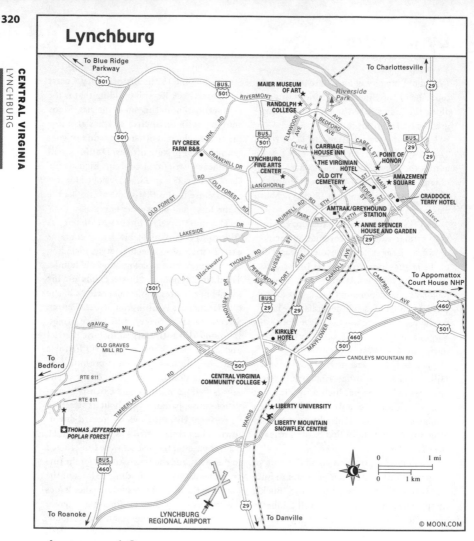

Amazement Square

Amazement Square (27 9th St., 434/845-1888, www.amazementsquare.org, Tues.-Sat. 10am-5pm, Sun. 1pm-5pm, $10.75, seniors 60 and over $7.75) is a hands-on museum for children with a happy atmosphere. It is the first multidisciplinary, interactive children's museum to be established in Central Virginia, and it has set a high standard. Kids make their way through four floors of exciting exhibits where they can climb, slide, and participate in a variety of programs and activities on the topics of art, the humanities, science, and health. Allow at least two hours to explore the museum. The staff is excellent.

Old City Cemetery

A fascinating historical spot in Lynchburg is the **Old City Cemetery** (401 Taylor St., 434/847-1465, www.gravegarden.org, daily dawn to dusk, free). It is the oldest public cemetery in Virginia that is still in use, and it has an estimated 20,000 "residents." Civil War notables, artists, inventors, civil servants—all are buried here, including 2,200 Confederate graves. A stroll through the grounds is a history lesson and a look at a who's who of Lynchburg. There are five small free museums on-site that interpret the history of the area, the city, and the cemetery itself. Four are designed for self-guided tours and can be viewed whenever the cemetery gates are open. The fifth, the **Mourning Museum,** is inside the Cemetery Center, a visitors center for the cemetery (Mon.-Sat. 10am-3pm). A scatter garden for human and pet ashes and a rose garden are also in the cemetery. A looped trail beginning at Taylor and 4th Streets takes visitors around the plots. Guided tours are available for a small fee and are by appointment only.

Point of Honor

Perched on a hill overlooking the James River is **Point of Honor** (112 Cabell St., 434/455-6226, www.pointofhonor.org, Mon.-Sat. 10am-4pm, Sun. noon-4pm, adults $6, children 6-17 $3, college students $4, seniors over 60 $5, under 6 free), a gorgeous Federal-style mansion. The home was built in 1815 and has been meticulously restored. It is not certain how it got its name, but there are two theories.

The first is that duels were fought here for honor, as was the custom in centuries past; the second theorizes that the name refers to the prominent point of land the home sits on looking out on the James River. The **Diggs Gallery** inside the home provides an orientation video and rotating exhibits. House tours are given daily and last 45 minutes.

Maier Museum of Art

A few blocks away from Point of Honor is the **Maier Museum of Art** (1 Quinlan St., 434/947-8136, www.maiermuseum.org, academic year schedule Tues.-Sun. 1pm-5pm, May-Aug. Wed.-Sun. 1pm-5pm, free, donations appreciated). This nationally recognized art museum at Randolph College features works by 19th to 21st-century American artists. The museum's permanent collection includes thousands of paintings, photographs, and drawings, with a focus on American impressionism and early 20th-century realism. They have a large collection of works by visionary modernist Arthur B. Davies and painter, printmaker, and photographer Ben Shahn. Special exhibits and programs are offered year-round as well as internships and class visits. The museum is located on campus, behind the athletic fields, and offers a

Point of Honor

great opportunity to see an amazing collection of artwork without the crowds.

Anne Spencer House and Garden

The **Anne Spencer House and Garden** (1313 Pierce St., 434/845-1313, www.annespencermuseum.com, adult tours $15, college students $5, children under 12 $3, seniors $10) is a two-story Queen Anne-style home that once belonged to poet Anne Spencer (1882-1975). Spencer's work is considered to be part of the Harlem Renaissance, and she wrote of love and beauty. While living in the home, the author entertained many famous guests, such as Martin Luther King Jr., Thurgood Marshall, and George Washington Carver. The gardens are open daily from dawn to dusk, and visitors can pick up a brochure at the garden cottage. There is no fee to visit the garden. Tours of the house are by appointment only and must be scheduled at least two weeks in advance. The house is closed November-March.

Lynchburg Museum

The **Lynchburg Museum** (901 Court St., 434/455-6226, www.lynchburgmuseum.org, Mon.-Sat. 10am-4pm, Sun. noon-4pm, free) is located in the old courthouse downtown. It relays a historical timeline of the people of Lynchburg in the main Court Room Gallery, more than 10,000 photos, an exhibit on African American education in Lynchburg, an exhibit on the courthouse itself, and two rotating exhibits.

Appomattox Court House National Historical Park

Twenty-two miles east of Lynchburg is **Appomattox Court House National Historical Park** (113 National Park Dr., 434/352-8987, ext. 226, www.nps.gov/apco, daily 9am-5pm, free). The park is the site of General Lee's surrender at the close of the Civil War on April 9, 1865. The park consists of numerous historic structures in the village of Appomattox and sits on 1,700 acres.

Begin your exploration at the visitors center, a reconstructed courthouse building that also serves as a museum offering exhibits that include artifacts from the surrender (including surrender documents and a pencil used by General Lee). The three-story **McLean House-Surrender Site** is the reconstructed house where the actual surrender took place approximately 150 yards west of the visitors center. The parlor inside the house, where the surrender meeting occurred, is furnished with both original and reproduced items. Park ranger interpretation is offered daily at the house, and tours are offered seasonally on the hour. Several outbuildings are also open to visitors, including the kitchen, outhouse, and slave quarters. Living-history programs are offered daily during the summer and feature historical interpretations from the 1860s.

Walton's Mountain Museum

Die-hard fans of *The Waltons* television series will enjoy the **Walton's Mountain Museum** (6484 Rockfish River Rd., Schuyler, 434/831-2000, www.walton-mountain.org, daily 10am-3:30pm, $10, under 5 free), 50 miles northeast of Lynchburg in Schuyler. See the childhood home of Earl Hamner (creator of *The Waltons*) and replicas of John Boy's bedroom, Ike Godsey's Store, the Waltons' kitchen, and the Waltons' living room. There's a good 30-minute video featuring Earl Hamner and stars of the television show.

RECREATION

Ski enthusiasts can indulge year-round at the **Liberty Mountain Snowflex Center** (4000 Candlers Mountain Rd., 434/582-3539, www.liberty.edu, skiing and snowboarding $8 per hour, tubing $13 per hour). This unusual ski complex opened on the campus of Liberty University six miles south of Lynchburg in 2009 as the first facility in the United States to offer skiing and snowboarding on simulated snow. The 5,000-acre mountain has a bunny slope, intermediate and advanced slopes, and even a freestyle park. A tubing chute and ski lodge complete the simulated ski experience.

Rental equipment is available ($14). They also offer an Olympic trampoline ($5).

Liberty Mountain also offers 50 miles of trails for mountain biking, hiking, and running. Trails are open to the public daily dawn to dusk. Visit www.liberty.edu for trail maps.

Another popular, well-marked trail is the **James River Heritage Trail,** a 9.5-mile trail combining two smaller trails, the **Blackwater Creek Trail & Bikeway** and the **RiverWalk Trail** (www.lynchburgparksandrec.com). The trail passes through downtown Lynchburg and also lush forest areas. The RiverWalk section is one of the most popular. Its 3.5 miles of paved trail begin on Jefferson Street and run east along the waterfront. To reach the Blackwater Creek Bikeway trailhead, take US 501 north from the Lynchburg Expressway. Turn right onto Old Langthore Road. The trailhead is on the right.

A favorite park in Lynchburg, **Riverside Park** (2238 Rivermont Ave., 434/455-5858, www.lynchburgparksandrec.com) offers more than 49 acres of recreation area with views of the James River. Walking trails, tennis, basketball, a large playground, and a seasonal "sprayground" are some of the main attractions. There is also a transportation exhibit that features a train locomotive, tender, and caboose.

The **James River Canoe Ramp** (7th St.) is a good place to launch hand-carried watercraft on the James River. It is located at the end of the 7th Street.

Running and cycling are popular in Lynchburg, and there are many local races and events throughout the year. For a rundown, visit www.localraces.com.

ENTERTAINMENT AND EVENTS

Options for live entertainment are less than abundant in Lynchburg. The **Academy of Fine Arts** (600 Main St., 434/846-8499, www. academycenter.org) offers live music, classes, and theatrical events. They have a list of their venues and upcoming events on their website. Live music can be found on most weekends

at **Phase 2 Dining & Entertainment** (4009 Murray Pl., 434/846-3206, www.phase2club. com). They offer a restaurant, concert hall, and banquet facilities. Concerts feature mostly country and rock. At the time of writing, the venue was for sale. The **Lynchburg Symphony Orchestra** (621 Court St., 434/845-6604, www.lynchburgsymphony. org) offers performances in a variety of locations in Lynchburg.

FOOD
American

You may not associate shoes with food, but at ★ **Shoemakers American Grille** (1312 Commerce St., 434/455-1510, www. shoemakersdining.com, Mon.-Sat. 5pm-9:30pm, $9-37) shoes are part of the history. The restaurant is housed in a building that used to be home to the largest shoe manufacturer in the country. The exposed brick is a nod to the building's factory roots, while the interior decor is modern and welcoming. The taste-bud-pleasing menu includes a wide variety of salads, steak, seafood, yummy sides (such as smoked gouda mac & cheese) and scrumptious desserts (try the Shoemaker's Candy Bar). They also have an extensive wine list. The restaurant is the perfect place for a date or to relax with friends. The atmosphere is lively and comfortable, and the service is some of the best in town. There's an outdoor patio that is perfect when the weather is nice.

The **Main Street Eatery & Catering Co.** (907 Main St., 434/847-2526, www. mainsteatery.com, Mon.-Sat. 4:30pm-9:30pm, $9-28) serves a delicious menu of seafood, pasta, beef, veal, and poultry. The menu isn't large, but they rotate offerings seasonally so there's always something new. In addition, each item is uniquely prepared with flavorful touches, and the wine and drink menus are extensive. Don't skip the dessert tray; it will tempt you even if you think you're full. Exposed brick and hardwood floors make a cozy atmosphere, and the owner frequently visits tables to check on his customers.

The sister eatery to the Texas Tavern

in Roanoke, the **Texas Inn** (422 Main St., 434/846-3823, www.texasinn.com, Mon.-Wed. 5am-midnight, Thurs.-Sat. 24 hours, Sun. closed, $1-8), also called "The T Room," is the oldest dining establishment in Virginia. It opened in 1935 and is a local icon that stays open late, is cheap, and serves greasy food. Grab a spot at the counter (it's your only choice for seating) and order the Cheesy Western. This signature dish is a hamburger with cheese and a fried egg topped with a delicious secret mustard relish. The chili is also legendary. Not a date place, not a business place, but a sacred institution nonetheless. There's a second location in Lynchburg at 110 Cornerstone Street.

Asian

Kings Island Restaurant (2804 Old Forest Rd., 434/384-0066, www.kingsislandrestaurant.com, Mon.-Thurs. 11:15am-10pm, Fri. 11:15am-10:45pm, Sat. 4:15pm-10:45pm, Sun. 11:15am-10pm, $8-28) is your best bet for Chinese and Japanese food in Lynchburg. It is also the oldest Chinese restaurant in town, first serving customers in 1977. The food is good, with the typical menu items for American Chinese restaurants, and the sushi is a step above. They earn extra points for the atmosphere, which is quiet and cozy without being dark and drab. The food is reasonably priced, and the service is excellent.

Italian

A great choice for pizza is **Waterstone Fire Roasted Pizza** (1309 Jefferson St., 434/455-1515, www.waterstonepizza.com, Mon.-Thurs. 11am-10pm, Fri.-Sat. 11am-11pm, Sun. 11am-9pm, $8-17). This popular pizza joint opened in 2010 and has a loyal following. Natural ingredients and wonderful flavor are the keys to their mouthwatering pizzas. They also have a brewery on-site. If you're lucky to go on a nice day or evening, grab a seat on the patio. The neighboring historic buildings offer a pleasant backdrop and make for an inviting atmosphere.

Mexican

Good Mexican food can be found at **La Carreta** (www.lacarretaonline.com, $7-14), a local chain that has seven locations within a 10-mile radius of Lynchburg. They serve flavorful, authentic fare at a very reasonable price. The salsa is fresh and delicious, and the beer is served in frosted mugs. This is a great place to bring a group, and it has a loyal local following. Consult their website for the most convenient location and hours.

ACCOMMODATIONS

$100-200

The ★ **Craddock Terry Hotel** (1312 Commerce St., 434/455-1500, www.craddockterryhotel.com, $138-197) may well be a first: This trendy boutique hotel is a converted turn-of-the-20th-century shoe factory. The large red lady's shoe out in front of the brick building might give that away, but the interior is far from its factory roots. The renovated space now offers 44 large modern rooms and suites with high ceilings, large windows, comfortable beds, luxurious bathrooms, and ecofriendly bath products. Views from the rooms include downtown, the James River, and the Blue Ridge Mountains. The decor is contemporary, with many historical artifacts from the Craddock-Terry Shoe Corporation and modern shoe-themed accents. They offer complimentary amenities such as parking, overnight shoeshine service, sedan service to the airport and Amtrak station, and high-speed Internet. Complimentary continental breakfast also arrives at your room each morning in a wooden shoeshine box. There are two restaurants, a fitness room, Tesla charging station, and business center on-site. The resident hotel dog, a wirehaired fox terrier, is named Penny Loafer, and guest pets are also welcome ($50).

The **Kirkley Hotel** (2900 Candlers Mountain Rd., 434/237-6333, www.kirkleyhotel.com, $102-149) is a reasonably priced hotel with many recent renovations. They have 168 rooms and suites with free wireless Internet, free parking and airport shuttle, comfortable beds, complimentary hot breakfast, indoor pool, fitness center, and business center. Suites have dining rooms, wet bars, and living rooms. This is a Wyndham hotel.

$200-300

A lovely bed-and-breakfast is the **Carriage House Inn** (404 Cabell St., 434/846-1388, www.thecarriagehouseinnbandb.com, $189-209) in the Daniel's Hill Historic District. This six-guest-room bed-and-breakfast offers comfortable accommodations in a beautifully renovated 1878 Italianate mansion featuring a grand spiral staircase and many original details such as molding, woodwork, and fixtures. The Carriage House Inn was the first lodging facility in Lynchburg to earn a "green" certification. Rooms are spacious with high ceilings, and the house has a nice porch with rocking chairs. Hiking and biking trails are just six blocks away. The entrance to the bed-and-breakfast is easy to miss from the road, so look carefully for the sign.

★ **The Virginian Lynchburg** (712 Church St., 434/329-3200, www. curiocollection3.hilton.com, $184-675) is an upscale and stately downtown hotel that is part of Hilton's Curio Collection. The building was erected in 1913 and has been beautifully restored. The hotel offers 115 large, modern, comfortable rooms/suites with free wireless Internet and a fitness center. The staff is friendly and helpful throughout. The hotel features a coffee shop and a rooftop restaurant and bar with great views. Self-parking and valet parking are available for $10. This is an excellent choice with a great location downtown.

INFORMATION AND SERVICES

The **Lynchburg Visitors Information Center** (216 12th St., 434/485-7290, www. discoverlynchburg.org, Mon.-Sat. 10am-4pm, Sun. noon-4pm) is a great additional resource for information and services in the city.

GETTING THERE

Lynchburg is 180 miles from Washington DC. **Lynchburg Regional Airport** (LYH) (350 Terminal Dr., no. 100, 434/455-6090, www. lynchburgva.gov) is a small, city-owned airport located about five miles southwest of downtown Lynchburg. The airport has a dozen arriving and departing flights a day through the regional carrier American Eagle.

Carriage House Inn

Rental cars are available on-site, and there is free wireless Internet.

Train service runs to the **Amtrak** station (825 Kemper St., 800/872-7245, www.amtrak. com). **Greyhound** (800/231-2222, www.

greyhound.com) bus service is also available in the same location.

Local bus service is provided by the **Greater Lynchburg Transit Company** (434/455-5080, www.gltconline.com, $2), with 37 buses traveling 14 routes Monday-Saturday.

Roanoke

Roanoke is the largest city in southwest Virginia. It sits in the picturesque Roanoke Valley and is bisected by the Roanoke River. The history of Roanoke dates back to the 1740s, when the area near natural salt marshes in the center of the valley was first settled. The marshes were called "licks" and served as gathering places for deer, elk, and buffalo. The first village was known as Big Lick.

When the Shenandoah Valley Railroad came to the area, Big Lick was renamed Roanoke, and in the late 1800s Roanoke became a crossroads for the railroad. This spurred the city's growth. A market opened not long after and remains the cornerstone of downtown commerce. Roanoke is now southwest Virginia's thriving center for transportation, manufacturing, trade, and entertainment.

Roanoke is known to offer residents a good quality of life. It is metropolitan, yet has a less stressful pace than many other cities. There is a vibrant downtown area with culture and business, and Roanoke has the largest airport in southwestern Virginia. Roanoke is also easily accessible via I-81.

SIGHTS
★ Taubman Museum of Art
The **Taubman Museum of Art** (110 Salem Ave. SE, 540/342-5760, www. taubmanmuseum.org, Wed.-Sat. 10am-5pm, Sun. noon-5pm, first Fri. of each month 10am-9pm, free) attracts visitors with its shiny, modern building that opened in 2008 on Salem Avenue. Between 100,000 and 130,000 people visit the museum each

year to take in exhibits on subjects such as art, crafts, dance, sculpture, graphic arts, photography, poetry, and film. The museum has 2,400 items in its permanent collection. Exhibits reflect cultural traditions throughout America as well as of a global nature, but also feature local culture from the Roanoke Valley and southern Virginia. There is an arts center at the museum called **Art Venture** ($5), where children and their families can create their own art and learn different artistic techniques. This hands-on gallery offers painting, drawing, theater, sculpture, music, and more. Exhibits change at the museum every six to eight weeks, so there is always something new to experience. The museum houses a store that showcases merchandise related to current exhibits and regional crafts and gifts from around the globe.

Virginia Museum of Transportation
The **Virginia Museum of Transportation** (303 Norfolk Ave. SW, Roanoke, 540/342-5670, www.vmt.org, Mon.-Sat. 10am-5pm, Sun. 1pm-5pm, adults $10, youth 13-18, students with ID, and seniors 60 and over $8, children 3-12 $6, under 3 free) is a unique, mostly outdoor museum featuring more than 50 exhibits. It provides a wonderful overview of the extensive railway heritage in Virginia and is best known for its exhibits on the Norfolk & Western Class J-611 and Class A-1218 modern steam locomotives. The museum's road exhibits take visitors through the history of road transportation starting

Downtown Roanoke

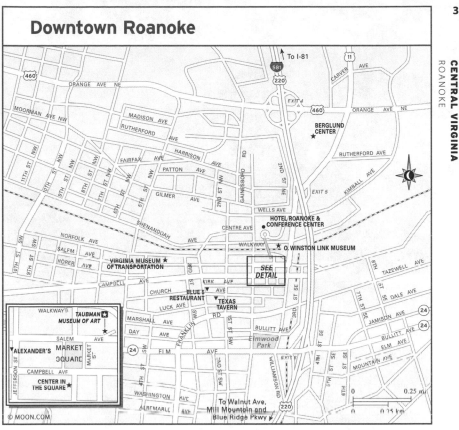

© MOON.COM

with the horse and buggy and ending with modern-day cars and trucks. Air exhibits discuss early aviation, commercial aviation, military aviation, and airports. The museum also features model trains and a gift shop.

Mill Mountain Star and Park

The **Mill Mountain Star and Park** (210 Reserve Ave., 540/853-2236) is famous for its huge illuminated star that sits on top of Mill Mountain. Roanoke is nicknamed "the Star City of the South," which was the inspiration for the construction of the massive star erected in 1949. It is the largest man-made illuminated star in the world. It is 88.5 feet tall and lit by 2,000 feet of neon tubes channeling 17,500 watts of power. The star is lit each evening, but is turned off at midnight.

O. Winston Link Museum

The **O. Winston Link Museum** (101 Shenandoah Ave., 540/982-5465, www.roanokehistory.org, Tues.-Sat. 10am-5pm, adults $6, children $5, seniors, students, and military $5.50) houses the largest exhibit of O. Winston Link's famous photographs depicting life in the 1950s along the railroad in Virginia. Even people who don't know anything about railroads can appreciate the talent of this photographer and the era that is represented in the museum. Each photograph captures a story, and many are accompanied by articles that appeared in a large variety of magazines and textbooks. The museum is housed in a restored historic passenger train station and shares space with the **Museum**

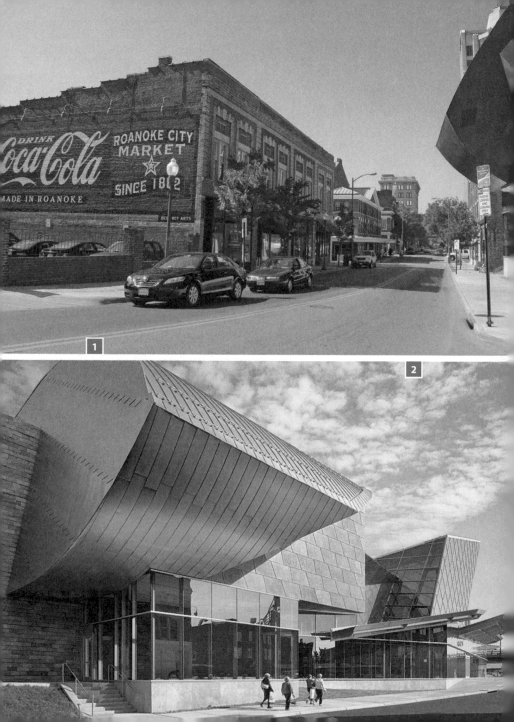

1

2

of Western Virginia, which features exhibits that share the history of western Virginia.

Center in the Square

In the southwest corner of Market Square (a historic market at the intersection of Campbell Avenue and Market Street) is a five-story cultural center called Center in the Square (1 Market Sq., 540/342-5700, www.centerinthesquare.org). The center opened in 1983 as the cornerstone of a redevelopment program in an urban area that was once facing economic decline. Several organizations focused on arts and science now call the center home: the Science Museum of Western Virginia (540/342-5710, www.smwv.org), Harrison Museum of African American Culture (540/857-4395, www.harrisonmuseum.com), Mill Mountain Theatre (540/342-5740, www.millmountain.org), and the Roanoke Pinball Museum (540/342-5746, www.roanokepinball.org). Visitors can now enjoy a thriving cultural community in the square and also visit private stores and restaurants. The most famous, perhaps, is the Roanoke Weiner Stand, which opened just after the original Center in the Square building (first called the McGuire Building) opened in 1915 and is a city landmark. As the name suggests, they serve outrageously good hot dogs and have a huge local following.

RECREATION

Outdoor recreation is a favorite pastime in Roanoke. Whether your preferred mode of transport is by mountain bike or foot, the Roanoke area has more than 600 miles of trails to explore. Virginia's Explore Park (mp 115, Blue Ridge Pkwy., 540/427-1800, www.explorepark.org) is about a 10-minute drive from downtown Roanoke on the Blue Ridge Parkway. This 1,200-acre park has nine miles of mountain bike trails, a one-mile interpretive trail, fishing, canoeing, and kayaking.

1: Roanoke 2: Taubman Museum of Art

Hikers can enjoy numerous trails near Roanoke and even explore parts of the Appalachian Trail. One of the most famous trails, the McAfee Knob Hike (www.visitroanokeva.com), is a challenging 8.8-mile round-trip hike that offers stunning views of the Catawba Valley and more than 1,700 feet of climbing (allow four hours). McAfee Knob itself, a large rocky outcrop, is one of the most photographed areas on the Appalachian Trail. To access the trail, take I-81 south from Roanoke to exit 141. Turn left at the light onto State Route 419 (Electric Rd.) and continue for less than a mile. Take State Route 311 north for 5.6 miles up the mountain. The trailhead parking lot is at the top of the mountain on the left. A great ending to this hike includes a stop at The Homeplace Restaurant (4968 Catawba Valley Dr., 540/384-7252) for dinner. To get there, continue north on State Route 311 for one mile to a large white farmhouse.

Another well-known local trail is Dragon's Tooth (www.roanokeoutside.com). This difficult, 4.5-mile out-and-back hike travels to its namesake geological feature, a collection of large Tuscarora quartzite spires that jut out of the top of Cove Mountain, the tallest being 35 feet. The Dragon's Tooth summit rewards hikers with great views year-round. The parking lot is about 20 minutes south of downtown Roanoke. Take I-81 south to exit 141. Turn left on State Route 419 (Electric Rd.) and then turn right on State Route 311. Continue for 10 miles to the Dragon's Tooth parking lot on the left.

Baseball fans will want to take in a Salem Red Sox (1004 Texas St., Salem, 540/389-3333, www.milb.com) home game in nearby Salem. This minor league baseball team is a Class A farm team for the Boston Red Sox. Virginia Tech fans can cheer on the Hokies just 45 minutes south of Roanoke in Blacksburg.

ENTERTAINMENT AND EVENTS

There's always something going on at the Berglund Center (710 Williamson Rd., 540/853-2241, www.theberglundcenter.com),

Getaway to Smith Mountain Lake

Smith Mountain Lake is the perfect mountain lake retreat and a favorite among Virginians. This is where the movie *What About Bob?* starring Richard Dreyfuss and Bill Murray was filmed, and it was also featured in the independent film *Lake Effects* in 2012.

Smith Mountain Lake is the largest artificial lake in Virginia; it covers 32 square miles and has 500 miles of shoreline. The average depth of the lake is 55 feet. The lake itself was created in the early 1960s when the Roanoke River was dammed at Smith Mountain Gap. It is equidistant from Lynchburg and Roanoke (about an hour's drive) and is a four-hour drive from Washington DC.

The community of Smith Mountain Lake has approximately 22,000 residents, but the area is a popular destination for vacationers. Residential growth was slow during the initial decades after the lake was created but has been increasing steadily since the mid-1980s. Upscale residences, condominiums, and golf course communities are the norm now, and commuters from Roanoke and Lynchburg also make their homes in the community. Retirees from Northern Virginia are part of the latest growth trend at Smith Mountain Lake, and the influx of new residents has contributed to recent retail and commercial development in the community.

State Route 122 is the only highway that crosses the lake. The area is accessed by State Routes 24, 116, and 40.

Smith Mountain Lake State Park (1235 State Park Rd., Huddleston, 540/297-6066, www. dcr.virginia.gov, daily 8:15am-dusk, $7/vehicle) provides a beach and public swimming on the lake, and there are a handful of public golf courses.

In addition to beautiful scenery and endless opportunities for outdoor recreation in the form of boating, biking, hiking, swimming, and fishing, Smith Mountain Lake offers shopping, antiquing, art, entertainment, and wonderful dining.

There are several marinas on Smith Mountain Lake, including **Parkway Marina** (16918 Smith Mountain Lake Pkwy., 540/297-4412, www.parkwaymarina.com), **Bridgewater Marina** (16410 BT Washington Hwy., 540/721-1639, www.bwmarina.com), and **Mitchells Point Marina** (3553 Trading Post Rd., 540/484-3980, www.mitchellspoint.com).

Vacation rentals can be booked through **Smith Mountain Lake Vacation Rentals** (877/773-2452, www.smithmountainlakerentals.com) and **Smith Mountain Lake Properties** (540/797-0477, www.smithmountainlakeproperties.org). For additional information on Smith Mountain Lake, visit www.smithmountainlake.com.

---

formerly known as the Roanoke Civic Center. This is the premier venue for concerts, ice hockey, expos, and even public ice-skating. For a more intimate setting, take in a performance at the **Jefferson Center** (541 Luck Ave., 540/345-2550, www.jeffcenter.org), a historic venue that hosts classical and contemporary performances.

The **Roanoke Festival in the Park** (www.roanokefestival.com) is the premier festival in Roanoke. It takes place annually over Memorial Day weekend and spans four days of art, music, and nightly concerts. Daytime events are free, but tickets are required for nighttime concerts ($15).

The **Salem Fair** (www.salemfair.com), in nearby Salem, is the largest fair in Virginia and features 10 days of rides, demos, and events that draw around 350,000 people. It takes place in early July. There is no admission fee.

The **Anthem GO Outside Festival** (www.roanokegofest.com) is a free festival that takes place over three days in October at the **Rivers Edge Sports Complex** (210 Reserve Ave.) and features approximately 125 outdoor events and activities with camping, music, competitions, and demos.

SHOPPING

The heart of downtown Roanoke is **Market Square** (213 Market St., 540/342-2028), where the **Historic Roanoke Street Market** first opened in 1882. It is the oldest continuously running open-air market in Virginia. It now has 40 permanent tables displaying an incredible selection of local fruits, vegetables, plants, meat, and handcrafted merchandise. The market is open year-round, its tables covered in festive white and yellow awnings. One vendor, Martin's Farm, has been a part of the market since 1905.

FOOD
American

For a special occasion, a celebration at ★ The Regency Room in the Hotel Roanoke & Conference Center (110 Shenandoah Ave., 540/985-5900, www.hotelroanoke.com, Mon.-Fri. 6:30am 10:30am, 11:30am-2pm, and 6pm-9pm, Sat.-Sun. 7am-10:30am, 11:30am-2pm, and 6pm-9pm, $22-45) can help make the evening memorable. This first-class restaurant first opened in 1938 and offers the same candlelit ambience as it did so many decades ago. White tablecloths, heavy drapery, and a baby grand piano give the dining room a cozy, upscale feel. The menu is simple and elegant, offering classics such as steak and lobster for entrées, but traditional Virginia menu items such as peanut soup, spoon bread, and bread pudding are also featured. They also offer a sensational crab cake with a Virginia twist. It is served with a corn-and-leek puree. The restaurant holds 150 people comfortably, and the tables are nicely spaced so you don't hear the conversation next door. Reservations are recommended.

The cosmopolitan atmosphere at Alexander's (105 S. Jefferson St., 540/982-6983, www.alexandersva.com, Wed. 11am-2pm, Tues.-Thurs. 5pm-9pm, Fri.-Sat. 5pm-10pm, $31-50) is unique in Roanoke, and the contemporary menu will impress most die-hard foodies. This intimate restaurant uses many ingredients from its own farm and gradually changes the menu with the growing season. Their seafood, steak, lamb, duck, and other entrées are masterfully prepared, and the staff is polite and knowledgeable. The wine list is impressive. Even the vases on their tables are filled with flowers and herbs from

their own garden. Small plates, wine, and cocktails are served Tuesday-Saturday at 4pm.

This author first discovered ★ The Homeplace Restaurant (4968 Catawba Valley Dr., Catawba, 540/384-7252, Thurs.-Fri. 4pm-8pm, Sat. 3pm-8pm, Sun. 11am-6pm, $15 for two meats, $16 for three, $3 extra for dessert) as a poor student at Virginia Tech. Groups of students would make a pilgrimage of sorts to seek out home-cooked meals sorely missed while living in student housing. The Homeplace is just as it sounds: a great place to dine on wonderful food like you would expect to be served at grandma's house and for a very reasonable price. The restaurant is even inside a beautiful old house on a large property. A set menu of classic Virginia fare is brought out to the entire table, family-style. There is roast beef or country ham, fried chicken, mashed potatoes, gravy, green beans, fresh biscuits, coleslaw, and cobbler for dessert. The best part is, the food keeps coming until you swear your pants will split. This place is an institution in the Roanoke area, but not just for students; friends, family, and even hikers detouring from the Appalachian Trail come together at this comfortable restaurant to share an old-fashioned home-cooked meal. The Homeplace is 16 miles northwest of Roanoke.

The Blue 5 Restaurant (312 2nd St., 540/904-5338, www.blue5restaurant.com, Tues.-Thurs. 11:30am-midnight, Fri. 11:30am-1am, Sat. 4pm-1am, $17-29) offers good food, craft beer, and live music. It's hard to argue with those offerings, and they do all three well. They serve Southern cuisine (the shrimp creole and grits is over-the-top delicious) and have 46 beers on tap. They offer live music four nights a week.

Pubs and Diners

The Texas Tavern (114 W. Church Ave., 540/342-4825, www.texastavern-inc.com, open 24/7, under $5) is the definition of a dive. This tiny tavern opened on Friday, February 13, 1930, and stays that way 24 hours a day every day of the year except for Christmas. This family business serves breakfast, lunch, and dinner and can seat a handful of people at the bar (there are also shelves by the window if you want to stand). If everyone is very familiar with each other, it might hold 15 people, but more than that would be pretty cozy. One of their slogans is "We seat 1,000 people, 10 at a time."

For a casual sandwich, salad, or burger, visit **Hollywood's Restaurant and Bakery** (7770 Williamson Rd., 540/362-1812, www.hollywoodsrestaurant.com, Mon.-Sat. 11am-10pm, $5-13). They offer a dine-in menu with a large variety of delicious salads and sandwiches served on freshly made bread. They have many vegetarian options and will also prepare tailgate packages when reserved the day before.

ACCOMMODATIONS
$100-200
The **SpringHill Suites Roanoke** (301 Reserve Ave., 540/400-6226, www.marriott.com, $179-239) is less than a mile from downtown Roanoke and has 127 nonsmoking suites. The rooms are large and have flat-screen LCD televisions, refrigerators, microwaves, and wireless Internet. There is a lovely indoor pool and fitness center at the hotel, and they offer complimentary shuttle service to the airport and to attractions within a 10-mile radius. There is an on-site bar. Breakfast is included.

For a good night's sleep in a historic bed-and-breakfast, book a room at the **King George Inn** (315 King George Ave. SW, 757/657-4034, www.kinggeorgeinnbandb.com, $145-160), a 1900s colonial revival home fully restored and within walking distance of downtown Roanoke. There are four spacious guest suites with private bathrooms, relaxing common areas, and a library. There are no televisions in the rooms. A gourmet breakfast as well as afternoon refreshments are included with all stays. The innkeepers are warm, helpful, and eager to make recommendations for things to do in the area. This establishment does not allow children.

$200-300
The ★ **Hotel Roanoke & Conference Center** (110 Shenandoah Ave., 540/985-5900, www.hotelroanoke.com, $175-408) is the most famous hotel in Roanoke and has been a prime destination since it was built in 1882. The restored historic Tudor hotel was originally supported by the railroad industry as a stop for rail travelers (it was owned by Norfolk and Western), but its popularity as a vacation

Hotel Roanoke & Conference Center

destination has kept it going long after the railroad heyday. As you stroll past the stunning facade, you will walk where numerous celebrities and presidents have trod, including Amelia Earhart and the King himself, Elvis Presley. The hotel is decorated with artifacts that showcase its long history and also American history. Portraits of two famous Virginians, George Washington and Robert E. Lee, adorn the lobby walls. Rooms are traditionally decorated but have modern amenities, and a business center is available to guests. The hotel is listed in the National Register of Historic Places and is part of the International Association of Conference Centers with its 34 meeting rooms and two ballrooms. There are 330 guest rooms and suites, which include many types of accommodations to choose from in a variety of price ranges. They also offer allergy-friendly guest rooms. Self-parking ($10) and valet parking ($16) are available.

The Hotel Roanoke is part of Hilton's Curio Collection. It's convenient to the Roanoke Regional Airport (with a free shuttle) and many local attractions. A walkway connects the hotel to Market Square. There are two restaurants on-site. **The Regency Room** and **The Pine Room**. There's a seasonal outdoor pool on the property and a fitness center. Spa services are also available in your room. The staff is exceptional at this hotel, and there are many fun little touches, such as the weekday-specific carpets in the elevators that say things like "Have a pleasant Friday!"

CAMPING

Visitors can pitch a tent at one of 74 tent sites in the **Roanoke Mountain Campground** (mp 120.4, Blue Ridge Dr., Roanoke, 540/342-3051, www.blueridgecampgrounds.com, $16). Facilities include 30 RV/trailer sites, comfort stations, water, flush toilets, and sinks (no showers).

INFORMATION AND SERVICES

For more information on the Roanoke area, visit www.visitroanokeva.com or stop by the Roanoke Valley Convention and Visitors Bureau (101 Shenandoah Ave., 540/342-6025, daily 9am-5pm).

GETTING THERE AND AROUND

Roanoke is 56 miles southwest of Lynchburg and 240 miles southwest of Washington DC. The **Roanoke-Blacksburg Regional Airport** (5202 Aviation Dr. NW, 540/362-1999, www.flyroa.com) is the primary regional airport in southwest Virginia. It is 5 miles north of downtown Roanoke. The airport has more than 40 scheduled daily flights and is served by commercial airlines such as American, Delta, and United. Car rentals are available at the airport.

The **Valley Metro** bus service (540/982-2222, www.valleymetro.com, Mon.-Sat. 6am-8:45pm, $1.75) provides bus transportation throughout Roanoke. Its main terminal is at Campbell Court (17 W. Campbell Ave.).

BLACKSBURG

Forty miles southwest of Roanoke near I-81 is Blacksburg, home of **Virginia Polytechnic Institute and State University, or Virginia Tech**. Blacksburg has a population of around 45,000, with approximately 34,000 students in attendance at Virginia Tech. Blacksburg is a cross between a charming mountain town and a technology-driven city. It offers endless outdoor recreation, beautiful scenery, diversity, culture, and opportunity while maintaining a small-town feel.

Blacksburg is known for the Blacksburg Electronic Village (BEV), a Virginia Tech project with the goal of linking the entire town through an online community. The project officially launched in 1993 and was the "first" in many aspects of networking.

Virginia Tech

Virginia Tech (210 Burruss Hall, 540/231-6000, www.vt.edu) was founded in 1872 as an agricultural and mechanical land-grant college and has long had a thriving cadet program. Today, the school is Virginia's leading research institution, with approximately 280 degree programs (both undergraduate and graduate) and a research portfolio over $531 million. One of the powerhouse universities in the state, its campus includes more than 2,600 beautiful acres, 125 buildings, and the enormous Lane Stadium (which seats more than 65,000). Most of the buildings are neo-Gothic limestone edifices. A large grassy drill field leads up to stately Burruss Hall, the main administration building on campus, which houses a 3,000-plus-seat auditorium where major events and concerts are held.

Danville

Danville was settled in 1793 and sits just a half hour's drive from the North Carolina border. It has a population of around 42,000 and was formerly one of the most important tobacco-auction centers in the country. It also had a thriving textile industry. Glimpses of its economic heyday are evident in several historic districts, including **The Danville Historic District,** where the popular **Millionaires' Row,** on River Park Drive, is located. Millionaires' Row is where those who were prosperous in the tobacco and textile industries resided in the late 19th century, and it has one of the premier collections of both Victorian and Edwardian architecture in the South. Five architecturally significant churches grace its streets and helped Danville earn the nickname "City of Churches."

The **Danville Tobacco Warehouse District** is the prime area for new development. Former tobacco warehouses are now home to new businesses, housing, and nanotechnology research. The focal point of the district is the **Crossing of the Dan** complex, which is a restored railroad station that now houses exhibits for the **Danville Science Center** and a community marketplace. The **Carrington Pavilion** is also there and features summer concerts.

The Dan River is a prominent feature in the city, and along both sides runs the **Dan River Historic District.** A historic canal, original textile factories from the 1880s, and several beautiful arch bridges can be found in the area.

SIGHTS

Danville Museum of Fine Arts & History

The **Danville Museum of Fine Arts & History** (975 Main St., 434/793-5644, www. danvillemuseum.org, Tues.-Sat. 10am-5pm, Sun. 2pm-5pm, adults $10, students age 7-college $4, seniors 62 and over $8, under 7 free) showcases nationally acclaimed and emerging artists, national traveling exhibits, and local and regional artists. The museum is housed in the Italianate Sutherlin Mansion in Millionaires' Row. The home served as the last capitol of the Confederacy for just nine days in April 1865, several weeks before the end of the Civil War. The museum has an impressive collection of Civil War memorabilia, and the history of the mansion itself will be of interest to Civil War buffs.

AAF Tank Museum

Take a trip back in time through the largest private collection of international tank and cavalry artifacts in the world. **The Tank Museum** (3401 US 29 N., 434/836-5323, www.aaftankmuseum.com, Jan.-Mar. Sat. 10am-4pm, Apr.-Dec. Fri.-Sat. 10am-4pm, adults $15, children 5-12 $10, seniors $12, veterans $10, under 4 free) has over 30,000 artifacts and 120 tanks and artillery pieces displayed spanning several hundred years. The museum is housed in a large warehouse, and the tanks are displayed on mini sets, complete with sand, woods, rice paddies, and plastic human figures. Additional items on display include helmets, guns, uniforms, and many

Danville

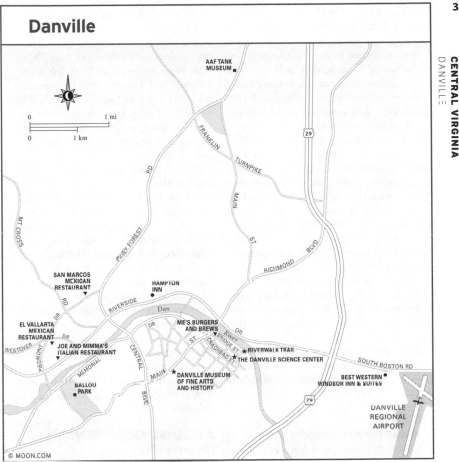

AAF TANK
MUSEUM

FRANKLIN
TURNPIKE

PD

MAIN

ST

29

RICHMOND

BLVD

MT CROSS

PINEY FOREST

SAN MARCOS
MEXICAN
RESTAURANT

HAMPTON
INN

RD

RIVERSIDE

Dan

DR

EL VALLARTA
MEXICAN
RESTAURANT

DR

WESTOVER

PIEDMONT

JOE AND MIMMA'S
ITALIAN RESTAURANT

MEMORIAL

CENTRAL

MAIN

BLVD

ME'S BURGERS
AND BREWS

River

DR

BRIDGE ST

ST

CRAGHEAD ST

★ RIVERWALK TRAIL
★ THE DANVILLE SCIENCE CENTER

SOUTH BOSTON RD

BALLOU
PARK

★ DANVILLE MUSEUM
OF FINE ARTS
AND HISTORY

29

BEST WESTERN
WINDSOR INN & SUITES

DANVILLE
REGIONAL
AIRPORT

0   1 mi
0   1 km

© MOON.COM

personal items. This is an interesting, one-of-a-kind museum.

The Danville Science Center

The Danville Science Center (677 Craghead St., 434/791-5160, www.dsc.smv.org, Mon.-Sat. 9:30am-5pm, Sun. 11:30am-5pm, admission and exhibits adults $7, youth and seniors $6, exhibits and digital dome adults $10, youth and seniors $9) is in the Danville Tobacco Warehouse District in the Crossing of the Dan complex. The center is part of the Science Museums of Virginia network, whose facilities aim to make science fun for kids of all ages by offering interactive exhibits and special programs. A butterfly station and garden are open between April and October.

A special collection at the Science Center is the **Estelle H. Womack Natural History Collection.** This exhibit is located in the Science Station (where the local Amtrak station is) and features artifacts donated by local residents of Danville over the years. The museum also features a **Digital Dome Theater** that takes viewers on a journey through the night sky and shows giant-screen films.

EVENTS AND RECREATION

Danville's **Festival in the Park** (760 W. Main St., Ballou Park, www.danvilleva.gov) is an annual event that's been held since 1974. The three-day festival takes place each May in historic Ballou Park. The festival includes arts and crafts, food, entertainment, a health fair, kids' activities, vendors, rides, and a 5K run/walk/wheelchair race.

The paved eight-mile **Riverwalk Trail** that runs along the Dan River is designed for walkers, runners, bikers, and inline skaters. Parking is available at the Crossing at the Dan, the Dan Daniel Memorial Park (302 River Park Dr.), Main Street at the Martin Luther King Bridge, and Anglers Park (350 Northside Dr.). A trail map and brochure can be downloaded at www.danvilleva.gov.

Mountain bikers should check out the **Anglers Ridge Mountain Bike Trail System** (www.danville-va.gov). This incredible network of 25 miles of single-track offers a technically challenging ride on sections such as Hot Tamale and Witchback, while novice riders will likely enjoy the more moderate terrain on Anglers Ridge and the Riverside Drive trails.

FOOD

★ **Me's Burgers and Brews** (215 Main St., 434/792-0123, www.mesburgers.com, Tues.-Thurs. 4pm-10pm, Fri.-Sat. 4pm-11pm, $9-16) is a trendy little surprise located downtown at the south end of the Main Street bridge. The mother-daughter owner duo artfully pulled together every little detail to make this beer-and-burger joint a step above the norm. They offer an ever-changing draft brew selection from local Virginia and North Carolina breweries, alongside a scrumptious menu of high-quality burgers named for classic authors. Burgers are served on potato rolls created by a Mennonite bakery with a sourdough starter. The mouthwatering sweet potato salad is made from a secret family recipe. Be sure to finish off the evening with their glazed doughnut bread pudding.

Tasty Mexican food can be found at **El Vallarta Mexican Restaurant** (418 Westover Dr., 434/799-0506, www.elvallartamexicanrestaurant.net, Mon.-Thurs. 11am-10pm, Fri.-Sat. 11am-11pm, Sun. 11am-9:30pm, $8-16). The cozy decor is upstaged by the friendly staff and delicious menu. With hundreds of choices for lunch and dinner, making a selection can be the hardest part. If you're stumped, try the fajitas, cheese dip, and a margarita.

Another good Mexican choice is **San Marcos Mexican Restaurant** (165 Holt Garrison Pkwy., 434/792-4202, www.sanmarcosrestaurant.com, Sun.-Thur. 11am-10pm, Fri.-Sat. 11am-11pm, $9-18). They have a large dining room and offer many traditional Mexican dishes along with a few surprises. This is a nice place to bring the family since there are so many menu options. They also make a decent margarita.

Joe and Mimma's Italian Restaurant (3336 Riverside Dr., 434/799-5763, www.joeandmimmasdanville.com, Mon.-Thurs. 11am-9:30pm, Fri.-Sat. 11am-10pm, $7-23) is a local favorite for delicious Italian food. They advertise "healthy" ingredients and serve a variety of entrées, pizzas, subs, pastas, and seafood.

ACCOMMODATIONS

Under $100

Fall Creek Farm (2556 Green Farm Rd., 434/791-3297, www.fall-creek-farm.com, $80-100) offers a unique bed-and-breakfast experience. Guests stay in individual log cabins, complete with fireplaces, period antiques, and continental breakfast delivered to their doorstep. The farm sits on 50 acres and offers a heated pool, hiking trails, and stream and pond fishing. There are also miniature donkeys at the farm.

$100-200

The **Courtyard Danville Marriott** (2136 Riverside Dr., 434/791-2661, www.marriott.com, $136-169) has 89 modern rooms, a fitness room, and an outdoor pool. The staff is

That Old-Time Bluegrass

The second week in August marks a very special time in the southern Virginia town of **Galax**. This town, 104 miles west of Danville and 90 miles east of Abingdon, near the North Carolina border, is the home of the largest old-time bluegrass fiddlers' convention in the country.

Galax is famous for a long history of "old-timey" music, and that tradition remains strong even with the younger crowd. The **Annual Old Fiddlers' Convention** (276/236-8541, www. oldfiddlersconvention.com) has been a main event in town since 1935. Hundreds of people from all over the country come with their instruments to compete for prize money totaling more than $10,000. Thousands more fans converge on the town to witness the contest and to hear up-and-coming bluegrass musicians.

The goal of the convention hasn't changed over time. It is dedicated to "Keeping alive the memories and sentiments of days gone by and make it possible for people of today to hear and enjoy the tunes of yesterday." Instruments featured in the competition include everything from mouth harps to bull fiddles. Some competitors have attended nearly every convention since 1935.

Tickets to the event are only sold at the gate and cost $7-13 per day. Attendees are advised to bring rain gear and boots since rain is common at that time of year and the fields where the performance stages are can get muddy.

Camping is available for $100, but spaces are only sold at the gate. Recordings of the highlights of each year's events are produced by Heritage Records and can be purchased by calling 276/236-9249.

exceptionally pleasant and helpful. This is one of the nicest hotels in the area and is good for business and leisure travel.

For a clean, quite stay, the **Best Western Windsor Inn & Suites** (1292 S. Boston Rd., 434/483-5000, www.bestwestern.com, $93-140) is a centrally located all-suite hotel. They offer 74 guest suites with refrigerators, microwaves, work desks, and sitting areas. The rooms are spacious, and there's a whirlpool, indoor pool, and fitness room on-site. Breakfast is included with your stay, and fresh-baked complimentary cookies are available in the evening.

Another good option is the 58-room **Hampton Inn Danville** (2130 Riverside Dr., 434/793-1111, www.hamptoninn3.hilton. com, $112-142). It offers free breakfast, a fitness room, business center, and outdoor pool.

INFORMATION

Additional information on Danville can be found at the **Welcome Center** (645 River Park Dr., www.danville-va.gov, Mon.-Fri. 8:30am-5pm, Sat.-Sun. 9am-5pm).

GETTING THERE

Danville is 80 miles southeast of Roanoke and 248 miles southwest of Washington DC. Most visitors arrive by car, but train service through **Amtrak** (677 Craghead St., 800/872-7245) and bus service through **Greyhound** (515 Spring St., 434/792-4722) are available.

Abingdon

Abingdon (named for Martha Washington's home parish in England) was incorporated in 1778 and is the oldest English-speaking town west of the Blue Ridge Mountains. It is hard to believe the town is still in Virginia, as it is a six-hour drive from Washington DC and is as far west as Cleveland. Abingdon, however, is a Virginia Historic Landmark and offers a 20-block historic district with beautiful tree-lined streets, brick sidewalks, and quaint 19th-century homes. The town is also known for its performing and visual arts.

Main Street in Abingdon is a collection of historic treasures. There are galleries, museums, inns, eateries, and a theater. The land the town occupies was originally surveyed in the mid-1700s. Daniel Boone named the area "Wolf Hill" after his hunting dogs were attacked by a pack of wolves nearby. The location of the attack is known as **Courthouse Hill.** In past years, 27 wolf sculptures could be seen around the town, but most have been sold and moved.

SIGHTS
The Arts Depot
One of the most popular sights in Abingdon is **The Arts Depot** (314 Depot St., 276/628-9091, www.abingdonartsdepot.org, Wed.-Sat. 10am-4pm and by appointment, free). Visitors can watch artists at work, walk through galleries, attend workshops, and listen to lectures in this former railroad freight station that is now dedicated to the arts.

William King Museum of Art
The **William King Museum of Art** (415 Academy Dr. NW, 276/628-5005, www.williamkingmuseum.org, Mon.-Sat. 10am-5pm, Sun. 1pm-5pm, first Thurs. of each month until 8pm, free) is a delightful visual arts museum and center that is located in a historic school building (from 1913). It offers fine world art, regional works, and exhibits

on cultural heritage. The exhibits change frequently. In addition to three main galleries (housing nine primary exhibits), the museum features a gallery with pieces from area school and college students and exhibits from local artists.

White's Mill
A short drive north of town brings you to **White's Mill** (12291 White's Mill Rd., 276/628-2960, www.whitesmill.org, Wed.-Thurs. 10am-3pm, Fri.-Sun. 10am-5pm, free), the only remaining water-powered gristmill in southwest Virginia. The mill was built in the late 18th century and provided flour and meal for the community. It was also a gathering place for local residents. The mercantile (store) at the mill sold goods to residents and now offers handmade arts and crafts, local books, and regional music.

Abingdon Vineyards
Wine enthusiasts can visit **Abingdon Vineyards** (20530 Alvarado Rd., 276/623-1255, www.abingdonvineyards.com, Wed.-Sun. 11am-6pm) to sample local wine in a welcoming, rustic atmosphere.

RECREATION
The **Virginia Creeper Trail** (www.vacreepertrail.org) is a 34-mile recreation trail that starts in Abingdon (off Pecan St. across the train tracks), runs through Damascus, Virginia, and ends at the North Carolina border. The trail is a former railroad bed and is now a shared-use trail, which means mountain bikers, hikers, and horses can all partake in the trail. There is a welcome center at the trailhead in Abingdon (300 Green Spring Rd.) and three visitors centers on the trail (Damascus Caboose, the Old Greene Cove Station, and the Whitetop Station) that are open on weekends May-October. Restrooms are provided in Damascus, the Straight

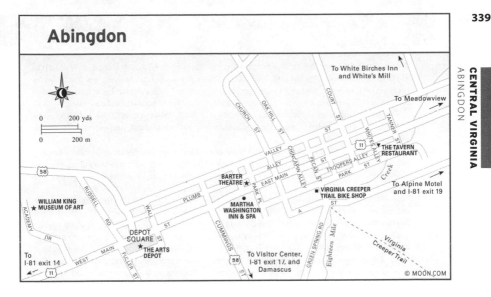

Abingdon

Branch parking lot, Creek Junction parking lot, Green Cove train station, Whitetop train station, and at the trail welcome center in Abingdon. The **Virginia Creeper Trail Bike Shop** (201 Pecan St. SE, 276/676-2552, www.vacreepertrailbikeshop.com, $17-27) is one shop that offers bike rentals. Several others offer rentals and shuttles and can be found on the trail website.

Twenty-four miles southwest of Abingdon, across the Tennessee state line in Bristol, is the **Bristol Motor Speedway** (151 Speedway Blvd., Bristol, 423/989-6900, www.bristolmotorspeedway.com), a NASCAR short-track venue and a highly popular one at that. The track is known for its steep banking as well as for being one of the loudest venues.

ENTERTAINMENT AND EVENTS

The **Barter Theatre** (127 W. Main St., 276/628-3991, www.bartertheatre.com) was opened in 1933 by a young actor named Robert Porterfield. Porterfield came up with a unique idea during the Depression to barter produce from local farms in exchange for a ticket to the theater. It opened under the slogan, "With vegetables you cannot sell, you can buy a good laugh." The price of a ticket was 40 cents or the equal in produce. Most patrons gained entrance in this manner and also bartered with dairy products and livestock. The town jail was beneath the stage and is now used for dressing rooms. Today, the theater hosts drama, comedy, musicals, and mystery performances much as it has done for more than 70 years, only it no longer accepts produce as payment.

Abingdon hosts one of the top 100 annual tourist events in the country. The **Virginia Highlands Festival** (www.vahighlandsfestival.org) is a 10-day event held in August that showcases music, art, crafts, and writing indigenous to the Appalachians. The festival began in 1948 and was founded by the same man who set up the Barter Theatre, Robert Porterfield. It started as a weeklong festival geared toward Appalachian arts and crafts and evolved into 10 days of festivities in a variety of venues. A large antiques market is also featured at the festival, and there is wine-tasting, gardening instruction, and even a hot-air-balloon rally.

Those who like ghost stories won't want to miss taking an **Abingdon Spirit Tour** (276/706-6093, www.visitabingdonvirginia.

Getaway to Mount Rogers

Thirty-five miles northeast of Abingdon is the beautiful **Mount Rogers National Recreation Area** (3714 Hwy. 16, Marion, 276/783-5196, www.fs.usda.gov). This 200,000-acre recreation paradise is part of the George Washington and Jefferson National Forests, which stretch from one end of Virginia to the other along the ancient Appalachian Mountains.

The area includes sprawling rural countryside and the 5,000-acre Crest Zone, which features mountains over 4,000 feet, large rock outcrops, mountain balds, forest, and even a herd of wild ponies.

The area also offers just about any kind of outdoor activity you can dream up in the mountains including camping, horseback riding (there are four horse camps), hiking, biking, cross-country skiing, and wildlife viewing. There are hundreds of miles of trails and seven campgrounds to choose from (call 877/444-6777 for reservations). Cabin rentals are also available.

Mount Rogers itself is the focal point of the region. This 5,729-foot-high mountain is the highest natural point in Virginia. The peak is named after the first Virginia state geologist, William Barton Rogers, who taught at both the College of William & Mary and the University of Virginia.

The **Mount Rogers Scenic Byway** runs through the Mount Rogers National Recreation Area. The first section of this scenic, curvy, hilly byway begins in Troutdale, Virginia. It runs west for 13.2 miles over State Route 603 and on to Konnarock, Virginia, as a paved, two-lane road. The second section runs 32.5 miles east from Damascus, Virginia, to Volney, Virginia, following US Route 58, also a two-lane paved road.

com). Since 1998, this popular two-hour walking tour has sent chills down visitors' spines as they learn Abingdon history including where skeletons are buried and local ghost lore. Tours are animated and fun and depart from many different locations (check website for more information).

SHOPPING

One of the oldest crafts cooperatives in the nation, **Holston Mountain Artisans** (214 Park St., 276/628-7721, www.holstonmtnarts.com) offers a large assortment of traditional arts and crafts from the region including home decor items, gifts, musical instruments, art, books, and photographs. The cooperative began in 1971 and represents more than 130 local artists. They are located in the historic jailhouse on Park Street.

A unique shopping stop on Main Street is the **Abingdon Olive Oil Company** (152 E. Main St., 276/525-1524). This fun tasting gallery and shop features a large variety of organic, extra-virgin, and naturally infused oils and balsamic vinegars. The friendly staff gives free tours and tastings.

FOOD
American

The **Rain Restaurant and Bar** (283 E. Main St., 276/739-2331, www.rainabingdon.com, Tues.-Sat. 11am-2pm and 5pm-9pm, the bar is open later with a limited menu, $22-29) is a wonderful place to spend an evening. This modern, colorful restaurant has good food, friendly and attentive staff, and lovely cocktails (try the cucumber martini). The menu includes steak, pasta, seafood, and chicken with an interesting and delicious assortment of soups and starters (try the buffalo crawfish).

Sisters at the Martha (150 W. Main St., 276/628-3161, www.themartha.com, daily 5pm-9pm, $18-40), within the Martha Washington Inn and Spa, has a lovely menu of Southern-style seafood, steaks, and poultry. This is a classy but casual setting, perfect for a quiet or romantic evening out. Reservations are recommended.

To sample local beer, go to **Wolf Hills**

1: Barter Theatre 2: Martha Washington Inn & Spa in Abingdon

Brewery (350 Park St., 276/451-5470, www. wolfhillsbrewing.com, Mon.-Fri. 5pm-9pm, Sat. 1pm-9pm, Sun. 1pm-6pm) in the old ice house near the Virginia Creeper Trail and the train tracks. They do not have a restaurant, but they hold special beer events.

Intercontinental

★ **The Tavern Restaurant** (222 E. Main St., 276/628-1118, www.abingdontavern.com, Mon.-Sat. 5pm-9pm, $16-44), housed in the oldest building in Abingdon, was originally a tavern and inn for stagecoach travelers. The doors and wood floors of this 1779 building lean a little, but that adds to the charm of this landmark. The delicious menu includes seafood, steak, and poultry with German, Austrian, and Swiss influences (the owner's background is German). There's a cozy bar on the first floor and nice dining areas upstairs. The beer menu is inspiring, as is the wine menu. This is a great place for families and a good place for a date, and the atmosphere is warm and inviting.

ACCOMMODATIONS
Under $100

For a classic, no-frills motel experience, the **Alpine Motel** (882 E. Main St., 276/628-3178, www.alpinemotelabingdon.com, $59-89) is a good choice. This well-maintained, clean motel sits against a hillside overlooking woods and farmland. It is comfortable and offers 19 spacious rooms.

A good-quality chain hotel near I-81 is the **Quality Inn & Suites** (930 E. Main St., 276/676-9090, www.choicehotels.com, $80-129). They offer 75 clean rooms with refrigerators, ironing boards, coffeemakers, hair dryers, and cable television. A free hot breakfast, a fitness center, and a seasonal outdoor pool are also available to guests.

$100-200

The five-guest-room **White Birches Inn** (268 White's Mill Rd., 276/676-2140, www.whitebirchesinn.com, $159-179) was Abingdon's first green bed-and-breakfast. It

is a lovely and reasonably priced choice for accommodations in Abingdon. All guest rooms are named after famous playwrights who bartered their work at Abingdon's Barter Theatre. There is a lovely porch out back and a small pond. Breakfast is included with your stay.

The **Hampton Inn Abingdon** (340 Commerce Dr., 276/619-4600, www.secure3hilton.com, $135-153) is another solid choice for a chain hotel in Abingdon. It is off I-81, within walking distance of the historic district. The property is nice, and the staff is warm and friendly. There are 68 guest rooms, and breakfast is included. The hotel offers walking trails, a fitness center, and an outdoor pool.

$200-300

The **Cooper Lantern Boutique Inn** (133 E. Valley St., 276/525-1919, www.copperlanterninn.com, $225-250) was built in 1873 and is conveniently located within walking distance of many attractions in Abingdon. Warm Southern hospitality comes with your room in this cozy bed-and-breakfast. The Georgian colonial-style home has a beautiful stained glass front door and offers eight individually named and furnished rooms, all with their own special history. Rooms are outfitted with Egyptian combed-cotton towels and fine bed linens with comfortable mattresses. Relax on the front porch or swing in the love seat in this friendly, comfortable setting. The food is also wonderful and homemade.

Over $300

The ★ **Martha Washington Inn & Spa** (150 W. Main St., 276/628-3161, www.themartha.com, $340-550) is a beautiful historic hotel with a lot of charm. Guests are drawn in by the attractive, sprawling front porch and the friendly staff, but they stay because of the relaxing atmosphere. The hotel has 55 rooms and eight suites and is decorated with some antiques but offers comfortable furnishings throughout. All rooms are fully renovated and have flat-screen TVs and wireless Internet. The hotel was once a private residence, then a women's college. It is across from the Barter Theatre on Main Street and convenient to many attractions. The rooms are nicely decorated and plenty large, and there is a spa, fitness room, heated saltwater pool, bikes, and tennis courts on-site. You can also schedule a carriage ride. A full hot breakfast is included, as is a glass of port wine each evening. The hotel offers bike rides on the Virginia Creeper Trail, where they will drive you out 17 miles, drop you off with a box lunch, and then let you ride downhill back to the inn. There is free valet parking for guests, a Tesla charging station, and free wireless Internet throughout the inn.

CAMPING

Scenic camping can be found approximately 10 miles south of Abingdon on the shores of South Holston Lake and in the surrounding area.

The **Lakeshore Campground** (19417 County Park Rd., 276/628-5394, www.virginia.org, Apr.-Nov., $30-45) on South Holston Lake offers 200 campsites, a sanitation facility, swimming, boating, boat storage, fishing, a game room, and telephones. Most of their sites are rented for a full season rather than nightly.

Seven miles north of Abingdon is **Riverside Campground** (18496 N. Fork River Rd., 276/623-0340, www.riversidecampground.org, Apr.-Oct., $29-42). They have more than 100 tent and RV sites along the North Fork of the Holston River. The campground is family oriented.

Washington County Park (19482 County Park Rd., 276/628-9677, Apr.-Sept., $25) is another campground on South Holston Lake. They offer 132 campsites with electric hookups, water, and sanitation facilities. They also offer 10 tent sites. They have a playground, picnic shelters, boating, fishing, and telephone access.

INFORMATION AND SERVICES

For additional information on Abingdon, stop by the **visitors center** (335 Cummings St., 276/676-2282, Mon.-Sat. 9am-5pm, Sun. 11am-5pm) or visit www.abingdon.com.

GETTING THERE

Most people arrive in Abingdon by car. It is just off I-81 in the southwestern corner of Virginia. The public **Tri-Cities Regional Airport** (2525 Hwy. 75, Blountville, TN, 423/325-6000, www.triflight.com) in Sullivan County, Tennessee, is 33 miles southwest of Abingdon. Carriers such as American and Delta offer service to the airport.

Background

The Landscape

GEOGRAPHY

The state of Virginia encompasses more than 42,000 square miles and stretches from the Atlantic Ocean to the Appalachian Mountains.

Virginia is divided into five geographic regions. The Atlantic coastal plain (also called Tidewater) is the easternmost portion of the state and is located east of Richmond. It includes salt marshes, coastal areas, the Eastern Shore, and the Atlantic beaches. The Piedmont is the low, rolling, fertile central region of the state and sits just west of the Atlantic coastal plain. It is the largest geographic region, extending from Richmond west to the Blue Ridge Mountains.

The Blue Ridge region sits just west of the Piedmont. It is a narrow band that is mostly mountainous (over 1,000 feet). The highest peak in Virginia, Mount Rogers (5,729 feet), is located in the Blue Ridge region in the southernmost part of the state, near the North Carolina border. West of the Blue Ridge is the Appalachian Ridge and Valley region, which is a series of valleys divided by mountains. This region includes the Shenandoah Valley. The far southwestern corner of Virginia is located in the Appalachian Plateau. This area is known for its forests, rivers, and streams.

CLIMATE

Virginia has what many residents feel is the perfect climate. There are four distinct seasons and the weather is seldom extreme. Having said this, most of the region—eastern and central Virginia—is considered subtropical, which is defined by hot, humid summers and mild, cool winters. The western portion of the state has a humid continental climate, which is defined by large seasonal temperature fluctuations with warm to hot summers and cold to severely cold winters.

The abundance of water on the East Coast, which includes the Atlantic Ocean, the Chesapeake Bay, and many large rivers and their tributaries, helps fuel the humidity commonly associated with the region. It's no surprise that the humidity is much higher in the coastal regions whereas the western mountain regions are typically 10 degrees cooler throughout the year and are considerably less "sticky."

Springtime in Virginia is fragrant and colorful. There are flowering fruit trees, blooming dogwoods, spring bulbs, and wildflowers throughout the state. Rivers swollen from melted winter snow rush by blankets of blooming bluebells and azaleas explode throughout suburban neighborhoods. Temperatures in the spring can vary greatly, but overall offer comfortable warm days with chilly nights.

Summer brings ample sunshine to the region with frequent afternoon thunderstorms. The humidity can be far more uncomfortable than the heat, but there are days, especially in August, where both seem unbearable and the air is so thick you'll think you can swim through it. The good news is, there are rare washout days in the summer when it rains continuously, and when it does it's a welcome break from the heat. The shore areas offer refuge during the summer as do the mountains, but neither is a close second to the comfort of modern air-conditioning.

Fall is brilliant in Virginia. Temperatures are cool, the humidity recedes, and the landscape explodes from exhausted greens to vibrant reds and yellows. The autumn foliage in the state is some of the best in the country, especially in the mountainous areas to the west. Peak foliage is normally in mid-October but varies year to year. The local news broadcasts usually keep tabs on the foliage and let people know the best days for leaf peeping. This spectacular natural display, coupled with crisp sunny days and chilly nights, makes fall the best time to visit the state.

When the leaves finally fall and the pumpkins are ripe on the vine, it's the first sign that winter is approaching. For most of Virginia, winter temperatures usually set in sometime in December and don't thaw until early March. Even so, the area receives minimal snowfall, normally a handful of snow events each season. Although it is possible to get a large snowstorm in Virginia, it does not happen every year. Likewise, temperatures can dip into the single digits, but that is not the norm. The thermometer normally rests somewhere between 25 and 40 degrees during the day in winter, but cold spells and also warm spells aren't unheard of. The exception to all

More Than Tasty Bivalves

Oyster lovers flock to the Chesapeake Bay region to feast on the famous eastern oyster. For more than 100 years, this delectable yet peculiar-looking creature flourished in the bay and was one of the most valuable commercial fishing commodities. However, in recent decades, overharvesting, disease, and pollution have severely reduced its numbers. This is more than just a bummer for oyster eaters; oysters are a vital piece of the Chesapeake Bay's ecosystem.

Oysters provide habitat for many aquatic animals. Their hard shells with many nooks and crannies act as much-needed reefs and are relied on by hundreds of underwater animals such as sponges, crabs, and fish. Oysters and their larvae are also an important food source for many aquatic residents and some shorebirds. In addition, oysters are filter feeders, which means they pump large amounts of water through their gills when they eat. This filters the water, removing chemical contaminants, nutrients, and sediments, which helps keep the water clean. One oyster can filter more than 50 gallons of water in a single day.

of this is Virginia's mountain areas, which can see more snow than their neighbors in the Piedmont, with snow totals averaging about 25 inches a year.

ENVIRONMENTAL ISSUES

One of the biggest environmental issues in Virginia is the health of the Chesapeake Bay. The bay faces many problems including nutrient and sediment pollution from agriculture, storm water runoff, wastewater treatment plants, and air pollution; contamination from chemicals; overharvesting; invasive species; and the effects of development on its shores and tributaries. All of these threats impact the health of the bay and its ability to maintain a viable aquatic ecosystem.

Excess nutrients are the primary pollutant in the Chesapeake Bay. They increase algae bloom growth, which blocks vital sunlight to aquatic grasses. These grasses are crucial to the bay's ecosystem since they provide food and habitat to aquatic animals, reduce erosion, and produce oxygen. In addition, when the algae die and decompose, it depletes the water of the oxygen that all aquatic animals need.

The issues facing the bay are not localized problems. The Chesapeake Bay's watershed covers 64,000 square miles through six states and DC. There are 17 million residents living in this area.

Mass media attention in recent years has led to a greater awareness of the issues facing the bay and its tributaries, but there is a still a very long way to go before the problems are solved.

The **Chesapeake Bay Foundation** (www.cbf.org), headquartered in Annapolis, Maryland, is the largest conservation organization dedicated to the well-being of the Chesapeake Bay watershed. Its famous "Save the Bay" slogan defines the continued quest to protect and restore the bay's natural resources.

Another environmental issue in Virginia is the need for healthy farming. Unsustainable farming practices have contributed to water and air pollution throughout the state and have also resulted in soil erosion, animal abuse, and poor human health. Organizations such as **Environment Virginia** (www.environmentvirginia.org) are looking for ways to expand opportunities for sustainable farmers that grow food in ways that don't pollute the environment.

PLANTS

The state of Virginia published a book titled *Flora of Virginia*, which is the only existing guide to nearly 3,200 species of trees, grasses, shrubs, flowers, and cacti that currently grow in the state. This huge book (weighing nearly seven pounds) took 11 years and $1.7 million to put together. It is a testament to the wide

Tree Trivia

- Black walnut trees give off a toxic chemical that inhibits other tree species from growing near them.

- The popular weeping willow is related to the black willow, but is native to Asia.

- Early settlers extracted the oil found in bitternut hickory nuts and used it as fuel for their oil lamps.

- Vessels in white oak wood are plugged with a substance that makes the wood watertight. This is why whiskey and wine barrels are made from the wood.

- The northern red oak is one of the most popular timber trees in the Atlantic region.

variety of plant life that has taken root in this region over the centuries.

Virginia's central location on the East Coast allows it to boast both southern and northern flora. Visitors can see northern tree species such as spruce and fir in the western mountain areas and then drive east to visit cypress swamps in the coastal regions.

Trees

Forest covers roughly two-thirds of Virginia. Much of the mountainous region in the western portion of the state is heavily forested and contains dozens of species of trees such as the eastern white pine (which can grow to 200 feet), Virginia pine, pond pine, eastern hemlock, and even red spruce. Forested areas can also be found in the Piedmont and coastal regions of the state. In fact, the loblolly pine, which is the most important commercial timber tree in Virginia, grows near the coast.

Other common trees found throughout the state include the eastern red cedar, black willow, black walnut, bitternut hickory (swamp hickory), American beech, American elm, yellow poplar, sycamore, northern red oak, and white oak.

Many ornamental trees are also native to

Virginia such as holly, red maple, magnolia, and the flowering dogwood (which is both the state tree and the state flower of Virginia).

Plants, Shrubs, and Flowers

Because of the mild climate, there are many flowering shrubs and 85 species of ferns in Virginia. Nothing announces the arrival of spring like the bright yellow blooms of the forsythia. This sprawling bush is a favorite of homeowners since it provides pretty blooms in the spring and a good screen in the summer. Several varieties of azaleas are native to the region, and in May residential neighborhoods are painted in their vibrant red, pink, purple, and white blooms. Rhododendrons are also native to the region, as are the butterfly bush (sometimes referred to as summer lilac) and the stunning hydrangea.

Spring and summer yield thousands of wildflowers across the state. Shenandoah National Park alone has 862 species, providing a breathtaking display from early spring through summer. Species include hepatica, violets, trillium, wild geraniums, mountain laurel, columbine, and wild sunflowers. In the coastal areas, wildflowers grow among marsh grasses and over sand dunes.

Although many native flowers grow quite well across Virginia, such as the woodland sunflower, hibiscus, lupine, lobelia, and phlox, some species are partial to either the eastern or western side of the state since the geography is so varied between the two. At least two types of asters are found primarily in the mountain regions, such as the smooth blue aster and the New England aster. The American lily of the valley is also partial to the mountainous region. The coastal region has its own share of plant species that exclusively call the area home, such as the New York aster and seaside goldenrod.

ANIMALS

Virginia is full of wildlife, and its mild climate and varied geography allow for many types of animals to flourish. Since the mountainous areas are heavily forested and less populated, they are home to the most animals. Although most are shy, there are often sightings of foxes, skunks, raccoons, rabbits, chipmunks, squirrels, and white-tailed deer. In some of the park areas, the deer have become too friendly with humans and will literally walk right up to you. Under no circumstances should you feed the wildlife, no matter how cute and convincing they are. Other animals that live in the western regions include the coyote, bobcat, and black bear.

The central regions of Virginia (dominated by the large Piedmont region) provide shelter for many species of animals that have learned to coexist well with nearby human populations. Raccoons, opossums, squirrels, chipmunks, beavers, and, more recently, coyotes can be found throughout the region.

The coastal regions' wetlands, marshes, and rivers entice populations of lizards, muskrats, butterflies, and snakes. Animals from the Piedmont can also be found in coastal areas, but less forest means fewer places to hide from predators and the harsh summer sunshine.

There are three types of venomous snakes in Virginia and 31 nonvenomous. The most common type of venomous snake is the northern copperhead. This snake can be found throughout Virginia and has dark-colored cross bands shaped like an hourglass. Next comes the timber rattlesnake, which is found in all the mountainous regions and in the southeastern corner of Virginia. It also has a patterned back with wavy cross bands. The eastern cottonmouth snake is only found in southeastern Virginia (south of Newport News). It can be yellowish olive to black in color and has approximately 13 black cross bands that are wide at the sides and narrow at the backbone.

Birds

A huge variety of birds live in Virginia, from migratory shorebirds to tiny songbirds—and even bald eagles. Virginia has 340 native bird species, but the number is much greater if you include seasonal birds that do not actually nest in the state. In spring and early summer, the woods are alive with the happy calls of songbirds, but during winter, many migrate south. On the flip side, some northern birds, such as snow geese, come down from Canada because the winters are milder here.

Many hawks live throughout Virginia, and the red-tailed variety can frequently be spotted (although they will surely see you before you see them). Another impressive and frequently seen bird is the turkey vulture, also known as a buzzard. They are huge and can have a wingspan up to six feet. Wild turkeys are also prevalent and look like they walked out of a children's Thanksgiving story. Game birds such as the grouse are also residents of the area and sometimes startle hikers by launching themselves in the air when they see someone approach.

Migratory birds such as warblers and jonquils frequent the mountain regions during the winter, and the Piedmont region offers sightings of bald eagles, pileated woodpeckers, great blue herons, cormorants, and bufflehead ducks. The coastal areas are prime for bird-watching. More than 40 types of ducks, geese, and swans alone have been documented in water-rich areas. This area is also home to ospreys, oystercatchers, plovers, peregrine falcons, black skimmers, and dozens of other shorebirds.

History

IN THE BEGINNING

It is believed that the first humans arrived in Virginia approximately 18,000 years ago. They were hunter-gatherers most likely organized into seminomadic bands. As time went on, hunting tools became more efficient, and delicacies from the Chesapeake Bay, such as oysters, became an important food source.

With new developments came the first Native American villages and the formation of social structures. Successive Native American cultures continued for thousands of years prior to the arrival of Europeans.

THE COLONIAL PERIOD

After many failed attempts at establishing a permanent settlement, in 1607 the first English settlers arrived at the mouth of the Chesapeake Bay in three ships and traveled 30 miles up the James River under the guidance of Captain John Smith. The settlers disembarked and promptly began to build a settlement at what later became Jamestown.

They found the coastal area inhabited by Algonquian natives (called the Powhatan Confederacy) who controlled land stretching from what is now North Carolina to the Potomac River. These native settlements included approximately 10,000 people who relied on hunting, fishing, and farming for survival.

The settlers were met with rich lands, many game animals, and initially friendly natives. Even so, they were not prepared for the physical labor and inevitable problems that came with starting a new settlement, and the colony nearly failed in the first few

years. Around 1612, a colonist named John Rolfe brought in the first tobacco seeds which he had gathered from an earlier voyage to Trinidad. The first tobacco crops were planted and were soon in high demand back in England. This provided an instant boost to the New World's economy.

Put mildly, life was very difficult for the early settlers. Disease, famine, and attacks from Native Americans wiped out much of the early population. Although the Native Americans were initially friendly, it didn't take long for their feelings to change when they realized the settlers intended to stay permanently. In just a couple of years, most of the Native American settlements had been seized, and it became unsafe for the settlers to venture past their settlement fences. A temporary truce resulted in 1614 from the marriage of the 13-year-old daughter of Chief Powhatan, named Pocahontas (who had earlier saved Captain John Smith's life when her father tried to kill him), to John Rolfe. The truce ended quickly with a surprise Powhatan attack that killed 400 settlers.

As land along the coast filled up, pioneers began to move farther inland toward the mountains. New immigrants continued

courthouse in Colonial Williamsburg

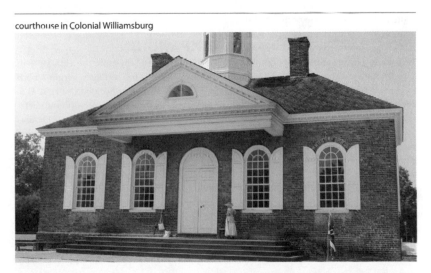

to arrive, including people from places such as Germany and Scotland. Virginia was a region of large plantations and minimal urban development. Since much of the plantation labor was supplied by indentured servants, few women came to the area. This, combined with a high rate of disease, made for the slow growth of the local population.

By 1700, most Native Americans had been driven out of Virginia. At the same time, the number of enslaved African people had grown rapidly in the region as the number of indentured servants declined. During this time, many colonists in Virginia began enjoying generous fortunes earned through growing tobacco.

The Church of England was the official church in Virginia, which differentiated it from the New England colonies. But the church became a secondary interest since there was a short supply of clergy and houses of worship. In 1705, Virginia's capital was moved from Jamestown to nearby Williamsburg.

Throughout the first half of the century, tensions between the colonies and their European motherland grew as England tried to squeeze as much money as possible out of the colonists through taxes while extending them far fewer rights than held by those living in the home country. One of the final straws came in 1763 with the passing of a ridiculous law prohibiting westward expansion of the colonies, which angered many colonists. A passionate and heated speech delivered by Patrick Henry in Williamsburg in 1765 implied publicly that the colonies might be better off without King George III. Tension between England and the colonies continued to grow, and rebellious outbreaks such as the Boston Tea Party in 1773 began to grow more frequent.

In 1775 Henry delivered his famous speech at St. John's Church in Richmond where he was quoted as saying, "I know not what course others may take; but as for me, give me liberty or give me death."

THE REVOLUTIONARY WAR

Virginia became a primary center of Revolutionary War activity since it was the largest and most populated colony. Virginia experienced fighting from the earliest days of the war, although it managed to escape much of the destruction for the first three years. Virginia's capital was moved to a safer location at Richmond in 1780 after British ships sailed into the Hampton Roads area, and the capital has remained there ever since.

Major Virginia confrontations included the Battle of Great Bridge, where British authorities were removed from the colony, and the Yorktown Campaign. The Yorktown Campaign moved through Petersburg when British forces landed along the James River in 1781 in order to support Lord Cornwallis's army, based in North Carolina. Twenty-five hundred British troops moved against Petersburg, and a clash with 1,200 militia occurred in what is now the neighborhood of Blanford.

The most well-known battle took place in Yorktown where 18,000 members of the Continental and French armies defeated British forces, causing their surrender in 1781. This battle was the final victory that secured America's independence.

EXPANSION

In 1788, Virginia became the 10th state in the new nation. One year later, Virginia-born George Washington became the first U.S. president. Many of the country's founding fathers came from Virginia, including Thomas Jefferson, James Madison, and George Mason. At the time, the state was home to 20 percent of the country's population and more than 30 percent of its commerce. A new law that enabled owners to free their enslaved people was also passed, and by 1790, there were more than 12,000 free African Americans in Virginia.

After the war, steam locomotives and clipper ships were developed, greatly expanding trade possibilities. A series of canals was built, including the Chesapeake & Ohio Canal along the Potomac River, and railroads were developed. This greatly increased access between East Coast ports and land west of the Appalachians. By the mid-1800s, railroad lines ran through Virginia bringing wealth and prosperity to many agricultural-based businesses, although it was not until after the Civil War that railroads connected all primary population centers in Virginia.

THE AMERICAN CIVIL WAR

Thomas Jefferson predicted a conflict regarding the issue of slavery. He felt that "God is just: that his justice cannot sleep forever" and a change in the current situation was very possible. Soon, calls for emancipation spread through the North, and scattered revolts against slavery gained momentum. In 1859, a raid on the federal arsenal in Harpers Ferry led by an American abolitionist named John Brown resulted in the death of 21 people—both free African Americans and whites—and the realization by the country that slavery opponents were willing to kill and die themselves for their cause.

In 1860, Abraham Lincoln was elected president and pledged to keep slavery out of the territories. In December that same year, South Carolina seceded from the Union and was followed shortly thereafter by Mississippi, Alabama, Georgia, Florida, Louisiana, and Texas. Virginia joined its southern neighbors and seceded from the nation in 1861, after which it became a prominent Confederate state.

Four years of bloody fighting took place on soil passionately defended less than a century before in the Revolutionary War. More than 600,000 Americans lost their lives in the war, more than those lost in both World Wars combined. Virginia suffered more casualties and witnessed more major battles than any other state. In just four years, the state was left in ruins. Some of the major battles fought in Virginia include the First and Second Battles of Bull Run (Manassas), the Battle of the Ironclads, the Seven Days' Battles, the Battle of Fredericksburg, and the Battle of Chancellorsville.

Richmond was burned on April 3, 1865. Six days later, General Robert E. Lee asked General Ulysses S. Grant for a meeting. Terms of the surrender were drafted and signed at Appomattox Court House, and the Confederate army turned over arms in a formal ceremony on April 12. Both armies saluted each other, and the Civil War was history.

MODERN TIMES

The 1900s brought a diversification of industry to Virginia. The state benefited from enormous expansion to the Newport News shipyard. The Great Depression slowed growth in some markets, but overall, the state fared well through that difficult time.

By the middle of the 20th century, Virginia had evolved from a rural state into an urban one. World War II had again given a boost to the Hampton Roads area in support of the Norfolk Naval Base and shipyard.

RECENT HISTORY

In recent decades, the Washington DC area has experienced an economic and technological boom, resulting in an increase in population, housing, and jobs in Northern Virginia. By the early 1990s, Virginia had a population of more than 6 million.

The early part of the new millennium was scarred by the terrorist attacks on 9/11 and by the sniper shootings in the DC area in 2002 that left 10 people dead. The resilient communities of DC and Virginia were actually united by these events, and today, they work together to tackle common issues such as rapid suburban development, economic fluctuations, and environmental preservation.

Government and Economy

GOVERNMENT

Virginia is traditionally a conservative state. It is governed by the Constitution of Virginia, which was adopted in 1971 and is the seventh constitution. There are three branches of government in Virginia: the legislative, executive, and judicial branches. The executive branch has three elected officials: the governor, lieutenant governor, and attorney general, who are elected individually statewide to four-year terms.

Virginia's governor is the chief executive officer of the Commonwealth and the commander in chief of the state militia. Governors can serve multiple terms, but they must be nonconsecutive. The lieutenant governor is the president of the Senate of Virginia and first in the line of succession to the governor. A lieutenant governor can run for reelection. The attorney general is second in the line of succession to the governor and the chief legal advisor to both the governor and the General Assembly. He or she is also the chief lawyer of the state and heads the Department of Law.

The legislative branch in Virginia is the General Assembly made up of 40 senators (serving four-year terms) and 100 delegates (serving two-year terms). The General Assembly claims to be the "oldest continuous law-making body in the New World" and traces its roots back to the House of Burgesses in Jamestown.

The Virginia judiciary is made up of the Supreme Court of Virginia and subordinate courts such as the Court of Appeals, the Circuit Courts, and the General District Courts. The judiciary is led by the chief justice of the Supreme Court, the Judicial Council, the Committee on District Courts, and Judicial Conferences.

Thomas Jefferson designed the State Capitol Building in Richmond, and Governor Patrick Henry laid the cornerstone in 1785.

ECONOMY

Virginia is traditionally a wealthy state and typically has the most counties and independent cities in the top 100 wealthiest jurisdictions in the country. Perhaps the wealthiest Southern state prior to the Civil War, Virginia recovered quickly from its Civil War scars and also weathered the Great Depression much better than the rest of the South. Much of the wealth is concentrated in the northern part of the state near Washington DC, where housing prices are sky-high. Loudoun and Fairfax Counties have two of the highest median household incomes out of all the counties in the nation. Virginia is one of 24 right-to-work states where union security agreements are prohibited.

Virginia's economy includes a balance of income from federal government-supported jobs, technology industries, military installations, and agriculture. The military plays a prominent role in the state's financial picture with facilities such as the Pentagon in Arlington, Marine Corps Base Quantico, and the privately owned shipyards in Newport News.

High-tech firms and government contractors have replaced dairy farms and now dominate Northern Virginia, which is home to 10 Fortune 500 companies and is the planned site of Amazon's East Coast headquarters. Richmond has an additional 7 Fortune 500 companies.

Although modern farming techniques have put many small farmers out of business and sent them to metropolitan areas in search of new careers, agriculture still plays a role in much of the state with crops such as tobacco, sweet potatoes, peanuts, tomatoes, apples, grains, hay, and soy. True to its roots, Virginia is still the third-largest tobacco producer in the country. Livestock is also a thriving commodity, and cattle fields can be seen along much of I-81 in the western part of the state. Despite the natural resources of the Chesapeake Bay, Virginia makes only a small portion of its revenue from the fishing industry.

The number of wineries is on the rise in Virginia with acres of vineyards in the Northern Neck, Charlottesville, and near the Blue Ridge Mountains. Predictions are that in decades to come, Virginia will rise through the ranks of the great wine-producing states.

People and Culture

DEMOGRAPHICS

Traditionally, the people in Virginia were hardworking farmers, political pioneers, and sailors. The early colonists came mostly from rural England but were soon joined by French, Irish, German, and Scots-Irish who immigrated from abroad and also came to the Shenandoah Valley through Pennsylvania and Maryland. African Americans were a large part of early culture in Virginia; many initially arrived as indentured servants, followed by larger numbers through the African slave trade. Native American populations were devastated by European disease to the point that just a very small population survived to see modern times.

Today Virginia is largely diversified with 85 percent of its residents living in metropolitan areas. Northern Virginia especially is a highly transient area with residents from all over the globe. Many households speak a language other than English at home, and many fabulous restaurants serving authentic international cuisine can be found.

African Americans make up the largest minority in Virginia, totaling nearly 20 percent. The African American population is heavily concentrated in the eastern portion of the state with the largest populations being in Richmond and Norfolk. Second is the Latino population, which comprises approximately 10 percent of the population (located primarily in Northern Virginia), followed by an Asian population of approximately 7 percent (also primarily in Northern Virginia).

RELIGION

The first colonists came to Virginia motivated primarily by material wealth rather than religious freedom. This is not to say that the colonists weren't religious; they just assumed religion and government went together and that the Anglican Church would be the designated church. There was some rivalry between Virginia and Catholic-established Maryland, although to attract settlers, the Anglicans of Virginia were flexible to newcomers. As such, they encouraged groups such as the Pennsylvania Dutch to move south into the Shenandoah Valley in part so they could alert eastern settlements of attacks by the French or Native Americans coming from bases in the Ohio River Valley. To this day, the German Mennonite heritage is still evident west of the Blue Ridge.

Thomas Jefferson and James Madison led first Virginia and then the nation to end government involvement in religion. This spread tolerance of religious freedom throughout the state and resulted in a permanent acceptance throughout the Commonwealth of various forms of religion and the option to follow no religion at all.

CULTURE

Many parts of southern and western Virginia embrace the culture of the southern United States. It is there you can find authentic Southern cuisine and Virginia-specific food such as Virginia ham (country ham produced in Virginia), Virginia barbecue (pork with a vinegar-based sauce, similar to North Carolina barbecue), marble cake, shoofly pie, Brunswick stew, and peanut soup.

It's almost impossible to summarize the attitudes of Virginians across the board because the state is so diverse. But in the smaller towns and rural areas, everyone waves, people ask strangers for directions, and you might get slipped a free piece of apple pie at a local diner for no apparent reason. Many areas in Virginia still offer a secure sense of community, although in some cities crime is unfortunately an issue.

THE ARTS

Virginia offers numerous opportunities for residents and visitors to not only enjoy the arts but to become part of them. In fact, the arts are an important part of many people's lives in this state, whether they realize it or not. Access to top-rated performances, historic architecture, quality handicrafts, and literature is often taken for granted by the people who live here. The **Virginians for The Arts** organization lists of more than 4,500 state organizations and individual advocates for the arts in Virginia.

Virginia's long history, diversified population, proximity to the nation's capital, and relative tolerance for religious and social beliefs open the state to many traditional and forward-thinking expressions of art, which in turn has created a thriving artistic community open to everyone who passes through its borders.

Countless theatrical venues throughout the region, including world-renowned venues in Washington DC, invite the highest-quality performances to the doorstep of many local communities, and specialized venues provide access to cutting-edge artistic advances.

Science Museum of Virginia in Richmond

Essentials

Transportation

Due in part to its close proximity to Washington DC, Virginia is an easily accessible destination from many parts of the United States and other countries.

AIR
Most major airlines serve the two major airports in Virginia. The first is **Ronald Reagan Washington National Airport (DCA)** (703/417-8000, www.flyreagan.com), just outside Washington DC in Arlington. It is a 15-minute drive from the airport to downtown Washington DC.

The airport is serviced by the Blue and Yellow Metrorail Lines. Taxi service is available at the Arrivals curb outside the baggage claim area of each terminal. Rental cars are available on the first floor in parking garage A. A shuttle to the rental car counter is available outside each baggage claim area. Rideshare services such as Uber and Lyft are also available.

The second is **Washington Dulles International Airport (IAD)** (703/572-2700, www.flydulles.com), 27 miles west of Washington DC in Dulles. It is a 35-minute drive to downtown Washington DC from Dulles. Bus service between Dulles Airport and Metrorail at the Wiehle Avenue Station in Reston (Silver Line) is available through **Washington Flyer Coach Service** (703/572-7661, www.flydulles.com, $5 one way, under 2 free). Tickets can be purchased at the ticket counter in the Main Terminal at Arrivals door 4 or at the Metrorail station at Wiehle Avenue. Buses depart approximately every 15-20 minutes. Passengers going from the Wiehle Avenue Metrorail station should follow signs for the Washington Flyer bus stop. Tickets can be purchased from the bus driver. At the time of publication, **Metrobus** (202/637-7000, www.wmata.com) operates an express bus (Route 5A) between Dulles Airport and the L'Enfant Plaza Metrorail station in Washington DC. Passengers can board the bus at the airport at the Ground Transportation Curb (on the Arrivals level) at curb location 2E. Metrobus has proposed the elimination of this route several times since the opening of the Metrorail Silver Line, so check their website before relying on this route. Rideshare services such as Uber and Lyft are also available.

The **Washington Dulles Taxi and Sedan** (703/554-3509, www.washingtondullestaxisedan.com) provides taxi and sedan service for passengers at both airports. Shuttle service is also available from both airports through **SuperShuttle** (800/258-3826, www.supershuttle.com).

There are also major airports near Richmond, Norfolk, Newport News/ Williamsburg, Charlottesville, and Roanoke.

CAR

Virginia, like most states in the country, is easiest to explore by car. The state encompasses a large amount of land. It can take six hours to drive from Washington DC to the southern end of Virginia and six hours to drive from Lexington to the Eastern Shore. Thankfully, a large network of interstate highways provides access throughout Virginia, even in the more rural areas on the western side of the state.

I-95 is the main north-south travel route along the East Coast and connects Washington DC and Richmond. I-81 is the main north-south travel route in the western portions of the state and connects Roanoke, Harrisonburg, and Winchester.

I-66 is a primary east-west route in the northern part of the state, starting at the Washington DC border in Arlington and ending past Front Royal at I-81. I-66 has High Occupancy Vehicle (HOV) restrictions and Express toll lanes during rush hour on weekdays. The other primary east-west route is I-64, which connects Norfolk, Richmond, and Charlottesville and ends near Staunton at I-81.

Washington DC is circled by I-495, also called the Beltway, which runs through both Virginia and Maryland as part of I-95. This massive highway has access points to many of the Virginia suburbs and can have extreme rush hour traffic.

Speed limits are posted throughout Virginia. The maximum allowable speed limit in the state is 70 miles per hour, although most roads have speed limits posted much below this maximum. Keep in mind that state-maintained roads can have both a name and a route number.

In Virginia, all drivers are banned by law from text messaging, and drivers under the age of 18 are prohibited from using cell phones and text messaging. In DC, text messaging and handheld cell phone usage are banned for all drivers. Drivers under 18 are prohibited from all cell phone use. Seatbelt laws are enforced throughout the state.

The Washington area is not known for its efficiency at clearing snow off the roads in winter, but for the most part, state-maintained roads are plowed fairly quickly. The biggest hazard in Virginia is ice, specifically black ice, especially when above freezing temperatures during the day melt ice and snow and then below freezing temperatures at night cause a refreeze. Fog can sometimes be an issue when driving in the mountains, especially along Skyline Drive.

Virginia's department of transportation is a good resource for maps, toll rates, webcams, road conditions, and details on HOV restrictions. Visit www.virginiadot.org.

TRAIN

Amtrak (800/872-7245, www.amtrak.com) offers rail service to 21 stations in Virginia. There is also 1 station in Washington DC—Union Station. Although a train ticket can rival the cost of airfare, it can also be more convenient and more comfortable to travel by train.

Amtrak connects to the **Virginia Railway Express (VRE)** (703/684-1001, www.vre.org) in Virginia. VRE runs commuter train service between the Northern Virginia suburbs along the I-66 and I-95 corridors, to Alexandria, Crystal City, and Washington DC. They have 19 stations and 16 trains.

BUS

Many cities in Virginia can be reached by **Greyhound** (800/231-2222, www.greyhound.com). Tickets are less expensive when purchased in advance, and discounts are often available to students, seniors, and military personnel.

Local bus service is available in many cities, with the most extensive being the **Metrobus** (202/637-7000, www.wmata.com/bus) service in and around Washington DC and its suburbs. Metrobus has an incredible 11,500 bus stops on 325 routes throughout Washington DC, Virginia, and Maryland and is the sixth busiest bus service provider in the nation. They have more than 1,500 buses.

There is also a tourist-friendly bus system in Washington DC with the **DC Circulator** (www.dccirculator.com, free).

SUBWAY

Washington DC and the surrounding area has a clean, reliable, and generally safe subway system called **Metrorail** (202/637-7000, www.wmata.com/rail) that is run by the **Washington Metropolitan Area Transit Authority (WMATA).** The Metrorail system is commonly known as the Metro and provides service to more than 600,000 customers a day. The system is number two in the country in terms of ticket sales and serves more than 91 stations throughout DC, Virginia, and Maryland.

There are six color-coded rail lines: the Red, Orange, Blue, Yellow, Green, and Silver. The system layout is easy to understand, as most stations are named for the neighborhood they serve, and getting from one station to another normally requires no more than a single transfer. Metrorail stations are marked with large "M" signs at the entrance that have colored stripes around them to show which line they serve. A complete list of fares and a map of each train line can be found on the website. Metrorail opens at 5am on weekdays, 7am on Saturday, and 8am on Sunday. It closes at 11:30pm Monday-Thursday, 1am Friday Saturday, and 11pm Sunday. Bicycles are permitted during non-peak hours.

WATER

If you're lucky enough to cruise into Virginia on a private boat, you'll have options for docking in marinas along the Chesapeake Bay, the

Intracoastal Waterway, and the Potomac River. Most towns on the water offer marina slips, but making plans ahead of time is advised, especially during the prime summer months and in popular areas.

Recreation

If you can dream it, you can do it in Virginia. Well, almost anyway. People in this state are crazy about getting outside, and with the mountains and seashore just a few hours apart, the opportunities are endless.

HIKING

Thousands of hiking trails are available throughout Virginia, including a large portion of the **Appalachian Trail.** The best part is, you only need a good pair of trail shoes or hiking boots and you're on your way. The **Shenandoah National Park** alone has more than 500 miles of trails, but other favorites include the Washington & Old Dominion Trail and the Virginia Creeper Trail.

The **Potomac Appalachian Trail Club** (www.potomacappalachian.org) is a wonderful resource for hikers throughout the state and offers maps, books, and trip information.

BIKING

Whether you like to road bike, mountain bike, or just toddle along on a cruiser enjoying the scenery, Virginia is the place to do it. From the flat Eastern Shore to the challenging mountains of the Shenandoah, there are endless choices for getting out and pedaling.

For those who are competitive, the racing scene is thriving in the region, and road races are held most weekends April through October. Mountain bike races are also very popular and run even later in the year.

Road Cycling

Many organized rides take place in Virginia. **Bike Virginia** (www.bikevirginia.org) is a six-day bike tour that goes through a different part of Virginia each year in June. Riders can choose from a variety of distances to pedal each day. A more challenging ride is the fierce **Mountains of Misery** (www.mountainsofmisery.com) ride in southern Virginia that takes place each May.

Not all roads are conducive to road cycling, given the extreme traffic conditions in many urban areas. Be wise about choosing a biking route; accidents do happen, and usually the bike is on the worse end of it.

Mountain Biking

Mountain biking is big in the mid-Atlantic, and Virginia is no exception. Charlottesville was even rated the eighth best dream town in the country for mountain bikers by *Mountain Bike* magazine. Mountain bike trails can be found near the cities, in the rural areas, and throughout the mountains. Fat-tire races are also held throughout the year. **MTB Project** (www.mtbproject.com) and **Singletracks** (www.singletracks.com) are good resources for mountain biking in the region.

ADVENTURE RACING

Adventure racing—contests that combine several activities such as running, mountain biking, kayaking, orienteering, etc.—has spread quickly through the East bringing new challenges to the physically fit and adventurous. Popular race organizations include **Odyssey Adventure Racing** (www.oarevents.com) and **EX2 Adventures** (www.ex2adventures.com).

Another organization that bills itself as the "Premier Obstacle Course Series in the World" is **Tough Mudder** (www.toughmudder.com). Its events are challenging 10-12-mile obstacle courses designed by British Special Forces.

Following the Appalachian Trail

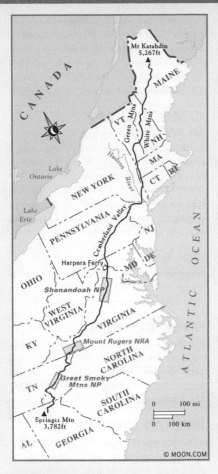

The Appalachian Trail passes through 14 states on the East Coast and is approximately 2,180 miles long. It is the longest continuously marked trail in the world. The trail's northern terminus is in Katahdin, Maine, and the southern terminus is at Springer Mountain in Georgia.

Each year, between 2 and 3 million people hike on the Appalachian Trail, and more than 2,500 people attempt to hike the entire trail in one season. These people are called "thru-hikers." About 25 percent who start hiking with the intent of completing the trail in one season finish each year. For those who hike it end to end, it normally takes between five and seven months. Thru-hikers normally adopt a "trail name" or are given one by other hikers they meet along the way. The names are often funny or descriptive such as "Iron Toothpick," "Thunder Chicken," or "Mr. Optimist."

The Appalachian Trail was completed in 1937 and is part of the national park system, although it is managed by a combination of public and private sectors. Although Harpers Ferry is home to the trail headquarters, only about four miles of the trail pass through West Virginia. Virginia claims the most miles along the trail at approximately 550.

There are literally hundreds of entrances to the Appalachian Trail, making it accessible to millions of people. Some people called "section-hikers" also hike the entire length of the trail, but do so in segments over several years. The total elevation gain on the Appalachian Trail equals the elevation gain of climbing Mt. Everest 16 times.

Additional information can be found on the Appalachian Trail Conservancy website at www.appalachiantrail.org.

CANOEING AND KAYAKING

Canoeing is one of the most popular ways to enjoy the multitude of rivers, creeks, and lakes throughout Virginia. Dozens of outfitters and liveries rent canoes and many offer guided trips.

Flat-water kayaking has become extremely popular in Virginia over the last decade. This part of the country may have lagged behind other water-influenced regions in the adoption of this sport, but it has fully caught on. Kayak tours and instruction are now available on many eastern rivers, lakes, the Chesapeake Bay, and at the beaches.

White-water kayaking is a much more

specialized sport enjoyed throughout the region on rivers such as the Potomac and James. A training center for racing is located on the Potomac River. Additional information can be obtained from the **Potomac Whitewater Racing Center** (www.potomacwhitewater. org).

BOATING AND SAILING

Saltwater, lakes, marinas, dock and dine restaurants—Virginia has them all. The Chesapeake Bay alone has 11,684 miles of shoreline, which is more than the West Coast of the United States. Every town on the bay has a marina and access can also be gained from public boat ramps in many locations. Many visitors even arrive from other regions by water.

Commercial and recreational powerboats must be registered in Virginia if that is where they are primarily used.

FISHING

Fishing is a favorite activity in Virginia. There are more than 2,800 miles of trout waters in the Blue Ridge alone. Whether you prefer fishing in a quiet lake, fly-fishing in a mountain stream, surf fishing, or taking a deep-sea fishing charter, you can do it all in this state. Most state parks offer fishing, and some areas are stocked through breeding programs.

Some favorite fishing spots in Virginia include Smith Mountain Lake (striped bass), the South Fork of the Shenandoah River (redbreast sunfish), the New River (yellow perch), the Chesapeake Bay (bluefish, flounder, and drum), and off the shore of Virginia Beach (marlin, sea bass, and sailfish).

Licenses are required in Virginia and Washington DC. Virginia fishing licenses can be purchased online from the **Virginia Department of Game and Inland Fisheries** (www.dgif.virginia.gov). Both "freshwater" licenses (resident $23, nonresident $47) and "freshwater and saltwater" licenses (resident $40, nonresident $71) are available. If you wish to fish in designated trout stocked waters, an additional trout license (resident $23, nonresident $47) is required. Licenses are good for one year from the date of purchase.

Fishing licenses in Washington DC can be purchased from the **District Department of Energy and the Environment** (www.doee. dc.gov). Licenses are $10 for residents and $13 for nonresidents and are valid from January 1 to December 31 of the same calendar year.

CRABBING AND CLAMMING

Getting dirty in the mud and risking losing a finger are free in Virginia if you are doing so to crab or clam for personal use only. Public access to beaches and marsh areas is prevalent, but keep in mind that limits and regulations apply. Current Virginia regulations can be found at http://mrc.virginia.gov.

GOLF

Hundreds of public golf courses are located in Virginia. A listing of courses in the state can be found at www.virginiagolf.com.

ROCK CLIMBING

A great rock climbing area located near Washington DC is **Great Falls Park,** with more than 200 climbing routes. There are also several dozen climbing areas along the Blue Ridge Mountains.

WINTER SPORTS

It's no surprise that winter sporting opportunities are concentrated in the western regions of Virginia. A handful of ski resorts, such as **Massanutten Resort** (www.massresort. com) near Harrisonburg, are open during the winter months. The **Liberty Mountain Snowflex Center** (www.liberty.edu) in Lynchburg offers year-round skiing on fabricated snow.

Cross-country skiing and snowmobiling are available on a limited basis when the weather cooperates on designated park trails. Ice-skating and hockey, however, are available throughout Virginia in indoor and seasonal outdoor facilities.

Travel Tips

DOMESTIC TRAVELERS

As of October 2020, US citizens over the age of 18 will need a passport, state-issued enhanced driver's license, or REAL ID for domestic air travel.

FOREIGN TRAVELERS

Visitors from other countries must present a valid passport and visa issued by a U.S. consular official unless they are a citizen of a country eligible for the Visa Waiver Program (such as Canada) in order to enter the United States. A foreign national entering the country by air that is a citizen of a country eligible for the Visa Waiver Program must present an approved Electronic System for Travel Authorization and a valid passport. A list of exceptions (38 total) can be found on the Department of Homeland Security website at www.cbp.gov.

ACCESS FOR TRAVELERS WITH DISABILITIES

Accessibility is in the eye of the beholder. Despite the Americans with Disabilities Act, it is unfortunate that universal access in public places is still not a reality in most parts of the country. Virginia is no exception. Although many restaurants, theaters, hotels, and museums offer ramps or elevators, some smaller, privately owned establishments (such as bed-and-breakfasts) do not always provide these necessities. It is best to call ahead and verify the type of access that is available.

Accessible Virginia (www.accessiblevir-ginia.org) is a great resource for information on access throughout Virginia.

GAY AND LESBIAN TRAVELERS

Virginia as a whole tends to be on the conservative side, but especially so south of the Washington DC suburbs. Some of the more densely populated areas such as Richmond, Charlottesville, Norfolk, and Virginia Beach have LGBTQ-friendly communities and businesses, but these are rarer in rural areas. Washington DC has a large LGBTQ population and readily accepts same-sex couples and families. The Gay and Lesbian Travel Center (www.gayjourney.com) is a great resource for travel.

TRAVELING WITH CHILDREN

Although most places don't make specific accommodations for children, in general, most tourist attractions throughout Virginia are family-friendly (except for obvious exceptions where noted). Some cities such as Charlottesville offer museums devoted specifically to children, but many other sights have a children's component to them. For a list of kid-oriented attractions in Virginia, visit the "Cool Places for Kids" section of the Virginia Is for Lovers website at www.virginia.org.

TRAVELING WITH PETS

In recent years more and more pet-friendly establishments have been popping up in Virginia. Many higher-end hotels (such as the Kimpton hotel chain) allow four-legged family members, and some establishments even host doggie happy hours. It's not uncommon for attractions, stores, historical sites, campgrounds, outdoor shopping malls, parks, beaches, and even the patios at some restaurants to welcome dogs with open arms. It is always best to call ahead before assuming an establishment is pet-friendly. Service and guide dogs are welcome nearly everywhere with their human companions.

DISCOUNTS

Numerous hotels, venues, and attractions offer discounts to seniors; all you have to do is ask when making your reservations or purchasing your tickets. The **American Association of Retired Persons (AARP)** (www.aarp.org) is the largest organization in the nation for seniors. They offer discounts to their members on hotels, tours, rental cars, airfare, and many other services. Membership in AARP is just $16 a year, so it's worth joining.

Many places also offer discounts to active **military** and/or veterans (and sometimes family members). Some require identification, so ask when making your reservations.

Students often get discounts as well. Some attractions require a student ID, so it's best to check the website before heading out.

TIPPING

A 15-20 percent tip is standard throughout Virginia on restaurant bills. Other service providers, such as taxi drivers and hairstylists, typically also receive 15-20 percent. Bellhops and airport personnel normally receive $1-2 per bag.

Information and Services

TOURIST INFORMATION

For information on tourism in Virginia, visit the **Virginia Is for Lovers site** (www.virginia.org) or the official **Virginia state site** (www.virginia.gov). For information on tourism in Washington DC, visit the official **DC tourism site** (www.washington.org).

COMMUNICATIONS AND MEDIA

Cell Phone Coverage

Cell phone coverage is generally available in most parts of Virginia. As with any state, there are scattered pockets of spotty coverage even near large cities, but overall, coverage is reliable. As a rule, the more rural the region you are traveling through (such as Central and Southern Virginia), the less coverage is available, but for the most part, the major highways have fairly consistent coverage. Once you leave the major highways, coverage can be a concern. Large parks, such as Shenandoah National Park, do not have reliable coverage, especially once you leave the main roads (such as Skyline Drive). Any time you head into the backcountry, be sure to bring supplies in case

Bring your best friend to Old Town Alexandria.

of an emergency instead of relying on your cell phone.

Internet Access

Internet access is readily available in hotels throughout Virginia and is very commonly included with the price of a room, but sometimes as an add-on. A few cities even offer wireless Internet access throughout their downtown areas, such as Roanoke and Charlottesville (on the pedestrian mall).

Media

Major city newspapers and magazines are available throughout Virginia. The most widely circulated daily newspaper in the Washington DC area (including Northern Virginia) is the *Washington Post* (www.washingtonpost.com). The paper features world news and local news and places an emphasis on national politics. The *Washington Times* (www.washingtontimes.com) is another daily newspaper that is widely circulated. Weekly and specialty newspapers include the *Washington City Paper* (www.washingtoncitypaper.com), an alternative weekly newspaper, and the *Washington Informer* (www.washingtoninformer.com), a weekly newspaper serving the DC area's African American population.

Many smaller cities offer daily local papers. They are typically found in convenience stores, grocery stores, and on newsstands.

Health and Safety

For emergencies anywhere in Virginia, dial 911 from any telephone (at no charge). From a cell phone, the state police can be reached by pressing #77. Generally speaking, hospitals in Virginia are very good, and excellent in the larger cities. Emergency room treatment is always costlier than a scheduled appointment, but emergency care facilities can also be found in most areas to treat minor conditions.

LYME DISEASE

Virginia is prime tick country, so Lyme disease, which is transmitted through the bites of deer-ticks, is a risk. Use insect repellent and check yourself thoroughly after spending time in the woods or walking through tall grass. If you are bitten, or find a red circular rash (similar to a bull's-eye), consult a physician. Lyme disease can be life-threatening if it goes untreated.

INSECTS

Mosquitoes are common throughout Virginia and aside from being annoying can carry diseases. Damp, low areas can harbor large populations of these little vampires, so use insect repellent and steer clear of stagnant water. Bees, wasps, yellow jackets, and hornets are all permanent residents of the region and are particularly active (and aggressive) in the fall.

Female black widow spiders are also found in the state and can be identified by a small red hourglass shape on their black abdomens. They live in dark places such as rotting logs and under patio furniture. Symptoms of their bite include severe abdominal pain and should be treated. The males are harmless. The brown recluse spider, contrary to common belief, is not native to Virginia. They can on occasion be found here, but only as a transplant.

ANIMALS

There are three types of venomous snakes in Virginia. The most common is the northern copperhead. This snake can be found across the state and has dark-colored cross bands shaped like an hourglass. The second type is the timber rattlesnake, which is found in all the mountainous regions of Virginia and in the southeastern corner of the state. It also has a patterned back with wavy cross bands. The eastern cottonmouth snake is only found in southeastern Virginia (south of Newport News). It can be yellowish olive to black in color and has approximately 13 black cross bands that are wide at the sides and narrow at the backbone.

Swimming in the Atlantic Ocean or the Chesapeake Bay could put you in contact with stinging **jellyfish** or **sea nettles** (especially in the Chesapeake Bay). **Sharks** are also found occasionally in both bodies of water.

PLANTS

Poison ivy, poison oak, and **poison sumac** are all native to Virginia and should be avoided even if you have never had a prior allergic reaction (you can develop one anytime). As the saying goes, "Leaves of three, let it be." Local mushrooms and berries can also be poisonous, so don't eat them unless you are 100 percent sure of their identification.

WEATHER

In addition to the obvious presence or prediction of a tornado, tropical storm, hurricane, or snowstorm (all of which are possible but rare in the state), be aware that **lightning** is a greater danger on exposed ridges, in fields, on golf courses, on the beach, or anywhere near water. Thunderstorms can pop up quickly, especially during the summer months, so check the weather before venturing out and be prepared with a plan B. Hypothermia can also be an issue. Being wet, tired, and cold is a dangerous combination. Symptoms include slurred speech, uncontrollable shivering, and loss of coordination.

CRIME

As in many states, downtown areas of larger cities such as Richmond and parts of Washington DC and Norfolk can be unsafe, especially at night. Ask hotel staff about the safety of the area you're staying in, lock your doors, take a cab or ride-hailing service instead of walking, and don't leave valuables in your car.

Resources

Suggested Reading

HISTORY
General History

Barbour, Philip, and Thad Tate, eds. *The Complete Works of Captain John Smith, 1580-1631.* Chapel Hill: University of North Carolina Press, 1986. Three volumes of Captain John Smith's work.

Dabney, Virginius. *Richmond: Story of a City.* Charlottesville: University of Virginia Press, 1990. Tells the story of Virginia's state capital.

Jefferson, Thomas. *Notes on the State of Virginia.* Chapel Hill: University of North Carolina Press, 1996. This classic shows Jefferson's personality and discusses life in the 18th century.

Kelly, C. Brian. *Best Little Stories from Virginia.* Nashville, TN: Cumberland House Publishing, Inc., 2003. A collection of more than 100 stories since Jamestown's founding.

Civil War History

Catton, Bruce. *America Goes to War: The Civil War and Its Meaning in American Culture.* Middletown, CT: Wesleyan University Press, 1992. An interesting study on the Civil War.

McPherson, James. *Battle Cry of Freedom: The Civil War Era.* New York: Ballantine Books, 1988. Perhaps the best single-volume history of the war.

SCIENCE AND NATURE

Duda, Mark Damian. *Virginia Wildlife Viewing Guide.* Helena, MT: Falcon Press, 1994. Provides information on 80 of Virginia's best wildlife-viewing areas.

Fergus, Charles. *Wildlife of Virginia and Maryland and Washington, D.C.* Mechanicsburg, PA: Stackpole Books, 2003. Provides details on the animals in the diverse habitats throughout Virginia and Maryland.

Frye, Keith. *Roadside Geology of Virginia.* Missoula, MT: Mountain Press, 2003. Provides general information on the state's geology.

Gupton, Oscar. *Wildflowers of the Shenandoah Valley and Blue Ridge Mountains.* Charlottesville: University of Virginia Press, 2002. A unique guide dedicated to wildflowers.

RECREATION
General Outdoor

Carrol, Steven, and Mark Miller. *Wild Virginia.* Helena, MT: Falcon Press, 2002. A guide to wilderness and special management areas throughout Virginia with a focus on the western and southern areas.

Hiking

Adkins, Leonard. *50 Hikes in Northern Virginia*. Woodstock, VT: The Countryman Press, 2015. A good resource for hiking in Northern Virginia.

Blackinton, Theresa Dowell. *Moon Take a Hike Washington DC: 80 Hikes within Two Hours of the City*. 2nd edition. Berkeley, CA: Avalon Travel, 2013. A terrific resource for hiking the Washington DC area including hikes in metropolitan DC, the Shenandoah, Western Maryland, Eastern Maryland, and Virginia's Piedmont and Coastal Plains.

Burnham, Bill, and Mary Burnham. *Hiking Virginia*. 4th edition. Guilford, CT: Falcon Guides, 2018. A lively and award-winning guide to hiking in Virginia.

de Hart, Allen. *The Trails of Virginia: Hiking the Old Dominion*. Chapel Hill: University of North Carolina Press, 2003. A very comprehensive resource for hiking in Virginia.

Bicycling

Adams, Scott. *Mountain Bike America: Virginia*. Guilford, CT: Globe Pequot, 2000. Scott Adams is one of the best guidebook writers for mountain biking and this is a great and informative read.

Adams, Scott, and Martin Fernandez. *Mountain Biking the Washington, D.C./Baltimore Area*. 5th edition. Guilford, CT: Falcon Guides, 2015. A great guide to mountain biking around Washington DC and Baltimore.

Eltringham, Scott, and Jim Wade. *Scott & Jim's Favorite Bike Rides*. Arlington, VA: S&J Cycling, 2006. A fun guide to biking in Northern Virginia and central Maryland.

Homerosky, Jim. *Road Biking Virginia*. Guilford, CT: Falcon Guides, 2002. Wonderful resource for road bikers in Virginia.

Fishing

Beasley, Beau. *Fly Fishing Virginia: A No Nonsense Guide to Top Waters*. Tucson, AZ: No Nonsense Fly Fishing Guidebooks, 2007. An award-winning guide to fly-fishing spots in Virginia.

Gooch, Bob. *Virginia Fishing Guide*. 2nd edition. Charlottesville: University of Virginia Press, 2011. A wonderful guide to fishing in Virginia.

Kayaking

Gaaserud, Michaela Riva. *AMC's Best Sea Kayaking in the Mid-Atlantic*. Boston: Appalachian Mountain Club Books, 2016. A great resource for coastal kayaking in Virginia.

Rock Climbing

Horst, Eric, and Stewart M. Green. *Rock Climbing Virginia, West Virginia, and Maryland*. Helena, MT: Falcon Press, 2013. Detailed information on climbs in Shenandoah National Park and Great Falls.

Internet Resources

STATE RESOURCES

www.virginia.gov
The official Commonwealth of Virginia website.

www.virginia.com
General travel information within Virginia.

www.virginia.org
The official visitor website for the Commonwealth of Virginia.

WASHINGTON DC

www.washington.org
Visitor information on Washington DC.

www.si.edu
Information on the Smithsonian Institution.

www.wmata.com
Information on Metrorail and Metrobus service.

www.historydc.org
The interesting and helpful website of the Historical Society of Washington, D.C.

RECREATION

www.nps.gov
The National Park Service website, a comprehensive guide to national parks throughout the country.

www.dcr.virginia.gov
Information on the Virginia Department of Conservation and Recreation.

www.hikingupward.com
Contains a wonderful interactive map of Virginia hikes.

www.baydreaming.com
Offers an excellent list of marinas and boating facilities in the Chesapeake Bay area.

www.thebayguide.com
A guide to boating in the Chesapeake Bay area.

www.findyourchesapeake.com
The Chesapeake Bay Gateways Network website provides information on public access parks around the bay.

LOCAL RESOURCES

www.mtnlaurel.com
A nice resource for life in Virginia's Blue Ridge.

www.virginialiving.com
Virginia Living Magazine has many fascinating articles on Virginia.

www.chesapeakebaymagazine.com
Chesapeake Bay Magazine is full of interesting articles on the bay area.

www.baydreaming.com
A guide to Chesapeake Bay events.

Index

XYZ

List of Maps

Photo Credits

All interior photos © Michaela Riva Gaaserud except: page 1 Virginia Museum of Fine Arts; page 3 NPS/ Neal Lewis; page 7 © (top) NPS/Neal Lewis; (bottom left) NPS/Katy Cain; page 8-9 NPS/Neal Lewis; page 10 (bottom) NPS/Neal Lewis; page 11 © George Washington's Mount Vernon; page 12 (top) Virginia; Museum; of the Civil; War; (bottom) page 17 © (bottom) Mark; Vandyke | Dreamstime.com, page 19 NPS/Neal Lewis; page 22 Konstantin Lobastov | Dreamstime.com; page 37 (top right) Kevin Tietz | Dreamstime.com; (bottom) Mariagroth | Dreamstime.com; (top right) page 40 Alan Karchmer/NMAAHC; (bottom right) Eric Long, National Air and Space Museum, Smithsonian Institution; (bottom) Dreamstime.com; page 55 © (top right) Faina Gurevich | Dreamstime.com; (bottom) Erik Lattwein | Dreamstime.com; (bottom) Amy Nicolai | Dreamstime.com; page 63 © (top) David Tulchinsky | Dreamstime.com; page 72 © (top) Richard Gunion | Dreamstime.com; (bottom) Cvandyke | Dreamstime.com; page 76 © Askoldsb | Dreamstime.com; page 83 © (bottom) Joe Sohm | Dreamstime.com; page 90 © George Washington's Mount Vernon; (top right) Jon Bilous | Dreamstime.com; page 121 © (top) Marybeth Charles | Dreamstime.com; (left middle) Diane Penland, National Air and Space Museum, Smithsonian Institution; page 148 © (top left) Christian Delbert | Dreamstime.com; (top right) Jamestown-Yorktown Foundation; page 179 © (top) Joe Sohm | Dreamstime. com; (left middle) Jamestown-Yorktown Foundation; page 189 © (top left) The Mariners' Museum and Park; page 199 © (bottom) Wangkun Jia | Dreamstime.com; page 224 © NPS/Katy Cain; page 225 © (top left) NPS/Neal Lewis; (top right) Zrf| Dreamstime.com; (bottom) Teresa Kenney | Dreamstime.com; page 231 © Winchester-Frederick County CVB; page 236 © (top left) NPS/Neal Lewis; (top right) NPS/Neal Lewis; page 244 © Jgorzynik | Dreamstime.com; page 258 (top right) Randall Stout/Taubman Museum of Art; page 264 (bottom) James Kirkikis | Dreamstime.com; page 266 © James Kirkikis | Dreamstime.com; page 276 © (top) Type01 | Dreamstime.com; (left middle) Jon Bilous | Dreamstime.com; (bottom) Liudmila Arsenteva Dreamstime.com; page 279 © (top) Virginia Museum of Fine Arts; (bottom) Virginia Museum of Fine Arts; page 287 The Jefferson Hotel; page 301 © (top) Bethany Snyder; page 302 © Wintergreen Resort; page 306 (right middle) Jill Lang | Dreamstime.com; (bottom) Larry Metayer | Dreamstime.com; (bottom) page 328 Tim Hursley/Taubman Museum of Art; page 344 NPS/Neal Lewis; page 347 © NPS/Neal Lewis; page 354 Sunny Nelson/Taubman Museum of Art; page 355 NPS/Neal Lewis

Craft a personalized journey through the top national parks in the U.S. and Canada with Moon Travel Guides.